THE ESSAYS OF
MONTAIGNE

Voyla pas vn plaidoyer d'vne hauteur inimaginable
& employe en quelle necessité. Certes vne si nonchallante &
molle consideration de sa mort, meritoit que la posterité la
considerast d'autant plus pour luy: Ce qu'elle fit, & il n'y a
rien en la iustice si iuste, que ce que la fortune a la recom-
mandation. Car les Atheniens eurent en telle abomination
ceux, qui en auoient esté cause, qu'on les fuyoit comme per-
sonnes excommuniées: On tenoit pollu tout ce, à quoy ils
auoient touché; personne à l'estuue ne lauoit auec eux; personne ne les faluoit ny accointoit: Si qu'en fin ne pouuant
plus porter cette hayne publique, ils se pendirent eux-mes-
mes. Si quelqu'vn estime, que parmy tant d'autres exemples
que i'auois à choisir pour le seruice de mon propos, és dicts
de Socrates, i'aye mal trié cettuy-cy, & qu'il iuge ce discours estre esleué au dessus des opinions communes, ie l'ay
faict à escient: Car ie iuge autrement, & tiens, que c'est
vn discours, en rang, & en naifueté, bien plus arriere, &
plus bas, que les opinions communes: Il represente la pure & premiere de nature. Car il est croyable que
nous auons naturellement craincte de la douleur; mais
non de la mort, à cause d'elle mesmes: C'est vne partie
de nostre estre, non moins essentielle que le viure: à quoy
faire, nous en auroit nature la hayne & l'horreur,
veu qu'elle luy tient rang de tres-grande vtilité, pour nourrir
la succession & vicissitude de ses ouurages: & qu'en cette be-
longue vniuerselle, elle sert plus de naissance & d'augmenta-
tion que de perte ou ruyne,

sic rerum summa nouatur.

La deffaillance d'vne vie, est le passage à mille autres vies.
Et voyons les bestes, non seulement la souffrir gayement:
la plus part des cheuaux hannissent en mourant; les ci-

Facsimile of a page of the 'Bordeaux Manuscript'
(Reprinted from the facsimile edition published by the Librairie Hachette)

THE ESSAYS OF
MONTAIGNE

TRANSLATED BY
E. J. TRECHMANN

WITH AN INTRODUCTION
BY THE RT. HON.
J. M. ROBERTSON
*Author of 'Montaigne
and Shakespeare'*

*In two volumes
Volume II*

London
OXFORD UNIVERSITY PRESS
HUMPHREY MILFORD
1927

Printed in Great Britain

BOOK III

CONTENTS

BOOK II (*continued*)

Book the Second

CHAPTER 12

APOLOGY OF RAYMOND SEBOND

(continued)

YOU,[1] for whom I have taken the pains, contrary to my usual habit, to stretch out my treatise to such a length, will not hesitate to defend your Sebond with the ordinary methods of argument in which you are every day instructed, and thus you will exercise your wit and learning ; for this final fencer's trick should not be employed except as a last resource. It is a desperate thrust, in which you have to abandon your weapon in order to disarm your adversary, and a secret ruse which should be practised seldom and with reserve. It is a very foolhardy thing to lose your life in order to kill another.

We must not wish to die in order to be revenged, as Gobrias did. For, being in close grips with a Persian lord, and Darius coming up with sword in hand, and fearing to strike lest he should brain Gobrias, the latter called him to lunge boldly, even though he should run them both through.

I have heard combats condemned, in which the weapons and conditions offered are so desperate that it was incredible that either could escape. The Portuguese captured fourteen Turks in the Indian Ocean, who, chafing at their captivity, resolved to reduce themselves and their captors and the vessel to ashes, by rubbing some ships' nails together, until a spark fell upon the kegs of gunpowder which they found ; and they carried out their resolution.

Here we are shaking the barriers and last fences of knowledge, wherein excess is to be condemned, as in virtue. Keep on the high road ; it will not do a crumb of good to be so subtle and clever. Remember the Tuscan proverb : *Chi troppo s'assottiglia, si scavezza.*[2]

---

[1] The lady Montaigne is addressing is supposed by some to have been Margaret of Valois, first wife of Henry IV, but this is uncertain.

[2] A line of Petrarch, which may have become proverbial in Montaigne's time. It might be rendered, using the words of the popular taunt, ' If you try to be too sharp, you will cut yourself.'

I advise you to be sober and reserved in your opinions
and expressions, as well as in your conduct of life and all
other things, and to flee all novelty and eccentricity. All
extravagant ways are a source of vexation to me. You
who, with the authority your lofty position gives you, and
still more with the advantages derived from your own
particular qualities, have all men at your beck and call,
could have given this charge to some professional man of
letters, who might have supported and enriched this rhapsody
with very much better arguments. However, I have lectured
you enough on your duty.

Epicurus said, speaking of the laws, that the worst of
them were so necessary to us, that without them men would
devour one another. And Plato comes near to saying that
but for the laws we should live like brute-beasts ; and he
tries to prove it.

Our mind is an erratic, dangerous and unthinking tool ;
it is difficult to reconcile it with order and moderation.
And in these days nearly all the men of exceptional eminence
above their fellows, and of extraordinary quickness of parts,
may be seen to get out of hand with their licentious opinions
and conduct. It is a miracle if you find one of them sober
and fit for society.

Men are right in setting up the strictest possible barriers
for the human mind. In study, as in all else, its steps
should be counted and regulated ; its hunting rights should
be artificially prescribed. They curb and fetter it with
religions, laws, customs, sciences, precepts, mortal and
immortal punishments and rewards ; and yet we see it, by
its versatility and licentiousness, escape all these bonds.
It is a shadowy body with nothing by which it may be
seized and directed ; a varying and shapeless body, incapable of being either bound or held. Indeed, there are few
minds so well-regulated, strong and well-born that they
may be trusted with their own guidance, and are able,
with moderation and without temerity, to sail in the freedom of their opinions, beyond those of the generality of
men. It is more expedient to place them under pupilage.

The mind is a formidable blade, even to its possessor,
if he cannot use it with judgement and discretion. And
there is no animal that is more in need of blinkers, to
control its eyes to look straight ahead, and keep it from

gadding about hither and thither, outside of the ruts that custom and the laws have traced.

Therefore it will be more becoming in you to confine yourself within the ordinary routine, whatever it be, than to soar aloft with such unbridled licence. But if any one of these new doctors [1] attempts to show off his cleverness in your presence, at the risk of his salvation and yours, to rid yourself of this dangerous pest, which is daily spreading in your courts, will be your best preservative, in extreme need, and will prevent the contagion of this poison from injuring either you or your environment.

The liberty, then, and wantonness of those ancient wits gave rise, in Philosophy and the Humanities, to several schools differing in their beliefs, each undertaking to choose and decide, in order to take sides. But now that men all go one pace, *who are so bound and devoted to certain fixed beliefs, that they are forced to defend even those they do not approve* (Cicero) ; now that we receive the arts and sciences in accordance with the decrees of the civil authorities, so that the schools are all after one pattern, and have a uniform and circumscribed system of education and discipline, they no longer regard the weight and value of coins, but every one in his turn accepts them according to the current price put upon them by general approval. They go to law, not about the standard, but the market-price ; so all things are regulated in like manner. They accept medicine as they do geometry, and they swallow wizardry, charms, ligatures,[2] correspondence with spirits and the dead, prognostications, domifications,[3] and even that absurd pursuit after the philosopher's stone ; all are accepted without question.

It is enough to know that the seat of Mars is in the middle of the triangle of the hand, that of Venus on the thumb, that of Mercury in the little finger ; and that when the table-line cuts across the tubercle of the forefinger it is a sign of cruelty ; when it falls short under the middle finger, and when the natural middle line forms an angle with the line of life under the same spot, it is a sign of a miserable death. That if, in a woman, the natural line

[1] The Reformers, according to Dr. Armaingaud.

[2] A spell to cause impotence in a man ; see the chapter on the Power of the Imagination.

[3] Dividing the heavens into twelve houses, to take a horoscope &c.

be open and does not close the angle with the line of life,
it means that she is unchaste. I call yourself to witness,
whether a man with this science may not be admitted, find
favour and make a reputation in any company.

Theophrastus said that human knowledge, guided by the
senses, could estimate the causes of things up to a certain
degree ; but that, having reached the ultimate and first
causes, it must stop and be turned back, by reason either
of its own weakness, or by the difficulty of things. It is
a belief soothing to the average mind, that our capacities
may guide us to the knowledge of some things, but that
there is a certain limit to their powers, beyond which it is
temerity to employ them. That is a plausible belief, suggested by people who are given to compromise.

But it is not easy to confine our mind ; it is curious and
insatiable to know, and has no more occasion to stop at
a thousand than at fifty paces. Having learned by experience that where one man has failed another has succeeded,
and that what was unknown to one century the following
century has made clear, and that the arts and sciences are
not cast in a mould, but that they are formed and shaped
by degrees, by repeated handling and polishing, as a she-
bear at her leisure licks her cubs into shape ; I do not cease
from testing and sounding what I have been unable to
discover, and by remanipulating and kneading this new
matter, by stirring and heating it, I make it easier for him
that shall succeed me, that he may enjoy it more at leisure,
and render it more pliable and manageable for him :

> As Hymettian wax grows softer in the sun,
> And moulded by the finger and the thumb,
> Will various forms and several shapes admit,
> Till for the present use 'tis rendered fit. (OVID.)

The second will do as much for the third ; for which
reason difficulties ought not to make me despair, any more
than my own incapacity, for it is only my own.

Man is as capable of all things as he is of some ; and if he
confesses, as Theophrastus says, ignorance of primary
causes and principles, let him boldly give me up all the rest
of his knowledge. If he lacks foundation his reason
sprawls on the ground. Disputes and investigations have
no other aim and limit but principles ; if this barrier do not
arrest his course, he falls into endless irresolution. *One*

thing can be neither more nor less comprehended than another,
since there is only one definition of the comprehension of
everything (Cicero).

Now it is probable that if the soul knew anything, she
would first of all know herself ; and if she knew anything
outside of herself, it would be before all things her body
and shell.

If to this day we still see the gods of the medical faculty
disputing about our anatomy,

Vulcan against, for Troy Apollo stood ;   (OVID.)

when can we expect them to agree ?   We are nearer to ourselves than the whiteness of snow and the weight of a stone
are to us.   If man does not know himself, how should he
know his functions and powers ?   It cannot be, perhaps,
but that we should harbour some real knowledge, but it is
by chance.   And since errors enter into our soul in the same
manner and guided through the same channel, she has no
means of distinguishing them, or of choosing between truth
and falsehood.

The Academics allowed the judgement to incline a little
to one side, and thought it too crude to say ' that it was
no more likely that snow was white than black, and that
we were no more certain of the motion of a stone thrown by
our hand than of that of the eighth sphere '.   And to avoid
this difficulty and strangeness, which indeed is hard to
imagine, although they conclude that we are in no sort
capable of knowing, and that the truth is engulfed in deep
abysses which human eyes cannot penetrate ;   yet they
allowed some things to be more likely than others, and
granted their judgement the option of inclining to one piece
of evidence more than to another.   This bias they permitted
themselves, but forbade the coming to any conclusion.

The Pyrrhonian attitude is bolder, and at the same time
more reasonable.   For that bias of the Academics, and their
leaning towards one proposition rather than to another,
what is it but an acknowledgement that one proposition is
more evidently true than another ?   If our understanding
is capable of taking in the shape, the lineaments, the face
and bearing of the truth, it would be just as likely to see it
full-grown as half-grown, incipient and imperfect.   That
apparent probability which makes them bear to the left

rather than to the right, you must increase ; that ounce of likelihood that turns the scales you must multiply by a hundred, by a thousand. In the end the scales will come to a definite decision, and fix on one choice and one absolute truth.

But how can they allow themselves to incline to a probability if they know not the truth ? How can they know the semblance of a thing of which they know not the essence ? We can either form an absolute judgement, or none at all. If the faculties of our intellect and senses lack foundation and foothold, if they only hover and are blown about by any wind, in vain do we allow our judgement to be carried away by any part of their operation, however apparent may be that which it sets before us ; and the surest and happiest attitude our understanding can take would be one of sobriety, justness, inflexibility, without any wavering and agitation. *As between things seen, whether true or false, it matters nothing to which the mind gives assent* (Cicero).

We can see clearly enough that our mind does not take in things in their form and essence, and that they do not enter therein by their own force and authority. Because, if that were so, we should all receive them in the same shape ; wine would taste the same to a sick man as to a sound. To a man with chapped or benumbed fingers the wood or iron he touches would seem as hard as to another. External objects therefore surrender to our mercy ; they dwell in us as we please.

Now, if for our part we took in anything without alteration, if the human grip were strong and capable enough to seize the truth by its own powers, these powers being common to all men, this truth would be bandied about from one to another, and there would be found at least some one thing in the world, out of so many as there are, that would be believed by all men with universal consent. But this fact, that there is no proposition that is not, or might not be, disputed and controverted among us, clearly proves that our innate judgement does not very clearly grasp that which it does grasp. For my judgement cannot force my neighbour's judgement to accept it ; which is a sign that I have become possessed of it by some other means than by a natural power that is in me and in all men.

We may pass over that endless confusion of beliefs that

we see among the philosophers themselves, and those perpetual and universal disputings concerning the knowledge of
things. For this is a very true presupposition, That on no
one thing are men in agreement, I mean the best-endowed
and most talented scholars, not even that the sky is over
our heads ; for they who doubt everything, doubt even
that. And they who deny that we are able to comprehend
anything, say that we have not comprehended that the sky
is above our heads ; and these two beliefs are without
comparison the most widely held.

Without considering this endless diversity and division,
it is easy to see, from the confusion that our judgement
causes ourselves, and the uncertainty that every man feels
in himself, that it has a very insecure seat. How variously
we judge of things ! How often we change our opinions !
What I hold and believe to-day I hold and believe with my
whole belief ; with all my tools and all my strength I grasp
that opinion, and they guarantee it with all the power at
their command.   There is no truth I could embrace and
keep more strongly than that. I am wholly and in very
truth possessed by it. But has it not happened, not once,
but a hundred, nay a thousand times, and every day, that,
with those same implements and under the same conditions,
I have embraced something else, which I have since concluded to be false ?

We must at least become wise at our own cost. If I have
often found myself betrayed marching under these colours ;
if my touchstone is usually at fault, and my scales uneven
and incorrect, what greater assurance can I have now than
at other times ?   Is it not folly to allow myself to be so
often misled by one guide ?

Nevertheless, though Fortune shift us five hundred times
from place to place, though she do nothing but unceasingly
empty and pour back into our belief, as into a vessel, other
and other opinions, the present and last one is ever the
certain and infallible one.   For this we must abandon
worldly goods, honour, life, salvation, and all :

> But then some later, likely better, find
> Destroys its worth and changes our desires
> Regarding good of yesterday. (LUCRETIUS.)

Whatever they preach to us, whatever we may learn, we

should still remember that it is a man that gives and a man
that takes. It is a mortal hand that offers it, it is a mortal
hand that accepts it. The things that come to us from
heaven have alone the right and authority to persuade,
they alone have the stamp of truth, which also we do not
see with our own eyes, nor receive by our own powers. That
great and holy image could not remain in so mean a habita-
tion, unless God prepared it for that purpose, unless God
repaired and strengthened it with his particular and supernatural grace and favour.

Our faulty condition should at least make us behave with
more moderation and discretion in our changes. We should
remember that whatever we receive into our understanding,
we often receive untruths, and that we receive them with
the aid of those same tools that often prove false and
deceptive.

Now it is no wonder if they prove false, being so easily
turned aside and twisted by the slightest events. It is
certain that our apprehension, our judgement, and the
faculties of our mind in general are affected by the movements and alterations of the body, which alterations are
continual. Is not our mind more wide-awake, our memory
more prompt, our reason more active, in health than in
sickness ? Do not things put on quite different faces when
we are in a gay and merry mood and when we are melancholy and oppressed by cares ? Do you think that the
verses of Catullus and Sappho smile upon a crabbed old
miser as they do upon a lusty and vigorous young man ?

Cleomenes, son of Anaxandridas, being sick, his friends
reproved him for his changed and unwonted humours and
fancies : ' I quite agree, he replied ; I am not the same
man I am in health. I being a different man, my opinions
and fancies are also different.'

The lawyers in our Palaces of Justice have a customary
saying, referring to a criminal who happens to have a judge
in good humour and an indulgent mood : *Gaudeat de bona
fortuna,* ' let him rejoice in his good fortune ! ' For it is
certain that we meet with judges who are at one time
harsher, more captious, more prone to convict, and at
another more easy-going, complaisant, and more inclined
to pardon. When Justice So-and-so leaves his house
suffering from the gout, from jealousy or from resentment

against his valet who has been robbing him, his whole soul
dyed and steeped in anger, we cannot doubt but that his
judgement will be warped accordingly.

That venerable Senate of the Areopagus used to sit in
judgement by night, lest the sight of the litigants might
corrupt their sense of justice. The very atmosphere and
the serenity of the sky have some power to change us,
according to these Greek lines, quoted by Cicero,

> The minds of men oft with the weather change,
> As the days, foul or fair, dark or serene. (HOMER.)

Not only do fevers, potions, and serious happenings upset
our judgement ; the least thing in the world will turn it
like a weather-cock. And there is no doubt, though we are
not conscious of it, that, if a continuous fever can prostrate
our soul, the tertian fever will impair it to a certain extent,
in proportion to its severity. If the apoplexy dims and
totally extinguishes the light of our intelligence, we cannot
doubt but that the influenza will blind it. And, consequently, hardly for a single hour in life will our judgement
chance to be in its proper trim, our body being subject to
so many continual changes, and stuffed with so many
different springs of action that (I take the word of the
physicians for it) it will be strange if there is not always
one that shoots wide of the mark.[1]

Moreover, this infirmity is not so easily detected, unless
it be extreme and quite past remedy ; inasmuch as reason
always walks crooked, lame and broken-hipped, and in the
company of falsehood as well as of the truth. Hence it is
difficult to discover her miscalculations and irregularities.

I always call by the name of Reason that semblance of it
which every man imagines himself to possess. This kind of
reason, which may have a hundred counterparts around
one and the same subject, all opposed to each other, is an
implement of lead and wax, that may be bent and stretched
and adapted to any bias and any measure ; it needs but
the skill to mould it. However well-meaning a judge may
be, if he does not closely hearken to his own conscience,
which few waste their time in doing, his leaning towards
friendship, kinship, the fair sex and revenge, and not only
things so weighty, but that fortuitous instinct which inclines

[1] Montaigne's mixed metaphors are often a little perplexing.

us to favour one thing more than another, and which, without the permission of reason, gives us the choice between two like objects, or some equally empty shadow, may imperceptibly creep into his judgement, and prompt him to allow or disallow a cause, and give a tip to the scales.

I, who watch myself more narrowly and have my eye continually bent on myself, as one that has no great business elsewhere,—

> I care not—not I—not a stiver,
>   Who in Scythia, frozen and drear,
> 'Neath the scourge of a tyrant may shiver,
>   Or who keeps Tiridates in fear,—(HORACE.)

I should hardly dare to tell of the vanity and weakness I am conscious of in myself. I am so unsteady and shaky on my feet, I am so inclined to trip and so apt to stumble, my sight is so irregular, that when fasting I am quite another man than after a meal. If health, and a fine, bright day smile upon me, behold me quite amiable ! If a corn trouble my toe, behold me sullen, disagreeable and quite unapproachable ! One and the same pace of my horse may appear to me now hard, now easy, the same road at one time shorter, at another longer, and the same shape now more now less agreeable. At this moment I am for doing anything, at another time for doing nothing. What is now a pleasure to me will sometimes be a drudgery. I am subject to a thousand rash and accidental impulses. I am possessed either by the melancholic or the choleric humour ; at this moment sadness predominates in me of its own accord, at another I am blithe and gay.

When I take up a book I may discover a charming and admirable passage, which strongly impresses my mind, whilst if I light upon the same passage on another occasion I may turn it over and over again in my mind, I may twist and bend it, but all in vain ; to me it is but a shapeless and unrecognizable mass.

Even in my own writings I cannot always recover the meaning of my former ideas ; I know not what I meant to say,[1] and often get into a regular heat, correcting and putting a new sense into it, having lost the first and better one.

[1] And no wonder !

I do nothing but come and go. My judgement does not always forge straight ahead ; it strays and wanders,

> Like a frail vessel caught on the mighty deep
> By stormy winds. (CATULLUS.)

Many a time having undertaken, by way of exercise or pastime, to support an opinion opposed to one I held (which I am fond of doing), my mind, turning and bending in the new direction, becomes so firmly attached to it, that I can no longer discover the reasons of my former belief, and so abandon it. I am dragged, as it were, the way I incline, whichever it may be, and am carried along by my own weight.

Every one almost could say the same of himself, if he looked into himself as I do. Preachers know that their own fervid eloquence in preaching animates their faith ; and that when angry we more hotly defend our proposition, we impress it upon ourselves and espouse it with greater vehemence and approval than we do in our cool and calm moments.

You state your case simply to a barrister, and he will answer you with doubts and hesitations ; you feel that it is a matter of indifference to him whether he takes up the one side or the other. If you have tempted him with a good fee to nibble at and take up your quarrel, will he not begin to take an interest in it and warm up his sympathy ? His reasoning powers and his learning are warmed up at the same time. See how his intelligence begins to discover an evident and indisputable truth ! He will detect an altogether new light thrown upon your case ; he honestly believes in it, and is convinced that he does so.

Nay, I know not if the ardour born of pique and obstinacy in his encounter with the violent attack of the law, and of his danger or the concern for his reputation, have not sent many a man to the stake in support of a belief for which, at liberty and among his friends, he would not have been willing to burn the tip of his finger.

The shocks and agitations that our soul receives through the bodily passions have a great influence upon her ; but still more have her own feelings, which have so strong a hold upon her, that it is perhaps tenable that she is only moved and propelled by the breath of her own winds, and that, unless stirred by them, she would remain inactive, like a ship becalmed on the open sea, to which the winds have denied their assistance. And whoever should maintain that belief (following therein the Peripatetics) would do us no great wrong, since it is a well-known fact that most of the noblest actions of the soul proceed from, and have need of, this impulsion of the feelings. Valour, they say, cannot become perfect without the aid of anger :

Ajax was ever brave, but bravest when in wrath. (CICERO.)

And we do not set upon the wicked, or our enemies, vigorously enough, unless we are angry. And they say that the barrister must provoke the judge to anger in order to obtain justice.

Strong passions moved Themistocles, moved Demosthenes, and have spurred the Philosophers to labour night and day, and to travel in distant countries ; they lead us to honour, to learning, to health : useful ends. And that faintheartedness with which we suffer grief and trouble helps to nourish remorse and repentance in the conscience, and make us feel that the scourges of God are for our chastisement, as well as the scourges of public correction.

Compassion acts as a spur to clemency ; and the wisdom to preserve and govern our lives is aroused by our fear. How many fine actions are due to ambition ! how many to presumption ! In short, no conspicuous and gallant valour but is caused by some unruly emotion.

Is it not possible that this is one of the reasons that moved the Epicureans to relieve God of all care and solicitude about our affairs, since his goodness cannot work its effects upon us without disturbing his repose through passions, which are so many spurs and incitements driving the soul to virtuous actions ? Or did they think otherwise, and regard them as tempests which shamefully seduce the soul out of her tranquillity ? *As we imagine the sea to be calm, when not the least breath of air stirs its waves ; so we judge the soul to be tranquil and at rest when no passion can stir her* (Cicero).

How variously our passions react upon our thoughts and reasoning faculties, and change our ideas to their very opposites ! What reliance then can we place in a thing so unstable and shifting, liable by its condition to be domineered by mental disturbances, and never going but a

forced and borrowed pace ? If our judgement be at the
mercy of sickness and violent emotions ; if folly and madness are bound to influence the impression we receive of
things, what reliance can we place in it ?

Is it not very rash on the part of Philosophy to suppose
that men perform their greatest actions, and those most
nearly approaching to divinity, when they are furious and
mad, and beside themselves ?   We are thought to become
better by the deadening and privation of our reason.   The
two natural ways by which to enter into the cabinet of the
gods, and there to foresee the course of destinies, are madness
and sleep. This is a quaint notion, that by the dislocation
of our reason through our passions we become virtuous ;
that by its annihilation in madness or sleep, the image of
death, we become soothsayers and prophets !

I was never more ready to believe it. It is a pure frenzy
which the sacred Truth has breathed into the spirit of
Philosophy, which wrests from it the confession, contrary
to its own standpoint, that the tranquil state of our soul,
the composed state, the healthiest state that philosophy
can win for her, is not her best state. Our waking state is
more asleep than sleep ; our wisdom is less wise than
madness. Our dreams are better than our reason. The
worst abode we can choose is in ourselves.

But does Philosophy think that we are not wise enough
to remark that the voice that renders the spirit, when
detached from man, so clear-sighted, so great, so perfect,
and, whilst it is in man, so earthly, ignorant, and cloudy,
is a voice proceeding from the spirit which is a part of
earthly, ignorant, and cloudy man ; and, for that reason,
a voice not to be trusted and believed ?

I, who am of a dull and easy disposition, have no great experience of those violent emotions, most of which suddenly
take our soul unawares, without giving her time to recollect
herself. But that passion which is said to arise in the hearts
of young men through idleness, although it walks with a
leisurely and measured step, very evidently manifests, to
those who have tried to resist its influence, the violence of
the alteration and subversion which our judgement suffers.

I have at other times attempted to arm myself to withstand and repel its advances (for I am so far from being one
of those who encourage vices, that I would not even follow

them, unless forcibly dragged by them). I would feel the beginning, the growth and increase of the passion in spite of my resistance, and in the end, quite alive and with open eyes, I would be seized and possessed by it, to such a degree that, as in drunkenness, things adopted quite a different appearance from the ordinary. The attractions of the desired object would visibly swell and increase ; they would be blown out and expanded by the breath of my imagination. The difficulties of the pursuit appeared to be smoothed and levelled, my reason and conscience appeared to withdraw into the background. But, this fire being damped all in an instant, as it were in the brilliance of a flash of lightning, my soul would recover another kind of sight, another state and another judgement ; the difficulties of retreat would appear great and insurmountable, and the same things would take on quite a different aspect and taste to that which they offered in the heat of desire.

Which had the more likelihood ? Pyrrho cannot tell.

We are never without sickness. Fevers have their hot and cold periods ; from the effects of a burning passion we fall back into the effects of a shivery passion.

As far as I had shot forward, so far do I recoil backwards :

> As when, with alternating ebb and flow,
> The advancing sea now rushes to the beach,
> Shoots o'er the crags in torrent foam, and bathes
> With curved billow all the sandy bourne,
> Now, with swift ebb, retreats, and sucking back
> The shingle, leaves the beach with gliding shoal. (VIRGIL.)

Now, being conscious of this my liability to change, I have accidentally cultivated in myself a certain steadfastness of belief, and have hardly altered my original and natural opinions. For, however much new fashions may appeal to me, I do not readily change, for fear of losing by the exchange. And since I am not capable of choosing for myself, I accept the choice of others, and remain in the state wherein God has placed me. Otherwise I could not keep from perpetual rolling. Thus, by the grace of God, I have kept wholly, without being stirred or troubled by conscience, within the ancient tenets of our religion, amidst the many sects and divisions that our times have brought forth.

The writings of the ancients, I mean the good, serious and pregnant works, allure and carry me almost whither they please ; the one I am listening to always appears to me the most forcible. I find each one right in his turn, although they contradict one another. The ease with which strong minds lend probability to whatever they please, and the fact that nothing is so strange but that they will try to colour it sufficiently to deceive a simplicity like mine, manifestly shows the weakness of their proof.

The heavens and the stars have been swinging round for three thousand years, as all the world had believed, until Cleanthes of Samos, or, according to Theophrastus, Nicetas of Syracuse, presumed to proclaim that it was the earth that moved, revolving about its axis, through the oblique circle of the zodiac. And, in our days, Copernicus has so well grounded this theory, that he very lawfully uses it for all astronomical conclusions. What can we make of that, except that we need not bother our heads about which of the two theories is right ? And who knows but that a third opinion, a thousand years hence, will overthrow the two former ?

Thus it is
That rolling ages change the times of things :
What erst was of a price, becomes at last
A discard of no honour ; whilst another
Succeeds to glory, issuing from contempt,
And day by day is sought for more and more,
And, when 'tis found, doth flower in men's praise,
Object of wondrous honour. (LUCRETIUS.)

Thus, when we are offered some new theory, we have great reason to distrust it, and to remember that before it was introduced the contrary was in vogue ; and as that was overthrown by this, a third discovery may start up, in time to come, which may knock the second on the head.

Before the principles which Aristotle introduced were in repute, other principles satisfied human reason, as his satisfy us at this moment. What letters-patent, what special privilege have these, that the course of our discoveries should stop at them, and that they should for all time to come possess our belief ? They are no more exempt from being thrust out of doors than their forerunners.

When I am driven into a corner by a new argument, I ought to consider that what I cannot answer satisfactorily, another will answer ; for to believe all the likely things we

cannot confute is great simplicity. It would follow therefrom that the belief of all common people (and we are all
common people) would be as versatile as a weather-cock.
For their minds, being soft and unresisting, would be continually forced to receive other and other impressions, the
last ever effacing the traces of the preceding one. He who
finds himself at a loss must answer, according to the usual
practice in law-suits, that he will confer with his counsel; or he
will refer to the wisest of those who have been his teachers.

How long has medicine been in the world ? It is said
that a new-comer, whom they call Paracelsus,[1] is changing
and reversing the whole order of ancient rules, and maintaining that to this hour that science has been of no service
but to kill men. I believe that he can easily verify that
statement. But I do not think it would be very wise to
stake my life on the proof of his novel experiments.

We must not believe every man, says the adage, because
any man may say anything.

One of those men who profess new and improved methods
in physics said to me not long ago that all the ancients had
evidently miscalculated the nature and motion of the winds,
which he would make very palpable to me if I would give
ear to him. After listening with some patience to his
arguments, which had all the appearance of likelihood,
' What ! I answered, did those who navigated under the
laws of Theophrastus go west when they were steering east ?
Did they go sideways or backwards ? ' ' That was chance,
he replied ; at all events they miscalculated.' I then
replied that I would rather believe facts than reasons.

Now those are things that often clash, and I have been
told that in Geometry (which thinks it has reached the
high-water mark of certainty among the sciences) may be
found irrefutable demonstrations that subvert the truth of
experience. For example, Jacques Pelletier said to me in
my house, that he had discovered two lines that started out
to meet, which nevertheless he proved could never meet
to all eternity. And the Pyrrhonians employ their argu-

---

[1] Theophrastus von Hohenheim, a Swiss physician who adopted the
rather pretentious name of Paracelsus (' greater than Celsus '). ' His
method and influence tended in the direction of the immediate observation
of nature, the discarding of antiquated theories, the encouragement of
independent research, experiments and innovation.'—*Chambers's Ency-
clopaedia*.

ments and their reason only to wreck the apparent facts of experience ; and it is marvellous how far the nimbleness of our reason has followed them in their design to resist the evidence of facts. For they demonstrate that we do not move, that we do not speak, that there is neither weight nor heat, with the same force of arguments with which we prove the most likely things.

Ptolemy, who was a great man, had fixed the limits of our world, and all the ancient philosophers thought they had taken its measure, excepting some remote islands which might have escaped their notice. A thousand years ago it would have been a case of Pyrrhonizing to question the science of cosmography, and its universally accepted conclusions. It was heresy to admit the existence of Antipodes. And behold ! in this century of ours there has just been discovered an infinite extent of terra firma, not merely an island or one particular country, but a hemisphere nearly equal in extent to the one we knew ! The geographers of our time do not stick at assuring us that to-day all is discovered, everything has been seen :

> For what we have at hand,
> That chiefly pleases and seems best of all. (LUCRETIUS.)

The question is, if Ptolemy, grounding his belief on reason, was once mistaken, whether it would not be foolish on my part now to trust the word of those geographers ; and whether it is not more likely that this great body which we call the World is quite another thing than we imagine.

Plato maintains that it changes its aspect in every way ; that the heavens, the stars and the sun at times reverse the motion we see, changing east to west. The Egyptian priests told Herodotus that since their first king, who lived eleven thousand and odd years before their time (and they showed him the effigies of all their kings, in the form of statues taken from the life), the sun had four times altered its course ; That the sea and the land alternately change into one another ; That the birth of the world has not been determined.

Aristotle and Cicero say the same. And some one [1] amongst us affirms, that the world has existed from all eternity ; that it is mortal, and comes to life again after

[1] Origen.

many changes, calling Solomon and Isaiah to witness, in
order to evade those objections, that God has at some time
been a creator without a creature ; that he has been idle ;
that he abandoned his idleness by setting his hand to this
work ; and that he is consequently subject to change.

In the most famous of the Greek schools [1] the World is
regarded as a god made by another and greater god, and
is composed of a body, and of a soul situated in the centre
of it, spreading, by musical numbers, to its circumference ;
divine, very happy, very great, very wise, eternal. In it
are other gods, the earth, the sea, the stars, which entertain
one another with a harmonious and perpetual motion and
divine dance ; now meeting, now parting, hiding, showing
themselves, changing their order, sometimes in front, sometimes behind.

Heraclitus declared that the World was composed by
fire ; and that, by order of the Fates, it would some day
be kindled and resolve itself into fire, and some day would be
born again. And of men Apuleius says, *Severally mortal,
as a body perpetual.*

Alexander wrote to his mother a story told to him by an
Egyptian priest, which the latter had gathered from their
monuments, and which evidenced the extreme antiquity of
that nation and comprised a true account of the birth and
progress of other countries.

Cicero and Diodorus say that in their day the Chaldeans
kept a record of four hundred thousand odd years ;

Aristotle, Pliny, and others, that Zoroaster lived six
thousand years before the age of Plato.

Plato says that the people of the city of Saïs possess
written records of eight thousand years, and that the city of
Athens was built a thousand years before the said city of Saïs ;

Epicurus, that whilst the things of this world are as we
see them, they are quite alike and after the same fashion
in many other worlds. Which he would have said with
greater assurance, if he had seen how the conditions of that
new world of the West Indies resemble and correspond to
those of our own in the present and the past, as shown by
such strange examples.

In truth, when we consider the things that have come to
our knowledge regarding the course of this terrestrial

---

[1] The Platonic School.

government, I have often marvelled to see, divided by great distances of time and place, so many coincidences in popular, fabulous ideas, so many uncivilized customs and beliefs, which, from whatever side we may look at them, seem to have no connexion with our inborn reason. The human mind is a great worker of miracles. But in this correspondence there is a something much more anomalous which I am unable to define. It shows itself also in names, in many incidents, and in a thousand other things.

For in that newly-discovered hemisphere were found nations who, as far as we know, had never heard of our world ; some that believed in circumcision ; regions in which great states were governed by women, without the help of men ; where our Lent and fastings were reflected, with the addition of abstinence from women. Where, as with us, the cross, in varying shapes, was held in honour. In one place tombs were adorned with it ; in another it was worn by people, especially the St. Andrew's cross, to protect themselves against nocturnal visions, or placed on the beds of children against enchantments. In another place they came upon a very tall wooden cross which was worshipped as the god of rain, and that very far inland.

There they found a very plain likeness of our shriving-priests, besides the wearing of mitres, the celibacy of the priesthood, the art of divining by the entrails of sacrificed animals, abstinence from every kind of flesh and fish in their diet ; the custom of the priests, when officiating, to use a special language in place of the vulgar tongue. And that fanciful notion that the first god was ousted by a second, his younger brother. That men were created with all kinds of advantages, which were afterwards taken from them for their sin ; that they were removed from their land and reduced to a worse condition.

That they were once submerged by an inundation of waters from heaven ; that only a few families escaped, who fled into the caves of high mountains, which caves they stopped up, so that the water could not come in, having shut up therein many kinds of animals ; that when they perceived the rain to be ceasing, they drove out some dogs, which returning clean and wet, they concluded that the waters had not yet quite subsided ; then sending out other dogs and seeing them return muddy, they issued forth to repeople the world, which they found full of nothing but snakes.

In one place they met with the belief in a Day of Judgement, so that the people took very great offence when the Spaniards scattered the bones of their dead in their search of the tombs for rich spoils, saying that those bones they had dispersed could not easily rejoin. They have trade by barter, and no other kind; fairs and markets for that purpose; dwarfs and misshapen persons to grace the tables of their princes; the practice of falconry according to the nature of their birds; tyrannical subsidies; refinements in horticulture; dancing and tumbling; the music of instruments; coats of arms; tennis-courts, dice and games of chance, at which they often become so excited that they will stake their persons and their freedom; no medicine but that of charms; the system of writing in pictures.

The belief of a single first man, father of all the nations; worship of a God who once lived as a man in perfect virginity, who, with fasting and penitence, preached the law of Nature and religious ceremonies, and who vanished from the world without dying a natural death. The belief in giants; the custom of drinking to excess and getting drunk with their liquor; religious ornaments with painted bones and deaths' heads; surplices, holy water, and sprinklers; the custom of wives and slaves vying in their eagerness to be burned or interred with their dead husbands or masters; the law by which the eldest son succeeds to the whole property, the younger having no portion but obedience; the custom, at the promotion to a certain office of great authority, of the promoted taking a new name and discarding his own; the custom of strewing lime on the knee of a new-born infant, with these words: ' From dust thou art come, to dust shalt thou return; ' the art of augury.

These empty shadows of our religion, which are seen in some of these examples, bear witness to its dignity and divinity. Not only has it insinuated itself to some extent into all the infidel nations on this side of the world, by a sort of imitation, but also into those barbarians, as by a universal and natural inspiration. For they also found a belief in a Purgatory, but in a new form : what we give to the fire they give to the cold, and imagine the souls to be both purged and punished by the severity of extreme cold.

And this example reminds me of another amusing diversity ; for, as there were some nations who found a satisfaction in unsheathing the end of their member, removing the skin after the manner of the Mahommedans and Jews, there were others who made so great a scruple about laying it bare, that, very carefully stretching the skin, they brought it up and fastened it with little cords, for fear lest the end might see the air.

And this diversity too, that, whereas we, in honour of kings and festivals, dress ourselves up in the handsomest clothes we possess, in some regions, to emphasize their disparity and their submission to their king, his subjects present themselves before him in their meanest attire, or on entering the palace throw some tattered old gown over their good one, that all the lustre and ornament may remain with their lord.

But let us continue. If Nature encloses within the bounds of her ordinary progress, besides all other things, the beliefs, judgements, and opinions of men ; if these beliefs have their revolving seasons, their birth, their death, like cabbages ; if heaven moves and rolls them about at its pleasure, what magisterial and permanent authority are we to attribute to them ? If experience makes it palpable to us that the form of our being depends on the atmosphere, the climate and the soil on which we are born, and not only our complexion, our stature, our constitution and countenance, but also the faculties of our mind—*the climate affects not only the vigour of the body, but also that of the soul,* says Vegetius— ; and if the goddess who founded the city of Athens chose for its situation a region whose temperature made men cunning, as the priests of Egypt told Solon :—*the air of Athens is light, wherefore the Athenians are reputed to be more astute ; that of Thebes is heavy, wherefore the Thebans are more dull-witted and more robust* (Cicero)— ; so that, as fruits and animals are born differing among one another, men are born more or less warlike, just, temperate and docile ; here given to wine, elsewhere to theft and lechery ; here inclined to superstition, elsewhere to unbelief ; here to freedom, there to slavery ; capable of one science or one art ; dull or clever ; obedient or rebellious ; good or bad, according as the place where they live inclines them ; and assume a new disposition if they change from one place to another, like the trees ; which was the reason why Cyrus would not grant the Persians permission to leave their rugged and hilly country and remove to another that was level and mild, saying that a fat and soft soil made men soft, and a fertile land made barren brains ; if at one time we see one art, one belief to flourish, at another time another, by virtue of some celestial influence ; if we see such or such an age produce such or such natures, and bend humankind to such or such a ply ; the minds of men now luxuriant, now lean, like our fields ; what becomes of all those fine prerogatives on which we flatter ourselves ? Since a wise man may go wrong, and a hundred men, and many nations ; nay, since even human nature, in our belief, may for many centuries go wrong in this thing or that ; what assurance can we have that it will at some time cease to go wrong, and that in this century it is not on the wrong track ?

Among other evidence of our imbecility I think that this deserves not to be forgotten, That even man's desire will not enable him to find out what he needs ; That, I will not say by enjoyment, but in imagination and wish, we are unable to agree about what we need for our satisfaction. Let our imagination cut out and sew at its pleasure, it cannot even desire what is meet for it, and be satisfied :

> For when does Reason guide desire or fear ?
> What plan dost thou conceive so happily,
> But that thou wilt repent of thy endeavour
> And of the granted prayer ? (JUVENAL.)

Therefore it was that Socrates prayed to the gods to give him nothing but what they knew to be good for him. And the import of the Lacedemonian's prayer, both public and private, was simply that he might be granted good and beautiful things, leaving the choice and selection of them to the discretion of the supreme powers :

> We pray for wife and child, but those above
> Are well aware what child and wife will prove. (JUVENAL.)

And the Christian prays to God that ' his will be done ', in order not to fall into the calamity that the poets invent for King Midas. He prayed the gods that everything he touched might turn to gold. His prayer was heard. His wine was gold, his bread gold, and the feathers of his bed, his shirt and clothes were all of gold, so that he found him-

self overwhelmed in the realization of his desire, and gifted
with a privilege that proved intolerable. He was fain to
unpray his prayer :

> Amazed at this calamity so rare,
> To be so rich, yet pitiably poor,
> He wishes now he could his wealth evade,
> And curses that for which before he prayed. (OVID.)

Take my own case. Being young, I desired of Fortune, as
much as anything else, the order of Saint Michael ; for at
that time it was the greatest mark of honour with the
French nobility, and very rare. She ironically gratified my
desire. Instead of raising and lifting me up from my station
to reach it, she treated me much more graciously : she
debased it and brought it down to the level of my shoulders,
and even below that.[1]

Cleobis and Bito, Triphonius and Agamedes, having be-
sought, the former of their goddess, the latter of their god,
a recompense worthy of their piety, received death for their
gift. So much do the gods differ from us as to what is good
for us !

God might sometimes grant us wealth, honours, life and
even health, to our prejudice ; for what is pleasing is not
always good for us. If, instead of a cure, he sends us death
or an aggravation of our ills—*thy rod and thy staff they
comfort me* (Psalms)—he does so for providential reasons, for
he takes account of what is our due much more unerringly
than we can do ; and we must accept it gladly, as from a
very wise and a very loving hand :

> Take my advice : allow the Gods themselves
> To weigh what is most meet we should receive,
> And to our state most profitable . . .
> Man is more dear to them than to himself. (JUVENAL.)

For to beg of them honours or offices is to beg of them to hurl
you into a battle, or a game of dice, or something of a like
nature, of which the issue is unknown to you, and the
advantage doubtful.

There is no strife among the Philosophers so violent and
so bitter as that which arises over the question of the

---

[1] This order was afterwards superseded as the greatest distinction by
the Order of the Holy Ghost, founded by Henri III, and it greatly fell in
estimation.

sovereign good of man, which, according to Varro's calculation, brought forth two hundred and eighty-eight sects. *But
whoever disagrees with me about the chief good, disagrees with
me about the whole principle of philosophy* (Cicero).

> I have three guests to dine. Alas for me,
> Their tastes about no single dish agree !
> What shall I give ? What not ? You can't abide
> The very thing for which another cried,
> And what I give as a *bonne bouche* to you
> Is sour and odious to the other two. (HORACE.)

Nature should give the same answer to all their disput-
tings and quarrellings.

Some say that our well-being lies in Virtue, others in
Pleasure, others again in conforming to Nature ; this man
in knowledge, that in freedom from pain, this other in not
allowing ourselves to be led away by appearances. (And
this last idea seems to come near to that of the ancient
Pythagoras :

> To wonder at naught is all the art I know
> To make men happy and to keep them so ; [HORACE.]

which is the aim of the Pyrrhonian school.)

Aristotle attributes this being amazed at nothing to greatness of soul. And Arcesilaus said that to suspend one's
judgement and to keep it upright and inflexible is good,
but to consent and yield is bad and deplorable. It is true
that in setting this up as a certain axiom he departed from
Pyrrhonism. The Pyrrhonians, when they say that the
sovereign good is Ataraxy, which is the immobility of the
judgement, do not mean it in an affirmative sense ; but the
same impulse of their soul which makes them shun a precipice and take shelter from the cool of the evening, itself
suggests this fancy and makes them reject any other.

How I could wish that, whilst I live, either another or
Justus Lipsius,[1] the most learned man still remaining to us,
a man of a most polished and judicious mind, true cousin-
german to my Turnebus, had the will, as well as the health
and sufficient leisure, carefully and honestly, and according
to our lights, to collect and make a divided and classified
list of all the theories of ancient philosophy on the subject

[1] Justus Lipsius, a Belgian scholar with whom Montaigne corresponded. He partially fulfilled this wish in a large work on Stoicism,
which appeared after Montaigne's death.

of our being and our conduct of life ; their controversies, showing how the different schools succeeded one another and in what repute they were held, how the founders and followers applied their own precepts on memorable and exemplary occasions in their lives ! What a fine and useful work that would be !

Moreover, if we ourselves determine the rule of our conduct, into what a confusion we are thrown ! For the counsel that our reason is most likely to give us is that every man generally shall obey the laws of his country, which was the advice of Socrates, inspired, as he says, by divine counsel. And what does reason mean thereby, if not that our duty is only guided by chance ?

Truth ought to have one face, always and everywhere the same. If a man's justice and equity had any substance and real existence, he would not let it be bound by the conditions and customs of this country or that. It would not be from the ideas of the Persians or Indians that virtue would take its shape.

There is nothing more subject to continual change than the laws. During my lifetime I have known the laws of our neighbours the English to change and change back again three or four times ; not only in political matters, wherein permanence may be dispensed with, but in the most important subject that can be, to wit, religion. Whereat I am the more shamed and grieved as they are a nation with whom the people of my district were once so intimately acquainted, that there yet remain in my household some traces of our old cousinship.[1]

And here at home I have known a thing to become lawful which used to be a capital offence ; [2] and we who hold other opinions may quite possibly one day, so uncertain are the fortunes of war, become guilty of high treason, both against men and God, should our justice fall under the mercy of injustice, and, after a few years' possession, assume a contrary character.

How could that ancient God [3] more clearly accuse human knowledge of ignorance of the divine being, and give men to understand that their religion was but a thing of their own

---

[1] Guienne belonged to England from 1152 to 1453.
[2] Montaigne is perhaps thinking of the Protestant faith.
[3] Apollo.

contrivance, and useful as a social bond, than by declaring, as he did to those who sought instruction of his tripod, ' That the true worship for every man was that which he found observed by the custom of the place where he lived ? '

O heavens ! how greatly we are under obligation to the goodness of our sovereign Creator for having purged our belief of those vagrant and arbitrary devotions, and fixed it on the eternal foundation of his holy word !

What then will Philosophy tell us in this strait ? ' That we must follow the laws of our country ? ' That is to say, that surging sea of the beliefs of a people or a ruler, who will paint me justice in so many colours, and reshape it into as many forms as there are changes of passion in themselves. I cannot have a judgement so flexible. What kind of good-ness can that be that was yesterday held in honour, and will cease to be so to-morrow, and which the mere crossing of a river turns into a crime ?

What kind of truth can that be that is bounded by these mountains, and that becomes a lie to the people on the other side of them ?

But those people amuse me who, to give some certainty to laws, say that there are some that are fixed, perpetual and immutable, which they call laws of Nature, and which, by the very condition of their being, are imprinted in humankind. And of these some say there are three, some four, some more, some less ; a sign that it is a mark as doubtful as the rest. Now, they are in such a hapless case (for what else can I call it but haplessness, that out of so infinite a number of laws there does not happen to be one at least that has been permitted by Fortune and the heed-lessness of chance to be universally accepted by the consent of all nations ?), they are, I say, so unhappy, that of those three or four selected laws there is not one that is not rejected and disowned, not by one nation, but by many.

Now the only likely token, by which they can argue some laws to be natural, is universality of approval. For what Nature has truly commanded us we should without doubt obey with universal consent. And not only every nation, but every individual, would resent the force and violence that any one should put upon him to drive him to oppose that law. Let them produce me a law of that kind, that I may prove it.

Protagoras and Aristo gave no other justification of the laws than the authority and judgement of the law-giver ; and held that, apart from this, the words ' good ' and ' honest ' would lose their meaning, and become empty names of indifferent things.

Thrasymachus, in Plato, thinks there is no other right but the convenience of the superior.

There is nothing in which the world varies so much as in customs and laws. Many a thing is abominable here that is commended elsewhere ; as in Sparta cleverness in stealing. Marriages with near relations are capital offences with us, and are in other countries held in honour :

> Some nations, so 'tis said, there are,
> Where fathers daughters, sons their mothers wed,
> And love is deepened by the double tie. (OVID.)

The murder of infants, the murder of fathers, community of wives, traffic in robberies, licence in all sorts of pleasures ; nothing in short is so outrageous but it may be allowed by the custom of some nation or other.

I can quite believe that there are laws of Nature, such as we may observe in other creatures ; but in us they have vanished, this fine human reason of ours thrusting itself into everything, commanding and domineering, confusing and distorting the face of things, in its vanity and inconsistency. *Nothing is any longer really ours ; what I call ours is the result of art* (Cicero).

Things may be considered from various points of view, which is the chief cause of diversity of opinions. One nation views a thing from one side, and stops there, another from another side.

Nothing more horrible can be imagined than to eat one's father. The people who formerly observed this custom, however, regarded it as evidence of piety and natural affection, as they thought by that means to give their progenitors the most honourable and worthy sepulture, harbouring in themselves, and as it were in their marrow, the bodies and remains of their fathers ; in some sort resuscitating and regenerating them by transmutation into their living flesh, by means of digestion and nourishment. We may easily imagine what cruelty and abomination it would have been to men steeped and imbued with this superstition, to throw their parents' mortal remains to the corruption of the earth, and to be food for beasts and worms.

Lycurgus considered theft from the point of view of the quickness, the agility, the impudence and skill with which a neighbour was done out of a thing, and the benefit which redounded to the people in general by every man looking more carefully to the safe keeping of what was his ; and believed that this double instruction in attack and defence was to the advantage of military discipline (which was the principal science and virtue in which he desired to train his people), and of much greater consideration than the disorder and injustice resulting from the purloining of others' property.

Dionysius the Tyrant offered Plato a long, figured, perfumed gown in the Persian fashion. Plato declined it, saying that, being born a man, he would not willingly dress in a woman's gown ; but Aristippus accepted it with this reply, ' that no apparel could corrupt a chaste heart.' His friends taunted him with want of spirit for being so unconcerned when Dionysius spat in his face. ' A fisherman, he said, will suffer himself to be dashed from head to foot by the sea-waves, to catch a gudgeon.' Diogenes was washing his cabbages and, seeing him pass, said, ' If you could live on cabbage, you would not fawn upon a tyrant ' ; to which Aristippus retorted, ' If you could live among men, you would not be washing cabbages.'

Thus does Reason provide a different point of view for different actions. It is a two-handled jug which can be grasped by the left or the right.

> War it is thou bringest,
> O stranger-country ! Steeds are armed for war,
> And war these herds portend us. Yet at times
> The same beasts use to bow them to the car,
> And, yoked together, bear the friendly rein ;
> Yes, there is hope for peace too. (VIRGIL.)

Some one was admonishing Solon not to shed vain and bootless tears for the death of his son. ' It is for that reason, he said, that I more rightly shed them, because they are bootless and vain.' Socrates' wife aggravated her grief by this consideration : ' Oh, how unjust of these wicked judges to put him to death ! ' ' Would you then rather that they should execute me justly ? ' he replied.

We have our ears bored ; the Greeks regarded that as a mark of slavery. We retire into privacy to enjoy our wives ; the Indians do it publicly. The Scythians immolated strangers in their temples ; elsewhere temples are a sanctuary :

> All peoples are with hate and fury filled
> For that their neighbours kneel to other Gods,
> Deeming none others can be recognized
> But their own deities. (JUVENAL.)

I have heard of a judge who, when he came across a sharp conflict between Bartolus and Baldus,[1] or some point discussed with many contradictions, was wont to write in the margin of his book, ' Question for a friend ' ; that is to say, that the truth was so entangled and debatable, that in a similar case he might favour whichever of the parties he thought fit. It needed but a little more wit and cleverness to write in all cases ' Question for a friend '. The lawyers and judges of our day discover in all cases enough bias to incline them to whichever side they please.

In a branch of learning of such infinite range, depending on the authority of so many opinions, and in so arbitrary a subject, there must necessarily be many conflicting judgements. And so we see that, be a law-suit never so clear, opinions regarding it will be found to differ. The judgement of one court is reversed by another, and on another occasion by itself. As a result of this licence, which is a marvellous blemish on the solemn authority and lustre of our courts of justice, it is quite usual to be dissatisfied with a sentence, and to run from court to court for a decision on the same case.

As to the freedom of philosophical thought concerning Vice and Virtue, that is a matter on which there is no need to expatiate, and on which there are many opinions which it would be better to hush up and not publish abroad for the weaker minds.

Arcesilaus said that in lechery it mattered little on which side or where it was committed. *As to lascivious pleasures, Epicurus thinks that, if nature requires them, we are not to regard birth, place or rank, but age, beauty and person* (Cicero). *Nor do we think virtuous love inconsistent with a wise man* (Cicero). *Let us consider up to what age youths are*

---

[1] Two eminent Italian lawyers of the fourteenth century.

to be loved (Seneca). These two last citations from the
Stoics, and the reproach of Dicaearchus to Plato himself on
this subject,[1] show what excessive and unnatural licence
even the soundest philosophy will tolerate.

The laws derive their authority from possession and use ;
it is dangerous to trace them back to their origin. They
grow and gather dignity as they roll on, like our rivers.
Follow them upstream to their source, it is but a little
spring of water scarce discernible, which thus grows in pride
and strength as it grows older. Look at the ancient motives
which gave the first start to this famous torrent, so authoritative, awe-inspiring and venerable ; you will find them so
trifling and slender that it is no wonder that these people,
who weigh and reduce everything to reason, and who accept
nothing by authority and on trust, find that their judgements are often very remote from those of the people.

It is no wonder if people who take their pattern from the
first image of Nature, in most of their opinions swerve from
the common path. As, for instance, few of them [2] would
have approved the strict conditions of our marriages ; and
most of them would have wished wives to be held in common
and without obligation. They rejected our proprieties.

[Everybody has heard of the want of shame shown by the
Cynic philosophers in their conduct.] Chrysippus said that
a philosopher will turn a dozen somersaults in public, even
without his breeches, for a dozen of olives. He would hardly
have advised Cleisthenes to refuse his daughter, the beautiful
Agarista, to Hippoclides, because he saw him stand on his
head with his legs apart on a table.

Metrocles broke wind rather indiscreetly while disputing
in presence of his school, and kept his house for shame, until
Crates went to see him, and, after consoling and reasoning
with him, set him an example of licence, urged him to a
competition in wind-breaking, and so cured him of his
scruples ; and besides, drew him over to his freer Stoical
sect, from the more urbane Peripatetic school of which he
had hitherto been a follower.

What we call Decency—not to dare to do that openly
which it is proper to do in private—they call Foolishness ;
and the affectation of concealing and condemning those of

[1] i. e., for countenancing pederasty.
[2] i. e., few of the ancient philosophers.

our actions which nature, custom, and our desire publish and proclaim, they reputed a vice. And they held that it was profaning the mysteries of Venus to remove them from the secluded sanctuary of her temple, and expose them to the people's gaze ; and that to draw her sports from behind the curtain was to cheapen them. (Shame is a weighty coin. Concealment, reservation, limitation, have their share in its estimation.) They held that voluptuousness very ingeniously protested, under the mask of virtue, against being prostituted in the middle of the highways, trodden under the feet and eyes of the crowd, prizing rather the dignity and convenience of its wonted cabinets.

Wherefore some say that to abolish the public brothels is not only to spread about everywhere the fornication that was assigned to those places, but also to spur men on to that vice, by making it difficult :

Thou, once her husband, art become her lover,
  Now that she is thy rival's spouse ;
Why should'st thou love another's, and not thine own ?
  Art impotent without the risk ? (MARTIAL.)

This experience is diversified in a thousand examples :

Scarce one in all the city would embrace
  Thy proffered wife, Cecilian, free to have ;
But now she's guarded and locked up, apace
  Thy custom comes. Oh, thou art a wily knave ! (MARTIAL.)

A philosopher who was surprised in the act, and was asked what he was doing, replied, ' I am planting a man ; ' no more blushing at being so caught than if he had been found planting garlic.[1]

I think it was out of over tenderness and respect that a great writer and monk [2] maintained that this action was so necessarily bound up with concealment and modesty, that he could not be persuaded that those shameless embraces of the Cynics were effectual ; but that they stopped short at imitating lascivious motions, in order to keep up the reputation for shamelessness which their school of philosophy professed ; and that it was still necessary for them to seek the shade to eject what shame had withheld and restrained.

[1] This story of Diogenes has had a wide circulation, but, according to Bayle, has never been traced. Give the devil his due !
[2] Saint Augustine, in his *City of God*.

He had not seen far enough into their debauchery. For Diogenes, behaving indecently in public, expressed a wish, in presence of the bystanders ' that he could as easily satisfy his hunger by rubbing his belly '. To those who asked him why he did not seek a more convenient place for eating than the open street, he answered, ' Because I am hungry in the open street.'

The women philosophers who mixed with their sect also mixed with their persons in all places and without discrimination ; and Hipparchia was received into the society of Crates only on condition of following in all things the uses and customs of his order.

These philosophers set an extreme price upon Virtue, and rejected any but a moral teaching. And yet in all their actions they attributed the chief authority to the choice of their sage, as being above the laws ; and placed no other check upon sensual pleasures but moderation and the preservation of others' liberty.

Heraclitus and Protagoras argued from the fact that wine seems bitter to the sick man and grateful to the sound, and that an oar appears bent in the water and straight outside of it, and from the like contradictory appearances in other things that all objects had in themselves the causes of their appearances : that in wine there was a certain bitterness which corresponded with the sick man's palate, and in the oar a certain bent quality which corresponds with the person who looks at it in the water. And so with all the rest. Which is as much as to say that everything is in all things, and consequently nothing in any ; for where all is, nothing is.

This theory puts me in mind of what we know by experience, that there is no meaning or aspect, either straight, or bitter, or sweet, or crooked, that the wit of man cannot find in the writings he may undertake to dig into. Into the clearest, simplest, and most perfect language imaginable, how many lies and falsehoods have not been read ! What heresy has not found in them sufficient grounds and evidence, both for attack and defence ? For this reason it is that the originators of such errors will never let go the proof and evidence afforded by their interpretation of words.

A certain dignitary, trying to justify to me by authority

the search for the philosopher's stone, in which he is
entirely absorbed, recently quoted to me five or six passages
from the Bible, on which he said he relied principally for
the discharge of his conscience (for he is an ecclesiastic by
profession) ; and indeed the discovery was not only amusing,
but also very properly suited to the defence of that pretty
branch of learning.

In this way do the diviners' fables gain credit. There is
no prophet of so great authority that people will think it
worth while turning over his pages and carefully examining
his words from every side and in their remotest meanings,
who cannot be made to say whatever we please, like the
Sibyls. For there are so many ways and means of interpreting a thing, that it can hardly be but that an ingenious
mind will discover in any subject, either obliquely or
directly, some meaning that will serve his turn.

Therefore it is that those people have so frequently and
from all times employed a cloudy and obscure style. Let
the writer succeed in attracting and busying posterity about
himself (which he may effect not only by the excellence of
his matter, but as much, and more, by the accidental favour
it enjoys), he need not care a rap if he expresses himself,
either through stupidity or subtlety, somewhat obscurely
and contradictorily. There will be any number of minds
that will sift and shake him, and squeeze out any number
of meanings, either his own, or beside the point, or contradictory, which will all redound to his honour. He will see
himself enriched through the means of his disciples, like the
tutor by the fees [1] of his scholars.

This it is that has given value to many worthless things,
that has made a reputation for many books, and filled them
with any kind of matter that the reader is pleased to put
into them. One and the same thing may be seen and considered from a thousand different points of view, or as many
as we please.

Can it be possible that Homer intended to say all that
he has been made to say ? And that he lent himself to so
many and so different shapes, that theologians, legislators,

---

[1] *Comme les regents du Lendit.* *Lendits*, according to Cotgrave, are
' gate-money, fairings, or yearly presents bestowed by the scholars of
Universities (especially those of Paris) on their tutors ' ; presumably at
the time of the *Lendit*, a great fair held annually near St. Denis.

generals, philosophers, people of every kind who treat of
sciences, be it ever so diversely and contradictorily, refer
to and rely upon him, as the Grand Master of all functions,
works and artists, General Adviser in all undertakings ?
Whoever had need of oracles and predictions found enough
of them in his work to serve his turn.

It is marvellous how many and wonderful passages a
learned friend of mine has lighted upon in Homer in support
of our religion ; and he cannot be easily persuaded that it
was not the poet's purpose (and yet he is as well acquainted
with him as any man of our time). And what he finds in
support of our religion many in ancient times found to
support theirs.

See how Plato is tumbled and tossed about ! Every man,
proud to think that he is on his side, bends him to the side
he would wish. They trot him about and ingraft upon him
all the new theories accepted by the world, and, as things
come to differ, make him differ from himself. To suit their
purpose they make him to disclaim the licit manners and
customs of his age, because they are illicit in ours. And all
this with the more keenness and power as the mind of the
interpreter is powerful and keen.

From the same ground on which Heraclitus took his
stand and gave out his maxim, ' That all things are as we
see them,' Democritus drew a quite opposite conclusion,
' That objects are in no wise as we see them.' And from
the fact that honey appears sweet to one and bitter to
another, he argued that it is neither sweet nor bitter.

The Pyrrhonians would say that they know not whether
it is sweet or bitter, or neither, or both ; for they always
reach the high water mark of doubt.

The Cyrenaics maintained that nothing was perceptible
from outside, and that that only was perceptible which
touched us by internal touch, as pain and pleasure ; admitting neither tone nor colour, but only certain impressions
that we received of them ; and that man's judgement had
no other seat.

Protagoras believed that ' what seems to every man is
true to every man '.

The Epicureans made the senses judges of all, both in the
cognisance of things and in pleasure.

Plato decided that the judgement of the truth, and the

truth itself, derived from opinions and the senses, belonged to the mind and thought.

This discussion has brought me to the consideration of the Senses, in which lie the greatest foundation and proof of our ignorance. Whatever is known is doubtless known by the faculty of the knower ; for since the judgement comes from the operation of him who judges, it is reasonable to suppose that this operation is performed by his means and will, not by the constraint of others, as would be the case if we knew things by the power and according to the law of their essence.

Now, all knowledge is conveyed to us through the senses ; they are our masters :

> Whereby the opened highways of belief
> Lead most directly into the human breast
> And temples of the mind. (LUCRETIUS.)

Knowledge begins through them and resolves itself into them.

After all we should know no more than a stone, if we did not know that there is sound, smell, light, taste, measure, weight, softness, hardness, roughness, smoothness, colour, breadth, depth. There you have the plan and groundwork of the whole edifice of our knowledge. And according to some, knowledge is nothing other than sensation. He who can drive me to confute the senses, has me by the throat ; he cannot make me recoil any further. The senses are the beginning and end of human knowledge :

> Thou'lt find
> That from the senses first hath been create
> Concept of truth, nor can the senses be
> Rebutted . . .
> What then than these our senses must there be
> Worthy a greater trust ? (LUCRETIUS.)

Allow them as little as we can, we must still grant them this, that all our instruction is conveyed by way of the senses and their agency. Cicero says that Chrysippus, having tried to discount the strength and power of the senses, raised up against himself arguments to the contrary, and such powerful objections, that he could not refute them. Whereupon Carneades, who supported the opposite side, boasted that he would use the very words and weapons of Chrysippus to fight him with, and therefore exclaimed against him, ' O wretched man, your strength has undone you ! '

There is no greater absurdity, in our opinion, than to maintain that fire does not warm, that light does not shine, that there is no weight nor solidity in iron, which are things brought to our notice by the senses ; nor is there any belief or knowledge in man which can compare with that for certainty.

The first observation I have to make on the subject of the Senses is that I doubt whether man be provided with all natural senses. I see that there are many creatures that live a full and perfect life, some without sight, and others without hearing ; who knows whether we too do not lack two, three, or many other senses ? For if any one is wanting, our reason cannot discover the want of it. It is the privilege of the senses to be the extreme limit of our perception. There is nothing beyond them that can help us to discover them. Nay, neither can one sense discover another.

> For shall the ears have power to blame the eyes,
> Or yet the touch the ears ? Again, should taste
> Accuse the touch, or shall the nose confute
> Or eyes defeat it ? (LUCRETIUS.)

They altogether form the extreme limit of our faculties :

> For unto each has been divided off
> Its functions quite apart, its power to each. (LUCRETIUS.)

It is impossible to make a man who is born blind understand that he does not see ; impossible to make him wish to see, and to regret his defect. Wherefore we should not take any assurance from the fact that our soul is contented and satisfied with those senses we possess ; seeing that it has not the means of feeling its infirmity and imperfection therein, if there be any. It is impossible to convey anything to this blind man, either by reason, argument, or comparison, that can arouse in his imagination any apprehension of light, colour, and sight. There is nothing behind that can push on the senses to evidence. If those born blind wish they could see, it is not because they understand what they require. They have heard us say that they lack something, that there is something in us which is desirable, and which, with its effects and consequences, they call good ; yet they know not what that is, and have neither a near or a distant apprehension of it.

I have seen a gentleman of good family, blind from his birth, or at least from such an early age that he knows not what sight is. He has so little understanding of what he lacks, that he makes use, as we do, of words which imply sight, and applies them in a way peculiarly his own. They brought him a boy, who was his godchild, and taking him in his arms he said, ' My word, what a fine boy ! it does one good to look at him ; what a merry face ! ' He will say, like any one of us, ' There is a fine view from this room ; it is a clear day ; the sun is shining bright.'

There is more to tell ; for having heard that hunting, tennis, and shooting at the mark are our sports, he takes a pleasure and a keen interest in them, and imagines that he can share in them as we do ; he delights in them, he becomes excited, and yet he only knows of them through his ears. Some one will call to him, ' Look, a hare ! ' when in the open country where he can clap on his spurs. They will tell him that a hare has been caught, and behold him as proud of the catch as he hears others say they are ! He will take a tennis-ball in his left hand and strike it with his racket. He will shoot at random with a musket, and is quite pleased when his men tell him that he is over or beside the mark.

Who knows but that mankind is committing a similar absurdity, through want of some sense or other, and that in consequence of this defect the face of things is for the most part hidden from us ? Who knows but that that is the reason why we are perplexed by many of the works of Nature, and that many of the actions of animals, which exceed our capacity, are the result of the exercise of some sense or other which we lack, and that some of them by this means live a fuller and more perfect life than we do ? We seize an apple wellnigh with all our senses ; we find in it redness, smoothness, smell, and sweetness. Besides these it may have other properties, as drying up or binding,[1] to which we have no corresponding sense.

As to what we call hidden properties in some things, as that of the magnet to attract iron, may we not believe that there are sentient faculties in Nature adapted to perceive

---

[1] *Comme d'asseicher ou restreindre.* I give W. C. Hazlitt's translation. Florio has ' either drying or binding ' ; Cotton ' as to heat or binding '.

and estimate them, and that the want of such faculties is the cause of our ignorance of the real essence of such things ? It is perhaps some special sense that enables the cock to know the morning and midnight hours, and incites him to crow. That teaches a hen, before all knowledge and experience, to fear a sparrow-hawk, and not a goose or a peacock, though birds of larger size. That warns a chicken of the natural hostility of the cat towards itself, and teaches it not to distrust a dog ; to be on its guard against the mewing, which is rather a wheedling sound, of the one, and not against the barking, a harsh and quarrelsome note, of the other. That teaches wasps, ants, and rats always to select the best pear and the best cheese before tasting them ; and guides the stag, the elephant, the snake to the knowledge of certain herbs that have curative properties.

There is no sense that does not exercise great dominion, and enable us by its means to know an infinite number of things. If we lacked the apprehension of sounds, of harmony and the voice, it would cause an inconceivable confusion in all our other knowledge. For, besides what attaches to the proper effect of each sense, how many arguments, consequences, and conclusions we draw with regard to other things, by comparing one sense with another ! Let an intelligent man imagine human nature to have been originally created without the sense of sight, and then consider how much ignorance and confusion such a defect would bring upon him, into what obscurity and blindness our soul would be sunk. From this we may see what an important difference it would make for the knowledge of the truth, should we be deprived of some other sense, or of two or three of them. We have built up a truth through the consultation and concurrence of our five senses ; but it would perhaps need the agreement and contribution of eight or ten to perceive it with certainty, and in its essence.

The schools that deny that we can know anything ground their denial chiefly on the uncertainty and weakness of the Senses. For, since all knowledge comes to us by and through them, if they fail in their report, if they alter and corrupt what they convey to us from without, if the light which through them shines into our soul be obscured on the way, we have nothing else to go by.

This extreme difficulty has given rise to these ideas :

' That every object has in itself all that we find in it ; That
it has nothing of what we think we find in it ' ; and that of
the Epicureans, ' That the sun is no bigger than it appears to
our sight ' :

> Whichever it be, she journeys with a form
> Naught larger than the form doth seem to be
> Which we with eyes of ours perceive ;   (LUCRETIUS.)

' That if a body appear large to one who is near, and smaller
to one who is at a distance, both appearances are real ' :

> And yet in this we don't at all concede
> That eyes be cheated. . . . And so
> Attach thou not this fault of mine to eyes ;   (LUCRETIUS.)

and this bolder idea, ' That there is no deception in the
senses ; that we must be at their mercy, and seek elsewhere
reasons to excuse the difference and contradiction we find
in them ; nay that we must invent any other false or
fanciful idea (for they go to that length) rather than accuse
the senses.'

Timagoras declared that he might squeeze and turn his
eyes ever so much, he had never been able to see the light of
a candle doubled ; and that that appearance was due to a
defect in the mind, not of the organ.

Of all absurdities the most absurd to the Epicureans is to
deny the power and effect of the senses.

> And therefore what
> At any time unto these senses showed,
> The same is true.   And if our reason be
> Unable to unravel to us the cause
> Why objects, which at hand were square, afar
> Seemed rounded, yet it more availeth us,
> Lacking the reason, to pretend a cause
> For each configuration, than to let
> From out our hands escape the obvious things,
> And injure primal faith in sense, and wreck
> All those foundations upon which do rest
> Our life and safety.   For not only Reason
> Would topple down ; but even our very life
> Would straightaway collapse, unless we dared
> To trust our Senses and to keep away
> From headlong heights and places to be shunned
> Of a like peril.   (LUCRETIUS.)

This desperate and so unphilosophical advice means

nothing more than that human knowledge can support itself only by unreasonable, foolish, and senseless Reason ; but that it is still better that man, in order to assert himself, should make use of it, and of any other remedy however fantastic, rather than confess his necessary stupidity : so unpalatable a truth ! He cannot run away from the fact that the Senses are the sovereign lords of his knowledge ; but that they are uncertain and liable to deception in all circumstances. It is there he must fight to the death, and, if his legitimate forces fail him, as they do, he must employ stubbornness, heedlessness, impudence.

Should it be true what the Epicureans say, namely, ' That we have no knowledge if the senses represent things falsely '; and also true what the Stoics say, ' That the senses represent things so falsely, that they cannot furnish us with any manner of knowledge,' we shall arrive at the conclusion, to the cost of these two great Dogmatic schools, That there is no such thing as knowledge.

With regard to the failure and uncertainty of the operation of the Senses, any man may provide himself with as many examples as he pleases : so commonly do they play us false. The sound of a trumpet re-echoing in a valley appears to come from in front of us, whilst it really comes from a league behind us :

> Between two mountains rising far away
> From midst the whirl of waters open lies
> A gaping exit for the fleet, and yet
> They seem conjoinèd in a single isle.

> And hills and fields
> Seem fleeing far astern, past which we urge
> The ship, and fly under the bellying sails.

> When in the middle of the stream
> Sticks fast our dashing horse, and down we gaze
> Into the river's rapid waves, some force
> Seems then to bear the body of the horse,
> Though standing still, reversely from its course,
> And swiftly push up-stream. (LUCRETIUS.)

When rolling a musket-ball under the forefinger, with the middle finger entwined over it, we have to force ourselves to admit that there is only one, so clearly does the sense of touch tell us that there are two. For we may observe at every turn that the senses are many a time masters of our reason, and force it to receive impressions which it knows and judges to be false. I leave aside the sense of touch, whose functions lie nearer, and are more alive and substantial, which so often, through the effect of the pain it imparts to the body, upsets all those fine Stoical resolutions, and compels that man to cry out with the belly-ache who has most resolutely established the doctrine in his soul, ' That the colic, like every other sickness and pain, is an indifferent thing, that has no power to diminish in any way the supreme happiness and felicity, in which the wise man lives by reason of his virtue.'

No heart is so faint that it does not beat the faster at the sound of our drums and trumpets, nor so hard that it will not be stirred and soothed by sweet music. No soul is so stubborn that it will not feel some touch of reverence when beholding the sombre vastness of our churches, the variety of ornaments and the order of our ceremonials, when hearing the devotion-inspiring notes of our organs, the harmony, so religious and solemn, of our voices. Even they who enter there disdainfully feel a certain thrill at their heart, and a certain awe which makes them distrust their opinions.

For my part, I do not feel strong enough to listen with equanimity to the lines of Horace or Catullus, ably sung by a young and beautiful voice.

And Zeno was right when he said that the voice is the flower of beauty.

Some one tried to make me believe that a man, well known to all of us Frenchmen, had unduly impressed me by his reciting of some lines he had composed ; that they were not the same on paper as in the air, and that my eyes would reverse the judgement of my ears : such is the power of utterance to lend value and shape to that which is left to its mercy ! Wherefore Philoxenus was to be excused when, hearing some one badly accentuating something he had composed, he began stamping on and breaking some tiles that belonged to him, saying, ' I break your property as you spoil mine.'

Why was it that those same men who had resolutely determined to die of their own free will would turn away their eyes, in order not to see the stroke they had ordered to be dealt them ; and that others who, for their cure, wish and order an incision or a cauterization, cannot endure the sight of the preparations, the surgical instruments and the operation itself, since the sight is to have no share in the pain ? Do not these examples sufficiently prove how the Senses dominate the reason ?

We may be quite aware that those tresses are borrowed of a page or a footman, that this blush is a product of Spain, and that this pallor and smoothness of skin has come out of the ocean-sea ; [1] yet must our eyes compel us, against all reason, to think the object more pleasing and lovely. For here there is nothing of her own.

> By dress we are beguiled ; defects are hid
> By gold and gems ; the girl is of herself
> The smallest part. And often when you seek
> The one you'd love mid all this outward show,
> Richness deceives the eye with Gorgon shield. (OVID.)

What a power the poets ascribe to the Senses, who make Narcissus distractedly in love with his own reflection !

> All things admires for which he is admired ;
> Fond youth, on self he dotes ; himself the lover,
> Himself alone he loves. He kindles passions
> Which do himself consume ; (OVID.)

and tell of Pygmalion's judgement so disturbed by the sight of his ivory statue, which he loves and worships as if it had life !

> He kisses gives, and thinks they are returned ;
> He speaks, and in his arms his love he strains,
> Believes the flesh to yield to his embrace,
> And fears the livid marks that may ensue. (OVID.)

Let a philosopher be placed in a cage of small thin-set iron wire, and suspend it at the top of one of the towers of Nôtre Dame de Paris ; by evident reason he will see that he cannot possibly fall out of it, and yet (unless he has been brought up to the trade of a steeplejack) he cannot help being paralysed with terror on looking down from that extreme height. For it is as much as we can do to feel secure in the galleries of our steeples, if they are guarded by an open-work parapet, although it be of stone. There are some who cannot bear even to think of it. Let these two towers be bridged by a beam of sufficient breadth to walk upon, no philosophic wisdom is so resolute that it can give

---

[1] Face-powder was perhaps made from the shel lof the cuttle-fish, now used for tooth-powder.

us courage to walk upon it, as we should do if it were on the ground.

I have often experienced this in our mountains on this side of the border (and yet I am not one who is easily frightened by such things), that I could not bear to look down into that bottomless depth without a shudder and a trembling in my hams and thighs ; even though I might be quite a body's length from the edge, and could not have fallen, unless I had purposely risked my life.

I have also observed that, however great the height, provided there be a tree or a jutting rock in the side of the precipice to catch the sight a little and break it, we are relieved and assured, as if those things might help to break our fall ; but that we cannot even look down a sheer and level precipice without a feeling of dizziness : *not to be looked down without giddiness both of eyes and mind* (Livy) ; which is an evident imposture of the sight.

That fine philosopher [1] put out his own eyes, to free his soul from the distractions which they caused him, and enable him to philosophize with greater freedom.

But by the same reckoning he should also have had his ears stopped up, which Theophrastus says are the most dangerous organs we have for receiving violent impressions that alter and disturb us ; and in short he ought to have deprived himself of all his other senses, that is to say, of his life and being. For they all have this power of overbearing our reason and our soul. *For it often happens that our mind is more vehemently struck by some sight, by a loud voice, or by singing ; often also by anxiety and fear* (Cicero).

Physicians hold that there are certain temperaments which are excited even to fury by certain sounds and instruments. I have known some who could not hear the gnawing of a bone under their table without losing patience ; and there is hardly a person who is not disturbed by the harsh and grating noise made by some one filing a piece of iron. So too some people are moved to anger and hatred if they hear any one chewing beside them, or speaking with an obstruction in the throat or nose.

Of what use was that piping prompter of Gracchus who softened, steadied, or modulated his master's voice when he

---

[1] Democritus, according to Cicero ; but Cicero doubts it, and Plutarch says positively that it was not true.

was haranguing at Rome, if the inflection and quality of the tone had not the power to move and alter the judgement of his audience ? [1] Truly a great thing to brag about is that fine firmness of judgement which suffers itself to be handled and swayed by the accidental stirring of so light a wind !

That same trickery with which the Senses deceive the understanding deceives them in their turn. Our soul sometimes gives tit for tat. They compete in lying and being deceived. What we see and hear when stirred by anger we do not hear as it is :

> A double sun, a twofold Thebes appear. (VIRGIL.)

The object we love appears to us more beautiful than it is :

> And thus we see
> Creatures in many a wise crooked and ugly
> The prosperous sweethearts in a high esteem, (LUCRETIUS.)

and that which we loathe appears more ill-favoured. To a man bowed down by grief and affliction the light of day appears dark and overclouded. Our senses are not only corrupted, but often quite deadened, by the passions of the soul. How many things we see which we do not take notice of when our mind is occupied with other thoughts !

> Yet thou canst know that, even in objects plain,
> If thou attendest not, 'tis just the same
> As if 'twere all the time removed and far. (LUCRETIUS.)

The soul seems to retire within itself, and the powers of the senses are kept in abeyance. Thus, both within and without, man is full of weakness and falsehood.

They who have compared our life to a dream were perhaps more in the right than they were aware of. When we dream, our soul lives, acts, exercises all her faculties neither more nor less than when we are awake. But if more inertly and obscurely, the difference is certainly not so great as between night and bright daylight ; rather as between night and shade. There she sleeps, here she slumbers. More and less it is always darkness, and Cimmerian darkness.

We wake sleeping, and waking sleep. I do not see so

---

[1] ' To guard against excesses, he ordered his servant Licinius, who was a sensible man, to stand with a pitch-pipe behind him when he spoke in public, and whenever he found him straining his voice or breaking out into anger, to give him a softer key, upon which his violence, both of tone and passion, immediately abated.'—Plutarch, *Life of T. Gracchus.*

clearly in sleep ; but as to my waking hours I never find them perfect and cloudless enough. Sleep, moreover, when it is deep, sometimes puts dreams to sleep. But our waking is never so wideawake as to thoroughly purge and dissipate reveries, which are the dreams of the waking, and worse than dreams.

Since our reason and our soul accept those fancies and opinions which arise in her while asleep, and authorize the actions of our dreams with the same approval as she does those of our day-dreams, why do we not question whether our thought and action be not another sort of dreaming, and our waking some kind of sleeping ?

If our Senses are our first judges, it is not only our own that must be consulted ; for in this faculty the animals are as much, and more, privileged than we are. It is certain that some of them have a more acute hearing than man, others a sharper sight, others a keener scent and others a finer touch and taste. Democritus said that gods and animals had the sensitive faculties much more perfect than man.

Now there is an extreme difference between the effects of their senses and ours. Our saliva cleanses and dries up our wounds ; it kills a snake :

> So great the distance and the difference is
> That what is food to one to some becomes
> Fierce poison, as a certain snake there is
> Which, touched by spittle of a man, will waste
> And end itself by gnawing up its coil. (LUCRETIUS.)

What property shall we attribute to saliva ? Shall it be from our point of view, or from that of the snake ? According to which point of view shall we prove its real essence, which we are seeking ? Pliny says that in the Indies there are certain sea-hares [1] which are poison to us, and we to them, so much so that we kill them by a mere touch. Which is really poisonous, the man or the fish ? Which are we to believe, the fish about the man, or the man about the fish ?

Air of a certain quality infects a man and does an ox no harm ; and a certain other quality infects an ox and does a man no harm. Which of the two shall, in reality and nature, be the pestilent quality ?

---

[1] Aplysia: sea-hare; a kind of snail or slug said to be poisonous.

To people who have the jaundice all things appear yellowish, and paler than to others :

> Again whatever jaundiced people view
> Becomes wan-yellow. (LUCRETIUS.)

Those who have the complaint which the physicians call Hyposphagma, which is a suffusion of blood under the skin, see everything red and bloody. How can we know but that these humours, which thus alter the action of our sight, predominate and are usual with animals ? For we may see some with yellow eyes like our jaundice-patients, others with bloodshot eyes. It is quite likely that to them the colour of objects appears other than to us. Which of us judges aright ? For it is not ordained that man alone shall be the referee with regard to the essence of things. Hardness, whiteness, depth, sourness, affect and are distinguished by the animals as they are by us ; by nature they exist for them as much as for us.

When we partially close the eye, the bodies we look at appear longer and more distended ; some of the animals have the eye thus half-closed. Those bodies are therefore perhaps really longer, and not as our eye normally perceives them. If we squeeze the eye from below, things appear double to us :

> Twin lights of torches blossoming with flames ;
> Twofold the face of man, and twain his body. (LUCRETIUS.)

If our ears are stopped with anything, or if the auricular passage is contracted, we receive the sound quite otherwise than we usually do. Animals with hair in their ears, or that have only a very little hole in place of an ear, do not consequently hear what we hear, and sounds appear different to them.

On feast-days and in theatres we may observe that when a pane of glass tinted with some colour is held before the candles, everything in the place appears green, yellow, or violet :

> .   This the crowd surveys
> Often in the theatre, whose curtain broad,
> Bedecked with crimson, yellow, or the tint
> Of steel cerulean, from their fluted heights
> Wave tremulous ; and, o'er the scene beneath
> Each marble statue, and the rising rows
> Of rank and beauty, fling their tint superb. (LUCRETIUS.)

It is likely that the eyes of animals, which we observe to vary in colour, cause bodies to appear to them of the same colour as their eyes.

We should therefore, to estimate rightly the action of the Senses, come to an agreement, in the first place with the animals, and secondly among ourselves. This we in no wise do, but ever and anon we fall to disputing, because one person differs from another as to what he hears, sees, or tastes ; and we wrangle about the different images that the senses put before us, as much as about anything else. By the ordinary rule of Nature a child hears, sees, and tastes differently to a man of thirty, and the latter otherwise than a sexagenarian.

In some people the Senses are more dim and cloudy, in others clearer and more acute. We take in things differently according to our nature, and as they seem to us. Now our seeming being so uncertain and open to controversy, it is no longer to be wondered at if we are told that we may admit that snow seems white to us, but that we cannot guarantee to prove that it is white by its essence and in reality ; and this principle being shaken, all the science in the world necessarily goes by the board.

What if our senses themselves hinder one another ? To the eyes a painting appears raised, to the touch it appears flat. Shall we say that musk, which delights our sense of smell and offends our taste, is agreeable or not ? There are herbs and unguents which agree with one part of the body and injure another. Honey is pleasant to the taste, unpleasant to look at. Of those rings which are cut in the form of feathers and are called in heraldry *Feathers without end*, there is no eye that can tell the width or escape the deception which makes them appear to grow wider on one side, and narrower and more pointed on the other, especially when we turn them round our finger ; and yet to the touch they appear equal in width and alike throughout.

When those persons who, in ancient times, enhanced their pleasure by using mirrors that enlarged and magnified the objects reflected in them, in order that the members they were about to busy might please the more by the ocular increase, which of the two senses carried the day, the sight which represented those members as big and long as they could wish, or the touch which made them appear small and contemptible ?

Is it our Senses that lend these different properties to objects, and have the objects nevertheless but one ? As we see in the bread that we eat ; it is only bread, but our use makes bones, blood, flesh, hair, and nails of it :

> For just as food, dispersed through all the pores
> Of body, and passed through limbs and all the frame,
> Perishes, supplying from itself the stuff
> For other nature. (LUCRETIUS.)

The moisture sucked up by the roots of a tree becomes trunk, leaf, and fruit ; and the air, being but one, driven through a trumpet, is diversified into a thousand kinds of sound. Is it our senses, I say, which in like manner give to those objects their different qualities, or have they really such ? And in the face of this doubt, what may we conclude with regard to their real essence ?

Moreover, since the conditions of sickness, delirium, or sleep make things appear to us otherwise than they appear to those in health and in their right mind, and to the waking ; is it not likely that there is something in our normal state and natural disposition that gives an essence to things corresponding and agreeing with our condition, as there is in our disordered state ? That our health, as well as our sickness, is capable of regarding things in its own way ? Why should not the temperate man have his own way of looking at things, as well as the intemperate, and in like manner stamp his own character upon them ?

The man with a fastidious taste charges wine with being insipid ; to the healthy man it has a bouquet ; the thirsty finds it delicious.

Now, since our condition accommodates things to itself, and transforms them according to itself, we no longer know things in their reality ; for nothing comes to us that is not altered and falsified by our Senses. When the compass, the square, and the rule are untrue, all the calculations drawn from them, all the buildings erected to their measure, are of necessity also defective and out of plumb. The uncertainty of our senses renders uncertain everything they produce :

> As in a building
> If the first plumb-line be askew, and if
> The square deceiving swerve from lines exact,

> And if the level waver but the least
> In any part, the whole construction then
> Must turn out faulty—shelving and askew,
> Leaning to back and front, incongruous,
> That now some portions seem about to fall,
> And falls the whole ere long—betrayed indeed
> By first deceiving estimates : so too
> Thy calculations in affairs of life
> Must be askew and false, if sprung for thee
> From Senses false. (LUCRETIUS.)

After all who will be a competent judge in these differences ? As we say that in discussions on religion we need a referee who is not attached to either one or the other side, one who has not made his choice and is free from partiality (a thing impossible among Christians) ; so it is in our case. For, if a man is old, he cannot be a judge of the feeling of old age, being himself a party in the controversy ; if he is young, the same ; if healthy, the same ; the same if sick, sleeping, or waking. We should need one who is exempt from all these conditions, to decide with unprejudiced mind these questions as if they were indifferent to him ; and by this rule we should need a judge who never has existed.

To judge the appearances we receive of things, we should need a judicatory instrument ; to verify this instrument, we should need demonstration ; to rectify this demonstration we should need an instrument : so here we are arguing in a circle !

Seeing that the Senses cannot decide our dispute, being themselves full of uncertainty, we must have recourse to Reason ; there is no reason but must be built upon another reason : so here we are retreating backwards to all eternity !

Our ideas are not due to direct contact with outside things, but are formed through the mediation of the Senses ; and the senses do not take in the outside objects, but only their own impressions. So the idea and image we form is not that of the object, but only of the impression and the feeling made by it on the senses ; which impression and the object are different things. Wherefore whoever judges by appearances, judges by something other than the object.

And if you say that the impressions of the senses convey to the soul the qualities of outside objects by resemblance, how can the soul and the understanding be assured of this resemblance, having of themselves no communication with outside objects? [Just as a man who does not know Socrates cannot, on seeing his portrait, say that it is like him.

Now, supposing a man nevertheless desires to judge by appearances. If it be by all, it is impossible ; for they hamper one another by their contradictions and discrepancies, as we know by experience. Shall some selected appearances govern the others ? We should need to verify the selection by another selection, the second by a third ; in this way we shall never make an end.

Finally, there is no permanent existence, either of our being or of that of the objects. And we, and our judgement, and all mortal things, incessantly go flowing and rolling on. So nothing certain can be proved of one thing by another, both the judging and the judged being in continual motion and change.

' We have no participation in Being, because all human nature is ever midway between being born and dying, giving off only a vague image and shadow of itself, and a weak and uncertain opinion. And if you chance to fix your thought on trying to grasp its essence, it would be neither more nor less than if you tried to clutch water. For the more you squeeze and press what by its nature runs through everything, the more surely will you lose what you would lay hold of. Hence, seeing that all things are liable to change from one thing to another, Reason, which seeks in them a real permanence, is deceived, being unable to apprehend anything that is subsistent and permanent. Because everything is either entering into being and does not yet fully exist, or is beginning to die before it is born.' [1]

Plato said that bodies never had existence, but only birth. He conceived that Homer made the Ocean father, and Thetis mother, of the gods, thereby to show us that all things are in a perpetual state of fluctuation, motion and variation ; an opinion held in common by all the philosophers before his time, as he says, excepting alone Parmenides, who denied that things had motion, of the power of which he made no small account.

---

[1] The above paragraph is taken word for word (with the exception of one word) from Amyot's translation of an essay of Plutarch ; a fact which appears to have escaped the notice of all the editors and commentators of Montaigne, until quite recently.

Pythagoras opined that all matter is flowing and unstable ;

The Stoics, that there is no present time, and that what we call Present is only the junction and meeting of the future and the past ;

Heraclitus, that no man ever entered twice into the same river ;

Epicharmus, that the man who borrowed money some time ago does not now owe it ; and that he who was overnight invited to come to dinner this morning, to-day comes unbidden, seeing that they are no longer themselves, but are become others, and ' That no mortal substance can be found twice in the same condition. For, through the suddenness and quickness of its change, it is now scattered, and now brought together again ; it comes, and then it is gone. Hence that which begins to be born never arrives at the perfection of being. Forasmuch as that birth is never finished and never stays, as being at an end ; but, even in the seed, is evermore changing and shifting from one to another. As the human seed first produces, in the mother's womb, a shapeless fruit, then a fully-formed infant, then, being out of the womb, a suckling, it afterwards becomes a boy, then in due course a stripling, then a full-grown man, an elderly man, and finally a decrepit old man. So that the subsequent age and generation is always undoing and destroying the preceding one ' :

> For lapsing aeons change the nature of
> The whole wide world, and all things needs must take
> One status after other, nor aught persists
> For ever like itself. All things depart ;
> Nature she changeth all, compelleth all
> To transformation. (LUCRETIUS.)

' And then we others foolishly fear one kind of death, when we have already passed and are still passing through so many others. For not only, as Heraclitus said, is the death of fire the birth of air, and the death of air the birth of water ; but we may see it much more clearly in ourselves. The man in his prime dies and passes when old age comes along, and youth comes to an end in the prime of the grown man, childhood in youth, and the early age dies in childhood. And yesterday dies in to-day, and to-day will die in to-morrow ; and there is nothing that stays and is ever One.

' For, as proof of this, if we always remain one and the same, how is it that we take pleasure now in one thing, now in another ? How is it that we love or hate opposite things, that we praise or blame them ? How is it that we have different affections, and that we do not retain the same feelings and thoughts ? For it is not likely that we should harbour other feelings without changing. And that which suffers change does not remain one and the same. And if it is not one and the same, neither does it then exist. But, with Being all one, it also simply changes its being, ever becoming one thing out of another. And, consequently, the senses by nature deceive and lie to themselves, taking that which seems for that which is, for want of really knowing what that which is, is.

' But what then really is ? That which is Eternal. That it to say, that which never had a birth, and will never have an end ; to which no time ever brings change. For Time is a thing which moves, and appears as in a shadow, with matter ever flowing and running, without ever remaining stable and permanent. Of which we use these words, Before, and After, and Has been, or Will be. Each of which at first sight gives clear evidence that it is not a thing that Is. For it would most evidently be wrong and absurd to say that that Is which is not yet in being, or which has already ceased to be. And as to these words, Present, or Here, or Now, on which our apprehension of time seems chiefly to be founded and to rest, Reason discovers the error and immediately destroys it, for she at once splits it up, and divides it into Future and Past, as though trying to see it of necessity divided into two.

' It is the same with Nature, which is measured, as with Time, which measures it. For no more is there anything in Nature that abides or is permanent, but all things in her are either born, or being born, or dying. According to which it would be a sin to say of God, who alone Is, that he Was, or Will be. For these words are changes, transitions or vicissitudes of that which cannot endure or remain in being. Whence we must conclude that God alone Is, not indeed according to any measure of time, but according to an immutable and immovable eternity, not measured by time nor subject to any decline ; before whom nothing is, nor will be after, neither more new nor more recent ; but one really being, which by one single Now fills the Ever ; and there is nothing that truly Is, except he alone, without our being able to say, He has been or He will be, without beginning and without end.' [1]

To this pious conclusion of a pagan I will only join these words of a witness in the same condition, and make an end of this long and wearisome treatise, which would furnish me with endless matter : ' O what a mean and abject thing is man, says Seneca, if he does not rise above humanity ! ' There we have a good word and a profitable desire, but at the same time an absurd one.[2] For to make the handful bigger than the hand, and the armful bigger than the arm, and to expect to stride further than our legs can reach, that is impossible and contrary to Nature. Neither is it possible for man to rise superior to himself and humanity. For he cannot see but with his eyes, nor grasp more than he can hold. He will rise if God extraordinarily lends him a hand. He will rise by abandoning and renouncing his own proper means, and by suffering himself to be raised and uplifted by purely celestial means.

It is for our Christian faith, and not his Stoical virtue, to aspire to that divine and miraculous metamorphosis.

CHAPTER 13

OF JUDGING OF ANOTHER'S DEATH

WHEN judging of another's assurance at the point of death, which is without doubt the moment in the life of a man that should be most carefully noted, we must take care to remember one thing, That it is difficult for a man to believe that he has reached that stage. Few people, when they are dying, have made up their minds that it is their last hour ; and at no point of our lives are we more deluded by deceptive hope. She keeps dinning into their ears,

---

[1] The whole of the above passage in inverted commas is copied, not word for word, as all the editors and commentators assert, but with alterations and omissions, from the aforesaid essay of Plutarch, in Amyot's translation.

[2] This sentence takes the place of the following, which originally stood in the edition of 1588 : ' In the whole of the Stoic school there is not a truer word than this.' Seneca was a Stoic, but Montaigne, though he did not like the Stoics, had a great admiration for Seneca.

' Others have been in a much worse condition, and have not died. Your case is not as hopeless as they think ; and, at the worst, God has worked greater miracles.'

And that comes of thinking too much of ourselves. We imagine that the universe will suffer some loss by our annihilation, and that it commiserates our condition. Our sight being disturbed, things appear to it equally disturbed, and we imagine that things are passing from us when we lose sight of them ; as to those who travel by sea, the mountains, fields, cities, heaven and earth appear to be tossed about in the same way as they are :

> From harbour fare we ; lands and cities fade. (VIRGIL.)

Who ever knew an old man who did not praise the past and blame the present, laying his troubles and misery to the charge of the world and the conduct of men ?

> The aged ploughman shakes his head and sighs ;
> And when he puts the present by the past,
> His father's fate he blesses, often prates
> How those of old with piety were filled. (LUCRETIUS.)

We drag everything along with us. As a consequence we look upon our death as a great matter, which does not come to pass lightly, nor without a solemn consultation of the stars ; *so many gods making a stir over one head* (Seneca). And of this we are more convinced the more we prize ourselves : ' What, is so much learning to be wasted, to the great detriment of the world, without the Fates being specially concerned about it ? Does it cost them no more to kill so rare and exemplary a mind than one that is common and of no use to the world ? This life of ours, that shelters so many others, on which so many other lives depend, which employs such a world of people, that fills so many places, is it to be dismissed like one that holds by its one single thread ? '

Not one of us lays it sufficiently to heart that he is but one.

Hence those words of Caesar to his pilot, more tumid than the sea which threatened him :

> If thou to sail to Italy decline
> Under the Gods' protection, trust to mine ;
> The only cause thou justly hast to fear
> Is that thou knowest not thy passenger ;
> But I being now aboard, slight Neptune's braves,
> And fearlessly cut through the swelling waves. (LUCAN.)

And these :

> But Caesar now
> Thinking the peril worthy of his Fates :
> ' Are such the labours of the gods ? exclaimed ;
> Bent on my downfall have they sought me thus,
> Here in this puny skiff in such a sea ? '

And that fantastic idea entertained by the people, that the sun for a whole year shrouded its face, in mourning for his death :

> Yea, he it was that showed
> At Caesar's death compassion upon Rome,
> Veiling in umber haze his dazzling head. (VIRGIL.)

And a thousand such, by which the world is so easily gulled, imagining that our loss changes the face of the heavens, and that they, in their infinity, take a keen interest in our paltry distinctions. *We are not so intimate with heaven that the light of its stars should die at our death* (Pliny).

Now it is not reasonable to judge of the resolution and firmness of a man who, though he be in certain danger, is not yet convinced of it ; and it is not enough that he dies in this frame of mind, unless he be really prepared for that event. In most cases they put on a brave face and utter brave words in order to acquire a reputation, which they still hope to live long enough to enjoy.

All those whose death I have observed were beholden to chance for their demeanour and not to their own design.

And even in the case of those who in ancient times took their own lives, we should carefully consider whether it was a sudden death, or a death that took time. That cruel Roman Emperor used to say of his prisoners that he wished to make them feel death ; and if one made away with himself in prison, he would say, ' That fellow has escaped me.' [1] He would rather he had felt the torments of a lingering death.

> His every limb
> Maimed, hacked and riven ; yet the fatal blow
> The murderers with savage purpose spared. (LUCAN.)

It is not indeed so great a matter, in a man in perfect health and in his right mind, to resolve to kill himself ; it is very easy to swagger before coming to grips. So we see

---

[1] The first part of the sentence applies to Caligula, the second to Tiberius, whose cruelty a certain Carvilius escaped by suicide.

the most effeminate man that the world has seen, Helio-gabalus, amid all his vulgar debaucheries, making prepara-tions for dying artistically, when occasion should force him to do so. And, that his death might not belie the rest of his life, he expressly built a sumptuous tower, the base and front of which was floored with boards enriched with gold and precious stones, from which to hurl himself. He also had cords made of gold and crimson silk threads to strangle himself ; a sword forged in gold wherewith to run himself through ; and kept poison in vessels of emerald and topaz to poison himself, according as the whim should seize him to choose between these different ways of dying :

> By a forced valour, resolute and brave. (LUCAN.)

Yet in respect of this man, the luxuriousness of his prepara-tions makes it more likely that he would have bled at the nose,[1] had he been put to the test.

But even in the case of those men of stouter heart who have resolved to dispatch themselves, we must consider (I say), whether it was with a stroke which left them no time to feel the effect of it. For it may be questioned whether, on feeling life draining away little by little, the body's senses mingling with those of the soul, and with the means at hand of undoing his action, a man would still obstinately persist in so dangerous an intent.

During Caesar's Civil wars, Lucius Domitius, who took poison after being made prisoner in the Abruzzi, afterwards repented. It has happened in our time that a man, having resolved to die, and not having struck deep enough at the first attempt, the itching of the flesh repelling his arm, after-wards dealt himself two or three very serious wounds, but could never screw up enough courage to thrust home.

Whilst Plantius Sylvanus was on his trial, Urgulania, his grandmother, sent him a poniard with which, having failed to kill himself outright, he made his slaves open his veins.

Albucilla, in the time of Tiberius, attempted to kill her-self, but struck half-heartedly, and still gave her adversaries the opportunity to imprison her and put her to death in their own way. The same thing happened to Demosthenes the General, after being routed in Sicily. And C. Fimbria,

---

[1] His courage would have failed him ; or, in the familiar phrase, he ' would have got cold feet '.

having struck himself too feeble a blow, entreated his slave to finish him.

On the other hand, Ostorius, unable to use his own arm, and disdaining to employ that of his slave except to hold the poniard with firm and steady hand, hurled himself forward, thrust his throat against the point, and so ran himself through.

It is indeed a meat that must be swallowed without chewing by one whose throat is not lined with paving-stones ; and so the Emperor Hadrian made his physician accurately mark and encircle the spot on his pap at which the man he had charged to kill him was to aim. For this reason it was that Caesar, when asked what death he thought the most desirable, replied, ' The least premeditated and the quickest.'

If Caesar had the courage to say so, it is no cowardice in me to believe it.

' A quick death, said Pliny, is the supreme good fortune in human life.' People are loath to acknowledge it. No man can say he is resolved on death who fears to reflect on it, and cannot bear to look on it with open eyes. They who, under sentence of death, in order to make a rapid end of it, urge and hasten on their execution, do so not because they are resolved, but because they would rather not have time to think it over. It is not death that troubles them, but very much the dying :

I fear not death, but dying gives me pause. (EPICHARMUS.)

That is a degree of firmness which I know by experience I could attain to, like those who plunge into danger, as into the sea, with eyes shut.

There is nothing, in my opinion, more illuminating in the life of Socrates, than that he had thirty whole days in which to ruminate over his death sentence, and that he digested it all that time in certain expectation of its being carried out, without dismay, without change, his train of words and actions rather depressed and languid than strained and exalted by the weight of such thoughts.

That Pomponius Atticus to whom Cicero wrote his letters, being ill, sent for Agrippa, his son-in-law, and two or three other friends, and said to them that, having found by experience that he gained nothing by trying to cure himself, and that all he did to prolong his life only prolonged and aggravated his pain, he was resolved to put an end to both, and begged them to approve of his determination, or, at the most, not to waste their labour in trying to dissuade him from it. Now, having chosen to die by abstaining from food, behold him accidentally cured of his disease ! The remedy he had employed to do away with himself restored him to health. When the physicians and his friends came to celebrate this happy event and rejoice with him, they were greatly disappointed, for, in spite of their efforts, they could not make him change his mind ; he said that some day he would in any case have to go through with it, and being now so far on his way, he would save himself the pains of beginning all over again on a future occasion.

This man, having made acquaintance with death at his full leisure, not only is not disheartened, but is eagerly bent on overtaking it ; for, being satisfied with the reason which made him enter into the combat, he makes it a point of bravery to see it out. There is a great distance between not fearing death and being ready to taste it and relish it.

The story of the philosopher Cleanthes is very similar. His gums were swollen and decayed. The physicians advised him to be very abstemious. After fasting for two days he is so much better that they pronounce him cured, and permit him to return to his usual diet. He, on the other hand, having already tasted the sweets of faintness, resolved not to go back, and ended the journey on which he was so far advanced.

Tullius Marcellinus, a young Roman, wishing to anticipate the hour of his destiny, to be rid of a disease which tyrannized over him more than he was minded to endure, although the physicians promised him a certain if not a speedy cure, called his friends together to discuss his case. Some, says Seneca, gave him the advice they would themselves have taken through faintheartedness. Others, to gratify him, that which they thought would be most acceptable to him. But a Stoic spoke as follows : ' Do not let it worry you, Marcellinus, as if you were considering a weighty matter. It is no great thing to live ; your slaves and animals live. But it is a great thing to die nobly, wisely and firmly. Think how long you have been doing the same things, eating, drinking, sleeping ; drinking, sleeping, and eating. We are continually going the same daily round ; not only evil and intolerable calamities, but the mere satiety of living, make a man wish to die.'

Marcellinus wanted no man to give him advice ; he wanted a man to help him. His slaves feared to meddle, but this philosopher explained to them that domestic slaves fall under suspicion only when it is doubtful whether the death of their master is voluntary ; that otherwise it would be as bad an example to prevent him as to kill him, seeing that

> To save a man against his will
> Is just the same as 'tis to kill. (HORACE.)

He then suggested to Marcellinus that, just as after a meal we give the dessert to the attendants, so when life is ended it would not be unbecoming to distribute something among those who have ministered to our needs. Now Marcellinus was of a free and generous disposition ; he divided a certain sum among his slaves, and comforted them. For the rest he needed neither steel nor blood. He resolved to walk out of this life, not to run away from it ; not to escape death, but to experience it. And, to give himself time to meditate over it, he gave up eating, and on the third day after, having had himself sprinkled with warm water, he became gradually weaker and weaker, and not, as he said, without a certain voluptuousness.

Indeed they who have experienced this failing of the heart due to weakness declare that they feel no pain, but rather a certain pleasure, as when passing into sleep and repose.

Those are studied and digested deaths.

But, in order that Cato alone might furnish an example of virtue in all respects, it would seem as if his kind destiny had injured the hand with which he dealt himself the blow, that he might have opportunity to meet death face to face, and hug him, fortifying his courage in the face of danger instead of abating it. And if it had been my lot to picture him in his most superb attitude, I should have represented him covered with blood and tearing out his bowels, rather than with sword in hand, as did the sculptors of his times. For this second murder was much more relentless than the first.

CHAPTER 14

HOW OUR MIND STANDS IN ITS OWN WAY

IT is an amusing idea, that of a man exactly balanced between two equally strong desires. For it is not to be doubted that he will never make up his mind, since choice and inclination would imply that things were unequally prized ; and if we were placed between the bottle and the ham, with an equal desire to eat and drink, there would doubtless be no help for it, but we must die of thirst and hunger.[1]

To provide against this dilemma, the Stoics, when asked how our mind comes to choose between two indifferent things, and why, from a large number of coins, we take one rather than another, when they are all alike, and there is no reason to incline us to any preference, reply that this movement of the soul is out of the common and irregular, coming to us by an outside, accidental, and fortuitous impulsion.

I think we might rather say that nothing meets our eyes which does not show some difference, however slight ; and that, either to the sight or the touch, there is always something additional which attracts us, however imperceptibly. Similarly, if we could imagine a piece of string equally strong in every part, it is impossible by all impossibility that it should snap ; for where would you have the break to begin ? And it is not in Nature that it should break everywhere at the same time.[2]

If we should add to this the geometrical propositions which conclude, by certain proofs, that the contents are greater than the containing, and the centre as great as its circumference ; and which discover two lines eternally approaching one another without ever meeting, and the philosopher's stone, and the squaring of the circle, where reason and experience are so opposed ; we might perhaps find some argument to support this bold saying of Pliny : *There is nothing certain but uncertainty, and nothing more miserable and arrogant than man.*[3]

[1] The classical instance of irresolution is that of Buridan's ass, which died of starvation standing between two bundles of hay.

[2] Save in fiction ; see Holmes's poem ' The Deacon's Masterpiece, or The Wonderful One-Hoss-Shay '.

[3] This is one of the sentences inscribed on the ceiling of Montaigne's library.

CHAPTER 15

THAT DIFFICULTIES INCREASE OUR DESIRES

THERE is no reason but has its opposite, says the wisest school of Philosophers.[1] I was just ruminating over that fine saying which one of the ancients adduces as a reason for despising life, ' No good thing can bring us pleasure but that for whose loss we are prepared : ' *Grief for a lost thing and the fear of losing it equally affect the mind* (Seneca) ; thinking to make clear thereby that we cannot truly enjoy life if we are in fear of losing it.

It might, however, be said, on the other hand, that we clasp and embrace this good thing the more closely and affectionately for seeing it to be less sure, and fearing to have it taken from us. For it is felt to be obvious that, as cold air helps to stir up a fire, our desire is also whetted by opposition :

> Ne'er had Danaë been by Jove embraced,
> Had she not been confined in brazen tower ; (OVID.)

and there is nothing that so naturally destroys an appetite as the satiety that comes of facility ; nothing that so whets it as rarity and difficulty. *In all things pleasure gains a new attraction from the very danger which should deter us* (Seneca).

> Deny thy favours, Galla ; love is cloyed
> When bliss is not with torment blent. (MARTIAL.)

To keep love in breath, Lycurgus decreed that married couples in Sparta should only meet by stealth, and that they should be as much ashamed at being discovered sleeping together as if they had been caught in adultery. The difficulty of assignations, the danger of surprise, the shame of the morrow,

> Silence and listlessness and piteous sighs
> Drawn from the inmost soul, (HORACE.)

these things it is that give piquancy to the sauce. How many most lasciviously pleasant sports are the result of the modest and shamefaced style of books on Love ! Lust even seeks an additional zest in pain. The pleasure is sweeter

---

[1] The Pyrrhonian.

when it smarts and scorches. The courtezan Flora [1] used to
say that she had never lain with Pompey but she made him
carry away the marks of her teeth :

> The parts they sought for, those they squeeze so tight,
> And pain the body ; implant their teeth upon
> The lips, and crush the mouth with kisses, yet
> Not unalloyed with joy ; for there are stings
> Which goad them on to hurt the very thing,
> Whate'er it be, from whence arise for them
> Those germs of frenzy. (LUCRETIUS.)

So it is in everything ; difficulty gives value to things.

The people of the March of Ancona prefer to pay their
devotions to Saint James, and the people of Galicia to Our
Lady of Loreto.[2] At Liège they have a high opinion of the
baths of Lucca, and in Tuscany they think as highly of those
at Spa. You rarely see a Roman in the fencing-school at
Rome, which is filled with Frenchmen.

The great Cato became as weary of his wife as any of us
might do, as long as she was his wife, and desired her when
she became another's.

I have turned an old horse into the stud, as he got quite
out of hand when he scented a mare. Facility presently
sated him towards his own ; but at sight of the first stranger
that passed along his paddock, he would neigh as im-
patiently, and become as hot and furious, as ever.

Our appetite despises and looks beyond what is at hand,
and runs after what it does not possess :

> He slights what 's near at hand, and longs
>   For what 's beyond his reach. (HORACE.)

To forbid us a thing is to make us long for it :

> If thou no better guard that girl of thine,
> She'll soon begin to be no longer mine. (OVID.)

To give it wholly into our possession is to breed in us
contempt for it. Want and abundance each have their disadvantages :

> You of your superfluity complain,
>   And I of want. (Adapted from TERENCE.)

[1] Dictes-moy où, n'en quel pays,
    Est Flora la bele Romaine.—Villon, *Ballade des Dames du temps
jadis.*
[2] Saint James of Compostella in Galicia. The Italians go on pilgrimage
to Spain, the Spaniards to Italy. Loreto is near Ancona.

Desire and enjoyment make us equally impatient. The severity of a mistress becomes a weariness, but an easy and yielding disposition becomes, to tell the truth, a greater ; seeing that dissatisfaction and anger are the result of the value which we put on the desired object, sharpening and kindling love. But satiety breeds distaste ; it is a blunt, dull, weary, and drowsy feeling.

> If you would keep your lover at your side,
> Treat him with scorn. (OVID.)

>> Treat your mistress with neglect ;
>> If yesterday she said you nay,
>> She'll come to you another day. (PROPERTIUS.)

What was Poppaea's intention, when she hid her beauty behind a mask, but to enhance it in the eyes of her lovers ? Why do they veil, even down to the heels, the beauties that every woman desires to show, and every man to see ? Why do they cover with so many obstacles, one on top of another, the parts on which are chiefly concentrated our desires and their own ? And what purpose is served by those great bastions which our ladies have recently adopted, to fortify their flanks, except to allure our appetites, and attract us to them by keeping us at a distance ?

> She hies her to the willows, hoping to be seen. (VIRGIL.)
> Her tunic interposed would ofttimes rouse my passion.
> (PROPERTIUS.)

What is the object of that maidenly modesty, that deliberate coolness, that severe expression, that profession of ignorance of things they know better than we who in-struct them, but to increase in us the longing to overcome, bear down, and trample upon all those affected airs and those obstacles to our desire ? For there is not only a pleasure, but a source of vainglory, in seducing that meek, mild and childlike bashfulness, in inflaming and goading it into mad-ness, and in subduing to our ardour a cool and calculated sternness. It is a matter for boasting, they say, to triumph over rigour, modesty, chastity and temperance ; and who-ever dissuades the ladies from those attitudes, betrays both them and himself. We are to believe that their hearts shudder with fright, that the sound of our words offends the purity of their ears, that they hate us for them, and yield to our importunities by a forced constraint. Beauty, all-powerful as it is, has no power to make itself relished without that interposition.

Look at Italy, where there is most beauty on sale, and the most perfect of its kind, and how they are obliged to seek extraneous means and other arts to make it acceptable ; and yet, to tell the truth, whatever they may do, being venal and public, it remains feeble and languid. Just as, even in the case of valour, when two deeds are alike, we hold that to be the nobler and more worthy, which offers the most difficulty and risk.

It is the work of divine Providence to suffer its holy Church to be disturbed, as we see it now, by so many troubles and storms, in order that pious souls may be roused up by this strife, and rescued from that drowsy lethargy in which they were plunged during a prolonged period of tranquillity. If we weigh the loss we have suffered by the many who have gone astray, against the gain that accrues to us through having recovered our breath, and resuscitated our zeal and our strength as the result of this strife, I know not whether the profit does not outweigh the loss.

We thought we had tied the knot of our marriages more firmly by removing all means of dissolving them ; but the bond of hearts and affections has become more loose and slack as that of constraint has been drawn closer. And, on the other hand, what made marriages to be so long honoured and so secure in Rome was the liberty to break them off at will. They loved their wives the better as long as there was the chance of losing them, and, with full liberty of divorce, five hundred years and more passed by before any took advantage of it.

> What's free we are disgusted at, and slight ;
> What is forbidden whets the appetite. (OVID.)

We might here mention the opinion of an ancient writer which is to the point, ' That punishments rather whet than dull the edge of sins ; That, instead of making us careful to do good, which is the work of reason and discipline, they only make us careful not to be caught doing ill ' :

> Though rooted out, the infection of the plague
> Spreads more luxuriantly. (RUTILIUS.)

I do not know whether that be true ; but I know this by experience, that never was a civil government reformed by that means. It needs some other power to make us orderly and regular in our morals.

Greek history makes mention of the Argippaeans, neighbours of the Scythians, who live without either rod or stick for striking ; yet not only does no one attempt to attack them, but any man who wishes to take refuge among them is safe, by reason of their virtue and sanctity of life, and there is no one who is so daring as to touch him. People of other regions have recourse to them to settle their differences.

There is a country where gardens and fields are made safe by being enclosed by a cotton thread only, which is found to be more firm and secure than our hedges and moats. *Things sealed up invite the thief. The burglar passes by an open door* (Seneca).

The easy access to my house is perhaps a reason among others why it has escaped the violence of our Civil wars. Defence allures the enterprising, and distrust provokes them. I have baffled the designs of the soldiery by depriving the exploit of all danger and all chance of military glory, which have usually provided them with an excuse and a pretext. Every courageous deed is an honourable deed in times when justice is dead. I have thus made the conquest of my house a cowardly action and a treachery. It is closed to nobody who knocks. It is provided with no other safeguard but a porter with old-fashioned ceremonious manners, whose office it is not to forbid my door, but rather to offer it with the more grace and decorum. I have no other sentinel nor watch but what the stars keep for me.

It is a mistake for a gentleman to make a show of defence, unless his defence be perfect. What is open on one side is open on all. Our fathers did not think of building frontier garrisons. The means of attacking, I mean without armies and artillery, and of falling upon our houses by surprise, every day grow greater than the means of guarding them. Men's wits generally are sharpened in that direction. Poor and rich alike are interested in invading, the rich alone in defending.

My house was strong for the time when it was built. I have added nothing to it in the way of strength, and should be afraid that its strength might be turned against me. Besides that a peaceful period would require it to be unfortified ; and there is the risk of being unable to recover it. And it is difficult to make sure of being safe. For in the matter of intestine wars, your own footman may be on the side you fear. And where religion serves as a pretext even kinship becomes unreliable, under the cloak of justice. The public exchequer will not support our domestic garrisons ; it would be drained thereby. We have not the means of doing so without ruin to ourselves, or, more unfitly and unjustly, without ruin to the people. My loss could hardly be greater.

Moreover, if you should ruin yourself, your friends will even go out of their way, rather than pity you, to accuse you of want of vigilance and caution, of ignorance and careless-ness in the exercise of your profession.

The fact that so many strongly guarded houses have been destroyed, whilst mine endures, makes me suspect that they were destroyed because they were strongly guarded. That arouses the assailant's desire, and provides him with an excuse. All defence wears the aspect of war. If God wills it, let them attack me ; but in any case I will not invite attack. It is my retreat and resting-place from wars. I try to keep this corner as a haven against the tempest outside, as I do another corner in my soul. Our war may well assume different forms, factions may vary and multiply ; for my part, I do not budge. When so many houses were fortified in France, I alone of my rank, so far as I know, simply entrusted mine to the protection of heaven. And I never removed even a silver spoon or a title-deed. I will neither fear nor save myself by halves. If by full gratitude I can gain the divine favour, it will remain with me to the end ; if not, I have still survived long enough to make my survival remarkable and fit to be recorded. How long ? For quite thirty years.[1]

CHAPTER 16

OF GLORY

THERE is the name and the thing ; the name is a sound which sets a mark on and denotes the thing. The name is no part of the thing nor of the substance ; it is an ex-traneous piece added to the thing, and outside of it.

God, who is all fullness in himself and the acme of all

[1] i. e., since the beginning of the Civil Wars, 1560 or 1562.

perfection, cannot grow and increase within ; but his name may grow and increase by the blessing and praise we bestow on his external works. Which praise, since it cannot be incorporated with him, because there can be in him no accession of good, we give to his name, which is the thing outside of him that is nearest to him. So it is that to God alone honour and glory are due ; and nothing can be more unreasonable than that we should seek them for ourselves. For, being indigent and necessitous within, being imperfect in essence, and continually in need of amendment, we should use all our endeavour to perfect ourselves.

We are all hollow and empty. Not with wind and words must we fill ourselves ; we need a more solid substance for our amendment. A famished man would be very foolish to think of providing himself with a fine coat instead of a good meal ; he should hasten to supply the more urgent need. As we say in our ordinary prayer, *Glory to God in the highest, and on earth peace towards men* (Saint Luke). We are suffering a dearth of beauty, health, wisdom, virtue and the like essential qualities. We must not think of external ornaments until we have provided the necessary things. Theology treats that subject fully and more pertinently ; but I am not well enough versed therein.

Chrysippus and Diogenes were the first to begin, and that most resolutely, to despise glory ; of all the gratifications they said there was none more dangerous, nor more to be avoided, than that which we derive from others' approbation. Indeed experience teaches us that we are often betrayed by it to our hurt. There is no worse poison for a prince than flattery, and nothing whereby a wicked man more easily wins their favour. Nor is there any fitter and more ordinary go-between to corrupt the chastity ·of a woman than to feed and entertain her with her praises.

The first charm the Sirens employed to seduce Ulysses was of this nature :

> Come here, thou worthy of a world of praise,
> That dost so high the Grecian glory raise. (HOMER.)

Those philosophers said that, to an intelligent man, all the fame in the world was not worth the stretching out of a finger to reach it :

> What 's glory in the highest degree,
> If it no more than glory be ? (JUVENAL.)

I mean for itself alone. For it is often attended with many advantages, for the sake of which it may become desirable. It brings us goodwill ; it leaves us less exposed to injuries and insults from others, and the like.

It was also among the principal teachings of Epicurus ; for this precept of his school, ' Conceal thy life ', which forbids a man to encumber himself with public offices and affairs, also necessarily presupposes a contempt for fame, which is the world's approval of actions by which we push ourselves into notoriety. The man who commands us to keep in the background and only mind our own business, and who would not have us make ourselves notorious, desires still less that we should seek to win honour and glory. So he advises Idomeneus to regulate his actions with no regard to public opinion or common renown, unless it were to avoid other incidental disadvantages which the contempt of men might bring upon him.

That view is, I should say, profoundly true and in accordance with reason. But we are, I know not how, double in ourselves, as a consequence of which we do not believe what we believe, and are unable to put aside what we condemn. Let us see the last words of Epicurus, written at the point of death ; they are great and worthy of such a philosopher, and yet they bear some signs that he was thinking of his renown, and that his mental attitude contradicted his teachings. Here follows a letter which he dictated shortly before breathing his last :

' EPICURUS to HERMACHUS, greeting.

' I write this letter while passing a happy day, which is also the last day of my life. And the pains of my bladder and bowels are so intense that nothing can be added to them which can make them greater. But still I have, to balance this, a joy in my mind, which I derive from the recollection of my philosophical teachings and discoveries. But do you, as becomes the goodwill which from your youth upwards you have constantly shown for me and for philosophy, protect the children of Metrodorus.'

That is his letter. And what makes me interpret the pleasure, which he says his soul feels in his discoveries, in the sense that he had some concern for the renown he hoped for after his death, is the injunction in his will and testament to Amynomachus and Timocrates, his heirs, ' to furnish every year what, in the opinion of Hermachus, shall be enough to keep his birthday in the month Gamelion, with all proper solemnity. And that they shall also every month, on the twentieth day of the month, supply money enough to furnish a banquet for those men who have studied philosophy with him, in order that his memory, and that of Metrodorus, may be duly honoured.'

Carneades was the chief upholder of the opposite view. He maintained that fame was desirable for itself ; just as we espouse the interests of our posthumous heirs, although we do not enjoy their acquaintance. This view has not failed to be more commonly followed, as those are apt to be which agree most with our inclinations.

Aristotle gives it the first place among external goods : ' Avoid, as two vicious extremes, immoderation either in running after it, or fleeing from it.'

I believe that, if we had the books that Cicero wrote on the subject, we should be hugely edified ; for that man was so infatuated with the passion for glory, that if he had dared, he would, I believe, have fallen into the excess into which others fell, who held, That virtue itself was only desirable for the honour which always attended it :

> Valour unsung shows in no nobler dress
> Than cowardice when dead. (HORACE.)

Which is so erroneous a view, that I am sorry it could ever have entered the mind of a man who was honoured with the name of philosopher.

If that were true, there would be no need to be virtuous except in public ; and there would be no object in keeping the operations of the soul, which is the true seat of virtue, in rule and order, except in so far as they might come to the knowledge of others.

Is it then only a question of sinning slyly and cunningly ? ' If you know, says Carneades, that a snake is concealed in a place where a person, by whose death you hope to gain, is about to sit down unsuspectingly, you do wickedly if you do not warn him of the danger. And the more so if the action can be known only to yourself.' If we do not find in ourselves the laws of well-doing, if impunity passes with us for justice, to how many kinds of wickedness shall we not yield every day !

What S. Peduceus did, in faithfully handing over to the widow the sum of money which C. Plotius had entrusted to his sole keeping and knowledge, a thing I have often done myself, seems to me not so praiseworthy as I should think it execrable if we had both failed in our trust.

And I think it a good and profitable thing to remember in these days the example of P. Sextilius Rufus, whom Cicero accuses of having received an inheritance against the grain of his conscience, and not only not contrary to the law, but with the consent of the law.

And M. Crassus and Q. Hortensius, who, by reason of their influence and authority, having been called in by a stranger to participate in the succession of a forged will, in order by that means to establish his own claim to a share, were content with having no hand in the forgery, whilst not refusing to enjoy the fruit of it ; feeling secure enough if they were sheltered from accusations, from witnesses and the laws. *Let them remember that they have God to witness, that is (as I understand it) their own conscience* (Cicero).

Virtue is a very vain and frivolous thing, if it derives its recommendation from glory. In vain should we undertake to make it keep its place apart, and separate it from fortune ; for what can be more fortuitous than reputation ? *Truly Fortune rules over all things ; she sheds a lustre on things, or obscures them, according to her own caprice rather than their merits* (Sallust).

It is purely the work of Fortune if actions are seen and become known. It is chance in its heedlessness that fastens glory upon us. I have often seen her marching in front of merit, and often outpacing merit by a long distance. The man who first thought of likening glory to a shadow made a better comparison than he was aware of. They are both pre-eminently empty of substance. The shadow too sometimes goes ahead of the body, and sometimes greatly exceeds it in length.

If you teach the nobility to seek in valour only honour, *as if nothing were virtuous unless noised abroad* (Cicero), what do you gain thereby except that you instruct them never to run into danger unless they are seen, and to take very good care that they have witnesses to carry news of their valour ; whilst they may have a thousand occasions to act bravely without being observed ? How many noble deeds of individuals are buried in the throng of battle ! Should any one in such a fray waste his time in checking the actions of others he cannot be very busy himself, and in giving testimony of his comrades' behaviour he would be furnishing evidence against himself. *The wise and truly great soul places honour, which is the chief aim of our nature, in deeds and not in glory* (Cicero).

All the fame I look for in life is to have lived it tranquilly ; tranquilly not as Metrodorus, or Arcesilaus, or Aristippus, understood it, but as I understand it. Since Philosophy has been unable to discover any way to tranquillity that is good for all, let every one seek it for himself.

To what do Caesar and Alexander owe the infinite greatness of their renown, if not to Fortune ? How many men has she not snuffed out in the beginning of their career, of whom we have no knowledge, who brought to their work the same courage as they, but whose ill luck stopped them short at the very birth of their enterprises ? In the course of the many and extreme dangers to which he was exposed, I do not remember having read that Caesar was ever wounded.[1] A thousand have fallen in lesser dangers than the least of those he passed through.

An endless number of noble deeds must be lost for want of witnesses, before one turns to account. A man is not always at the top of a breach, or in the forefront of an army, in the sight of his general, as on a stage. He is taken unawares between the hedge and the ditch ; he must tempt fortune in attacking a hen-roost ; he must dislodge four wretched musketeers out of a barn ; he must separate from his company, and attack on his own account, as necessity provides the occasion. And if we look into the matter, we shall find by experience that the least brilliant occasions happen to be the most dangerous ; and that in the wars of our own times more good men have been lost on slight and unimportant occasions, and in disputing some paltry fort, than in worthy and honourable places.

He who thinks his death wasted except on some signal occasion, instead of throwing a lustre on his death, is more likely to cast a shadow over his life ; in the meantime

---

[1] The edition of 1588 adds these words : ' but I know very well that that is said of Hannibal and of Scanderbeg ; ' i. e., that they were never wounded.

allowing many a fitting opportunity for venturing his life to escape him. And there is lustre enough in every fitting opportunity, each man's conscience sufficiently trumpeting them. *Our glory is the testimony of our conscience* (Saint Paul).

He who is only good because his goodness will be known, and because he will be the better thought of after it is known ; he who will only do good on condition of his goodness coming to the knowledge of men, is not one from whom much service is to be expected.

> The remnant of the winter, he with shield
> And spear achieved things worthy to be shown,
> I ween ; but these were then so well concealed,
> It is no fault of mine they were not blown ;
> For good Orlando was in fighting field
> Prompter to do than make his prowess known.
> Nor e'er was bruited action of the knight,
> Save when some faithful witness was in sight. (ARIOSTO.)

A man must go to the wars as a matter of duty, and expect this reward which cannot fail every noble deed, however hidden it may be, or even a valiant thought, that is, the inward satisfaction that a well-regulated conscience reaps from well-doing. A man must be valiant for himself and for the advantage he derives from having his courage firmly based, and secure against the assaults of Fortune :

> Worth, all indifferent to the spurns
>   Of vulgar souls profane,
> The honours wears it proudly earns,
>   Unclouded by a stain ;
> Nor grasps nor lays the fasces down
> As fickle mobs applaud or frown. (HORACE.)

Nor for outward show must our soul play her part, but within ourselves, where no eyes but our own can penetrate. There she will shelter us from the fear of death, of pain, and even of shame ; there she will arm us against the loss of our children, of our friends and fortunes, and when opportunity offers, she will also lead us on to the hazards of war ; *not for any profit, but for the beauty attached to virtue* (Cicero). This is a much greater gain, and much more worthy of being coveted and hoped for, than honour and glory, which are no more than a favourable judgement passed upon us by others.

We must needs select a dozen men out of a whole nation to decide a question about an acre of land ; and the judgement of our inclinations and actions, the most difficult and important matter that can be, we refer to the voice of the people, to the rabble, the mother of ignorance, injustice, and fickleness. Is it reasonable to make the life of a wise man dependent on the judgement of fools ? *Can anything be more foolish than to rate highly as a body those whom singly we despise ?* (Cicero). Whoever aims at pleasing them will never have done ; it is a butt we can neither see nor hit. *Nothing can be so little counted upon as the mind of the multitude* (Livy).

Demetrius said wittily of the voice of the people that he set no more store by that which issued from above than on that which issued from below. Cicero goes still farther : *My opinion is that, though a thing be not disgraceful in itself, it cannot be free from suspicion when it is commended by the multitude.*

No skill, no mental cunning, could direct our steps to follow so misleading and erratic a guide. In this windy chaos of rumours, reports, and vulgar opinions, in which we are blown about, we can fix upon no road that is likely to lead anywhere.

Let us set up a goal that is not so unsteady and wavering ; let us consistently follow reason. Let public approval then follow us, if it will ; and, as it is entirely dependent on chance, we have no more reason to expect it by any other way rather than that. Even should I not follow the straight road for its straightness, I should follow it because I had learned by experience that at the end of the reckoning it is usually the happiest and most profitable. *Providence has given this gift to mortals, that honesty is the best policy* (Quintilian). The ancient mariner spoke thus to Neptune in a great storm : ' O God, you can save me if you will, and if you will you can destroy me ; yet will I always keep my rudder straight.'

In my time I have seen a thousand supple-minded, double-faced, and equivocating men whom nobody doubted to be more worldly-wise than myself, and who were lost where I was saved :

I laughed to see that wit no better sped. (OVID, altered.)

Paulus Emilius, on setting out upon his famous expedition against Macedonia, especially warned the people of Rome ' to restrain their tongues during his absence with regard to his actions '. What a disturbing element in great affairs is freedom of opinion ! seeing that not every one has the firmness of Fabius who, in face of the hostile and abusive tongues of the people, suffered his authority to be pulled to pieces by the idle fancies of men rather than carry out his charge less well, with a favourable reputation and with the approval of the populace.

There is naturally something indescribably pleasant in hearing oneself praised ; but we attach far too much importance to it :

> I'm not afraid of praise, I must confess,
> My heart is not of horn, but ne'ertheless
> I must deny the only end and aim
> Of doing well is to hear men exclaim :
> ' O worthy man, O noble deed ! ' (PERSIUS.)

I care not so much what I am in the opinion of others as what I am in my own. I would be rich of myself, and not by borrowing. Strangers see only actions and outside appearances. Any man can put on a bold face outside, though in a fever of fright within. They do not see my heart, they only see my countenance.

With good reason do people denounce the hypocrisy we see in war-time ; for what is easier for the practised soldier than to shirk the dangers, and to bluster, although he may be but a faint-hearted fellow ? For the individual there are so many ways of avoiding risks, that we may deceive the world a thousand times before we are involved in a dangerous undertaking ; and even then, finding ourselves entangled in it, we are well able for the time being to hide our game behind a bold face and brave words, though our heart be all in a tremble within.

And if they had the use of Plato's ring which made him invisible who wore it on his finger, by giving it a turn towards the palm of the hand, many people would often conceal themselves when they should show themselves most openly, and would be sorry to be placed in so honourable a position, where necessity must make them bold.

> None but knaves and liars can be charmed
> By groundless praise, by slanders be alarmed. (HORACE.)

Thus we see how marvellously uncertain and doubtful are all those judgements that are founded on external appearance ; and no witness is so reliable as each man is to himself.

On those occasions how many camp-followers have we to share our glory ? When a man stands firm in an open trench, what more does he do than fifty wretched pioneers have done before him, in clearing the way and sheltering him with their bodies for a daily pay of twopence-halfpenny ?

> For if thick-headed Rome should aught condemn,
> Pay thou no heed, nor take upon thyself
> To mend her faulty scales. Go thine own way ! (PERSIUS.)

To disperse and scatter our name into many mouths we call aggrandizing it ; we should like it to be favourably thought of, and profit by this aggrandizement ; that is the best excuse for this desire. But this craving is carried to so great an excess that many seek to become notorious in any way whatsoever. Trogus Pompeius said of Herostratus, and Livy of Manlius Capitolinus, that they were more ambitious of a world-wide than of a good reputation.[1] It is a common fault. We are more anxious that people *should* talk about us, than *how* they talk about us ; it is enough if our name be on men's lips, whether for good or evil. To be known seems in some sort to have our lives and duration in others' keeping.

For my own part, I consider that I exist only in myself ; and of that other life of mine, which lies in the knowledge of my friends, considering it naked and simply in itself, I know very well that I am sensible of no fruit or enjoyment from it, but by the vanity of a fantastic opinion. And when I am dead I shall be still less sensible of it ; and so I shall absolutely lose the enjoyment of the real advantages which sometimes accidentally attend it. I shall then have no handle by which to take hold of reputation, nor will it have any means of reaching or touching me.

For, supposing that I should expect my name to become famous : in the first place I have no name which I can sufficiently call my own. Of the two that I have, one is

---

[1] Herostratus successfully sought to gain immortality by burning the magnificent Temple of Diana, one of the seven wonders of the world. Manlius was ambitious of becoming, by fair means or foul, the greatest man in Rome.

common to all my family, and indeed to other families besides. There is a family with the surname of Montaigne at Paris and at Montpellier, another in Brittany, another in Saintonge, who call themselves La Montaigne. The removal of a single syllable will so entangle our threads that I may share in their glory, and they perchance in my shame. And besides, my family formerly bore the surname Eyquem, a name which still attaches to a well-known house in England.

As to my other name,[1] anybody that pleases is at liberty to take it. So a street-porter may perhaps succeed to the honour that is due to me. And then, though I had a particular mark to myself, what can it mark when I am no more ? Can it designate and bring into prominence a thing of no substance ?

> What though posterity should laud his name,
> The tomb will press no lighter on his bones.
> No violets will spring from his remains. (PERSIUS.)

But of this I have spoken elsewhere.[2]

After all, in a whole battle, in which ten thousand men are maimed or killed, not fifteen will be noticed. It must be some great and outstanding deed, or one that is accidently followed by important consequences, that will bring into prominence not merely a musketeer's, but a general's exploit. For to kill a man or two, or ten, to face death courageously, is indeed something for each one of us, for we hazard everything. But for the world they are such common and every-day occurrences, and it needs so many of the same kind to produce any noteworthy result, that we cannot expect to be particularly commended for them :

> That fate is shared by many, it is trite,
> As picked at random out of Fortune's heap. (JUVENAL.)

Of so many myriads of valiant men who have died these last fifteen hundred years in France, with their weapons in their hands, not a hundred have come to our knowledge. The memory, not only of the leaders, but of the battles and victories, is buried.

The happenings of more than half the world, for want of record, are confined to one spot, and vanish without duration. If I possessed the knowledge of all unrecorded events,

---

[1] Michel.
[2] In the chapter Of Names, in the First Book.

I think I could very easily furnish examples of every kind that would supplant those that have been recorded.

Why, even of the Romans and Greeks consider how few names have been handed down to us, in spite of the many rare and noble exploits they performed, and all their writers and witnesses !

> Scarcely to our ears
> Floats through the ages a thin breath of Fame. (VIRGIL.)

It will be a wonder if, a hundred years hence, it is remembered in a general way that there were civil wars in our time in France.

The Lacedemonians, on entering into battle, sacrificed to the Muses, that their deeds might be well and worthily written down, thinking it to be a divine and no common favour if their noble actions should find witnesses able to give them life and memory.

Do we imagine that at every musket-shot we receive, and every danger we run into, there will suddenly appear a notary to record it ? And a hundred notaries besides may write them down, and their comments will endure only three days and be seen by nobody.

We do not possess a thousandth part of the works of the ancients. Fortune has given them a shorter or longer life, according to her favour ; and, not having seen the remainder, we are at liberty to question whether those we have are not the worst. History is not written on every small trifle. A man must have been a leader and conquered an empire or a kingdom ; he must have won fifty-two pitched battles, and always with inferior numbers, like Caesar. Ten thousand good fellows and many great captains valiantly and courageously died in his service, whose names endured only as long as their wives and children lived :

> Whom Rumour doth in darkness hide. (VIRGIL.)

Even those whose brave deeds we have witnessed, three months or three years after they are left on the field of battle, are no more spoken of than if they had never been.

If you consider, in due measure and proportion, the people and the deeds whose fame is preserved in the memory of books, you will find that there are very few actions and very few persons in our time that may claim any right to such fame. How many valorous men have we not seen to survive their own reputation, men who have seen and suffered the honour and glory they had justly acquired in their younger days to be snuffed out in their presence ! And for three years of this fanciful and imaginary life shall we throw away our real and essential life, and be plunged into a perpetual death ? The wise man sets up a much fairer and more fitting goal to such an important enterprise as life. *The reward of a good deed is to have done it* (Seneca). *The fruit of a service is the service itself* (Cicero).

It would be excusable perhaps in a painter or any other artist, or even in a rhetorician or grammarian, to labour to make a name by his works ; but the actions of Virtue are too noble in themselves to seek any other reward but from their own worth, and especially to seek it in the vanity of human estimation.

And yet if this erroneous notion is of such service to the community as to keep men within their duty ; if the people are thereby instigated to virtue ; if rulers are moved when they hear the world blessing the memory of Trajan and execrating that of Nero ; if it stirs them up to hear the name of that great scoundrel, once held in such fear and dread, freely cursed and reviled by the first schoolboy who attacks his memory ; let it wax bravely, and let us nourish it to the best of our power !

And Plato, employing every means to make his citizens virtuous, advises them amongst other things not to despise the good repute and esteem of the people. He declares that by some divine inspiration it happens that even the wicked man is often able, not only by words but in thought, to distinguish rightly between the good and the bad. This great man and his schoolmaster [1] are marvellously bold craftsmen in the art of bringing in the operations and revelations of the gods whenever the power of man fails ; *after the example of the tragic poets, who have recourse to a god when they are unable to unravel their plot* (Cicero). That is perhaps why Timon called him abusively ' the great forger of miracles '.

Since man, on account of his shortcomings, will not be satisfied with good money, let us also pay him in spurious coin. This expedient has been practised by all the law-givers ; and there is no body of laws that is not mixed up

[1] Socrates.

with some empty ceremonies or lying legends, to serve as
a curb to keep the people to their duties. For this reason
it is that to most legislators is given a fabulous origin and
beginning, with a wealth of mysteries and superstitions. It
is this that has brought spurious religions into credit, and
made them to be countenanced by men of intelligence. For
this reason too did Numa and Sertorius, the better to impose
on the credulity of their people, feed them with this foolish
idea, the one that the nymph Egeria, the other that a white
fawn, conveyed to them from the gods all the decisions they
adopted.

And the same authority that Numa claimed for his laws,
on the pretence of being patronized by the aforesaid goddess, Zoroaster, the legislator of the Bactrians and Persians,
claimed for his, in the name of the god Oromazis ; Trisme-
gistus of the Egyptians, in the name of Mercury ; Zamolxis
of the Scythians, in the name of Vesta ; Charondas of the
Chalcidians, of Saturn ; Minos of the Candiots, of Jupiter ;
Lycurgus of the Lacedemonians, of Apollo ; Draco and
Solon of the Athenians, of Minerva. So every code of laws
has a god as its fountain-head ; falsely so the others, but
truly so that which Moses established for the people of
Judea when they were come out of Egypt.

The religion of the Bedouins, as the Lord of Joinville tells
us, taught, among other things, that the soul of any one of
them who died for his prince entered into another body
that was happier, stronger, and handsomer than the first.
This belief made them much more ready to risk their lives :

> They covet wounds and seek their deaths ; 'tis base
> To save a life so soon to come again. (LUCAN.)

There we see a very wholesome belief, however groundless
it may be. Every nation has many examples of the
same kind. But this subject would deserve an essay by
itself.

To add a few more words on my first theme, neither
will I advise the ladies to call their duty honour. *In
ordinary parlance that only is called honourable which enjoys
popular favour* (Cicero). Their duty is the pith, their honour
is but the rind. Nor do I advise them to give us this excuse
for payment of their refusal. For I take it for granted that
their intentions, their desire, and their will, with which

honour has nothing to do, since they do not appear on the surface, are still better regulated than their deeds :

> She sins who but abstains from fear of sin. (OVID.)

Towards God and the conscience the desire would be as great an offence as the deed. And, besides, they are actions which are of themselves hidden and secret ; it would be very easy to keep an action, on which honour depends, from the knowledge of others, if they had no other consideration for their duty and the affection in which they hold their chastity for its own sake.

Every woman of honour will choose to lose her honour rather than her conscience.

CHAPTER 17

OF PRESUMPTION

THERE is another kind of glory,[1] which is to have too high an opinion of our own worth. It is an unthinking self-love which we nourish, and which makes us appear to ourselves other than we are ; like the passion of love, which lends charm and beauty to the object it embraces, which disturbs and corrupts the judgement of the man in love, and makes him think his lady other and more perfect than she is.

Yet I would not have a man, through fear of sinning in that direction, mis-know himself, and think himself worse than he is ; the judgement should maintain its rights always and everywhere. It is right that here, as in all things, he should see what the truth sets before him. If he is a Caesar, let him boldly think himself the greatest general the world has seen.

We are all convention ; conventions carry us away, and we neglect the substance of things. We hang on to the branches, and leave the trunk and body. We have taught the ladies to blush at the mere mention of things they have no fear of doing. We dare not call our members by their right names, yet we are not afraid to employ them in all kinds of debauchery. Convention forbids our expressing in words things that are allowed and natural, and we obey her. Reason forbids our doing illicit and wicked things, and

[1] Vainglory.

nobody obeys her. Here I am fettered by the laws of
convention ; for she allows a man to speak neither well
nor ill of himself. We will leave her alone for the time being.

The man whom Fortune (call it good or ill, as you please)
has enabled to live in some position of eminence may by
his public actions testify to what he is. But he who is only
one of the herd (and of whom no man will speak unless he
speak of himself) is to be excused if he has the hardihood
to speak of himself, especially to those who are interested
in knowing him, after the example of Lucilius :

> As unto loyal friends and tried
> He to his notebook would confide
> His secrets ; thither turning still,
> Went Fortune with him well or ill ;
> Hence all the old man's life is known
> As on a votive tablet shown. (HORACE.)

He committed to his paper his actions and thoughts, and
there portrayed himself as he felt himself to be. *Nor did
any one doubt the honesty or question the motives of Rutilius
or Scaurus in writing their memoirs* (Tacitus).

So I remember that, from my tenderest childhood, there
was observed in me a certain indefinable carriage of the
body and certain gestures which testified to some empty and
silly pride.

I may say this, in the first place, that there is no harm
in certain qualities and propensities which are so much
a part of ourselves that we have no means of perceiving
and recognizing them. And of such natural inclinations
the body may easily, without our knowledge or consent,
retain a certain bent.

It was a kind of affectation sorting with his beauty that
made Alexander carry his head a little on one side, and
caused Alcibiades to lisp. Julius Caesar used to scratch
his head with one finger, which is the action of a man full
of troublesome thoughts ; and Cicero, I think, was wont to
wrinkle his nose, which is a sign of a scornful disposition.
Such motions may arise without our noticing them.

Others there are that do not come naturally, of which
I will not speak, such as our bows and salutations, whereby
one gains credit, wrongfully for the most part, for being
very humble and polite ; a man may be humble through
vainglory. I am rather prodigal of bonnetings, especially

in summer, and never take a salute without returning it, whatever the rank of the person, unless he be in my pay.

I could wish that some princes I know would be more sparing and discriminating in dispensing these marks of courtesy. For, thus unwisely bestowed, they are thrown away ; if they are given without respect of persons, they lose their effect.

Among different kinds of irregular deportment let us not forget the haughty bearing of the Emperor Constantius, who in public always held his head erect, without turning it or bending it this way or that way, not even to look at those who saluted him from the side ; keeping his body rigid and motionless in spite of the jolting of his coach, and daring neither to spit, blow his nose, nor wipe his face before the people.

I do not know whether those gestures they remarked in me were of this first kind, and whether I had indeed some hidden propensity to the fault in question, as may well have been the case. And I cannot answer for the motions of my body ; but as regards the motions of the soul, I will here confess what I think about myself.

This vainglory consists of two parts, namely, To think too highly of ourselves, and Not to think highly enough of other people. With regard to the one, I think that in the first place these considerations should be taken into account :

That I feel oppressed by an error of the soul, which displeases me, both as being unjust, and still more as being troublesome. I try to correct it, but eradicate it I cannot. This fault is that the mere fact of possessing a thing makes me undervalue it, and that I attach too high a value to things that are not mine, that belong to another and are out of my reach. This habit of mind is very common. As the privileged authority which men have over their wives makes some regard their own, and some fathers their children, with a wicked disdain ; so it is with me, and of two works that are equal I should always think less of my own. It is not so much that zeal for my progress and improvement disturbs my judgement and prevents my being satisfied with myself, as that the fact of being master of itself breeds contempt of what we hold and control.

The governments, customs, and languages of distant countries are my delight; and I am aware that Latin, by reason of its dignity, fascinates me more than it should, as it does boys and the common sort of people. My neighbour's husbandry, his house, his horse, though no better than my own, I value more than my own, just because they are not mine. I am besides very ignorant of my own affairs. I admire the cheerful self-assurance and optimism of other people, whilst there is scarcely anything I am sure of knowing, or that I can answer for being able to do. I have no exact idea in advance of the means at my disposal, and only know of them after the event. I am as doubtful of myself as of everything else; whence it comes that if I happen to succeed in any business, I attribute it more to my luck than to my ability, seeing that in all my plans I am haphazard and diffident.

So another general characteristic of mine is this, that of all the estimates of mankind in the gross expressed by the ancient writers, I most readily embrace and most strongly adhere to those that are most contemptuous, most humiliating and most crushing. To me Philosophy never seems to have so easy a game as when she attacks our presumption and vanity, when she sincerely admits her own indecision, weakness, and ignorance. It seems to me that the nursing-mother of the most erroneous ideas, both of men in general and of the individual, is the exaggerated opinion man has of himself.

Those men who bestraddle the epicycle of Mercury and see so far into the heavens get on my nerves.[1] For when in my studies, whose subject is Man, I find so great a variety of opinions, so inextricable a maze of obscurities one on top of the other, so great variance and uncertainty in the very school of Wisdom, you may judge (since those men have been unable to agree in their knowledge of themselves and their own condition, which is ever present to their eyes, which is within them; since they do not know how those things move which they themselves set in motion, nor how to describe and explain the springs of action which they themselves hold and manage), you may imagine, I say, how far I can believe them when they explain the causes of the flow and ebb of the river Nile. The curiosity

[1] Lit., pull out my teeth.

to know things has been given to man for a scourge, says Holy Scripture.[1]

But to come to my own particular case, I think it would be very difficult to find a man who has a smaller opinion of himself, nay, a man who has a smaller opinion of me, than I have of myself.

I regard myself as a very ordinary person, except in this respect, that I do regard myself in that light. I plead guilty to the meanest and commonest defects ; I neither disclaim nor excuse them. The only value that I set upon myself is that I know my own value.

If I have any vainglory, it is superficially poured upon me, through the treachery of my nature, and has not so much body that my judgement can perceive it ; I am sprinkled but not dyed with it.

For indeed, with regard to intellectual achievements of any kind, I never produced anything that filled me with satisfaction. And the approval of others does not repay me. My taste is delicate and hard to please, and especially with regard to my own work. I continually repudiate myself, and feel myself at all times fluctuating and bending by reason of my weakness. I have nothing of my own that satisfies my judgement. My sight is clear and normal enough, but when at work it becomes blurred.

This I experience most evidently in the case of poetry. I am extremely fond of it, and I can form a pretty good judgement of others' work ; but when I try to set my hand to it I am indeed but a child, and the result is something I cannot tolerate. We may play the fool in anything else, but not in poetry :

> For Gods and men and booksellers refuse
> To countenance a mediocre Muse. (HORACE.)

Would to Heaven that these lines were inscribed over the doors of all our printers' shops, to forbid the entrance of so many versifiers !

> None more conceited than a sorry poet. (MARTIAL.)

Why are not our people like this ? Dionysius the father valued nothing of his so highly as his poetry. At the season of the Olympian games, with chariots surpassing all others

---

[1] A translation of one of the Latin sentences inscribed on the ceiling in Montaigne's library.

in magnificence, he also sent poets and musicians to present his verses, together with tents and pavilions royally gilt and tapestried. When they began to recite his lines, the charm and excellence of the delivery at first attracted the attention of the people ; but after considering the inanity of the composition, they first showed disdain, then, becoming more and more exasperated, they soon fell into a fury and angrily rushed his tents and tore them all in pieces. And when his chariots failed to make a show in the races, and the vessel which carried back his people missed the coast of Sicily and was driven before the gale and dashed against the rocks at Tarentum, they took it for a certain sign that the gods, like themselves, were incensed against the badness of his poem. And even the sailors who escaped from the shipwreck backed up the opinion of the people, with which also the oracle that predicted his death seemed in some sort to agree.

This was to the effect ' that Dionysius should be near his end when he had vanquished those who were better than himself '. These he interpreted to be the Carthaginians, whose forces were greater than his own. Being at war with them he often dodged the victory, or qualified it, in order not to incur the fate intended by that oracle. But he misunderstood it ; for the God was thinking of the occasion when, by favour and injustice, he gained the advantage at Athens over the tragic poets who were better than he, and in competition with whom he had his play, called ' The Leneians ',[1] acted. He died immediately after this victory, partly in consequence of the excessive joy he felt at his success.

What I find tolerable in my own work is not so really and in itself, but by comparison with other and worse things which I observe to be well received. I envy the happiness of those who are able to rejoice and find a satisfaction in their productions ; for that is an easy way of indulging oneself, since the source of our pleasure is in ourselves, especially if we are strong in our self-conceit.

I know a poet against whom everybody, the strong and the weak, in the crowd and in the chamber, against whom

---

[1] Not quite accurate. The play had another name, but was acted at the Leneian games. As to Dionysius's death, it was not the excessive joy, but the deep potations with which he celebrated his victory, that brought t on.

heaven and earth cry out that he is no poet. For all that
he will not abate a jot of the measure to which he has cut
himself ; ever beginning again, ever persisting, ever recon-
sidering, he is all the stronger and more stubborn in his
good opinion of himself for being the only one who holds it.

My works are so far from pleasing me that, as often as
I peruse them, so often do they annoy me :

> When I re-read I blush at what I've written ;
> For many things I see which even I,
> Being judge, account but fit to be erased. (OVID.)

I have always an idea in my mind, a sort of blurred
picture, which shows me, as in a dream, a better form than
that I have framed ; but I cannot grasp it and turn it to
account. And yet that idea is but on a middle plane.
From this I conclude that the productions of those great
and fertile minds of the past are very far beyond the utmost
stretch of my imagination and desire. Their writings not
only satisfy me to the full, but they excite my astonished
and rapturous admiration. I see and appreciate their
beauty, if not so far as they are capable of being appreciated,
at least so far that I cannot possibly aspire to equal them.

Whatever I take in hand, I owe a sacrifice to the Graces,
as Plutarch says of some one, to conciliate their favour :

> If anything should please that I indite,
> Into men's minds if it infuse delight,
> I owe it to the charming Graces. (Poet unknown.)

But they always leave me in the lurch. All that I write
is rude ; it lacks grace and beauty. I am unable to make
the most of things. My style adds nothing to the matter.[1]
Therefore I need a strong matter, with plenty of grip, and
one that shines by its own light. When I take up a popular
theme and one of a more sprightly nature, I do so in obedience to my own instinct, as I do not affect a solemn and
gloomy wisdom, like the world in general ; to enliven myself, not my style, which is rather suited to a grave and
austere subject (at least if I may call that a style which is
a way of speaking without form or rule, a popular jargon,

---

[1] A commentator points out that Montaigne here seems to flatly
contradict what he said in another place : ' Do not look to the matter,
but to the shape that I give it. My humour is to regard the form more
than the substance.'

proceeding without definitions, without divisions, without conclusions, hazy, like that of Amafanius and Rabirius).[1]

I can neither please, nor delight, nor tickle. The best story in the world becomes dull and dry by my handling. I can only speak in real earnest and am entirely without that facility which I observe in many of my friends of entertaining any chance people and keeping a whole company amused, or of holding the attention of a prince with all kinds of small talk, without boring him. Those people never run short of matter, by reason of their gift in laying hold of the first that comes to hand, and adapting it to the humour and capacity of those they are talking with.

Princes are not very fond of serious talk ; nor am I of telling stories. The first and most obvious arguments, which are usually the most readily accepted, I am unable to hit upon ; a poor preacher for the gentry ! When once I start a subject I am apt to exhaust it.

Cicero thinks that in philosophical treatises the most difficult part is the exordium. If that be so, I confine myself to the conclusion.

And yet we must tune the string to every kind of note ; and the sharpest is that which comes least often into play. It needs at least as much perfection to develop an empty theme as to sustain a weighty one. At times one needs to handle a matter superficially, at other times to dig deeply into it. I know well that most people keep to that lower stage, being unable to see beneath the outer rind. But I also know that the greatest masters, both Xenophon and Plato, often unbend and employ that lower and popular manner of speaking and treating of matters, enhancing them however with the charm that never fails them.

Now in my style there is no ease and polish ; it is harsh and disdainful, disposed to be free and unrestrained. And as such it flatters my inclination, if not my judgement. But I am very sensible of the fact that I sometimes allow myself to go too far, and that by endeavouring to avoid art and affectation, I drop into them on another side :

> I grow obscure in trying to be brief. (HORACE.)

Plato says that length and brevity are not qualities that either take from or give value to style.

[1] Two men mentioned by Cicero. The former was one of the earlier Roman writers of the Epicurean school. Of the latter nothing is known.

I could not, though I tried, attain to that even, smooth and correct style of other writers. And, although the concise and rhythmic style of Sallust best suits my humour, yet I find Caesar both greater and less easy to copy. And if my inclination prompts me rather to imitate the style of Seneca, I have yet a higher estimation of that of Plutarch.

As in doing, so also in speaking, I simply follow my natural bent ; which is perhaps the reason why I am better at speaking than at writing. Movement and action put life into words, especially with those who, like me, move briskly and become heated. Demeanour, face, voice, attitude, and the gown may set off a speech, which in itself is mere twaddle. Messala complains, in Tacitus, of some tight garments or other worn in his time, and of the arrangement of the benches from which the orators had to speak, and which impaired their eloquence.

My French is corrupt, both in pronunciation and in other respects, through the barbarism of my native place. I have never known a man of the hither provinces [1] whose native speech did not show a very perceptible twang, and offend purely French ears. Not however that I am very expert in my Périgord patois, for I can speak it no better than I can German. Nor do I much care ; for (like the other dialects around me, going from district to district, those of Poitou, Saintonge, Angoumois, Limoges, and Auvergne) it is a languid, drawling, long-winded language.

There is certainly above us, towards the mountains, a Gascon dialect which I consider singularly fine, blunt, concise, expressive, and indeed a more virile and soldier-like language than any I know ; as sinewy, forcible, and direct as the French is graceful, neat, and fluent.

As for Latin, which was given me for my mother-tongue, I have, through want of practice, lost the ready use of it in speaking ; nay, in writing too, though at one time I could be called a master-hand at it. There you may see how much I fall short in that direction.

Beauty is a highly commendable quality in human intercourse. It is the first means of winning the favour of other people, and no man is so barbarous and surly as not to feel the attraction of it in some degree. The body has a great part in our being, and holds an eminent place in it ; hence

[1] i. e., south of the Charente, the boundary of the Languedoc.

its structure and composition are well worthy of consideration.

They are to blame who would disunite our two principal parts and keep them apart. They should on the contrary be coupled and joined together. We should bid the soul, not to stand aside and entertain herself alone, not to despise and forsake the body (nor can she do so, except by some pretence and hypocrisy), but to become allied with him, to embrace him, cherish him, assist him, control him, advise him, correct him and bring him back when he goes astray; in short marry him and become his spouse, that they may not appear to be pulling in different and opposite directions, but to live together in unity and harmony.

Christians have a particular instruction concerning this bond. For they know that the divine justice embraces this union and fellowship of body and soul, to the extent of making the body capable of everlasting rewards; and that God looks at the actions of the whole man, and wills that he shall receive, as one whole, his punishment or his wage, according to his deserts.

The Peripatetic school, of all sects the most sociable, makes this the sole care of Wisdom, to provide for and procure the common good of these two associated parts. And they point out that the other sects, through not giving sufficient consideration to this admixture, took sides, one for the body, another for the soul, with equal error on both sides; and that they lost sight of their subject, which is Man, and their guide, which they generally admit to be Nature.

It is probable that the first of human distinctions, and the first consideration which gave to some men a pre-eminence over others, was the advantage of beauty:

> They portioned out their flocks and fields,
> And gave to each according to his beauty,
> Or strength or sense. For beauty then was prized,
> And strength was valued. (LUCRETIUS.)

Well, I am a little below the middle height. This is not only an ugly defect, but it is also a disadvantage, especially in those who are in office and command. For the authority given by a fine presence and bodily dignity is lacking. C. Marius was unwilling to enlist soldiers under six feet.

The Courtier[1] is quite right when, in the gentleman he is training, he prefers a moderate stature rather than any other ; and objects to anything unusual that would make him too noticeable. But if he fails to be of the right middle height, I should prefer, in a military man, that he should exceed it.

Little men, says Aristotle, are very pretty, but not handsome ; and as a great soul connotes greatness, so a big and tall body connotes beauty. The Ethiopians and the Indians, he says, when they elected their kings or magistrates, had regard to the beauty and lofty stature of the candidates. They were right. For the sight of a tall and handsome leader marching at the head of his army inspires his followers with respect and his enemies with terror :

> Himself too Turnus, of surpassing mould,
> Amid the foremost moving, arms in hand,
> By a whole head o'ertops them. (VIRGIL.)

Our great, divine, and heavenly King, about whom everything should be carefully, religiously, and reverently remarked, did not despise bodily advantages : *thou art fairer than the children of men* (Psalms). And Plato desires beauty, as well as temperance and courage, in the guardians of his Republic.

It is very humiliating, if you are standing among your servants, to be addressed with the question, ' Where is your master ? ' and to receive only the fag-end of a salute made to your secretary or your barber. As happened to poor Philopoemen.[2] Being the first of his company to arrive at a house where he was expected, his hostess, who did not know him and received him rather coldly, made use of him to help her maids draw water and stir the fire against Philopoemen's coming. When the gentlemen of his suite appeared, and caught him busily engaged in this pleasant occupation (for he had not failed to obey the lady's orders), they asked him what he was doing there. ' I am paying the penalty of my ugliness,' he replied.

Other kinds of beauty are for the women ; beauty of stature is the only beauty of man. When a man is small, neither a broad and round forehead, nor clear and soft eyes,

---

[1] *The Courtier ;* see vol. i., p. 286.
[2] The 1580 edition has Phocion, with the remark, ' I can easily mistake a name, but not the substance.'

nor an average nose, nor small ears and mouth, nor white
and regular teeth, nor a thick, smooth, auburn beard, nor
curly hair, nor a properly rounded head, nor a fresh complexion, nor a pleasant face, nor an odourless body, nor a
correct symmetry of limbs, will make him handsome.

As to myself, I have a sturdy, thick-set figure ; my face
is full without being fat ; my disposition between the jovial
and the melancholy, moderately warm and sanguine ;

> My legs are stiff with bristles,
> And hair is on my chest. (MARTIAL.)

I enjoyed a robust and vigorous health until I was well on
in years, and was rarely troubled by illness.

Such I was, for I am not portraying myself now that I
have entered the avenues of old age, being long past forty :

> And now by slow degrees
> Years break my strength, my vigorous growth destroy,
> And drag me downward to a dull decay. (LUCRETIUS.)

Henceforth I shall be only half a man, and no longer
myself. I escape and steal away from myself every day :

> Then too the years they rob us, as they run,
> Of all things we delight in, one by one. (HORACE.)

Skill and agility I have never had ; and yet I am the son
of a very nimble father, who retained his sprightliness to an
extreme old age. He could scarcely find a man in his station
of life to equal him in all bodily exercises ; whilst I have
hardly come across one who did not surpass me, except in
running, at which I was middling good. Of music, either
vocal, for which my voice is very ill-adapted, or instrumental, they could never teach me anything. In dancing,
tennis, wrestling, I was never able to acquire more than a
very slight and ordinary skill ; in swimming, fencing, vault-
ing, and leaping, none at all.

My hands are so awkward, that I cannot even write
legibly enough for myself ; so that I prefer to re-write what
I have scribbled rather than give myself the trouble of
deciphering it.[1] And I can hardly read any better. I feel

---

[1] On this point we can at least flatly contradict Montaigne. His hand-
writing, which is open to all the world to see, never gave anybody any
trouble.

that I bore my listeners. Otherwise, a good scholar.[1] I
cannot fold a letter correctly, nor could I ever cut a pen,
nor carve at table worth a rap, nor saddle and bridle a horse,
nor properly carry a hawk and let it fly, nor speak with
hound, hawk, or horse.

In short, my bodily and mental faculties are very much
on a par. There is no briskness, only perfect strength and
vigour. I can stand hard work, but only when it is voluntary, and as long as my desire prompts me,

> Where the zest and the sport
> Makes the labour seem light, and the long hours short. (HORACE.)

Otherwise, unless I am allured by some pleasure, and have
no guide except my free will and inclination, I am good for
nothing. For I have arrived at that stage when, excepting
health and life, there is nothing for which I would bite my
nails and that I would purchase at the price of mental
torment and constraint :

> For all the sands and all the golden wealth
> That shady Tagus rolls into the sea. (JUVENAL.)

Extremely idle, extremely independent, both by nature
and habit, I would as willingly lend my blood as my pains.

I have a soul that belongs wholly to itself and is accustomed to go its own way. Having had, to this hour, neither
master nor governor forced upon me, I have gone ahead as
far as I pleased, and at my own pace. This has made me
slack and unfit in the service of others, and of no use to any
but myself.

And, as far as I am concerned, there was no need to force
my heavy, lazy, and do-nothing disposition. For, having
enjoyed from my birth such a degree of fortune that I had
reason to be satisfied with it [a reason, however, which a
thousand others of my acquaintance would rather have used
as a plank over which to pass in quest of fortune, worries,
and anxieties] ; and being endowed with as much sense as
I felt I had occasion for, I have neither sought nor taken
anything :

[1] A reminiscence of a well-known line of Marot, who, after enumerating
all his vices and shortcomings, ends up with

> Au demourant, le meilleur fils du monde,

' otherwise, the best son in the world.'

Fair winds we may not have, nor swelling sails,
Yet neither have we always adverse gales.
In strength, in worth, in influence, powers of mind,
In rank and fortune though I were behind
The very foremost, many yet there be
That in their turn come lagging after me.　(HORACE.)

A sufficiency was all I needed to make me content ; that, however, if rightly considered, implies a well-ordered state of mind, equally difficult in every station of life, and, as we see by experience, more often found with want than with plenty. Since, as with our other passions, the hunger for wealth is perhaps whetted more by its enjoyment than by its scarcity, and the virtue of moderation is rarer than that of patience. And all I needed was to enjoy in tranquillity the good things that God in his bounty placed in my hands.

I have never fancied any kind of tiresome labour. I have hardly ever [1] had any but my own affairs to manage ; or, if I have, it has been on condition of managing them at my own times and in my own way, when they were committed to me by people who trusted me, who knew me and did not hustle me. For expert horsemen will get some service out of even a restive and broken-winded nag.

Even in childhood my training was relaxed and free, and I was not subjected to a rigorous discipline. All this has produced in me a sensitive disposition that is impatient of anxieties ; to such a degree that I prefer any losses or irregularities that concern me to be kept from my knowledge. I put down under the heading of my expenses what it costs me to feed and maintain my negligence :

Poor is the house wherein there 's not a deal
Which masters never miss, and varlets steal.　(HORACE.)

I prefer not to take count of what I have, that I may be the less sensible of what I lose. I pray those that live with me, if they are wanting in attachment to me and treat me accordingly, to cheat me with all outward decency. For want of sufficient fortitude to endure the troubles, misfortunes, and crosses that we are liable to, and being unable to keep up the strain of regulating and managing my affairs,

---

[1] The editions previous to that of 1588 had ' never ', which was altered to ' hardly ever ' after Montaigne had been Mayor of Bordeaux for four years.

I leave myself entirely in the hands of Fortune, and to the best of my power foster this notion in myself, ' to be prepared for the worst in all things, and to resolve to bear that worst meekly and patiently.' For that alone do I strive ; that is the aim to which I direct all my thoughts.

In face of a danger I do not so much consider how I shall escape it as how little it matters whether I escape it or not. Even though I should succumb, what would it matter ? Not being able to control events, I control myself ; and I adapt myself to them, if they do not adapt themselves to me. I am hardly cunning enough to dodge Fortune, to escape from her or to compel her, and wisely to direct and incline matters to serve my purpose. Still less have I the patience to suffer the hard and painful anxiety needed to do so. And the most painful position for me is to be kept in suspense in urgent affairs, and tossed between fear and hope.

Deliberation, even in the most indifferent things, is a trouble to me ; and my mind is more put to it to suffer the various shocks and shakes of doubt and deliberation than to settle down and acquiesce in any course whatever, after the die is cast. My sleep has been disturbed by few passions ; but the slightest deliberation will disturb it. So too, having the choice of ways, I generally avoid the steep and slippery hill-side, and take the high road, however deep the mud, where I can sink no lower, and feel secure. And I prefer a misfortune pure and simple, in which I am no longer tormented and worried after feeling certain that it cannot be mended ; and which at the first push plunges me directly into suffering :

The ills that plague me most are those half-known. (SENECA.)

When a thing has happened, I bear myself like a man ; when it has to be carried through, like a boy. The dread of falling throws me into a greater fever than the fall itself. The game is not worth the candle. The miser suffers more from his passion than the pauper, and the jealous man than the cuckold. And it is often better to lose your vineyard than to go to law about it. The lowest step is the firmest. There lies safety. There you have need but of yourself. There it is grounded and rests solely upon itself.

Is there not something philosophical in the attitude of a certain gentleman who was well-known ? He married when he was well on in years, having spent his youth in convivial company ; moreover, great at telling merry tales. Remembering how often he had had occasion to laugh at others who ' wore the horns ', he resolved to be safe and under cover, and married a woman whom he picked up in a place where any man could have what he needed for his money, and made a match of it with her. ' How d'ye do, Mistress Whore ? '—' How d'ye do, Master Cuckold ? ' And he was always ready to talk openly about his venture to anybody who came to see him, and so took the wind out of the sails of any would-be scandal-monger or tale-bearer, and the point off their sting.

With regard to ambition, which is neighbour, or rather daughter, to presumption, Fortune, to advance me, would have had to come and take me by the hand. For I could never have gone to any trouble for an uncertain hope, or submitted to all the difficulties which attend those who try to push themselves into favour at the beginning of their career :

> I will not purchase hope at any price. (TERENCE.)

I cling to what I see and have, and keep the harbour well in view :

> Into the sea one oar I plunge,
> And with the other rake the sands. (PROPERTIUS.)

And, besides, we seldom advance very far unless we first risk what we have. And I am of opinion that if we have sufficient to keep up the state we are born and accustomed to, it is foolish to let it go in the uncertain hope of increasing it. The man to whom Fortune has denied a foothold and the means of settling down into a calm and peaceful life, may be excused if he risks what he has, since in any case necessity sends him out to seek a living :

> In evil we must take the boldest step. (SENECA.)

And I could more readily excuse a younger son for scattering his portion to the winds, than one who has the honour of his family in his keeping, and cannot become necessitous except by his own fault.

With the advice of my good friends in the past I have

found the shorter and easier way of being rid of that
ambition and sitting still :

> Who would not win the palm of victory
> Without the sweat and dust of the arena ?　(HORACE.)

Besides, having a very sound judgement of my own
powers, and knowing that I am not capable of great things,
and remembering that saying of the late Chancellor Olivier
that ' the French are like apes, climbing up a tree from
branch to branch, and, having reached the topmost bough,
showing their backsides ' :

> 'Tis base to take a load one cannot bear,
> And, fainting 'neath it, bend the knee and yield.　(PROPERTIUS.)

Even the irreproachable qualities I possess have been
useless in this age. My easy-going ways would have been
called slackness and weakness ; my fidelity and conscien-
tiousness would have been deemed scrupulous and squeamish, my frankness and independence troublesome, rash and
inconsiderate.

Ill luck is of some good. It is not amiss to be born in
a very depraved age ; for, by comparison with others you
may earn a cheap reputation for goodness. The man who
in our days is only guilty of parricide and sacrilege is a good
man, and an honourable :

> If now a friend do not deny a trust,
> If he restore a purse with all its rust,
> His faith is deemed prodigious, fit to be
> Enrolled in sacred books of Tuscany,
> Or celebrated by some sacrifice
> Of lambs with garlands decked.　(JUVENAL.)

And there never was a time and place when a ruler could
expect a greater and more certain reward for goodness and
justice. I shall be much mistaken if the first who makes it
his business to push himself into favour and influence by
that path, does not easily outstrip his fellows. Force and
violence can do something, but not always everything.

We see tradesmen, village justices, artisans, holding their
own with the nobles in valour and military knowledge.
They give a good account of themselves both in public
battles and in private combats ; they fight, they defend
cities in our wars. A Prince's special qualities are eclipsed
in this crowd. Let him shine by his humanity, his truth,

his loyalty, his moderation, and especially in his justice :
marks rarely seen, unknown and banished. Only by the
goodwill of the people can he carry out his functions ; and
no other qualities gain their affection as do those, being much
more beneficial to them than the others. *There is nothing
so popular as goodness* (Cicero).

By this standard [1] I should be as great and out of the
common as I am dwarf-like and common by the standard
of some of the past ages, when, if no other stronger qualities
concurred, it was usual to find a man moderate in his
revenge, slow to resent an insult, religiously scrupulous in
keeping his word, neither double-faced nor cunning, nor
accommodating his faith to others' wishes or to every
occasion.[2] Rather would I allow a transaction to break its
neck than twist my words in order to further it.

For, with regard to this new-fangled virtue of hypocrisy
and dissimulation, which is now held in so great honour,
I have a deadly hatred of it. Of all vices I know of none
that gives more evidence of a mean and craven spirit. It
shows a cowardly and servile disposition to disguise ourselves and hide behind a mask, and not to dare to show
ourselves as we are. By that means the men of our day
train themselves to perfidy. Being accustomed to speak
untruths, they make no scruple of breaking their word.

A generous heart should not belie its thoughts, but should
be ready to show its inmost depths. It is either all good,
or at least all human.

Aristotle regards it as the duty of a great soul to hate
and love openly, to judge, to speak in all freedom, and,
when the truth is in question, to pay no attention to the
approval or disapproval of others.

Apollonius said it was for slaves to lie, and for free men
to speak truth.

That is the first and fundamental part of virtue. We
must love her for herself. He who tells the truth because
he is obliged to do so, and because it serves his turn, and
who is not afraid of telling an untruth when it is of no
importance to anybody, is not truthful enough.

---

[1] i. e., by comparing myself with my contemporaries.
[2] By these words Montaigne originally intended to characterize himself. The earlier editions have : ' By this standard I should have been
moderate in *my* revenge, &c.'

My soul naturally abominates a lie, and hates even to think one. I feel an inward shame and a pricking remorse if one happens to escape me, as sometimes it does, if the occasion is unexpected and I am taken unawares.

It is not always necessary to say everything ; that would be foolishness. But what we say should be what we think ; the contrary would be knavery. I do not know what advantage people expect who continually feign and dissemble, except it be not to be believed even when they speak the truth. That may deceive men once or twice, but to make a profession of secrecy, and to boast, as some of our rulers have done, ' that they would throw their shirt into the fire, if it were privy to their real intentions ' (which was a saying of the ancient Metellus of Macedon) ; and ' that the man who cannot dissemble cannot rule '.[1] is to warn those who have to deal with them, that what they say is but lying and deceit. *The more artful and cunning a man is the more is he hated and suspected, when he loses his reputation for honesty* (Cicero).

A man would be very simple who allowed himself to be beguiled either by the looks or the words of one who relies upon never being the same outside and within, as Tiberius did. And I cannot see how such people can share in human transactions, as they never utter anything that can be accepted as current coin.

He who is disloyal to the truth is also disloyal to falsehood.

Those men of our time who, in drawing up the duties of a Prince,[2] considered only his advantage, without any regard for his good faith and conscience, might perhaps have been in the right, supposing the affairs of the Prince had been so disposed by Fortune that he could settle them once for all by a single breach of faith. But that is not the way things happen. He often has occasion to enter upon the same transaction. He has to draw up more than one peace, more than one treaty, in his life. The gain which allures him to the first breach of faith (and gain is almost always the end in view, as it is of every other kind of villainy ; sacrilege, murder, rebellion, treachery, are all committed for profit of some kind or other), this first gain is

---

[1] A favourite saying of Louis XI. The other was also attributed to Charles VIII.

[2] Macchiavelli, author of *The Prince*, and his followers.

followed by endless losses, and the Prince, after this example of his faithlessness, is barred from every opportunity of treating and negotiating.

When, during my boyhood, Solyman, of the Ottoman race, a race that is not over-scrupulous in the keeping of promises and pacts, after making a raid with his army on Otranto, was told that Mercurino de Gratinare and the inhabitants of Castro were kept prisoners after having surrendered the place, in contravention of the terms of capitulation, he sent word that they should be released ; for, as he said, having some other great enterprises on hand in those parts, such a breach of faith, although it might appear to be a present gain, would in the future bring upon him a disrepute and distrust of infinite prejudice.

Now for my part, I would rather be a troublesome and indiscreet bore than a fawner and dissembler.

I allow that there may be a little touch of pride and obstinacy mixed with my integrity and candour, that takes no consideration of others. And methinks I tend to grow a little more outspoken where I should be less so, and that, where I should show the more respect, I become the more heated in upholding my opinion. It may also be that, for want of tact, I let Nature have her own way. Using the same freedom of speech and demeanour with men in high position that I have used in my own house, I am sensible of how much it inclines to indiscretion and incivility. But, besides that I was born that way, I am not quick-witted enough to dodge a sudden question, and escape by some shift, or to invent a truth. Nor is my memory good enough to keep to a truth I have thus invented, and I certainly lack the assurance to stick to it.

Wherefore through feebleness I put on a bold face. I take refuge in candour and always say what I think, both by nature and design, leaving it to Fortune to guide the issue.

Aristippus said that the best fruit he had gathered from Philosophy was that he spoke freely and openly to every man.

The memory is a wonderfully serviceable implement, without which the judgement does its duty very laboriously ; in me it is entirely wanting. If a matter is expounded to me, it must be done piece-meal. For it is not in my power to answer a proposition with several different heads. I cannot carry a message without noting it in my tablets. And if I have to make a long-winded speech of any importance, I am reduced to the poor and miserable necessity of getting by heart, word for word, what I have to say ; otherwise I should have neither method nor assurance, being afraid of my memory playing me a trick. But with this expedient I find it no less difficult. It takes me three hours to learn three lines. And besides, in a composition of my own, the freedom and authority whith which I change the order and alter a word, continually varying the matter, makes it the more difficult to keep it in mind.

Now, the more I distrust my memory the more muddled does she become ; she serves me best by chance, and I have to woo her unconcernedly. For if I hustle her she is put out ; when she once begins to totter, the more I sound her the more perplexed and entangled does she become. She waits upon me at her own time, not at mine.

The same defect I find in my memory I find also in several other parts. I shun all command, obligation, and constraint. What at other times I can do easily and naturally I am unable to do if I strictly and expressly command myself to do it. Even those parts of my body that have any particular freedom and authority over themselves sometimes refuse to obey me, if I intend them to do me a necessary service at a fixed time and place. They spurn such a compulsory and tyrannical order. They shrink through fear and spite, and become paralysed.

One day, being in a place where it is considered a barbarous piece of discourtesy not to pledge those who invite you to drink, although they allowed me every freedom, I tried to play the part of a good boon companion, out of respect to the ladies who were of the company, according to the custom of the country.[1] But there was compensation ; for, as I was preparing, under threats, to force myself beyond my habit and inclination, my gullet became so stopped that I was unable to swallow a single drop, and was debarred from drinking even as much as I needed for my meal. And my thirst was fully quenched by the great amount of drink that my imagination had anticipated.

[1] Probably a reminiscence of his travels, which took him through part of Germany.

This effect is most apparent in those who have the most powerful and vivid imagination ; yet it is natural, and there is no one who does not in some degree feel it. An eminent archer, who had been condemned to death, was offered the chance of saving his life if he would give a signal proof of his skill ; he declined to attempt it, fearing lest the too great strain on his will might misdirect his aim, and that, instead of saving his life, he might also forfeit the reputation he had acquired in shooting with the bow.

A man whose thoughts are elsewhere will not fail, when he is walking, to take every time the same number and length of steps, within an inch ; but if he gives his attention to measuring and counting them, he will find that what he did naturally and by chance he will not do so exactly by design.

My library, which is a handsome one among country libraries, is situated at one corner of my house.[1] If anything enters my head that I wish to look up or to write down there, I am obliged, for fear of its escaping me while merely crossing the courtyard, to communicate it to some other person. If, in speaking, I am so bold as to digress ever so little from the thread, I never fail to lose it ; for which reason I force myself to be short, concise, and sparing of words. My servants I am obliged to call after the name of their occupation or their province,[2] for I have great difficulty in remembering names. I can tell indeed that it has three syllables, that it has a harsh sound, that it begins or ends with such and such a letter. And if I should live long, I am not sure that I shall not forget my own name, as others have done.

Messala Corvinus was two years without a trace of memory, and the same is said of George of Trebizond. And in my own interest I often reflect what kind of a life was theirs, and whether without this faculty I shall have enough left to support me in easy circumstances. And, if I look closely into the matter, I fear that this privation, if complete, will be attended with the loss of all the functions of the mind.

---

[1] More precisely, in a tower which forms an angle of the large courtyard, where it still stands.

[2] This, however, appears to have been a common practice. In the comedies of Molière and others we find such names of valets as Basque, Champagne, Picard, &c.

*It is certain that the memory is the only receptacle, not only of
Philosophy, but of all that concerns the conduct of life, and
of all the arts* (Cicero).

I'm full of cracks, and leak out every way. (TERENCE.)

More than once it has happened to me to forget the
watchword which I had given out three hours before, or
received from another ; to forget where I had hidden my
purse, whatever Cicero may say.[1] I help myself to lose
what I have carefully locked up.

Memory is the receptacle and coffer of knowledge. Mine
being so defective I have no great cause to complain if I know
so little. I know in a general way the names of the arts, and of
what they treat, but nothing more. I turn over the leaves
of books ; I do not study them. What I retain of them
I no longer recognize as another's. Only my judgement
has profited by the thoughts and ideas it has imbibed from
them. The author, the place, the words, and other circumstances, are immediately forgotten.

And I am so eminent in forgetfulness that I forget my
own writings and compositions no less than the rest. At
every turn people quote my Essays to me without my
being aware of it. If any one would know where to find
the lines and examples I have here accumulated, I should
be at a great loss to tell him.[2] And yet I have begged them
only at well-known and famous doors, not satisfied with
their being rich unless they also came from rich and honourable hands. Authority and reason there co-operate with
one another.

It will be no great wonder if my book follows the fortune
of other books, and if my memory loses its hold of what
I write, as it does of what I read ; of what I give as well as
of what I receive.

Besides the defect of memory I have others which greatly
contribute to my ignorance. My mind is slow and blunt ;
the least cloud will arrest its point, so that (for example)
I never set it any problem, however easy, that it could
unravel. Any idle subtlety will perplex me. Of games in

[1] 'I have never heard of any old man forgetting where he has hidden
his treasure.'—Cicero, *Of Old Age*.

[2] Montaigne gave no references, and his editors, beginning with Mlle
de Gournay, have no doubt had great trouble in identifying the twelve
hundred and more quotations.

which the intellect has its part, as chess, cards, draughts, and others, I have only the rudest idea.

My apprehension is slow and muddled ; but what it once grasps it grasps thoroughly, and embraces very closely, very deeply and very comprehensively, for as long as it does grasp it. I have a long, sound and perfect sight, but it is soon tired by work and becomes dim ; for which reason I cannot converse for any length of time with my book except with another's help.

The younger Pliny will tell those who have not experienced it how important [1] is this delay to those who are fond of reading.

No mind is so feeble and brute-like that it does not give plain evidence of some particular faculty ; none is so deeply buried but that it will start up at one place or another. And how it comes to pass that a mind that is blind and asleep to all else is found to be clear, wide-awake, and excelling all others in one particular direction, is a question for the masters. But the best minds are those which are far-reaching, open, and ready to embrace all things ; if not educated, at least capable of education.

What I say is a condemnation of my own. For, whether from weakness or indifference (and I am far from approving indifference to what lies at our feet, what we have in hand, what most nearly concerns the employment of our time), no mind is so absurdly ignorant as mine of many such ordinary things, of which it is a disgrace to be ignorant. I must relate a few examples.

I was born and bred in the country and among field-labourers ; I have had the business of husbandry in my own hands ever since my predecessors in the possession of the property I enjoy left me to succeed to it. And yet I can add up neither with counters nor with a pen. Most of our coins are unknown to me.[2] I cannot differentiate

---

[1] Perhaps Montaigne intended to say ' vexatious ' (*importun*), and had in mind an anecdote which Pliny tells of his uncle : ' I remember once, his reader having pronounced a word wrongly, somebody at the table made him repeat it ; upon which my uncle asked him if he understood it ? He acknowledged that he did : ' Why then, said he, would you make him go back again ? We have lost, by this interruption, above ten lines ' : so covetous was this great man of time.

[2] It must be remembered that coinage was in Montaigne's time not so simple as it is now. Every important city appears to have had its own.

between one grain and another, either in the ground or in
the barn, unless the difference be too glaring ; and can
scarcely distinguish between the cabbages and lettuces in
my garden. I do not even know the names of the chief
implements of husbandry, nor the rudest principles of
agriculture, which the boys know. I know still less of the
mechanical arts, of trade and merchandise, of the nature
and diversity of fruits, wines, and foodstuffs, of training
a hawk or physicking a horse or a hound. And, to complete my disgrace, only a month ago I was caught in ignorance of the fact that leaven is used in making bread, and
of the meaning of allowing wine to ferment.

Somebody at Athens once conjectured an aptitude for
mathematics in a man he saw cleverly arranging a load of
brushwood and making it up into faggots. Truly in my
case one could draw quite the opposite conclusion ; for give
me a whole kitchen-battery and you will see me starving.

From this outline of my confession you may imagine
other things to my prejudice. But whatever I make myself
out to be, provided it be such as I am, I attain my purpose.
So I will not apologize for daring to put in writing such
paltry and trivial details as these. The meanness of the
subject [1] compels me to do it. You may condemn my purpose, but not my treatment of it. After all I see well
enough, without being informed of the fact by another,
how unimportant and worthless all this is, and how foolish
my design. It is enough if my judgement is not put out, of
which these are the essays :

> Be nosy, be all nose, till your nose appear
> So big that Atlas it refuse to bear ;
> Though even against Latinus you inveigh,
> Against my trifles you no more can say
> Than I have said myself. Then to what end
> Should you to render tooth for tooth contend ?
> You must have meat if you'd be full, my friend.
> Lose not your labour ; but on those that so
> Admire themselves your deadliest venom throw.
> That these things nothing are full well I know. (MARTIAL.)

I am not obliged to refrain from saying absurd things,
provided I do not deceive myself and know them to be such.
And to trip knowingly is so usual with me that I seldom

---

[1] Meaning himself, as stated in earlier editions.

trip any other way ; I never trip by accident. It is a slight accusation to attribute my foolish actions to heedlessness, since I cannot deny that I usually attribute my vicious actions to the same.

One day at Bar-le-Duc I saw King Francis the Second being presented with a portrait which King René of Sicily had painted of himself, and sent to him to recall him to his memory. Why should not every one be allowed, in like manner, to portray himself with his pen, as he did with his brush ? I will not then omit also this scar, which is very unfit to be published : my want of resolution, a very serious drawback in transacting the business of the world. In dubious enterprises I am at a loss which side to take :

> Nor yes nor no my inmost heart will say. (PETRARCH.)

I can maintain an opinion, but I cannot choose one.

For in human affairs, to whatever side we lean, we are confronted by many probabilities which confirm our opinions (and the philosopher Chrysippus said that he wished to learn of Zeno and Cleanthes, his masters, only their doctrines, for, as to proofs and reasons, he could furnish enough himself) ; so, whichever way I turn, I can always provide myself with grounds and probabilities enough to keep me there. Hence I hold myself in suspense, with freedom to choose, until the occasion urges me. And then, to confess the truth, I most often throw the feather into the wind, as the saying goes, and commit myself to the mercy of Fortune. A very slight turn and circumstance will carry me along :

> When the mind doubts and oscillates,
> A pin will turn the scales. (TERENCE.)

The uncertainty of my judgement is so evenly balanced on most occasions, that I could readily decide it by a throw of the dice. And, when I ponder over our human disabilities, I note that even sacred history gives examples of that custom of leaving it to chance and Fortune to determine the choice in doubtful cases : *The lot fell upon Matthias* (Acts).

Human reason is a two-edged and dangerous sword. And even in the hand of Socrates, her most intimate and familiar friend, observe that it is a stick with many ends.

Thus I am fitted only for following and am easily carried

away with the crowd. I have not sufficient confidence in my own strength to take upon me to command and lead ; I am quite content to find my steps marked out by others. If I must run the risk of a doubtful choice, I prefer that it be under one who is more assured of his opinions, and espouses them more strongly, than I do mine, the ground and foundation of which I find to be very slippery.

And yet I am not too easily imposed upon, since I perceive a like weakness in the contrary opinions. *The mere habit of assenting seems to be dangerous and slippery* (Cicero). Especially in political matters there is a large field for hesitation and conflict :

> As scales correct and pressed by equal weights,
> Nor rise, nor dip, but keep an even poise. (TIBULLUS.)

Macchiavelli's reasons, for example, were sound enough for the subject they treated of, yet it was very easy to combat them ; and they who did so made it no less easy to combat theirs. In that kind of argument there can never be wanting matter for answers, rejoinders, replications, triplications, quadruplications,[1] and that endless chain of disputes which our lawyers draw out to as great a length as they can in favour of law-suits :

> We lunge and parry, dodging in and out,
> Like Samnites at a tedious fencing-bout ; (HORACE.)

since the reasons have little other foundation than experience, and human actions and passions take on such an endless variety of forms.

A shrewd person of our days says that if, when our almanacs say cold, you say hot, and wet when they say dry, and always put the opposite of what they predict, you might lay a wager upon either event, without caring which side you take ; except in cases that admit of no uncertainty, as if you promised extreme heat at Christmas, or the rigours of winter at Midsummer.

I should say the same about these political controversies ; whatever part they set you to play, you will have as fair a prospect as your adversary, provided that you do not run counter to principles that are too solid and obvious. And yet, according to my way of thinking, in public matters

---

[1] *Dupliques, répliques, tripliques,* like their English equivalents, seem to be legal terms. Montaigne goes one better and adds a *quadruplique.*

no course of proceeding is so bad, provided it have age and continuity to recommend it, but that it is better than change and uncertainty. Our morals are extremely corrupt, and wonderfully incline to the worse. Many of our laws and customs are barbarous and monstrous ; yet, by reason of the difficulty of improving our condition, and the danger of the whole State toppling to pieces, if I could put a spoke into our wheel and stop it at this point, I would do it with a light heart :

> No acts so foul and shameful could I tell,
> But that far worse remain behind. (JUVENAL.)

The worst thing I observe in our State is instability ; our laws cannot, any more than our clothes, settle down to any fixed shape. It is very easy to condemn a government for its imperfection, for all mortal things are full of it. It is very easy to generate in a people a contempt for their ancient observances ; no man ever attempted it without succeeding. But many have come to grief in their attempt to establish a better state of things in place of what they have destroyed.

I seldom consult my prudence in my conduct ; I generally allow myself to follow the ordinary routine of the world. Happy are the people who do what they are commanded better than they who command, without troubling their heads about reasons ; who allow themselves gently to roll according to the heavenly rolling. Obedience is never pure and simple in one who talks and argues.

In fine, to return to myself, the only quality for which I take some credit to myself is that in which no man ever thought himself deficient. My self-approbation is common and vulgar, and shared by all ; for what man ever imagined he was lacking in Sense ? That would be a self-contra-dictory proposition. It is a disease that never exists where it is seen ; it is very strong and tenacious, but at the first glimmer the patient has of it it is seen through and dis-persed, as a thick fog is dispersed by the sunbeams.

To accuse oneself in this case would be to excuse, and to condemn oneself would be to absolve. There never was a street-porter or any silly woman who did not think they had enough sense for their needs. We are ready enough to acknowledge others to have the advantage over us in courage, bodily strength, experience, agility, beauty ; but the advantage in judgement we yield to none. And we think we could have discovered the reasons which naturally occur to the mind of another, if we had adopted his point of view.

We quite readily admit the learning, style, and such other qualities as we see in the works of another, if he excels us therein ; but regarding them as mere products of the understanding, each one of us thinks he could have discovered the same in himself. And he does not easily perceive the importance and difficulty of them, unless they be at an extreme and incomparable distance, and scarcely even then.

[And he who could very clearly discern the height of another's judgement would be able to raise his own to the same pitch.]

So it is a kind of exercise for which I must expect very little praise and commendation, and a kind of composition which promises little reputation.

And then, for whom do you write ? The scholars, to whom it falls to sit in judgement on books, value them only for their learning, and will admit no procedure in the mind but along the lines of art and erudition. If you have mistaken one of the Scipios for the other, can you say anything worth saying ? According to them, the man who is ignorant of Aristotle is at the same time ignorant of himself. Vulgar and common-place minds, on the other hand, cannot discern the charm and power of a lofty and elegant style. Now, these two classes of people are in possession of the world. The third class by whom it is your lot to be judged, that of men of naturally strong and well-regulated intellect, is so small, that for that reason they have neither name nor position with us. It is time half wasted to aspire and endeavour to please them.

It is commonly said that the fairest portion of her favours that Nature has given us is that of Sense ; for there is no man who is not contented with his share of it. Is not that reasonable ? He who should see beyond would see beyond his sight.

I think my opinions are good and sound ; but who does not think the same of his ? One of the best proofs I have of this is the small estimation in which I hold myself. For

if I had not been very sure of those opinions they might
easily have been led astray by the singular affection I bear
myself ; as one who concentrates it almost all upon himself,
and does not squander much of it on others. All the love
that others distribute among an infinite number of friends
and acquaintances, upon their glory and their grandeur,
I dedicate entirely to the tranquillity of my mind and to
myself. If any escapes me in other directions, it is not
really with my deliberate consent :

> By instinct trained for self to thrive and live. (LUCRETIUS.)

Well, I seem to be very bold in so persistently condemning
my own littleness. It is indeed a subject on which I exercise
my judgement as much as on any other. The world always
looks over the way ; I turn my eyes inwards. There I fix
them and keep them fixed. Every one looks in front of
him ; I look within myself. I have no business but with
myself, I continually reflect upon myself, examine and
analyse myself. Other men, if they will but see it, always
go abroad ; they always go straight ahead :

> No man attempts to dive into himself. (PERSIUS.)

As for me, I revolve in myself.

This capacity which I have, whatever it may be worth,
for sifting the truth, and my independence in not readily
subjecting my belief, I owe chiefly to myself. For the most
abiding and general ideas I have are those which, so to say,
were born with me ; they are natural and entirely my own.
When I begat them, with a strong and bold, but rather hazy
and imperfect begetting, they were crude and simple ;
I have since confirmed and established them with the
authority of others, and the sound reasonings of those
ancient writers with whom I found myself to agree. They
strengthened my hold upon them, and enabled me more
fully to possess and enjoy them.

Whilst all others seek to recommend themselves by an
active and ready wit, I lay claim to steadiness ; the satisfaction they seek in conspicuous and signal deeds, or in
some particular talent, I find in the order, the consistency,
and moderation of my opinions and conduct. *Now it is
certain that, if anything in the world is becoming, it is a constant uniformity in our whole lives and particular actions ;
which it is impossible we should ever maintain so long as we*

run counter to our inclinations, and follow after those of other people (Cicero).

Here then you see to what degree I am guilty of what I called the first kind of Presumption. Of the second, which consists in not having a sufficiently high opinion of others, I know not whether I can so fully exonerate myself ; for, at whatever cost to myself, I am resolved to speak the truth.

Whether it be perhaps that my continual intercourse with the habits of mind of the ancient writers, and the picture I have formed of those richly-endowed minds of the past, have put me out of humour with others, and with myself ; or that we do in truth live in an age which produces only very indifferent things, the fact remains that I see nothing worthy of great admiration. At the same time I know few men so intimately that I am qualified to pass judgement upon them ; and those with whom my station in life brings me most frequently into contact are, for the most part, men who pay little attention to their mental culture, and to whom the greatest blessing is honour, and valour the greatest perfection.

Whatever I see that is fine in others I am very ready to praise and esteem. Nay, I often express more admiration than I feel, and that is the extent to which I allow myself to be untruthful. For I am unable to originate anything untrue. I willingly testify to the laudable qualities I see in my friends, and of a foot of merit I generally make a foot and a half. But attribute to them qualities they do not possess I cannot, nor can I openly defend their imperfections.

Even to my enemies I honestly concede the honour that is their due. My feelings may change, but not my judgement. I do not confuse my animosity with other circumstances that are foreign to it ; and I am so jealous of the independence of my judgement that I can very hardly part with it for any passion whatever. I do myself more injury by lying than I do the man about whom I lie.

This laudable and generous custom has been observed in the Persian nation, that they speak of their deadly enemies, and at the same time wage war to the death with them, fairly and honourably, in so far as they deserve it by their valour.

I know men enough who have divers fine qualities, the

one wit, the other courage, another skill, another conscience, another eloquence, one, one science, another, another. But as for a man great in all respects, combining all those fine qualities, or possessing one in so eminent a degree as to excite wonder or be comparable with those we honour in the past, it has not been my fortune to meet with him. The greatest I have known in the flesh, I mean for natural qualities of the soul, and of the best disposition, was Étienne de La Boëtie. His was a full mind indeed that appeared beautiful from every point of view, a soul of the old stamp, which would have produced great things if Fortune had so willed it. And he added greatly to his rich nature by learning and study.

But I know not how it is, and it is undoubtedly the case, that there is as much vanity and as little intelligence in those men who lay claim to the highest abilities, who meddle with literary pursuits and bookish occupations, as in any other class of people ; whether it is that more is required and expected of them, and common defects are inexcusable in them, or, perhaps, because the conceit they have of their learning makes them bolder to show off and push themselves too far forward, the result being that they betray and give themselves away.

As an artist gives more evidence of his dullness when working upon a rich material that he has in hand, by applying and mixing it stupidly and against the rules of his work, than when using a baser material ; and as we are more shocked by a fault in a statue of gold than in a plaster model : so do these men when they quote things which would be good in themselves and in their proper place ; for they serve them up without discrimination, doing honour to their memory at the expense of their intelligence. They do honour to Cicero, to Galen, to Ulpian and Saint Jerome, and bring ridicule upon themselves.

I readily return to that subject of our absurd educational system ; its aim has been to make us, not good and wise, but learned ; and it has succeeded. It has not taught us to follow and embrace Virtue or Wisdom, but has impressed upon us their derivation and etymology. We can decline Virtue, if we cannot love it. If we do not know what Wisdom is by practice and experience, we know it by jargon and by heart. We are not content with knowing the origin of our neighbours, their kindred and their inter-marriages ; we wish to be friends with them, to establish some intercourse and understanding with them. This education has taught us the definition, the divisions, and sub-divisions of Virtue, as we know the surnames and branches of a genealogical tree, without further caring to become familiar and intimate with her. It has selected, for our instruction, not those books which contain the soundest and truest opinions, but those which speak the best Greek and Latin ; and with all those fine words has poured into our minds the most unprofitable ideas of the ancients.

A good education changes one's outlook and character, as in the case of Polemo. This dissipated young Greek, happening to hear Xenocrates lecture, was struck not only by the eloquence and learning of the professor, and carried home not only the knowledge of some noble matter, but a more substantial and palpable fruit, which was a sudden change and amendment of his former life. Who was ever affected in that way by our education ?

> Say, will you act like Polemo
> On his conversion long ago ?
> The signs discard of your disease,—
> Your mits, the swathings of your knees,
> Your mufflers too,—as he, 'tis said,
> Slipped off the chaplets from his head
> Which, flushed with revel, still he wore
> When he was stricken to the core
> By the undinner'd sage's lore. (HORACE.)

To me the least contemptible class of people are those who, by reason of their simplicity, stand on the lowest rung ; their relations with each other are better regulated. I generally find the morals and the language of the peasants more in accordance with the teachings of true Philosophy than those of our philosophers. *The common people are wiser, because they are as wise as they need be* (Lactantius).

In my opinion, the most remarkable men judging by outward appearance (for to judge them in my own way I should need more light thrown upon them) have been, for eminence in war and soldier-like qualities, the Duke of Guise,[1] who died at Orleans, and the late Marshal Strozzi ; [1]

---

[1] François de Guise, 1519–63 ; Piero Strozzi, d. 1558.

for great ability and uncommon merit, Olivier and l'Hôpital, Chancellors of France. Poetry too I think has flourished in our century ; we have an abundance of good craftsmen in that trade,[1] Daurat, Bèze, Buchanan, l'Hôpital, Montdoré, Turnebus. As to the French poets, I think they have raised their art to the highest pitch it will ever attain ; and in those qualities in which Ronsard and Du Bellay excel, I do not think they fall far short of the perfection of ancient poetry. Adrianus Turnebus knew more, and knew better what he did know, than any man of his time, and long before his time.

The lives of the Duke of Alva, lately dead, and of our Constable de Montmorency were noble lives, and in several respects their fortunes were uncommonly alike. But the beauty and lustre of the latter's death, in the sight of Paris and of his King, and in their service, fighting against his nearest relations, at the head of an army victorious through his leadership, and coming so suddenly in an advanced old age, deserves, in my opinion, to rank among the noteworthy events of my time.

The same may be said of the constant goodness, the gentle manners and the scrupulous affability of Monsieur de la Nouë, who lived all his life surrounded by violent deeds of armed factions (a real school of treachery, inhumanity, and brigandage), a great and most experienced warrior.

[I have taken pleasure in proclaiming, in several places, the hopes I entertain of Marie de Gournay le Jars, my *fille d'alliance*, whom I truly love, with a more than paternal affection, and whom in my solitude and retreat I cherish as one of the best parts of my own being. She is now my chief concern in this world. If I may presage from her youth, her soul will be some day capable of the finest things, and amongst others, of the perfection of that very sacred friendship, to which, as far as my reading goes, none of her sex has yet been able to rise. Her sincerity and steadfast character are quite equal to it. Her affection for me is more than superabundant, and such in short that it leaves nothing to be desired. I could wish, however, that she were not so cruelly troubled by apprehensions of my end, since we first met when I was fifty-five years of age. Her appreciation, as a woman, and of this century, and so

[1] Montaigne means writers of Latin poetry.

young, and alone in her district, of the first Essays, and the wonderful impetuosity of her love and desire to make my acquaintance, long before setting eyes on me, merely on the strength of her esteem, are circumstances well worthy of consideration.] [1]

Other virtues have been little, if at all, prized in this age ; but valour is become common through our Civil wars. And in this respect we have souls brave even to perfection, and so numerous that it is impossible to sift them out.

Those are all I have known hitherto who have shown any extraordinary and uncommon greatness.

CHAPTER 18

OF GIVING THE LIE

YES, but, some will tell me, this idea of using oneself as a subject to write about would be pardonable in a famous and eminent person, whose reputation had aroused a desire to become acquainted with him. That is certain ; I admit it. And I know very well that a mechanic will hardly raise his eyes from his work to see a man of the common run ; whilst to see a great and distinguished person arriving in a town, shops and workrooms will be deserted. It ill becomes any other to make himself known unless he have qualities worthy of imitation ; unless his life and opinions may serve as a pattern.

Caesar and Xenophon had a real and solid foundation whereon to base their histories, in the greatness of their own deeds. And it were to be wished that we had the written journals of the great Alexander, and the commentaries on their exploits which Augustus, Cato, Sylla, Brutus, and others left behind them. One loves and studies the statues of such men, even in bronze and marble.

This objection is very true, but it affects me very little :

I ne'er recite except to friends ; and even from that forbear
Unless implored ; to everyone I can't, nor everywhere.

---

[1] This passage does not appear in the ' Bordeaux Manuscript ' ; which omission, in the opinion of at least one commentator, casts some doubt upon its authenticity.

In open Forum some recite their works, and some for choice
Within the baths, whose vaulted space rings sweetly back the voice.
                                                (HORACE.)

I am here not erecting a statue to be stuck up at the street
corner of a town, or in a church or market-place :

> No aim of mine to swell my page
> With such pretentious trifles . . .
> With you alone I mean to talk
> In secret converse. (PERSIUS.)

It is intended for a nook in the library, and to entertain a
neighbour, a kinsman, a friend, who may take a pleasure
in renewing his acquaintance and intimacy with me by
means of this portrait. Others have taken heart to speak
of themselves because they thought the subject worthy and
fruitful ; I, on the other hand, because I thought it too
meagre and barren to incur the suspicion of ostentation.

I am ready enough to judge the actions of others ; of my
own I give little to judge of, by reason of their insignificance.
I do not find so much good in myself that I cannot tell it
without blushing.

What a satisfaction it would be to hear somebody thus
tell me of the habits, the faces, the behaviour, the everyday
words, and the fortunes of my ancestors ! How attentively
I would listen to it ! Truly it would show a bad nature to
despise even the portraits of our friends and forbears, the
fashion of their clothes and their armour. I treasure the
inkstand, the seal, the breviary, and a peculiar sword which
they used ; and have not banished from my cabinet certain
long switches which my father usually carried in his hand.
*A father's coat and his ring are the more dear to his children
the more they loved him* (St. Augustine).

If my posterity should, however, be of another mind, I
shall have the means of being revenged upon them ; for
they cannot care less for me than I shall then care for them.[1]

All the traffic I have in this with the public is that I
borrow the implements of their writing, as being easier to

---

[1] This was probably not intended to be taken seriously, but if it means
anything it would mean that he would be beyond caring, since he did not
believe in immortality. That his posterity were not of his mind seems
certain, as his daughter appears to have soon disposed of his library of
about a thousand books, which were afterwards dispersed. Only about
seventy of them have since been recovered.

read and more speedy. In requital of it I shall perhaps keep some pat of butter from melting in the market-place : [1]

> Lest tunny-fish and olives lack a coat. (MARTIAL.)
> And mackerel shall have a roomy shirt. (CATULLUS.)

And if nobody reads me, shall I have wasted my time, when I have beguiled so many idle hours with such pleasant and profitable reflections ? In modelling this figure after myself, I have so often been obliged to adjust and compose it, in order to get at myself, that the copy has in some sort become shaped and consolidated of itself. In portraying myself for others I have portrayed myself in more distinct colours than were mine originally. I have no more made my book than my book has made me ; a book consubstantial with its author, concerned with me alone, a part of my life ; not dealing with and aimed at other and third persons, like all other books.

Have I wasted my time in so continually and carefully rendering an account of myself ? For they who only occasionally survey themselves in thought and speech do not examine themselves so closely, they do not penetrate so far beneath the skin, as one who makes it his study, his work and his trade, who is engaged, with all his faith, with all his strength, on a record that will endure.

The most delightful pleasures are indeed digested inwardly, leaving no trace of themselves, and avoiding the sight not only of the public, but of any other person.

How often has not this work diverted me from troublesome thoughts ? And all frivolous thoughts ought to be accounted troublesome. Nature has amply endowed us with the faculty for entertaining ourselves with our own thoughts ; and often invites us to do so, to remind us that we owe ourselves in part to society, but for the best part to ourselves.

For compelling my fancy to indulge even its reveries in some order and according to some plan, and to keep it from wandering aimlessly and losing itself, there is nothing like giving a body to and recording all the trifling thoughts that

---

[1] By the ' implements of their writing ' Montaigne seems to mean the printing-press. He was not a good prophet when he suggested that his books might be used for wrapping butter.

present themselves. I give ear to my reveries because I have to record them.

How many a time, when annoyed by some action which civility and good sense forbade my openly reproving, have I not disgorged myself here, not without an eye to the instruction of the public ? And then these poetical lashes :

> Zon dessus l'euil, zon sur le groin,
> Zon sur le dos du Sagoin ! [1]

make a still deeper impression on paper than on the living flesh. What if I lend ear a little more attentively to books, since I am on the look out to pilfer any little thing, to enamel and prop up my own ?

I have by no means studied in order to make a book ; but I have to some extent studied because I had made one, if we may call it studying to skim and to lay hold, by the head or the feet, now of one author, now another. Not by any means to form my opinions, but certainly to support, confirm, and serve those formed long ago.

But whom are we to believe when speaking of himself in so corrupt an age, seeing there are few, if any, whom we can believe when speaking of others, when there is less to be gained by lying ? The first stage in the corruption of morals is the banishing of the truth ; for, as Pindar said, to be truthful is the beginning of a great virtue, and it is the first article that Plato requires in the ruler of his Republic.

Our truth nowadays is not what is, but what we can persuade others to believe ; just as we call Money not only that which is legal, but also any spurious coin that will pass. Our nation has long been taxed with this vice ; for Salvianus of Massilia, who lived in the time of the Emperor Valentinian, says, ' that with the Franks lying and perjury are not vice, but a way of speaking.' If you would overbid this testimony, you might say that they now regard them as a virtue. We are trained, we are fashioned to it as to an honourable practice ; for dissimulation is among the most notorious qualities of this century.

Wherefore I have often considered whence could have arisen that custom we so religiously observe, of being more

---

[1] ' One in the eye, one on the snout, one on the back of the pig '. From a poem of Marot in reply to a violent attack upon him by a priest named Sagon. Their quarrel, in which others joined, lasted for quite a year.

deeply offended when taxed with this vice, which is so common with us, than with any other ; and that to be accused of lying is the last insult that can be put upon us in words. From this it seems to me to be natural to deny most strongly the faults with which we are most strongly tainted. It would seem as if, by hotly resenting the accusation, we in some sort acquit ourselves of the guilt. If we have it in fact, we at least condemn it in appearance.

May it not also be because this reproach seems to imply cowardice and a craven heart ? Can there be any more manifest cowardice than to deny what we have said ? Then how much more cowardly to deny what we know !

Lying is an ugly vice, which is painted in its most shameful colours by an ancient writer when he says that ' to lie is evidence that we despise God and at the same time fear men '. It would be impossible to declare more fully what a vile, detestable, and outrageous a thing it is. For what more infamous can we imagine than to be a coward before men and to stand up against God ? As speech is the only means that men have of understanding one another, the man who violates it is a traitor to society. It is the only instrument for communicating our wishes and thoughts ; it is the interpreter of our soul. If it fails us we can no longer hold together, we shall cease to know one another. If it deceives us, it breaks off all our intercourse and dissolves all the ties of our government.

Certain nations of the new Indies (there is no object in mentioning their names, which no longer exist ; for the desolation attending their conquest went so far as to utterly abolish the names, and all knowledge of the old places—a monstrous and unheard-of example !) made offerings to their gods of human blood, but only such as was drawn from the tongue and ears, to atone for the sin of lying, both heard and uttered.

That good old Greek [1] said that boys play with knucklebones and men with words.

With regard to the different ways in which we give the lie, and our laws of honour on this point, and the changes which have taken place in them, I will defer saying what I know of them to another occasion. Meanwhile I will learn, if I can, when that habit arose of so exactly weighing and

[1] Lysander.

measuring our words, and making it a point of honour to do so. For we may easily imagine it was not in the time of the old Romans and Greeks. And I have often thought it strange and novel to see them abuse and accuse one another of lying, without any further quarrel. Their laws of duty steered some other course than ours. Caesar is called, now a robber, now a drunkard, to his face. We see how free they were in their mutual invectives ; I mean the greatest war-lords of both nations, among whom words are only avenged with words, and that was the end of it.

CHAPTER 19

OF FREEDOM OF CONSCIENCE

IT is a common thing to see good intentions, unless guided by moderation, driving men to very mischievous acts. In this conflict which has now stirred up France to civil wars, the best and the soundest side is no doubt that which up-holds both the old religion and the old government of the country. Yet amongst the honourable men who follow that side (for I do not mean those men who make a pretence of it, either to wreak their private vengeance, or to gratify their avarice, or to court the favour of princes ; but those who follow it out of true zeal to their religion and a godly desire to maintain the peace and the present state of their country), among these, I say, we see many who are driven by passion beyond the bounds of reason, and sometimes adopting unjust, violent, and even foolhardy measures.

It is certain that in those early days when our religion first gained authority with the laws, many armed themselves with zeal against pagan books of every kind, in consequence of which men of letters have suffered an enormous loss. In my estimation this devastation has done more harm to Letters than all the fires of the Barbarians. A good witness to this is Cornelius Tacitus ; for although the Emperor Tacitus, his kinsman, had, by express command, furnished all the libraries in the world with his works, not a single complete copy was able to escape the careful search of those who desired to destroy them, on account of five or six insignificant sentences adverse to our religion.

Another characteristic of theirs was their readiness to

lend undeserved praise to all the Emperors who were on our side, and to condemn generally all the actions of those who were hostile to us ; as we may plainly see in the case of the Emperor Julian, surnamed the Apostate.[1]

He was indeed a very great and very uncommon man, with a mind deeply imbued with the teachings of Philosophy, by which he professed to regulate all his actions. And indeed there is no kind of virtue of which he has not left behind some very notable examples. In respect of chastity (of which in the course of his life he gives very clear evidence), they tell of him a similar story to that related of Alexander and Scipio, that of a number of very beautiful captive girls he would not even look at one, although he was then in the prime of life, for he was killed by the Parthians at the early age of thirty-one.

As to his justice, he went to the trouble of personally hearing the parties to a suit ; and, although out of curiosity he would inquire of what religion they were who appeared before him, yet the hostility he bore to ours never weighed down the scales. He himself made sundry good laws and cut down a great number of the subsidies and imposts which his predecessors had levied.

We have two good historians who were eye-witnesses of his actions. One of them, Marcellinus, strongly condemns, in several passages of his history, that edict of his which forbade all Christian rhetoricians and grammarians to keep school and teach ; and he adds that he could wish this action of his to be buried in silence. It is probable that, had Julian adopted any harsher measures against the Christians, Marcellinus would not have omitted to mention them, being very favourably inclined to our religion.

He was indeed a harsh, but not a cruel, enemy to us ; for our own people tell this story of him : One day, as he was walking about the city of Chalcedon, Maris, the Bishop of the place, had the temerity to call him ' wicked traitor to Christ ', to which he merely answered, ' Go, wretched man,

---

[1] The character of the Emperor Julian was censured, when Montaigne was in Rome in 1581, by the Master of the Sacred Palace, who, however, as Montaigne tells us in his Travel journal, referred it to his conscience to alter it. This he did not do, and this chapter supplied Voltaire with the greater part of the praises he bestowed upon that Emperor.—*Note by Leclerc.*

and deplore the loss of your eyes.' To which the Bishop retorted, ' I thank Jesus Christ for having deprived me of sight, that I might not see your insolent face.' Wherein they say he affected a philosophic tolerance. It is at least true that this action cannot be reconciled with the cruelties he is reported to have exercised against the Christians. He was (says Eutropius, my other witness) an enemy to Christianity, but without touching blood.

And, to return to his justice, there is nothing to be brought up against him except the severity he exercised, in the beginning of his reign, against those who had sided with Constantius, his predecessor.

As to his sobriety, he always lived a soldier's life ; and even in peace times he dieted himself like a man who is preparing and training for the hardships of war.

His vigilance was such that he divided the night into three or four parts, the least part of which was allotted to sleep ; the rest of it was spent either in supervising in person the state of his army and his bodyguard, or in study ; for, among other rare qualities of his, he was a very eminent scholar in all branches of literature.

They tell of Alexander the Great that, having gone to rest, lest sleep should divert him from his thoughts and studies, he had a basin placed at his bedside, and grasping a copper ball in one hand held it over the basin, in order that, should sleep overtake him and cause his fingers to relax their hold, the noise of the ball dropping into the basin might awaken him. Our man had his mind so bent on what he was about, and so little disturbed by the fumes of wine, by reason of his singular abstinence, that he was able to dispense with that artifice.

As to his eminence in military matters, he was wonderfully endowed with all the qualities appertaining to a great general, and no wonder, since he was nearly all his life continually engaged in warfare, for the most part with us in France, against the Germans and Franks. We have hardly any record of a man who looked on more dangers, or more often gave proof of his personal valour.

His death has something in common with that of Epaminondas ; for he was pierced by an arrow and tried to pull it out, and would have done so but that, the arrow having a sharp edge, he cut and disabled his hand. He incessantly requested to be carried back, as he was, into the thick of the battle, to encourage his soldiers, who very bravely held their own without him, until night separated the armies.

To philosophy he was indebted for the singular contempt in which he held his life and things human. He had a firm belief in the eternity of the soul.

In the matter of religion he was wrong throughout. He was called the Apostate for having abandoned ours ; yet there seems to be more likelihood in this explanation : That he never had Christianity at heart, but that, in obedience to the laws, he dissembled until he held the Empire in his own hands.

He was so superstitious in his own religion that even his co-religionists of the time ridiculed him ; they said that if he had gained the victory over the Parthians, he would have drained the world of oxen to satisfy his sacrifices. He was also infatuated with the art of Divination, and encouraged all kinds of prognostications.

He said at his death, among other things, that he was grateful to the gods, and thanked them, for having decreed that he should not be surprised by death, since they had long before apprised him of the time and place of his end, and that he should neither die a soft and ignominious death, more suitable to idle and effeminate persons, nor a prolonged, lingering, and painful death ; that they had held him worthy of dying in this noble way, in the full tide of his victories and at the height of his fame. He had had a vision like Marcus Brutus, which first threatened him in Gaul and afterwards reappeared to him in Persia, at the point of his death.

These words that they have put into his mouth when he felt himself wounded, ' You have vanquished, Nazarene,' or, according to others, ' Be satisfied, Nazarene,' would not have been forgotten, if they had been believed, by my witnesses, who, being present in the army, observed his slightest movements and words at the end ; any more than certain other miracles attached to his name.

And, to come back to the subject of my essay, he had, according to Marcellinus, long cherished Paganism in his heart. But since his army was wholly composed of Christians, he did not dare to disclose it. In the end, when he found himself strong enough to venture to proclaim his change of mind, he caused the temples of the gods to be thrown open, and did his utmost to restore idolatry. To effect his purpose, having found the people at Constantinople at loggerheads, and the prelates of the Christian church divided among themselves, he summoned them to his palace, and earnestly admonished them to suppress their civil dissensions, promising that every man should, without fear or hindrance, follow his own religion. He was very careful to urge this point, in the hope that this liberty would strengthen the factions and the schisms which divided them, and would prevent the people from becoming reunited, and consequently fortifying themselves against him by unanimous concord and mutual understanding ; having learned by experience, from the cruelty of some of the Christians, ' That there is no beast in the world so much to be feared by man, as man.'

Those are very nearly his words. Wherein this is worthy of consideration, that the Emperor Julian, to stir up civil troubles and dissensions, uses the same remedy of freedom of conscience that our Kings have lately employed to stifle them. It may be said, on the one side, that to give a loose rein to the factions to hold to their opinions, is to sow and scatter division, and almost to lend a hand to increase it, there being no barrier and restraint of the laws to check and impede its course. But, on the other side, it might also be said that to give the factions the reins to hold to their beliefs is to render them soft and lax through ease and facility, and to blunt the edge which is sharpened by rarity, novelty and difficulty. And so I think it is better, for the honour of the piety of our kings, that, not having been able to do what they would, they have made a show of willing what they could.

CHAPTER 20

THAT OUR ENJOYMENTS ARE NEVER UNMIXED

WE are naturally so feeble that we cannot enjoy things in their native purity and simplicity. The elements we live on are corrupted ; and so are the metals : even gold must be debased with some other matter to fit it for our use.

Neither the virtue, simple as it seemed, which Aristo and Pyrrho, as well as the Stoics, made the ' end of life ', nor the hedonism of the Cyrenaics and Aristippus, were of any practical use without being compounded.

Of the pleasures and good things we enjoy not one is exempt from some mixture of evil and discomfort :

> Since from the very heart of these delights
> A bitter something springs, something to sting
> Even amid the flowers. (LUCRETIUS.)

Our keenest pleasure appears, as it were, to groan and lament. Would you not think it were dying of anguish ? Nay, when we compose a picture of it at its highest point ; we deck it out with sickly and painful epithets and qualities, languor, softness, weakness, faintness, *morbidezza* ; a great testimony to their consanguinity and consubstantiality.

In profound joy there is more seriousness than gaiety ; in the highest and fullest contentment more soberness than merriment. *Even felicity, unless it be tempered, overwhelms* (Seneca). Happiness grinds us down.

That is the meaning of an old Greek line which says that ' the gods sell us all the good things they give us ' ; that is to say, that they give us none pure and perfect, and that we do not buy at the price of some evil.

Toil and pleasure, very unlike by nature, are however joined together by some sort of natural connexion.

Socrates said that some god tried to mix in one lump and to confound pain and pleasure ; but that, unable to succeed, he bethought himself to couple them at least by the tail.

Metrodorus said that in sadness there is some alloy of pleasure. I know not whether he meant something else, but for my part I imagine there is a certain amount of purpose, acquiescence, and satisfaction in nursing one's melancholy ; I mean besides the desire for approval which may be mixed up with it. There is a little shade of daintiness and delicacy that smiles upon and flatters us in the very lap of melancholy. Are there not some natures that feed upon it ?

> A certain kind of pleasure 'tis to weep. (OVID.)

And one Attalus, in Seneca, says that the memory of our lost friends is grateful to us, like the bitterness of wine that is too old :

> O ministering slave, of old Falernian
> Pour out a bitterer cup ; (CATULLUS.)

and like sour-sweet apples.

Nature discloses to us this confusion. Painters hold that we work the same facial muscles and wrinkles both in crying and laughing. In fact, if you watch the progress of a picture before either expression is fully developed, you will be in doubt which of the two the artist is aiming at. And the merriest laughter is mingled with tears. *There is no evil without its compensation* (Seneca).

When I think of a man besieged by every desirable felicity (let us put the case that all the parts of his body are constantly seized with a pleasure equal to that of generation at its highest point), I can imagine him sinking under the weight of his pleasure, and see that he is utterly unable to support a delight so unmixed, so constant and universal. Indeed, he will run away from it when he is in it, and will naturally make haste to escape, as from a place where he can find no foothold, and is afraid of sinking.

When I make a rigorous self-confession I find that the best virtue I have has some taint of vice. And I am afraid that Plato, in his greenest virtue (I who am as sincere and faithful an admirer of it, and of other virtues of the same stamp, as any man can be), if he had lent an attentive ear to it, and he did lend an attentive ear to it, would have detected some sinister note of a human admixture ; but it would be a faint sound and perceptible only to himself. In all things and throughout man is but patchwork and motley.

Even the laws of Justice cannot subsist without some blending of injustice. And Plato says that they who imagine they can remove from the laws all their defects and unfairness, are undertaking to cut off the Hydra's heads. *In every exemplary punishment there is a certain amount of injustice towards the individual which is counterbalanced by public utility*, says Tacitus.

It is likewise true that for the ordinary conduct of life and service in public affairs our minds may be too clear and perspicacious. This penetrating clearness of vision is too subtle and curious. These qualities should be weighted and blunted to make them more obedient to example and practice ; they should be thickened and obscured to adapt them to this cloudy and terrestrial life.

Therefore it is that commonplace and less highly-strung minds are more proper and more successful in managing affairs. The lofty and exquisite ideas of Philosophy are unsuited to practical purposes. That mental acuteness and vivacity, that supple and restless volubility, are a disturbing factor in our negotiations. Human enterprises must be handled more roughly and superficially ; and a good and great part must be left to the guidance of Fortune. It is not necessary to pry so deeply and cunningly into things. We lose our way when we view matters in so many contrary aspects and in such divers shapes. *Turning over in their minds things so contradictory they became quite dazed* (Livy).

This is what the ancients say of Simonides : Because his imagination suggested to him (upon the question King Hiero had put to him, to answer which he had many days to meditate in) so many different subtle and ingenious solutions, that he doubted which was the most probable, and totally despaired of finding the true.[1]

He who inquires into and embraces all the circumstances and consequences, impedes his choice. An average mind will suffice equally well for conducting operations of great or little weight. Observe that the best managers of their own affairs are those who are least able to say how they came to be so ; and that those self-sufficient talkers can generally do nothing to the purpose.

I know a man, a great talker and most excellent at describing every kind of husbandry, who has allowed a yearly revenue of a hundred thousand livres to slip through his fingers, more's the pity ! I know another who can prate, and give better advice than any man of his counsel, and there is not a man in the world who makes a better show of mental gifts ; yet when it comes to deeds, his servants can tell quite a different tale. I mean without taking his ill-luck into account.

CHAPTER 21

AGAINST IDLENESS

THE Emperor Vespasian, though sick of the disease which brought on his death, did not cease to take an interest in the state of the Empire ; and, even lying in bed, continually dispatched many affairs of importance. When his physician rated him for it, as a thing prejudicial to his health, he replied, ' An Emperor must die standing.' A fine saying, in my opinion, and worthy of a great ruler !

[1] The question was : ' What is God ? '

The Emperor Hadrian afterwards made use of the same expression on a similar occasion, and it ought to be frequently recalled to the minds of kings, to make them feel that the great charge that is laid upon them, of ruling so many men, is not an idle charge. And that there is nothing that can so justly disgust a subject, and make him unwilling to expose himself to hardships and dangers in the service of his Prince, as to see him all the while lolling in idleness, or busy over paltry and frivolous things ; and to look after the safety of one who is so neglectful of ours.[1]

If anyone should wish to maintain that it is better for a ruler to conduct his wars through others than himself, Fortune will furnish him with examples enough of princes whose lieutenants have brought great enterprises to a happy issue in their service, and even of kings whose presence in war would have done more harm than good. But no brave and valorous prince could patiently listen to such a shameful suggestion. Under colour of preserving his head, like the statue of a saint, for the happiness of his kingdom, they just degrade him from his office, which lies entirely in military activity, and declare him incapable of it.

I know one who would much rather be defeated than sleep whilst others are fighting for him, and who was never without jealousy when he knew that even his own men were doing great things in his absence.[2]

And Selim the First said very rightly, it seems to me, ' that victories which are won without the master are not complete.' How much more he would have been inclined to say that that same master should blush for shame to claim a share in the honour when he had busied only his voice and his thoughts in the matter ! And not even that, since, in that kind of business, the only direction and command which deserve honour are those which are given on the spot and in the midst of the fray.

No pilot can perform his duty on dry land.

The rulers of the Ottoman race, the first race in the world in military fortunes, warmly espoused this opinion. And Bajazet the Second, with his son, who departed from this principle, spending their time in the sciences and other

---

[1] The last word, ' ours ', if used intentionally, appears to confirm the view that this was a hint for the reigning monarch, Henry III.

[2] It appears probable that Henry IV was here meant.

stay-at-home occupations, gave to their empire a good slap in
the face ; and the present ruler, Amurath the Third, following their example, is pretty well beginning to find himself
in the same pickle.

Was it not the King of England, Edward the Third, who,
speaking of our Charles the Fifth, made this remark, ' There
was never a king who armed less ; and yet there was never
a king who gave me so much to do ? ' He was right to
think it strange, as a result of chance rather than of reason.

Those who would number the Kings of Castile and Portugal among warlike and great-hearted conquerors, because
at twelve hundred leagues distance from their abodes of
idleness, by the skin of their agents, they made themselves
masters of the East and West Indies, may seek some other
than myself to agree with them ; since it is doubtful
whether they would even have had the courage to go in
person to take possession of their conquests.

The Emperor Julian said even more, ' that a philosopher
and a gallant soldier should not so much as breathe ' ; that
is to say, that they should yield no more to their bodily
needs than what cannot be refused, ever keeping soul and
body busied about great, noble and virtuous things. He
felt ashamed to be seen spitting and sweating in public
(which is also said of the Spartan youths and by Xenophon
of the young men of Persia), because he thought that
exercise, continual labour and sobriety should have burned
and dried up all those superfluities. What Seneca said will
not be out of place here, that the old Romans kept their
young men standing on their feet : ' They taught their boys
nothing, he says, that had to be learned sitting.'

It is a noble desire to wish even to die usefully and like
a man ; but the realization lies not so much in our good
resolution as in our good fortune. Thousands have resolved
to vanquish or to die in battle, who have failed in either
design ; wounds, imprisonment, cross their purpose, and
force them to live. There are diseases which prostrate even
our desires and our understanding.

[Fortune was not allowed to second the vanity of the
Roman legionaries who bound themselves by oath to die or
vanquish. *I will return a victor from the combat, O Marcus
Fabius ; if I fail, I call down upon myself the wrath of Father
Jupiter, Mars Gradivus, and the other Gods* (Livy).

The Portuguese tell that in a certain part of the conquered Indies they came across soldiers who had doomed themselves, with horrible execrations, to accept no alternative but to be killed or remain victorious ; and, as a token of this vow, they shaved their heads and beards. In vain do we obstinately rush into danger. It would seem as if blows avoid those who confront them too cheerfully, and are loath to reach the man who offers himself too willingly and spoils their design.

Many a man, after vainly trying every means to be killed by the hand of the enemy, has been constrained to take his own life in the very heat of the battle, in order to make good his resolution to return with honour or not to return alive. I could cite other examples, but here is one : Philistus, head of the naval forces of Dionysius the younger against the Syracusans, offered them battle, which was fiercely contested, the forces being equal. In this engagement, by reason of his prowess, he had the best of it at the beginning. But when the Syracusans drew up and surrounded his galley, after performing great deeds of valour in his own person, in trying to extricate himself, and despairing of relief, with his own hand he took away the life he had so freely and so vainly exposed to the enemy.]

Muley Moloch, King of Fez, who has lately won, against Sebastian, King of Portugal, that battle made famous by the death of three Kings, and the transference of that great kingdom to the crown of Castile, happened to be seriously ill when the Portuguese invaded his state with an armed force ; and he grew daily worse until his death, which he foresaw. Never did a man more strenuously and more gloriously use up his strength. He felt too weak to endure the pompous and ceremonious entry into his camp, which, according to their custom, is attended with much magnificence, and necessitates great activity. This honour he resigned to his brother, but it was the only function of a general that he resigned. All the other necessary and useful duties he carried out very rigorously and with much labour, his body reclining, but his understanding and courage upright and firm to the last gasp, and a little beyond.

He was able to wear down his enemies, who had imprudently advanced into his territory, and it was a great grief to him that for want of a little life and of somebody to replace him in the conduct of this war and the management of a troubled kingdom, he was obliged to seek a doubtful and bloody victory, when he had it in his power to make it clean and sure.

However, he husbanded his strength in miraculous fashion, in spite of his illness, wearing down the enemy, and drawing them far away from their naval forces and the seaports they held on the coast of Africa, until the last day of his life, which he purposely reserved and employed for that great battle.

He disposed his troops in circular form, investing the camp of the Portuguese from all sides, and this circle, bending and closing in, hindered the enemy not only in the battle (which was very furious owing to the valour of the young assailant King), seeing they had to offer a front in every direction, but also prevented their flight after their rout. And, finding all the outlets seized and closed, they were obliged to fall back upon themselves—*piled up not only by the slaughter, but by their flight* (Livy)—and were heaped up one on top of the other, enabling the conquerors to gain a very murderous and very complete victory.

Dying as he was, he had himself borne and hurried from place to place whither necessity called him, and, passing along the ranks, he encouraged his captains and men one after another. But when one wedge of his line of battle was broken, he was not to be kept from mounting his charger with sword in hand. He strove with all his power to enter the fray, his men trying to hold him, some by the bridle, others by his gown or his stirrups. This effort finished the little life that was left in him. They laid him down again. Then, recovering with a start from his swoon, unable in any other way to advise his people to hush up his death, which was the most necessary command he had then to give, that his soldiers might not be driven to despair by the news, he expired with his finger on his closed lips, the usual sign for enjoining silence.

What man ever lived so long and so far into death ? What man ever died so erect ?

The highest degree, and the most natural, of bravely meeting death, is to look upon her not only without dismay, but unconcernedly, freely continuing one's wonted course of life even into her very lap. Like Cato, who passed his time in sleep and study, all the while having a violent and bloody death in his mind and in his heart, and holding it in his hand.

CHAPTER 22

OF RIDING POST

I HAVE not been among the least able in this exercise, which is suited for men of my build, short and sturdy. But I have given up the business ; it is too trying in the long run.

I was just now reading that King Cyrus, the more speedily to obtain news from all parts of his empire, which was of very great extent, ascertained how far a horse could go at a stretch in one day ; and at that distance from one another he posted men whose business it was to keep horses in readiness to mount those who were coming to him. And some say that this speed amounts to the measure of the flight of cranes.

Caesar says that Lucius Vibulus Rufus, being in haste to bring information to Pompey, rode night and day, changing his horses for greater dispatch. And he himself, according to Suetonius, travelled a hundred miles a day in a hired coach. But he was a furious courier, for whenever a river cut across his road he would swim it, and never turned out of his way to look for a bridge or ford.

Tiberius Nero, going to see his brother Drusus, who was ill in Germany, made two hundred miles in twenty-four hours, having three coaches.

In the war of the Romans against King Antiochus, T. Sempronius Gracchus, says Livy, *with almost incredible speed rode in three days from Amphissa to Pella on relay horses* ; and it appears, looking at the journey, that they were fixed posts, not freshly commanded for that ride.

Cecinna's contrivance for sending news to his family was much speedier ; he carried swallows with him, and released them to fly to their nests when he wished to send back news of himself, having marked them with some colour, according to pre-arrangement with his people, to signify his meaning. At the theatre in Rome the paterfamilias would keep a pigeon in his bosom and tie a letter to it when he desired to send a message to his people at home ; and it was trained to bring back an answer. D. Brutus also employed pigeons when besieged in Mutina ; and others elsewhere.

In Peru they rode post upon men, who carried them on their shoulders by means of litters ; and they were so agile that, in full career, the first porters would transfer their load to the second, without stopping a moment.

I understand that the Wallachians, who are the Grand Sultan's couriers, make wonderful speed, since they are authorized to change mounts with any rider they meet on the way, leaving him their jaded horse. And that, to guard against weariness, they compress their waist very tightly with a broad bandage [as do many others. I have not found it to give any relief].

CHAPTER 23

OF EVIL MEANS EMPLOYED TO A GOOD END

THERE is a wonderful relation and correspondence in that general scheme of the works of Nature, which clearly proves that it is neither accidental nor carried out by divers masters. The diseases and conditions of our body are reflected in states and governments ; kingdoms, republics are born, flourish and decay with old age, as we do. We are subject to a useless and harmful superabundance of humours ; either of good humours (for even this the physicians fear ; and because there is no stability in us, they say that a too brisk, robust and perfect state of health must be artificially reduced and lowered, lest our nature, unable to settle down to any certain condition, there being no room for improvement, might make a disorderly and too sudden retreat ; and therefore they prescribe purgings and bloodlettings for athletes, to save them from that superabundance of health), or a superabundance of evil humours, which is the usual cause of diseases.

We may observe that States are often sick of a like superabundance, and it has been the custom to purge them in different ways. Sometimes a large number of families are allowed to leave a country for its relief, and seek settlements in other regions at the expense of strangers. So it was that our ancestors the Franks came from the heart of Germany, took possession of Gaul, and drove out its first inhabitants. So was created that endless tide of people that poured into

Italy under Brennus and others. So the Goths and Vandals, as well as the people who are now in possession of Greece, quitted their native country to settle elsewhere, where they had more elbow-room ; and there are scarcely two or three corners of the world that have not felt the effects of these removals.

In this way the Romans established their colonies ; for, perceiving their city to be growing beyond measure, they drained it of the least necessary people, and sent them to inhabit and cultivate their conquered territories. At times too they purposely fomented war with some of their enemies, not only to keep their soldiers in breath, lest idleness, the mother of corruption, should bring worse evils upon them :

> A lengthy peace has been our bane, for war
> Is less disastrous than are ease and sloth ;   (JUVENAL.)

but also to bleed their Commonwealth, to vent a little the too exuberant heat of their young men, and to prune and thin out the branches of that too lustily growing stock. To serve this end they once made war upon the Carthaginians.

By the treaty of Bretigny, Edward the Third, King of England, refused to include, in that general peace he made with our King, the difference regarding the Duchy of Brittany, in order that he might keep a place upon which to unload his soldiers, and that the crowd of Englishmen he had employed in his affairs on this side of the Channel might not pour back into England. It was one of the reasons why our King Philip consented to send his son John to war overseas, that he might take along with him a great number of young hot-bloods who were among his armed troops.

There are many nowadays who argue in this manner, and would like the heated and turbulent spirits among us to be drained into some war with our neighbours, lest those peccant humours which are now predominant in our body, if not allowed to flow out in other directions, should keep our fever at its present height, and end by causing our total ruin. And indeed a foreign war is a much milder disease than a civil war. But I do not believe that God would look with favour upon so iniquitous a design as to insult and pick a quarrel with others for our convenience :

> Grant me no fierce desire, Rhamnusian maid,
> To rob a lawful owner of his wealth. (CATULLUS.)

Yet we are so feeble by nature that we are often driven to the necessity of using bad means to a good end. Lycurgus, the most virtuous and perfect legislator that ever was, contrived this most iniquitous plan for teaching his people to be temperate, of forcibly making the Helots, who were their slaves, drunk, in order that the sight of these men, so lost and buried in wine, might inspire the Spartans with a horror of that vice carried to excess.

They were still more in the wrong who, in ancient times, allowed criminals, whatever kind of death they were condemned to suffer, to be cut up alive by the physicians, in order to see our internal parts in their natural state, and obtain a greater certainty in their art. For if we must run to excess, it is more excusable to do so for the health of the soul than for that of the body ; as the Romans trained the people to valour and contempt of dangers and death by means of those outrageous exhibitions of gladiators, who were pledged to fight to the death, cutting up and killing each other in their presence ;

> What other object has this savage sport,
> This death of youths, this blood-fed lust ? (PRUDENTIUS.)

And this custom continued till the time of the Emperor Theodosius :

> Seize now the honour destined for thy reign,
> O Prince, and to the glory of thy sire
> Add all that now remains to thee to gain.
> Henceforth let none in Rome be slain for sport,
> Condemned to please the rabble by his pain.
> Let blood of beasts alone henceforth be shed ;
> No homicides permit with cruel arms. (PRUDENTIUS.)

It was, forsooth, a wonderful example, and highly edifying for the populace, to see every day a hundred, two hundred, nay a thousand couples of men armed against one another, hacking each other to pieces, with such intense courage and fortitude, that they were never heard to utter a word indicating weakness or pity, never seen to turn their backs, nor as much as to take one cowardly step to dodge their adversary's stroke, but rather to extend their neck to the sword and offer to receive the death-blow !

Many of them, when covered with wounds and at death's door, sent to ask the spectators whether they were satisfied that they had done their duty, before lying down to give up the ghost in the arena. It was not enough to fight and die bravely, but they must also do it cheerfully ; for if they were seen to show any reluctance to die, they were howled down and cursed.

The very girls egged them on :

> The gentle maid jumps up at every blow ;
> And every time the victor thrusts his blade
> Into his rival's gorge, shrieks with delight,
> And with extended thumb urges him on
> To kill his prostrate foe. (PRUDENTIUS.)

The early Romans employed criminals for this exemplary exhibition. But afterwards they used innocent slaves, and even freemen who sold themselves for the purpose ; nay, Roman senators and knights, and, what is more, women :

> They sell their heads to die in the arena ;
> Though peace prevails, each seeks an enemy. (MANILIUS.)

> Amid these tumults and new sports
> The tender sex, unskilled in arms,
> Immodestly their weakness test
> In fights for men intended. (STATIUS.)

All this I should think very strange and incredible, were it not that we are daily accustomed to see, in our wars, many myriads of foreigners staking, in return for money payment, their blood and their life in quarrels in which they have no concern.

CHAPTER 24

OF THE GREATNESS OF ROME

I WILL say only a word on this inexhaustible subject, in order to show up the simplicity of those who couple the pitiful greatness of these times with that of Rome. In the seventh book of Cicero's *Familiar Letters* (the grammarians may, if they please, drop the epithet ' familiar ', for it is not really very appropriate ; those who, in place of ' familiar ', have substituted *ad familiares*,[1] may be justified by the fact that Suetonius, in his *Life of Caesar*, states that there was a volume of letters of his *ad familiares*), there is one addressed to Caesar, who was then in Gaul, in which Cicero

---

[1] To his friends.

repeats these words which appeared at the end of another
letter that Caesar had written to him : ' With regard to
Marcus Furius, whom you have recommended to me, I will
make him King of Gaul ; and if you want me to advance
some other friend of yours, send him to me.'

It was no new thing for a simple Roman citizen, as Caesar
was at the time, to dispose of kingdoms ; for indeed he
deprived King Deiotarus of his to give it to a nobleman of
the town of Pergamus, by name Mithridates. And those
who write his Life record several other kingdoms sold by
him ; and Suetonius says that at one stroke he squeezed
out of King Ptolemy three million six hundred thousand
crowns, which was very like selling him his kingdom :

> So much Galatia cost ; so much for Pontus,
> So much for Lydia was paid. (CLAUDIAN.)

Mark Antony said that the greatness of the Roman people
showed itself not so much in what they took as in what they
gave. And yet, about a century before Antony, they ousted
one, among others, with so marvellous a show of authority,
that in the whole history of Rome I know of no example
that throws so strong a light on her reputation and power.
Antiochus possessed the whole of Egypt, and was engaged
in the conquest of Cyprus and other appendages of the
empire. During the progress of his victories, C. Popilius
came to him in the name of the Senate, and at first refused
to take him by the hand until he had read the letters he was
bringing. The King, having read them and saying he would
consider the matter, Popilius with his staff drew a circle
around the spot on which he was standing, and said,
' Return me an answer to carry back to the Senate before
you step outside of this circle.' Antiochus, astonished at
this rude and peremptory command, replied after a little
thought, ' I will do as the Senate commands me.' Then
Popilius greeted him as a friend of the Roman people.

To give up so great a monarchy and so fortunate and
prosperous a career, because of the impression made by
three lines of writing ! He had good reason indeed to send
word to the Senate, as he afterwards did by his ambassadors,
that he had received their command with the same respect
as if it had come from the immortal gods.

All the kingdoms that Augustus won by the right of war

he restored to those who had lost them, or presented them to strangers.

And, in this connexion, Tacitus, speaking of the King of England, Cogidunus, by a wonderful touch gives us an inkling of this immense power. 'The Romans, he says, had from time immemorial been wont to leave the kings they vanquished in possession of their kingdoms, subject to their authority, *that they might have even kings to be the tools of their slavery.*'

It is very likely that Solyman, whom we have seen generously bestowing the kingdom of Hungary and other states, had more regard to this consideration than the one he was accustomed to allege, 'That he was glutted and overburdened with so many kingdoms and so much power [which had been acquired by his own valour or that of his ancestors.]'

CHAPTER 25

OF NOT MALINGERING

THERE is an epigram of Martial, which is among his good ones (for they are of all sorts), and in which he tells in a humorous way the story of Cælius who, to avoid paying his court to several of the great men in Rome, assisting at their levee, following and attending upon them, pretended to have the gout ; and, to make his excuse the more plausible, had his legs rubbed with ointment and swathed, and in all respects assumed the behaviour and looks of a gouty person. In the end Fortune gratified him by making him really so :

> What may not man with care and art obtain ;
> He feigned the gout, and now has ceased to feign.   (MARTIAL.)

I have read, somewhere in Appian, I think, a similar story of one who, wishing to escape the proscriptions of the Triumvirs at Rome, and to evade recognition by those who were in pursuit of him, disguised and hid himself, pretending in addition to be blind in one eye. When he came to recover a little more liberty, and removed the plaster he had so long worn over that eye, he found that under the disguise he had really lost the sight of it.

It may be that the action of sight had become dulled through having been so long without exercise, and that the

visual power had wholly transferred itself to the other eye.
For if we keep one eye covered we can very plainly feel it
conveying some part of its virtue to its fellow, with the
result that the eye which remains free dilates and grows
bigger. So also idleness, combined with the heat of the
bandages and medicaments, might very well have attracted
some podagric humour to the gouty man of Martial's
epigram.

Having read in Froissart of the vow taken by a band of
young English noblemen to keep their left eye covered until
they had crossed over into France and distinguished themselves in fighting against us, I have often been tickled by
the idea that they might have been caught, like the above-
mentioned, and might have returned with only one good
eye to the mistresses for whom they had taken this rash vow.

Mothers are right to scold their children when they mimic
blindness, lameness, squinting, and other personal infirmities of the same kind. For besides that their body at that
tender age might take on some evil ply, Fortune somehow
seems to deride us and take us at our word. I have heard
of many instances of people becoming ill after pretending
to be so.

I have always been accustomed, when riding or walking,
to burden my hand with a switch or stick, even affecting
an air of elegance by using it as a support. Several have
warned me that Fortune might one day turn this foppery
into a necessity. I rely upon the fact that I should be the
very first of my clan to have the gout.

But let us prolong this chapter and checker it with another
story on the subject of blindness. Pliny tells of a man who,
dreaming in his sleep that he was blind, next morning found
himself really so, though he had not previously suffered any
infirmity. The power of imagination may easily be a con-
tributing cause, as I have explained elsewhere ; and Pliny
seems to be of that opinion. But it is more probable that
the agitation which the body felt within (of which the
physicians may, if they please, discover the cause), and
which deprived him of his sight, occasioned the dream.

We will add one more story, akin to this subject, which
Seneca relates in one of his letters : ' You know, he says,
writing to Lucilius, that Harpaste, my wife's idiot, has been
thrown upon my hands as a hereditary burden ; for I have

a natural aversion to these freaks ; and if I have a mind to laugh at a fool, I have not far to go, for I can laugh at myself. This idiot has suddenly lost her sight. I am telling you something strange but true. She is not conscious of being blind, and keeps urging her keeper to take her out, because she says my house is dark.

'What we laugh at in her I pray you to believe happens to every one of us : no man knows that he is avaricious or covetous. The blind at least ask for a guide ; we go astray of our own accord. I am not ambitious, we say ; but at Rome a man cannot live otherwise. I am not a spendthrift, but the city requires a great outlay. It is not my fault if I am choleric, if I have not yet laid down a certain plan of life ; it is the fault of youth.

'Let us not seek our evil outside of us ; it is within us, it is rooted in our entrails. And the mere fact that we are not conscious of being sick makes the cure more difficult. If we do not begin in good time to look after ourselves, when shall we have time to attend to so many sores and maladies ? And yet we have a very sweet medicine in Philosophy ; for of the others we do not feel the pleasure until after the cure. This one pleases and cures at the same time.'

Those are the words of Seneca, who has carried me away from my theme. But there is profit in change.

CHAPTER 26

OF THUMBS

TACITUS relates that it was the custom of certain barbarian kings, when entering into a firm covenant, to clasp their right hands tightly, with the thumbs interlocked ; and when by dint of squeezing, the blood rose to the tips, they pricked them lightly, and each sucked the other's.

Physicians say that the thumb is the master-finger of the hand, and that the word (*pouce*) is derived from the Latin word *pollere*.[1] The Greeks call it ἀντίχειρ, as who should say ' another hand '. And the Latins sometimes appear to take it in this sense of the whole hand :

> No soft persuasion, whether of voice or thumb,
> Will make him rise to the occasion. (MARTIAL.)

[1] To be strong or powerful.

At Rome, to close and hold down the thumbs was meant to signify approval :

> Admirers now applaud your play
> With both their thumbs turned in. (HORACE.)

and disapproval to raise and turn them up :

> They kill their man to win applause
> When the assembled mob turn up their thumbs. (JUVENAL.)

The Romans excused from military service those whose thumbs were injured, as not having sufficient strength to grasp their weapons. Augustus confiscated the estates of a Roman knight who had cunningly cut off the thumbs of his two young sons, to excuse them from joining the army. And before his time the Senate, during the Italian wars, sentenced Caius Vatienus to perpetual imprisonment, and confiscated all his property, for having purposely cut off the thumb of his left hand, to exempt himself from that expedition.

Some person whose name I no longer remember,[1] having won a battle at sea, ordered the thumbs of all his vanquished enemies to be cut off, to render them incapable of fighting or rowing. The Athenians did the same to those of Aegina, to deprive them of their superiority in the art of navigation.

In Lacedemon the schoolmaster punished his boys by biting their thumbs.

CHAPTER 27

COWARDICE IS THE MOTHER OF CRUELTY

I HAVE often heard it said that cowardice is the mother of cruelty. And I have found by experience that this malevolent and inhuman ferocity and heartlessness are usually accompanied by a feminine weakness. I have observed that some of the most cruel men are easily moved to tears, and for trivial reasons. Alexander, the Tyrant of Pheres, dared not witness a tragedy in the theatre, lest his citizens should see him groaning over the misfortunes of Hecuba and Andromache, although he himself every day cruelly murdered, without any pity, so many of his subjects. Can it be weak-mindedness that makes them so easily liable to every kind of extreme ?

[1] Philocles, one of the Athenian generals in the Peloponnesian war.

Valour, which only manifests itself when there is resistance to be overcome :

To fight
An unresisting bull gives no delight, (CLAUDIAN.)

restrains itself when it sees the enemy at its mercy.   But pusillanimity, to be able to say that she too has acted, unable to assume the leading rôle, takes a secondary one, that of bloodshed and massacre.   The killing after a victory is usually done by the rabble and the baggage-officials. And what causes so many unexampled cruelties in civil wars is that the dregs of the army become callous, and imagine themselves to be heroes when steeped up to the elbows in blood after ripping up a body at their feet, since that is their only idea of valour :

The wolves, the filthy bears, and all
The more ignoble beasts will fall
Upon the dying foe. (OVID.)

They are like a cowardly house-cur worrying and tearing the skin of a wild beast it would not have dared to attack in the open.

What is it that in these days makes our quarrels altogether deadly ; and that, whilst our fathers observed some degrees in revenge, we now begin with the last, and at the very outset speak of nothing but killing ?   What is that if not cowardice ?

Every one is well aware that it needs a more scornful courage to defeat one's enemy than to finish him off, to make him lick the dust than to kill him.   Besides that the craving for vengeance is more completely assuaged and satisfied, for it only aims at making itself felt.   That is why we do not attack an animal or a stone when they hurt us, since they are incapable of feeling our revenge.   And to kill a man is to save him from further injury on our part.

And as Bias called out to a wicked man, ' I know that soon or late you will be punished for it, but I am afraid I shall not be there to see ; ' and pitied the Orchomenians because the penalty which Lyciscus paid for the treason committed against them was not exacted until there was nobody alive of those who had been injured by it, and who should have been gratified by his punishment ; so revenge is to be pitied, when he upon whom it is executed has lost the power of feeling it. For, as the avenger desires to witness his vengeance in order to derive pleasure from it, so must he upon whom it is carried out witness it, in order to suffer pain, and repent.

' He will repent it,' we say. And when we have shot him through the head with a pistol, do we think that he will repent ? On the contrary, if we watch him closely, we shall see that he is making a face at us as he falls. He does not even begrudge us our revenge, which is very far from repenting. And we are doing him the greatest favour possible by making him die suddenly and painlessly.

As for us, we are driven to scuttle about and hide like a rabbit, and fly from the officers of justice who are at our heels, whilst he is at rest. To kill a man is a good means of avoiding future injury, but not of avenging one already committed. It is an action dictated by fear rather than bravery, an act of precaution rather than courage, an act of defence rather than of aggression. It is obvious that by that action we abandon both the real object of our revenge, and care for our reputation. We are afraid, if he lives, that he will return to the charge. You rid yourself of him, not to his prejudice, but in your interest.

In the kingdom of Narsinga this expedient would avail us naught. There not only military men but even artisans settle their quarrels with the sword. The king never denies the field to those who wish to fight, and in the case of persons of quality he looks on, and rewards the victor with a gold chain. But to win this chain any man who has a mind to it is at liberty to cross swords with the wearer. So that, having settled with one adversary, he may have several on his hands.

If we thought that by our valour we should always master our enemy and crow over him at our pleasure, we should be sorry for him to escape us, as he does by dying. We desire to vanquish, but with safety rather than honour. And in our quarrel we look to the end rather than the glory.

For an honourable man the case of Asinius Pollio illustrated a like error. Having written an invective against Plancus, he awaited his death before publishing it. That was like ' biting his thumb ' at a blind man, casting filthy abuse at a deaf man or wounding one who has no feeling, rather than run the risk of his resentment. And it was in

reference to him that somebody said that ' it was only for
ghosts to strive with the dead '. As for the man who awaits
the death of an author before attacking his writings, what
does he do but confess himself a feeble brawler ?

Someone said to Aristotle that a man had spoken ill of
him. ' Let him do more, he said, let him flog me, provided
I am not there.'

Our fathers were content to answer an insult with a
contradiction, a contradiction with a blow, and so on, in
regular order. They were brave enough not to fear an
adversary, alive and insulted. We tremble with fright as
long as we see him with a leg to stand on. And that that
is so, is it not shown in our noble practice nowadays of
pursuing to the death both the man we have insulted and
the man who has insulted us ?

It was also by a kind of cowardice that the custom was
introduced of being attended in our single combats by
seconds and thirds and fourths. Formerly they were duels ;
now they are encounters and battles. Those who initiated
this practice were afraid of being alone, *because neither had
any confidence in himself*. For naturally any kind of company is a comfort and a solace in danger. Formerly they
called in third persons to guard against irregularity and foul
play, and as witnesses to the hazard of the combat. But
now that it has assumed this form that the witnesses themselves engage with one another, whoever is called upon
cannot honourably stand aside as a spectator, for fear lest
he might be suspected either of want of feeling or of
courage.

Besides the iniquity and the vileness of this action of
engaging another strength and valour not your own for the
defence of your honour, it seems to me that, for a good man
who has full confidence in himself, it is a disadvantage to
go and mix up his fortune with that of a second. Each one
incurs a sufficient risk for himself without also incurring it
for another, and has enough to do to safeguard his own
valour in defence of his life, without committing a thing so
dear to the hands of a third party. For, unless the contrary
has been expressly agreed upon, the four form a combined
party. If your second is down, you have two adversaries
to deal with, and rightly so. And if you say that it is not
fair play, that is indeed so, just as it is unfair, if you are

well armed, to attack a man who has only the stump of a sword, or, if you are sound, a man who is already badly wounded. But if these are advantages you have won in the fight, you may use them without fear of reproach.

The disparity and inequality are weighed and considered only from the point of view of the condition of the combatants at the beginning of the fight ; as for the rest you must take your chance. And when single-handed you have three men to deal with, your two companions having been killed, you would have no more wrong done you than I should do if, with equal chances in a battle, I cut down an enemy with my sword whom I saw fiercely attacking one of my own side.

It is in the nature of fellowship that, when a body of men is opposed to another (as when our Duke of Orleans challenged King Henry of England, a hundred against a hundred ; three hundred against the same number, as in the case of the Argives against the Lacedemonians ; three against three, as in the case of the Horatii against the Curiatii), the number on either side is regarded but as a single man. Wherever there is company the hazard is confounded and mixed.

I am interested in this discussion for family reasons. For my brother, the Sieur de Matecoulom, was called upon at Rome to second a gentleman whom he hardly knew and who was the defender, having been challenged by another. In this duel he happened to be matched against one whom he knew better and who was nearer to his heart. (I should like to hear somebody justify by reason these laws of honour which so often contradict and collide with the laws of reason.) Having disposed of his man, and seeing the two principals in the quarrel still on their feet and unhurt, he went to the relief of his own. What less could he do ? Was he to keep quiet and look on whilst the man for whose defence he had come was defeated, if Fate had so willed it ? What he had so far done had not advanced the business ; the quarrel was still unsettled.

That courtesy which you can and certainly ought to show your enemy, when you have brought him to his knees and have a great advantage over him, cannot be exercised, as far as I can see, when another's interest is at stake, when you are only an assistant, when the quarrel is none of yours. He could not afford to be either just or courteous at the risk of the man to whom he had lent his assistance. He was therefore released from the Italian prisons upon a very speedy and solemn recommendation of our King.

What a hare-brained people we are ! We are not satisfied with making our vices and follies known to the world by repute, but we must go among foreign nations and let them see them with their own eyes. Put three Frenchmen in the Lybian deserts, and they will not be a month together without annoying and scratching each other. You would imagine that this peregrination of our countrymen were specially organized to give foreigners the satisfaction of witnessing our tragedies, and most often to those who rejoice over and laugh at our misfortunes.

We go to Italy to learn to fence, and practise at the expense of our lives before we have acquired any skill. And yet by the rule of discipline we should put theory before practice. We betray ourselves as mere tyros :

> O bitter first-fruits of a youth so fair !
> O war's stern prelude ! promise dashed to scorn ! (VIRGIL.)

I know well that it is an art that is very useful for the end it has in view (in the duel between the two Princes,[1] who were cousins-german, in Spain, the elder, says Livy, by skill in the use of his weapon and by cunning, easily got the better of the more reckless strength of the younger) ; and, as I know by experience, an art the knowledge of which has swelled the hearts of some beyond their natural measure. But it is not valour, properly speaking, since it derives its support from skill, and relies upon something other than itself.

The honour of the combat consists in the jealousy of courage, not of science. And so I have seen a friend of mine, famed as a past master in this exercise, choose in his quarrels weapons which deprived him of the power of exercising this advantage, and wholly depended on good fortune and assurance, in order that his victory might not be put down to his skill in fencing rather than his valour. In my boyhood the nobles shunned the reputation of good fencers as offensive, and retired from public view if they

---

[1] Corbis and Orsua ; see Livy, xxviii. 21.

wished to learn the art, as a cunning trade, derogating from true and natural valour :

> They shrink not, trifle not, strive not to smite
> By artificial rules, with wary will;
> Stand not on postures or on points, the night
> And their blind rage forbid the tricks of skill;
> But swords crash horribly with swords, and shrill
> The mountain echo shrieks along the plain;
> Not a foot stirs,—where stood, there stand they still;
> But aye their hands in motion they maintain;
> And not a lunge, or foin, or slash descends in vain. (TASSO.)

Shooting at the target, tournaments, tilting-matches and suchlike mimic warfare, were the exercises of our fore-fathers. This other exercise is the more ignoble since it has only a private end in view, and teaches us to destroy one another against the laws and justice, and in every way produces only harmful results. It is much more meritorious and becoming to practice things which strengthen instead of injuring our government, which tend to public security and the common glory.

Publius Rutilius, the Consul, was the first to instruct the soldier in handling his weapon with skill and science, who joined art and valour ; not to employ them in private quarrels, but in war and the quarrels of the Roman people. An art of fence for the people and the citizen.

And, not to mention the example of Caesar, who com-manded his men to aim chiefly at the faces of Pompey's legionaries at the battle of Pharsalia, a thousand other army generals have bethought themselves of contriving new forms of weapons, and new ways of striking and defending, accord-ing to the needs of the moment.

But just as Philopoemen condemned wrestling, in which he excelled, since the training for that exercise differed from that appropriate to military discipline, to which he thought that men of honour should alone devote themselves, so it seems to me that this agility to which we now form our limbs, those feints and movements which the young men are taught in this new school, are not only useless, but rather contrary and harmful to the military style of fighting.

Besides, our people commonly use particular weapons specially intended for that purpose. And I have known the time when it was hardly considered the right thing for a gentleman, when challenged to fight with rapier and dagger, to appear in military equipment [or that any should offer to come with his cloak instead of a dagger].

It is worthy of consideration that Laches, in Plato, speaking of an apprenticeship in the handling of weapons agreeing with ours, said he had never known a great soldier to come out of that school, especially from among the masters of it. As to these our experience tells us the same. In any case we may at least maintain that they are talents that have no relation or correspondence with one another. And Plato, in the educational system of his Republic, forbids the art of using the fists, introduced by Amycus and Epeius, as well as that of wrestling, invented by Antaeus and Cercyon, because they have another aim than that of making youths more fit for military service, and do not contribute to it.

But I am straying a little aside from my theme.

The Emperor Maurice, being warned by dreams and several divinations that one Phocas, a soldier then unknown to him, was to kill him, questioned his son-in-law Philip with regard to this Phocas, his disposition, his circumstances and habits ; and when Philip told him, amongst other things, that he was cowardly and timorous, the Emperor at once concluded that he was murderous and cruel.

What is it that makes tyrants so bloodthirsty ? It is anxiety for their safety, and because their faint hearts can suggest to them no other means of ensuring it than to exterminate those who have the power to injure them ; even the women, for fear of a scratch.

> He strikes at all, for every man he fears.   (CLAUDIAN.)

The first cruelties are practised for their own sake ; thence springs the fear of a just revenge, which afterwards gives rise to a string of fresh cruelties, in order to stifle the first by means of others.

Philip, King of Macedon, the one who had so many bones to pick with the Roman people, moved by horror of the murders committed by his orders, finding himself unable to decide what precautions to take against the many families he had at different times injured, resolved to seize all the children of those he had put to death, in order, from day to day, to destroy them one after the other, and thus set his mind at rest.

A beautiful matter will always be in place, wherever it is sown. I, who am more solicitous about the weight and utility of what I say than of its order and connexion, should not be afraid of bringing in here, though a little out of the way, a very pretty story. [When they are rich in their own beauty and are able to justify themselves only too well, I am satisfied with the end of a hair to join them to my matter.]

Among those condemned by Philip was one Herodicus, a Prince of the Thessalians. After killing him he later put to death also his two sons-in-law, each of whom left a very young son. Theoxena and Archo were the two widows. Theoxena could not be induced to marry again, although she was much sought after. Archo married Poris, the leading man among the Aenians ; she had by him a number of children, but died leaving them all very young. Theoxena, spurred by a motherly love for her nephews, in order to take them under her care and guidance, married Poris.

Then came the proclamation of the King's edict. This brave mother, fearing both Philip's cruelty and the excesses of his satellites directed against these fair and tender children, boldly declared that she would rather kill them with her own hands than give them up. Poris, alarmed by this declaration, promises her to convey them secretly to Athens, and place them in charge of some trusted guest-friends of his. They take the opportunity afforded by an annual festival which was celebrated at Aenia in honour of Aeneas, and thither they go. After assisting during the day at the ceremonies and a public banquet, they stole away by night in a ship that lay ready to escape by sea.

The wind was against them, and finding themselves next morning in sight of the land whence they had put to sea, they were pursued by the harbour guards. As these approached, and while Poris was busy urging the sailors to make all speed, Theoxena, frantic with love and revenge, in pursuance of her first resolution, prepared weapons and poison, and showing them to the boys, said, ' Come, my children, death is henceforth the only means of your defence and freedom, and will be an occasion for the Gods to exercise their sacred justice. These drawn swords, and these cups, will open the door to it. Courage ! And you, my son, who are the eldest, grasp this blade and die the braver death ! '

Having on one side so energetic a counsellor and on the other the enemy at their throats, each of them wildly rushed at the weapon that was nearest at hand, and half dead they were thrown into the sea. Theoxena, proud of having so gloriously provided for the safety of all her children, warmly embraced her husband with the words, ' Let us follow these boys, my friend, and enjoy the same grave with them.' And locked in each others' arms they leapt into the sea, and the vessel was taken back to land without its masters.

Tyrants, in order both to kill and make their anger felt, have used all their wits to find the means of prolonging death. They wish their enemies to be gone, but not so quickly that they may not have leisure to taste their revenge. Herein they are greatly perplexed, for if the tortures are violent, they are short ; if they are prolonged, they are not sufficiently painful for their liking. So we see them carefully contriving their implements. We see thousands of examples of this in antiquity ; and I do not know whether we have not unwittingly retained some traces of this barbarity.

All that is over and above simple death appears to me pure cruelty.[1] Our justice cannot hope that the man who is not deterred from wrong-doing by the fear of being hanged or beheaded, will be prevented by the idea of a slow fire, or the pincers, or the wheel. And I know not but that he is meanwhile driven to desperation. For what can be the condition of a man's soul, who is awaiting twenty-four hours of death, broken on the wheel, or, after the old fashion, nailed to a cross ?

Josephus relates that during the wars of the Romans in Judea, passing by a place where, three days before, several Jews had been crucified, he recognized three of his friends, and obtained permission to remove them. Two of them died, he says, the other lived since that time.

Chalcondylas, a man worthy of belief, in the memoirs that he left of events which happened in his days and in his neighbourhood, records as the worst of punishments that which was often inflicted by the Emperor Mahomet of having a man cut in two, with one stroke of a scimetar, at the diaphragm, just below the ribs ; the result being that

[1] This sentence was censured by the Papal authorities in Rome, when Montaigne was there in 1581 ; but he defied the censure by retaining it.

they died as it were two deaths at once. He adds that both parts could be seen long after, full of life and writhing in torment.

I do not suppose that these movements implied that there was much feeling left in those bodies. The most ghastly torments to look at are not always the hardest to endure. To my mind there is more atrocity in those he inflicted, according to other historians, upon some lords of Epirus, who were flayed piecemeal, by a dispensation so malignantly devised, that they endured that agony for fifteen days.

And here are two other examples. Croesus had a nobleman, a favourite of his brother Pantaleon, seized and carried into a fuller's shop, where he was scratched and carded with the cards and combs used in the trade, until he died.

George Sechel, leader of those Polish peasants who, under the cloak of a crusade, did so much mischief, being defeated and taken prisoner in battle by the Voivode of Transylvania, was for three days bound naked to a wooden horse, exposed to all manner of tortures that anybody might devise against him. During this time the other prisoners were given nothing to eat or drink. In the end, while he was still alive and able to see, they gave his blood to drink to his beloved brother Lucat, whom he entreated them to spare, drawing upon himself all the hatred for their misdeeds. Twenty of his most favoured captains were made to feed upon him, tearing his flesh with their teeth and swallowing the morsels. After he was dead the rest of his body, with the entrails, was boiled and given to others of his followers to eat.

CHAPTER 28

THERE IS A TIME FOR ALL THINGS

THOSE who compare Cato the Censor with the younger Cato, who was his own murderer, compare two fine characters that are much akin. The former displayed his in more ways, and surpassed the other in military exploits and in the usefulness of his public services. But the virtue of the younger, besides that it would be blasphemy to compare any other with it in vigour, was much more unblemished. For who could acquit the Censor of envy and ambition, when he presumed to attack the honour of

Scipio, who in goodness and all eminent qualities was very much greater than he and any man of his time ?

What they tell of him, among other things, that in his extreme old age he began to learn Greek with a greedy appetite, as if to quench a long-standing thirst, does not appear to me very greatly to his honour. It is properly speaking what we should call falling into second childhood.

There is a time for all things, good and all. I may say my Paternoster at the wrong moment ; and T. Quintus Flaminius was denounced for having been seen standing apart, wasting his time in praying to God during the course of a battle which he won as army general.

> The sage sets bounds to even virtuous things. (JUVENAL.)

Eudemonidas, seeing Xenocrates in his old age very busy over his school lessons, said, ' When will this man know, if he is still learning ? ' And Philopoemen replied to those who were extolling King Ptolemy because he daily hardened his body in warlike exercises, ' It is not commendable in a king of his age to practise them ; he should henceforth actually apply them.'

The young should make their preparations ; the old should reap the fruits of them, say the sages. And the greatest defect they observe in our nature is that our desires incessantly renew their youth. We are ever beginning to live over again. Our studies and desires should sometimes savour of old age. We have a foot in the grave, and our appetites and pursuits are but new-born :

> So you, upon death's very brink,
> Of cutting marbles only think,
> That yet are in the quarry's womb,
> And, all unmindful of the tomb,
> Rear gorgeous mansions everywhere. (HORACE.)

The most far-seeing of my plans have no more than a year in view ; henceforth I think of nothing but the end. I shake off all fresh hopes and enterprises, take my last leave of all the places I shall quit, and every day dispossess myself of my belongings. *For a long time I have neither lost nor gained ; I have more than enough provisions for my journey* (Seneca).

> My life is lived ; the course by Fortune given
> I have fulfilled. (VIRGIL.)

This is in fact all the comfort I have in my old age, that it deadens in me many desires and cares which trouble our life ; care about how the world wags, care for wealth, greatness, knowledge, health, myself. This man learns to speak [1] when he ought to learn to hold his peace for ever.

We may continue our studies at all times, but not our schooling. What a foolish thing is an old man learning his ABC !

> For different things do different men delight ;
> And all things are not for all ages right. (PSEUDO-GALLUS.)

If we must study let us take up a study that is suitable to our present condition, that we may answer as he did who was asked for what purpose he was studying in his decrepitude, ' that I may depart this world a better man, and a happier.'

Of this kind were the studies of the younger Cato, when he felt his end to be near and came across Plato's Discourse *Of the Eternity of the Soul.* Not but that, as we may well believe, he had long been furnished with every kind of provision for that departure. Of confidence, a resolute will and learning, he had more than Plato had in his writings. His knowledge and his courage were in this respect ahead of Philosophy. He applied himself to this study, not that it might be serviceable to him in death, but, like a man whose sleep is not even disturbed when important matters are under consideration, he also continued, without choice or change, his studies with the other wonted actions of his life.

The night which followed his rejection for the Pretorship he spent in play ; that in which he was to die he spent in reading. The loss of either life or office was all one to him.

CHAPTER 29

OF VALOUR

I HAVE learned by experience that there is a great difference between the flights and sallies of the soul and a firm and constant habit of mind ; and very well perceive that there is nothing we cannot do, even, as somebody says,[2] to

---

[1] A reference to the above-mentioned Cato, who learned to read Greek in his old age, in order to improve his eloquence.

[2] Seneca.

surpassing the Deity itself, since it is a greater thing to become immune to passion by our efforts than to be so by our original condition ; and even to be able to combine our human frailty with a godlike firmness and assurance. But it is by fits and starts. And in the lives of those heroes of olden times there are sometimes seen miraculous flashes, which seem by a long way to exceed our natural powers ; but they are indeed flashes, and it is hard to believe that it is possible for the soul to be so dyed and steeped in these exalted conditions that they become usual and as it were natural to her.

It may even befall ourselves, who are but human abortions, that our soul, aroused by others' examples and teachings, will sometimes shoot up far beyond her ordinary range ; but it is some kind of passion which stirs and drives her, and carries her some way outside of herself. For, when that whirlwind has blown over, we see that she unconsciously flags and slackens of herself, if not to the lowest key, at least so far as to be no longer the same ; so that upon any occasion, for a lost hawk or a broken glass, we suffer ourselves to be moved almost like any one of the vulgar sort.

Saving order, moderation and firmness, I think all things are possible to a man who is generally very defective and infirm.

For that reason, say the sages, to form a correct judgement of a man, we must in the first place examine his ordinary actions, and surprise him in his everyday habit.

Pyrrho, who built up such an amusing theory of ignorance, endeavoured, like all other true philosophers, to make his life correspond to his teaching. And, because he held that man's judgement was so extremely weak that he could not make up his mind to choose, and would keep it perpetually on the balance, regarding and accepting all things as indifferent, they say of him that he always preserved the same demeanour and countenance. If he had begun to speak he would not stop till he had finished, when the man he was speaking to was gone. If he was walking he would not be turned from his path for any impediment he came across, and his friends had to save him from precipices, from colliding with carts, and from other accidents. For, to fear or avoid a thing would have been to run counter to his propositions, according to which even the senses were deprived of all choice and certainty. Sometimes he suffered the surgeon's lancet or the caustic with such stolidity that he was never seen even to wink his eyes.

It is something to bring the mind to these ideas. It is something more to translate them into action ; yet it is not impossible. But it is almost incredible that a man can do so habitually, in things so far removed from common usage, with so much constancy and perseverance.

So we hear that he was once discovered in his house sharply scolding somebody for his sister, and, when it was pointed out to him that he was sinning against his theory of indifference, he replied, ' What, may I not break my rules in the cause of this weak woman ? ' On another occasion, when he was seen defending himself from a dog, he said, ' It is very difficult entirely to strip off the man ; we must endeavour to make it our duty to combat things, in the first place by deeds, but, as a last resource, by reason and argument.'

About seven or eight years ago, a man living in a village about two leagues from here, who is still alive, having been long plagued by his wife's jealousy, returning one day from his labour, was welcomed with her customary screechings. He became so furious that suddenly, with the bill-hook he still held in his hand, he clean mowed off the parts which were the cause of her heat, and threw them into her face. And it is said that an amorous and lusty young gentleman of our nation, having at length by his perseverance softened the heart of his fair mistress, was thrown into despair because, at the moment of attack, he found that he himself was soft and a weakling, and that

Languidly the member raised his head. (TIBULLUS.)

When he returned home he immediately stripped himself of it and sent it, a cruel and bloody sacrifice, for the expiation of his offence. If this had been done from religious motives and deliberately, as the priests of Cybele did, what should we not say of so sublime an action ?

Not many days ago a woman living at Bergerac, five leagues from my house up the river Dordogne, having been the night before beaten and ill-used by her husband, a surly man of uncertain temper, resolved to escape from his violence at the price of her life. On rising next morning she had a few words with her neighbours as usual, and let fall a few words in recommendation of her affairs ; then taking a sister of hers by the hand she took her to the bridge, and after taking leave of her as if in jest, without showing any other alteration of manner she threw herself headlong into the river, where she perished. What is more remarkable in this case is that her plan was maturing a whole night in her head.

But it is quite another thing with the Hindu women. For, it being the custom for the men to have several wives, and for the best beloved of them to kill herself after her husband, each of them makes it the aim of her whole life to gain this point and advantage over her companions ; and for the good offices they render their husbands they expect no other reward but to be preferred to accompany him in death :

> For when above the bier the death-fires gleam,
> Round crowd the loving wives with locks astream ;
> Strive which shall first her husband's footsteps trace,
> And deem refusal bitterest disgrace.
> The favoured seeks the flames with dauntless breast
> And dies, her scorched lips to her husband's prest. (PROPERTIUS.)

A man still living writes of having observed this custom, which is still held in honour among those Eastern nations, of not only the wives being interred after their husbands' death, but also the slave-girls he has enjoyed. It is done in this manner. The husband being dead, the widow may, if she desires (but few desire it), demand two or three months respite to arrange her affairs. The day being come, decked out as if for her wedding, she mounts a horse, and that with a cheerful countenance, as if going, as she says, to sleep with her spouse, holding a mirror in her left hand and an arrow in her right. After riding about in state, attended by friends and relations and a concourse of people in festal garb, she presently returns to the public place appointed for these shows. This is a large square, in the middle of which is a pit filled with wood, and adjoining it a raised place with four or five steps, to which she is led and served with a sumptuous repast. After partaking of it she begins to dance and sing and, when she thinks fit, gives the word for the fire to be kindled. This being done she steps down, and, taking the nearest of her husband's relations by the hand, they repair together to the river which is near by, where she strips herself naked, and, having distributed her clothes and jewels among her friends, plunges into the water as if to wash away her sins. On leaving the water she wraps herself in a yellow linen cloth about fourteen French fathoms long, and again giving her hand to this kinsman of her husband, they return to the mound, from which she makes a speech to the people, and recommends her children, if she has any. Between the pit and the mound they usually draw a curtain, to shut out the burning furnace from their sight ; but some wives forbid it, to show the greater courage. When she has finished her speech a woman presents her with a vessel full of oil to anoint her head and whole body ; which done, she throws it into the fire and immediately leaps in after it. The people at once cover her with a great many faggots to prevent a lingering death ; and all their joy is converted into sorrow and mourning.

If they are persons of meaner stuff, the body of the defunct husband is taken to the place where it is to be buried, and there placed in a sitting posture ; the widow, on her knees before him, closely embraces him and remains there whilst they build a wall around them, and, when it has reached the height of the woman's shoulders, one of her relations, taking hold of her head from behind, wrings her neck. As soon as she has given up the ghost the wall is at once built higher and closed, and there they remain entombed.

A similar custom was observed in the same country by their Gymnosophists.[1] For, not under outside constraint, nor from a sudden impetuous caprice, but by express profession of their order, their custom was, as soon as they had reached a certain age, or if they found themselves threatened by some disease, to have a funeral pile erected, and on the top of it a richly decorated couch. After joyously feasting their friends and acquaintances, they remained lying on this couch with such determination that, when the fire was applied, they were not seen to move either hand or foot.

Thus died one of them, by name Calanus, in presence of the whole army of Alexander the Great. And he who did not thus commit suicide and dismiss his soul purged and purified by fire, after all that was mortal and earthly in him had been

[1] A hermit class of ancient Hindu philosophers, who wore little or no clothing and were addicted to mysticism and asceticism.

consumed, was reputed neither a saint nor blessed. It is this constant premeditation of a whole life that excites our wonder.

Among our other questions under dispute that of *Fatum* has entered in. To bind future events and even our will to predetermined and inevitable necessity, they still employ this time-honoured argument : ' Since God foresees that all things shall happen in such and such a way, as no doubt he does, they must therefore so happen.' To this our masters reply : ' That to see a thing happen, as we do, and God likewise (for, as everything is present to him, he sees rather than foresees), is not to force it to happen ; nay, we see because things happen, and things do not happen because we see. The happening causes the knowledge, and not the knowledge the happening. What we see happen, happens ; but it might have happened otherwise. And God, in the catalogue of the causes of happenings which he has in his prescience also has those which are called fortuitous, and the voluntary ones which depend on the freedom of the will he has given us ; and he knows that we shall sin, because we shall have willed to sin.'

Now I have known a good many men who encouraged their troops with this necessity of Fate. For if our last hour is fixed to a certain point, neither the musket-shots of our enemies, nor our boldness, nor our flight and cowardice, can either advance or retard it.

That is easily said, but find a man who will act upon it. And if it is the case that a strong and lively belief will be followed by actions of a like nature, truly this faith, of which our mouths are so full, is marvellously little in our days. Unless it be that the contempt in which works are held by Faith makes her disdain their company.[1]

So much is true that, apropos of this, the Lord of Join-ville, as credible a witness as any other, tells us of the Bedouins, a race associated with the Saracens with whom Saint Louis had to deal in the Holy Land, that in their religion they so firmly believed that every man's days have been from all eternity prefixed and numbered by an inevit-able preordination, that they went to war bare of armour except a sword in the Turkish fashion, their bodies covered

---

[1] An allusion to the question whether salvation is won by faith or by works.

only by a white linen garment. And their strongest curse, which they were always ready to utter when angered by their own men, was : ' Accursed be thou as he who arms himself for fear of death ! ' Here we see a proof of faith and belief very different from ours.

And with this may be classed the faith of those two Florentine monks in our fathers' days. Being engaged in some learned controversy, they both agreed to enter the fire in the market-place in sight of all the people, to prove their argument. All the preparations had been already made, and the matter was about to be carried into execution, when it was interrupted by an unforeseen accident.

A young Turkish lord signalized himself by some feat of arms in full view of the two armies of Amurath and Huniades when on the point of engaging. When asked by Amurath what it was that had filled him, so young and inexperienced (for it was the first war he had witnessed) with such a noble and undaunted courage, he replied that he had learned his best lesson in valour of a hare. ' Being out hunting one day, he said, I descried a hare lying in her forme, and, though I had with me two excellent greyhounds, I thought it advisable, to be sure of my quarry to use my bow, for she offered a very good mark. I began to discharge my arrows and shot as many as forty I had in my quiver, not only without touching, but without rousing her. After all I slipped my dogs upon her, but they were no more successful. From this I learned that she was covered by her Destiny, and that neither arrows nor swords will avail without permission of our fate, which it is not in our power either to retard or to advance.'

This tale may serve to teach us, by the way, how much our reason may be influenced by a sight of any kind.

A man advanced in years, of great repute, dignity and learning, was boasting to me that he had been led to alter his faith on a very important point by a strange incentive, so fantastic and moreover so inconclusive that I thought it a stronger argument to the contrary. He called it a miracle, and so did I, but in a different sense.

Their historians [1] say that the conviction so widely dispersed among the Turks of the fatal and inflexible pre-

[1] i. e., the Turkish historians.

determination of their days visibly helps to inspire them with confidence in danger.

And I know a great Prince who gains by it greatly to his honour [whether it be that he believes in it, or that he makes it an excuse for risking his life to such an extraordinary degree], if Fortune continues to lend him a helping hand.[1]

There has not been seen within our memory a more wonderful example of determination than that of the two who plotted the death of the Prince of Orange.[2] It is a marvel how the second, who dispatched him, could screw up sufficient courage to repeat an attempt in which his fellow-assassin had so miscarried, although he did his utmost. For, following in his footsteps and using the same weapon, he attacked a lord armed with so recent a lesson of distrust, powerful in his friendly following and his bodily strength, in his own hall, in the midst of his body-guards, in a town wholly devoted to him. Assuredly he employed a very resolute hand and a heart moved by strong passion. A dagger is a surer weapon for striking home, but since it needs more movement and strength of arm than a pistol, it is more liable to be turned aside or intercepted. I make little doubt that this man ran the risk of a certain death ; for any hopes that might have been held out to him could not have deceived a man of sober intelligence. And the manner of his execution shows that he had no lack of it, any more than of courage. A conviction so powerful may be grounded on various motives, for our imagination does what it will, both with itself and with us.

The assassination which took place near Orleans [3] is not to be compared with it ; there was more chance than vigour in it. The stroke was not fatal if Fortune had not made it so ; the act of shooting from horseback and from a distance, at a man whose motion followed that of his horse, was the act of a man who would rather have failed in his attempt than failed to escape. This was proved by the sequel. For he was so dazed and intoxicated by the thought of killing so exalted a personage, that he entirely lost his head in

[1] Probably an allusion to Henry IV.
[2] Jean de Jaureguy, who wounded the Prince at Antwerp in 1582, and Balthazar Gérard, who killed him in his house at Delft in 1584, both using pistols.
[3] The murder of the Duc de Guise in 1563 by Poltrot.

managing both his flight and his tongue when answering questions.

What more need he have done but rejoin his friends across a river ? It is a means I have often resorted to in lesser dangers, and is of little risk, in my opinion, however broad the crossing, provided that your horse can enter the water easily and that you can calculate upon a safe landing-place on the other bank, taking account of the current. The other, when hearing his dreadful sentence read out to him, said, ' I was prepared for this, and will astonish you by my endurance.'

The Assassins, a people subject to Phoenicia, are reputed among the Mahommedans to be supremely religious and pure in morals. They hold that the surest way to deserve Paradise is to kill someone of a different religion. Wherefore, despising all personal danger in carrying out so useful a purpose, one or two of them have often been known to offer, with the expectation of certain death, to assassinate (we have taken this word from their name) their enemies in their strongholds. Thus was killed our Count Raymond of Tripoli in his own city [during our conduct of the Holy war ; and likewise Conrad, Marquis of Montferrat. The murderers were led to execution, puffed up with pride for their fine masterpiece].

CHAPTER 30

OF A YOUNG MONSTROSITY

THIS tale shall be told quite simply ; for I leave it to the doctors to discuss it. Two days ago I saw a boy that was being carried about by two men and a nurse, who said they were his father, his uncle and aunt, to make a few coppers by exhibiting him on account of his strangeness. In all other respects he was of ordinary shape ; he could stand on his feet, walk and chatter much as other boys of the same age. He had not yet taken to any food except his nurse's milk, and when, in my presence, they tried to put something into his mouth, he chewed it a little and spat it out without swallowing it. There was certainly something unusual in his crying. He was just fourteen months old.

Below the paps he was fast stuck to another boy that had no head, the spinal canal being stopped up ; the rest of the body was entire. One arm was indeed shorter than the other, but it had been broken by accident at birth. They were joined face to face, as if a smaller child were trying to embrace one a little bigger. The juncture and the space where they held together was only four fingers' breadth or thereabouts, so that if you turned up the imperfect child you could see below it the navel of the other ; so the joining was between the paps and his navel. The navel of the smaller child could not be seen, but you could see all the rest of his belly. Thus the unattached parts of the imperfect child, as the arms, the rump, the thighs and legs, remained hanging and dangling from the other, and might reach half-way down his legs. The nurse told us besides that he urined from both places ; also that the limbs of this other were nourished and living, and throve as well as his own, except that they were smaller and thinner.

This double body and its several limbs corresponding to a single head might indeed serve as a favourable augury to the King, that he will maintain those several parties and factions of our State under the union of his laws. But, lest the issue might belie the prophecy, it will be better to let it go on before ; for there is no prophesying except in things already past. *So that, when things have come to pass, we may interpret them as prophecies* (Cicero). So they said of Epimenides that he prophesied backwards.

I have just seen a shepherd at Medoc, thirty years of age or thereabouts, who has no show of genital parts. He has three holes from which he continually drops his water. He is bearded, has desires, and readily seeks contact with women.

What we call monstrosities are not so to God, who sees in the immensity of his work the infinity of shapes which he has comprehended within it ; and it may be believed that this figure which arouses our astonishment corresponds to and resembles some other figure of the same kind unknown to man. From his all-wisdom there proceeds nothing that is not good, usual and regular ; but we do not see the relationship and the harmony. *What he often sees does not excite his wonder, even though he knows not the cause of it. But if a thing happen that he has not already seen, he regards it as a prodigy* (Cicero).

We call contrary to Nature what happens contrary to

what is customary ; there is nothing whatsoever that is contrary to Nature. This universal and natural reason should dispel from our minds the errors and the wonder caused by what is new and strange.[1]

CHAPTER 31

OF ANGER

PLUTARCH is admirable throughout, but especially when he judges human actions. In his comparison of Lycurgus and Numa we may read the excellent things that he says on the subject of our great folly in leaving children in the charge and under the rule of their fathers.

In most of our States, as Aristotle says, the guidance of his wives and children is left to each man, after the manner of the Cyclops,[2] according to his foolish and unthinking caprice ; and the Lacedemonian and Cretan are almost the only states where the direction of childhood is entrusted to the laws. Who does not see that everything in a state depends upon their nurture and bringing up ? And yet, without any discrimination, they are left to the mercy of their parents, however foolish and wicked they may be.

Among other things, how often have I felt a desire, when passing along our streets, to play some trick, to avenge the little boys I saw being belaboured, knocked down and bruised by some father or mother in a mad frenzy of anger ! You may see their eyes flashing with fire and rage :

> By burning fury they are headlong borne,
> As when great rocks are from the mountain torn,
> By which the cliffs deprived and lessened are,
> And their steep sides are naked left and bare, (JUVENAL.)

(and, according to Hippocrates, the most dangerous diseases are those which disfigure the face), with shrill, piercing voice often directed against a child that has just left its mother's breast. And then see how they are stunned and crippled

---

[1] Nowhere perhaps does Montaigne show how far he is in advance of his age than in his attitude to deformities and monstrosities, which in his day and long after were usually regarded as a judgement of God and a punishment of sins.

[2] ' Each the law gives out to his own wives and children.' Hom., *Od.* ix. 114.

with blows, and our justice taking no notice of it, as if they were not members of our Commonwealth that were being thus maimed and dislocated !

> Most grateful 'tis to people and to State
> To give a citizen, if he be fit
> To till the earth, or serve his fatherland
> In peace or war. (JUVENAL.)

There is no passion that so disturbs the clearness of our judgement as anger. No one would hesitate to punish with death a judge who had sentenced his criminal in anger. Why should fathers and pedagogues be any more allowed to flog and chastise the boys in anger ? It ceases to be correction and becomes vengeance. Chastisement takes the place of medicine with children ; and should we tolerate a physician who was moved to anger against his patient ?

We masters, if we wish to act rightly, should never raise our hand against a servant as long as we are angry. While the pulse beats and we are sensible of passion we should defer the business. The matter will indeed appear to us in a different light when we have recovered and cooled down. It is passion that then rules, it is passion that speaks ; it is not we ourselves.

Faults, when seen through passion, appear greater to us, like bodies seen through a mist. A man uses meat to appease his hunger ; but when he would use punishment he must neither hunger nor thirst for it.

And besides, a punishment that is administered deliberately and with discrimination is taken in better part by him who suffers it, and with more benefit. Otherwise he will think he has been unjustly condemned by a master who is moved by anger and fury ; and will plead, for his justification, the extraordinary conduct of his master, his inflamed countenance, his unaccustomed oaths, his excitement and inconsiderate hastiness :

> With anger faces swollen show,
>   The veins turn black with rush of blood,
>   The eyes with Gorgon fires glow. (OVID.)

Suetonius relates that, Lucius Saturninus [1] having been condemned by Caesar, what most prevailed with the people

---

[1] More correctly Caius Rabirius, as corrected in all the later editions. L. Saturninus was a Tribune whom he had opposed.

(to whom he appealed) to declare in his favour was the fierce animosity which Caesar had exhibited in that sentence.

Saying is one thing and doing is another. We must consider the sermon apart from the preacher. Those who in our days have tried to shake the truth of our Church by attacking the vices of her ministers, have had an easy game ; she draws her testimony from elsewhere. Theirs is a foolish line of argument which would throw everything into confusion. A man may have an erroneous belief though his morals be good ; and a wicked man may preach the truth, nay, even though he does not believe it. When doing and saying go together it is indeed a beautiful harmony ; and I will not deny that words, when followed by deeds, are of greater authority and efficacy.

As Eudamidas said, on hearing a philosopher holding forth on war, ' The language is fine, but the man who is speaking is not to be believed, for his ears are not accustomed to the sound of the trumpet.' And Cleomenes, hearing an orator declaiming on valour, burst out laughing, at which the other taking great offence, he said, ' I should do the same if I heard a swallow talking of valour ; but an eagle I would readily listen to.'

I think I can gather from the writings of the ancients that the man who says what he thinks drives it home much more forcibly than he who dissembles. Listen to Cicero speaking of the love of freedom, and then listen to Brutus. From the mere written words of the latter you hear the note of a man who was ready to buy it at the price of his life. Let Cicero, the father of eloquence, treat of the contempt of death, and then let Seneca treat of the same ; in the former the words drag feebly, and you feel that he is trying to persuade you of a thing of which he himself is not persuaded. He gives you no heart, for he has none himself. The other excites and inflames you. I never read an author, especially one who treats of virtue and duties, without carefully endeavouring to find out what kind of a man he was.

For the Ephors at Sparta, hearing a dissolute man offering a wholesome piece of advice, ordered him to hold his tongue, and requested a respectable man to appropriate the idea and propound it.

Plutarch's writings, if we taste them aright, sufficiently disclose their author, and I think I am able to see into his soul ; and yet I could wish that we had some memoirs of his life. After digressing a little in this Essay I am obliged to Aul. Gellius for having left us in writing this story reflecting on his character, which brings me back to the subject of Anger.

One of his slaves, a bad and vicious man, but whose ears had drunk in a few of the teachings of Philosophy, having been, for some fault or other, stripped and flogged by Plutarch's orders, at first muttered that he was being punished without reason, since he had done nothing. But at last he began to shout and roundly abuse his master, saying, ' that he was no philosopher, as he boasted of being ; that he had often heard him say that it was an ugly thing to get angry, and he had even written a book on the subject ; and that to have him so cruelly beaten, when plunged in anger, was completely to belie his writings.' To which Plutarch replied quite coldly and tranquilly, ' What, you clown, from what do you argue that I am angry at this moment ? Do my face, my voice, my colour, my words give you any indication of my being in a passion ? I do not think my eyes are rolling wildly, that my countenance is disturbed, or that I am shouting very terribly. Am I red ? Do I foam at the mouth ? Have I allowed a word to escape me of which I might repent ? Am I shaking and trembling with fury ? For these, I may tell you, are the true marks of anger.' Then, turning to the man who was flogging him, ' Go on with your work, he said, whilst he and I are having our little argument.' That is the story.

Archytas of Tarentum, returning from a war in which he had been commander-in-chief, found his household affairs in a state of great disorder, and his lands lying fallow, through the mismanagement of his steward. Having sent for him, he said, ' Go ; If I were not angry I should give you a good thrashing.' Plato too, being greatly incensed against one of his slaves, charged Speusippus to chastise him, excusing himself from laying hands upon him on the ground that he was angry. Charillus, a Lacedemonian, said to a Helot whose behaviour was too bold and insolent, ' By the Gods, if I were not angry, I should have you put to death on the spot.'

It is a self-complacent and self-flattering passion. How often, when we have been put out under a wrong impression, and the offending person offers a good defence or excuse, we are vexed even at the truth and his innocence! In connexion with which I remember a remarkable example in antiquity.

Piso, in all other respects a most worthy man, being greatly angered against one of his soldiers because, returning alone from foraging, he was unable to explain the absence of his companion, took it for granted that he had murdered him, and forthwith condemned him to death. He was no sooner on the gibbet than the missing man turned up. The whole army was in high glee, and after much kissing and embracing on the part of the two fellows, the executioner conducts them both into the presence of Piso, all the bystanders expecting that he would be equally pleased. But it fell out quite otherwise; for shame and vexation increased his fury, which was still at its height, and, with a craftiness which his passion instantly suggested to him, he made three guilty men of one, because one had been found innocent, and had them all three dispatched: the first soldier because he was under sentence; the second, who had lost his way, because he was the cause of his comrade's death; and the executioner, because he had not carried out his orders.

Those who have to deal with headstrong women may have experienced how furious they become if we meet their excitement with a cool silence, and disdain to add fuel to their rage.

The orator Celius was by nature exceedingly choleric. Supping in the company of a man of a mild and gentle disposition, who, in order not to excite him, had decided to approve and agree with everything he said, he exclaimed, unable any longer to suffer his ill humour not to be fed, ' By all the Gods, do contradict something I say, that there may be two of us ! ' So the women only lose their temper in order that we may lose ours, therein following the laws of love.

Phocion, when interrupted in a speech by a man who began to insult him with opprobrious words, merely stopped speaking, to give the man time to exhaust his anger; then, without any mention of the disturbance, he continued his speech at the place where he had left off. There is no retort so stinging as a contempt of that kind.

Of the most hot-tempered man in France (it is always a fault, but more excusable in a soldier, for in that profession there certainly are occasions when it cannot be dispensed with) I often say that he is the most patient man to curb his anger that I know ; it stirs him to such violence and fury :

> As when a wood-fire crackles with such fierce roar,
> Heaped round a cauldron, and the simmering stream
> Foams, fumes and bubbles, and at last boils o'er,
> And upward shoots the mingled smoke and steam,   (VIRGIL.)

that, to moderate it, he is obliged to exercise a cruel restraint. And, for my part, I know of no passion to conceal and restrain which I were capable of making such an effort. I would not set wisdom at so high a price. I do not so much consider what he does, as what it costs him to do no worse.

Another was boasting to me of his mildness and self-control, which is indeed out of the common. I said to him that it was certainly something, especially in a man of high standing like himself, on whom all eyes are directed, always to show great moderation to the world ; but that the main thing was to be well provided inwardly, and that to eat his heart out was not, in my opinion, the right way to husband his resources. And I was afraid that he was doing so in order to keep up that mask and outward appearance of self-control.

Anger, by being concealed, becomes incorporated. Hence Diogenes said to Demosthenes who, for fear of being seen in a tavern, was withdrawing into it, ' The further you retire into it, the more you are in it.'

I should advise you rather to give your footman a slap on the cheek, even though it were undeserved, than to strain your inclination to put on the airs of a sage. I would rather show my feelings than brood over them at my own expense. To vent and give expression to them makes them flag. It is better that their point should be turned away from us than against ourselves. *All vices are less serious when they appear in the open ; they are most dangerous when concealed under an appearance of discretion* (Seneca).

I admonish those of my family who are authorized to get angry ; Firstly, to husband their anger, and not to pour it out at any cost, since that lessens its effect and weight.

Unpremeditated and continual brawling becomes a habit, and is set at naught by everybody. Your scolding of a servant for theft will lose its effect, if you have scolded him in the same way a hundred times for a dirty glass or a misplaced footstool. Secondly, not to vent their anger at random, but see that their reproof reaches the ears of the delinquent ; for people commonly begin to shout before the guilty person has entered their presence, and continue to shout for an age after he is gone :

> And petulant madness contends with itself. (CLAUDIAN.)

They fall out with their shadow and continue their bluster in a place where nobody is punished or affected except by the racket of their voice, which many have to suffer who have done nothing to deserve it. I also condemn those one-sided quarrels in which a man fumes and blusters without any antagonist ; he should keep his rodomontades for those they are intended for :

> As when a bull, against some battle-bout
> Uplifts a fearful bellowing, and for proof
> Flings wrath into his horns, and butts against
> A tree-trunk, and provokes the air with blows,
> Or, scattering sand, makes prelude of the fray. (VIRGIL.)

When I get angry my outbursts are quick, but as brief and subdued as I can make them. I am indeed hasty and violent, but I do not so lose my head that I fling about any kind of insulting words, at random and without choice, and without considering whether they are pertinently placed where I think they will hurt most ; for my tongue is usually my only weapon. My serving-men come off better in great matters than in small. The small ones take me unawares, and the mischief is that when you are once over the precipice it matters not who has given you the push, you will reach the bottom all the same ; the fall accelerates its own speed without any more pushing.

When the matter is important it pays me that my cause is so just that all expect me to be reasonably angry ; for I have a sense of triumph in disappointing their expectation. Against the great occasion I brace and prepare myself, for if I give way to it I lose my head and am in danger of going too far. I find it easy to be on my guard against falling into a great rage, and am strong enough to repel its attack if I expect it, however great the cause. But if it takes me unawares and has once got a fair grip on me, it will carry me away, be the cause ever so small.

This is how I bargain with those who are able to stand up against me : ' When you feel that I am the first to get excited, let me have my say, whether I am right or wrong ; I will do the same for you in my turn.' The storm is bred only from the clashing of two passions, which usually produce one another, and are not born simultaneously. Let each run its course and we shall always be at peace ! A useful arrangement, but difficult to carry out !

It sometimes happens that I simulate anger for the better government of my household, without any real emotion. As I become more crabbed with advancing years I study to resist my temper, and, if I am able, I will try henceforth to be less peevish and hard to please as I shall have more excuse and inclination to be so ; although I have hitherto been one of the least impatient.

One more word to close this chapter. Aristotle says that ' anger is sometimes a weapon in the hands of virtue and valour '. That is very likely ; yet they who deny it wittily reply that it is a weapon of novel use. For we move the other arms, whilst this one moves us ; our hand does not guide it, it guides our hand ; it holds us, we do not hold it.

CHAPTER 32

DEFENCE OF SENECA AND PLUTARCH

MY familiarity with these two men, and the help they give me in my old age, and to my book, which is purely built up of their spoils, oblige me to espouse their honour.

With regard to Seneca, among a myriad of pamphlets which the adherents of the religion which calls itself Reformed circulate in defence of their cause (and which sometimes proceed from such good hands that it is a great pity they were not busied upon a better subject), I once read one in which, to supplement and complete the similarity which he thinks he sees between the rule of our late poor King Charles the Ninth and that of Nero, the writer compares the late Cardinal de Lorraine with Seneca ; their fortunes, each of them having been at the head of the government of his

Prince, and at the same time their character, their circumstances and their conduct. By this comparison he pays, in
my opinion, a very great compliment to the said Lord
Cardinal. For, although I am of those who have as high an
opinion as anybody of his intelligence, his eloquence, his
zeal in the cause of his faith and in his service to his King,
as well as his good fortune to have been born at a time when
it was so novel and rare a thing, and at the same time so
necessary for the public weal, to have a Churchman of such
high rank and dignity sufficient and capable of undertaking
so weighty a charge ; yet, to confess the truth, I do not
think that in capability he comes anything near to Seneca,
or that his virtue was so entirely strong and pure.

Now, in this book I speak of, the author, to justify his
comparison, gives a very opprobrious description of Seneca,
having borrowed his strictures of Dion the historian, to
whose testimony I attach no importance whatever. For,
besides that he is inconsistent in calling him now a very
wise man, now a deadly enemy of Nero's vices, and elsewhere makes him out to be a miser, a usurer, ambitious,
effeminate, voluptuous and claiming to be a philosopher
on false pretences, Seneca's virtues show forth so clear and
strong in his writings, and he vindicates himself so clearly
from some of these imputations, such as his wealth and his
excessive expenditure, that I should believe no testimony
to the contrary. And moreover it is much more reasonable
in these matters to believe the Roman historians than the
Greeks and foreigners. Now Tacitus and the others speak
in very honourable terms of his life and death, and depict
him in all respects as a very excellent and a very virtuous
man. And I will urge no other accusation against Dion's
judgement than this, which is irrefutable, that his ideas
with regard to Roman affairs are so unsound that he dares
to maintain the cause of Julius Caesar against Pompey, and
that of Antony against Cicero.

We will come to Plutarch.

Jean Bodin is a good author of our day, who is endowed
with much more judgement than the crowd of scribblers of
his time, and merits consideration and appreciation. I find
him a little bold in that passage of his *Method of History* in
which he not only accuses Plutarch of ignorance (on which
I should have allowed him to have his say, as that does not

come within my province), but also remarks that that author often writes of ' incredible and wholly fabulous things ' (those are his words). If he had simply said ' things otherwise than they are ', it would have been no great reproach, for what we have not seen we take at the hands of others and on trust, and I have observed that he sometimes knowingly tells the same story differently, such as Hannibal's opinion as to the three best generals that ever lived, which appears differently in the Life of Flaminius and in that of Pyrrhus. But to charge him with having taken for current coin incredible and impossible things is to accuse the most judicious author in the world of want of judgement.

And this is his example : ' As, he says, when he tells us that a Spartan boy suffered all his bowels to be torn out by a young fox he had stolen and was hiding under his garment, choosing rather to die than disclose his theft.' In the first place I think this example is badly chosen, since it is very difficult to set bounds to the power of the mental faculties, whereas we are more at liberty to assume a limit to our knowledge of the bodily powers: And for that reason, if it had lain with me, I should rather have chosen an example of this second kind. And there are some that are less credible, as, among others, what he tells of Pyrrhus ' that, wounded as he was, he dealt an enemy who was armed at all points such a stroke with his sword that he clove him from the head downwards, so that the two parts of the body fell asunder.'

In Bodin's example I see no great miracle, and I cannot accept the excuse with which he shelters Plutarch that he added the words, ' as the story goes ', in order to put us on our guard and curb our belief. For, except on things received on good authority, or in reverence to religion or antiquity, he would not have been willing either himself to accept or expect us to believe things incredible in themselves. And it may be easily seen that he does not there use these words ' as the story goes ' for the purpose suggested ; for in connexion with the endurance of the Spartan boys, he himself tells us, in another place, of other examples which happened in his own time, and which are much more difficult to believe. That, for instance, to which Cicero before him also testified, ' having, as he said, been on the spot,' that even

in their time there were boys who, in the test of endurance
to which they were subjected before the altar of Diana,
endured being flogged until the blood ran down their whole
body, not only without shouting, but without even moaning, and some until they voluntarily gave up their
lives.

And there is that other story which Plutarch tells,
together with a hundred other witnesses, of a Spartan boy
who, as he was burning incense during a sacrifice, suffered
a red-hot ember which had fallen into his sleeve to burn his
whole arm until the smell of the broiling flesh reached the
bystanders.

There was nothing, according to their custom, in which
their reputation was more concerned, nor for which they
had to suffer more blame and disgrace, than being caught
in a theft. I am so impressed by the greatness of those
people, that not only does that story of Plutarch not appear
incredible to me, as it does to Bodin, but I do not find it
even strange and uncommon.

Spartan history is full of a thousand more cruel and more
uncommon examples ; it is, in this respect, all miracle.

Marcellinus relates, on this subject of theft, that in his
time they had not yet discovered any kind of torture that
could compel the Egyptians, when detected in this crime,
which was very prevalent with them, even to reveal their
names.

A Spanish peasant, being put to the rack to make him
betray his accomplices in the murder of the Praetor Lucius
Piso, exclaimed in the midst of his torments ' that his
friends need not stir, but might look on in all security, and
that no pain had the power of wresting a word of confession
from him.' And that was all they could get out of him on
the first day. On the following day, as they were again
dragging him to the torture, he vigorously shook himself
free from the hands of his jailors and killed himself by
dashing his head against a wall.

Epicharis, having exhausted and glutted the cruelty of
Nero's satellites by enduring for a whole day their fires,
their stripes, their instruments, without a word that could
reveal her conspiracy, the next day, as she was being
carried back to the torture, her limbs all broken, she tied
the girdle of her garment round an arm of her chair with

a running knot, and, thrusting her head into it, was strangled by the weight of her body.[1]

Having had the courage to die in this manner after surviving the first torments, does it not appear as if she had purposely lent her life to that test of her endurance, in order to flout the tyrant, and to encourage others to a like attempt against his life ?

And if any one will question our mounted musketeers on their experiences in these Civil wars, he will discover deeds of endurance, obstinacy, and stubbornness in this our miserable age, and in this rabble sunk in a more than Egyptian indolence and effeminacy, that will bear comparison with those we have just told of Spartan courage.

I know that there have been simple peasants who have suffered the soles of their feet to be grilled, the ends of their fingers to be crushed with the cock of a pistol, their bleeding eyes to be squeezed out of their heads by means of a thick cord twisted around their brows, before they would allow themselves even to be ransomed. I have seen one, left for dead naked in a ditch, his neck all bruised and swollen from a halter still hanging to it, by which they had dragged him all night at a horse's tail, his body pierced in a hundred places by dagger-thrusts, which had been dealt him, not to kill, but to cause pain and terrify him ; who had suffered all this, and even lost all speech and feeling, resolved, as he told me, to die a thousand deaths (and indeed, as far as suffering goes, he had passed through a complete death) rather than make any promise. Yet he was one of the wealthiest labourers in the whole district.

How many of them have been seen patiently to endure burning and roasting for opinions borrowed of others, which they neither knew nor understood !

I have known hundreds of women, for they say that Gascon heads have a certain prerogative in this respect, who would rather bite into red-hot iron than let go their bite of anything they have said in anger. Beating and violence exasperate them only the more. And the man who made up the story of the woman who, in defiance of all threats and cudgellings, kept on calling her husband ' Lousy ' ; and, when plunged into a pond, and on the point

---

[1] Montaigne's account of this feat is not very clear ; but that of Tacitus is hardly more so.

of drowning, still raised her hands above her head and imitated the action of killing lice, invented a tale that plainly illustrates the obstinacy of woman, as we may see it any day. And obstinacy is the sister of constancy, at least in strength and firmness.

We must not judge of what is possible and what is not so, according to what is credible and incredible in our judgement, as I have said elsewhere ; [1] and it is quite an error, into which, however, most men fall (this is no reflexion on Bodin), to make a difficulty about believing of others what they themselves could not, or would not, do. Every man believes that he represents Nature's masterpiece ; by this he tests, as if it were the touchstone, all other pieces. The conduct that does not square with his is counterfeit and artificial. What brutal stupidity ! [If you tell him something about another person's doings or abilities, the first thing he does is to compare him with himself ; as he is, so must the world be. O dangerous, intolerable and asinine folly !]

For my part, I regard some men as very far above me, especially among the ancients, and, although I clearly recognize my inability to follow in their footsteps, I yet follow them with my eyes and can estimate the powers that raise them to such a height, and of which I feel I have some of the seeds in myself ; just as I can estimate the depths to which a mind can sink, which I am neither astonished at nor refuse to believe. I can very well detect the proceeding whereby those great souls raise themselves, and wonder at their greatness. I understand their aspirations, which appear to me very noble, and if my strength is not equal to it, my judgement at least readily goes along with them.

The other example which Bodin cites of ' things incredible and entirely fabulous ' mentioned by Plutarch is ' that Agesilaus was fined by the Ephors for having drawn to himself alone the hearts and good-will of his citizens '. I know not what mark of falsehood he sees in it, but surely Plutarch is here speaking of things that he must have known much better than we do ; and it was no new thing in Greece to see men punished and exiled for being too acceptable to their fellow-citizens. Witness Ostracism and Petalism.[2]

---

[1] Book I, chapter 27.

[2] Ostracism, banishment for ten years from Athens ; Petalism, the

There is in the same place another accusation which annoys me on Plutarch's account, namely, that he was honest in his comparison of Romans with Romans, and Greeks with Greeks, but not of Romans with Greeks ; witness, he says, Demosthenes and Cicero, Cato and Aristides, Sylla and Lysander, Marcellus and Pelopidas, Pompey and Agesilaus, holding that he favoured the Greeks by giving them such unequal mates. That is really to attack what is most excellent and commendable in Plutarch. For in his parallels (which are the most admirable part of his work, and in which I think he took a particular pride) the fidelity and sincerity of his judgements equals their weight and profundity. He is a philosopher who is teaching us virtue.

Let us see if we can defend him from this reproach of prevarication and falsehood.

What I think may have given rise to this censure is the great and brilliant lustre which in our imagination falls upon those Roman names. It does not appear possible to us that Demosthenes should rival the glory of a man who was a Consul, Proconsul, and Quaestor of the great Republic. But if we consider the truth of the matter, and the men in themselves, and compare their nature, their moral qualities, their genius, rather than their fortunes, which was Plutarch's chief aim, I think, in contradiction to Bodin, that Cicero and the elder Cato fall short of their parallels. For his purpose I should sooner have chosen the example of the younger Cato compared with Phocion ; for in this parallel there would have been a more likely disparity, to the advantage of the Roman.

As to Marcellus, Sylla, and Pompey, I quite see that their exploits in war are more inflated, more glorious and pompous than those of the Greeks with whom Plutarch compares them ; but the noblest and most valorous actions are not always, either in war or elsewhere, the most famous. I often see the names of generals smothered under the splendour of less meritorious names ; witness Labienus, Ventidius, Telesinus, and many others.

And, to adopt Bodin's argument, if I had reason to

same for five years from Syracuse. They were so-called respectively from the earthen tablets and the olive-leaf on which the citizens recorded their votes.

complain on behalf of the Greeks, might I not say that Camillus is much less to be compared with Themistocles, the Gracchi with Agis and Cleomenes, Numa with Lycurgus ?

But it is foolishness to try to estimate things at one glance, from so many points of view. When Plutarch compares them, he does not on that account make them equal. Who was able more eloquently and conscientiously to mark their differences ? When he comes to parallel the victories, the martial exploits, the forces led by Pompey, and his triumphs, to those of Agesilaus, ' I do not believe, he says, that even Xenophon, if he were alive, though he were allowed to write whatever he pleased to the advantage of Agesilaus, would dare to bring them into comparison.' Does he speak of equalling Lysander to Sylla ? ' There is no comparison, he says, either in the number of victories, or in the hazard of battles ; for Lysander won only two naval battles, &c.'

This is not robbing the Romans of any glory ; by merely confronting them with the Greeks, he can have done them no wrong, whatever disparity there may have been between them. And Plutarch does not weigh them all together ; he does not indicate any preference for either as a whole ; he compares actions and circumstances, one after another, and estimates them separately. Wherefore, if we would convict him of partiality, we should have to pull one particular judgement to pieces ; or we should have to say, in a general way, that he was mistaken in matching this Greek with that Roman, since there were others more suitable for comparison and more resembling each other.

CHAPTER 33

THE CASE OF SPURINA

PHILOSOPHY is not conscious of having made a bad use of her resources in giving Reason the sovereign mastery over our soul, and authority to keep our appetites in check. They who hold that there is no desire more violent than that engendered by love, have this argument in their favour, that it affects both body and soul, and that the whole man is possessed by it ; to such an extent that health itself depends on it, and medicine is sometimes obliged to be its broker.

But we might also say, on the other hand, that the inter-ference of the body abates and weakens it ; for this desire is subject to satiety and susceptible to material remedies.

Many, wishing to rid their soul of the continual restless-ness caused by this appetite, have had recourse to incisions and amputation of the disturbed and ravenous parts. Others have quite subdued its strength and ardour by frequent application of cold objects, as snow and vinegar. The *haire* of our ancestors was applied to this purpose ; this was a fabric woven of horse-hair, of which some of them made shirts and others belts to chafe their reins.

A Prince not long ago told me that in his younger days, on the occasion of a solemn festival at the court of King Francis the First, when everybody was dressed in his best, a fancy took him to put on his father's hair-shirt, which is still in his house. But, in spite of his devotion, he had not patience enough to await the night to strip himself of it ; and he was ill for a long time after. He added that he did not think that any heat of youth could be so fierce but that the use of this remedy would damp it. It may be, however, that he never felt that heat at its strongest ; for experience shows that that disturbance will often survive under rough and beggarly garments, and that the *haire* does not always make him a *hère* who wears it.[1]

Xenocrates went more rigorously about it ; for his dis-ciples having, to test his continence, smuggled into his bed the famous and beauteous courtesan Laïs, quite bare but for the arms of her beauty and those philters, her wanton charms ; he, feeling, in spite of his teachings and rules, his body, usually so hard, beginning to rebel, had those mem-bers burned that had lent ear to this rebellion.

Whereas, when the passions are all in the soul, as ambi-tion, avarice, and the rest, they give the reason much more to do ; for she cannot find any help but in herself. Nor are they appetites which are capable of being satiated, but rather become whetted and increased by gratification.

The example of Julius Caesar alone may suffice to illus-trate the disparity of these appetites ; for no man was ever more addicted to amorous delights. One testimony of this is the meticulous care which he devoted to his person, which

---

[1] A very bad pun, which Montaigne drags in by the shoulders. *Un pauvre hère* means a ' poor, feeble creature '.

he carried so far as to adopt the most lascivious devices then in vogue, such as having his whole body depilated with tweezers and dressed with exquisitely choice perfumes. And he was naturally a handsome man, fair, tall, and active, with a full face and dark, bright eyes, if we are to believe Suetonius ; for the statues we see of him in Rome do not always correspond with this picture.

Besides his wives, whom he changed four times, and without counting his youthful amours with Nicomedes, King of Bithynia, he had the maidenhead of the so renowned Queen of Egypt, Cleopatra ; witness the little Cesarion, who was the result of it. He also ' made love ' with Eunoë, Queen of Mauritania, and at Rome with Posthumia, wife of Servius Sulpitius ; with Lollia, wife of Gabinius ; with Tertulla, wife of Crassus ; and even with Mutia, wife of the great Pompey ; which was the reason, say the Roman historians, why her husband repudiated her, but which Plutarch confesses he does not know. And the Curios, father and son, afterwards, when Pompey married Caesar's daughter, twitted him with becoming the son-in-law of the man who had made him cuckold, and whom he himself was wont to call Aegisthus.[1]

Besides all this crowd he kept Servilia, the sister of Cato and mother of Marcus Brutus, which, as every one supposes, explains the great affection he had for Brutus, because he was born at a time which made it likely that he was the father.

Hence I think I am justified in regarding him as a man who was in a high degree given to that excess, and of a very amorous disposition. But the other passion of ambition, with which he was also afflicted in a very high degree, coming in conflict with the other, soon made it yield the first place.

Recalling to mind, on this subject, Mahomet, the one who subjugated Constantinople and brought about the final extermination of the Greek name, I can think of no case in which these two passions were more evenly balanced ; he was equally indefatigable as a lecher and a soldier. But when the two compete with one another in his life, the quarrelsome spirit always dominates the amorous. And the

[1] Lover of Clytemnestra, and murderer of her husband King Agamemnon.

latter (although out of its natural season) did not fully regain the absolute power until he was in his extreme old age, and no longer able to support the burden of war.

What is related, as an example in the opposite direction, of Ladislaus, King of Naples, is noteworthy : That, a good general, brave and ambitious, he made it the chief aim of his ambition to satisfy his sensuality and enjoy some rare beauty. His death was in keeping. Having, after a closely conducted siege, reduced the city of Florence to such straits that the inhabitants were on the point of capitulating, he left them in possession on condition that they delivered up to him a girl of exceeding beauty of that city whom he had heard of. They were forced to grant his wish, and avert the public ruin by a private wrong.

She was the daughter of a physician famous in his day, who, seeing himself reduced to so foul a necessity, resolved on a desperate expedient. As all were busy dressing his daughter and bedecking her with jewels and ornaments, to render her pleasing to this new kind of lover, he also gave her a handkerchief, exquisite in workmanship and perfume, which she was to use at their first embraces. It was an article they seldom neglect to use in those parts. This handkerchief, poisoned with all the skill he was capable of, rubbed over the inflamed flesh and open pores, so quickly infused its venom, that, suddenly converting their warm into a cold sweat, they expired in each other's arms.

I come back to Caesar.

His pleasures never permitted him to steal a single moment of time, nor turn one step aside from any occasion that offered for his aggrandizement. His ambition exercised such sovereign sway over all his other passions, and possessed his soul with such absolute authority, that it carried him wherever it pleased. It vexes me indeed when I consider the greatness, in all other respects, of this man, and the wonderful talents wherewith he was endowed ; so eminent was he in every kind of learning, that there was hardly any branch of science on which he had not written. He was so great an orator that many preferred his eloquence to Cicero's ; and he himself, as I conceive, did not think he owed him much in that respect. He wrote his two *Anti-Catos* chiefly to counterbalance the fine style that Cicero had used in his *Cato*.

As for the rest, was there ever a mind so vigilant, so active, so patient of labour as his ? And without doubt it was adorned with many uncommon seeds of virtue, I mean living, natural, not counterfeit. He was singularly sober, and so far from being dainty in his eating that Oppius relates that one day at table, when he was handed some sauce made with medicinal [1] instead of ordinary oil, he ate of it copiously, in order not to shame his host. On another occasion he had his baker whipped for serving him with other than the ordinary bread.

Cato himself was wont to say of him that he was the first sober man who had set out to ruin his country. And as to the same Cato one day calling him ' drunkard ', it happened in this way. Both of them being in the Senate, whilst Catiline's conspiracy was being discussed, in which Caesar was suspected of having a share, some one from outside secretly handed him a note. Cato, thinking it was some warning from the conspirators, challenged him to hand it over, which Caesar was obliged to do to avoid a greater suspicion. It happened to be an affectionate letter from Servilia, Cato's sister. Cato, after reading it, threw it back at him with the words, ' There, drunkard ! ' That, I should say, was rather a word uttered in anger and contempt than an explicit accusation of that vice ; as we often use the first insulting words that come to our lips against one that has angered us, although by no means deserved by the person we apply them to. Besides, that vice that Cato cast in his teeth is wonderfully akin to that in which he had detected Caesar, for Venus and Bacchus, according to the proverb, are usually on good terms.

But with me Venus is much more sprightly when accompanied with sobriety.

The examples of his mildness and clemency towards those who offended him are endless ; I mean besides those he gave during the time when the Civil War was still in progress, the purpose of which was, as he himself makes sufficiently clear in his writings, to cajole his enemies, and make them less afraid of his future dominion and victory. Yet we must say that, if those examples are not sufficient evidence

[1] This seems to suggest the favourite remedy of the Fascisti ; but, according to Suetonius, it was ' stale instead of fresh oil ', and according to Plutarch, ' sweet ointment poured upon the asparagus instead of oil '.

of his natural mildness, they prove at least that this man possessed wonderful trust and magnanimous courage. It often happened that he sent back to the enemy whole armies, after vanquishing them, not even deigning to bind them by oath, if not to befriend him, at least to refrain from making war upon him. Three or four times he captured certain captains of Pompey, and as often set them free. Pompey declared all those to be his enemies who did not accompany him to the war ; and Caesar proclaimed all those to be friendly who did not stir, and did not actually take up arms against him. If his captains deserted from him to take other service, he sent them their arms, horses, and accoutrements. The towns he had taken by force he left at liberty to follow which side they pleased, leaving them no other garrison but the memory of his mildness and clemency. And on the day of his great battle of Pharsalia, he forbade any man to lay hands on a Roman citizen, except as a last resource.

There we see, in my judgement, some very risky steps ; and it is not to be wondered at if, in the Civil Wars we are suffering from, those who, like him, are fighting against the old institutions of their country, do not imitate his example. They were extraordinary methods, which Caesar's fortune alone and his wonderful foresight were allowed to employ successfully. When I reflect upon his incomparable greatness of soul, I can excuse victory for not having been able to shake off his fetters, even in that very unjust and very iniquitous cause.

To return to his clemency, we may see many genuine examples of it at the time of his rule, when, everything being subjected to his power, he had no more need to dissemble. Caius Memmius had published a very biting satire against him, to which he very sharply replied ; but that did not prevent him from soon after helping him to the Consulship. Caius Calvus, who had composed several insulting epigrams upon him, having employed some of his friends to reconcile them, Caesar was prompted to write to him first. And our good Catullus, who had given him such a rude dressing under the name of Mamurra, coming one day to make his excuses to him, Caesar invited him to stay to supper at his table. Having been informed of some who spoke ill of him, he merely announced in one of his public speeches that he had been informed of it. If he did not hate his enemies, still less did he fear them. Certain conspiracies and meetings organized against his life having been discovered, he contented himself with publishing by edict that he knew of them, without further prosecuting the ringleaders.

With regard to the consideration he had for his friends, Caius Oppius travelling with him and feeling indisposed, he relinquished to him the only lodging there was, and slept all night in the open on the hard ground.

As to his justice, he put to death one of his freedmen of whom he was particularly fond, for having lain with the wife of a Roman knight, although nobody had made any complaint of it. No man ever showed more moderation in his victory, nor more fortitude in his adverse fortunes.

But all these noble inclinations were stifled and corrupted by that furious passion of ambition by which he was so forcibly carried away, that we may safely declare that it held the rudder and steered all his actions. It turned a generous man into a public robber, to provide for that profusion and liberality, and made him utter that vile and most iniquitous saying, ' that if the most wicked and degraded men in the world had been faithful in serving him towards his aggrandizement, he would cherish and advance them to the best of his power, as well as the most honourable.' It intoxicated him with so excessive a vanity that he dared to boast, in presence of his fellow-citizens, ' that he had made the great Roman Republic a name, without shape and without body ', to declare that his answers must henceforth be taken as laws, to remain seated when he received the Senate in a body in his house, and to allow himself to be worshipped, and divine honours to be paid him in his own presence.

To sum up, this single vice, in my opinion, destroyed in him the richest and most beautiful nature that ever was, and made his memory abominable to all good men, since it led him to seek his glory in the ruin of his country and the subversion of the most powerful and flourishing Republic the world will ever see.

We could, on the other hand, find many examples of great men whose sensuality caused them to neglect the conduct of their affairs, as Mark Antony and others ; but where love and ambition are equally balanced and clash together with equal forces, I make no doubt but that the latter will win the prize of mastery.

Now, to retrace my steps, it is a great thing to be able to curb our appetites with the arguments of reason, or violently to force our members to keep within the bounds of duty. But as to punishing ourselves for the good of our neighbours ; not only ridding ourselves of that sweet passion that tickles us, of the pleasure we feel in being agreeable to others, and beloved and sought after by all ; but conceiving a hatred and loathing of the charms which are the cause of it, and blaming our beauty because another is inflamed by it, of this I have met with few examples ; but here is one.

Spurina, a young Tuscan,

> Glittering like a gem that cleaves
> The red gold round it, to deck head or throat,
> Or as gleams ivory, cunningly inlaid
> In boxwood or Orician terebinth, (VIRGIL.)

being endowed with a beauty so uncommon and surpassing that the most continent eyes could not continently resist its brilliance, not content to leave so much flame and fever, which he kindled on all sides, without relief, conceived such a furious spite against himself and the rich gifts which Nature had bestowed upon him, as if they were to be blamed for others' faults, that he purposely slashed and disfigured with wounds and scars the perfect proportion and symmetry that Nature had so carefully observed in his face.

To give my own opinion, I do not so much admire as wonder at actions of that kind. Such excesses outrage my sense of order. The purpose was noble and conscientious, but, to my mind, a little wanting in wisdom. What if his subsequent deformity resulted in making others guilty of the sin of hatred and contempt, or of envy of the glory of such uncommon merit, or of calumny, by attributing this whim to a frantic ambition ? Is there anything on which malice cannot, if it will, find an occasion, one way or another, to vent itself ? It would have been better and at the same time more glorious to have made these gifts of God an occasion for exemplary virtue and right conduct.

Those who try to escape from the common duties, and

that endless number of rules, difficult from so many points of view, which bind a strictly honest man to civil life, practise, to my mind, a fine economy, whatever degree of special rigour they impose upon themselves. It is, in a sense, dying in order to avoid the trouble of living well. They may have some other reward, but it never seemed to me that they could have the reward of difficulty. Nor do I think there is anything more difficult than for a man to keep straight amid the rushing waters of this world, loyally responding to and satisfactorily performing every part of his charge.

It is perhaps easier to keep clear of the whole sex than to behave entirely as we should in companionship with our wives. And a man may pass a more easy and careless life in poverty than in a rightly dispensed abundance. To employ one's wealth according to reason is harder than abstinence. Moderation is a virtue that gives us more trouble than suffering does. The right living of the younger Scipio may assume a thousand forms ; the right living of Diogenes only one. The latter surpasses in harmlessness the life of the ordinary man as much as it is itself surpassed in usefulness and power by the most perfect and uncommon lives.

CHAPTER 34

OBSERVATIONS ON JULIUS CAESAR'S METHODS IN WAR

IT is told of several war-chiefs that they had a particular regard for certain books, as the great Alexander for Homer ; Scipio Africanus for Xenophon ; Marcus Brutus for Polybius ; Charles the Fifth for Philip de Commines. And we are told that Macchiavelli is still held in repute in other countries. But the late Marshal Strozzi without doubt made a much better choice in adopting Caesar as his favourite ; for that book should indeed be the breviary of every soldier, as being the true and supreme model of the art of warfare. And God knows besides with what charm and beauty he has overlaid that rich matter, expressed in so pure, delicate, and perfect a style, that to my taste there are no writings in the world comparable to his on that subject.

I will here record certain individual and uncommon features, in connexion with his warfare, that have remained in my memory.

His army being somewhat intimidated by a rumour which was circulating of the numerous forces which King Juba was leading against him, instead of diminishing the apprehension of his soldiers and minimizing the enemy's resources, having called them together to reassure them and give them courage, he adopted the opposite course to that we are accustomed to. For he told them that they need no more trouble to inquire about the forces the enemy was leading, and that he had very certain information about them. Then he gave them a number greatly exceeding both the truth and the report that was circulating in his army, herein following the advice of Cyrus in Xenophon ; since the deception is not so important when it is found that the enemy is in fact weaker than was expected, as when he is found to be very strong after having been reported weak.

He trained his soldiers above all to simple obedience, and not to presume to criticize or even speak of their general's plans, which he never communicated to them until they were about to be carried out. And if they happened to get wind of them, he delighted in changing his mind on the spur of the moment, in order to deceive them. And often, with the same end in view, having fixed upon an encampment at a certain spot, he would pass on and prolong the day's march, especially in bad and rainy weather.

At the commencement of his Gallic wars, the Swiss having sent to ask permission to cross over the Roman territory, although determined to stop them by force, he yet pretended to favour their request, and put off his answer for several days to give himself time to collect his army. Those poor men did not know how excellent a hand he was at husbanding his time ; for many a time he repeats that the supreme qualification for a general is to be able to seize his opportunity at the right moment, and to be ever on the spot. And his exploits show that he possessed this quality in an unexampled and incredible degree.

If he did not show much scruple in taking advantage of an enemy under colour of a treaty of agreement, he had as little in requiring in his soldiers no other quality but valour, and he seldom punished any faults except mutiny and disobedience. Often, after a victory, he would give them a free hand to revel at pleasure, releasing them for a time from the rules of military discipline ; and, what is more, he had trained his soldiers so well that, perfumed and oiled though they were, they would none the less rush into battle with great fury. Indeed he liked them to be richly armed, and encouraged them to wear engraved, gilded and plated armour, that they might be the more anxious to save it, and consequently more resolute in their defence.

When he spoke to them he called them ' Fellow-soldiers ', as we do now, a practice which his successor Augustus discontinued, holding that Caesar had done so when his affairs made it necessary, and to gratify the hearts of men who only followed him as volunteers ;

> At crossing of the Rhine great Caesar was
> My general ; in Rome he is my fellow.
> So crime does equalize those it pollutes ;   (LUCAN.)

but that this mode of address was beneath the dignity of an Emperor and army-general ; and he revived the custom of calling them merely ' Soldiers '.

With this courtesy, however, Caesar combined great severity in keeping them in check. The Ninth legion having mutinied near Placentia, he ignominiously disbanded it, although Pompey was still afoot at the time, and only after many entreaties did he receive them back into favour. He appeased them more by authority and audacity than by soft words.

In the passage where he speaks of his crossing of the river Rhine into Germany, he says that he thought it unworthy of the honour of the Roman people to convey his army across in boats, and built a bridge that they might pass over firm-footed. It was there that he built that wonderful bridge, the construction of which he describes in all its details. For he never dwells with so much complacency on his exploits as he does in explaining the ingenuity of his inventions in this kind of manual works.

I have also observed this, that he attaches great importance to his addresses to his troops before battle. For when he wishes to show how much he was surprised and hard pressed, he always mentions the fact that he had no time even to harangue his army. Before that great battle with the forces of Tournay, he writes, ' Caesar, having given all necessary orders, immediately hastened to that part of the army whither chance led him, to exhort his soldiers, and coming across the Tenth legion he had only time to tell them to remember their pristine valour, not to be taken aback, and boldly to resist the enemy's onslaught. And, the enemy having already approached to within a dart's throw, he gave the signal for battle ; and forthwith proceeding to another part to encourage the others, he found them already engaged in fighting.'

That is what he says there. In truth his tongue did him very notable service in many places, and, even in his own day, his military eloquence was so highly thought of, that several in his army took down his speeches ; by this means there arose a collection of volumes that existed long after his time. He had a peculiar charm in speaking, and so characteristic of him, that his familiar friends, among whom was Augustus, hearing those speeches read which had been collected, detected even words and phrases which were not his.

The first time he left Rome with a public command, he reached the river Rhone in a week, having a secretary or two in front of him in his coach, whom he kept continually writing, and behind him the man who carried his sword. And indeed, if one were merely travelling, one could hardly attain the speed with which he advanced from victory to victory. For, leaving Gaul and pursuing Pompey to Brindisi, he subdued Italy in eighteen days ; returned from Brindisi to Rome ; from Rome he penetrated into the heart of Spain, where he surmounted the greatest difficulties in the war against Afranius and Petreius, and at the prolonged siege of Marseilles. From thence he returned to Macedonia, defeated the Roman army at Pharsalia ; passed thence, still in pursuit of Pompey, into Egypt, which he subdued ; from Egypt he came to Syria and the region of the Pontus, where he fought against Pharnaces ; thence to Africa, where he defeated Scipio and Juba ; and again retraced his steps, through Italy, into Spain, where he defeated Pompey's sons :

> Fleeter than flames of heaven, or tigress newly-delivered.
>
> (LUCAN.)

> As when a boulder, from a hill-top borne,
> Which rains have washed, or blustering winds have torn,
> Or creeping years have loosened, down the steep,
> From crag to crag, leaps headlong, and in scorn
> Goes bounding on, and with resistless sweep
> Lays waste the woods, and whelms the shepherd and his sheep.
>
> (VIRGIL.)

Writing of the siege of Avaricum he says it was his custom to remain night and day with the workmen he was employing. In every important undertaking he always reconnoitred in person, and never brought his army to a place that he had not first thoroughly explored. And, if we are to believe Suetonius, when he invaded England, he was the first to sound the ford.[1]

He was wont to say that he would rather gain a victory by thought than by strength. And in the war against Petreius and Afranius, when Fortune offered him a very obvious advantage, he refused it, hoping, as he says, to get the better of his enemies with less risk by prolonging the operation.

There too he performed a wonderful feat when he commanded his whole host, without any necessity, to swim the river :

> Eager to fight they plunged into the stream
> They would have feared if close pursued in flight.
> Their armour donned, their frozen limbs restore
> By running to and fro. (LUCAN.)

To me he appears to have been rather more cautious and deliberate in his enterprises than Alexander ; for the latter seems to have looked for dangers and rushed headlong into them, like an impetuous torrent which attacks and collides with everything that comes into its way, without choice or discrimination :

> So rolls the flood of horned Aufidus,
>   That flows beside Apulian Daunus' realm,
> When he designs in mood tumultuous
>   With deluge dread the fields of tilth to whelm.
>   (HORACE.)

And then too he was busy at that work in the bloom and first ardour of youth ; whilst Caesar set about it when he was already mature and well on in years. Besides that Alexander was of a more sanguine temperament, hot and choleric, and he aggravated this disposition by drinking wine, of which Caesar was very abstemious.

But in case of need and when the occasion required it, never did any man hold his life more cheaply. For my own

[1] Montaigne's knowledge of the Channel appears to be a little at fault. Suetonius says ' he did not cross to Britain until he had himself explored the harbours and the navigation, and the access to the island '.

part I seem to read in divers of his exploits a determined resolve to throw his life away, to avoid the shame of being vanquished. In that great battle which he fought against those of Tournay, seeing the vanguard of his army wavering, he hastened to the front of the enemy, without a buckler, just as he was ; and the same happened on several other occasions. Hearing that his men were besieged, he passed through the enemy's forces in disguise, to go and encourage them by his presence.

After crossing the sea to Dyrrhachium with a very small force, and seeing that the remainder of his army, which he had left in Antony's charge, was slow in following him, he dared alone to recross the sea in a violent storm, and, the ports on the other side and the whole sea being in Pompey's possession, he slipped through to fetch the rest of his army himself.

As to the expeditions he carried out with armed forces, some of them exceeded in risk all the rules of military art ; for with what feeble resources he undertook to subdue the kingdom of Egypt, and afterwards attacked the armies of Scipio and Juba, ten times greater than his own ! Men of his kind have had an unaccountable and superhuman confidence in their fortune.

He used to say that one should embark, and not deliberate, upon great enterprises.

After the battle of Pharsalia, having sent his army before him into Asia, and crossing with a single ship the strait of the Hellespont, he met Lucius Cassius at sea, with ten great ships of war ; he had the pluck, not merely to await his coming, but to steer straight for him and call upon him to surrender ; and he was successful.

Having undertaken that mad siege of Alesia, which was defended by a garrison of eighty thousand men, the whole of Gaul having risen in arms to come down upon him and raise the siege, with an army of 109,000 [1] horse and 240,000 foot, what maniacal foolhardiness it was to refuse to give up the attempt and to be determined to perform two such difficult feats at the same time ! And yet he carried them through. After winning that great battle against the army

---

[1] 8,000 according to Caesar himself. The mistake was perhaps due to Montaigne's misreading of Caesar's number *IIX milibus* (*De Bel. Gall.* vii. 76).

outside, he soon brought those he was besieging to their knees.

Lucullus performed a similar feat at the siege of Tigrano-certa, against King Tigranes ; but the conditions were not the same, considering the want of energy shown by the enemy with whom Lucullus had to do.

I must here note two rare and extraordinary circum-stances in connexion with the siege of Alesia. The one is that the Gauls, assembling together for the purpose of encountering Caesar, after a calculation of all their forces, decided in council to cut down a good part of that great multitude, lest they might fall into confusion. This was a new thing, to be afraid of being too many ; but looking at it rightly, it is probably true that an army-corps should be of moderate size, and regulated within certain limits, either on account of the difficulty of feeding it, or of the difficulty of handling it and keeping it in order. It would be very easy at least to prove by examples that those immense armies have seldom done anything worth speak-ing of.

According to the saying of Cyrus, in Xenophon, it is not the number of men, but the number of good men, that gives the advantage. The rest are a hindrance rather than a help.

And Bajazet grounded his decision to give battle to Tamerlane, against the advice of all his captains, chiefly on the consideration that the numberless number of the enemy army gave him an assured hope of throwing them into confusion.

Scanderbeg, a good and very expert judge, was wont to say that ten or twelve thousand reliable fighting-men should suffice a competent leader to guarantee his reputation in any kind of military emergency.

The other circumstance, which appears to be contrary to usage and reason in warfare, is that Vercingetorix, who was elected general-in-chief over all the parts of the revolted Gauls, decided to shut himself up in Alesia. For the man in command of a whole country should never shackle him-self except in the extreme case of his last stronghold being in danger, and of there being no hope but in defending it. Otherwise he should hold himself free, in order to have the full power of protecting all the regions under his command.

To come back to Caesar. With advancing years he became rather less active and more deliberate, as his friend Oppius testifies ; thinking it wise not lightly to risk the honour of so many victories which a single disaster might cause him to lose. The Italians, when they wish to reprove their young men for their foolhardiness, call them *bisognosi di honore*, ' hard up for honour'. When they still hunger and thirst after fame they are right to seek it at any price ; but, having already acquired a sufficiency of it, they should renounce it. There may be some reasonable moderation in this craving for honour, and this appetite, like any other, may be glutted. Many men have had this experience.

He had outgrown the scruples of the ancient Romans, who would take no unfair advantage in their warfare, but relied upon pure and native valour alone ; and yet he was more conscientious than we should be in these days, and did not approve of every kind of means to gain a victory. In the war against Ariovistus, whilst he was parleying with him, some trouble arose between the two armies, of which the fault at first lay with Ariovistus' horsemen. This tumult gave Caesar a great advantage over his enemy, yet he would make no use of it, for fear of being accused of bad faith.

When he went to battle he was usually richly dressed, and in bright colours, to make himself conspicuous.

In presence of the enemy he kept a tighter rein on his soldiers, and kept them more strictly in hand.

When the ancient Greeks wished to accuse a man of extreme incompetence, they used a proverbial saying : ' That he could neither read nor swim.' Caesar held the same opinion, that the art of swimming was very useful in war, and it gave him many advantages. When he was in great haste he usually swam the rivers he came across ; for he loved to travel on foot, like the great Alexander. In Egypt, having been obliged to save himself by entering a little skiff, and so many men leaping in after him that it was in danger of foundering, he chose rather to commit himself to the sea and gained his fleet by swimming, although it was more than two hundred yards away, holding his tablets above the water in his left hand, with his military cloak, which he held with his teeth, trailing after him, that it might not fall into the hands of the enemy ; and he was already well advanced in years.

No general ever inspired such trust in his soldiers. At the beginning of his Civil wars, his centurions offered to pay a horseman each, out of their own purses ; and the foot-soldiers offered to serve him at their own expense, those who were better off also undertaking to defray the cost of the more needy.

The late Admiral de Chatillon recently showed us a similar case in our Civil wars ; for the Frenchmen of his army furnished the money out of their own purses to pay the foreigners who accompanied him. We could not find many examples of so warm and ready an affection among those who march under the old colours, under the old government of the laws.[1]

Passion rules us much more strongly than reason. And so it happened, in the war against Hannibal, that, after the generous example of the Roman people in the city, the men-at-arms and captains refused their pay ; and those who took it in Marcellus' camp were called Mercenaries.

After suffering a check near Dyrrhachium, his soldiers came of their own accord and offered themselves for chastisement and punishment, so that there was more need to comfort than to scold them. A single cohort of his held their own against four of Pompey's legions for more than four hours, until nearly the whole cohort was shot down with arrows, of which 130,000 [2] were found in the trenches.

A soldier named Scaeva, who commanded one of the approaches, invincibly maintained his ground, having lost one eye, one shoulder and thigh being shot through, and his shield pierced in two hundred and thirty places. Many of his soldiers, being taken prisoner, chose death rather than promise to join the other side. Granius Petronius, having been captured by Scipio in Africa, the latter, after putting his comrades to death, sent word to him that he gave him his life, as he was a man of rank and a quaestor. Petronius replied that the soldiers of Caesar were wont to grant life to others, not to receive it, and immediately killed himself with his own hand.

---

[1] i.e. in the Catholic army. Montaigne was nothing if not impartial. The Admiral de Chatillon is better known as Gaspard de Coligny.

[2] According to Suetonius ; but Caesar himself makes the number 30,000.

Of their fidelity we have endless examples. We must not forget the conduct of the men who were besieged at Salona, a town that held with Caesar against Pompey, on account of an uncommon incident which occurred there. Marcus Octavius held them in siege ; those within were reduced to such extreme necessity in all things, that, in order to supply the want of men, most of them having been killed or wounded, they manumitted all their slaves, and were constrained to cut off the hair of all the women to make ropes for their catapults ; not to speak of a great shortage of food. Yet they were determined never to surrender.

This siege having dragged out to a great length and Octavius having become in consequence more negligent and less attentive to his operations, they chose a day about noon, and, after ranging the women and children on the walls to make a good show, they sallied out with such fury against the besiegers that, having broken through the first, the second, and the third body of guards, and the fourth, and then all the remainder, and forced them to abandon all their trenches, they drove them to their ships ; and Octavius himself escaped to Dyrrhachium, where Pompey was.

I cannot at this moment call to mind another example of the besieged beating the besiegers wholesale, and gaining the upper hand in the campaign ; nor of a sortie being converted into a real and entirely victorious battle.

CHAPTER 35
OF THREE GOOD WIVES

GOOD women are not found by the dozen, as everybody knows, and especially in the duties of marriage ; for that is a bargain fraught with so many difficulties, that a woman's will is strained to keep to it entirely for long. The men, although they enter into it under somewhat better conditions, yet have enough to do to keep to it.

The touchstone of a good marriage, and its real proof, is the duration of the partnership, and whether it has been constantly pleasant, loyal, and smooth. In our days the women more commonly reserve the display of their good offices and the strength of their affection for their husbands until after they have lost them ; then at least they seek to give evidence of their goodwill. A tardy and unseasonable testimony ! They prove thereby rather that they only love them when dead.

Life is full of tumult ; death, of love and courtesy. As fathers conceal their affection for their children, so the wives likewise are wont to conceal their affection for their husbands, in order to keep up a modest respect. That mystery is not to my liking. In vain do they tear their hair and lacerate their faces ; I should go to the lady's maid or the secretary and whisper in their ear, ' How did they get on ? how did they live together ? '

I am always reminded of that wise saying : *They make most ostentation of sorrow who grieve the least.*[1] Their glum looks are offensive to the living and useless to the dead. We should willingly give them leave to smile after, if only they smile on us during life. Is it not enough to bring one back to life in vexation to find her who spat in his face when alive coming and rubbing his feet when he is hardly dead ? If there is any honour in weeping over a husband, it is only for one who has smiled upon him ; let those who have wept during his life smile at his death, outwardly as well as inwardly.

Therefore pay no heed to those tear-stained eyes and that pitiful voice ; observe rather her bearing, her colour and the plumpness of her cheeks under those thick veils ; it is by them that they speak plain French. There are few who do not improve in health, an infallible sign. That ceremonious demeanour looks not so much backward as forward ; it means acquisition more than payment. When I was a boy, an honest and very fair lady, the widow of a Prince and still living, dressed a little more ornamentally than is permitted by our laws of widowhood ; to those who reproved her for it, she replied, ' The meaning of it is that I am not on the look-out for a new lover, and have no desire to marry again.'

In order not to be quite out of harmony with our customs, I have here made choice of three women whose extreme tenderness and affection also centred around their husbands' death. Yet they are examples of a somewhat different kind, and of a love so convincing that they bravely threw life into the scale.

---

[1] Altered from Tacitus.

Pliny the Younger had a neighbour living near one of his houses in Italy who was grievously afflicted with ulcers on his private parts. His wife, seeing his prolonged anguish, entreated him to allow her to examine at leisure the condition of his malady, that she might tell him more frankly than any other what hopes he had. His permission being obtained, and having carefully considered his case, she found that a cure was impossible, and that all he could hope for was to drag out a painful and lingering life. Therefore she advised him, as the surest and most sovereign remedy, to kill himself ; and finding him a little reluctant to adopt so heroic a measure, she said, ' Do not think, my friend, that the pain I see you suffering does not touch me as much as yourself, and that I am not willing to use, to rid myself of it, the same medicine I am prescribing for you. I will accompany you in the cure as I have done in the disease. Put away your fear, and believe me that we shall derive only pleasure from this passage which is to deliver us from such torments. We will depart happily together.'

Having said that, and warmed up her husband's courage, she resolved that they should leap into the lake [1] through a window of their house that overlooked it. And, to preserve to the last that loyal and vehement affection with which she had embraced him during life, she desired that he should die in her arms. But, lest they should fail her and the closeness of her embrace be relaxed in the fall through fear, she had herself fast bound to him by the waist ; and so gave up her own life for the repose of her husband's. [2]

This was a woman of humble origin ; and in this class of people it is not so unusual to see occasional acts of uncommon goodness :

> When Justice fled this world of wickedness,
> 'Twas in their midst that last her steps were seen. (VIRGIL.)

The other two are noble and rich, among whom examples of virtue are rarely found.

---

[1] Lake Larius, the modern Como.
[2] Montaigne rather elaborates the story, which Pliny tells in a third as many words ; introducing it with the remark : ' How much does the fame of human actions depend upon the station of those who perform them ! '

Arria, wife of Cecinna Paetus, a man of consular rank, was the mother of another Arria, the wife of Thrasea Paetus, so renowned for his virtue in Nero's time, and through this son-in-law, grandmother of Fannia ; for the resemblance between the names and fortunes of these men and women has led many to confuse them. When Cecinna Paetus, her husband, was taken prisoner by the Emperor Claudius' soldiers, after the defeat of Scribonianus, whose party he had joined, this first Arria entreated those who were leading him captive to Rome, to take her into their ship, where she would be of much less expense and trouble to them than a number of persons they would need to wait upon her husband, since she alone would undertake the whole charge of his cabin, his cooking, and all other services. They refused her request. She embarked in a small fishing-vessel which she hired on the spot, and in this craft followed him from Sclavonia.

One day, when they were at Rome, in presence of the Emperor, Junia, the widow of Scribonianus, having fami-liarly accosted her on the strength of their similar fortunes, she repulsed her rudely with these words, ' I, speak to you, or listen to anything you say ! you, in whose lap Scribo-nianus was killed, and you still alive ! ' These words, together with several other indications, made her relations suspect that, unable to endure her husband's fate, she was designing to do away with herself. And when Thrasea, her son-in-law, on hearing those words, entreated her not to throw her life away, saying, ' What ! if I incurred the same fate as Cecinna, would you expect my wife, your daughter, to do the same ? ' ' Would I ? she replied, most certainly I would, if she had lived as long and in such har-mony with you as I have done with my husband.' These answers increased their solicitude about her, and made them watch her conduct more carefully.

One day she said to those who were keeping guard over her, ' You may do what you please, you may drive me to a much more painful death, but prevent me from dying you cannot ; ' and thereupon, rushing madly from the chair on which she was seated, she dashed her head with all her might against the nearest wall, so that sorely bruised she fell down in a swoon. After they had with great trouble brought her round, she said, ' I told you that if you refused me some easy way of dying, I would choose another, however painful it might be.'

The end of so admirable a virtue was this : When her husband Paetus was sentenced to death by the Emperor's cruelty, he had not sufficient courage of his own to take his life.   One day, among others, after employing all the arguments and persuasions which she thought best calculated to prevail upon him to do her bidding, she snatched the dagger which her husband was wearing and, holding it naked in her hand, said, as a last exhortation, ' Do this, Paetus,' and at the same instant dealt herself a fatal stab in the heart.   Then, tearing it out of the wound, she offered it to him, at the same time ending her life with these noble, generous, and immortal words, *Paete, non dolet*.   She had only time to utter those three words of such beautiful meaning, ' See, Paetus, it does not hurt me.'

> When from her breast chaste Arria snatched the sword,
> And gave the fatal weapon to her lord,
> ' My wound, she said, believe me, does not smart ;
> 'Tis thine alone, my Paetus, pains my heart.'   (MARTIAL.)

The words are much more alive in the original, and richer in meaning ; for both her husband's and her own wound and death were so small a matter to her, since it was she who advised and instigated them.   But having taken this bold and heroic step solely for her husband's benefit, she had no thoughts except for him in the last gasp of her life, and for removing his fear of following her in death.   Paetus immediately stabbed himself with the same blade ; ashamed, as I think, of having needed so dear and precious a lesson.

Pompeia Paulina, a young and very noble Roman lady, had married Seneca in his extreme old age.   Nero, his precious pupil, sent his satellites to announce to him his death decree, which was done in this wise : When the Roman Emperors of that time had sentenced any man of rank, they sent him word by their officers to choose what death he pleased, and to take his life within such and such a prescribed time, which was shorter or longer according to the temper of their choler ; giving him leisure to arrange his affairs during that time, or sometimes making the interval so short that he was deprived of the opportunity of doing so.   And, if the condemned resisted the order,

they sent special men to execute it, either by cutting the
veins of his arms and legs, or forcibly making him take
poison. But a man of honour did not abide this necessity
and employed his own physician and surgeon to that end.

Seneca heard their charge with calm and confident demeanour, and then asked for paper to make his will;
which being refused by the centurion, he turned to his
friends. ' Since I cannot, he said, leave you anything else
in requital of what I owe you, I leave you at least the best
thing I possess, which is the example of my life and character, which I pray you to cherish in your memory, that
by doing so you may acquire the name of true and sincere
friends.' At the same time, now with gentle words assuaging
the bitterness of the grief he saw they were suffering, now
hardening his voice to chide them, ' Where, he said, are
those brave precepts of philosophy ? What has become
of the provisions that for so many years we have laid up
against the accidents of Fortune ? Was Nero's cruelty
unknown to us ? What could we expect of a man who has
killed his mother and his brother, if not that he would also
put to death the tutor who has fostered and brought
him up ? '

Having spoken these words to the company, he turned
to his wife, and, closely embracing her, whose heart and
strength were sinking under the weight of her grief, he
entreated her for the love of him to bear this misfortune
a little more patiently, and said to her that the hour was
come when he had to show, no longer by words and arguments, but by deeds, the fruit he had gathered from his
studies ; and that he really embraced death, not only
without pain, but cheerfully. ' Wherefore, my love, he
added, do not dishonour it by your tears, that you may
not seem to love yourself more than my reputation ;
moderate your grief, and comfort yourself with the knowledge you have had of me and my actions, and pass the
remainder of your life in the honest occupations to which
you are devoted.'

To this Paulina, having a little recovered her spirits and
warmed her great heart by a very noble affection, replied,
' No, Seneca, I am not the woman to leave you without my
company in such a need ; I will not have you think that
the virtuous examples you have set by your life have not

also taught me how to die well; and how could I do so better
and more honourably, or more to my own desire, than in
your company ? So be assured that I am departing with
you.' Then Seneca, approving this noble and glorious
resolution of his wife, and glad to be delivered of the fear
of leaving her after his death at the mercy and cruelty of
his enemies, said, ' I have advised you how to lead your
life more happily ; you prefer then the honour of death.
Truly I will not begrudge it you ; the fortitude and resolution in our common end may be alike, but the beauty and
glory will be greater on your part.'

When he had said that, the veins of their arms were
opened at the same time, but Seneca's being shrunk both
through old age and abstinence, and the blood flowing too
long and too sluggishly, he ordered them also to cut the
veins of his thighs ; and lest the anguish he was suffering
might pierce his wife's heart, and to be delivered from the
affliction he felt at seeing her in so pitiable a condition,
after taking a very tender leave of her, he prayed her to
allow herself to be carried into the adjoining room ; which
was done.

But all these incisions being still insufficient to cause his
death, he ordered his physician, Statius Annaeus, to give
him a poisonous draught, which had scarcely more effect ;
for, by reason of the feebleness and chilliness of the limbs,
it could not reach the heart. Therefore they prepared in
addition a very hot bath ; and then, feeling his end to be
near, as long as he had any breath he continued to talk
very excellently on the subject of his present condition,
his secretaries taking down his words as long as they were
able to hear his voice. And his last words were long after
treasured and held in honour by men (it is a grievous loss
to us that they have not been preserved to this day). As
he felt the last pangs of death, with some of the bath-water
mixed with blood he wetted his head,[1] saying, ' I make
libation of this water to Jove the Deliverer.'

When Nero was informed of all this, fearing lest he might
incur the blame of Paulina's death, who was a lady allied
to some of the best families in Rome, and towards whom he
felt no particular enmity, he sent in all haste to command her

[1] According to Tacitus, who appears to be Montaigne's authority, he
did not wet his head, but ' sprinkled ' some of his slaves.

wounds to be bound up ; which her people did without her knowledge, she being already half dead and unconscious. And, though she continued to live against her design, she lived very honourably and as befitted her virtue ; her wan complexion testifying how much life had flowed from her wounds.

Those are my three very true stories, which I find as entertaining and as tragic as any of those that we make up out of our heads to please the public. And I wonder that it does not occur to those who are devoted to that kind of composition to choose rather one of ten thousand very fine stories which are found in books, which would give them less trouble and bring more pleasure and profit. And if any man should wish to build up a whole and connected body of them, he need provide nothing of his own but the link, like the solder of some other kind of metal ; by this means he might accumulate a store of true incidents of all sorts, arranging and varying them as the beauty of the work may require, pretty much as Ovid sewed and pieced together, from that great number of different fables, his *Metamorphoses*.

In respect of the last couple, this is also worthy of consideration, that Paulina voluntarily offers to relinquish this life for love of her husband, and that her husband had once also relinquished death for the love of her. To us there is no great equivalence in this exchange, but, according to his Stoic way of thinking, it seems to me that he thought he had done as much for her in prolonging his life for her sake, as if he had died for her.

In one of the letters he wrote to Lucilius, after giving him to understand that, having caught a fever at Rome, he immediately took coach to retire to one of his country houses, against his wife's advice, who tried to make him stay ; and that he had replied that his fever was not a fever of the body, but of the place, he continues as follows : ' She allowed me to go, strongly recommending me to look after my health. Now I, knowing that her life is involved in mine, begin to look after myself in order to look after her. I lose the privilege which my old age had given me of being more firm and resolute in many things, when I remember that in this old life there is a young life to which I am of some use. Since I cannot bring her to love me more

courageously, she brings me to love myself more carefully ;
for we must allow something to honest affections. And at
times, although occasions urge us to the contrary, we must
call back our life, even though it be a torture. We must
arrest the soul between our teeth, since with men of honour
the law of living is determined not by their pleasure but by
their duty.

' The man who does not value his wife or one of his friends
sufficiently to prolong his life for them, and obstinately
persists in dying, is too squeamish and lax in his love. The
soul must command itself to do this, when it is requisite
to serve our dear ones. We must sometimes lend ourselves
to our friends, and, when we would rather die for our own
sake, renounce our intention for theirs. It is evidence of
a great heart to return to life out of consideration for others,
as many eminent men have done. And it is a sign of a
singular good nature to preserve old age (the greatest
advantage of which is that it makes us less solicitous about
prolonging it, and more courageous and disdainful in the
conduct of life), if we feel we are doing some sweet, agreeable, and profitable service to one to whom we are very
dear. And we reap a very pleasant reward ; for what is
sweeter than to be so dear to your wife that for her sake
you become dearer to yourself ? So my Paulina has charged
me not only with her fear, but also with my own. It was not
enough for me to consider with how much fortitude I might
die, but I have also considered with how little fortitude
she might bear my death. I have forced myself to live,
and to live is sometimes the mark of a great soul.'

Those are his words, excellent as they always are.

CHAPTER 36

OF THE GREATEST MEN

IF I were asked to make a selection from among all the
men who have come to my knowledge, I think I could
pick out three who excel all the rest.

The first is Homer. Not but that Aristotle or Varro (for
instance) was perhaps as learned as he, and that possibly
in his art itself Virgil may be compared with him. I leave
that question to be decided by those who know them both.

Knowing only one of them, I can say only this, that as far
as my range goes I do not think that the Muses themselves
could outstrip the Roman :

> So sweetly to his tuneful lyre he sings ;
> His only rival is the Cynthian God.   (PROPERTIUS.)

We must not forget, however, in judging him, that it is
chiefly from Homer that Virgil derives his inspiration, that
he was his guide and schoolmaster,[1] and that a single
incident in the Iliad provided both body and matter for
that great and divine *Aeneid*.   That does not come into my
reckoning ; I bring in several other circumstances which
make this man a source of wonder to me, and almost above
human conditions.   And in truth I often wonder that he
who introduced many gods into the world and by his
authority brought them to honour, did not himself gain
the rank of a god.   Being blind and poor, living before the
sciences were reduced to rules by certain observations, he
knew them so well, that all who have since taken upon
them to set up governments, to conduct wars, and to write
either on religion and philosophy, of whatever sect or
school, or on the arts, have made use of him as of a very
perfect master in the knowledge of all things, and of his
books as of a nursery of every kind of excellence :

> Whose rich and storied page
> Better than Crantor or Chrysippus sage
> Shows what is base, what noble, to man's lot
> What is of true advantage, and what not ;   (HORACE.)

and, as another says,

> From whose perennial spring the poet sips,
> And in Pierian waters wets his lips ;   (OVID.)

and another,

> 'Mid comrades of the Heliconian maids
> The peerless Homer holds his sceptre high ;   (LUCRETIUS.)

and another,

> From whose full-flowing lips, all later poets
> Have filched their lines, and turned the mighty stream,
> Sole source of eloquence, into their little
> Rivulets.   (MANILIUS.)

---

[1] *Tu duca, tu signor, et tu maestro*, in the words of Dante saluting
Virgil in Hell.

His creation of the most excellent work it was possible to produce was against the order of Nature. For ordinarily things are born in an imperfect condition ; they increase, and gather strength in their growth. In him, the infancy of poetry and several other sciences is mature, perfect, and accomplished. For this reason he may be called the first and last of the poets, in accordance with that noble testimony which antiquity has left us of him, ' that, as there was no one before him whom he could imitate, so there has been none since who could imitate him '. His words, according to Aristotle, are the only words that have movement and action ; they are the only substantial words.

Alexander the Great, having lighted upon a rich casket among the spoils of Darius, commanded it to be kept for him as a receptacle for his Homer, saying that ' he was the best and most faithful counsellor he had in military matters'. For the same reason Cleomenes, son of Anaxandridas, said that ' he was the poet of the Lacedemonians, because he was a very good master for the teaching of warfare'. This singular and remarkable eulogy has also been bestowed upon him by Plutarch, ' that he was the only author in the world who never cloys the appetite, appearing ever new to the reader, and ever blooming with a new charm.' That madcap Alcibiades, having asked one who professed to be a man of letters for a book of Homer, gave him a box on the ear because he had none ; as who should find that one of our priests was without a breviary.

Xenophanes one day lamented before Hiero, Tyrant of Syracuse, his being so poor that he had not enough to feed two slaves. ' What ! he replied, Homer, who was much poorer than you, can feed more than ten thousand, dead though he be.'

What more could Panaetius say of Plato than to call him the ' Homer of Philosophers ' ?

Besides, what fame can be compared to his ? There is nothing that will live so long on men's lips as his name and his works ; nothing will ever be better known or more acceptable than Troy, Helen, and his wars, which perhaps never took place. Our children are still called by the names he invented more than three thousand years ago. Who does not know a Hector or an Achilles ? Not only a few individual families, but most of the nations seek their origin in his fictions. Mahomet, the second of that name, Emperor of the Turks, writing to our Pope Pius the Second, says, ' I wonder that the Italians should league themselves against me, seeing that we have our common origin in the Trojans, and that I, as well as they, have an interest in avenging the blood of Hector on the Greeks, whom they are backing up in opposition to me.' Is it not a noble drama in which kings, commonwealths, and emperors have been playing their parts for so many centuries, and for which all this great world has been the stage ? Seven Greek cities disputed the honour of being his birthplace ; so much honour did his very obscurity bring him !

Smyrna, Rhodos, Colophon, Salamis, Chios, Argos, Athenae.[1]

The second is Alexander the Great. For, if we consider the early age at which he commenced his career ; the small means with which he carried out his glorious designs ; the authority which he gained in his boyhood among the greatest and most experienced captains in the world, whom he led ; the extraordinary favour with which Fortune embraced and seconded many of his hazardous, I might almost say foolhardy, exploits ;

> He bore down all that his high aims withstood,
> And joyed to force a way across the ruins ; (LUCAN.)

his greatness in having, at the age of thirty-three, victoriously traversed the whole of the habitable globe, and in having, in half a lifetime, attained to the utmost that human nature is capable of, so thât you cannot imagine his full term of life, and the continuation of his growth in valour and fortune until a ripe age, without imagining something superhuman ; in having made so many lines of kings to spring from his soldiers, leaving the world after his death allotted among four successors, mere captains in his army, whose descendants have so long remained in possession of that great inheritance.

If we consider his many great virtues, justice, temperance, liberality, integrity in keeping his word, love for his men, humanity to the vanquished ; for his character appears to have been indeed above just reproach, although some of his individual actions were uncommon and extraordinary. But

[1] Aulus Gellius. The names are so arranged as to form a hexameter line.

it is impossible to conduct such great movements according to the rules of justice ; such men as he need to be weighed in the gross, with an eye to the chief end of their actions. The destruction of Thebes [and Persepolis], the murder of Menander and Hephaestion's physician, of so many Persian prisoners at one time, of a troop of Indian soldiers, not without prejudice to his good faith, of the Cosseians, even their little children ; these are outstanding excesses which can hardly be condoned. For, with regard to Clytus, he made amends for his mistake beyond its weight ; and this action, as much as any other, is evidence of the mildness of his disposition : it shows a nature in itself eminently formed for goodness, and it was wittily said of him ' that Nature gave him his virtues, and Fortune his vices '.

As to his being rather boastful, a little too impatient of hearing himself spoken ill of, and with regard to the mangers, weapons, and bridles that he had scattered about the Indies,[1] all these things, it seems to me, may be excused in consideration of his age and the remarkable prosperity of his fortunes.

If we consider withal his many military qualities, his diligence, foresight, patience, discipline, subtlety, magnanimity, resolution, and his good fortune, wherein, even though we had not Hannibal's authority for saying so, he was the first of men ; the uncommon beauty and symmetry of his person, which amounted to the marvellous ; his carriage and imposing mien, in a face so young, ruddy, and radiant :

> As when the dawn-star, washed in Ocean's wave,
> Dearer to Venus than all stellar fires,
> Uplifts in heaven his sacred head and melts
> The darkness ; (VIRGIL.)

his eminent learning and abilities ; his great and enduring fame, pure and untainted, free from blemish and envy ; and the fact besides, that long after his death it was religiously believed that his medallions were lucky to those who wore them, and that more kings and princes have written of his exploits than other historians have written of the exploits of any other king or prince whatever ; and

---

[1] ' He contrived many ingenious devices to impress the natives, as, e. g., he caused arms, bridles and mangers for horses to be made of much more than the usual size, and left them scattered about.'—PLUTARCH.

that to this day the Mahommedans, who despise all other histories, by a special privilege accept and honour his alone.

Considering all these things together, I think it will be admitted that I am right in putting him even before Caesar, who alone could have made me doubtful of my choice. And it cannot be denied that there was more of his own in Caesar's exploits, and more of Fortune's in Alexander's. In many things they were equal, and Caesar perhaps had some greater qualities.

They were two fires, or two torrents, that ravaged the world by several ways :

> Lo, as fierce flames drive in from left to right
> Through woodlands parched and groves of crackling bay ;
> As sweep impetuous from a mountain height
> Loud, foaming torrents, that withouten stay
> Cleave to the sea their devastating way. (VIRGIL.)

But, though Caesar's ambition might have been of its nature more moderate, it was so unfortunate in having for its abominable object the ruin of his country and the humiliation of the world in general, that, all things raked together and placed in the scales, I cannot but incline to the side of Alexander.

The third and, to my mind, the greatest, is Epaminondas.

Of fame he has not nearly so much as others (which, for that matter, is not a part of the substance of the thing). Of fortitude and valour, I mean, not that which is whetted by ambition, but that which wisdom and reason may implant in a well-ordered soul, he had as much as it is possible to imagine. Of this particular virtue of his he has, in my opinion, given as many proofs as Alexander himself, and as Caesar. For, although his warlike exploits were not so frequent, nor on so large a scale, they were nevertheless, if duly considered with all their surrounding circumstances, as important and as stoutly carried out, and bear evidence of as much bravery and military genius.

The Greeks have done him the honour, which has not been disputed, to call him the first man of their nation ; but to be the first man in Greece is to be an easy first in the world.

With regard to his knowledge and abilities, this estimate of the ancients has come down to us, ' that no man ever knew so much and spoke so little as he.' For he was by sect a Pythagorean. And what he said no man ever said better. An excellent and very persuasive speaker.

But in character and conscience he surpassed by a very long distance all who have ever undertaken the management of affairs. For in this respect, which ought to be considered in the first place, which alone really shows what we are, and which alone I place in the scales against all other things together, he yields to no philosopher, not even to Socrates. In him blamelessness is a natural, dominating, constant, uniform, incorruptible quality, in comparison with which it appears in Alexander subordinate, uncertain, capricious, sentimental, and accidental.

The ancients thought that if you minutely analyse all the other great generals, you will find in each some special quality that makes him illustrious. In Epaminondas alone we see a virtue and excellence everywhere the same and complete, which in all offices of human life leave nothing to be desired, whether in public or private employment, in peace or war, whether in living or in dying greatly and gloriously. I know of no man whom for his personal qualities and his career I look upon with so much love and honour.

It is certainly true that I consider his persistence in poverty, as described by his best friends, as rather too scrupulous. This attitude alone, though lofty and very worthy of admiration, appears to me a little too acid to make me even desire to imitate it [in the same degree].

Scipio Emilianus alone, if we could give him as sublime and magnificent an end, as deep and comprehensive a knowledge and learning, could make me doubtful about the choice. O, what an ill turn Time has done me in withholding from our eyes, at the very time when they are most needed, and among the first, the Lives of this pair of men, precisely the most noble pair in Plutarch, and by common agreement of the world, one the first of the Greeks, the other of the Romans ! What a subject ! What a craftsman ! [1]

For a man who was no saint, but rather a man of the world, of average social habits and moderate eminence, the richest life I know of to have been lived among the living, as they say, and stored with more rich and desirable parts

[1] It appears that Epaminondas was Plutarch's favourite hero, as he was Montaigne's. His parallel lives of the two men are lost.

than any, was, everything considered, to my mind, that of Alcibiades.

But with regard to Epaminondas, to exemplify his exceeding goodness, I will add here some of his opinions.

He declared that the sweetest satisfaction he had had in all his life was the pleasure he gave his father and mother by his victory at Leuctra. It is saying a great deal that he thought more of their pleasure than of his own, so full and so just, in so glorious an action.

He did not regard it as permissible, even to recover the freedom of his country, to kill a man without just cause. For that reason he was so lukewarm towards the enterprise of his companion Pelopidas, for the relief of Thebes.

He also maintained ' that in battle we should avoid encountering a friend who was on the opposite side, and we should spare him '.

And his humanity, even towards the enemy, having made him suspected by the Boeotians, because, after miraculously forcing the Lacedemonians to open the pass to him which they had attempted to defend at the entrance to the Morea, near Corinth, he contented himself with charging through them without pursuing them to the death, he was deposed from the rank of commander-in-chief : very honourably upon such an account, and for the shame it was to them to be obliged soon after to restore him to his place of honour, and to acknowledge how much their glory and safety depended upon him ; victory attending him like his shadow wherever he led. The prosperity of his country died, as it was born, with him.

CHAPTER 37

OF THE RESEMBLANCE OF CHILDREN TO THEIR FATHERS [1]

IN making up this bundle of so many diverse pieces, I never set my hand to it unless driven by an idleness that has become unbearable, and nowhere but at home. So it has built itself up with divers intervals and interruptions, which vary according to my occasional absences, sometimes for months together.

For the rest, I do not correct my first impressions by my

[1] Or, as we should say, Heredity.

second, except perhaps a word or two ; but only to vary the phrase, not to expunge. My intention is to show the progress of my opinions, and that each part may be seen in its original state. I should like to have begun earlier, that I might follow the course of my changes. A valet whom I employed to write at my dictation thought he had made a rich booty by filching several of my essays, chosen according to his liking. I am consoled by the thought that he will gain no more than I lose.

I have grown older by seven or eight years since I began ; not without some new acquisitions. These years have been so generous as to make me familiarized with the stone in the bladder. A long intercourse and acquaintance with Time is not often made without some such fruit. I could have wished that, of the many gifts he has in store for those who have long known him, he had chosen a more acceptable one. For he could not have selected one of which I have had a greater horror since my childhood. Of all the misfortunes of old age it is just the one I dreaded most. Many a time have I thought to myself that I was travelling too far, and that in thus prolonging my journey I should not fail in the end to be involved in some unpleasant adventure. Often enough I felt and protested, That it was time to depart, and that life ought to be cut short when sound and healthy, following the rule of the surgeons when they have to amputate a limb ; That of the man who did not pay in good time Nature was wont to exact a very stiff usury.

But those were idle speculations. So far was I from being ready at the time that in the eighteen months or thereabouts that I have been in this disagreeable plight I have already learned to put up with it. I am already compounding with this colicky existence. I am finding a source of comfort and hope in it. Men are so accustomed to hug their miserable existence, that no state is so wretched that they will not accept it, provided they live.

Listen to Maecenas :

> Though I be lame in hand and foot,
> Though every tooth in my head be loose,
> So long as life remains, 'tis well. (cited by SENECA.)

And Tamerlane cloaked under a foolish kind of humanity the fantastic cruelty which he exercised upon the lepers, by putting to death all he heard of, ' to deliver them, as he said, from the painful life they were living '. For there was not one among them who would not rather have been a leper three times over than not to live.

And Antisthenes the Stoic being very ill and calling out, ' Who will deliver me from these evils ? ' Diogenes, who had come to see him, offered him a knife, saying, ' This, if you mean it, and that very quickly.' ' I do not mean life, he replied, I mean my evils.'

The sufferings that merely affect us through the soul afflict me much less than they do most others. Partly by estimation, for the world deems many things to be dreadful, or avoidable at the cost of life, which to me are wellnigh a matter of indifference. Partly from a dull insensibility to accidents which do not hit me point-blank ; and that insensibility I regard as one of the best parts of my nature. But bodily and really essential sufferings I feel very acutely. And yet, when formerly I dimly foresaw them, with a sight enfeebled and mollified by the enjoyment of the happy and prolonged health and repose that God had given me, for the best part of my life, I conceived them in imagination to be so unbearable that in truth my fear of them was greater than my present suffering. Wherefore I am ever more confirmed in this belief, that most of the faculties of the soul, as we exercise them, disturb the peace of life more than they promote it.

I am at grips with the worst, the most sudden, the most painful, the most fatal and most irremediable of all diseases. I have already experienced five or six very long and painful attacks of it. And yet, unless I flatter myself, even in this condition there is something endurable for a man whose soul is free from the fear of death, and free from the menaces, conclusions, and consequences which the doctors keep dinning into our ears. But the pain itself is not so violent, so sharp and piercing, as to drive a sober-minded man to rage and despair. I derive at least this advantage from the colic, that it will accomplish what I had not hitherto been able to bring myself to do, that is, to become wholly reconciled and familiarized with death. For, the more it oppresses and troubles me, the less shall I fear to die. I had already gained this much, that I was attached to life only for the sake of life ; my pain will dissolve also this idea.

And God grant that, if its violence exceeds my powers, it
will not in the end drive me to the other, and not less
wicked extreme, to love and desire death !

> Pray not for death, but feel no fear
> When the last hour of life draws near. (MARTIAL.)

Those are two feelings to be dreaded, but the one has its
remedy much more ready to hand than the other.

Moreover, I have always regarded as affectation that
precept that so sternly and precisely tells us to put on
a good face, a disdainful and indifferent mien, when suffering
pain. Why does Philosophy, who is concerned only with
what is vital and effective, waste her time over these
external appearances ? [1] Let her leave that charge to
actors and teachers of rhetoric, who set so great a value on
our gestures. Let her boldly condone this cowardice of the
vocal organs, and lay the blame on the pain, as long as it
does not come from the heart or the seat of the passions ;
let her place those voluntary lamentations in the same
category with sighs, sobs, palpitations, pallors, which
Nature has put beyond our control. As long as the heart
shows no fear, words no despair, let her rest content !
What matter whether we wring our hands, as long as we do
not wring our thoughts ? She trains us for ourselves, not
for others ; to be, not to seem. Let her stop short at
governing our understanding, which she has taken upon
herself to instruct. During the attacks of the colic let her
keep our minds capable of self-control, and of going their
accustomed way, combating and subduing pain, and not
shamefully grovelling at its feet ; excited and heated, not

[1] The earlier editions had this passage in place of what follows : As if
she were training men for the acts of a comedy, or as if it were within
her jurisdiction to hinder the movements and alterations which we are
by Nature forced to accept. Let her then prevent Socrates from blushing
with shame or emotion, from winking his eyes when threatened by a blow,
from shaking and sweating in a fever. The painting of Poetry, which is
free and does what it pleases, dares not forbid even tears in the persons
she wishes to represent as perfect and accomplished :

> Who are so pained,
> They bite their hands, they bite their lips,
> Bedew their cheeks with plenteous tears. (ARIOSTO.)

They should leave this charge to those who make a profession of regulating our expressions and demeanour.

subdued and overthrown, in the struggle ; able, to a certain degree, to converse and communicate with others.

In so extreme a calamity it is cruelty to expect so composed a bearing. If we play the game it is no great matter that we make a wry face. If the body finds a relief in lamenting, let it lament. If agitation pleases it, let it tumble and toss at its pleasure. If by raising the voice with greater violence the pain appears to evaporate a little (as some physicians say that it helps a woman in child-birth), or if it distracts its anguish, let it shout at the top of its voice. We need not command our voice to shout, but let us not forbid it. Epicurus not only permits his sage to shout in pain, but he advises it. *Even the pugilists groan when they strike with the cestus, because in throwing out the voice the whole body is on the stretch, and the blow is driven home with greater force* (Cicero). We have enough to do to contend with the evil, without labouring over these superfluous rules.

I have said all this in excuse of those we generally see raging and storming under the shocks and attacks of this disease. For my part I have hitherto suffered them a little more patiently [and I stop short at groaning, without braying]. Not, however, that I put any great constraint upon myself to maintain this seemly exterior, for I make little account of such an advantage. In this respect I yield to the pain as much as it requires ; but either my pangs are not so excessive, or I bring more fortitude to them than the average man. I moan, I fret and fume when I am in the throes of a sharp attack, but I never yield to despair, like this man :

> Whose groans, bewailings, and whose bitter cries
> With grief incessant rend the very skies.
>
> (ATTIUS, quoted by Cicero.)

I watch myself in the thick of the onslaught, and I have always found that I was capable of speaking, thinking, and answering as sanely as at any other time, but not so consistently, the pain disturbing and distracting my thoughts. When those present think I am most stricken, and refrain from troubling me, I often test my powers, and myself broach a subject most remote from my condition. I can do anything by a sudden effort, but it must not continue long.

O why have I not the faculty of that dreamer in Cicero, who, dreaming he was embracing a young girl, found that he had discharged his stone in the sheets ! Mine strangely diswenches me !

In the intervals of excessive pain, when my ureters languish without stinging so sharply, I immediately return to my normal condition ; [1] since it is only my body and senses that have been alarmed, and not my soul. And this I certainly owe to the care with which, with the help of reason, I prepare my mind for such attacks :

> To me no toil strange or unlooked-for comes.
> All things have I forecast, and in my mind
> Traversed ere seen. (VIRGIL.)

Yet I have been rather rudely tried, for a beginner, and with a very sudden and very violent change for the worse, having dropped all at once, from a very easy and very happy state of life, into the most painful and uneasy that can be imagined. For, besides that it is a disease that is in itself greatly to be dreaded, its beginnings have been much ruder and harder in me than they are wont to be. The attacks recur so frequently that I hardly ever feel in perfect health. Yet I have hitherto kept myself in such good spirits that, so long as they continue so, I am in rather better condition of life than a thousand others, who have neither fever nor any other infirmity except those that, for lack of judgement, they bring upon themselves.

There is a certain kind of subtle humility, which is born of presumption, as for instance, this, That we confess our ignorance in some things, and are so polite as to admit that there are, in the works of Nature, certain properties and conditions of which we do not perceive, the means and causes of which we are unable to discover. By this honest and conscientious declaration we hope to gain the advantage of being believed in respect of those things we say we do understand. We have no need to go and sift miracles and things that appear strange and obscure ; it appears to me that among the things we commonly see there are some so strange and incomprehensible that they surpass all the mysteries of miracles.

[1] The earlier editions add : I talk, I laugh, I study, without emotion or alteration.

What a wonderful thing it is that that drop of seed, from which we are produced, bears in itself the impressions, not only of the bodily shape, but of the thoughts and inclinations of our fathers ! Where can that drop of fluid harbour such an infinite number of forms ? And how do they convey those resemblances, so heedless and irregular in their progress, that the great-grandson shall be like his great-grandfather, the nephew like his uncle ?

In the family of Lepidus, at Rome, there were three, not consecutive but at intervals, who were born with the same eye covered with a cartilage. At Thebes there was a family who from their mothers' womb bore the picture of a lance-head ; and he who was not born so was regarded as illegitimate.[1] Aristotle tells of a certain nation among whom wives were held in common, that they allotted the children to the fathers by their resemblance.

It may be supposed that I owe this stony propensity to my father, for he died grievously tormented with a large stone in the bladder. He was not sensible of his disease until the sixty-seventh year of his age. Before then he had neither menace nor symptom of it, either in his kidneys, sides, or any other part, having lived till that time in a happy state of health, and very little subject to infirmities. He lived another seven years with this malady, dragging out to the end a very painful existence. I was born twenty-five years or more before his disease came on, and during the time of his best state, the third of his children in order of birth.

Where was the propensity to this defect hatching all this time ? And when he was so far from the infirmity, how could that small part of his substance, of which I was constructed, carry for its part so great an impression ? And how did it remain so concealed that I did not begin to be sensible of it until forty-five years after, the only one hitherto among so many brothers and sisters, and all of one mother ? If any man will enlighten me about the course of this mischief, I will believe him in any other miracles he pleases ; provided that he does not put me off with a theory, as they generally do, that is much more obscure and fantastic than the thing itself.

[1] This last touch was evidently imagined by Montaigne, for Plutarch, his authority for the tale, makes no mention of illegitimacy.

I hope the doctors will excuse my freedom a little, for it is by this same fatal infusion and insinuation that I have inherited my hatred and contempt of their science. My antipathy to their art is hereditary. My father lived to be seventy-four, my grandfather sixty-nine, my great-grand-father to nearly eighty, without ever tasting any kind of physic ; and with them, whatever was not in ordinary use took the place of a drug.

Medicine is built up on examples and experience ; so is my theory.

Is not that a very positive and very serviceable experi-ence ? I doubt whether they will find me three on their case-books, who were born and bred, and who died at the same hearth, under the same roof, and lived so long under their directions. They must grant me this, that, if not reason, at least Fortune is on my side. Well, with the physicians, Fortune is stronger than reason. Let them not take me at a disadvantage, let them not threaten me, pros-trate as I am at this moment ; that would be foul play. Besides, to tell the truth, I have gained sufficient advantage over them by my family examples, although they stop there. In human affairs there is not usually so much constancy.

This experience of ours has endured for two centuries, wanting but eighteen years ; for the first of them was born in the year 1402. It is indeed but reasonable that this experience should begin to fail us. They cannot now upbraid me for the calamity that has now seized me by the throat ; is it not enough for me to have lived in good health for forty-seven years ? Though it should be the end of my career, it is one of the longest.

My ancestors, by some natural and mysterious instinct, loathed physic ; for my father was horrified at the very sight of drugs. The Seigneur de Gaviac, my uncle on the father's side, an ecclesiastic, who was delicate from his birth and yet made his sickly life hold for sixty-seven years, having once been taken with a violent and dangerous con-tinued fever, the doctors ordered him to be plainly told that unless he called in their aid (they call Aid what is more often Hindrance), he would infallibly be a dead man. The good man, terrified though he was by that dreadful sentence, replied, ' Then I am a dead man.' But God soon after falsified the prognostic.

The last of the brothers (there were four of them), the Sieur de Bussaguet, and the last by many years, alone submitted himself to their art, by reason, I think, of his connexion with the other arts, for he was a Councillor in the Court of Parliament ; but with so little success that, although he seemed to be of a stronger constitution, he died long before the others, with the exception of one, the Sieur de Saint-Michel.

It may be that I have inherited from them this natural antipathy to medicine ; but if that was the only reason, I should have tried to overcome it. For all those unreasonable prejudices we are born with are unsound ; they are a kind of disease we must combat. It may be that I had this propensity, but I have supported and fortified it by arguments, which have confirmed me in my opinions. For I also hate that idea of rejecting medicine on account of its bitter taste. That would hardly be in accordance with my mental attitude, since I hold health to be worth purchasing at the price of all the most painful cauteries and incisions that can be applied.

And I agree with Epicurus when he says that sensual pleasures are to be shunned if they are succeeded by greater pains, and that those pains are to be sought that are followed by greater pleasures.

Health is a precious thing, the only thing indeed that deserves to be pursued at the expense not only of time, sweat, labour, worldly goods, but of life itself ; since without it life becomes a burden and an affliction. Without it, pleasures, wisdom, knowledge, and virtue lose their colour and fade away ; and to the most forcible and laboured arguments that Philosophy would impress upon us to the contrary, we have but to oppose the idea of Plato stricken with the falling sickness or an apoplexy, and, on this supposition, challenge him to call to his aid the rich and noble faculties of his mind. To my mind no way that leads us to health can be rugged, no means dearly bought.

But I have several other ways of looking at it, which make me strangely distrustful of all that lumber. I do not deny that there may be some art in it ; that there are, among the many works of Nature, things proper for the preservation of our health ; that is certain. I know well that there are certain simples that moisten, certain others that dry up ; I know by experience both that horse-radish induces flatulence, and that senna-leaves relax the bowels. I have several other experiences of the same kind, as I know that mutton nourishes and wine heats me ; and Solon said, ' that eating, like the other drugs, is a physic against the disease of hunger '. I do not deny the use we derive from the things of this world, nor do I doubt the power and fecundity of Nature, and that it may be applied to our needs. I can clearly see that pikes and swallows are well off under her protection.

I distrust the inventions of our mind, of our learning and art, for whose sake we have abandoned Nature and her rules, and are unable to keep within the bounds of moderation.

As we call Justice the fortuitous hotch-potch of the first laws that come to hand, and the practical dispensing of them, which is often very foolish and unjust ; and as they who ridicule and condemn the application of them have no intention of disparaging that noble virtue, but only condemn the abuse and profanation of that sacred name, so, in medicine, I indeed honour that glorious name, its intentions, its promises, so useful to the human race ; but, as it is understood with us, I neither honour nor esteem it.

In the first place experience makes me dread it ; for there is no sort of people, as far as my knowledge of them goes, who are so liable to fall ill, and take so long to cure, as those who are under the thumb of medicine. Their very health is impaired and undermined by the constraint of diet. The doctors are not content with dominating sickness ; they make health sickly, to guard against their patients' ever escaping from their authority. Do they not argue that perfect and continuous good health means a great sickness in the future ?

I have been ill pretty often, and without their help my illnesses (and I have experienced nearly every kind) have been as easy to bear and as short as those of any other person ; and yet I have never interfered with them by taking their bitter prescriptions. My health, when I have it, is full and free, without any rules, and without any other schooling than that of my habits and my pleasure. Any place suits me to stay in, for I need no other comforts when ill than those I need when I am well. I am not frightened at the idea of being without a physician, apothecary, and medical aid, which to most men is a greater affliction than the illness. What ! do the doctors themselves give any evidence, by living longer and happier, of any manifest effect of their skill ?

There is no nation that has not existed many centuries without medicine, and those the first ages, that is to say, the best and happiest. And to this day a tenth part of the world has no use for it. There is a vast number of people who have no knowledge of it, and they live longer and in better health than they do here. And with us the common people can happily dispense with it. The Romans had existed six hundred years before they received it ; but after making trial of it they drove it from their city at the instance of Cato the Censor, who demonstrated how easily he could do without it, having lived for eighty-five years and kept his wife alive to an extreme old age, not indeed without physic, but certainly without a physician. For everything we find conducive to a healthy life may be called physic.

He kept his family in health, it seems, according to Plutarch, by the use of hare ; [1] as the Arcadians, according to Pliny, cured all maladies with cows' milk. And the Libyans, says Herodotus, generally enjoy an uncommon good health by observing this custom that, when their children have reached the age of four, they cauterize and burn the veins of the head and temples, by which means they cut off all the defluxions of rheum for their whole lives.

And the villagers of this neighbourhood, for all emergencies, use only the strongest wine they can procure, mixed with plenty of saffron and spice ; all this with a like result.

And, to tell the truth, what after all is the end and result of all this diversity and confusion of prescriptions but to void the bowels, which a thousand household simples will do ? And yet I do not know that this is so beneficial as they declare, and that our nature does not require that the excrements should remain for a certain part, as do the lees

[1] I quote, without comment, the passage from Plutarch : He himself had a book full of recipes, according to which he used to physic and regulate the diet of any who fell sick in his house, being careful never to allow the patient to fast, but making him eat salad, with ducks, pigeons and hares, which he said were light food and suitable for sick persons, except that it often happened that those who ate of them suffered from nightmare.

of wine for its preservation.[1] You often see healthy people, through some strange accident, taken with a sudden attack of vomiting and diarrhoea, attended with a copious evacuation of the bowels, without any preceding need and without any succeeding benefit, but rather feeling much the worse for it.

It was from the great Plato that I lately learned that of three kinds of motions that are natural to us, the last and worst is a purge, and that no man who is not a fool ought to undergo it except in the extremest necessity. We disturb and irritate the evil by contrary oppositions. It should be gradually diminished and brought to an end by our manner of living. The violent gripings caused by the drug and the illness are always to our prejudice, since the two fight it out in our bodies, and the drug is an unreliable aid, naturally inimical to our health, and having no access in our domain except through disturbance.

Let us leave things to go their own way. The Order which takes care of fleas and moles will also take care of men, if they have the same patience to allow themselves to be governed as fleas and moles. In vain do we shout ' Gee up ' ; we shall only make ourselves hoarse and not advance a step. That Order is proud and pitiless. Our fear and despair disgust her and keep her from coming to our relief, instead of inviting her. She owes it to the malady, as well as to health, to let it take its course. She will not allow herself to be bribed in favour of the one, to the prejudice of the other's rights ; that would mean disorder. Let us follow, in God's name, let us follow ! She guides those who follow ; those who will not follow she will drag along together with their fury and their physic. Get a purge prescribed for your brain ; it will be better employed than in your stomach.

A Lacedemonian was asked what had made him live so long in good health : ' Ignorance of medicine,' he replied. And the Emperor Hadrian kept exclaiming on his death-bed, ' that the crowd of doctors had killed him '. A poor wrestler took up medicine. ' Bravo, said Diogenes, you are right ; you can now throw those who once threw you.'

But they have this good fortune, according to Nicocles,

---

[1] This is of course rank heresy to the Faculty ; but after nearly seventy years' experience of life the translator has come to the conclusion that there is at least something in what Montaigne says.

that ' the sun shines on their successes, and the earth hides their failures '. And besides, they have a very useful knack of taking advantage of all kinds of happenings ; for it is the privilege of the Faculty to take the credit for the good and salutary things that Fortune or Nature, or some other extraneous cause (and there is an endless number of them) produces in us. All the happy effects that the patient feels, who is under their care, is due to them. The causes which have cured me, which cure a thousand others who do not call in the doctors, they usurp in the case of their subjects.

When an unfortunate accident occurs, either they will disclaim all responsibility, and lay the blame on the patient ; and they take care never to be at a loss for any number of frivolous reasons, such as, ' he must have left his arm uncovered ; he has heard the rattling of a coach,

> The wagons crossing in the narrow streets ; (JUVENAL.)

somebody has opened the window ; he has been lying on his left side ; he has been thinking of something painful '. In short, a word, a look, a dream, appear to them a safe excuse for shifting the blame.

Or, if they so please, they will even take advantage of this relapse and turn it to their account, by this other trick which can never fail them : When the disease has become aggravated by their applications, they put us off with the assurance that it would have been very much worse but for their remedies. If they have precipitated them out of a chill into a quotidian fever, ' he might have had a continued fever, but for me '. There is no risk of their doing their business badly, since the loss turns to their profit. In truth they are right to require their patients to place an implicit trust in them ; and it must indeed be a really very compliant trust that will believe things so hard to swallow.

Plato said very appropriately that Physicians were the only men that might lie in all freedom, since our health depends on the falsity and emptiness of their promises.

Aesop, an author of most rare excellence, of whom few people discover all the charm, humorously illustrates the tyrannical authority which they usurp over poor souls enfeebled and cast down by sickness and fear. He tells of a doctor questioning his patient about the operation of his physic. ' I have been sweating a great deal.' ' That 's good,' said the doctor. Another time, when he asked him how he felt after his medicine, he said, ' I have been very cold and shivery.' ' That 's very good,' said the doctor. He asked him a third time how he was. ' I am all swollen and puffed up, as if I had dropsy.' ' That 's splendid ! ' said the doctor. One of his friends presently coming to inquire after his condition : ' Really, my friend, I am getting on so well that I am on the point of death.'

In Egypt they had a juster law, which compelled the physician to take a patient under his care, for the first three days, at the latter's risk and chance ; when the three days were over, it was at his own risk. For why was Aesculapius, their patron, struck by a thunderbolt for having brought the dead Helen [1] back to life :

> Then, wroth that mortal should from shades of hell
> Rise to the light of life, the Almighty Sire
> With his own levin-bolt to Stygian wave
> Thrust down the finder of such craft and cure,
> The Phoebus-born ; (VIRGIL.)

when his followers are absolved, who dispatch so many living souls to death ?

A physician was boasting to Nicocles of the great authority of his art. ' It must be so indeed, said Nicocles, when it can kill so many people with impunity.'

For the rest, if they had consulted me, they would have enveloped their art in more sanctity and mystery. They began well enough, but they did not end as well. It was a good beginning to make gods and demons the originators of their science, to adopt a language of their own, and a writing of their own ; although Philosophy may think that it is folly to advise a man for his good by a way that is unintelligible. *As if a physician should order his patient to take ' an earth-born, grass-crawling, house-bearing, bloodless creature ' * [2] (Cicero).

It was a good rule of their art, and one that accompanies all fantastic, empty, and supernatural arts, that the patient's faith must anticipate, by good hope and confidence, the

---

[1] The editions published after 1588 substitute Hippolytus, who was brought back to life at the request of Diana. According to another account, Aesculapius was killed by Zeus at the bidding of Pluto, who found that the inhabitants of Hades were dwindling.

[2] i.e. a decoction of snails.

efficacity of their treatment. And they cling so firmly to this rule that they regard the most ignorant and incompetent doctor as more fit to treat one who has confidence in him, than the most experienced, if he is a stranger.

Even the choice of most of their drugs is in some sort mysterious and divine : the left foot of a tortoise, the urine of a lizard, an elephant's dung, a mole's liver, blood drawn from under the right wing of a white pigeon ; and for us who have the stone (so scornfully do they take advantage of our misery !), the pulverized droppings of a rat, and other such tomfooleries that are more suggestive of magic and spells than of a serious science. Not to mention their pills, to be taken in uneven numbers, the setting apart of certain days and festivals in the year, of certain hours for gathering the herbs of their ingredients, the grim scowl, the wise and learned looks and demeanour which they put on, and which even Pliny remarked upon with derision.

But what I mean to say is that, having made so good a beginning, they were wrong in not making their meetings and consultations more mysterious and secret. No profane person should be admitted to them, any more than to the secret ceremonies of Aesculapius. The result of this error is that their irresolution, the weakness of their arguments, their guesses and grounds, the fierceness of their disputes, revealing nothing but hatred, jealousy, and self-consideration, coming to the knowledge of all the world, a man must be marvellously blind not to see that he runs great risks at their hands.

Who ever heard of a doctor using a colleague's prescription without taking something from, or adding something to it ? Thereby they sufficiently betray their practice, and make it plain to us that they consider their reputation, and consequently their profit, more than their patient's interests.

He was a wiser physician who in ancient times laid down the rule that only one doctor should undertake to treat a patient ; for, if he does no good, the failure of a single man cannot be a very great reproach to the medical faculty. And, on the other hand, if he happens to make a lucky guess, his glory will be the greater. Whilst if there are many of them, they bring the profession into disrepute at every turn, since they more frequently do harm than good.

They ought to be satisfied with the perpetual discord we

find in the theories of the chief masters and the ancient writers on this science, which is known only to people who are well read in books, without betraying to the people the controversies and inconsistencies of judgement which they still keep alive among themselves.

Would you like an example of the ancient controversy in medicine ?

Herophilus places the original cause of diseases in the humours ;

Erasistratus, in the blood of the arteries ;

Asclepiades, in the invisible atoms gliding through our pores ;

Alcmaeon, in the exuberance or deficiency of the bodily powers ;

Diocles, in the inequality of the elements of the body, and in the quality of the air we breathe ;

Strato, in the abundance, crudity, and corruption of the food we take ; and

Hippocrates lodges it in the spirits.

There is a friend of theirs, whom they know better than I, who exclaims in this connexion, ' That the most important science we practise, as having charge of our health and preservation, is unfortunately the most uncertain and most confused, and is more disturbed by changes than any other.' [1]

There is no great danger in miscalculating the height of the sun or the fraction of some astronomical computation ; but here, where our whole being is at stake, it is not a mark of wisdom to abandon ourselves to the mercy of so many winds blowing from different quarters.

Before the Peloponnesian war not much was heard of this science. Hippocrates brought it into repute. All that he established Chrysippus overthrew. After him, Erasistratus, Aristotle's grandson, overthrew all that Chrysippus had written about it. After them appeared the Empirics, who adopted quite a different method from that of their predecessors in their practice of the art. When the credit of these latter began to grow stale, Herophilus set another sort of practice on foot, which Asclepiades in his turn combated and annihilated. By turns the theories of Themison gained authority, then Musa's, and after them those of Vectius

[1] Pliny.

Valens, a physician who became famous through his intimacy with Messalina. In Nero's time the empire of medicine fell into the hands of Thessalus, who condemned and abolished all that had been accepted before him. The latter's theories were upset by Crinas of Marseilles, who reintroduced the practice of regulating all medicinal operations by the Ephemerides, and motions of the stars ; of eating, drinking, and sleeping at such times as were pleasing to the Moon and Mercury. His authority was soon after supplanted by Charinus, a physician of the same city of Marseilles. This man opposed not only the older science of medicine, but also the hot baths which had been generally in use for so many centuries. He made the men bathe in cold water, even in winter, and plunged his patients into the natural water of streams.

Until Pliny's day no Roman had ever deigned to practise medicine ; it was in the hands of foreigners and Greeks, as, among us French, it is practised by Latinists.[1] For, as a very great physician has said, we are loath to take the medicine we understand, or the drugs we gather. If those countries from which we import our guaiacum, sarsaparilla, and China root have any physicians, we may imagine, if they follow our example of valuing a thing for its strangeness, rarity, and dearness, how greatly they must prize our cabbages and parsley. For who would dare to despise things brought from such a distance, at the risk of so long and perilous a voyage ?

Since those ancient changes in medicine there has been an endless number of others even to our days, and for the most part complete and universal changes, like those introduced in our time by Paracelsus, Fioravanti, and Argenterius. For they alter not only a prescription, but, as I am told, the whole disposition and order of the body of physic, accusing all who have professed it hitherto of ignorance and imposture. I leave you to imagine where the poor patient comes in.

If only we were sure, when they make mistakes, that they do us no harm, even if they do us no good, it would be quite a reasonable bargain to risk gaining something, without incurring the danger of losing.

[1] Perhaps those who assumed Latin names, like Paracelsus—whose real name was von Hohenheim—or who used a Latin jargon.

Aesop in one of his Fables tells how a man who had bought a Moorish slave, thinking his colour was accidental and brought on by the ill usage of his former master, had him very carefully medicined with many baths and potions. The result was that the Moor was not a whit cured of his swarthy complexion, but entirely lost his previous good health.

How often we hear the doctors charging one another with the death of their patients! I remember an epidemic disease, of a very dangerous and fatal nature, raging in the towns round about me a few years ago. When the storm, which had swept away an endless number of people, had passed over, one of the most reputed physicians of the whole district published a pamphlet on the subject, in which he changed his mind about the blood-lettings which had been practised, and confessed that that was one of the chief causes of the mortality which ensued. Moreover, the writers of the faculty hold that there is no medicine that does not contain some hurtful ingredients; hence, if those which benefit us also do us some harm, what must those do that are totally misapplied?

For my own part, though there were nothing else to be considered, I am of opinion that for those who loathe the taste of medicine, to force it down at such inconvenient times and with so much aversion, must have a very danger-ous and prejudicial effect. And I believe it must try the patient's constitution to an alarming degree at a time when he has so much need of rest. Besides, when we consider the grounds on which they generally diagnose the cause of our maladies, they are so slight and so ticklish that I argue therefrom that a very little error in the dispensing of their drugs may do us a great deal of mischief.

Now, if the doctor's mistake is dangerous, we are in a very bad way; for it is very unlikely but he will often fall into the same error. He has too many details and circumstances to consider before deciding upon his treatment: he should know his patient's constitution, his temperament, his hu-mours, his inclinations, his actions, even his thoughts and ideas. He must make sure of external circumstances, of the nature of the place, of the atmospherical and weather con-ditions, of the position of the planets and their influences. He must know the causes of the disease, the symptoms, the effects, and the critical days.

In the matter of drugs he must know their weight, their strength, the place of their origin, their appearance, their age, and the right way to administer them ; and he must know how all the parts are to be proportioned and related to each other to create a perfect symmetry. Wherein if he makes the slightest error, if there is a single one of these springs that is twisted awry, it is enough to kill us.

Heaven knows how difficult it is to know most of these details ; for how will he discover, for example, the true symptom of the disease, when every disease is capable of showing an infinite number of symptoms ? How often do they not doubt and dispute together about the interpretation of the urine ! Otherwise, why all those continual altercations over the diagnosis of the malady ? How can we excuse the error they so often fall into of taking fox for sable ? In the diseases that I have had, when there was the slightest doubt, I have never found three of them to agree. I am readier to note examples which concern myself.

Recently at Paris a gentleman was operated upon by order of the physicians, and in the bladder they found no more stone than in the palm of his hand. And in the same city a Bishop, with whom I was very friendly, was strongly urged by most of the doctors he consulted to allow himself to be cut ; and I myself helped to persuade him, on the faith of others. When he was dead and opened it was found that he only had kidney trouble. They have less excuse in the case of this malady, since it is in some sort palpable. Hence it appears to me that surgery is much more certain, since it can see and feel what it is doing. There is less conjecture and guess-work ; whereas the physicians have nothing in the way of a vaginal speculum which might enable them to look into our brain, our lungs, and liver.

The very promises of medicine are incredible. For, as they have to provide against different and contrary ills which often afflict us at the same time and are almost necessarily related together, such as inflammation of the liver and a chill on the stomach, they would make us believe that one of the ingredients of the physic will warm the stomach and another cool the liver. One of them has received its orders to proceed directly to the kidneys, nay even to the bladder, without spreading its action elsewhere, and, by its occult property, to preserve its power and virtue on that long journey, fraught with obstacles, until it reaches the place it is intended to benefit. One will dry the brain, another moisten the lungs.

Having made up a potion of all that bundle of ingredients, is it not a kind of delusion to expect that the different virtues will divide and sort themselves from out that mixture and confusion, to hasten on their different errands ? I should very much fear that they would lose or exchange their labels, and mistake their quarters. And who can suppose that in this liquid confusion those properties will not corrupt, disturb, and vitiate one another ? To make matters worse, the making up of this prescription is entrusted to another functionary, to whose mercy and good faith we have again to abandon our lives !

As we have our doublet-makers and our breeches-makers to clothe us, and are the better served by them because each of them meddles only with his own province, and his skill is more restricted and concentrated than that of an all-round tailor ; and as, in the matter of food, the nobles, in order to be better served, have distinct functionaries for making their soups and roasting their meats, which a cook who takes the whole charge could not succeed in doing so perfectly ; so the Egyptians were right to reject this trade of general practitioner, and to break up the profession. To each disease and each part of the body its own workman ; for it was more properly and less confusedly treated when each one was concerned only with his own specialty.

It never occurs to our doctors that he who sees to all sees to nothing ; that the entire government of this little world is beyond their digestion. Whilst they were afraid to arrest the progress of a dysentery, in order not to bring on a fever, they killed me a friend [1] who was better than the whole pack of them put together. They place their own guesses in the scales against the present evils ; and in order not to cure the brain to the prejudice of the stomach, they injure the stomach and make the brain worse by jumbling up their quarrelsome drugs.

With regard to the variety and feebleness of the reasonings of this profession, they are more apparent than in any other :

Aperients are beneficial to a man with the stone, because

[1] Étienne de la Boëtie.

by opening and dilating the passages they help forward the sticky matter of which the gravel and calculi are formed, and convey downward the matter that is beginning to collect and harden in the kidneys.

Aperients are dangerous to a man with the stone, because by opening and dilating the passages they convey the matter that forms the gravel towards the kidneys, which by their nature are apt to seize upon it, so that they must necessarily arrest a great part of that which was carried to them.

Moreover, if there happens to be some body that is a little too big to pass through all those narrows that still have to be passed in order to be expelled, that body, being stirred up by the aperient and thrown into those narrow channels, will stop them up and bring on a certain and very painful death.

Their advice with regard to regimen is equally wobbly :

It is a good thing to pass water frequently, for we know by experience that by allowing it to stagnate, the excrements and lees which form the matter of which the stone is built up in the bladder, have time to settle.

It is a good thing not to pass water frequently ; for the heavy excrements it drags along with it will not be carried away without violence, as we see by experience that a swiftly rolling torrent sweeps and cleans the places it passes over much more effectually than a gently flowing and sluggish river.

Similarly, it is a good thing to have frequent intercourse with women, for that opens the passages and carries away the gravel and sand ; it is also very bad, because it inflames, wearies and weakens the kidneys.

It is a good thing to take hot baths, since that relaxes and softens the places where the sand and stone settle ; it is also a bad thing, because the application of external heat assists the kidneys in baking, hardening, and petrifying, the matter there stored up.

For those who are taking the baths it is more wholesome to eat little in the evening, that the waters they have to drink next morning may act more effectually when the stomach is empty and unhampered.

On the other hand it is better to eat little at dinner, in order not to hinder the action of the water, which has not yet had its due effect, and not to overload the stomach so immediately after that other labour, and to leave the duty of digestion to the night, which is more equal to it than the day, when body and mind are in perpetual movement and action.

That is how they go on trifling and juggling with their reasons at our expense. And they cannot provide me with a proposition to which I could not construct a contrary one of equal force.

Let them no longer rail against those who, in their troubles, allow themselves to be gently guided by their appetites and the counsel of Nature, and resign themselves to the common lot.

In the course of my travels I have seen almost all the famed baths in Christendom ; and for some years past have begun to make use of them. For I look upon bathing as generally salubrious, and believe that we suffer in health to no small degree through having left off the custom, which was universally observed in former times by almost all nations, and is still observed by many, of washing the body every day. And I cannot imagine but that we are much the worse for having our limbs so encrusted and our pores stopped up with grime.

And with regard to the drinking of the waters, it is in the first place fortunate for me that they are in no way hostile to my taste ; in the second place they are simple and natural, and are at least attended with no danger, even if they do no good. Which is warranted, I take it, by the large number of people of every sort and constitution who are gathered together at the baths. And, although I have not felt any extraordinary or miraculous effects from them, but rather, after investigating a little more carefully than is usually done, I have found all such reports of miraculous cures which circulate in those places, and are believed (the world generally being easily gulled into believing what it wishes to believe), to be ill-grounded and untrue ; yet I have hardly met any people who have been the worse for taking the waters, and nobody can, without malice, deny them this, that they stimulate the appetite, help the digestion, and inspire us with fresh energy, unless we go there in too weak a condition, which I would dissuade anybody from doing. They are not supposed to restore a heavy ruin, but they may prop up a slight leaning, or prevent a threatening deterioration.

He who does not bring with him sufficient energy to be able to enjoy the pleasure of the society he will find there, and the promenades and exercises to which the beauty of the places where these springs are usually situated invites us, will no doubt lose the best and surest part of their effect. For this reason I have hitherto selected, for residence and use of the waters, those baths which are most pleasantly situated, and which offer the most advantages in the way of lodging, food and society. Such are, in France, the baths of Bagnères ; on the frontier between Germany and Lorraine, those of Plombières ; in Switzerland, those of Baden ; in Tuscany those of Lucca, and especially those of Della Villa, which I have used most often and at different seasons.

Each nation has its own ideas regarding their use, and their rules and methods of taking advantage of them, all different, and, as far as my experience goes, with about the same result. In Germany the drinking of them is not practised at all ; the Germans bathe for all maladies, and will lie in the water like frogs almost from sun to sun. In Italy, when they drink nine days, they will bathe at least for thirty ; and they usually drink the water mixed with other drugs, to assist its operation. Here we are ordered to take exercise, to digest the water ; there they are kept in bed, where they have taken it, until they have voided it, the stomach and feet being kept continually warm. As the Germans are peculiar in their general practice of blood-letting, by means of leeches or cupping-glasses after scarification, in the bath ; so the Italians have their *doccie*,[1] which are certain drops of hot water which are conducted through pipes, and will bathe, for an hour in the morning, another hour after dinner, for the space of a month, either the head or the stomach, or some other part of the body that is under treatment.

There is an endless variety of other customs in each country ; or, more correctly speaking, there is hardly any resemblance between the different customs.

So we see that this branch of medicine, to which alone I have submitted myself, although it is the least artificial, yet has its good share in the confusion and uncertainty which is seen in all the other branches of the art.

[1] Anglice, shower-baths.

The poets are able to express all their meaning with greater emphasis and charm ; witness these two epigrams :

A doctor touched the statue of great Jove ;
No marble could withstand the awful shock.
To-day, removed from out the sacred fane,
They buried him, though God he was, and stone.   (AUSONIUS.)

And the other :

He bathed and dined with me, he seemed so bright.
Next morn they found him dead, the luckless wight.
Would'st know what was the cause of his decease ?
He dreamed he saw the quack Hermocrates.   (MARTIAL.)

And now I will tell a couple of stories.

The Baron de Caupene in Chalosse and I share the right of presentation to a benefice in a parish of great extent, called Lahontan, at the foot of our mountains.   It is with the inhabitants of this corner of the world as it is said to be with those in the valley of Angrougne.   They formerly lived their own life, had their own manners, habits, and dress ; they were ruled and governed by certain particular laws and customs handed down from father to son, to which they submitted without any other compulsion than reverence to established usage.   This little state had continued from time immemorial in so happy a condition that no neighbouring judge had ever been put to the trouble of inquiring into their doings, no lawyer had ever been consulted to give them advice, no stranger had ever been called in to settle their quarrels.   And no man in the district had ever been known to beg alms.

They avoided any relations or intercourse with the outer world, in order not to impair the purity of their government, until, as the story goes, one of their number, within living memory, his soul spurred by a noble ambition to bring his name into credit and renown, took it into his head to make one of his sons a Maître Jean or a Maître Pierre,[1] and, having had him taught to write in some neighbouring town, succeeded in turning him into a fine village attorney.

This man, having outgrown himself, began to sneer at the old customs, and to fill the heads of his neighbours with

---

[1] *Maître* is the form of address of all lawyers in France.

stories of the magnificence of the world this side the mountains. The first of his cronies whose goat had lost a horn he advised to demand satisfaction at the hands of the royal justices in the neighbourhood ; and, what with one thing and another, he soon had the whole place corrupted.

On the heels of this mischief they say that another presently followed, of worse consequence, through a doctor who conceived a desire to marry one of their daughters and settle among them. This fellow began by teaching them the names of fevers, colds, and abscesses, the situation of the heart, the liver, and the intestines, of all which they had hitherto been very ignorant. And, in place of the garlic with which they had learned to drive away every kind of disease, however violent or extreme, he led them into the way of taking, for any cough or cold, strange mixtures, and began to trade, not only on their health, but on their death. They declare that only since then have they observed that the night air made their heads heavy, that drinking when they were heated was injurious, that the autumn winds were more unhealthy than those of spring ; that since taking physic they find themselves overwhelmed by a legion of unwonted infirmities, that they are conscious of a general decline in their former vigour, and live only half as long as before. That is the first of my tales.

The other is that, before my gravelly tyranny, having heard several people speak highly of the blood of a he-goat as a heavenly manna sent down in these latter ages for the protection and preservation of the life of man, and hearing it spoken of by intelligent people as a wonderful drug and infallible in its action ; having, moreover, always imagined myself to be liable to any accident that may befall any other man, I took a satisfaction, although I was in perfect health, in providing myself with this miracle. I gave orders for a he-goat to be fed on my estate in accordance with the recipe ; for he has to be removed during the hottest days of summer, and be given nothing but laxative herbs to eat and white wine to drink.

I happened to return home on the day he was to be killed. They came and told me that my cook was finding two or three big balls in the paunch, which rattled against each other among the stuff he had eaten. I was curious, and had all this tripe and guts brought to me, and had the large,

thick skin opened in my presence. There came out three
big lumps, light as sponges, so that they appeared to be
hollow ; hard and firm however on the outside, and spotted
with several dull colours. One was perfectly round, the size
of a short bowl ; [1] the other two rather smaller, not so
perfectly round, but apparently becoming so. Having made
inquiries of people accustomed to open those animals, I
found that the case was unusual and rare. It is probable
that these stones are cousins to ours ; and, if that is so, it is
very hopeless for those afflicted with gravel to expect a cure
from the blood of an animal that is itself about to die of a like
disease. For to say that the blood does not share the infection, and that its wonted virtue is not corrupted thereby,
is not to be believed, but rather that nothing is engendered
in a body but by the concurrence and communication of all
the parts. The whole mass works together, although one
part may contribute to it more than another, according to
the diversity of the action. Wherefore it appears very clear
that there was some petrifying property in all the parts of
that goat.

It was not so much from fear of the future, and for myself,
that I felt a curiosity about this experiment ; but it happens
in my household, as in many others, that the women store
up petty drugs of that kind for the benefit of the people
round about, using the same recipe for fifty diseases, and of
such a kind that they do not themselves take, and yet are
triumphant when they turn out successful.

On the whole I honour the physicians ; not in accordance
with the precept,[2] because they are necessary (for to this
text we may oppose another where the prophet reproved
King Asa for having recourse to a physician), but for love
of themselves, having met many honest and likeable men
among them. It is not them I attack, but their art ; and
I do not greatly blame them for taking advantage of our
folly, for the greater part of the world does so. Many professions, both of greater and less repute than theirs, are
built up and rely upon the deception of the public.

---

[1] *Courte boule,* according to Cotgrave ' our round bowle '.   Perhaps
he means the jack, in the game of bowls.

[2] Honour the physician with the honour due unto him for the use
which ye may have of him : for the Lord hath created him.—Ecclesi-
asticus xxxviii. 1.

I call them in to keep me company when I am ill, if they happen to be near at hand, and expect them to talk to me ; and I pay them as others do. I give them leave to order me to cover myself up warm, if I would rather be warm than not ; they may, if they please, choose between lettuces and leeks to make my broth, and order me to drink white wine or claret. And so with all other things that are indifferent to my palate or habit. I know very well that I am doing them no favour, since bitterness and strangeness are incidental to and of the very essence of physic.

Lycurgus ordered the Spartans to drink wine when they were ill. Why ? because they hated the use of it when well. Like a gentleman, a neighbour of mine, who takes it as a very wholesome drug when he has a fever, because naturally he has a deadly hatred of the taste of it.

How many doctors we see who are of my mind, who despise physic for their own account, who adopt a liberal diet, quite contrary to that they prescribe for others ! What is that but shamelessly abusing our simplicity ? For their life and health are no less dear to them than ours is to us, and they would adapt their practice to their preaching, if they did not themselves know its falsity.

It is the fear of death and pain, inability to bear sickness, a frantic and unthinking thirst for cure, that so blinds us ; it is pure cowardice that makes us so credulous and ready to be imposed upon. Yet most people do not so much believe as merely acquiesce. For I hear them finding fault and speaking of it as we do. But in the end they become resigned. ' What should I do ? ' As if impatience were of itself a better remedy than patience ! Is there any one of those who have submitted to this wretched tyranny who does not equally submit to any kind of imposture, who does not put himself at the mercy of any man who has the impudence to promise a cure ?

The Babylonians carried their sick to the public square. The people were the physicians ; every one who passed by was obliged by humanity and civility [1] to inquire into their case, and give them some salutary advice according to his experience. We do pretty much the same. We are ready to believe the mumblings and charms of any old woman of the people ; and for my own part, if I had to take physic, I

[1] Obliged by law, according to Herodotus.

should more readily take this than any other, the more so as there is at least no fear of being harmed by it.

What Homer and Plato said of the Egyptians, that they were all physicians, should be said of all people. There is nobody who does not crack up some remedy and experiment with it upon his neighbour, if he will take his advice. The other day I was in a company where some one or other of my confraternity [1] brought news of a kind of pill made up of a hundred odd ingredients, accurately calculated. There was great rejoicing, and we felt singularly comforted ; for what rock could withstand so numerous a battery ? I understand, however, from those who have tried it, that even the smallest little pebble disdained to be stirred by it.

I cannot take my hand from this paper without adding a word or two upon the claim they make that their experience is a warrant of the infallibility of their drugs. The greater part and, as I think, more than two-thirds of the medicinal virtues consist in the quintessence or occult property of simples, which we can only know by use. For quintessence is no other than a quality of which we cannot, by our reason, find out the cause. Those of their proofs which they say they have acquired by the inspiration of some demon I am content to accept (for, as to miracles, I never touch upon them) ; or again the proofs which are derived from things which we often employ for some other purpose ; as when in the wool in which we are usually clothed they accidentally find some occult dessicative property which cures chilblains on our heels, or when in the radishes we eat for our food they detect some aperient action.

Galen tells us that a leper happened to be cured by drinking some wine out of a vessel into which a viper had crept by chance. In this example we may discover the means and a likely guide to that kind of experiment, as also in those to which the physicians say they have been led by the example of certain animals. But in most of the other experiments to which they say they were led by fortune, and had no other guide but chance, I find it impossible to believe in the progressive course of their investigation.

I imagine a man looking at the endless number of things around him, plants, animals, metals. I cannot think where to make him begin his experiments ; and if his first fancy

[1] The confraternity of sufferers from stone in the bladder.

should light upon an elk's horn, which would need a very pliant and easy faith, he will yet find himself equally perplexed in his second operation. He is confronted with so many diseases and so many circumstances, that, before he has arrived at any certainty as to whither the perfection of his experiments should lead him, human wit will be at the end of its tether. And before he has discovered, among that endless number of things, that it is this horn ; among so many diseases, that it is epilepsy ; so many constitutions, the melancholic ; so many seasons, in winter ; so many nations, the French ; so many ages, old age ; so many celestial changes, the conjunction of Venus and Saturn ; so many parts of the body, the finger ; [1] being guided in all this neither by reason, nor by conjecture, nor by example, nor by divine inspiration, but solely by the movement of chance, it must be a chance that is perfectly artificial, regular and methodical.

And then, even should the cure be effected, how can he be assured that it was not because the disease had reached its crisis, or that it was not the result of chance, or that it was not due to something else he had eaten or drunk or touched on that day, or to the power of his grandmother's prayers ?

Besides, supposing this proof to have been perfect, how many times was it repeated ? How often was this long bead-roll of chances and coincidences strung anew, to infer a certain rule therefrom ? Should it be inferred, by whom ? Among so many millions there will be but three men who trouble about recording their experiments ; will chance have lighted upon just one of these three ? What if another or even a hundred others have had the contrary experiences ? We might perhaps see some daylight if all the reasonings and all the decisions of men were known to us ; but that three witnesses, and those three doctors, should lord it over mankind is against reason. They would have to be chosen and deputed by human nature, and declared our judges by express power of attorney.

[1] To understand the above sentence we may suppose that Montaigne was thinking of an imaginary case, namely, that of an elderly Frenchman of a melancholic temperament who is afflicted with epilepsy. The question is, how did the physicians discover that it could be cured by a preparation of elkshorn to be applied to the finger, in winter and at the conjunction of Venus and Saturn ?

To Madame de Duras

Madame, you found me at work on this chapter when you came to see me the other day. As these trifles may some day fall into your hands, I wish them also to bear witness that the author feels very highly honoured by the favour you will show them. You will find in them the same air and manner that you observed in his conversation. Even though I had been able to adopt some other than my ordinary garb, and some better and more honourable shape, I would not have done so ; for I wish to derive no advantage from these writings but that they shall recall me to your memory as Nature made me. These same qualities and faculties which you are familiar with and have received, Madame, with much more honour and courtesy than they deserve, I will lodge (but without change and alteration) in a compact body which may survive me a few years, or a few days, where you will find them again when you are pleased to refresh your memory of them, without taking too much pains to recall them ; for they are not worth it. I desire you to continue the favour of your friendship for me, for the same qualities by which it was acquired.

It is by no means my aim to be better loved and esteemed dead than living. Tiberius's whim was ridiculous, and yet is shared by many : he was more anxious to extend his fame to posterity than to win the goodwill and esteem of his contemporaries.

If I were one of those to whom the world could owe commendation, I would acquit it, and be paid in advance. Let their praises come quick and heaped-up around me, more thick than long, more full than lasting ; and let them boldly vanish with my knowledge of them, and when their sweet sound shall no longer reach my ears. It would be a foolish fancy, now that I am about to sever my connexion with humanity, to introduce myself to them by a new recommendation.

I make no account of the gifts I have been unable to employ in the conduct of my life. Whatever I may be I wish to be elsewhere than on paper. My skill and industry have been employed to make myself worthy ; my studies, to teach me to do, not to write. I have used all my endeavours to shape my life. That has been my trade and my work. I am less a maker of books than of any other commodity. I have wished for talents in order to gain present and essential advantages, not to store them up and keep them for my heirs.

If a man has any good in him, let it appear in his conduct, in his ordinary talk, in his love affairs and his quarrels, in play, in bed, at table, in the management of his business and household economy. If I saw a man wearing tattered hose and writing good books, I should advise him first to mend his hose. Ask a Spartan whether he would rather be a good speaker than a good soldier ; do not ask me, who would rather be a good cook, if I were not provided with one.

Good heavens, Madame, how I should hate to be commended for a clever writer and looked upon as an insignificant fool in other respects ! Yet would I rather be a fool, both here and there, than to have made so ill a choice in using my talents. And I am so far from expecting to earn any new honour with these foolish fancies, that it will be as much as I can do not to lose the little I have acquired. For, besides what this dead and dumb picture will take from my natural being, it does not resemble me at my best ; it shows me greatly fallen off from my former vigour and sprightliness, and verging on the decayed and mouldy. I have come to the end of the cask, which begins to taste of the lees.

For the rest, Madame, I should not have dared so boldly to stir up the mysteries of medicine, considering the esteem in which you and so many others hold it, if I had not been shown the way by the writers on the art. Among the ancient Latins I think there are only two, Pliny and Celsus. If some day you will look into them, you will find that they treat their art much more roughly than I do. I only pinch it ; they kill it outright. Pliny, among other things, twits them with this, that when they are at the end of their tether, they have hit upon this pretty shift, to send the patients they have teased and tormented to no purpose with their drugs and dietings, some to seek assistance in prayers and miracles, others to the hot springs. (Be not offended, Madame, he does not speak of those on this side of the frontier which are under the patronage of your family, and all belong to the Gramonts). They have a third device for getting rid of us and avoiding our reproaches for the small improvement in our infirmities, which they have had so long under their charge that they can think of nothing more to put us off with ; that is to send us for change of air to some other country.

Enough, Madame ; you will give me permission to resume the thread of my discourse, from which I turned aside to talk with you.

It was, I think, Pericles who, being asked how he was, replied, ' You may judge by this,' pointing to the amulets he had tied about his neck and arm. He wished to imply that he was in a very bad way, since he was reduced to have recourse to such vanities, and had allowed himself to be so equipped. I do not guarantee that I may not some day be borne away to this absurd notion of committing my life and health to the mercy and government of the doctors. I may fall into such a frenzy. I cannot answer for my future firmness. I too, should anybody ask me how I am, may answer with Pericles, ' You may judge by this,' showing my hand filled with six drachms of electuary. That will be a very evident symptom of a severe illness. My judgement will be marvellously unhinged. If fretfulness and fright obtain such a hold upon me, you may conclude that my soul is in a very violent fever.

I have taken the trouble to plead this cause, of which I have little enough understanding, to support and fortify a little the natural aversion to drugs and medicine as practised by our physicians, which I have derived from my ancestors ; that it may not appear to be merely a stupid and thoughtless bent, but to have a little better foundation. And also that they who see me standing so firm against exhortations and threats when in the throes of sickness, may not think that it is mere stubbornness ; or in case any one should be so ill-natured as to think that I were being spurred by vainglory. It would be a well-aimed ambition forsooth to try to gain honour by an attitude that I share with my gardener and my muleteer ! My heart is indeed not so puffed up and windy that I should wish to exchange so solid, so fleshy and marrowy a pleasure as health for a pleasure that is imaginary, spiritual and airy. Fame, even that of the four sons of Aymon, is too dearly bought by a man of my humour, if it costs him three good attacks of the colic. Give me health, in God's name !

They who love our medicine may also have their good, great, and strong reasons ; I have no hatred of ideas that contradict my own. I am so far from being exasperated by seeing a disagreement between my opinions and others', and from being unfit for the society of men because their sentiments and party differ from my own, that on the contrary (the most general path that Nature has followed being that of variety, and more in minds than bodies, the former being of a more pliant substance and susceptible of taking on more shapes) I have found that opinions and views disagree much more often than they agree. Never in the world were two opinions alike, any more than two hairs or two grains. Their most universal quality is diversity.

BOOK THE THIRD

CHAPTER 1

OF THE USEFUL AND THE HONEST

NO man is exempt from saying silly things ; the mischief is to say them deliberately :

> With all his pains he says most foolish things. (TERENCE.)

That does not touch me ; mine slip from me as heedlessly as they deserve. All the better for them. I would part with them at once for the little they are worth. And I neither buy nor sell them except for what they weigh. I speak to my paper as I speak to the first person I meet. That this is true, observe what follows.

To whom should not treachery be detestable, when Tiberius refused it when it was so much to his interest ? They sent him word from Germany that, if he approved, they could rid him of Arminius by poison. He was the most powerful enemy the Romans had, since he had treated them so villainously under Varus, and was the only obstacle to the expansion of their dominion in those parts. Tiberius replied, ' that the Roman people were accustomed to take revenge on their enemies by open means, with arms in their hands, not by fraud and stratagem.' He renounced the profitable for the honest.

He was (you will tell me) an impostor. I believe it ; it is no great miracle in men of his profession. But the recognition of Virtue carries no less weight in the mouth of one who hates it, since truth forcibly wrests it from him, and, if he will not receive it into his heart, he at least covers himself with it, as with an ornament.

Our structure, both public and private, is full of imperfection. But there is nothing useless in Nature ; not even uselessness itself. Nothing has thrust itself into this universe that has not its fitting place. Our being is cemented with diseased qualities : ambition, jealousy, envy, vindictiveness, superstition, despair, quarter themselves upon us with so natural a possession, that we recognize the semblance of them even in animals. Nay, cruelty too, so unnatural a vice ; for, with all our compassion, we feel within us a kind of bitter-sweet pricking of malicious pleasure in witnessing the sufferings of others ; and the children feel it :

> 'Tis sweet when, down the mighty main, the winds
> Roll up its waste of waters, from the land
> To watch another's labouring anguish far. (LUCRETIUS.)

Whoever would root out the seeds of those qualities in man would destroy the fundamental conditions of our life. Similarly, in every government there are necessary offices which are not only base but wicked. Wickedness finds a place there, and is employed in sewing and binding us together ; as poison is used for the preservation of our health. If it becomes pardonable, since we are in need of it and the common necessity blots out its real quality, we must allow that part to be played by the stoutest and least timorous citizens, who will sacrifice their honour and their conscience ; as those others, in ancient times, sacrificed their lives for the good of their country. We others who are more feeble will assume easier and less dangerous parts. The public weal requires men to betray, to lie, and to massacre ; let us resign that charge to men who are more obedient and more compliant.

It has often really angered me to see a judge, by deceit and false hopes of favour or pardon, alluring a criminal to betray his offence, using to that end a shameless trickery. It would be a good service to justice, and to Plato even who countenances that custom, to furnish me with other means more to my liking. It is a mischievous kind of justice, and is wronged, in my opinion, no less by itself than by others. Not long ago I answered that I could hardly betray my Prince for a private individual, since I should be very sorry to betray any private person for the Prince ; and I hate not only to deceive, but I also hate that any one should be deceived in me. I will not even provide matter and occasion thereto.

On the few occasions I have had to negotiate between our Princes, in these divisions and subdivisions by which we are to-day rent in pieces, I have carefully avoided that they should be mistaken in me, or deceived by my face. The

men of the trade ¹ are the least open ; they profess and
pretend to be as unbiassed and as near to you as they can.
For my part I recommend myself by my readiest opinions
and by a manner that is most my own. A mild negotiator
and a novice, I would rather fail in the business than be
untrue to myself. And yet I have followed that course to
this day with so much luck (for indeed Fortune has the
chief share in it) that few men have been bandied from one
to another with less suspicion and with greater favour and
familiarity.

I have an open and easily ingratiating manner that inspires confidence at the first acquaintance. Naturalness
and the simple truth will always find their opportunity and
pass current, in any age whatever. Besides, the freedom of
speech of the man who acts without any self-interest
attracts little suspicion and odium. He may truly make
use of the answer of Hyperides to the Athenians who
complained of the bluntness of his speech : ' Good sirs, do
not consider whether I am free-spoken, but whether I am
so without accepting anything and without thereby advancing my own affairs.' My candour has also readily
cleared me from all suspicion of dissembling by its vigour
(leaving nothing unsaid, however painful and bitter ; I
could not have said worse behind their backs), and by its
evident show of simplicity and indifference. I expect no
other result from acting than to act, and look to no far-
reaching consequences or projects. Every action plays its
own particular game ; let it strike home if it can.

Moreover I am not swayed by any passion, either of love
or hatred, towards the great ; nor is my will strangled by
offence or obligation for particular favours. I look upon
our Kings simply with the loyal affection of a citizen, which
is neither stimulated nor cooled by private interest ; for
which I think the better of myself. To the general and
rightful cause I have only a moderate attachment, without
any heat. I am not subject to those close and deep-seated
pledges and engagements. Anger and hatred go beyond the
duty of justice, and are feelings which are useful only to
those who are not sufficiently kept to their duty by simple
reason. [*Let him employ his passion who can make no use
of his reason* (Cicero).] All fair and lawful intentions are of

¹ The diplomats.

themselves equable and temperate ; if not, they degenerate and become seditious and unlawful. This it is that makes me walk ever with head erect, with open face and heart.

Indeed, and I am not afraid of confessing it, I could readily, in case of need, follow the example of the old woman and offer a candle to St. Michael and another to his serpent.[1] I will follow the good side as far as the fire, but exclusively, if I can.[2] Let Montaigne [2] be engulfed in the general ruin, if need be ; but, if there is no need, I shall be grateful to Fortune if it escapes, and I will make use of all the length of rope my duty allows me, to save it.

Was it not Atticus who, holding to the right side, which was the losing side, in that general shipwreck of the world, amid so many changes and divisions, saved himself by his moderation ? It is easier for a private citizen, as he was ; and I think one may be justified in not being ambitious to thrust oneself uninvited into that kind of business.

When one's country is disturbed and the people are divided I think it neither handsome nor honourable to be a wobbler and a hybrid, to be unmoved in one's affections and to incline to neither side. *That is not to steer a middle course ; it is to steer no course at all. It is to await events, in order to join the fortunate side* (Livy).

That may be allowed in the case of affairs with neighbours. And so Gelo, Tyrant of Syracuse, in the war between the barbarians and Greeks, so suspended his inclination, keeping an ambassador with presents at Delphi, to be on the watch and see to which side Fortune should turn, and seize the right opportunity to make up to the victors. It would be a kind of treachery to act in this manner in the home affairs of one's own country, in which a man must necessarily and designedly make up his mind to join one side or the other.

But for a man to hold aloof from affairs who is not in public service, or driven by express command, I hold to be more excusable (and yet I do not accept this excuse for my

---

[1] To propitiate both parties. St. Michael, who was presumably Montaigne's patron saint, was usually represented on altar-pieces in the act of slaying a dragon.

[2] Montaigne is not in the habit of striking heroic attitudes, and we must not take him too literally. The words *jusqu'au feu exclusivement* are playfully adopted from Rabelais, who uses them several times. In the next sentence Montaigne means the château of that name.

own part) than not to join in foreign wars, in which, however, by our laws, no one need be engaged against his will. Nevertheless, even those who are wholly engaged in them may conduct themselves with such order and moderation that the storm will pass over their heads without injury to themselves. Had we not reason to expect this in the case of the late Bishop of Orleans, the Sieur' de Morvilliers ? And among those who at this moment are valiantly labouring at it, I know some of such even and mild temper that they are likely to remain standing, however great the ruin and desolation that Heaven has in store for us.

I am of opinion that it properly belongs to kings alone to quarrel with kings, and can see the absurdity of those spirited persons who gaily stand up to so uneven a contest. For to march openly and bravely against a Prince in defence of our honour and at the call of duty is not to pick a private quarrel with him. If he does not love such a man, he does better, he esteems him. And especially the cause of the laws and of the defence of the old State has always this privilege, that even those who, for private ends, attack the same, excuse, if they do not honour, the defenders.

But we must not call by the name of duty, as we do every day, a bitterness and asperity of the soul that is born of private interest and passion ; nor must we call a treacherous and malicious conduct by the name of courage. Their mischievous and violent propensities they call zeal. It is not the cause that excites them but their self-interest. They stir up war, not because it is just, but because it is war.

There is nothing to prevent a man acting in an accommodating manner between men who are enemies, without being disloyal. Bear yourself with an affection, if not altogether equal (for it may be of different degrees), at least moderate, and which will not so pledge you to one of them that he can require everything at your hands. Content yourself too with a moderate measure of their favours, and with swimming in troubled waters without trying to fish in them.

The other way, that of offering to do one's best for both parties shows imprudence rather than want of conscience. Does not the man to whom you betray another, who receives you with equal favour, know that you will treat him in the same way, when his turn comes ? He regards you as a scoundrel; meanwhile he will listen to you, he will draw what he can out of you and turn your disloyalty to his own account. For double-dealers are useful for what they bring; but you must take good care that they carry away as little as they can.

I say nothing to the one that I could not say to the other at the right moment, with only a little change of accent; and I report only things that are either indifferent, or known, or which are serviceable to both sides. For no useful end would I permit myself to lie to them. What is entrusted to my silence I religiously keep; but I receive as few secrets as I can. The secrets of princes are an awkward trust to one who has no use for them. I willingly offer them this bargain, that they trust me with little, but that they confidently trust me in what I bring them. I have always known more than I wished.

Open speaking opens the way to another's speaking, and draws it out, like wine and love.

Philippides replied wisely to King Lysimachus, who asked him, ' Which of my goods do you wish me to hand over to you? ' ' Whatever you please, provided it is not one of your secrets.' I have observed that men generally grumble if you keep from them the gist of the business on which you employ them, and if you conceal something that lies at the back of it. For my part, I am satisfied if they tell me no more than what they wish me to do; and do not desire that my knowledge of the business should exceed or restrict what I have to say. If I am to serve as a tool of deceit let me at least salve my conscience. I would not be thought either so affectionate or so loyal a servant as to be judged fit to betray any man. He who is untrue to himself is excusably so to his master.

But the Princes I have in my mind will not accept men by halves, and scorn limited and conditional services. There is no way out of it; I tell them frankly how far I will go. For if I must be a slave I will be so to Reason alone; and yet I can hardly compass even that. And they too are wrong to demand of a free man the same submission and obligation to their service, as they do of a man they have created and bought, or whose fortunes are particularly and expressly bound up with theirs.

The laws have saved me great pains; they have chosen

a side for me and given me a master. All other authority and obligation should be relative to that of the laws, and restricted. That does not mean however that, if my affection should otherwise incline me, my hand would immediately obey it.[1] Will and desire make their own laws ; actions have to submit to the law of public policy.

My method of negotiating as a whole, as here described, is a little out of harmony with that practised in our country. It would produce neither great nor lasting results. Innocence itself could not negotiate between our parties without dissimulation, nor strike a bargain without lying. And besides, public employments are not in my line ; what my profession requires I perform in as private a manner as I can.

As a youth I was plunged up to the ears in public affairs, and that not without success ; and yet I let go of them in good time. Since then I have often declined, seldom consented, and never volunteered to meddle with them ; keeping my back turned upon ambition, but, if not like rowers who thus advance backwards, yet so that I owe it more to my good fortune than to my resolution that I am not wholly embarked in them. For there are ways less inimical to my taste, and more within my capacity, by which, if Fortune had at one time invited me to take public service and to seek advancement in the world's honours, I know that I should have stepped over my better judgement, and followed her.

Those who usually declare, in contradiction to what I profess, what I call frankness, simplicity, and ingenuousness in my conduct to be art and cunning, and discretion rather than goodness, cleverness than naturalness, good sense than good luck, do me more honour than they rob me of. But indeed they make my subtlety too subtle ; and if any one has closely followed and spied upon me, I will own myself beaten, if he does not confess that there is no rule in their school [2] that could, on such various and tortuous roads, produce this natural impulse, and keep up an appearance of freedom and independence so uniformly inflexible ; and that all their ingenuity and watchfulness are unable to bring them to it.

The way of truth is one and simple ; that of private gain

---

[1] That if my affections inclined to the Protestants I should act with them.   [2] The school of diplomacy.

and of advantage, in the conduct of affairs a man is charged with, is double, uneven, and accidental. I have often seen that counterfeit and artificial freedom in practice, but for the most part without success. It is often too suggestive of the ass in Aesop's fable who, in imitation of the little dog, quite happily planted his two hoofs on his master's shoulders ; but, whilst the little dog received caresses in abundance, the poor ass was treated to twice as many bastinadoes. *That best becomes a man which is most natural to him* (Cicero).

I will not deprive deceit of its place ; that would be to misunderstand the world. I know that it has often been of profitable service, and that it supports and feeds most of the avocations of men. There are lawful sins, just as there are many either good or pardonable actions which are unlawful.

True justice, which is natural and universal, is otherwise regulated, and more nobly, than that other special, national justice, which is restricted by the necessities of our governments. *Of true right and real justice we have no solid and positive model ; we practise only the shadow and image of it* (Cicero). The sage Dandamis,[1] hearing tell of the lives of Socrates, Pythagoras, and Diogenes, judged them to be great men in every other respect except that they were too much enslaved to reverence of the laws, to justify and support which true virtue must abate much of its original vigour ; and added that many wicked actions are done not only with their permission, but by their instigation. *There are crimes authorized by the decrees of the Senate and the popular vote* (Seneca). I follow the ordinary language which makes a distinction between things that are profitable and things that are honest ; so that some natural actions, which are not only profitable but necessary, are called dishonest and unclean.

But let us continue our examples of treachery. Two pretenders to the kingdom of Thrace had started a quarrel about their rights. The Emperor[2] prevented their coming to blows ; but one of them, under colour of bringing things to a friendly issue by a conference, having invited his competitor to an entertainment in his own house, had him imprisoned and killed. Justice required that the Romans

---

[1] A Hindu sage who lived in the time of Alexander the Great.

[2] Tiberius ; the pretenders were Rhescuporis and Cotys, the brother and son of Rhemetalces, the last King of Thrace.

should demand satisfaction for this crime. There was a difficulty in obtaining it by ordinary means. What they could not lawfully do without war and risk, they attempted to do by treachery. What they could not do honestly they did profitably. For this they found a fit and proper instrument in Pomponius Flaccus. This man, having drawn the other into his nets by feigned words and assurances, instead of the honours and favours he promised him, sent him bound hand and foot to Rome.

Here one traitor betrays another, contrary to the usual custom ; for traitors are full of distrust, and it is difficult to catch them with their own wiles ; witness the sad experience we have lately had.[1]

Let who will be a Pomponius Flaccus, and there are men enough who are willing. For my part, both my word and my good faith are, like the rest of me, parts of this common body.[2] The best they are capable of is at the public service ; I take that as a matter of course. But just as, if I were commanded to take charge of the Palace of Justice and the lawsuits, I should answer, ' I know nothing about them ' ; or, if commissioned to be a leader of pioneers, I should say, ' I am called to play a worthier part ' ; so also, if any man proposed to employ me to lie, to betray, commit perjury, not to speak of assassinating and poisoning, for some important end, I should say, ' If I have stolen or robbed from any man, send me rather to the galleys.' For a man of honour may be allowed to say as did the Lacedemonians, when, after their defeat by Antipater, they were arranging terms, ' You may put upon us as many heavy and ruinous burdens as you please, but if you command us to do shameful and dishonourable things, you will waste your time.'

Every man should take to himself the oath which the Kings of Egypt made their judges solemnly take, ' that they would not deviate from their conscience, though they themselves should command them to do so.'

In a command to act dishonestly there is an evident mark of ignominy and condemnation. The man who gives it you, accuses you ; and he gives it to you, if you understand him

---

[1] Montaigne here perhaps refers to the feigned reconciliation between Catherine de' Medici and Henry, Duke of Guise, in 1588.

[2] The State.

rightly, for a burden and a punishment. In the same
degree that public affairs are bettered by your action your
own state has become worse. The better you do in it, so
much the worse do you do for yourself. And it will be no
new thing, nor perhaps without some colour of justice, if
the very same man who has set you to the work punishes
you for it.

If perfidy can ever be excusable it is only so when it is
employed to punish and betray perfidy.

There are examples enough not only of treachery being
disowned, but of its being punished by those on whose
behalf it was practised. Who does not know of Fabricius'
denunciation of Pyrrhus' physician ? [1]

But this also we find, that some person has commanded
an act of treachery, and has rigorously avenged the victim
of it upon the man he had employed to carry it out ; dis-
claiming such unbridled authority and power, and refusing
an obedience so abject, slavish, and unprincipled.

Jaropelc, Duke of Russia, suborned a Hungarian nobleman to betray Boleslaus, King of Poland, either by killing
him or by putting the Russians in the way of doing him
some notable injury. This man set to work with great
cunning ; he became more assiduous than ever in that
King's service, contriving to become his counsellor and one
of his most trusted servants. With these advantages,
taking an opportune occasion of his master's absence, he
betrayed Vislicza to the Russians, a great and rich city,
which was completely sacked and burned by them, with
total slaughter, not only of the inhabitants of whatever age
or sex, but of a great number of the nobles of the neighbourhood, whom he had assembled to that end.

Jaropelc, his vengeance and anger being assuaged, for
which he was, however, not without justification (for Boleslaus had done him great injury, and in the same way), sated
with the fruit of this treachery, when he came to consider
the foulness of it, naked and by itself, and to look upon it
with sane vision no longer blinded by passion, was seized with

[1] When Pyrrhus, King of Epirus, was at war with the Romans, his
physician wrote to Fabricius, the Roman Consul, offering to poison the
King and so put an end to the war. Fabricius denounced him to Pyrrhus,
' lest your death, he wrote, should bring a disgrace upon us, and we
should seem to have put a period to the war by treachery when we could
not do it by valour.'

so great remorse and disgust, that he commanded his agent to be blinded, and his tongue and privy parts to be cut off.

Antigonus persuaded the Argyraspides [1] to betray to him Eumenes, their commander-in-chief and his adversary ; but no sooner had he put him to death after they had delivered him into his hands, than he himself desired to be the agent of the divine justice, for the punishment of so detestable a crime. He handed them over to the Governor of the province, with most express command to destroy them and bring them to an evil end in any manner whatsoever. So that not one of them, although so numerous a body, ever again saw the air of Macedonia. The better he had been served by them the more wickedly he judged it to be, and the more punishably.

The slave who betrayed the hiding-place of his master, P. Sulpicius, was given his freedom, in accordance with the promise of Sylla's proscription ; but in accordance with the promise of public justice, freeman though he was, he was hurled from the Tarpeian rock. They hang them, so to say, with the purse of their payment around their necks. After carrying out their second and special promise, they satisfy their general and primary conscience.

Mahomet the Second, wishing to be rid of his brother, by reason of his jealousy as a ruler, so common in that race, employed for the purpose one of his officers, who choked him by pouring too suddenly a great quantity of water down his throat. That being done, to expiate the murder he delivered the murderer into the hands of the dead man's mother (for they were brothers only on the father's side). She, in his presence, opened the murderer's stomach, and, whilst still quite warm, with her own hands searched for his heart, tore it out and threw it to the dogs to eat.

And our King Clovis, instead of the golden arms he had promised the three slaves of Cannacre, hanged them after they had, at his own instigation, betrayed their master.

And even to the most abandoned person it is so pleasant a feeling, after profiting by a wicked deed, subsequently to be able to sew upon it, in all security, a stitch of goodness and justice, as by way of compensation and conscientious correction. To which may be added that they look upon the ministers of such horrible crimes as a living reproach,

[1] A body of soldiers who carried silver shields.

and seek by their death to smother the knowledge and testimony of such proceedings.

Now, if by chance you are rewarded for it, in order that the public necessity for such extreme and desperate remedies may not be frustrated, the man who rewards you cannot but regard you as an accursed and execrable fellow, unless he be so himself, and as more treacherous than does the man you have betrayed ; for he tests the wickedness of your heart by your own hands, which act without disapproval and without object. But he employs you as they do hopelessly degraded men to be the executors of high justice,[1] an office as necessary as it is dishonourable ; not to speak of the vileness of such commissions, there is a prostitution of conscience.

Since the daughter of Sejanus could not, by a certain provision of the laws at Rome, be punished with death, because she was a virgin, in order to allow the law to take its course, she was violated by the hangman before being strangled. Not only his hand, but his soul, is a slave to public convenience.

When the first Amurath, to aggravate the punishment of his subjects who had given their support in the parricidal rebellion of his son against him, commanded their nearest relations to lend their assistance in the execution, I think it highly honourable in some of them to have rather chosen to be unjustly thought guilty of another's parricide than to serve justice by parricide of their own.

And when, after the storming of some wretched fortress in my time, I have seen a rascal consenting, in order to save his own life, to hang his friends and comrades, I thought him worse off than the hanged.

It is said that Witolde, Prince of the Lithuanians, once made it a law that the condemned criminal should with his own hand carry out his execution. He thought it strange that a third person, innocent of the fault, should be employed and laden with the guilt of homicide.

When, by urgent circumstances, or some sudden and unexpected event, a ruler is obliged, for reasons of state necessity, to shuffle out of his word and break his faith, or is otherwise forced out of the ordinary path of duty,

[1] i. e., hangmen ; now sometimes euphemistically referred to as the ' exécuteurs des hautes œuvres '.

he must regard this necessity as a stroke of the divine rod. A sin it is not, for he has abandoned his own reason to a more universal and powerful reason ; but it is indeed a misfortune. So that to some one who asked me, ' What remedy ? ' ' No remedy, I replied ; if he was really squeezed between those two extremes—*but let him beware of seeking a pretext for his faithlessness* (Cicero)—he was obliged to do it ; but if he did it without regret, if it did not weigh upon his mind, it is a sign that his conscience is in a bad way.'

Even if there were any ruler of so tender a conscience as to think no cure worth so serious a remedy, I should not esteem him the less. He could not ruin himself more excusably and more becomingly. We cannot do everything. In any case we must often entrust the protection of our vessel to the simple guidance of Heaven, as to our last anchorage. For what more justifiable necessity does he reserve himself ? What is less possible for him to do than what he can do only at the price of his good faith and honour, things which should perhaps be dearer to him than his own safety, nay, than the safety of his people? Though he should stand with folded arms and merely call God to his aid, may he not hope that the divine goodness will not refuse exceptional favours from its hand to a hand that is so clean and just ?

Those are dangerous examples, rare and sickly exceptions to our natural laws. We must yield to them, but with great moderation and circumspection. No private interest is worth so great a strain upon our conscience ; public interest certainly, when it is both very apparent and very important.

Timoleon fitly expiated his extraordinary deed by the tears he shed when he called to mind that it was with a brother's hand that he had killed the tyrant ; and his conscience justly pricked him that he should have been put to the necessity of purchasing the public weal at so high a price as his honesty of character. Even the Senate, delivered from thraldom by his means, did not venture roundly to pass judgement upon a deed so sublime and split into two so important and contrary aspects. But the Syracusans having, very opportunely at that moment, sent to the Corinthians to solicit their protection by sending them a leader able to restore their city to its former dignity and cleanse Sicily of a number of petty tyrants by whom it was being oppressed, they deputed Timoleon, with this new-fangled quibble and declaration, ' That according as he bore himself well or ill in his charge, they would decide to pardon him as the liberator of his country, or disgrace him as his brother's murderer.' This fantastic decision is some-what to be excused, by reason of the danger of the example and the seriousness of so singular a deed. And they did well to throw off the burden of passing sentence, and to make it depend on other and extraneous considerations.

Now the conduct of Timoleon on this mission soon made his cause more clear, so worthily and virtuously did he bear himself in every way. And the good fortune which attended him in the difficulties he had to overcome in this noble business seemed to have been sent to him by the gods conspiring in favour of his vindication.

This man's aim was excusable, if ever any could be. But the advantage of increasing the public revenue, which served the Roman Senate as a pretext for that unsavoury decision which I am about to tell of, is not great enough to warrant any such injustice.

Certain cities had by a money payment redeemed them-selves and regained their freedom, by the order and per-mission of the Senate, from the hands of L. Sylla. The matter having come up again for decision, the Senate condemned them to be taxable as before, and decided that the money they had paid for their redemption should remain lost to them.

Civil wars often give rise to such villainous cases, as when we punish private individuals for following the advice we gave them when we were other than we are now, and the self-same judge lays the penalty for his own change of mind upon one who is innocent of it. The master whips his pupil for his docility, and the leader his blind charge. A horrible counterfeit of justice !

There are rules in Philosophy which are both false and weak. The example that is proposed to us to make private advantage to prevail over a given promise, does not receive sufficient weight from the circumstance they mix up with it. Robbers have seized you ; they have set you at liberty after extracting an oath from you to pay a certain sum. They are very wrong who say that a man of honour, once out of their power, will be quit of his word without paying. Nothing of the kind. What fear has once made me will I am bound still to will when the fear is past. And even though fear forced only my tongue without my will, I am still bound to pay to the last farthing what I have promised. For my part, when my tongue has sometimes heedlessly outstripped my thoughts, I have yet scrupled to disown it. Otherwise we shall, little by little, come to upset all the claims that a third person has upon us on the strength of our oaths and promises. *As though a man of courage could be wrought upon by force !* (Cicero.)

In this case only does private interest justify us in failing to keep our promise : when we have promised a thing that is in itself wicked and iniquitous. For the right of virtue should prevail over the right of our obligation.

I erstwhile placed Epaminondas in the front rank of great men ; and I do not retract it. To how high a pitch this man raised the consideration of his private duty, who never killed a man he had vanquished, who, for the inestimable blessing of restoring freedom to his country, scrupled to put a tyrant or his accomplices to death without the forms of justice, and who regarded him as a wicked man, however good a citizen he might be, who, among the enemy and in battle, did not spare his guest-friend ! There we have a richly compounded soul ! To the rudest and most violent human actions he wedded goodness and humanity, even the most delicate that may be found in the school of Philosophy.

Was it Nature or Art that softened this heart, so big, so full, so obstinate against pain, death, and poverty, to such an extreme degree of sweetness and gentleness of disposition ? A dreaded man of blood and iron, he goes breaking and shattering a people invincible against any but himself, and, in the midst of such a fray, turns aside to avoid an encounter with a guest-friend. Truly he was a fit and proper man to control war, who forced it to submit to the curb of loving-kindness in the very heat of battle, when, all inflamed, it foamed with fury and slaughter. It is wonderful to be able to mingle with such actions any semblance of justice ; but only a man as strong as Epaminondas was able to mingle with them the most gentle and affable manners and pure innocence.

And whereas one [1] said to the Mamertines that ' laws
were powerless when opposed to armed men ' ; another,[1]
to the Tribune of the People,' that the time of justice and
the time of war were two ' ; and a third,[1] ' that the noise
of arms drowned the voice of the laws ' : this man was not
deaf even to the voice of urbanity and pure courtesy. Had
he not borrowed from his enemies [2] the custom of sacrificing
to the Muses when he went to war, to dilute its martial fury
and fierceness with their sweetness and gaiety ?

After so great a teacher let us not be afraid of concluding
that there are things which should not be allowed even in
fighting the enemy, and that the common interest should
not require all things of all men, against their private
interest : *the memory of private right continuing even in the
midst of public dissensions* (Livy) ;

> No power on earth can sanction treachery
> Against a friend ; (OVID.)

and that not all things are permissible to a man of honour,
in the service of his king, the general cause and the laws.
*For duty to one's country does not override all other duties ;
she herself requires that we be dutiful towards our parents*
(Cicero).[3]

This teaching befits our times ; we have no need to
harden our hearts with these steel blades. It is enough
that our shoulders are hardened by them. It is enough to
dip our pens in ink, without dipping them in blood. If it is
the sign of a great heart and the effect of a singular and rare
virtue to despise friendship, private obligations, one's word
and one's kinsmen, for the common good and obedience to
authority, we are truly sufficiently excused from showing
it by the consideration that it is a greatness that can have
no place in the great heart of Epaminondas.

I abominate those crazy exhortations of this other unruly
spirit : [4]

> When weapons flash, let no fond thoughts of love,
> Friendship and piety compassion move ;
> But boldly strike the venerable face
> Of your own fathers, if opposed in place. (LUCAN.)

[1] Respectively Pompey, Caesar, and Marius.   [2] The Spartans.
[3] The first clause is put interrogatively by Cicero ; and his answer does
not agree with Montaigne's.
[4] Julius Caesar. It is within the recollection of all how these words

Let us deprive wicked, bloodthirsty, and treacherous natures of this pretence of reason ; let us thrust aside that atrocious and insane justice, and imitate more humane examples. How much cannot time and example bring to pass ! In an encounter during the civil war against Cinna, one of Pompey's soldiers, having unwittingly killed his brother who was on the opposite side, immediately took his own life for shame and sorrow ; and a few years later, in another civil war of the same nation, a soldier demanded a reward from his captains for having killed his brother.

To judge an action to be fine and honourable because it is useful is a poor argument ; as also to hold that every man is obliged to perform such an action, and that it becomes him as long at it is useful :

All things are not alike for all men fit. (PROPERTIUS.)

Let us take that action which is most necessary and useful for human society ; which will surely be marriage. And yet the council of the saints has concluded the contrary to be more honourable, and excludes from it the most venerable profession of men ; as we destine for our studs the least valuable of our cattle.

CHAPTER 2

OF REPENTANCE

OTHERS [1] form man ; I describe him, and portray a particular, very ill-made one, who, if I had to fashion him anew, should indeed be very different from what he is. But now it is done.

Now the features of my painting do not err, although they change and vary. The world is but a perennial see-saw. All things in it are incessantly on the swing, the earth, the rocks of the Caucasus, the Egyptian pyramids, both with the common movement and their own particular movement. Even fixedness is nothing but a more sluggish motion.

were re-echoed before the Great War by another and lesser Caesar (pro nounced by the Romans *Kaiser*).

[1] The other moralists.

I cannot fix my object;[1] it is befogged, and reels with a natural intoxication. I seize it at this point, as it is at the moment when I beguile myself with it. I do not portray the thing in itself. I portray the passage; not a passing from one age to another, or, as the people put it, from seven years to seven years,[2] but from day to day, from minute to minute. I must adapt my history to the moment. I may presently change, not only by chance, but also by intention. It is a record of diverse and changeable events, of undecided, and, when the occasion arises, contradictory ideas; whether it be that I am another self, or that I grasp a subject in different circumstances and see it from a different point of view. So it may be that I contradict myself, but, as Demades said, the truth I never contradict.[3] If my mind could find a firm footing, I should not speak tentatively, I should decide; it is always in a state of apprenticeship, and on trial.

I am holding up to view a humble and lustreless life; that is all one. Moral philosophy, in any degree, may apply to an ordinary and secluded life as well as to one of richer stuff; every man carries within him the entire form of the human constitution.

Authors communicate themselves to the world by some special and extrinsic mark; I am the first to do so by my general being, as Michel de Montaigne, not as a grammarian or a poet or a lawyer. If the world finds fault with me for speaking too much of myself, I find fault with the world for not even thinking of itself.

But is it reasonable that I, who am so retired in actual life, should aspire to make myself known to the public? And is it reasonable that I should show up to the world, where artifice and ceremony enjoy so much credit and authority, the crude and simple results of nature, and of a nature besides very feeble? Is it not like making a wall without stone or a similar material, thus to build a book without learning or art? The ideas of music are guided by

---

[1] i. e., myself.

[2] Alluding to a popular notion that the human body is entirely renewed every seven years.

[3] Not quite accurate: Demades said, according to Plutarch, that he may have often contradicted himself, but that he had never said anything contrary to the public weal.

art, mine by chance. This I have at least in conformity
with rules, that no man ever treated of a subject that he
knew and understood better than I do this that I have
taken up ; and that in this I am the most learned man
alive. Secondly, that no man ever penetrated more deeply
into his matter, nor more minutely analysed its parts and
consequences, nor more fully and exactly reached the goal
he had made it his business to set up. To accomplish it
I need only bring fidelity to it ; and that is here, as pure
and sincere as may be found.

I speak the truth, not enough to satisfy myself, but as
much as I dare to speak. And I become a little more
daring as I grow older ; for it would seem that custom
allows this age more freedom to prate, and more indiscretion
in speaking of oneself. It cannot be the case here, as I often
see elsewhere, that the craftsman and his work contradict
each other. 'How could a man who shows to such advantage in company write so foolish a book ? ' or, 'Are these
learned writings the work of a man of such feeble conversation ? '

When a man of ordinary conversation writes uncommon
things, it means that his talent lies in the place from which
he borrows them, and not in himself. A learned man is not
learned in all things ; but the accomplished man is accomplished in all things, even in ignorance.

Here, my book and I go hand in hand together, and keep
one pace. In other cases we may commend or censure the
work apart from the workman ; not so here. Who touches
the one touches the other. He who judges the one without
knowing the other will wrong himself more than he does
me ; he who has come to know the work will completely
satisfy me. Happy beyond my deserts if I have only this
share of public approval, that intelligent persons will be
made to feel that I was capable of profiting by learning,
if I had had any ; and that I deserved more assistance from
my memory !

In this place let me offer an excuse for what I often
repeat, that I seldom repent, and that my conscience is
satisfied with itself, not as the conscience of an angel or
a horse, but as the conscience of a man ; always with the
addition of this refrain, not a formal or conventional refrain,
but prompted by a real and natural modesty, 'that I speak

as an inquirer and an ignoramus, leaving the decision purely
and simply to the common and authorized beliefs.'   I do
not teach, I relate.

There is no vice, that is really a vice, which is not hurtful
and which a sound judgement does not condemn ;   for its
ugliness and evil consequences are so apparent that they
are perhaps right who say that it is chiefly begotten of
stupidity and ignorance. So hard it is to imagine that a man
may know it and not hate it !

Wickedness sucks in the greater part of its own venom,
and poisons itself with it.

Vice, like an ulcer in the flesh, leaves a repentance in the
soul, which is always scratching itself and drawing blood.
For Reason blots out all other grief and sorrow, but begets
that of repentance, which is the more hard to bear since
it is born from within ;   as the chill and heat of a fever are
more acutely felt than those which are external. I regard
as vices (but each according to its measure), not only those
which are condemned by reason and Nature, but those too
which have been created by human opinion, even false and
erroneous opinion, if it is authorized by laws and custom.

There is likewise no goodness in which a well-born nature
does not delight. We feel indeed a certain self-congratula-
tion when we do a good deed, which gives us inward satisfaction, and that generous pride which accompanies a good
conscience. A boldly wicked soul may perhaps arm itself
with assurance ;   but with that complacency and satisfaction it cannot provide itself.

There is no small pleasure in feeling oneself preserved
from the contagion of so corrupt an age, and saying to
oneself, ' Should any one look into my very soul, he would
yet not find me guilty of the affliction or ruin of any man
or of revenge or envy, of publicly offending against the laws
of innovation or disturbance, or of failing to keep my word.
And whatever the licence of the times may permit or
suggest to any man, I have laid hands on no Frenchman'
property nor dived into his purse. I have never lived but
on what is my own, either in war or peace time ;   and have
never used another man's labour without hire.'   These
testimonies of a good conscience please ;   and this natural
satisfaction is a great boon to us, and the only payment
that will never fail us.

To ground the reward of virtuous actions on others' approval is to choose a too uncertain and shaky foundation. Especially in an age so corrupt and ignorant as this, the good opinion of the people is harmful. Whom can you trust to see what is praiseworthy ? God defend me from being an honest man according to the ideas of honesty which men every day ascribe to themselves ! *What was once vicious is now become moral* (Seneca).

Some of my friends have at times attempted to lecture and censure me unreservedly, either of their own accord or at my invitation, as a service which, to a well-regulated mind, exceeds all services of friendship, not only in usefulness but in kindness. I have always welcomed it with the most open arms of courtesy and gratitude. But when I come now to speak of it candidly, I have often discovered in their blame or praise such a want of proportion, that I should hardly have gone wrong if I had sinned, rather than done a good deed, according to their way of thinking.

We especially who live a retired life, not exposed to any view but our own, must have a fixed pattern within ourselves by which to test our actions, and, according to this pattern, now pat ourselves on the back, now kick ourselves. I have my own laws and my own court to judge me, and I appeal to them more than to others. I do indeed restrict my actions according to others, but extend them only according to myself. You alone know whether you are cruel and cowardly, or loyal and devout. Others do not see you, they guess you by uncertain conjectures ; they see not so much your nature as your art. Therefore pay no heed to their sentence, pay heed only to your own. *Use your own judgement with regard to yourself . . . The conscience weighs heavy in deciding your virtues and vices. Take that away, and all falls to the ground* (Cicero).

But when they say that repentance follows close upon the heels of sin, they do not seem to consider the sin which is in its corslet, which dwells in us as in its own domicile. We may disown and retract the sins that take us unawares, and to which we are carried away by passion. But those which, by long habit, are rooted and anchored in a strong and powerful will, are not capable of being resisted. Repentance is no other but a recanting of our will and an opposition

to our fancies, which leads us about in all directions. It
makes this man [1] disown his past virtue and continence :

> Alas ! alas !
> Why feel I not to-day
> As in my youthful bloom, when I
> Unmoved heard others moan,
> Or, now that I would win them, why
> Is all my beauty flown ?   (Horace.)

It is a life in a thousand that is consistently well-ordered
even in private.   Any man may play his part in the mummery, and act the honest man on the scaffolding ; but to be
right within, in his own bosom, where all is allowed, where
all is concealed—there's the point !   The next step is to
be so in our own home, in our ordinary actions, of which
we need render no account to any man, where there is no
study, no make-believe.   Wherefore Bias, describing an
exquisite state of family life, says : ' of which the master is
the same within, before his own conscience, as he is abroad,
under fear of the laws and the tongues of men'.   And that
was a worthy saying of Julius Drusus to the workmen who
offered, for three thousand crowns, to rebuild his house in
such a way that his neighbours could no longer overlook
him as before : ' I will give you six thousand, he said, to
build it in such a way that any one may see into it from all
sides.'   They make honourable mention of Agesilaus' habit,
when travelling, of lodging in the churches, that the people
and the gods themselves might see into his private actions.

Many a man has been a wonder in the eyes of the world
in whom neither his wife nor his valet have ever detected
anything even remarkable.   Few men have been admired
by their own household.

No man has been a prophet not only in his own house,
but in his own country ; such is the experience of history.
It is the same in things of no account.   In the following
humble example you may see a reflection of greater ones.
In my clime of Gascony they think it droll to see me in print.
The farther from my own home that the knowledge of me extends, the more am I valued.   In Guienne I buy the printers ;
elsewhere they buy me.   On this eventuality do they found
their hopes who keep in concealment when alive and present,

---

[1] Horace imagines Ligurinus, when he is old, repenting of not having
made a better use of his beauty.

to make a name when dead and absent. I would rather have
less. I launch myself upon the world only for the portion of
it that I actually gain. When I leave it, I will hold it quit.

This man,[1] after playing his part in public, is escorted to
his door by an enthusiastic rabble. With his gown he drops
this part ; the higher he had risen, the lower does he now
fall. Within, in his house, all is confusion and sordidness.
And even if order should prevail there, it needs a keen and
well-sifting judgement to perceive it in those humble and
private acts. Besides, orderliness is a dull and obscure
virtue. To enter a breach, conduct an embassy, rule a
people, are conspicuous actions. To chide, laugh, sell, pay,
love, hate, to live in communion with one's people and
oneself, pleasantly and correctly, not to give way to passion,
not to contradict oneself ; that is more rarely seen, more
difficult and less remarked.

Wherefore, whatever they may say, a retired life is
burdened with as difficult and strenuous duties, if not more
so, than other lives. And private individuals, says Aristotle, do a higher and more difficult service to virtue than
those in authority. We prepare ourselves for eminent
occasions more for glory than for conscience's sake. The
shortest way to arrive at fame would be to do for conscience's sake what we do for glory. And the virtue of
Alexander appears to me to reflect much less vigour on his
stage, than that of Socrates in his humble and obscure
actions. I easily conceive Socrates in Alexander's place ;
Alexander in that of Socrates, I cannot. If you ask the
former what he can do, he will reply, ' Subdue the world ; '
if you ask the latter, he will say, ' Lead a human life conformably with its natural condition ; '[2] a much more
general, more important, and more legitimate art.

The worth of the soul lies not in flying high, but in
walking in an orderly manner. Its greatness is not brought
into play in greatness, but in a middle state. As those who
judge and probe our hearts think but little of the brilliance
of our public acts, and see that they are but thin threads
and sprays of water spurting from an otherwise thick and

---

[1] i. e., the man who is not a hero in his own home. The previous
paragraph was an interpolation.

[2] Montaigne here added in the margin, but deleted, the words : ' do
for the world that for which he is in the world.'

muddy depth ; so likewise those who judge us by this brave outward show conclude the like of our inner nature ; being unable to reconcile common faculties, resembling their own, with those other faculties that astonish them, that are so far beyond their vision.

So it is that we give to demons uncouth shapes. And who does not endow Tamerlane with raised eyebrows, open nostrils, a fear-inspiring visage, and a huge stature, in accordance with the imaginary stature we have conceived from report of his fame ? At one time, if I had been introduced to Erasmus, I could hardly have believed but that he spoke only in adages and apothegms to his servant and landlady. We can much more fitly imagine an artisan upon his stool or on his wife than a great President, of venerable demeanour and sufficiency. We imagine that from those lofty thrones they will not even condescend to live.

As wicked souls are often stirred by some outside impulse to do a good action, so are virtuous souls to do evil. We must judge them therefore in their settled state, when they are at home, if ever they are ; or at least when they are more nearly in repose, and in their natural seat.

Natural inclinations are assisted and strengthened by education, but they seldom change and are seldom mastered. In my time a thousand natures have escaped towards virtue, or towards vice, in spite of a contrary training.

> As jungle beasts, in cages long confined,
> Tamed and subdued to suffer man's control,
> Are by a single taste of blood transformed.
> Their native rage and fury then returns ;
> They thirst for more, and scarcely can be stayed
> From onslaught on their trembling lord. (LUCAN.)

These original qualities are not to be extirpated ; they may be covered and concealed. Latin is to me like a native tongue ; I understand it better than French. But for these forty years past I have made no use of it either for speaking or writing. And yet on two or three occasions in my life, under sudden and violent emotion (once, when my father, although in good health, fell back into my arms in a swoon), the first words I uttered, coming from the depth of my heart, were always in Latin ; Nature, in spite of so long a disuse, springing up and finding forcible expression. And this is said to have occurred to many others.

Those who, in my time, have attempted to correct the morals of the world by new beliefs, have reformed the surface vices ; the essential ones they have left as before, if they have not increased them ; and it is to be feared that they will increase. We are apt to rest from all other well-doing on the strength of these external, arbitrary improvements, which cost less and earn greater esteem. And we thereby cheaply satisfy the other natural, consubstantial, and inherent vices.

Just see what our own experience teaches. There is no man, if he listen to himself, who will not discover in himself a particular nature, a dominant nature, that struggles against his education and against the tempestuous passions that oppose it. For my part I am seldom stirred by fits and starts ; I am nearly always in my place, like a heavy and unwieldy body. If I am not at home, I am always very near it. My excesses do not carry me very far. There is nothing extreme or uncommon in them. And besides I have healthy and vigorous recoveries.

The real condemnation, which touches the common run of men in our time, is that even their recantation is altogether corrupt and unclean ; their idea of amendment smudged, their penitence as sick and faulty almost as their sin. Some, from being glued to vice either by a natural adhesion or by long habit, have lost all sense of its ugliness. In others (to which regiment I belong) sin is a burden, but they counterbalance it with pleasure, or some other need ; they suffer and give way to it, at a certain price ; viciously however, and basely. Yet we might perhaps imagine a disproportion of degree so remote that pleasure might with justice excuse the sin, as we say of usefulness ; not only if it were accidental and apart from the sin, as in larceny, but in the very exercise of sin, as in intercourse with a woman, where the incitement is violent and, so they say, sometimes unconquerable.

Being the other day at Armagnac, on the estate of a kinsman of mine, I saw a country fellow whom everybody nicknamed the Thief. He gave us this account of his life : That being born a beggar and discovering that, by earning his bread with the labour of his hands, he would never be sufficiently armed against want, he decided to take to thieving ; and, being of great bodily strength, he practised

that trade in all security throughout his younger days.
For he reaped his harvest and vintage on other men's lands,
but at such a distance and in so great stacks that it is
incredible how one man could have carried away so much
on his shoulders in a single night. And he took care besides
to equalize and distribute the damage he did, so that the
total loss became less serious for each individual.

He is now, in his old age, rich for a man of his rank in
life, thanks to this traffic, which he openly confesses. And
to make his peace with God out of his winnings, he says
that it is his daily task to compensate, in charity, the heirs
of those he robbed ; and, if he does not finish his good work
(for he cannot see to it all at once), he will charge his heirs
to repay them, proportionally to the wrong he did to each,
which he alone knows.

From this declaration, whether it be true or false, it
appears that this man regards theft as a dishonest action
and hates it, but less than he does poverty ; he repents of
it very simply, but in so far as it is thus counterbalanced
and compensated, he does not repent of it.

This is not a case of that habit by which we are incorporated with vice, when even our understanding is brought
into conformity with it ; nor is it the case of an impetuous
wind that in gusts disturbs and blinds our soul, and for the
time being hurls us, judgement and all, into the power of sin.

What I do I do thoroughly, as a matter of habit, and
make one step of it ; and I seldom take any step that
steals away and hides from my reason, and that is not very
nearly guided by all my faculties in agreement, without
division or inner revolt. My judgement takes all the blame
or all the praise for it ; and the blame it once takes it takes
always, for almost from birth it has been one : the same
inclination, the same direction, the same strength. And in
the matter of general opinions, I have since my childhood
occupied the position I had to hold.

Some sins there are which are impetuous, quick, and
sudden ; let us leave them on one side. But with regard
to those other sins, so often repeated, deliberately, ad-
visedly, whether constitutional sins, or even professional or
vocational sins, I cannot imagine them to have been so long
implanted in one and the same heart, unless the reason and
conscience of the man who has them constantly wills them,

and intends them to be so. And I find it somewhat hard to form a mental image of the repentance which, as he is apt to boast, comes upon him at a certain prescribed moment.

I do not share the opinion of the Pythagorean school, ' that men take up a new soul when they approach the images of the Gods to receive their oracles.' Unless he meant this, that it must be extrinsic, new, and lent for the occasion ; since their own soul shows so little sign of the purification and cleanness befitting such an office.

They do just the opposite to what the Stoics teach, who command us indeed to correct the imperfections and vices we know to be in us, but forbid us to grieve and trouble ourselves about them. They make us believe that they feel great regret and remorse within ; but of improvement and correction, or of discontinuance, they show no signs. Hence it is no cure, if the disease be not thrown off. If repentance were placed in the scale of the balance, it would weigh down the sin. I know of no virtue that is so easy to copy as piety, if life and morals are not in conformity with it ; its essence is hidden and abstruse ; the imitation easy and showy.

For my part, I may desire in general to be different ; I may dislike and condemn my whole being, and beseech God to reform me throughout and pardon my natural infirmity. But I should not, I think, call that repentance, any more than my being dissatisfied that I am not an angel or a Cato. My actions are orderly, and conformable with what I am and my condition ; I can do no better. And repentance does not properly concern the things that are not in our power ; but regret certainly does. I can imagine an endless number of natures on a higher plane and better governed than mine, and yet I do not improve my powers ; just as neither my arm nor my mind becomes any stronger by conceiving those of another to be so. If to imagine and desire a nobler conduct than ours led to our repenting of our own, we should have to repent of our most innocent actions, since we rightly suppose that a superior nature would have performed them with greater perfection and dignity ; and we should wish to do equally well.

When, with the eyes of old age, I look upon the conduct of my younger days, I find that I generally behaved in an orderly manner, according to my lights ; that is all that my power of resistance can do. I do not deceive myself ; in like circumstances I should always do the same. It is not a smutch, it is rather a universal tincture with which I am stained. I know no superficial, half-way, and formal repentance. It must touch me in every part before I can call it so ; it must grip my heart and distress it as deeply and thoroughly as God sees into me.

With regard to business, I have allowed many good ventures to slip through my fingers for lack of successful management. Yet my plans were well chosen, considering the opportunities I was offered. It is my habit to take always the easiest and safest course. I have found that in my former decisions, following my own rule, I proceeded wisely, considering the nature of the matter proposed to me, and I should do the same a thousand years hence on the like occasions. I do not consider what it is at this moment, but what it was when I deliberated upon it.

The importance of every decision lies in the moment ; opportunities and matters roll on and change incessantly. I have in my life run into some serious and clumsy mistakes, not for want of good judgement, but for want of good luck. There are hidden and undreamt of springs in objects we have to handle, especially in human nature ; mute conditions that make no show, sometimes unknown even to their possessor, that are manifested and aroused by unexpected occasions. If my prudence was unable to penetrate into and foresee them, I cannot blame it in the least ; its office is limited. If the issue beats me, and if it favours the course I have refused, there is no help for it ; I do not blame myself, I accuse my luck, not my work. That cannot be called repentance.

Phocion had given the Athenians certain advice which was not followed. When, however, the affair turned out happily against his expectation, somebody said to him, ' Well, Phocion, are you pleased that the things have gone so well ? ' ' Indeed I am pleased, he replied, that it has happened in this way, but I do not repent of having counselled the other course.'

When my friends refer to me for my advice, I give it to them freely and frankly, without being deterred, as most people are, by the consideration that, the matter being risky, it may turn out quite contrary to what I expected, and that I may be blamed for my advice ; that does not trouble me in the least. For they will be in the wrong, and I felt obliged not to refuse them that office.

I have generally only myself to blame for my errors or my misfortunes. For, as a matter of fact, I seldom ask another's advice, except formally and as a· compliment, saving when I have need of scientific instruction and knowledge of facts. But, in things in which I have but to use my judgement, others' reasons may serve to confirm it, but not often to divert me. I lend a favourable and courteous ear to them all. But I cannot remember to this hour having ever followed any but my own counsel. To me they are but flies and specks that distract my will. I set little store by my own opinions, but I set as little by others'. Fortune pays me as I deserve.

If I take little advice, I give still less. It is very seldom asked, and still more seldom is it followed ; and I know of no undertaking, public or private, that has been set right and mended by my advice. Even those who chanced to be somewhat dependent upon it have been more ready to follow the directions of anybody else's brains. And, as I regard the rights of my repose as jealously as the rights of my authority, I would rather have it so ; by leaving me in peace they humour what I profess, which is to be set up in myself and wholly self-contained. It is a satisfaction to me to be disinterested in others' affairs and free of responsibility with regard to them.

When an affair is over, however badly it has turned out, I seldom fret. For I am soothed by the reflection that things were bound to happen thus ; I see that they follow the great stream of the universe, and are involved in the concatenation of Stoical causes. Your imagination cannot conceive or wish the slightest alteration without upsetting the whole order of things, both past and future.

For the rest, I hate that repentance which is incidental to old age. The man who said of old [1] that he was obliged to his years for having rid him of sensuality was not of my opinion ; I can never be beholden to impotence for any good it can do me. *Nor can Providence ever be so hostile to her own work that debility should be ranked with the best things* (Quintilian). Our passions are seldom excited in old age ; we are seized with an extreme satiety after the

[1] Sophocles.

act. In that I can see no sign of conscience ; vexation and weakness imprint upon us a mean-spirited, rheumatic virtue. We must not allow ourselves to be so wholly carried away by our natural alterations as to warp our judgement. Youth and pleasure did not in former years so overpower me that I did not recognize the face of vice in sensual pleasure ; nor does the distaste that years bring with it so overpower me now, that I do not recognize the face of sensual pleasure in vice. Now that I am no longer in it I judge as if I were still in it.

If I rudely shake up my reason and examine it attentively, I find it to be the same as in my most licentious years, except perhaps in so far as it has become enfeebled and impaired by age. And I find that the pleasure it refuses me in the interest of my bodily health, it would not refuse me, any more than formerly, for my spiritual health. I do not esteem her to be any more valiant for being *hors de combat*. My temptations are so broken and mortified that they are not worth being resisted by her. I exorcize them by merely spreading out my hands in front of me. Should she be face to face with that old lust, I fear she would have less power to resist it than she once had. I cannot see that she thinks any differently about it than she did then, or that she has acquired any new light. Wherefore if there is any convalescence, it is a broken-down convalescence.

A miserable kind of cure to owe one's health to disease ! It is not the part of our misfortune, but of the good fortune of our judgement, to do this office. Ills and afflictions can make me do no more than curse them ; they are good enough for people who can only be stirred up by the whip. My reason runs a nimbler course in prosperity. She is much more absorbed and put to it to digest pains than pleasures. I see much more clearly in fair weather. Health admonishes me more cheerfully and to better purpose than sickness. I approached as nearly as I could to an amended and orderly life when I had health to enjoy. I should feel ashamed and mortified that the misery and misfortune of my shaky old age should be thought more estimable than my good, healthy, sprightly, vigorous years ; and that I should be honoured, not for what I have been, but for what I have ceased to be.

In my opinion human felicity lies in the happy life, not

in the happy death, as Antisthenes declared. I never expected to be that monstrosity, a philosopher's tail attached to the head and body of a libertine ; nor that that miserable appendage should disclaim and belie the fairest, fullest, and longest part of my life. I wish to show and present myself uniformly throughout. If I had to live my life over again I would live it as I have lived it ; I neither regret the past nor fear the future. And if I do not deceive myself, I have been nearly the same inwardly as outwardly. It is one of the chief things that I owe to my fortune, that my bodily state has run its course, each part in its due season. I have seen it in the herb, in the flower, and in the fruit ; and now I see it in decay. Happily, however, since it was according to Nature, I bear my present infirmities much the more patiently because they are in season, and because they invoke a more kindly recollection of the long happiness of my past life.

So also my wisdom may well have been of the same stature at the one time as at the other. But it was capable of achieving much more and had a better grace when green, gay, natural, than now that it is broken down, morose, painful. I repudiate therefore those casual and dolorous conversions.

God must touch our hearts. Our conscience must amend of itself, with the reinforcement of our reason, and not through the weakening of our passions. Sensual pleasures are in themselves neither pale nor discoloured because they appear so to dim and bleared eyes. We ought to love temperance for its own sake, and for our reverence to God who commanded it, as well as chastity ; if they are lent to us by a catarrh, or if I owe them to the favour of my stone, they are neither chastity nor temperance. We have no right to boast of despising and combating carnal pleasure, if we cannot feel it, if we know nothing of it, of its charms and power, and its most alluring beauties. I know both, and so have a right to speak.

But it seems to me that in old age our souls are subject to maladies and infirmities more troublesome than those of youth. I used to say so when I was a young man ; at that time they would cast my beardless chin in my teeth. I say so still, now that my grey hairs give me authority to speak. We call by the name of wisdom our austere humours, our distaste for present things. But to tell the truth, we do not so much abandon our vices as change them, and, in my opinion, for the worse. Besides a silly and feeble pride, a wearisome garrulousness, a captious and unsociable temper, and superstition, and a ridiculous anxiety about money after we have lost the use of it, I find there more envy, injustice, and malice. Old age sets more wrinkles on the mind than on the face ; and we never, or very seldom, see a soul that does not, as it grows old, smell sour or musty. The whole man waxes and wanes.

When I look at the wisdom of Socrates, and several circumstances connected with his condemnation, I should venture to believe that he in some sort purposely contributed towards it himself by prevarication, seeing that he was so soon, at the age of seventy years, to suffer his richly-endowed mind to become more sluggish, and to see its wonted clearness becoming dimmed.

What metamorphoses I see many of my acquaintances undergoing every day through old age ! It is a powerful disease that steals upon us naturally and imperceptibly ; it needs a great store of study, and great precaution, to avoid the infirmities that it lays upon us, or at least to retard their progress. I feel that, notwithstanding all my intrenchments, it is gaining upon me foot by foot. I hold out as long as I am able. But after all I do not know to what it will reduce even me. Happen what may, I am satisfied that the world may know from what height I have fallen.

CHAPTER 3

OF THREE KINDS OF INTERCOURSE

WE must not rivet ourselves too firmly to our humours and dispositions. Our chief talent lies in our being able to adapt ourselves to different fashions. To keep oneself tied and bound by necessity to a single course is to exist, not to live. The best minds are those which show most variety and versatility. Here we have an honourable testimony to the elder Cato : *His mind was so equally versatile for all purposes that, whatever he was doing, you would have thought he had been born for that alone* (Livy). If it lay with me to dress myself up in my own fashion,

I should not like to be so firmly modelled to any pattern, however good, as not to be able to get away from it.

Life is an unequal, irregular, multiform movement. To follow incessantly one's own inclinations, to be so held by them as not to be able to deviate from them or twist them out of their course, is to be, not our own friend, still less our own master, but our own slave. I say this now, because I find it difficult to shake myself free from the tyranny of my soul, who cannot interest herself in a thing without being absorbed in it, nor occupy herself with any subject without devoting her full powers to it. However trifling the subject given to her, she is apt to magnify and stretch it to such a point as to require her utmost strength. For that reason her idleness is to me very distressing, and prejudicial to my health.

Most minds need a matter outside of themselves in order to quicken and exercise them; mine needs it rather to enable it to settle down and rest : *the vice of idleness must be shaken off by occupation* (Seneca) ; for its chief and most laborious study is the study of itself.

Books are for my mind one of the occupations which distract her from her study. At the first thoughts that come to her she is aroused, she makes trial of her vigour in all directions, exercising her power of handling the subject, now in a forcible, now in an orderly and graceful manner ; she becomes steady, moderate, and strong. She has the means within her of rousing her faculties. Nature has given her, as to all other minds, matter enough of her own to utilize, subjects enough of her own on which to exercise her imagination and judgement.

Meditation is a powerful and ample exercise for a man who is able to search his mind and employ it vigorously. I would rather fashion my mind than furnish it. There is no exercise that is either more feeble or more strenuous, according to the nature of the mind, than that of entertaining one's thoughts. The greatest make it their profession, *for whom to live is to think* (Cicero). Besides, Nature has gifted it with this privilege, that there is nothing we can do for so long a time, nor any activity to which we can devote ourselves more frequently and easily. It is the business of the Gods, says Aristotle, from which comes their happiness and ours.

Reading serves especially to wake up my reasoning power by suggesting various subjects for meditation ; it busies my judgement, not my memory.

Therefore few conversations are able to hold my attention that are carried on without a mental effort. It is true that charm and beauty sometimes hold and satisfy me no less, if not more, than weight and profundity. And since I become sleepy in any other kind of converse, and only give the rind of my attention to it, it often happens that, in such languid and indolent talk, which we keep up for appearances, I say silly things and make absurd replies, unworthy of a child, or, still more rudely and foolishly, observe an obstinate silence. I have a dreamy way of withdrawing into myself, and on the other hand a gross and childish ignorance of many common things. These two peculiarities have earned me five or six anecdotes, true ones, which people tell of me, as silly as those told of any man.

Now, to follow up my subject, this difficult propensity makes me particular in choosing my company. I have to pick them out on the sorting-board. And it unfits me for ordinary actions. We live and deal with ordinary people. If we are bored by associating with them, if we disdain to adapt ourselves to humble and vulgar minds—and the humble and vulgar are often as well regulated as the most refined (and all sapience is insipid that does not adapt itself to ordinary insipience)—we must cease to meddle either with our own or with others' business. And both public and private business has to be negotiated with such people.

The least strained and most natural pace of our soul is the finest ; the least forced occupations are the best. Good heavens, how well wisdom serves those whose desires she regulates according to their power ! There is no more useful knowledge than this : ' According to one's power,' which was the refrain and favourite saying of Socrates ; a word of great substance.

We must direct and fix our desires on the easiest and nearest objects. Is it not a foolish humour in me to be out of sympathy with a thousand to whom I am joined by Fortune, without whom I cannot live, and to cling to one or two who are outside of my circle, or rather, to a fanciful desire for a thing I cannot obtain ? My easy-going ways, adverse to all bitterness and austerity, may easily have saved me from envy and hostility ; no man ever gave more occasion, I will not say to be loved, but not to be hated. But the coolness of my demeanour towards others has, and rightly so, deprived me of the goodwill of many, who are to be excused if they interpret it in another and worse sense.

I am very capable of contracting and keeping up rare and chosen friendships. Since I grasp so hungrily at any acquaintance that promises to be to my liking, I make such advances, I rush forward so eagerly, that I rarely fail to become attached, and to make an impression where I hit. I have often made happy proof of this. In ordinary friendships I am rather dry and cool ; for my motion is not natural if not with full sail.

Besides, Fortune, having in my younger days spoiled me and made me dainty, as the result of a unique and perfect friendship, has in fact given me a slight distaste for others, and has too deeply imprinted on my fancy that, as that ancient [1] said, it is a ' beast of company, not of the herd '. And then I find it naturally hard to communicate myself in a half-hearted and reserved manner, and with that slavish and suspicious caution which intercourse with numerous and imperfect friends enjoins ; and enjoins especially in these days when we cannot speak of the world without risk and without dissembling.

I see very well, however, that one who, like me, has the amenities of life (I mean the essential amenities) for his end, ought to avoid like the plague those difficult and particular humours. I should commend a soul of several degrees, that can both wind and unwind itself ; that is well wherever its Fortune bears it, that can chat with its neighbour about his building operations, about his hunting and his quarrels, and take a pleasure in talking with a carpenter and a gardener. I envy those who can be familiar with the meanest of their retinue, and begin a conversation among their own staff of servants.

Plato's advice is not to my liking, that we should always speak in a masterful tone to our servants, whether male or female, without any jests, without any familiarity. For, besides the reason I have already given, it is inhuman and unjust to assert so strongly that privilege, such as it is, that we owe to Fortune. And that household dominion

[1] Plutarch.

appears to me the most equitable which admits the least disparity between masters and men.

Others study how to elevate their minds and raise them on stilts ; I, to humble mine and bring it low. It is refractory only in expansion.

> The race of Aeacus
> You tell, and wars 'neath Ilion's sacred wall.
> Of Chian wine the cost,
> Who at the fire shall make our water hot,
> When and with whom for host
> To 'scape the cold Pelignian, that you tell not. (HORACE.)

Thus, as the Lacedemonian valour needed moderating and soothing in war by the soft and pleasing notes of the flute, lest it should turn to fury and madness ; whereas all other nations generally use loud and shrill sounds and voices, which stir and inflame the hearts of the soldiers to the last degree ; so it appears to me, contrary to the usual opinion, that in using our minds, we have for the most part more need of lead than of wings, of coolness and repose rather than of heat and agitation. It is especially foolish, to my mind, to put on wise and knowing airs before simple people, always to speak in a stilted manner, *on the point of a fork*.[1] You must come down to the level of those in whose company you are, and sometimes affect ignorance. Lay aside your strength and cunning ; in ordinary converse it is enough to preserve order. For the rest crawl on the ground, if they like it.

The savants generally stumble over this stone ; they keep parading their pedantry, and scatter their book-learning right and left. In these days they have poured out so much of it into the boudoirs and ears of the ladies, that if the fair creatures have not retained the substance of it, they at least try to appear as if they had. On every kind of subject and in all conversation, however shallow and commonplace, our womenkind affect a novel and scholarly style of writing and speaking :

> In this same language they express their fears,
> Their anger and their joys, their griefs and troubles,
> And all the secrets of their soul pour out.
> What more ? Their love is done in learned style. (JUVENAL.)

They will quote Plato and Saint Thomas as witnesses,

[1] As the Italians say, *favellar in punta di forchetta*.

when any chance comer could serve as well. The learning that cannot reach their mind remains on their tongue.

If the well-bred ladies will take my advice, they will content themselves with making the best of their own natural wealth. They cover and conceal their beauties under borrowed beauties. It is a great sign of simplicity to extinguish one's own light in order to shine with a borrowed lustre. They are buried and entombed under artifice : *they look as if they had come out of a band-box* (Seneca).

The fact is they do not sufficiently know themselves. The world has nothing more beautiful. It is for them to honour the arts and to paint the lily. What need they do but live beloved and honoured ? They have and know more than enough to do that. They need but revive a little and rekindle the faculties that are in them. When I see them intent on rhetoric, astrology, logic, and the like drugs, so futile and useless for their needs, I begin to suspect that the men who urge them to these studies do so as a means of getting them into their power. For what other excuse can I find for them ?

Enough that they can, without our instruction, train their charming eyes to look merry, severe, or soft, season a ' No, no ' with cruelty, hesitation, or encouragement, and need no interpreter for the speeches we make in our wooing. With this knowledge they can command with the switch and master their schoolmasters and the school.

If, however, it irks them to acknowledge their inferiority to us in anything, and if they insist, out of curiosity, on having their share in book-learning, poetry is a diversion suited to their needs ; it is a wanton, subtle, dressed-up and talkative art, all pleasure and show, like themselves. They will also derive various advantages from history. In Philosophy, that part of it which is useful in the conduct of life, they may choose the dissertations that will teach them to judge of our humours and dispositions, to protect themselves against our treacheries, to regulate the boldness of their own desires, to husband their freedom, to prolong the pleasures of life, and meekly to bear the inconstancy of a lover, the rudeness of a husband, the unwelcome encroachments of years and wrinkles, and the like things. That is the utmost share I should allot to them in the matter of learning.

There are peculiar natures that retire into their own shells. It is of the essence of my nature to be communicative, to come out of myself. I am all outside and in evidence, born for society and friendship. The solitude that I love and preach shows itself chiefly in leading my thoughts and feelings back to myself, in restraining and confining, not my steps, but my desires and cares, in eschewing any solicitude about outside things, in avoiding with mortal dread any subjection and obligation, and not so much the throng of men as the throng of business. Local solitude, to tell the truth, makes me rather expand outwardly and sets me more at large ; I am more ready to devote myself to affairs of state and to the world when I am alone. At the Louvre [1] and in the crowd I shrink and retire into my skin ; the crowd thrusts me back upon myself, and my thoughts are nowhere so mad, so licentious and so personal as in places where respect, discretion, and ceremoniousness should be observed. It is not human follies that make me laugh, but our displays of wisdom.

By nature I am not adverse to the bustle of courts ; I have spent a part of my life in them, and am accustomed to bear myself cheerfully in grand company, provided it be at intervals and at my own times.

But that fastidiousness of taste, of which I was speaking, forcibly attaches me to solitude, even at home, amid a numerous household, where visitors are as frequent as elsewhere. I see enough people there, but seldom of the kind that I like to converse with ; and I there reserve, both for myself and others, an unusual liberty. There is a truce to ceremony, dancing attendance on people and showing them off the premises, and such other laborious rites enjoined by politeness (a slavish and tiresome custom !). Every one there behaves as he pleases ; whoever likes may commune with his own thoughts. I may hold my peace, dreamy and absorbed, without offence to my guests.

The people whose society and intimacy I court are those they call refined and talented men, the idea of whom puts me out of liking for others. It is, if rightly understood, the rarest type with us, a type that is chiefly due to Nature. The aim of this intercourse is simply frequent and intimate forgathering and conversation ; the exercise of wits, with-

[1] The Royal Court.

out any other fruit. In our talks all subjects are alike to me ; it matters little to me if there be neither gravity nor profundity in them ; charm and pertinency are never wanting. All is tinted with mature and consistent good sense, mingled with kindliness, freedom, gaiety, and friendship. Not only on the subject of substitutions and the affairs of kings does our mind disclose its beauty and power ; it shows it no less in intimate chat. I know my sort even by their silence and their smiles, and discover them perhaps more easily at the dining-table than at the council-board.

Hippomachus said truly that ' he could tell a good wrestler by merely seeing him walk in the street '.

If Learning is pleased to intrude into our conversation, she will not be shown the door, provided she be not, as she usually is, overbearing and obtrusive, and does not attempt to lay down the law ; but modest and ready to learn herself. We only seek to pass the time ; when it is time to be instructed and preached at we will go and seek her on her throne. Let her stoop to our level for the nonce, if she will so please ; for, useful and desirable as she may be, I imagine that at a pinch we shall very well dispense with her presence, and manage our business without her. The mind of a well-bred person, who has come into frequent contact with the world of men, is in itself sufficiently agreeable. Art is nothing other than the record and register of the productions of such minds.

I also take pleasure in the society of beautiful and honest women. *For we also have eyes that are learned in the matter* (Cicero). If the mind has not the same enjoyment in this as in the other, the bodily senses, which also have a greater share in this, bring it to a proportion near to, although, in my opinion, not equal to the other. But it is an intercourse in which we men must be a little on our guard, especially those, like myself, in whom the body counts for much. In my youth I burned myself at that fire, and suffered all the torments that, according to the poets, befall those who abandon themselves to it without order or judgement. It is true that that whipping has since taught me better :

> The fleet that once escaped Capharean rocks
> Will evermore avoid Euboean seas. (OVID.)

It is madness to give one's whole thoughts to it, and

become entangled in a furious and senseless passion. But, on the other hand, to associate with them without any love or bond of affection, after the manner of actors ; to play an ordinary stage-part, assuming the appropriate age and costume, to contribute nothing of our own except the words, is indeed to keep on the safe side, but in a mean-spirited way, like a man who abandons his honour, or his profit, or his pleasure, in fear of danger. For it is certain that those who contract an intimacy of that kind can expect to reap no fruit from it that will move or satisfy a noble mind.

A man must have earnestly desired what he wishes earnestly to enjoy ; I mean when Fortune should unjustly favour their mask, which often happens, for there is not one of them, however ill-favoured she may be, who does not think herself very attractive, who has not some point to recommend her, her age, or her smile, or her graceful movements (for there are no entirely ugly, as there are no entirely beautiful women) ; and the Brahmin maidens who have no other recommendation go to the market-place, after the people have been assembled by the public crier to see them, and show their matrimonial parts, to see if they at least have not the power of procuring them husbands.

Consequently there is not one who is not easily won over by the first vow a man takes to be her lover. Now, the necessary consequence of these common and ordinary betrayals by the men of to-day is, as we already know by experience, either that they rally together and stand upon the defensive in order to avoid us ; or that they too follow the example that we set them, play their part in the comedy, and lend themselves to the transaction, without passion, without care, without love. *Incapable of attachment, she requires none from others* (Tacitus). They think, following the persuasion of Lysias in Plato, that they may the more profitably and advantageously surrender to us the less we love them.

It will be the same as in a stage-play : the spectators will take as much or more pleasure in it than the actors.

For my part, I can no more recognize Venus without Cupid than maternity without offspring ; these are things that mutually lend and owe their essence to one another. So this cheat recoils upon the man who is guilty of it. It costs him little, but he also gains nothing worth having. Those who made Venus a goddess saw to it that her chief beauty was incorporeal and spiritual ; but the Venus that these people are after is not only not human, it is not even animal.

The animals will not have it so gross and earthy. We often see that imagination and desire kindle and excite them, before the body ; we may observe in both sexes that, among the herd, they make a choice and selection in their affections, and that their mutual intimacies and likings are enduring. Even those to whom old age denies bodily strength will still tremble, neigh, and thrill with love. We may see them, before the deed, filled with hope and ardour, and when the body has played its part, still gratified by the sweetness of the remembrance ; and some there are that are afterwards puffed up with pride and, though weary and sated, crow with triumph and glee.

He who has but to relieve his body of a natural necessity, has no need to trouble others with such careful preparations ; it is no meat for a coarse and gross appetite.

As I have no expectation of being thought better than I am, I will tell this of the errors of my youth. Not only on account of the danger to health (and yet I did not manage so well but I have had two touches, slight, however, and transitory),[1] but also out of contempt, I have seldom had recourse to venal and public connexions. I preferred to whet the pleasure by difficulty, by desire, and by some vain-glory. I shared the tastes of the Emperor Tiberius, who in his amours was as much taken with modesty and noble birth as with any other quality ; and the inclination of the courtezan Flora, who gave herself to no man below the rank of a Dictator, a Consul, or a Censor, and found her delight in the dignity of her lovers. No doubt pearls and brocades, titles and retinues, contribute their part to the pleasure.

For the rest, I used to set great store by mental qualities, but only provided that there was no fault to be found with the body. For, to answer conscientiously, if one or the other of these two attractions must of necessity be wanting,

---

[1] We may observe how Montaigne becomes more indiscreet as he grows older. This parenthesis was a marginal addition to the 1588 edition.

I would have chosen rather to renounce the spiritual ; it has its use in better things. But in the matter of love, which chiefly concerns sight and touch, something may be done without the charms of the mind, nothing without the charms of the body. Beauty is the real advantage of the ladies. It is so peculiarly their own that ours, though it requires somewhat different characteristics, is never at its best but when confounded with theirs, boyish and beardless. It is said that at the court of the Grand Turk the youths that serve him on the score of beauty, who are of endless number, are dismissed at the latest when they are twenty-two years of age.

Reason, wisdom, and the offices of friendship are found better among men ; therefore they govern the affairs of the world.

These two kinds of intercourse are accidental and depend upon others. The one is annoyingly rare, the other withers with age ; so they could not sufficiently satisfy the needs of my life. Intercourse with books, which is the third, is much surer and more in our power. To the first two it yields the other advantages, but it has for its share the constancy and facility of its service. This goes side by side with me in my whole course and accompanies me everywhere. It is my comfort in old age and solitude. It relieves me of the burden of a wearisome idleness, and at all times delivers me from unwelcome company. It blunts the edge of grief, unless it be extreme and overmastering. For diverting my troublesome fancies there is no resource like that of books ; they easily turn my thoughts to themselves and drive out the others. And yet they do not grumble when they see that I only seek their company for want of those more real, more lively, and natural pastimes ; they always receive me with the same welcome.

He may well go on foot, as they say, who leads his horse by the bridle ; and our James, King of Naples and Sicily, who, though young, handsome and robust, was carried about the country on a stretcher, lying on a wretched feather-pillow, clothed in a gown of grey cloth and a bonnet of the same, attended at the same time by a numerous retinue and royal pomp, litters, hand-led horses of all kinds, gentlemen and officers, formed a picture of a still delicate and hesitating asceticism.

The sick man is not to be pitied who has his cure in his sleeve.

In my experience and application of this maxim, which is a very true one, lies all the benefit I reap from books. As a matter of fact I hardly make more use of them than those who have no knowledge of them. I enjoy them as a miser enjoys his treasure, knowing that I can enjoy them when I please ; my mind is satisfied to the full with this right of possession.

I never travel without books, either in peace or in wartime. Yet many days, and even months, will pass without my using them. It will be presently, I say, or to-morrow, or when I please. Meanwhile time flies, and is gone, and I am none the worse. For it cannot be imagined what a restful and comforting thought it is to me, that they are at my side to give me pleasure at my own time, and to feel how much they help me in life. It is the best provision I have found for this human journey ; and I greatly pity any intelligent man who is deprived of it. I am more inclined to accept any other kind of diversion, however trivial, since this can never fail me.

When at home I resort a little more frequently to my library, from which I can quite easily overlook my household. It is over the entry, and I see below me my garden, my farm-yard, my court-yard, and into most parts of my house. There I turn over now one book, now another, without order or plan, in a desultory way. At one time I muse, at another I make notes and dictate, walking to and fro, my fancies, such as these.

It is on the third story of a tower ; on the first is my chapel, on the second a bedroom with its accompaniment, where I often lie down, to be alone. Above it is a large wardrobe. Formerly this was the most useless place in my establishment. There I spend most of the days of my life, and most of the hours of the day ; I am never there at night. Adjoining the library is a rather neat study, in which a fire may be kindled in winter, very pleasantly lighted by a window. And if I did not fear the trouble more than the expense, the trouble that drives me from every kind of business, I could easily join to each side, on the same level, a gallery, a hundred paces long and twelve broad, having found all the walls raised, for another purpose, to the necessary height.

Every place of retirement requires a place for walking. My thoughts go to sleep if I sit still. My mind will not move unless stirred by my legs. All who study without a book are in the same plight.

My library is circular in shape, the only flat side being that needed for my table and chair ; it being rounded, I can see all my books at a glance, arranged about me on five rows of shelves. From this room I have three open and extensive views ; and it offers sixteen paces of empty space in diameter.

In winter I am not there so continually, for my house is perched upon an eminence, as its name implies, and no room is more exposed to the winds than this, which, being rather difficult of access and a little out of the way, I like, both for the benefit of the exercise and because I can keep people at a distance.

Here is my throne ; here I endeavour to make my rule absolute, and to sequester this one corner from all society, conjugal, filial, and social. Everywhere else my authority is only verbal, and doubtful in reality.

Miserable, to my mind, is he who has not in his home a place to himself, where he may give all his attention to himself ; where he may hide ! Ambition is forsooth a great satisfaction to its devotees, since it keeps them always in evidence, like a statue in a market-place. *A great fortune is a great slavery* (Seneca). Not even their privy is private. Nothing appears to me so intolerable in the austere life which our monks affect as the rule I have observed in one of their communities of being perpetually in company, and performing no action whatever except in presence of numbers of others. I find it rather more supportable to be always alone than never to be able to be alone.

If any one tells me that it is degrading to the Muses to use them only for a toy and pastime, he does not know, as I do, the value of pleasure, sport, and pastime. I can hardly help saying that any other aim is ridiculous. I live from day to day, and, speaking in reverence, I live only for myself ; I aim no further.

In my youth I studied for ostentation ; after that a little to gain wisdom ; now for diversion ; never for gain. I have long given up a vain and expensive hobby I had for acquiring that kind of furniture, not only to supply my needs, but to go a little further, to cover and adorn my walls.

Books have many charming qualities for those who know how to choose them. But no good thing without a drawback : it is no more than any other a pure and unadulterated pleasure. It has its disadvantages, and very weighty ones. The mind is exercised by them, but the body, the care of which I have likewise not neglected, meanwhile remains inactive, and becomes heavy and dull. I know of no excess more prejudicial to me, and more to be shunned, in these my declining years.

Those are my three favourite and particular occupations. I will not speak of those civil duties I owe to the world.

CHAPTER 4

OF DIVERSION

I WAS once engaged in comforting a lady who was really afflicted ; for most of their mourning is put on and formal :

> A plenteous gush of tears is ever at hand,
> Ready to flow at will. (JUVENAL.)

We go the wrong way to work when we oppose this grief ; for opposition goads them and drives them further into their sadness. The heat of discussion exasperates the evil. We may observe, in ordinary conversation, if I have made a casual remark and somebody disputes what I say, I resent his contradiction and stoutly defend what I have said ; and still more so that in which I take an interest.

And besides, by proceeding in this way, you enter upon your task too abruptly ; whereas the first greeting of a patient by his physician should be pleasant, cheerful, and encouraging. A grumpy and disagreeable doctor never did any good. On the contrary, then, we must at first encourage and second their grief, and appear to approve and excuse it. By this understanding you will be authorized to proceed further, and, by easy and imperceptible degrees, you will pass over to more solid arguments, and such as are more likely to cure them.

My chief desire being to delude the bystanders who had their eyes upon me, I bethought myself of palliating the evil. And I have found by experience that I am a poor and unsuccessful hand at persuading. My reasons are offered too dryly and pointedly, or too brusquely, or too carelessly.

After having for some time touched upon her anguish, I did not attempt to cure her by strong and powerful reasons, because I have a lack of them, or because I thought I could better effect my purpose in a different way. Nor did I choose the different methods of consolation which Philosophy prescribes : That what we complain of is no evil, with Cleanthes ; That it is a slight evil, with the Peripatetics ; That this lamenting is neither a right nor a praiseworthy action, with Chrysippus ; nor that of Epicurus, more near to my style, That we should shift our thoughts from unpleasant to pleasant things ; nor that of Cicero, To make a bundle of all this mass of cures, and dispense them as occasion offers.

But, quite imperceptibly changing our subject and diverting it gradually to more adjacent ones, and then to others a little more remote, according as she gave me more attention, I insensibly drew her out of her painful thoughts, and kept her in good spirits and quite calm as long as I was there. I made use of diversion.

Those who succeeded me in the same service found no improvement, for I had not laid the axe to the roots.

I have perhaps touched elsewhere upon some kinds of diversion in public affairs. And the use of it in military matters by Pericles in the Peloponnesian war, and by a thousand others at other times, for enticing hostile forces from their own country, is too frequent in history.

That was an ingenious shift with which the Sieur d'Himbercourt saved both himself and others in the city of Liège, which the Duke of Burgundy, who held it besieged, had commanded him to enter, to carry out the terms of surrender agreed upon. The people of the town, assembled together by night to take the necessary measures, began to revolt against those agreements which had been passed, and a number of them decided to fall upon the negotiators whom they had in their power. He, getting wind of the first wave of people who were coming to storm his lodgings, immediately let loose upon them two of the inhabitants of the town (for some of them were on his side), charged with fresh and milder terms to be proposed in their council, which in his need he had there and then invented. These two arrested the first storm and led back the excited rabble to the town hall to hear their message and discuss it. The discussion was short, and now a second storm burst loose, as violent as the other ; and he immediately dispatched four new mediators of the same kind to meet them, with protestations that they now had fatter terms to offer them, which would absolutely content and satisfy them. By this means the people were again turned back to their conclave. In fine, by thus dispensing out delays, diverting their fury and dissipating it in fruitless discussions, he at length laid it to sleep until daylight appeared, which was his main purpose.

This other story falls into the same category. Atalanta, a maiden of exceeding beauty and marvellously agile, to be rid of the throng of a thousand suitors who sought her in marriage, issued this decree, ' that she would accept the man who was her match in running, on the understanding that those who failed should lose their lives.' There were many who thought the prize was worth the risk, and who suffered the penalty of the cruel bargain.

Hippomenes, whose trial was to come after that of the others, addressed himself to the tutelary goddess of this amorous ardour, and invoked her aid ; and she, lending a favourable ear to his prayers, provided him with three golden apples, with instructions how to use them. The race-track being cleared, as Hippomenes perceived that his mistress was gaining upon him, he dropped, as if by accident, one of these apples, and the girl, beguiled by the beauty of it, did not fail to step out of her way to pick it up :

> The maiden, dazzled by the glittering gold,
> Stops in her course to seize the rolling fruit. (OVID.)

He did the same, when he saw his opportunity, with the second and the third, until, by thus diverting her and making her lose ground, he won the race.

When the doctors are unable to purge the catarrh, they divert it and guide it into some less dangerous part. I have observed that that is also the most usual cure for mental ailments. *Sometimes the mind should be guided to other interests, other preoccupations, other cares, other business ;*

*often it will be cured by change of place, as in the case of sick
people who are slow in recovering* (Cicero). Little good is
done by making a direct onslaught on the disease ; we do
not make the patient sustain or ward off the attack, we
draw it off and turn it aside.

This other lesson is too high and too difficult. It is only
for men of the highest order to dwell simply upon the thing,
to consider and estimate it. It belongs to a Socrates alone
to meet death with an everyday countenance, to become
familiar and trifle with it. He seeks no consolation outside
of the thing. Dying appears to him a natural occurrence
and a matter of indifference ; he just fixes his eyes upon
it, he is prepared for it without looking elsewhere.

The disciples of Hegesias who, inflamed by the splendid
eloquence of his lectures, starved themselves to death, and
so thickly that King Ptolemy forbad him again to entertain
his school with these homicidal discourses, do not consider
death in itself ; they do not appreciate it. It is not on
death that they fix their thoughts ; they aim and rush at
a new existence.

These poor wretches we see on the scaffold, filled with
a burning piety, doing their utmost to devote all their
senses to it, their ears to the instructions given to them,
their eyes and hands lifted up to heaven, their voices in loud
prayers, under violent and continual excitement, no doubt
do a thing very commendable and proper in such a strait.
We ought to commend their devotion, but strictly speaking
not their fortitude. They shun the struggle, they turn
their thoughts from death, as we try to amuse children
when they are about to be lanced. I have seen some who,
if they happened to cast their eyes on the dreadful preparations for death going on around them, became paralysed,
and frantically cast their thoughts elsewhere.

We recommend those who are passing along a dreadful
precipice to close their eyes or turn them aside.

When Subrius Flavius, sentenced by Nero's command
to lose his life, and that at the hands of Niger (both com-
manders in war), was led to the place of execution, he
observed that the hole that Niger had had dug for his
burial was badly and unevenly made, and said, turning to
the soldiers present, ' Not even this is according to military
discipline.' And to Niger, who exhorted him to keep his

head steady, ' I only wish that you may strike as steadily.'
And he divined correctly, for Niger's arm trembled so that
he needed several blows to sever it. This man appears to
have had his thoughts directly fixed upon the matter in
hand.

The man who dies in the fray, sword in hand, does not
then give his mind to death ; he does not feel it, or even
think of it. He is carried away in the heat of battle.

A gentleman of my acquaintance, having fallen to the
ground when fighting in the lists, and feeling himself
stabbed nine or ten times with a dagger by his enemy,
whilst every one present was calling upon him to think of
his conscience, told me afterwards that, although those
voices reached his ears, they did not move him in the least,
and that he thought of nothing but how to disengage and
avenge himself. He killed his man in this same combat.

The man who brought L. Silanus his death-sentence did
him a good turn in that, having heard his reply, ' that he
was indeed ready to die, but not at the hands of a criminal,'
he hastened with his soldiers to lay forcible hands upon him,
and when Silanus, unarmed as he was, offered a stubborn
defence with fists and feet, he killed him in the struggle,
thus drowning in a sudden and tumultuous rage the painful
apprehension of the lingering death that was in store
for him.

Our thoughts are always elsewhere ; we are stayed and
supported by the hope for a better life, or by the hope that
our children will turn out well, or that our name will be
famous in the future, or that we shall escape the evils of
this life, or that vengeance threatens those who are the
cause of our death :

> I hope indeed that on the mid-sea rocks,
> If aught the good powers can, thy lips will drain
> The cup of suffering, and oft cry aloud
> On Dido's name. O graceless, thou shalt rue it,
> And I shall hear thereof, yea, for the tale
> Will reach me, even among the nether dead. (VIRGIL.)

As Xenophon was sacrificing, crowned with a garland,
news was brought to him of the death of his son Gryllus,
killed at the battle of Mantinea. On first hearing the news
he threw his wreath to the ground ; but when they subse-

quently told him of the manner of his death, which was most brave, he picked it up and replaced it on his head.

Epicurus himself, drawing near to his end, is comforted by thoughts of the immortality and usefulness of his writings. *All labours are easy to bear, if followed by fame and reputation* (Cicero). And the same wound, the same fatigue, says Xenophon, does not bear so hard upon an army general, as upon a common soldier.

Epaminondas accepted his death much more cheerfully when he was informed that the victory remained with him. *This is a solace, this is a fomentation in the greatest sorrow* (Cicero). And other like circumstances delay, divert, and turn our thoughts from the consideration of the thing in itself.

Nay, even the arguments of Philosophy keep on skimming over and dodging the matter, hardly ever rubbing the crust of it. The first man of the first school of Philosophy, which superintended the others, the great Zeno, against death : ' No evil is honourable ; death is honourable : therefore death is no evil.' Against drunkenness : ' No man entrusts his secret to the drunkard ; every one entrusts it to the wise man : therefore the wise man will not be a drunkard.' Is that hitting the bull's eye ? I love to see that those leading minds cannot escape our common lot. Perfect men as they are, they are still men in a very dull and heavy way.

A sweet feeling is revenge, and deeply implanted in our nature. I can see that well enough, although I have no experience of it in myself. Endeavouring recently to turn a young Prince's thoughts from revenge I did not tell him that he should turn his other cheek to the man who had struck him, for charity's sake ; nor did I picture to him the tragic results that poetry attributes to that passion. I did not touch that string ; but I tried to make him relish the beauty of a picture of a contrary kind, the honour, the favour, the goodwill he would gain by goodness and clemency. I diverted his thoughts to ambition. That is how it is done.

When passion in love gets the better of you, disperse it, they say ; and they say true, for I have often tried it with advantage. Break it up into several desires, of which one may be ruler and master, if you please ; but lest it be domineering and tyrannical, weaken it, arrest its progress, by dividing and diverting it :

> When fretful throbs the vein, then vent the sperm
> Within thee gathered, into sundry bodies.
>
> (PERSIUS and LUCRETIUS.)

And look to it in good time, lest it torment you when once it has taken hold of you :

> Unless thou dost destroy even by new blows
> The former wounds of love, and curest them
> While yet they're fresh, by wandering freely round
> After the freely-wandering Venus. (LUCRETIUS.)

I was once stricken with an overpowering grief for one of my nature ; and yet it was more justified than powerful. I might perhaps have sunk under it, if I had simply trusted to my own strength. Having need of a powerful diversion to take my thoughts from it, I made myself, by art and study, fall in love, wherein I was assisted by my youth ; love solaced me and withdrew me from the evil caused by friendship.

It is the same in all things. A painful fancy takes possession of me ; I find it shorter to change than to subdue it ; if I cannot replace it by another contrary idea, I replace it at least by a different one. Variety always solaces, dissolves, and scatters. If I cannot combat it, I run away from it ; and in running away I double and change my direction. By changing place, occupation, company, I escape into the crowd of other thoughts and diversions, where it loses my trace, and leaves me safe.

In this way does Nature proceed, with the help of inconstancy ; for Time, which she has given us for the sovereign physician of our passions, chiefly obtains its result in this way : by supplying our imagination with other and still other matter, it dissolves and destroys the first feeling, strong as it may be.

A wise man has a hardly less vivid picture of his dying friend after twenty-five years [1] than in the first year ; and according to Epicurus it is no less vivid. For he attributed no alleviation of afflictions either to the anticipation or to the age of his grief. But so many other thoughts cross this one, that in the end it languishes and wearies.

To turn aside the stream of popular gossip, Alcibiades cut

[1] This was written about twenty-five years after La Boëtie's death.

off the ears and tail of his handsome dog, and drove him into the market-place, in order that the people might have something to talk about, and leave his other actions in peace. I have also observed that, for the same purpose of diverting people's suspicions and conjectures and putting the gossips off the scent, some women conceal their real amours by pretending to be in love with some other man. But I knew one who, whilst merely making believe, became seriously smitten, and left the real and original lover for the pretended one. She taught me that the man who has found a soft place is a fool to acquiesce in this dissimulation. When the lady keeps her smiles and favours in public for this suborned wooer, believe me when I say that he is not very clever if he does not in the end usurp your place and dismiss you to his. This is properly speaking to cut out and sew a shoe for another to put on.

It takes very little to divert and turn us aside ; for it takes little to hold us. We seldom consider things in the gross and singly ; it is the minute and superficial surroundings and pictures that strike us, and the empty husks that peel off from the things :

> As nowadays in summer tree-crickets
> Do leave their shiny husks. (LUCRETIUS.)

Even Plutarch bewails his daughter on account of her pretty childish tricks. The recollection of a farewell, of an action, of a particular charm, of a last recommendation, will revive our sorrow. Caesar's toga stirred all Rome as his death had not been able to do. The mere sound of a name buzzing in our ears : ' My poor master ! or My good friend ! Alas, my dear father ! or My kind daughter ! ' When I am distressed by these repeated lamentations, and look closely into them, they appear to me nothing but words and phrases. The word and the tone offend me, as the shouting of a preacher will often arouse his congregation more than his reasons, and as we are moved by the piteous cries of an animal killed for our use ; so that I am meanwhile unable to weigh and penetrate into the true and solid essence of my subject :

> With these incitements Grief provokes herself. (LUCRETIUS.)

These are the foundations of our mourning.

The obstinacy of my stones, especially as affecting the

penis, has sometimes caused so long a suppression of the urine, for three, even four days, and brought me so near death, that, considering the cruel strain this state puts upon me, it would have been madness to hope, nay to desire, to avoid it.

O what a past master in the hangman's trade was that good Emperor [1] who had the yards of his criminals tied fast, that they might die through being unable to pass water !

When I found myself in this plight, I would reflect how trivial were the reasons and objects that imagination fed me with to make me cling to life ; what atoms go to the building up in my soul of the importance and difficulty of departing this life ; for how many frivolous thoughts we find room in so great an affair. A dog, a horse, a book, a glass, and what not, counted for something in my loss. With others it is their ambitious hopes, their purse, their learning, no less foolishly to my mind. I looked upon death with indifference when I saw it in a general way, as the end of life. I master it in the lump ; in detail it worries me. The tears of a lackey, the disposing of my old clothes, the touch of a well-known hand, a commonplace word of comfort, make me soft and sorry for myself.

In like manner our hearts are touched by the laments of fiction ; the tears of Dido and Ariadne strongly affect even those who do not believe in their existence in Virgil and Catullus. It is the sign of a hard and unbending nature not to be stirred to emotion by them, as is related of Polemon, as if it were a something to wonder at ; but he did not even turn pale when bitten by a mad dog that carried away the calf of his leg. And no man is wise enough to picture in his mind the cause of so sharp and overwhelming a grief, that it will not be enhanced by its actual presence, when eyes and ears have a share in it ; parts which are not to be moved only by unreal incidents.

Is it reasonable that even the arts should take advantage of and profit by our natural stupidity and feebleness of mind ? The barrister, says Rhetoric, in that farce they call pleading, will be moved by the sound of his own voice and his feigned emotion, and will suffer himself to be cozened by the passion he is acting. He will affect a real and substantial grief in this mummery he is playing, to transmit

[1] Tiberius.

it to the jury who are still less concerned in the matter than he. Like those men who are hired at funerals to assist in the ceremonial of mourning, who sell their tears and grief by weight and measure ; for, although they are stirred by borrowed emotions, it is certain that, through the habit of settling their countenance to suit the occasion, they are often quite carried away and affected with genuine melancholy.

I assisted, with several others of his friends, in escorting the body of Monsieur de Grammont to Soissons, from the siege of La Fère, where he was killed. I observed that, in all the places we passed through, the people we met with were moved to tears and lamentations by the mere solemn pomp of our convoy ; for they did not know even the name of the departed.

Quintilian relates that he saw actors who entered so deeply into a tragic part that they still wept after reaching home ; and of himself he tells that, having undertaken to work upon others' feelings, he was so carried away by his own that he detected himself not only in tears, but with the paleness of countenance and behaviour of a man really overwhelmed with grief.

In a region near our mountains the women play the part of Prester Martin,[1] for whilst magnifying their grief for their deceased husband by recalling his good and agreeable qualities, in the same breath they summon up and proclaim his imperfections ; as if to strike a balance with themselves and turn away from pity to contempt. This they do with a much better grace than we who, on losing any chance acquaintance, take a pride in praising him for newly dis-covered and unreal qualities, and make him out quite another man when we have lost sight of him than he appeared when we saw him in the flesh ; as if grief were something instructive, or as if tears cleared up our under-standing by washing it.

For my part I renounce from this time forward the testi-mony any man will give in my favour, not because I shall deserve it, but because I shall be dead.

If you ask this man, ' What interest have you in this siege ? ' he will say, ' The interest of example and of

---

[1] Some legendary priest who when celebrating Mass took the parts both of priest and clerk.

common obedience to the Prince ; I expect to gain nothing whatever by it, and as for glory, I know how small a share will fall to an individual like myself. I have neither feeling nor quarrel in the matter.' And yet look at him on the following day, quite another man, red and boiling with fury, in the battle-ranks and ready for the attack. It is the gleam of so much steel, the fire and din of our cannon and drums, that have cast this new hardness and hatred into his veins.

A frivolous cause, you will say. Why a cause ? None is needed to stir our souls ; any idle fancy, without body or object, will rule and stir them. Let me take to building castles in Spain, my imagination will invent pleasures and delights in them, by which my soul will be really tickled and rejoiced. How often we darken our minds with anger and sadness by means of such shadows, and give ourselves up to chimerical feelings which alter both our body and soul !

What astonished, grinning, perplexed grimaces we put on when we indulge in day-dreams ! How limbs and voice start and tremble ! Would you not think that this man, although all alone, falsely imagines that he is conversing with a crowd of other men, or that he has some devil inside him and persecuting him ?

Search within yourself where is the object of this change. Is there anything in Nature except man that feeds on unrealities, and upon which they have any power ?

Cambyses, because he dreamed in sleep that his brother was to become King of Persia, put him to death ; a brother whom he loved and had always trusted ! Aristodemus, King of the Messenians, killed himself for some fancied ill-omen which he drew from the meaningless howling of his dogs. And King Midas did the same, being disturbed and upset by some unpleasant dream he had dreamed.

To abandon life for a dream is to appraise it at its true value. And yet listen to our soul exulting over the wretchedness of the body and its weakness, and because it is exposed to every kind of injury and corruption ! Truly it has a right to speak !

O wretched clay, first by Prometheus shaped !
How little wisdom showed he in his work !
In moulding body he heeded not the soul,
The soul which should have been his art's first care. (PROPERTIUS.)

CHAPTER 5

ON SOME LINES OF VIRGIL

AN edifying thought is engrossing and burdensome in proportion to its fullness and substance. Sin, death, poverty, disease, are solemn and depressing subjects. Our minds should be taught the means to support and combat evils, and the rules of right living and right thinking, and should be often stirred up and exercised in that noble study. But by a mind of ordinary stamp it should be done intermittently and with moderation; if it is too continually strained it will become deranged.

In my younger days I needed self-exhortations and urgings to keep myself in moral trim; a cheerful and healthy nature does not go very well, so they say, with such wise and serious reflexions. I am now differently situated; the conditions attending old age are only too ready to give me warnings and preach me wisdom. From an excess of high spirits I have dropped into the more regrettable excess of seriousness.

For that reason I now purposely indulge myself a little in licence, and sometimes occupy my mind, to give it a rest, with youthful and wanton thoughts. I am at this age only too sober, too heavy and too mature. Every day my years read me lessons in coldness and temperance. This body flees irregularities and dreads them. It is taking its turn in guiding my mind towards reformation. In its turn it is beginning to domineer, and that more rudely and imperiously. It leaves me not an hour of respite, either sleeping or waking, from preaching to me about death, patience, and repentance. I am now on the defensive against temperance, as I was once against sensuality. It pulls me back too much, to the extent of making me insensible.

Now, I desire to master myself in every way. Wisdom has its excesses, and, no less than folly, needs to be moderated. So, lest I should dry up and wither, and be weighed down with prudence, in the intervals that my infirmities allow me,

Lest mind be too intent upon my ills, (OVID.)

I gently turn aside, and avert my eyes from that stormy
and cloudy sky that faces me, which, thanks be to God,
I can regard indeed without terror, but not without effort
and study ; and I divert my thoughts with recollections of
my youthful follies :

> My Soul would have again what she has lost,
> And revels but in memories of the past. (PETRONIUS.)

Let childhood look ahead, and old age behind it ; was
that not the meaning of Janus' double face ? Let years
drag me along, if they will, but backward ! As long as my
eyes are able to distinguish that lovely expired season of
life, I turn them off and on in that direction. If it escapes
from my blood and my veins, I will not at least tear the
picture of it out of my memory :

> The man lives twice who can the gift retain
> Of memory, to enjoy past life again. (MARTIAL.)

Plato recommends old men to look on at the exercises,
dances and games of youth, to enjoy in others the beauty
and suppleness of body which they no longer possess, and
recall to their mind the gracefulness and charm of their
prime ; and would have them award the honour of victory
in those sports to the youth who has provided most recrea-
tion and amusement to the greatest number of people.

Formerly I used to mark the dull and cloudy days as
extraordinary ; these are now almost ordinary with me,
and the extraordinary are the fine and bright days. I shall
soon have come to such a pass that I shall leap for joy,
and regard it as an unwonted favour, to be without pain.
Though I tickle myself I cannot force a poor laugh out of
this wretched body. I am merry only in fancy and in day-
dreams, to divert by artifice the chagrin of old age. But,
in faith, it would require another remedy than that of a
dream. A feeble struggle of art against nature !

It shows great simplicity to prolong and anticipate human
discomforts, as most men do. I would rather be old for
a shorter time than be old before my time. I eagerly grasp
even the slightest occasions for pleasure that I meet with.

I know indeed, from hearsay, several kinds of delights
that are discreet, powerful, ostentatious ; but I am not
such a slave to public opinion as to wish to acquire an
appetite for them. I prefer them not so much grand,

brilliant and showy as luscious, easy and ready to hand. *We depart from Nature ; we follow the people, who are never a good guide* (Seneca).

My philosophy lies in action, in natural and present practice ; little in imagination. O that I could take a pleasure in playing at cobnut or spinning a top !

> For he regarded not the foolish prate
> Of idle people—but his own good health. (ENNIUS adapted.)

Pleasure is an unambitious pursuit ; it is rich enough in its own estimation without adding to it the reward of fame, and prefers to be in the shade. A young man who spends his time in acquiring a taste for choice wines and sauces deserves a thrashing. There is nothing I have known so little about and valued so little. I am now beginning to learn. I am greatly ashamed of it, but what can I do ? I am still more ashamed and vexed at the occasions which drive me to it.

It is our part to dote and trifle ; it is for the young to gain a reputation and climb the ladder. They are going into the world and the world's opinion ; we are withdrawing from it. *Let them keep arms, horses, spears, clubs, tennis, swimming, and races. Of so many sports let them leave the dice-box to us old men* (Cicero). Even the laws send us home. I cannot do less, to gratify this wretched condition into which my age is forcing me, than to provide it with toys and playthings, as we do children ; and after all it is a second childhood that we fall into. And wisdom and folly will have a hard task to prop and succour me with alternate services in this calamity of old age :

> Mingle your wisdom with glimpses of folly ;
> 'Tis delightful at times the fool to play. (HORACE.)

And I try to escape the lightest punctures ; and those that once would not have left a scratch now pierce me through and through. My habit of body begins to be so easily susceptible to pain. *To a frail body every shock is intolerable* (Cicero) :

> A sickly mind can suffer nought that 's hard. (OVID.)

I have always been delicately sensitive and susceptible to injuries : I am now still more tender and exposed to them on all sides : ·

> It needs no force to break a dish that 's cracked. (OVID.)

My judgement certainly keeps me from kicking and murmuring against the discomforts that Nature commands me to suffer ; but it cannot keep me from feeling them. I, who have no other aim but to live and be merry, would travel from one end of the world to the other in search of one good year of agreeable and cheerful tranquillity. A dull and melancholy tranquillity may suffice me, but it benumbs and stupefies me ; and that is not to my liking. If there is any person, any good company, in country or town, in France or elsewhere, whether stay-at-home or travellers, who like my humours, whose humours I like, they have but to whistle in their palms, and I will come and provide them with Essays in flesh and bone.

Seeing that it is the privilege of the mind to escape from old age, I advise mine to do so to the best of its power ; let it bud, let it flower meanwhile, if it can, like the mistletoe on a dead tree !

But I fear my mind is a traitor ; he has formed so close a tie with the body that he forsakes me at every turn, and leaves me to follow him in his need. I take him aside to coax him, I make up to him, but to no purpose. In vain do I try to wean him from this intimacy, and offer him Seneca and Catullus, the ladies and royal dances ; if his comrade has the colic he seems to have it too. Even the activities which are peculiarly and essentially his own cannot then be stirred ; they so evidently smack of a cold in the head. In his productions there is no joy if it is not shared by the body.

Our masters are wrong in this : when seeking the causes of the extraordinary soarings of our soul, besides those they attribute to a divine rapture, to love, to martial fierceness, to poetry, to wine, they have not given its due share to health ; a full, lusty, exuberant, lazy health, such as once the verdure of youth and the feeling of security provided me with in increasing measure. That fire of good humour kindles in the mind bright and vivid flashes beyond our natural capacity, and some of the most joyous, not to say extravagant, enthusiasms.

It is no wonder then if a contrary state depresses my spirits, nails them down, and produces a contrary effect :

When body flags 'twill rise to no achievement. (PSEUDO-GALLUS.)

And yet my mind expects me to be grateful to it because, as it tells me, it acquiesces much less in this languor than is usual with most men. Let us at least, while we are under truce, drive away the evils and difficulties of our partnership :

> While yet we may,
> We'll drive old age with clouded brow away. (HORACE.)

'*Tis good to sweeten black cares with pleasantries* (Sidonius Apollinaris). I love a gay and sociable wisdom, and steer clear of all sour and austere morality ; I suspect a forbidding mien,

> The arrogant gloom of a scowling face. (BUCHANAN.)
> Austerity hides many a debauchee. (MARTIAL.)

I heartily agree with Plato when he says that an easy or difficult humour contributes much towards making a soul either good or wicked. Socrates had a settled expression, but serene and smiling ; not settled like that of the elder Crassus, who was never seen to laugh.

Virtue is a pleasant and cheerful quality.

I know well that very few people will frown at the looseness of my writings who will not have more reason to frown at the looseness of their own thoughts. My sentiments agree with theirs, but I offend their eyes.

It shows a nice habit of mind indeed to cavil at Plato's writings, and glide over his supposed relations with Phaedo, Dion, Stella,[1] Archeanassa ! *Let us not be ashamed to say what we are not ashamed to think.* I hate a gloomy and dismal person who allows the pleasures of life to pass him by, and fastens and browses on its miseries. Like flies that cannot fasten on a very smooth and polished surface, but fix and rest on rough and uneven places ; or like leeches that suck and crave only for bad blood.

For the rest I have made it a rule to dare to say all that I dare to do ; and I dislike even unpublishable thoughts. The worst of my actions and qualities does not appear to me so ugly at it appears ugly and base not to dare to own it.

Every man is discreet in confession ; we should be the same in action.

Boldness to sin is somewhat compensated and curbed by the boldness to confess it. If a man forced himself to tell

---

[1] i. e., Aster, of which Stella is the Latin equivalent.

everything, he would force himself not to do anything that he is obliged to conceal.

God grant that my extreme outspokenness should induce our men to be more free, and to be above those timorous and affected virtues, born of our imperfections ; that at the cost of my immodesty I may lead them on to the point of good sense !

A man must see and study his faults before he can criticize them. They who conceal them from others usually conceal them from themselves. And they do not think them sufficiently hidden if they can see them ; they disguise them and withdraw them from their own consciousness.

Why does no man confess his faults ? Because he is still a slave to them. We must be awake to tell our dreams (Seneca).

The diseases of the body become more distinct as they increase. What we thought was a cold or a sprain turns out to be gout. The diseases of the mind become more obscure as they increase ; the most sick are least sensible of them. Therefore we must often, with pitiless hand, bring them to the light of day, lay them bare, and tear them out of the hollow of our bosom.

As in the case of good deeds, so also in the case of evil deeds, the mere confession is sometimes a reparation. Is any sin so ugly that one can be excused the duty of confessing it ?

It is so painful to me to conceal anything that I shun being trusted with another's secrets, not having the assurance to deny what I know. I am able to keep it to myself ; but deny it I cannot without effort and great reluctance. To be really secretive, one must be so by nature, and not by obligation. In the service of a prince it is of little use to be secretive if one is not also a liar.

If the man who asked Thales of Miletus whether he should solemnly deny having committed adultery had referred to me I should have told him not to do so. For lying appears to me still worse than adultery. Thales advised him quite otherwise, that he should swear in order to shield the greater by the lesser sin.[1] Yet he advised him not so much a choice as a multiplication of sins.

[1] Either Montaigne's memory here played him false, or he was misled, as Coste suggests, by the absence of a note of interrogation in his Greek

Whereupon let us say this by the way, that we make it easy to a conscientious man when we offer him some difficulty to counterbalance a sin ; but when we hem him in between two sins, we put him to a rude choice, as in the case of Origen. He was given the alternative of either practising idolatry or suffering himself to be carnally enjoyed by a big ruffian of an Ethiopian who was brought before him. He submitted to the former condition ; and sinfully, according to one writer. On this assumption, those ladies would not be in the wrong, according to their erroneous views, who *protest* to us in these days that they would rather charge their conscience with ten men than one mass.[1]

If it is an indiscretion thus to publish abroad one's errors, there is no great danger that it will become a precedent and custom ; for Aristo said that the winds that people fear most are those which uncover them. We must tuck up this silly rag that covers our manners. They send their conscience to the brothel and preserve a starched countenance. Even traitors and murderers observe the laws of decorum, and make it a matter of duty. Yet neither can injustice complain of incivility [2] nor knavery of indiscretion. It is a pity that a wicked man is not at the same time a fool, and that outward decency should palliate his sin. Such a rough-cast is only suitable to a good and sound wall, that deserves to be preserved or whitewashed.

In common with the Huguenots, who condemn our auricular and private confession, I confess in public, simply and scrupulously. St. Augustine, Origen, and Hippocrates published the errors of their belief ; I, besides, those of my morals. I am hungering to make myself known ; and I care not to how many, provided I do so truly ; or, to speak more correctly, I hunger for nothing, but I have a deadly fear of being thought other than I am by those who come to know me by name.

What does that man who will do anything for honour

text of Diogenes Laertius. His answer was, ' Is not perjury worse than adultery ? '

[1] Montaigne will have his little joke, though it may not be in the best taste. He felt, however, neither ill-will nor intolerance towards the Protestants.

[2] i.e., perhaps : a man who violates the laws is not entitled to rebuke a man for rude behaviour.

and glory think to gain by showing himself to the world with a mask, hiding his real nature from public knowledge ? Praise a hunchback for his handsome figure, and he must take it for an insult. If you are a coward and some one compliments you on being a man of valour, is it you he is speaking of ? He takes you for another. I should as soon commend him who was pleased with the bonnetings that somebody bestowed upon him, thinking he was master of the company, when he was the meanest of the retinue.

As Archelaus, King of Macedon, was passing along the street, some one poured water upon him ; his attendants said he ought to be punished. ' Yes, but, said he, it was not me he poured the water upon, but the man he took me for.'

Socrates said to one who informed him that people were speaking ill of him, ' Not of me ; there is nothing in me of what they say.'

For my part, if any man commended me for a good pilot, or as very modest, or as very chaste, I should owe him no thanks. And, on the other hand, if one called me a traitor, a thief, a drunkard, I should just as little take offence. Those who misknow themselves may feed on undeserved approbation. Not I, who can see myself, who can search my very heart, and know very well what is due to me. I am content to be less commended, provided I be better known. I might be thought wise in such a sort of wisdom as I take to be folly.

It annoys me that the ladies use my Essays merely as a common piece of furniture, furniture for the reception-room. This chapter will make me suitable for the boudoir. I love their society when it is a little private ; in public it is without favour or savour.

In taking farewell we warm up, more than ordinarily, our affection for the things we are leaving. I am taking my last leave of the sports of the world. These are our last embraces. But let us come to my theme.

What harm has the genital act, so natural, so necessary, and so lawful, done to humanity, that we dare not speak of it without shame, and exclude it from serious and orderly conversation ? We boldly utter the words, *kill*, *rob*, *betray* ; and the other we only dare to utter under our breath. Does this mean that the less of it we breathe in words, the more are we at liberty to swell our thoughts with it ? For it is amusing that the words which are least used, least written, and most hushed up, should be the best known and the most generally understood. There is no person of any age or morals but knows them as well as he knows the word *bread*. They are impressed upon each of us, without being expressed, without voice and without form. [And the sex that does it most is charged to hush it up.]

It is also amusing that it is an action we have placed in the sanctuary of silence, from which to tear it by force is a crime, even for the purpose of accusing it and bringing it to justice. And we do not dare to scourge it but in round-about and figurative terms. A great favour indeed for a criminal to be so execrable that justice thinks it wrong to touch and see him ; free and saved by the favour of the severity of his sentence ! Is it not the same as with books, that sell better and become more public for being suppressed ? For my part I will take Aristotle's word for it, who says, ' To be shamefaced is an ornament of youth, but a reproach to old age.'

These lines are preached in the old school, a school with which I hold much more than with the modern ; its virtues appear to me greater, its vices less :

> Who strives too much to shun fair Venus' wiles
> Sins equally with him who is too keen
> In her pursuit. (AMYOT after PLUTARCH.)

> Thou, Goddess,
> Dost rule the world alone, and without thee
> Naught rises to the shining shores of light,
> Nor aught of joyful or of lovely is born. (LUCRETIUS.)

I know not who could have set Pallas and the Muses at variance with Venus, and made them cool towards Cupid ; but I know of no deities that agree so well together, and are more indebted to one another. Take from the Muses their amorous fancies and you will rob them of the best entertainment they have, and of the noblest matter of their work. And if you deprive Cupid of the society and service of Poetry you will blunt his best weapons. In this way you charge the god of sweet intimacy and amity, and the patron goddesses of humanity and justice, with the sin of ingratitude and forgetfulness.[1]

---

[1] In writing the above, Montaigne might have been reminiscent of a

I have not been so long cashiered from the staff and
retinue of this god but that I still retain a memory of his
power and worth :

> Too plain
> I know the traces of the long-quenched flame. (VIRGIL.)

There is still some remnant of heat and emotion after the
fever :

> In wintry age let not this love grow cool ! (JOHANNES SECUNDUS.)

Withered and drooping though I be, I still feel a few
tepid remains of that past ardour :

> As the deep Aegean, when no more blow the winds,
> That rolled its tumbling waves with troublous blasts,
> Doth yet of tempests passed some show retain,
> And here and there its swelling billows casts. (TASSO.)

But, if I understand the matter, the power and importance of this god, as portrayed in poetry, are much greater
and more alive than they are in reality :

> And Poetry has fingers too
> To titillate and please. (Adapted from JUVENAL.)

Her pictures are somehow more amorous than Amor himself. Venus is not so beautiful, quite naked and alive and
panting, as she is in these lines of Virgil :

> The Goddess ceased, and with the soft embrace
> Of snowy arms about his body wound
> Fondled him as he faltered. Quick he caught
> The wonted fire ; the old heat pierced his heart,
> Ran through his melting frame : as oftentimes
> A fiery rift, burst by the thunder-clap,
> Runs quivering down the cloud, with flash of light.
> .   .   .   .   So saying, he gave
> The embrace she longed for, on her bosom sank,
> And wooed calm slumber to o'erglide his limbs. [1] (VIRGIL.)

pretty passage in Rabelais : ' I remember having read that Cupid on a
time being asked of his mother, Venus, why he did not assault the Muses,
his answer was, That he found them so fair, so neat, so modest, so
virtuous, and so continually occupied, that approaching near unto them
he unbent his bow, shut his quiver and extinguished his torch, through
mere shame and fear that he might do them some hurt. Which done he
thereafter put off his fillet wherewith his eyes were bound, to look them
in the face, and to hear their melody and poetic odes. There took he the
greatest pleasure in the world, that many times he was transported with
their beauty and pretty behaviour, and charmed asleep by the harmony ;
so far was he from assaulting them, or interrupting their studies.'

[1] As probably no translation can do full justice to the original, another

What strikes me is that he depicts her a little too passionate for a married Venus. In this sober contract the desires are not generally so wanton; they are dull and more blunted. Love hates to be held by any tie but himself, and goes feebly to work in intimacies formed and continued under a different name, such as marriage. Family and fortune are there rightly accounted as important, or more so, than charm and beauty. We do not marry for ourselves, whatever they may say; we marry as much, or more, for posterity, for the family. The custom and interest of marriage concern our stock, long after we are dead.

For this reason I approve of its being arranged by a third hand rather than by our own, by others' good sense rather than our own. How totally different is all this to a love compact! Besides, it is a kind of incest in this sacred and time-honoured alliance to employ the extravagant actions of amorous licence, as I think I have said elsewhere.[1] We should, says Aristotle, approach our wives discreetly and soberly, lest the pleasure of being touched too lasciviously should transport them beyond the bounds of reason. What he says upon the account of conscience the physicians say upon the account of health, ' that an over-heated, voluptuous and assiduous pleasure corrupts the seed and hinders conception.' They say, on the other hand, ' that in a languid intercourse, as this is by its nature, the man should offer himself rarely and at considerable intervals, in order that a proper and fertile heat may be stored up ' :

> To eagerly absorb
> Their fill of love, and deeply entertain. (VIRGIL.)

I know of no marriages that are so soon troubled and that version may be appended, that of the late E. Fairfax Taylor. The translation in the text is by Mr. James Rhoades :

> She spoke, and both her snowy arms outflung
> Around him doubting, and embraced the Sire,
> And, softly fondling, kissed him as she clung.
> Through bones and veins her melting charms inspire
> The well-known heat, and reawake desire.
> So, riven by the thunder, through the pile
> Of storm-clouds runs the glittering cleft of fire.
> . . . . He said,
> And gave the love she longed for ; on her breast
> Outpoured at length he slept, and loosed his limbs with rest.

[1] Book I, chapter 30.

so soon come to grief as those which are contracted on
account of beauty and amorous desires. It needs more solid
and permanent foundations, and we should proceed circum-
spectly ; such an exuberant vivacity serves no purpose.

They who think to do honour to marriage by the addition
of love are in the same case, it seems to me, as those who,
thinking to honour virtue, maintain that virtue and nobility
are the same thing. They are qualities which have some
affinity, but there is a great difference between them. There
is no need to confuse their names and titles, whereby both
of them are wronged. Nobility is a fine quality and introduced with good reason ; but as it is a quality dependent
on others, and may fall to the share of any vicious or worthless person, in estimation it falls far short of virtue. If it
can be called a virtue, it is an artificial and visible virtue,
depending on time and fortune, varying in its nature according to country, of this life and mortal, with no more source
than the river Nile, genealogical and common to many, a
thing of succession and resemblance, derived by inference,
and a very weak inference.

Knowledge, strength, goodness, beauty, wealth, all other
qualities, have their value in intercourse and commerce ;
this is self-centred, and of no use in the service of others.

One of our kings was offered the choice of two competitors
for the same office, one of whom was a nobleman, and the
other not. He ordered them to elect the man of greatest
merit, without regard to that kind of quality ; but in case
of their being of exactly equal merit, that they should take
nobility into consideration. This was to give it its proper
place.

Antigonus said to a young man who was a stranger to
him, and who entreated him to be allowed to succeed to his
father's command, a man of valour, lately dead, ' My friend,
in such preferments I regard not so much the noble birth
of my soldiers as their prowess.'

In truth it should not be as with the functionaries of the
Kings of Sparta, trumpeters, musicians, cooks, who were
succeeded in their office by their sons, however incompetent
they might be, in preference to the most experienced in the
profession.

The people of Calicut look upon their nobles as a superhuman species. They are forbidden to marry, or adopt any

profession except war. Of concubines they may have their fill, and the women as many gallants, without any mutual jealousy. But it is a capital and unpardonable crime to mate with a person of different rank to their own. They think themselves contaminated if they have been merely touched by them in passing, and, as their nobility is damaged and injured thereby to a remarkable degree, they will kill any who have only come a little too near them. So the ignoble are obliged to shout as they walk, like the gondoliers at Venice, at the street-corners, for fear of collisions ; and the nobles order them, as they choose, to step to one side or the other. By this means the one avoids what they regard as a perpetual disgrace, and the other a certain death. No length of time, no princely favour, no office, no virtue, no wealth, can ever make a noble of a plebeian. To which the custom contributes that marriages between different trades are forbidden. A girl of shoemaker stock may not marry a carpenter ; and the parents are rigorously obliged to train a son to his father's calling, and to no other, by which means the distinction and continuity of their fortunes is preserved.

A good marriage, if there is such a thing, rejects the company and conditions of love. It tries to imitate those of friendship. It is a sweet partnership for life, full of constancy, trust, and an endless number of useful and substantial services and mutual obligations. No woman who relishes the taste of it,

On whom the nuptial torch has shed a welcome light,   (CATULLUS.)

would like to hold the position of her husband's mistress or leman. If she is lodged in his affections as a wife she is much more honourably and securely lodged. Even if he is paying ardent attentions to another, let any one ask him ' on which of the two, his wife or his mistress, he would rather a disgrace should fall ? whose misfortune would grieve him most ? for whom he would desire the greatest honour ? ' These questions would admit of no doubt in a sound marriage.

It is a sign of the value and excellence of marriage that we see so few good ones. If rightly established and properly understood, there is no better institution in modern society. We cannot dispense with it, and we continue to dishonour it. It may be compared to a cage ; the birds outside are desperately anxious to get in, and those that are in it are equally anxious to get out.

Socrates, when asked whether it was better to take a wife than not, replied, ' Whichever you do, you will repent it.' It is a compact to which the saying fitly applies, ' Man is to man either a god or a wolf.' It needs the conjunction of many qualities to build it up. In these days it is better adapted for simple souls, those of the people, who are not so much disturbed by pleasures, curiosity and idleness. Men of loose morals, like myself, who hate any kind of tie or obligation, are not so well fitted for it :

To me 'tis sweeter far to live with neck unyoked. (PSEUDO-GALLUS.)

If I had followed my own bent, I would have shunned wedlock with Wisdom herself, if she would have had me. But, say what we please, custom and the uses of everyday life carry us along. Most of my actions are guided by example, not by choice. In any case it was not properly at my own prompting that I married. I was led and brought to it by outside occasions. For not only inconvenient things, but anything, however offensive, wicked and repulsive, may be rendered acceptable by some condition or circumstance ; so unsteady are we on our feet !

And I certainly was drawn into it at the time more ill-prepared and more reluctantly than I should be at present, after having made trial of it. And, however loose I may be thought, I have in truth observed the laws of wedlock more strictly than I either promised or expected. It is too late to kick when once we have been hobbled. We must manage our freedom wisely ; but, having once submitted to bondage, we must keep within the laws of common duty, or at least make an effort to do so.

Those men who enter into this bond with the intention of behaving with hatred and contempt act wrongly and improperly ; and this pretty rule which passes from hand to hand among the ladies, like a sacred oracle,

> Serve your husband as a master ;
> Trust him not, for he betrays you,

which is as much as to say, ' Bear yourself towards him with a constrained, hostile and distrustful reverence,' as if it were a war-cry and a challenge, is equally hard and unjust.

I am too mild to harbour such repellent intentions. To tell the truth, I have not yet arrived at such perfection of cleverness and refinement of wit as to confound reason with injustice, and make a mockery of all rule and order that does not fall in with my desires. Though I may hate superstition I do not forthwith take refuge in irreligion. If we do not always do our duty, we should at least always love and acknowledge it. To marry without being wedded is treachery. Let us proceed.

Our poet depicts a marriage in which there is perfect harmony and propriety, in which there is, however, not much loyalty. Did he mean to imply that it is not impossible to yield to the power of love, and yet reserve some duty towards marriage ; and that it may be bruised without being altogether broken ? Many a serving man shoes his masters' mule [1] without necessarily hating him. Beauty, opportunity, fate (for Fate also has a hand in it),

> There is a Fate that rules our hidden parts ;
> For if the stars be not propitious,
> Virility will not avail thee aught,   (JUVENAL.)

have attached her to a stranger ; not so wholly perhaps but that there remains some tie by which she is still held to her husband. It is like two plans, with distinct routes, not to be confounded with one another. A woman may surrender to a certain man whom she would in no case have married ; I do not mean on account of the state of his fortune, but for his personal qualities. Few men have married their mistresses without repenting it.

And even in the other world, what a poor match Jupiter made of it with the wife whom he had first seduced and enjoyed in love's dalliance ! That is, as the proverb puts it, ' to cack in the basket, and then put it on your head.'

I have seen in my time, in a good family, love shamefully and indecently cured by marriage ; the considerations are too different. We love, without pledging ourselves, two different and contradictory things.

Isocrates said that the city of Athens pleased after the manner of the ladies we serve for love. Every man loved to go there, to saunter and pass the time ; but no one loved it so well as to marry it, that is to say, to reside and settle there.

---

[1] Pilfers from him.

I have been annoyed to see husbands hate their wives merely because they themselves have wronged them. We should at all events not love them less for our own faults ; pity and repentance should at least make them more dear to us.

They are different ends, he says,[1] and yet in some sort compatible. Marriage has, for its share, usefulness, justice, honour and constancy ; a stale but more durable pleasure. Love is grounded on pleasure alone, and it is indeed more gratifying to the senses, keener and more acute ; a pleasure stirred and kept alive by difficulties. There must be a sting and a smart in it. It ceases to be love if it have no shafts and no fire. The liberality of the ladies is too profuse in marriage, and blunts the edge of affection and desire. Observe what pains Lycurgus and Plato take, in their Laws, to avoid that disadvantage.

Women are not by any means to blame when they reject the rules of life which have been introduced into the world, seeing that it is the men who made them without their consent. Intrigues and wranglings between them and ourselves are only natural ; the closest agreement we enjoy with them is still attended with tumults and storms.

In the opinion of our author we treat them without consideration in this respect : After knowing that they are incomparably more capable and ardent in the sexual act than we, of which that priest of antiquity was a witness, who was first a man and then a woman :

> Tiresias must decide
> The difference, who both delights has tried ; (OVID.)

after hearing moreover from their own lips the proof that was given, in different centuries, by an Emperor and an Empress of Rome,[2] both famous master-workers in the art (he indeed deflowered in one night ten Sarmatian virgins, his captives, but she actually suffered in one night twenty-five assaults, changing her company according to need and liking :

> Still burning with unconquerable lust,
> Weary she gave up, but still unsatisfied ; [JUVENAL].)

and after the dispute which took place in Catalonia, when a woman complaining of her husband's too unremitting

---

[1] Isocrates.   [2] Proculus and Messalina.

attentions, not so much, I take it, because she was inconvenienced by them (for I believe in no miracles, except in
matters of faith), as, under this pretext, to restrict and
curb, in this the most fundamental act of marriage, the
authority of husbands over their wives, and to show that
their perverseness and ill-will extend beyond the nuptial
couch and tread under foot even the sweets and delights
of Venus ; and the husband, certainly an unnatural brute,
replying that even on fast-days he could not do with less
than ten, the Queen of Aragon interposed with that notable
sentence, by which, after mature deliberation with her
Council, that good Queen, to establish for all times a rule
and example of the moderation and modesty required in a
rightful marriage, prescribed as a lawful and necessary
limit the number of six per diem ; thus renouncing and
surrendering a great part of her sex's needs and desires, to
set up, as she said, ' an easy and consequently permanent
and immutable formula ; ' against which the doctors exclaim, ' what must be the appetite and lust of women, when
their reason, their amendment and virtue are taxed at such
a rate ! '

Considering these varying estimates of our sexual needs,
and seeing that Solon, head of the school of lawgivers,
assesses this conjugal intercourse, if we are not to be found
wanting, at no more than three times a month ; after believing and preaching all this, we have gone and allotted
them continence for their particular portion, at the risk of
the last and extreme penalties.

There is no passion more exacting than this, which we
expect them alone to resist, as being not simply an ordinary
vice, but an abominable and accursed thing, and worse
than irreligion and parricide ; whilst we men at the same
time yield to it without blame or reproach. Even those of
us who have tried to master it have often enough had to
admit how difficult, or rather how impossible it was, by the
use of material remedies, to deaden, to weaken and cool the
body.

On the other hand, we expect them to be healthy, robust,
plump, well nourished and chaste at the same time ; that
is to say, both hot and cold. For marriage, whose function
we say it is to keep them from burning, brings them but
little relief, as we live nowadays. If they take a husband

who is still exuberant with the vigour of youth, he will make
a boast of expending it on others :

> If you don't mend your ways, we'll go to law.
> Your vigour, bought with many thousand crowns,
> No longer's yours, my Bassus ; you have sold it. (MARTIAL.)

The philosopher Polemon was rightly haled before justice
by his wife, for sowing in a barren field the fruit that was
meant for the genital field.

If on the other hand, they take one of the worn-out kind,
behold them in full wedlock worse off than virgins and
widows ! We think they are well provided for because they
have a man at their side. By the same reasoning the
Romans held Clodia Laeta, a Vestal virgin, to have been
violated, because Caligula had approached her, although
it was averred that he had no more than approached her.
Their need is, on the contrary, thereby redoubled, since
the contact and company of any male whatever excites
their heat, which in solitude would remain more dormant.

And, in order, in all probability, to render their chastity
the more meritorious by this circumstance and consideration, Boleslas and Kinge, his wife, King and Queen of
Poland, by mutual agreement consecrated it by a vow,
while lying together on their very wedding-night, and kept
it in the teeth of conjugal opportunities.

We train them from childhood in the service of love ;
their charm, their dressing up, their knowledge, their language, all their instruction, have only this end in view.
Their governesses keep suggesting amorous ideas to them,
though always with the intention of exciting their disgust. My daughter (who is the only child I have) is at an
age when the most precocious of them are allowed by the
laws to marry ; she is constitutionally backward, thin and
delicate, and has accordingly been brought up by her
mother in a retired and particular manner, so that she is
only now beginning to put off her childish naïveté.

She was reading a French book when I was present, and
came across the word *fouteau*, the name of a well-known
tree (beech). The woman to whose care she was entrusted
rather rudely stopped her short and made her pass over the
danger spot. I let her have her way in order not to disturb
their rules, for I never meddle with that government ;

feminine policy has a mysterious procedure, and we must leave it to them. But, if I am not mistaken, the conversation of twenty lackeys could not, in six months, have implanted in her imagination, the meaning and use and all the consequences of the sound of those criminating syllables, as this good old lady did by her reprimand and interdict.

> The ripening virgin joys to learn
> In the Ionic dance to turn
>   And bend with plastic limb ;
> Still but a child, with evil gleams
> Incestuous love's unhallowed dreams
>   Before her fancy swim. (HORACE.)

Let them but drop their formal modesty a little, give them occasion to talk freely ; compared with them we are but children in that science. Only hear them describing our pursuits and our conversation ; they will very soon let you know that we can bring them nothing they have not known and digested without our help. Can it be, as Plato says, that they have once been dissolute boys ?

My ear once happened to be in a place where it was able, without being suspected, to snatch a little of their talk. Why cannot I repeat it ? By our Lady, said I, what need is there to study the phrases of Amadis and the books of Boccaccio and Aretino, and think ourselves so knowing ? It is a mere waste of time. There is no word, no example, no proceeding, that they know not better than our books ; it is an instruction that is born in the veins,

> By Venus herself inspired of old, (VIRGIL.)

which those good schoolmasters, Nature, Youth and Health, continually breathe into their souls. They have no need to learn it ; they breed it :

> Not more delighted is the snow-white dove,
> Or if there be a thing more prone to love,
> Still to be billing with her male than is
> Woman with every man she meets to kiss. (CATULLUS.)

If the natural violence of their desire were not held a little in check by the fear and honour with which they have been provided, we should be shamed. The whole movement of the world resolves itself into and leads to this pairing ; it is a matter infused throughout ; it is a centre to which all things are directed. We may still see some of

the laws of old and wise Rome, drawn up for the service
of Love ; and Socrates' precepts for the instruction of
courtezans :

> On silken cushions they love to lie,
> Those little books the Stoics write. (HORACE.)

Zeno, amongst his laws, gives rules for the spreading and
the attack in deflowering. What was the drift of the philosopher Strato's book, Of Carnal Conjunction ? Of what did
Theophrastus treat in those he called, one The Lover, the
other Of Love ? Of what Aristippus, in his work Of Ancient
Delights ? What was the aim of Plato's so lengthy and
lively descriptions of the boldest amours of his time ? And
of the book Of the Lover, by Demetrius of Phalera ? And
Clinias, or the Ravished Lover, of Heraclides of Pontus ?
And Antisthenes' Of Begetting Children, or Of Weddings,
or his other, Of the Master or the Lover ? And Aristo's Of
Amorous Exercises ? Those of Cleanthes, one Of Love,
the other Of the Art of Loving ? The Amorous Dialogues
of Sphaerus ? And the Fable of Jupiter and Juno, by
Chrysippus, which is shameless beyond all bearing, and of
his fifty so lascivious Epistles ? For I must omit the writings of the philosophers who followed the Epicurean school
[the protectors of sensuality].

In ancient times fifty deities were subservient to this
business. And there were countries where, to assuage the
lust of those who came to pay their devotions, they kept
girls and boys in the churches for enjoyment, and it was
a ceremonious act to use them before going to service.
*Doubtless incontinence is necessary for continence, as a fire is
extinguished by fire.*

In most parts of the world that part of the body was
deified. In one and the same province some flayed off the
skin to offer and consecrate a piece of it, and others offered
and consecrated their semen. In another province the
young men publicly pierced and opened it in several places
between the flesh and skin, and through the openings thrust
skewers, as long and thick as they could bear them ; and of
these skewers they afterwards made a fire, as an offering
to the gods. They were reputed weak and unchaste if they
were dismayed by the force of this cruel pain. In another
place the most sacred magistrate was revered and known

by that member ; and in some ceremonies an effigy of it was carried about in state, to the honour of various divinities.

At the festival of the Bacchanals the Egyptian ladies carried about their necks a wooden effigy of it, exquisitely carved, big and heavy according to their capacity ; besides which the statue of their god exhibited one which exceeded in size the rest of the body.[1]

In my neighbourhood the married women twist their kerchief over their forehead into the shape of one, to boast of the enjoyment they have out of it ; and when they become widows they turn it behind them and hide it under their coif.

The most sedate of Roman matrons thought it an honour to offer flowers and garlands to the god Priapus ; and the virgins at the time of their nuptials were made to sit upon his least seemly parts. And I know not but that I have seen something of the like devotion in my time.

What was the meaning of that ridiculous part of the hose our fathers wore, and which is still seen on our Swiss ? [2] What is the idea of the show we still make of our pieces, in effigy under our galligaskins ; and, what is worse, often, by falsehood and imposture, above their natural size ?

I am inclined to think that a dress of this kind was invented in the best and most conscientious ages in order not to deceive the world, and that every man might, publicly and boldly, render an account of his capacity. The most simple nations still have it, nearly corresponding to the real thing. In those days the workman was taught the art, as it is practised in taking the measure of an arm or a foot.

That good man who, when I was young, castrated so many beautiful and antique statues in his great city, that the eye might not be offended, following the advice of that other ancient worthy :

> The censure of this shame [3] to those is due
> Who naked bodies first exposed to view,
>
> (ENNIUS, quoted by Cicero.)

---

[1] More correctly, according to Herodotus, ' nearly as large as the rest of the body.'

[2] Probably the Swiss mercenaries quartered in the neighbourhood.

[3] The ' shame ' Ennius refers to is the widely prevailing vice of sodomy.

should have considered that, as in the mysteries of the Good Goddess [1] all male semblance was precluded, nothing would be gained unless he also had horses and asses, and in short nature, castrated :

> All things terrestrial, whether man or brute,
> The ocean tribes, tame beasts, gay-feathered birds,
> Rush on to passion's pyre. (VIRGIL.)

The Gods, says Plato, have furnished us with a disobedient and tyrannical member, which, like an animal in its fury, attempts, in the violence of its desire, to subdue everything to its power. So also to the women they have given a greedy and voracious animal which, if denied its food in due season, goes mad in its impatience of delay ; and, breathing its rage into their bodies, stops up the conduits, arrests breathing, and causes a thousand kinds of ills, till, having imbibed the fruit of the common thirst, it has copiously bedewed and sown the ground of their matrix.

Now my legislator [2] should also have considered that it is perhaps a more chaste and salutary practice to let them know betimes the living reality, than to leave them to guess it according to the licence and heat of their imagination. In place of the real parts their desire and hope substitute others triply magnified. And a certain man of my acquaintance ruined his chances by openly disclosing his in a place where he was not yet enabled to put them to their proper and more serious use.

What mischief is not done by these pictures of enormous size that the boys scatter all over the galleries and staircases of the royal houses ! From them they derive a cruel contempt for our natural capacity.

How do we know that Plato had not an eye to this when he ordained, following other well-established republics, that men and women, young and old, should appear naked in view of one another in his gymnasiums ?

The Indian women, who see their men undressed, have at

---

[1] The *Bona Dea*, worshipped by the women of Rome as the goddess of chastity and fidelity, whose temple no man was permitted to enter. In later times it became the resort of unchaste women, and the scene of licence.

[2] The ' good man ' who treated the statues at Rome in the aforementioned manner, supposed to have been Pope Paul III.

least cooled their sense of sight. And, although the women
of that great kingdom of Pegu, who have nothing to cover
them below the waist but a cloth slit in front, and so skimp
that, however much modesty they may try to observe, they
reveal themselves at every step they take, may tell us that
is a device for attracting the men to their sides and wean
them from intercourse with their own sex, a practice to
which that nation is universally addicted, we might reply
that they lose thereby more than they gain, and that a
complete hunger is sharper than one that has been satisfied
at least by the eyes.

Besides, Livia said ' that to an honest woman a naked
man is no more than a statue '.

The Lacedemonian women, more virginal as wives than
our maidens are, every day saw the young men of their city
stripped for their exercises, and were not very particular
themselves to cover their thighs as they walked, esteeming
themselves, as Plato says, sufficiently covered by their
virtue without a farthingale.[1]

But those men, mentioned by Saint Augustine, who raised
a doubt whether the women, at the universal judgement,
will rise again in their own sex, and not rather in ours, lest
they should tempt us in that holy state, have ascribed a
wonderful power of temptation to nudity.

In short we lure and flesh them by every means ; we incessantly heat and excite their imagination, and then we
shout when we are hurt. Let us confess the truth : there is
hardly one of us who does not fear the disgrace his wife's
misdeeds may bring upon him more than his own ; who
does not look more tenderly after his good spouse's conscience than his own (wonderful charity !) ; who would not
rather be a thief and guilty of sacrilege, and that his wife
were a heretic and murderess, than that she should be less
chaste than her husband.

And they would willingly offer to seek a livelihood in the
law-courts, or a reputation in war, rather than be obliged,
in the midst of pleasures and idleness, to keep so difficult
a guard. Do you think they do not see that there is not a

---

[1] *Assez couvertes de leur vertu sans vertugade.* This pun perhaps
suggested the ingenious derivation *vertugarde,* ' virtue-guard '. The
farthingale (actually a corruption of *vertugade,* which is of Spanish origin)
was certainly well contrived to keep men at a distance.

tradesman, or an attorney, or a soldier, who will not leave his business to run after this other ; nor even a street-porter or cobbler, weary and jaded as they are with labour and hunger ?

> For all that did Achaemenes possess,
>   Or wealth Mygdonian of rich Phrygia,
> Or Arab treasure-house, would'st give one tress
>   Of thy Licymnia,
>
> While to thy burning kiss her neck she bends,
>   Or with feigned cruelty that kiss denies
> Which ravished then the thief she more commends,
>   Sometimes to ravish tries ? (HORACE.)

What an iniquitous balancing of sins ! Both we and they are capable of a thousand more mischievous and unnatural depravities than lasciviousness. But we create and weigh sins not according to Nature, but according to our interest ; wherefore they assume such unequal shapes. The harshness of our decrees makes the addiction of the women to that sin more serious and sinful than its nature admits of, and involves it in consequences which are worse than their cause.

I doubt if the achievements of an Alexander or a Caesar surpass in difficulty the steadfastness of a handsome young woman, brought up after our fashion, in the open view and in contact with the world, assailed by so many contrary examples, keeping herself entire in the midst of a thousand powerful and persistent solicitations. There is no activity more abounding in thorny difficulties, nor more active, than this inactivity. I should think it easier to wear a suit of armour all one's life than a virginity. And the vow of chastity is the most noble of all vows, as being the hardest. *The power of the Devil is in the loins,* says Saint Jerome.

Certainly the most arduous and rigorous of human duties is that we have resigned to the ladies, and we leave them the glory of it. That should serve them as a particular spur to persist in it ; it offers them a fine occasion to challenge us, and to tread under foot that vain pre-eminence in courage and valour that we claim over them. They will find, if they take notice, that they will be not only very highly esteemed for it, but also better loved.

A gallant man does not give up his pursuit for a refusal, provided it be a refusal of chastity, not of choice. Though

we swear and threaten and complain ever so much, we lie ;
we love them the better for it.   There is no greater allure-
ment than a chastity that is not hard and forbidding.   It is
stupid and vulgar to persist obstinately in the face of hatred
and contempt ; but to do so against a virtuous and constant
resolution, accompanied by a grateful disposition, is the
action of a noble and generous spirit.   They may gratefully
accept our services to a certain degree, and with due
modesty make us feel that they do not disdain us.

For it is indeed a cruel law, if only for its difficulty, which
commands them to abhor us because we adore them, and
hate us because we love them.   Why should they not listen
to our offers and requests, so long as they keep within the
bounds of modesty ?   Why should they try to detect the
note of some more licentious meaning under our words ?
A Queen of our time wittily said that ' to repel these
approaches was a testimony of weakness, and an accusation
of her own facility ; and that a lady who had not been
tempted could not vaunt her chastity '.

The bounds of honour are not by any means cut so
closely ; it is quite able, without transgressing, to relax its
severity, and give itself a freer rein.   Beyond its frontier
there is some expanse of land, free, indifferent and neuter.
He who has hunted and forcibly run it home, even into its
corner and stronghold, is wanting in tact if he is not satisfied
with his fortune.   The prize of victory is estimated by its
difficulty.

Would you know what impression your assiduity and
your merit have made on her heart ?   Judge of it by her
character.   Many a woman may give more without giving so
much.   The obligation of a benefit is entirely in proportion
to the will of him who gives.   Other circumstances which
accompany the conferring of a benefit are dumb, dead and
fortuitous.   This little may cost her dearer to give than it
may cost her companion to give her all.   If ever rarity was
a sign of esteem it must be so in this case ; do not consider
how little it is, but how few have it.   The value of a coin
changes according to the stamp and the place where it is
minted.

Whatever the spite and indiscretion of some men, at the
height of their discontent, may drive them to say, virtue
and truth always recover their ground.   I have known

women, whose reputation had long been unjustly com-
promised, to recover their good name in the eyes of the
world by their constancy alone, without any effort or cunning. All did penance and took back what they had once
believed. From being a little under suspicion as girls they
have risen to the first rank among good and honourable
ladies.

Somebody said to Plato, ' All the world is maligning
you.' ' Let them say, he said, I will live in such a way that
they shall change their tone.'

Besides the fear of God and the reward of so rare a fame,
which should incite them to keep themselves unspotted, the
corruption of the world we live in compels them to do so ;
and if I were in their place, there is nothing I would not
rather do than entrust my reputation in such dangerous
hands.

In my time the pleasure of telling (a pleasure which in
sweetness falls little short of that of doing) was only permitted to those who had some trusty and unique friend.
Nowadays, when men come together at table or elsewhere,
their ordinary talk consists of boasts of favours received and
the secret liberality of the ladies. Truly it shows too mean
and vulgar a spirit to allow those tender charms to be so
cruelly followed up, pounded and tumbled about by ungrateful, indiscreet, and empty-headed fops.

This our intemperate and unjustifiable exasperation
against that sin is born of the most futile and turbulent disease that afflicts the mind of man, which is Jealousy.

> Who'd shrink from torch to take a light ?
> Whate'er they give, they nothing lose. (OVID and another.)

She and her sister Envy appear to me the most foolish of
the tribe. Of the latter I can say little ; though described
as a strong and powerful passion, she has had the good grace
never to come my way. As to the other, I know her, at
least by sight. The animals have a sense of it : the shepherd
Crastis, having become enamoured of a goat, her ram, in a
fit of jealousy, came and butted his head as he was asleep,
and crushed it.

We have exceeded in this passion, after the example of
some barbarian nations ; the best disciplined have not

escaped, which is reasonable, but they have not been driven
to extremes by it :

> Ne'er did adulterer, by sword of husband slain,
> The purple blood of Stygian waters stain. (JOHANNES SECUNDUS.)

Lucullus, Caesar, Pompey, Antony, Cato, and other brave
men were cuckolds and knew it without making a fuss about
it.   In those times there was only a fool of a Lepidus who
died of grief for that reason :

> Ah, wretch ! if you are taken in the act,
> They'll drag you feet first through the open door,
> And make you food for turnips and red mullets. (CATULLUS.)

And the god of our poet, when he surprised one of his
fellow-gods with his wife, was satisfied with putting them to
shame ;

> And one of the Gods, not of the most austere,
> Wished he could share the shame ; (OVID.)

yet none the less is he warmed by the sweet caresses she
offers him, and complains that for such a trifle she should
distrust his affection :

> Why, Goddess mine, invent
> Such far-fetched pleas ? Dost thou thy faith remove,
> And cease to trust in Vulcan ?   (VIRGIL.)

Nay, she asks a favour of him for a bastard of hers,

> Thine arms I ask, a mother for her son ; (IBID.)

which is generously granted by him ; and Vulcan speaks
honourably of Aeneas :

> Arms for a hero must the forge prepare. (IBID.)

Truly a superhuman humanity ! And I am willing to
leave this excess of kindness to the gods :

> Nor is it meet to equal men with Gods. (CATULLUS.)

With respect to the confusion of children, besides that
the most thoughtful legislators consider it desirable and
ordain it in their republics, it does not trouble the women,
in whom, however, that feeling [1] is, for some reason or
other, still more justified :

> Even the stately Juno, Queen of heaven,
> Was maddened by the oft-repeated faults
> Of her poor erring spouse. (CATULLUS.)

---

[1] Jealousy.

When jealousy seizes those poor weak and unresisting souls, it is pitiful to see how cruelly it catches them in its toils and masters them. It worms itself into them under the cloak of affection, but when it once possesses them, the same causes which served as the foundation of kindness, serve as the foundation of a deadly hatred. Of all mental diseases it is the most easily fed and the most difficult to cure. The virtue, the health, the merit, the reputation of the husband are the firebrands of their fury and malevolence :

> No hate implacable except the hate of love. (PROPERTIUS.)

This feverish passion disfigures and corrupts all that is otherwise good and beautiful in them ; and there is no act of a jealous woman, however chaste and however good a housewife she may be, that does not reveal a bitter and nagging spirit. It is a furious perturbation of mind, which will drive them to an extreme the very opposite to its cause.

This was absurdly exemplified by one Octavius in Rome : Having lain with Pontia Posthumia, his affection was so much increased by enjoyment, that he pestered her with entreaties to marry him. Being unable to persuade her, his excessive love hurled him to the opposite extreme of the most cruel and deadly hatred, and he killed her.

In like manner the ordinary symptoms of that other love-malady are intestine hatreds, plots, and conspiracies :

> We know what frantic woman scorned can do, (VIRGIL.)

and a rage which eats into itself the more it is obliged to shield itself under the cloak of kindness.

Now the duty of chastity is far-reaching. Is it their will that we would have them curb ? That is a very supple and active thing. It is too nimble to be stayed. What if dreams sometimes carry them so far that they cannot deny them ? It is not in them, nor perhaps in Chastity herself, since she is a female, to guard against lust and desire. If their will alone had the power of injuring us, where should we be ? Imagine the great scramble, supposing any man had the privilege of being borne, fully equipped, without eyes to see or tongue to tell, to every one who had the opportunity to receive him !

The Scythian women put out the eyes of all their slaves

and prisoners of war, to make use of them more freely and more secretly.

O what a tremendous advantage is opportunity ! Should any one ask me what is the first advantage in love, I should reply that it is to be able to make one's opportunity ; likewise the second, and the third as well. There you have the key to everything.

I have often wanted luck, but sometimes I have also wanted enterprise ; God shield him from harm who can laugh at this ! It needs greater temerity in these days, which our young men excuse under the name of ardour ; but if the ladies looked closely into it, they would find that it rather proceeds from contempt. I used to be scrupulously afraid of giving offence, and am inclined to respect where I love. Besides, in this traffic, if you leave out the esteem, you will destroy the glamour. I like the lover to be something of a boy, timid, and a slave. If not quite in this, I have in other situations something of the foolish bashfulness that Plutarch speaks of, and which at various times in the course of my life has been to me a blemish and a source of harm. It is a quality that is not in keeping with my nature as a whole.

But what are we if not a bundle of rebellions and discrepancies ? My eyes are as sensitive to suffer a refusal as they are to refuse ; and it troubles me so much to be troublesome to others, that, on occasions where duty compels me to ask a favour of another when the granting of it is doubtful and would put him to any cost, I do so sparingly and reluctantly. But if it is for my own particular benefit (although Homer truly says, ' that in a poor man bashfulness is a foolish virtue ') I usually commission a third person to blush for me. And if another requests a favour of me, I find it equally difficult to show him the door ; so that I have sometimes had the inclination, but not the strength of will, to deny.

It is folly therefore to try to curb in women a desire that is so acute and so natural to them. And when I hear them boast of having so cold and virginal a disposition, I laugh at them ; I tell them they are too backward. If she is a toothless and decrepit old woman, or, if young, sapless and consumptive, though it is not altogether credible, there may at least be a semblance of truth in it. But those who still

move and breathe only make the matter worse, seeing that
he who excuses himself incautiously accuses himself. Like
a gentleman of my neighbourhood who was suspected of
impotence,

> Whose dagger, hanging limp as well-cooked beet,
> Could never rise to middle height. (CATULLUS.)

Three or four days after his wedding, to vindicate his reputation, he went about boldly declaring that he had ridden
twenty stages the night before. His own words were afterwards used to convict him of pure ignorance, and to un-
marry him.

Besides, when the women make the aforesaid boast they
prove nothing ; for there can be neither continence nor
virtue where there is no temptation to resist. ' That is true,
they should say, but I am not one to make an easy surrender.' Even the saints say the same. I am speaking of
those who boast in good earnest of their coldness and insensibility, and expect to be believed with a serious countenance. For when they say it with an affected air, when
their eyes belie their words, when they talk the cant of the
profession, which must be taken against the grain, I find
it amusing. I am a great admirer of naturalness and plain-
ness of speech ; but there is no hope for them. If it is not
wholly simple and childish, it is improper for ladies, and
out of place in that kind of intercourse ; it very soon
inclines to effrontery.

Only fools are taken in by their masks and faces. Lying
is there in the seat of honour ; it is a roundabout way, and
leads to the truth by the postern-gate. If we cannot curb
their imagination, what do we expect of them ?   Deeds ?
There are enough of these that avoid all outside communication, by which chastity may be corrupted :

> That 's often done that 's done without a witness. (MARTIAL.)

And the people we fear least are perhaps the most to be
feared ; their silent sins are the worst :

> I confess,
> A simple prostitute offends me less. (MARTIAL.)

There are acts which, without immodesty on their part,
may cost them their virginity, and, what is more, without
their intention. *Sometimes a midwife, on pretence of examin-*

*ing a virgin's integrity, by evil-mindedness, unskilfulness or
accident, has destroyed it* (St. Augustine). Many a one, in
seeking her maidenhead, has lost it ; many a one has killed
it in sport.

We cannot precisely circumscribe the actions we would
forbid them. Our rules must be worded in general and
ambiguous terms. The very idea we create of their chastity
is ridiculous ; for, among the extreme patterns I have are
Fatua, wife of Faunus, who never allowed any man to see
her after her wedding, and the wife of Hiero, who did not
realize the fact that her husband had a stinking breath,
thinking it was a characteristic of all men. To satisfy us,
they must become invisible and devoid of senses.

Now we must confess that our difficulty in estimating
this duty lies chiefly in the disposition. There have been
husbands who have suffered that mishap, not only without
blaming their wives or feeling injured by them, but under
a sense of singular obligation and acknowledgement of their
virtue. Many a woman there has been who, though she
loved honour more than life, has prostituted herself to the
furious appetite of a deadly enemy, to save her husband's
life ; doing for him what she would never have done for
herself. This is not the place to enlarge upon these examples : they are too sublime and too precious to be set
off by this foil ; let us reserve them for a nobler setting.

But for examples of more commonplace distinction, are
there not women amongst us who every day lend themselves
out for their husbands' sole benefit, and by their express
command and mediation ? And, in ancient times, Phaulius
of Argos offered his wife to King Philip out of ambition. The
same was done out of civility by that Galbus, who, entertaining Maecenas to supper, and seeing his wife and him
beginning to conspire together by signs and oglings, sank
down upon his couch, pretending to be overcome with sleep,
in order to help on their understanding. And he very
graciously gave himself away ; for when, at this point,
one of his slaves made bold to lay hands on the plate which
was on the table, he called out, ' Don't you see, you rascal,
that I am only asleep for Maecenas ? '

This woman may be of loose conduct, and yet of a more
moral disposition than that other whose behaviour appears
more correct. As we hear some lamenting the fact that

they had made a vow of chastity before the age of discretion, I have also heard others truly complain of having been given over to a dissolute life before the age of discretion. This may be due to the sin of the parents, or to the force of necessity, who is a rude counsellor. In the East Indies, although chastity was there held in singular esteem, yet custom permitted a married woman to abandon herself to any man who presented her with an elephant ; and it reflected a certain glory to have been valued at so high a price.

Phaedo the philosopher, a man of good family, after the capture of his country Elis, made it his trade to prostitute his youthful beauty, as long as it endured, to any man who would pay the price, and thereby gained a livelihood.

And Solon is said to have been the first in Greece who by his laws gave women the liberty, at the cost of their chastity, to provide for the necessities of life ; a custom which Herodotus asserts to have been usual, before his time, in several states.

And then, what do we gain by this painful anxiety ? For, however justified this feeling [1] may be, it still remains to be considered whether it carries us very far. Does any man think he can confine them, with all his ingenuity ?

> Hang bolts and bars ; keep her in close confinement.
> But who will watch the guards ? The crafty wife
> Begins with them. (JUVENAL.)

Will they ever lack opportunities in so knowing an age ?

Curiosity is mischievous in all things ; but here it is fatal. It is madness to seek enlightenment on a disease for which there is no physic that does not aggravate it and make it worse, the disgrace of which grows greater and becomes public chiefly through jealousy ; revenge for which wounds our children more than it heals us. You will pine away and die whilst searching in the dark for proofs.

How pitifully they have fared who in my time have succeeded in this quest ! If the informer does not offer a remedy and relief together with the information, he will only make mischief, and deserves the poniard more than if he kept back the truth. The man who is at pains to prevent it is laughed at no less than the man who is in

[1] Jealousy.

ignorance. The mark of cuckoldry is indelible ; the man who is once stamped with it will always carry it ; the punishment makes it more visible than the guilt. It is a fine thing to see our private misfortunes dragged out of doubt and obscurity, to be trumpeted on the tragic boards ; and especially misfortunes that only pinch us by being told. For we say ' Good wife ' and ' Happy marriage ' not of those that are so, but of those no man speaks of.

We must exercise our ingenuity to prevent that awkward and useless knowledge from reaching us. It was customary with the Romans, when returning from a journey, to send a messenger before them to the house, to give their wives notice of their coming, in order not to surprise them. And for the same reason a certain nation arranged that the priest should ' open the ball ' with the bride on the wedding night, to relieve the bridegroom of doubt and curiosity, on his first trial, as to whether she comes to him a virgin, or bruised by another's love.

But the world will be talking. I know a hundred respectable men who are cuckolded, respectably and not discreditably. A gentleman is pitied for it, but not held in less esteem. See to it that your worth drowns your misfortune, that good men curse the occasion ; and that he who wrongs you trembles at the mere thought of it. And besides, does any one escape being talked of in that sense, from the little man to the greatest ?

> Many a man who mighty empires ruled,
> And was by far a better man than you
> In many things, you miserable wretch ! (LUCRETIUS.)

When you hear so many decent men involved in this reproach in your presence, remember that neither will you be spared in other quarters. But even the ladies will laugh at it ; and what are they more ready to laugh at in these days than a tranquil and well-settled married life ?

There is not a man of you [1] who has not made some one a cuckold ; now, Nature runs quite on parallel lines, in compensation, and turn for turn.

The frequency of this mishap must by this time have

---

[1] Montaigne originally wrote on the margin of the 1588 edition, ' There is not one of *us*,' but he deleted *us*, and substituted *you*. A significant alteration !

tempered the bitterness of it ; it will soon have become the rule.

A miserable passion ! which has this also, that it is incommunicable :

> And spiteful Fortune too denies
> An ear to our laments. (CATULLUS.)

For where will you find a friend to whom you dare confide your doleful complaints, who, if he does not laugh at them, may not use them as a stepping-stone and an instruction to take his share in the quarry ? Both the bitter and the sweet of marriage the wise man keeps to himself. And among its other awkward conditions one of the chief, to a communicative man like myself, is this, that custom makes it improper and prejudicial to confide to anybody all we know and feel about it.

To give the women the same advice, in order to disgust them with jealousy, would be a waste of time ; their nature is so steeped in suspicion, vanity, and curiosity, that to cure them by legitimate means is not to be expected. They often recover from this infirmity by a form of health much more to be feared than the malady itself. For, as there are spells which cannot remove a disease except by laying it upon another, so they are apt, when they lose this fever, to transfer it to their husbands.

Yet I know not, to tell the truth, that a man can suffer worse at their hands than jealousy ; it is the most dangerous of their conditions, as the head is of their members. Pittacus said, ' that every man had his trouble, and that his was his wife's jealous temper, but for which he would be perfectly happy.' It must be very hard to bear, when a man so just, so wise, so valiant, felt his whole life poisoned by it ; what are we other little fellows to do ?

The Senate of Marseilles was right to grant the request of the man who asked permission to kill himself, that he might be delivered from his wife's tempestuous temper ; [1] for it is a disease which is only removed by removing the whole piece, and has no effectual remedy but flight or suffering, both, however, very difficult.

---

[1] The example seems to be of Montaigne's invention ; but it is recorded that the Senate of Marseilles permitted that course to any who was the victim of adversity or too great prosperity.

That man, I think, knew something about it who said ' that a happy marriage might be arranged between a blind wife and a deaf husband.'

We must also see to it that that great and violent strictness of obligation we lay upon them does not produce two results that may run counter to our purpose ; to wit, that it may spur on the followers, and make the women more ready to surrender. For, as to the first point, by enhancing the value of the fortress, we enhance the value and desire of conquest. Might not Venus herself have thus cunningly raised the price of her wares by making the laws her brokers ; knowing how insipid a pastime it would be, if not heightened by the imagination and by its dearness ? In short, it is all swine's flesh, varied by sauces, as Flaminius' host said. Cupid is a rogue of a god, who makes it his sport to wrestle with religion and justice ; it is his glory that his power battles with every other power, and that all other laws give way to his :

He ever seeks out victims for his guilt. (OVID.)

And with regard to the second point : Should we not be less often cuckolded if we were less afraid of it, considering the nature of woman ? For prohibition incites and invites them :

You will, they won't ; you will not, they insist. (TERENCE.)

They think it shame to go where we permit. (LUCAN.)

How could we better interpret Messalina's behaviour ? At first she conceals her amours from her husband, as they commonly do ; but finding that, by reason of his dullness, she could carry on her intrigues too easily, she soon disdained that customary way. Behold her then making love openly, owning her admirers, entertaining and favouring them in the sight of all. She wished to make him resent it. When that animal was not to be roused by all this ; when her pleasure was rendered flat and tasteless by his weak and easy-going nature, which appeared to authorize and legalize her conduct, what did she do ? Wife of an Emperor still living and in good health, and at Rome, the theatre of the world, at full noon, with public pomp and ceremony, and to Silius, whom she had already long enjoyed, she is married on a day when her husband was outside the city.

Does it not appear as if she were on the way to becoming

chaste through her husband's nonchalance, or as if she were seeking another husband who might whet her appetite with his jealousy and rouse her by opposition ? But the first difficulty she encountered was also the last. The beast woke up with a start. We often drive the worst bargain with those who appear to be deaf or asleep. I have found by experience that this extreme long-suffering, when once dissolved, will vent itself in the most cruel acts of revenge ; for anger and fury, being heaped up in a mass and suddenly taking fire, discharge all their energy at the first attack :

> And so let loose the reins of wrath. (VIRGIL.)

He put her to death, together with a large number of those who were intimate with her ; even some who had been guilty against their will, having been invited to her bed with scourges.

What Virgil says of Venus and Vulcan, Lucretius more fitly said of a stolen enjoyment between her and Mars :

> Thou on whose breast, consumed with eager love,
> Mars throws himself, who rules with powerful sway
> O'er war's wild works, and then with gaze upturned
> All open-mouthed, with shapely neck flung back,
> Feeds his love-greedy eyes on thy dear face,
> While all his soul hangs quivering on thy lips.
> Oh, while he lies within thy fond embrace,
> With all thy godlike charms around him shed,
> Pour low sweet words from thy sweet lips.

When I reflect upon those words *rejicit* (throws), *pascit* (feeds), *inhians* (open-mouthed), *molli* (soft), *fovet* (fondles), *medullas* (marrow), *labefacta* (melting), *pendet* (hangs), *percurrit* (runs through), and that noble *circumfusa* (shed around), mother of the pretty *infusus* (infused),[1] I despise those little conceits and verbal triflings, which have since cropped up. Those simple poets had no need of that clever and ingenious playing upon words ; their language is quite full-bodied, and big with a natural and constant vigour. They are all epigram ; not only the tail, but the head, stomach, and feet. There is nothing far-fetched, nothing that drags ; it all proceeds at an even pace. *It is a texture of manly beauties ; they are not concerned about flowers of rhetoric* (Seneca).

[1] Some of these words occur in the passage from Virgil which forms the theme of the chapter.

It is not merely a tame eloquence, where nothing offends. It is nervous and substantial, and does not so much please the palate, as it fills the mind with rapture, and especially the greatest minds. When I see those bold forms of expression, so vivid, so deep, I do not say ' This is well said ', but ' This is well thought '. It is the healthy freshness of the imagination that elevates and swells the words. *It is the heart which makes one eloquent* (Quintilian). We moderns confound language with judgement, and fine words with full conceptions.

This painting is not so much the result of manual dexterity as of having the object more vividly imprinted on the soul. Gallus [1] speaks simply because he conceives simply. Horace is not content with a superficial expression ; it would betray him. He sees more clearly and more deeply into the matter. His mind unlocks and ransacks the whole storehouse of words and figures wherewith to express itself ; and he needs them beyond the commonplace, because his conceptions are beyond the commonplace.

Plutarch said that he saw the Latin language through things.[2] It is the same here ; the sense illuminates and brings forth the words, which are not mere wind, but flesh and bone. They mean more than they say. Even the feeble-minded show some reflection of this ; for when I was in Italy I could say what I pleased in ordinary talk, but in serious conversation I should not have dared to trust myself with an idiom that I could not wind and turn out of its ordinary course. I like to be able to introduce something of my own.

It is the use and the handling of language by men of genius that sets it off ; not so much by innovations as by putting it to more vigorous and varied services, by stretching and bending it. They do not contribute words to it, but they enrich their own, giving more weight and depth to their meaning and their use, teaching them unaccustomed movements, but discreetly and skilfully.

---

[1] Cornelius Gallus or the Pseudo-Gallus, an elegiac poet, a friend of Virgil and Propertius.

[2] ' In the reading of Latin books, singular as it may appear, I did not find that the words assisted me to discover the meaning, but rather that my knowledge of the history enabled me to find out the meaning of the words.'—Plutarch, *Life of Demosthenes*.

And how little that is given to all may be seen in the numerous French writers of our time. They are so bold and disdainful that they will not follow the common high-road ; but want of inventiveness and of judgement is their ruin. We see in them only a miserable affectation of singularity, of frigid and absurd disguises which, instead of elevating, lower the matter. As long as they can strut about in new things, they care little about the effect ; if they can grasp at a new word, they will drop the usual one, which is often more forcible and energetic.

In our language I find plenty of stuff, but rather a want of style. For there is nothing that might not be done with our jargon of the chase and our military terms, which are a fruitful soil to borrow from. And forms of speech, like plants, improve and grow stronger by being transplanted. I find it sufficiently abundant, but not sufficiently pliable and vigorous. It usually succumbs under a powerful conception. If you try to strain it you will often feel it drooping and bending under you ; and when it fails you, Latin comes to your aid, as Greek does to others.

Of some of those words I have picked out we find it harder to realize the energy, because the frequent use of them has somewhat debased and vulgarized their beauty for us ; as in our vernacular we meet with excellent phrases and metaphors whose charm has withered with age, and whose colour is tarnished by too general handling. But that does not take away from their flavour for one who has a good nose, nor does it lessen the glory of those old authors who in all probability brought these words to their present prominence.

The scholars treat of things too subtly, in too artificial a manner, differing from the common and natural. My page makes love, and understands it. Read to him Leo Hebreus and Ficino ; [1] they speak of him, his thoughts and actions, and yet he will not understand a word of it. I do

---

[1] Juda Leon, or Leo Hebreus, a Portuguese Rabbi, who lived under Ferdinand the Catholic, author of *Dialoghi d' Amore*, translated from Italian into French, and evidently widely read in the sixteenth century. Four dialogues between a youth and a maiden, in which there is more subtlety than love-making. Marsilio Ficino, who lived about the same time, was an Italian philosopher and theologian who entered the Church rather late in life. He translated from Plato and other classical works, and wrote on metaphysics and theology, but I have seen no mention of any work on Love that he wrote.

not recognize in Aristotle most of my ordinary motions ; they have been covered and clothed in another gown, for the use of the school. God grant that they be right ! If I were of the trade, I should naturalize art as much as they artialize nature. Let us leave Bembo and Equicola [1] alone.

When I write I can dispense very well with the company and remembrance of books, lest they should interfere with my style. Also because, in truth, the good authors humble me too much, and dishearten me. I would gladly do like the painter who, having made a wretchedly bad picture of some cocks, gave his boys strict injunctions to allow no natural cock into his shop. And to set myself off a little, I should rather have to adopt the idea of Antigenidas the musician, who, when he had to perform, took care that, before or after him, his audience was drenched by some other poor singers.

But I can more hardly do without Plutarch. He is so universal and so full, that on all occasions, and however extravagant the subject you have taken in hand, he will thrust himself into your business, and hold out to you a liberal, an inexhaustible handful of treasures and orna-ments. I feel vexed that he should be so exposed to plunder by those who resort to him. I can hardly come near him without purloining a leg or a wing.

And it suits my present purpose to write at home, in these uncivilized parts, where I have nobody to assist or correct me ; while I associate with no man who understands the Latin of his Paternoster, and who does not know even less French.[2] I might have done it better elsewhere, but the work would have been less my own ; and its chief aim and perfection is to be precisely my own. I might indeed correct an incidental error, and these abound with me whenever I run on carelessly ; but the imperfections which are common and constant with me it would be a treachery to remove.

[1] Cardinal Pietro Bembo (1470–1547), a celebrated Italian scholar who wrote among other things *Gli Asolani*, supposed to be a licentious dialogue on Platonic love. Equicola, a theologian and philosopher of the sixteenth century, wrote a book *Della Natura d' Amore*.

[2] Montaigne probably means the French of Paris, which would be very different from that of Gascony.

When another tells me, or I say to myself, 'You are too thick in metaphors; here is a word of Gascon growth; there is a risky expression' (I avoid none that are used in the streets of France; those who would oppose grammar to usage are queer people); 'this is ignorant reasoning; that is paradoxical reasoning; this is too foolish; you often jest; people will think you are serious when you are pretending.' 'Yes, I reply, but I correct the faults of inadvertence, not those which are customary with me. Do I not speak like that throughout? Do I not portray myself to the life? Enough. I have done what I intended; all the world will recognize me in my book, and my book in me.'

Now it is in my nature to ape and copy. When I presumed to write verse (and I never wrote any except in Latin), they openly betrayed the poet I had last been reading; and some of my first Essays smell rather exotic. At Paris I speak a language somewhat differing from that I speak at Montaigne. If I look upon any one attentively I easily take some impression of him. What I consider I usurp: a foolish deportment, a disagreeable grimace, a ridiculous way of speaking. Still more vices; as soon as they prick me they stick, and will not let go without shaking. I have more often been heard to swear by imitation than naturally.

It is a murderous imitation, like that of those terribly big and strong apes that King Alexander came across in a certain region of the Indies, and which he would have found it difficult to master if they had not afforded him the means by that propensity of theirs to copy everything they saw done. For this gave the hunters the idea of putting on shoes when they were looking, and tying them with many laces and knots, of wrapping their heads in some contrivance provided with running nooses, and pretending to anoint their eyes with bird-lime. So these poor beasts incautiously followed their ape-nature to their own ruin: they glued up their own eyes, hobbled their own feet and strangled themselves.

That other accomplishment of cleverly and purposely mimicking the words and actions of another, which often affords amusement and is much admired, I have no more than a log.

When I swear in my own way, it is only *Perdy*, which is

the most straightforward of all oaths. They say that
Socrates swore by a dog, that Zeno used the same inter-
jection now used by Italians, *Cappari*, and that Pythagoras
swore by water and air.

I am so apt unthinkingly to take those superficial impressions that if I have had the words ' Sire ' or ' Your
Highness ' on my lips for three days in succession, they
will slip from me for a week after instead of ' Your Excel-
lency ' or ' Your Lordship '. And if I begin to say a thing
in sport or jest, I am likely to say it next day in earnest.
Wherefore in writing I am more loath to choose a thrashed-
out subject, lest I should treat of it at another's expense.

Every theme is equally pregnant for me. A fly will serve
my purpose ; and God grant that this I have now in hand
has not been taken up at the bidding of too flighty a disposition ! I need only begin with a subject that I fancy, for
all subjects are linked to one another.

But I am dissatisfied with my mind in that it usually
brings forth its profoundest ideas, as well as its maddest
and those I like best, unexpectedly, and when I least look
for them, for they will instantly vanish if I have no means
at hand for fixing them ; on horseback, at table, in bed,
but mostly on horseback, where my thoughts wander most
widely.

When speaking I am rather sensitively jealous of attention and silence, if I am speaking forcibly ; whoever inter-
rupts me, stops me. When travelling, the necessities incidental to the road will cut conversation short ; besides that
I most frequently travel without company fit for connected
discourse. Wherefore I take every opportunity to commune
with my own thoughts.

It is the same with my dreams ; when dreaming I recommend them to my memory (for I am apt to dream that I am
dreaming) ; but next morning I can indeed call to mind
what colour they were of, whether gay, or sad, or strange,
but as to what they were besides, the more I labour to
recover them, the more deeply do I plunge them into
oblivion. So of those ideas that come accidentally into my
mind I retain only a vague outline ; only enough to make
me worry and fret in pursuit of them, and all to no purpose.

Well then, setting books aside and speaking more materi-
ally and simply, I find after all that Love is nothing else but

the thirst for enjoying the desired object, and that Venus is but the pleasure of discharging one's vessels [like the pleasure Nature gives us in discharging other parts], which becomes vicious by immoderation or indiscretion. For Socrates Love is the appetite for generation, by the mediation of beauty.

And when I think, as I have done many a time, of the ridiculous titillation of this pleasure, the absurd, giddy, crack-brained emotions which it stirs up in Zeno and Cratippus, of that unreasonable rage, that countenance inflamed with fury and cruelty at the most delightful moment of love, and then that solemn, stern, ecstatic mien in so extravagant an action ; when I consider besides that our joys and excrements are lodged together pell-mell, and that sensual pleasure at its height is attended, like pain, with faintness and moaning, I believe it is true what Plato says, that man is the plaything of the gods :

> Truly a cruel way to sport with us ! (CLAUDIAN.)

and that Nature was in a mocking mood when she left us that most common and most disturbing of our actions to make us all alike and put us on the same level, wise men and fools, men and beasts. The most contemplative and wisest of men, when I picture him in that attitude, appears to me a humbug with his wise and contemplative airs ; it is the peacock's feet that humble his pride :

> Why may not truth in laughing guise be dressed ? (HORACE.)

Those who refuse to discuss serious matters playfully act, as somebody says, like the man who fears to worship the statue of a saint unless it has an apron.

We eat indeed, and drink like the animals ; but these are not actions that hinder the workings of the mind. In these we maintain an advantage over them ; the other brings every other thought under its yoke, brutifies and bestializes, by its imperious authority, all the theology and philosophy that is in Plato ; and yet he does not lament it. In all other things you may observe some decorum. All other operations may be subjected to the rules of decency ; this one cannot even be imagined other than vicious and ridiculous. Try to find, if you can, some modest and sober way of doing it.

Alexander said that he knew himself to be mortal chiefly by this action, and by sleeping. Sleep stifles and suppresses the faculties of our mind. The sexual act similarly absorbs and dissipates them. Truly it is a mark, not only of our original corruption, but also of our inanity and deformity.

On the one hand Nature pushes us on to it, having connected with this desire the noblest, most useful, and pleasant of all her operations ; and on the other hand she allows us to condemn and fly from it as from a shameless and immodest action, to blush at it and recommend abstinence.

Are we not indeed brutes to call brutish the operation that makes us ?

The nations, in their religions, have met together in a number of conventions, as sacrifices, candles, incense, fasts, offerings and, among other things, in their condemnation of this action. All opinions tend that way, as well as to the widespread custom of cutting off the foreskin, which is a punishment of it.

We are perhaps right in blaming ourselves for producing so foolish a thing as man ; in calling the action shameful, and shameful the parts that serve that purpose. (At present mine are really shameful and shamefaced.)

The Essenians, of whom Pliny speaks, kept up their numbers for several centuries without nurses or baby-clothes, through the influx of foreigners who, following that pretty humour, continually joined them : a whole nation risking extermination rather than become entangled in a woman's embrace, and breaking the continuity of men rather than create one.

It is said that Zeno never had to do with a woman but once in his life, and then only out of civility, that he might not seem too obstinately to disdain the sex.

Every one avoids seeing a man born ; every one runs to see him die. For his destruction they seek out a spacious field, in the full light of day ; for his construction they creep into some dark little corner. It is a duty to hide and blush when making him ; and it is a glory, and the source of many virtues, to be able to unmake him. The one is offence, the other is grace ; for Aristotle says that in a certain phrase of his country, to benefit some one is to kill him. The Athenians, to equalize the disgrace of these two actions, having to purify the island of Delos and justify themselves to Apollo, forbade at once all burials and births within its territory. *We are ashamed of ourselves* (Terence) ; we regard our being as a sin.

There are countries where they cover themselves when they eat. I know a lady, and one of the greatest, who holds the same view, that a woman masticating is an unpleasant sight, as it takes away much of her charm and beauty ; and she does not care to appear in public with an appetite. And I know a man who cannot bear to see another, or to be seen, eating, and is more shy of company when filling than when emptying himself.

In the empire of the Turk there are many who, to show their superiority over others, are never seen at their meals, and only take one a week ; who cut and disfigure their face and limbs ; who never speak to any man : all of them [fanatic] people who think they honour their nature by de-naturalizing themselves, who prize themselves for their mis-prision, and think they become better by becoming worse. What an unnatural animal to be a horror to himself, to grieve at his pleasures, to regard himself as a misfortune ! There are some who conceal their lives,

> And change the sweets of home
> For exile kingdoms 'neath an alien sky ; (VIRGIL.)

and withdraw from the sight of other men ; who shun health and cheerfulness as if they were hurtful enemies. There are not only many sects, but many nations, that curse their birth and bless their death. There are countries where the sun is abominated and the darkness worshipped.

We show no skill except in ill-treating ourselves ; that is the true quarry for our powerful intellect : a dangerous tool when misapplied !

O wretched men, whose pleasures are a crime ! (PSEUDO-GALLUS.)

Alas, poor human ! you have sufficient necessary evils, without adding to them by your own invention ; you are miserable enough by nature without being so by art. You have real and essential deformities in abundance without forging imaginary ones. Do you think you are too well off unless you find [the half of] your well-being an affliction ? Do you think you have fulfilled all the necessary duties to which Nature binds you, and that she is wanting and idle

in you, if you do not force yourself to create fresh duties ?
You are not afraid of sinning against her universal and
unquestionable laws, and spur yourself to obey your own,
which are partial and fanciful ; and the more partial, uncertain and questionable they are the more do you persist in
obeying them. You are possessed and bound by the positive
orders of your own invention and the rules of your parish ;
those of God and the world leave you unconcerned. Consider for a moment the examples of this kind ; all your life
is reflected in them.

The lines of these two poets, treating lasciviousness as
they do with so much reserve and discretion, appear to me
to disclose it more fully and cast a strong light upon it. The
ladies cover their bosoms with open-work lace, the priests
keep many sacred things hidden, painters put shadows
into their work to set off the light, and they say that the
sun's rays and the wind are harder to bear when reflected
than direct. The Egyptian who was asked, ' What are you
hiding under your cloak ? ' answered discreetly, ' I am
hiding it under my cloak that you may not know what it
is.' But there are certain other things that are hidden to
be shown. Listen to this man, who is more unreserved :

> And pressed her naked body unto mine.[1]   (Ovid.)

I feel as if he were caponizing me. Let Martial gather up
Venus's skirts as high as he pleases, he will not succeed in
making her appear so entire. He who says all sates and
disgusts us. He who fears to be explicit leads us on to thinking more than is meant. There is treachery in this kind of
modesty, and especially when they half open, as these do,
so fair a path to imagination. And the action and the
painting should smack of theft.

I like the Spanish and Italian methods of making love,
which are more respectful, more timid, more affected and
discreet. Somebody in ancient times, I forget who, wished
for a gullet as long as a crane's neck, that he might the
longer relish what he was gulping down. This wish is more
appropriate to this quick and hasty pleasure, especially in

---

[1] The commentator Coste, after quoting Cotton's translation of this
line, remarks, ' We cannot say the same thing so openly in French ; and
if more disguised, it would form a ridiculous contrast with what Montaigne
adds immediately after.'

a nature like mine, whose failing it is to be too sudden.
To arrest its flight and lengthen out the preliminaries, everything serves as a favour and recompense between them : a
look, a nod, a word, a sign. If we could dine off the steam
of a roast joint, what an expense we could save !

It is a passion in which very little solid reality is mingled
with much more unreality and feverish imagination ; it
should be paid and served accordingly. Let us teach the
ladies to make the most of themselves, to observe self-
respect, to keep us in suspense ånd fool us. We begin with
the final attack, and always show our French impetuosity.
When they spin out their favours and spread them out in
small portions, each of us, even miserable old age, will find
a little to glean, according to his substance and merit.

He who finds no enjoyment except in enjoyment, who
wins nothing unless he sweeps the stakes, who loves the
chase only for the sake of the quarry, has no business to
intrude into our school. The more steps and degrees there
are, so much higher is the uppermost seat, and so much
more honourable it is to reach it. We should take a pleasure
in being led to it, as into a magnificent palace, through
divers porticoes and passages, long and pleasant galleries
and many turnings. This dispensation would turn to our
advantage ; we should dwell there the longer, and love the
longer. Without hope and without desire we can make no
progress worth a rap.

They should infinitely dread our mastery and entire
possession of them. As soon as they have wholly surrendered to the mercy of our fidelity and constancy, their
position is a little too risky ; for those virtues are rare and
hard to find. No sooner are they ours than we are no more
theirs.

> The lust of greedy soul once satisfied,
> Nor oaths nor promises they reck. (CATULLUS.)

And Thrasonides, a young Greek, was so much in love
with his love that, having won his mistress's heart, he refused to enjoy her, that he might not thereby deaden, sate,
and weaken that restless ardour on which he fed and so
prided himself.

Dearness gives relish to the meat. See how the form of
salutation, which is peculiar to our nation, spoils by its

cheapness the charms of the kiss which, as Socrates says,
is so powerful and dangerous a stealer of hearts. It is a
disagreeable and offensive custom for a lady to have to lend
her lips to any man, however disgusting, who has three
lackeys at his heels : [1]

> As from his snout, so like a dog's,
> Hangs the rime of frozen fogs,
> And the beard it fairly clogs
> Around his throat. . . .
> A hundred times I'd rather kiss his ———. (MARTIAL.)

And we ourselves do not gain much by it ; for the world
is so divided that for three pretty women we must kiss fifty
plain ones. And for a tender stomach, such as we have at
my age, a bad kiss is too high a price to pay for a good one.

In Italy they act the part of the languishing suitor even
with the ladies who are for sale, and defend this practice as
follows : ' that there are degrees in enjoyment, and that by
paying them homage we try to procure for ourselves the most
complete. For these ladies sell only their bodies ; their
good will cannot be on sale, it is too free and too much at its
own disposal.' Hence they say that it is the will they lay
siege to ; and they are right. It is the will we must serve
and win by our attentions. To me it is a horrible idea that
a body void of affection should belong to me. It can only
be compared to the mania of that youth who defiled by his
love the beautiful statue of Venus that Praxiteles made ;
or of that raving Egyptian whose lust was kindled by a
dead body he was embalming and shrouding, which was the
occasion of the law since made in Egypt, which ordained
that the bodies of beautiful young women and those of good
family should be kept for three days before being delivered
into the hands of the undertakers. Periander acted still
more unnaturally by carrying his conjugal affection (although more regular and lawful) to the point of enjoying
his wife Melissa after she was dead.

Does it not appear a lunatic humour in Luna, when she
could not otherwise enjoy her darling Endymion, to put him
to sleep for several months, and browse in the enjoyment of
a youth who stirred only in his dreams ?

[1] Sir John Falstaff, with his three retainers, is a case in point ; see
Merry Wives, Act I. sc. i. Evidently the custom was not peculiar to
France.

So I say that we love a body without a soul, or without feeling, when we love a body without its consent and desire. All enjoyments are not alike ; some are hectic and some languid. A thousand other causes besides goodwill may win us this favour of the ladies ; it is not a sufficient evidence of affection. Treachery may lurk there, as elsewhere ; sometimes they respond with only one buttock :

> As cool as at a sacrifice, you'ld think
> Her marble, or in quite another place. (MARTIAL.)

I know some who would rather lend that than their coach, and who have nothing else to communicate. You must observe whether she enjoys your company on any other account, or on that alone, as if you were some burly stable-boy ; in what degree of favour or esteem you are housed :

> Whether she gives herself to thee alone,
> And marks thy day out with the whiter stone. (CATULLUS.)

What if she eats your bread with the sauce of a more pleasing imagination :

> She holds you in her arms,
> But sighs for other loves. (TIBULLUS.)

What ! Have we not heard of some one, in our time, who turned this action to a horrible revenge, to poison and kill, as he did, an honest woman ? They who know Italy will never think it strange if, in this connexion, I do not go elsewhere for examples. For that nation may be said to be the school-master of the world in this practice.

Handsome women are more commonly met with in that nation, and fewer plain ones than here ; but in rare and surpassing beauties I think we are on a par. And I judge the same of their intellects ; of commonplace minds they have many more. A brutish stupidity, as may be plainly seen, is with them incomparably more rare. In exceptional minds and those of the highest degree we can hold our own with them.

If I were to carry this comparison further, I think I may say, on the other hand, that, as compared with them, valour is common and natural with us ; but sometimes we may see it on their side in so full and powerful a degree, that it exceeds all the boldest examples we can produce.

The marriages in that country are lame in this respect :

their custom commonly imposes so rude and slavish a law upon the wife, that the most distant acquaintance with a stranger is for her as capital an offence as the most intimate. The result of this law is that every approach is necessarily of a substantial nature ; and, since all comes to the same with them, they have a very easy choice. And, once they have broken through this partition, you may imagine that they catch fire. *Lust, like a wild beast, angered by its chains, breaks loose* (Livy).

We must give them a little more rein :

> Of late I saw, with firm bit held, a colt
> Rush headlong like a mighty thunderbolt. (OVID.)

The desire for company is assuaged by giving it a little liberty.

We are pretty much in the same case ; they go too far in restraint, we in licence. It is a pleasing custom we have in this country that our sons are received into good families to be brought up and trained as pages, as in a school of nobility ; and it is regarded as a piece of discourtesy and an affront to refuse one of gentle birth.

I have perceived (for so many houses, so many different styles and methods) that those ladies who have tried to lay down the strictest rules for the maids of their retinue have not had the best luck. It needs moderation, and we must leave a good part of their conduct to their own discretion ; for, taking all in all, there is no discipline that will curb them at every point. But it is most true that one who has come safe, with bag and baggage, out of a free schooling, inspires much more confidence than one who comes safely out of a school in which she has been kept a strict prisoner.

Our fathers trained their daughters to look bashful and timid (hearts and desires were the same) ; we train ours to put on an air of assurance. We understand nothing of the matter. That is all very well for the Sarmatian women, who are not allowed to lie with a man until they have with their own hands killed another in war.

For me, who have no authority over them except through the ears, it is enough if they retain me for their counsel, in accordance with the privilege of my age. So I counsel them, as well as ourselves, abstinence ; but, if this generation is too hostile to it, at least discretion and modesty.

For, as Aristippus, according to the tale, said to some young men who blushed to see him enter the house of a courtesan, ' The sin is not in entering, but in not coming out again.' If she has no care for her conscience, let her have some regard to her good name. Though the substance be not worth much, let the appearance hold good.

I commend gradation and delay in the dispensation of their favours. Plato points out that in every kind of love an easy and prompt surrender is forbidden in those who hold the fort. It is a sign of gluttony, which they should conceal with all their cunning, to surrender so heedlessly and impetuously all they have. By observing order and measure in granting their favours, they fool our desire the better, and conceal their own. Let them ever flee before us. I mean even if they wish to be caught. They will conquer us the better in flight, like the Scythians. Indeed, according to the law that Nature has given them, it is not properly their part to will and desire ; their part is to suffer, obey, and consent. That is why Nature has given them a perpetual capacity ; to us a rare and uncertain one. They always have their hour, that they may always be ready for ours ; *born to be passive* (Seneca). And, whilst she has decreed that our appetites should show and declare themselves prominently, she has arranged for theirs to be hidden away and inward, and has provided them with parts fitted simply for the defensive, and not for show.

They must leave pranks like the following to Amazonian licence : when Alexander was marching through Hyrcania, Thalestris, Queen of the Amazons, came to see him with three hundred troopers of her own sex, well mounted and well armed, having left the remainder of a large army that was following her beyond the neighbouring mountains, and said to him aloud and publicly, ' that the reports of his victories and his valour had brought her thither to see him and offer her power and resources to help him in his enterprise ; and that, seeing he was so handsome, young and strong, she, who was perfect in all his qualities, proposed to him that they should cohabit, that there might be born, of the most valiant woman in the world and the most valiant man then living, something great and rare for the time to come.' Alexander thanked her for the rest ; but to gain time for the accomplishment of her last request, he stayed thirteen days at that place, which he spent in feasting and jollity to the best of his powers, to welcome so courageous a princess.

We are, in almost all things, unjust judges of their actions, as they are of ours. I confess the truth when it tells against me as when it is on my side. It is an infamous and badly ordered state of things that so often drives them to change, and prevents them from fixing their affections on any object whatever ; as we see in that goddess to whom we attribute so much fickleness and so many lovers. Yet it is true that it is contrary to the nature of love not to be violent, and contrary to the nature of violence to be constant. And they who wonder at it, who exclaim against it and look for the causes of this frailty in them, as if it were unnatural and incredible, why can they not see how often they themselves share it, without being amazed and crying ' miracle ' ? It would perhaps be more strange to see them attached to one object. It is not a merely bodily passion. If there is no end to avarice and ambition, neither is there to lechery. It still lives after satiety ; and neither constant satisfaction nor limit can be set to it ; it ever outlives possession.

And besides, inconstancy is perhaps rather more pardonable in them than in us. They may plead, as we do, the inclination to variety and novelty common to both sexes ; and secondly they may plead, as we do not, that they buy a cat in a poke.

Joan, Queen of Naples, had her first husband Andreasso hanged at the bars of her window with a cord of silk and gold thread twisted with her own hands, because in the matrimonial fatigue-duties she found that neither his parts nor his performances answered the expectations she had formed of him when she saw his stature, his beauty, his youth and activity, by which she had been caught and deceived.

They may plead that the active part needs more effort than the passive, so that on their part the effort is always equal to the occasion, whilst on our part it may fall out otherwise. For this reason it was that Plato wisely made a law that, in order to decide upon the expediency of a marriage, the judges should see the youths who contemplated it stark naked, and the girls nude only down to the girdle.

When they come to try us they do not perhaps find us worthy of their choice :

> All efforts vain to excite his vigour dead,
> The married virgin flies the unjoyous bed. (MARTIAL.)

It is not enough that the will should drive straight. Weakness and incapacity lawfully dissolve a marriage :

> A lover much more vigorous she needs
> To undo her virgin zone. (CATULLUS.)

Why not ? and, according to her standard, a more licentious and more active capacity for love :

> Lest to his pleasing toil he prove unequal. (VIRGIL.)

But is it not a great impudence to bring our imperfections and weaknesses where we desire to please and leave a good opinion and recommendation of ourselves ? For the little that I now need,

> —For one encounter only am I fit,—(HORACE.)

I would not trouble a person I have to respect and fear :

> Let me not suspicion rouse
> Who now, alas, have passed my fiftieth year. (HORACE.)

Nature should be satisfied with making this age miserable, without also making it ridiculous. I should hate to see it, for one inch of pitiful vigour that inflames it three times a week, strutting and swaggering as fiercely as if it had some big and lawful day's work in its belly : a regular straw-fire. What wonder if, after leaping up into a sudden and crackling flame, it dies down in a moment and becomes cold and lifeless !

That desire should only be found in the prime of youth and beauty. Trust your age, if you would be convinced, to back up that indefatigable, full, constant and courageous ardour you feel in yourself ; it will leave you nicely in the lurch. Better to boldly hand on your experience to some nerveless, wide-eyed, ignorant boy, who still trembles under the rod, and will blush at it :

> A crimson blush her glowing face o'erspread,
> As Indian ivory, when stained with red,
> Or lilies mixed with roses in a bed. (VIRGIL.)

He who can await, in the morning, without dying of

shame, the contempt of those beautiful eyes that have witnessed his slackness and impertinence,

> And truly eloquent with dumb reproof,   (OVID.)

has never felt the satisfaction and pride of wearying them
and setting dark rims around them by the vigorous exercise
of an active and busy night.

When I have seen one dissatisfied with me, I did not at
once accuse her of fickleness ; I began to wonder whether
I should not rather blame Nature, who has certainly treated
me unfairly and unkindly :

> He is not very tall, and not very stout.   (PRIAPEA.)

> The very matrons look with much disfavour
> Upon a man with little parts ;   (IBID.)

and done me a most enormous hurt. Every part of me
makes me what I am, as much as any other. And no other
makes me more properly a man than this.

I owe it to the public to give them my full-length portrait.
The wisdom I have learned lies wholly in truth, freedom of
speech, reality. It disdains to include in the catalogue of
its real duties those petty, invented, customary provincial
rules. It is entirely natural, constant, universal. Its
daughters, but bastard daughters, are civility and con-
ventionality.

We shall easily get the better of the sins of appearance
when we have conquered those of reality. When we have
done with the latter, we may run full tilt at the others, if
we find it necessary to run at them. For there is danger of
our setting up new duties in our imagination, to excuse our
neglect of our natural duties, and to obscure them. As a
proof of this we may see that in places where faults are
crimes, crimes are no more than faults ; that with the
nations where the laws of propriety are more uncommon
and more laxly kept, the primitive and common laws are
better observed ; since the innumerable crowd of so many
duties stifles, deadens, and scatters our attention. Our
application to little things withdraws us from more urgent
ones.

O what an easy and pleasant path do those superficial
men take, in comparison with ours ! They are shadowy
things wherewith we plaster our conscience and pay one

another's debts. But we do not pay, but rather pile up, our debts to that great judge, who pulls up our rags and tatters around our shameful parts, and does not pretend not to see through us, even to our inmost and most secret impurities. Our virginal modesty would be usefully covered if it could keep this discovery from him.

In short, whoever could sharpen the wits of man and rid him of these over-nice verbal superstitions would do the world no great harm. Our life is part folly, part wisdom. He who only treats of it reverently and canonically will leave more than half unsaid. I do not indulge in self-excuses, and if I did, I should rather excuse myself for my excuses than for any other fault. I excuse myself to those of a certain way of thinking, whom I hold to be more numerous than those on my side. For their consideration I will say this besides—for I wish to please every one ; though it is a difficult thing *for a single man to conform to that great variety of manners, discourses and wills* (Q. Cicero)— that they ought not strictly to blame me for the things I quote from authorities accepted and approved by many centuries ; and that there is no reason why, because I do not write in verse, they should deny me the freedom that is enjoyed, in our days, even by church dignitaries, and those of our nation and the most tufted. Here are two specimens :

Rimula, dispeream, ni monogramma tua est.[1]

Un vit d'ami la contente et bien traite.

And what about so many others ? I love modesty, and it is not judgement that prompts me to choose this scandalous way of speaking. It is Nature who has chosen for me. I do not commend it any more than I do all methods that are contrary to accepted custom ; but I excuse it, and, by particular and general circumstances, lighten the accusation.

---

[1] Which a commentator translates : ' Que je meure si ta fente n'est pas légère.' The line is by Theodore de Bèze, born 1519 in Burgundy, one of the most influential of the Genevese reformers, who in his youth wrote witty but indecent poetry, the publication of which caused him bitter regrets in his after days. The second line is by Mellin de Saint-Gelais, who was Chaplain to the Dauphin, and whose poems, published after his death, were remarkable only for the absence of poetic feeling, and for the continual blending of pious and erotic phrases. The meaning of the word *vit* may be guessed.

But to proceed. Whence too comes that sovereign authority you usurp over one who grants you favours at her own cost,

> Who in the dead of night has given you
> Many a little present; (CATULLUS.)

and whom you immediately treat with the self-interest, coolness, and authority of a husband ? It is a free compact ; why do you not keep it as you would hold her by it ? There is no law to bind voluntary actions.

It is contrary to custom, but it is true none the less that in my time I have carried out this bargain, as far as the nature of it would permit, as conscientiously as any other bargain, and with some appearance of justice ; that I never pretended more affection than I felt ; and that I gave simple expression to its decline, its vigour and birth, its outbursts and slack periods. One does not always go at the same pace. I was so sparing of promises that I think I did more than I promised or owed. They found me faithful to the point of serving their interest when they were inconstant to me, I mean avowedly and sometimes repeatedly inconstant. I never broke with them as long as I was attached to them even by a thread ; and whatever cause they may have given me I never broke with them so far as to hate and despise them. For those intimacies, even when gained on the most shameful terms, still oblige me to have some kindly feeling for them.

At times I have given way to anger and somewhat unwise impatience on detecting their tricks and shifts, and in our quarrels ; for I am naturally liable to sudden fits of temper which, though fleeting and soon over, are often prejudicial to my interest. If they were minded to test the freedom of my judgement, I did not shirk giving them some sharp paternal advice, and pinching them where they smarted. If I gave them any cause for complaint, it was rather because they found me too foolishly conscientious in my love, compared with modern ways. I have kept my word when I might easily have been excused from doing so ; they would then sometimes surrender with credit to themselves, and on conditions which they would readily have allowed the victor to break.

More than once I have made the pleasure at its highest

point to yield to the interest of their honour. And when urged by reason I have armed them against myself, so that they acted more securely and decorously by my rules, when they freely submitted to them, than they would have done by their own.

As often as I could I took upon myself all the risks of our rendezvous, to relieve them of responsibility ; and always contrived our meetings at the most difficult and unexpected times and places, because they arouse less suspicion and are besides, I think, more accessible. A place is chiefly open at a spot which is supposed to be of itself covered. The less we fear a thing the less are we on the defensive and on the watch for it. You may more easily dare a thing that nobody thinks you will dare, so that it becomes easy through its difficulty.

No man ever acted with more regard to consequences.[1] This way of loving is more correct ; but who knows better than I how ridiculous it appears nowadays, and how little it is practised ? Yet I shall not repent of it ; I have nothing more to lose there :

> My votive tablet, in the temple set,
> Proclaims that I to Ocean's God have hung
> The garments from my latest shipwreck wet. (HORACE.)

I can now speak openly about it. But, just as I might perhaps say to another, ' My friend, you are dreaming ; love, these days, has little to do with faith and honesty ' :

> Now if you try to make unstable counsel
> Stable by reason's rules, you only add
> To madness, and are reasonably mad ; (TERENCE.)

so, on the contrary, if I had to begin anew I should certainly pursue the same path and the same course of proceeding, however fruitless it might be to me.

Incapacity and folly are praiseworthy in an unpraise-worthy action. The further I depart from their point of view in this, the nearer I keep to my own.

For the rest, in this traffic, I did not let myself go entirely ; I took pleasure, but I did not forget myself, in it ; I kept entire the little sense and judgement that Nature has given

---

[1] On the margin of the edition of 1588 was written, and then deleted : ' The desire to generate should be purely legitimate.'

me, for their sake as well as for my own ; a little excitement, but no delirium. My conscience was also involved to the point of making me licentious and dissolute ; but ungrateful, treacherous, malicious or cruel, never. I was not reckless in pursuing the pleasure of this vice, but bought it for what it cost and nothing more. *There is no vice that is self-contained* (Seneca).

I hate a stagnant and sleepy idleness almost as much as a toilsome and thorny activity ; the latter pinches me, the other makes me drowsy. I like a wound as well as a bruise, a cut as well as a dry blow. I found in this traffic, when I was fitter for it, a right moderation between those two extremes. Love is an excitement, wideawake, lively and gay ; it did not disturb or afflict me, but it made me warm and thirsty for more. One should stop there ; it is hurtful only to fools.

A young man asked the philosopher Panaetius whether it was becoming in a wise man to be in love. ' Let us leave the wise man out of the question, he replied ; but you and I, who are far from being wise, must not become entangled in so violent and exciting a business, which enslaves us to another and makes us contemptible to ourselves.' He spoke truth, that a soul is not to be trusted that has not the strength to withstand the attack of a thing that comes so suddenly, and that is not able practically to disprove the saying of Agesilaus ' that wisdom and love cannot go abreast '.

True, it is a vain pastime, unbecoming, shameful and unlawful ; but, conducted in this fashion, I regard it as salubrious, proper to enliven a dull body and soul. And, as a physician I would prescribe it for a man of my temperament and condition as readily as any other remedy, to stir him up and keep him robust till well on in years, and to ward off the attacks of senility. Whilst we are yet but in the suburbs and the pulse still beats ;

> Whilst hair is yet but grey, and age still stands upright,
> While yet remain some threads for Lachesis to spin,
> While on my feet I walk and need no staff to help,   (JUVENAL.)

we need to be solicited and tickled by some such biting excitation as this. See what youth, vigour and sprightliness it put into the wise Anacreon. And Socrates, when older than I now am, said, speaking of a girl he fell in love with, ' With her shoulder touching mine, and my head near to hers, as we were looking together into a book, I suddenly felt a pricking in the shoulder, if you will believe me, like the bite of an insect ; and for more than five days it tingled, and through my heart ran a continual itching pain.' What ! a touch, and that an accidental one, and of a shoulder, disturb and kindle a soul cooled and weakened by age, and of all human souls the most chastened ! Why not, in heaven's name ? Socrates was a man, and desired neither to be nor seem anything else.

Philosophy does not strive against natural pleasures, as long as due measure be observed ; she preaches moderation, not flight. Her power of resistance is used against exotic and bastard pleasures. She says that bodily desires must not be heightened by the mind, and wittily warns us not to try to excite hunger by surfeiting, not to stuff instead of merely filling the belly ; to avoid all enjoyment that may bring us to want, and all food and drink that makes us thirsty and hungry.

So in the service of love she bids us to choose an object that simply satisfies the body's need, that does not stir the soul, which must not look to its own satisfaction, but should simply follow and assist the body.

But am I not right in thinking that these precepts, which by the way are in my opinion a little too rigorous, concern a body that is equal to its functions ; and that when a body is in a low condition, like a disordered stomach, it is excusable to warm and sustain it artificially, and by means of the imagination to restore the appetite and cheerfulness which it loses when left to itself ? .

May we not say that there is nothing in us, during this earthly imprisonment, that is purely either corporeal or spiritual ; that we wrongfully tear a living man to pieces, and that it seems but reasonable that we should look upon pleasure with at least the same favour as upon pain ? The latter (for example) was violent to the point of perfection in the souls of the Saints, by means of penitence ; the body naturally, by virtue of their alliance, shared the pain, and yet could have little share in the cause. And still they were not satisfied that it should simply follow and assist the ill-used soul ; they tormented the body itself with atrocious and appropriate tortures, in order that soul and body might vie together in plunging man into anguish, the more cruel, the more salutary.

So in the case of bodily pleasures, is it not wrong to cool the soul with regard to them, and to say that she must be dragged to them as to some enforced and slavish obligation and necessity ? It is her part rather to cherish and promote them, to offer and invite herself to share them, since it is her office to rule. As it is also, I think, her part, in respect of her own pleasures, to breathe and instil into the body all the feeling they are capable of arousing, and study to make them sweet and wholesome. For it is reasonable, as they say, that the body should not follow its appetites to the prejudice of the mind.

But why is it not also right that the mind should not follow hers to the prejudice of the body ?

I have no other passion to keep me in breath. What avarice, ambition, quarrels, lawsuits, do for other men who, like myself, have no fixed occupation, love would do more beneficially. It would wake me up again, make me more sober, pleasing and careful of my person ; it would recompose my countenance and prevent the grimaces of old age, those ugly and pitiful grimaces, from spoiling it ; it would bring me back to wise and healthy studies, whereby I might become better loved and esteemed, driving from my mind its hopelessness in itself and its employment, and restoring it to itself ; it would divert me from a thousand troublesome thoughts, a thousand melancholy humours, which idleness and the poor state of our health impose upon us at this age ; would warm up, at least in dreams, this blood that Nature forsakes, would raise the chin and stretch out a little the nerves and the vigour and the gaiety in the soul of this poor man who is moving full speed towards disintregration.

But I know well that it is a blessing very hard to recover. Through failing strength and long experience our taste has become more delicate and fastidious. We demand more when we can bring less ; we are more anxious to choose when we least deserve to be accepted. Knowing ourselves for what we are, we are less confident and more distrustful of our powers ; nothing can make us sure of being loved, knowing our condition and theirs.

I am ashamed of being found in the midst of these green and exuberant young people,

> In whom undaunted vigour stands more firm
> Than sapling on the mountain-side. (HORACE.)

Why should we go and intrude our misery into that gay throng,

> That fervid youngsters may behold,
> With laughter loud and long,
> The burnt-out torch into the ashes flung ? (HORACE.)

They have strength and reason on their side ; let us give place to them ; we can only look on.

And that germ of budding beauty will not be touched by such stiff old hands, nor won by mere material means. For, as the old philosopher replied to the man who jeered at him for being unable to win the good graces of a tender lass he was pursuing, ' My friend, the hook will not bite in such fresh cheese.'

Now, it is an intercourse that needs reciprocity and mutual exchange. The other pleasures we receive may be acknowledged by returns of a different nature ; but this can only be paid for in the same kind of coin. Indeed in this pastime the pleasure I give tickles my imagination more agreeably than that which I feel. Now there is no generosity in the man who can receive pleasure where he confers none ; it is a mean soul that would be beholden for everything, and is content to keep up relations with a person to whom he is a charge. There is no beauty, favour or intimacy so exquisite that a gentleman should desire it at that price. If they can be kind to us only out of pity, I would much rather not live, than live on alms. I would like to have the right to ask it of them in the way in which I heard them beg in Italy : *Fate ben per voi* ; [1] or after the manner of Cyrus exhorting his troops : ' Who loves himself, follow me ! '

You may tell me to consort with persons in my own state, who, sharing the same fortune, will be more easy of access. O foolish and insipid compromise !

> I will not pluck the beard of lion dead. (MARTIAL.)

Xenophon makes it the ground of his objection and accusation against Menon, that in his amours he set to work on faded flowers.

---

[1] Charity, for the good of your soul.

I find more sensual pleasure in merely witnessing, or even in only imagining, the sweet and honest pairing of two fair young people, than in myself making a second in a pitiful and imperfect conjunction. I leave that fantastic appetite to the Emperor Galba, who preferred his meat when it was old and tough ; and to this poor wretch :

> O that the Gods would grant me yet to see
> And kiss thy own dear self with changed locks,
> And clasp thy withered body to my arms ! [1]

And among the chief disfigurements I count a forced and artificial beauty. Emonez, a young boy of Chios, thinking by pretty ornaments to acquire the beauty that Nature had denied him, appeared before the philosopher Archesilaus and asked him whether a wise man might fall in love. ' Yes, by heaven, he replied, as long as it is not with a dressed up and sophisticated beauty like yours.' The confessed ugliness of old age is less old and less ugly, to my mind, than when it is painted and polished.

Shall I say it ? Provided you do not seize me by the throat. Love, in my opinion, is not properly and naturally in season except in the age next to childhood :

> Him should you, with dishevelled hair
> And that ambiguous face bring in
> Among a troop of pretty girls,
> He would deceive the subtlest there,
> So smooth, so rosy is his skin. (HORACE.)

Nor beauty either. For while Homer extends it until the chin begins to be shaded, Plato himself remarked that that was rare. And the reason is notorious why the Sophist Bion so wittily called the downy hairs of adolescence Aristogeitons and Harmodians'.[2] In manhood I think it already out of date ; not to speak of old age.

> Ruthless is Love, for past the withered oak
> He flies. (HORACE.)

And Margaret, Queen of Navarre, being a woman, greatly extends the privileges of her sex, ordaining that thirty is the season for them to exchange the name of ' beautiful ' for that of ' good '.

[1] Ovid, writing in exile to his wife at Rome.
[2] As Harmodius and Aristogeiton delivered their country from the tyrant, so the first signs of virility delivered the Greek youth from a persecution of a different kind.

The shorter the possession we grant Cupid over our lives, the better we are for it. Look at his bearing, and his boyish chin ! Who knows not how, in his school, all goes backward, against all rule ? Study, exercise, use, are the ways that lead to inefficiency ; there the novices are the teachers. *Love knows no order* (St. Jerome). Truly his conduct is much more charming when blended with heedlessness and irregularities ; mistakes and checks give point and grace to it. Provided it be eager and hungry, it matters little whether it be prudent. See how he goes reeling, tripping and wantoning ; you put him in the stocks when you guide him by art and discretion, and he is restrained in his divine freedom when put under those hirsute and callous hands.

For the rest, I have often heard the ladies describing this intercourse as entirely spiritual, and disdaining to consider the part the senses play in it. Everything serves, and I may say that I have often observed that we pardon their intellectual shortcomings in consideration of their bodily charms ; but I have not yet observed any of them to be willing to favour intellectual beauty in us, however wise and mature, when joined to a body that shows the least signs of decay. Why does not one of them feel a desire to make that noble Socratic exchange of body for soul, purchasing a spiritual and philosophical generation and intelligence at the price of her thighs, the highest rate at which she can value them ?

Plato, in his Laws, ordains that one who has performed a signal and useful exploit in war shall, as long as it is being waged, not be denied, however old or ill-favoured he may be, a kiss or any other amorous favour from any woman he may choose. Can that which he thinks so fair in consideration of military worth not also be fair in consideration of some other kind of worth ? And why does not one of them seek to forestall her sisters and win the glory of so chaste a love ? I may well say chaste :

> A horse grown old,
> Slow kindling unto love, in vain prolongs
> The fruitless task, and, to the encounter come,
> As fire in stubble blusters without strength,
> He rages idly. (VIRGIL.)

The vices that are confined to thought are not the worst.

To conclude this remarkable commentary, which has slipped from me in a torrent of babble, a torrent sometimes impetuous and hurtful :

> Like the red apple, her lover's secret gift,
> In the chaste bosom of the maiden fair,
> Where hidden it lies in tunic soft forgot ;
> Soon as she hears her mother's step she starts ;
> Away it rolls, and conscious of her crime
> Her cheeks are steeped in red. (CATULLUS.)

I say that male and female are cast in the same mould ; saving education and habits, the difference is not great. Plato, in his Republic, invites all indiscriminately to share all studies, exercises, charges and occupations, in peace and war ; and the philosopher Antisthenes rejected all distinction between their virtue and ours. It is much easier to accuse one sex than to excuse the other ; it is, in the words of the proverb, ' the poker calling the shovel black '.

CHAPTER 6

OF COACHES

IT may very easily be verified that the great authors, when they write of causes, make use not only of those they think true, but also of those they do not believe in, provided there be some originality and beauty in them. They speak truly and usefully enough, if they speak judiciously. We cannot make sure of the master-cause ; we accumulate a number of them, to see if by chance it may not be found among them :

> There are besides some things
> Of which 'tis not enough one only cause
> To state—but rather several, whereof one
> Will be the true. (LUCRETIUS.)

Do you ask me whence comes that custom of saying ' God bless you ! ' when a person sneezes ? We produce wind of three sorts. That which comes from below is too foul ; that which issues from the mouth brings with it some reproach of gluttony. The third is the sneeze, and because it comes from the head and is without offence we give it that civil greeting. Do not smile at this subtle distinction ; it is said to have been made by Aristotle.

I think I have read in Plutarch (who, of all writers I know, has best blended art with nature, and judgement with knowledge) that he gives as a reason for the heaving of the stomach in those who travel by sea, that it is caused by fear ; having first discovered some reason by which he proves that fear may produce some such effect. I, who am very liable to sea-sickness, know very well that that is not the case with me ; and I know it, not by reasoning, but by necessary experience. Not to mention, what I have been told, that the same thing often happens to animals, and especially pigs, that have no idea of danger ; and the testimony of an acquaintance of mine, that, though very subject to it, on two or three occasions, being in a very stormy sea and very much afraid, the inclination to vomit passed away. So it happened to that ancient writer : *I was too much upset to think of danger* (Seneca).

I have never had any fear on the water, nor indeed anywhere else (and I have often enough had just cause to be afraid, if death be one), at least to such a degree as to be disturbed or bewildered by it.

Fear is sometimes due to want of judgement, as well as to want of courage. All the dangers I have seen, I have seen with open eyes, with free, sound, and entire sight ; besides, it needs courage to be afraid. Mine once stood me in good stead, compared with others, in conducting my flight in an orderly manner, since it was done, if not without fear, at least without alarm and dismay ; I was excited, but not stunned or distracted.[1]

Great souls go yet much further, and offer us a picture of flight not merely correct and steady, but proud. I will quote what Alcibiades relates of Socrates, his comrade in arms : ' I found him (he says), after the rout of our army, him and Lachez, among the last of the fugitives, and I was able to observe him at leisure and from a safe place, for I was mounted on a good horse, and he on foot, as we had been in the battle. I noted first how much presence of mind and determination he displayed when compared with Lachez, and then how boldly he marched, never exceeding his ordinary pace ; how firm and steady his glance when

---

[1] Montaigne is here perhaps referring to the time when the plague was ravaging the district, and he found great difficulty in finding a refuge for his family.

observing and taking in the situation, looking now at one, now at another, friends and enemies, in such a way as to encourage the former and signify to the latter that he was the man to sell his blood and life very dearly to any who had a mind to take them. And so they got away ; for men like that are not readily attacked ; it is the terrified who are pursued.'

There we have the testimony of that great captain, and it teaches us, what we may learn any day by experience, that nothing is so likely to bring us into danger as a frantic eagerness to escape from it. *Where there is less fear there is generally less danger* (Livy).

Our common people are wrong to say ' so-and-so fears death ', when they mean to say that he ponders over it and foresees it. Foresight is equally proper in all that concerns us, whether for good or ill. To consider and appreciate the danger is in some sort the reverse of being alarmed by it.

I do not feel myself strong enough to withstand the force and impetuosity of that passion of fear, or of any other violent passion. If I were once vanquished and beaten down by it, I should never entirely recover. Whoever should make my soul lose her footing would never again set her upright. She probes and searches herself too deeply and too closely, and therefore would never allow the wound that has pierced her to close up and heal. It has been fortunate for me that no sickness has yet prostrated her. To every attack made upon me I stand up and defend myself in my corslet. So the first that should sweep me off my feet would leave me without resources. I have no second defence. Wherever the torrent should break my dike I should be defenceless and drowned without help.

Epicurus says that the wise man can never pass into a contrary state. Reading it backwards I rather agree with that sentence, and say, That he who has once been a very fool, will never after be very wise.

God tempers the wind to the shorn lamb, and gives me passions in proportion to my means of resistance. Nature, having uncovered me on one side, has covered me on the other : having disarmed me of strength, she has armed me with insensibility and a moderate or dull power of apprehension.

Now, I cannot bear for any length of time (and much less could I bear them in my younger days) either coach, or litter, or boat, and I hate any other conveyance but on horseback, both in town and country. But I can bear a litter less than a coach ; and for the same reason I can more easily bear a rough tossing on the water, which usually causes fear, than the motion we feel in calm weather. That slight concussion caused by the oars, that makes the craft slip from under us, somehow disturbs my head and stomach ; neither can I endure a tottering chair under me. When the sail or the current carries us along smoothly, or when we are towed, the even motion causes me no discomfort whatever. It is an intermittent motion that upsets me, and more so when it is slow. I cannot exactly describe its effect. The doctors have recommended me to bind and compress the bowels with a towel, to remedy the discomfort ; but I have not tried it, being accustomed to wrestle with my defects and overcome them by self-control.

If my memory were sufficiently stored, I would not spare my time in telling here of the infinite variety that history offers of the use of coaches in the service of war, varying according to nations and according to the age ; of great effect, in my opinion, and very necessary, so that it is a wonder that we have lost all knowledge of them. I will only say this, that quite recently, in the time of our fathers, the Hungarians worked them to great advantage against the Turks ; each of them occupied by a targeteer and a musketeer, a number of muskets lying in a row, ready loaded, wholly protected by a fence of shields, like a galiot. These coaches formed the battle-front to the number of three thousand, and, after the cannon had played, they were made to advance, and the enemy had to swallow that volley before tasting the rest, which was no small advantage. Or they rushed them into the squadrons to break them and open a way ; besides the assistance they could derive from them by flanking in a ticklish place the troops marching into the field, or by hastily covering a camp and fortifying it.

In my time a gentleman on one of our frontiers, who was unwieldy of body and unable to find a horse equal to his weight, having a feud, used to travel the country in a coach like those described above, and felt quite safe. But enough of these war-coaches. [As if their sloth had not been sufficiently notorious by better proofs,] the [last] kings of our first dynasty travelled the country in a cart drawn by four oxen.

Mark Antony was the first who had himself drawn in Rome by lions harnessed to a chariot, with a female musician at his side. Heliogabalus did the same later, calling himself Cybele, mother of the gods ; he was also drawn by tigers in imitation of the god Bacchus, and on occasion had a pair of stags harnessed to his chariot ; and again, four hounds ; and again he was dragged in state by four young nude girls, he also being naked. The Emperor Firmus had his chariot drawn by ostriches of prodigious size, so that it seemed to fly rather than roll.

The strangeness of these inventions has put this other idea into my head, That it is a kind of small-mindedness in a monarch, and a sign that he is not sufficiently sensible of his power, when he labours to enhance his importance, and show off by excessive expenditure. It might be excusable in a foreign country ; but among his own subjects, where he is all-powerful, he derives from his dignity the highest degree of honour he is able to reach.

So it appears to me superfluous in a gentleman to dress with studied elegance in his own home. His household, his retinue, and his table are sufficient guarantee of his station.

The advice that Isocrates gave to his king appears to me not unreasonable, ' That he may be sumptuous in furniture and utensils, since he spends on durable things that are handed on to his heirs ; but that he should avoid all extravagance on things that will presently drop out of use and memory.'

When I was a young fellow I was fond of dress, for want of other attractions ; and it sat well on me. There are some on whom fine clothes weep.

We have wonderful tales of the frugality of our kings in regard to their person and their gifts, kings great in renown, in valour and fortune.

Demosthenes fought tooth and nail against the law of his city which allotted public money to be spent on ostentatious games and feasts ; he thought the greatness of the city should show itself in the number of well equipped ships and good, well furnished armies. And Theophrastus was rightly condemned for setting up a contrary opinion, in his book on Riches, and maintaining that an expenditure of that kind was the true fruit of opulence. 'Those are pleasures, says Aristotle, that only appeal to the meanest of the people, and vanish from memory as soon as they have been satiated with them. No serious and sensible man can value them.'

The expense would, it seems to me, be more royally as well as more justly, usefully and durably devoted to ports, harbours, fortifications, and walls ; to sumptuous buildings, churches, hospitals, colleges, the improvement of streets and roads, for which Pope Gregory the Thirteenth is held in praiseworthy memory in my time, and wherein our Queen Catherine might for many long years testify to her natural liberality and munificence, if her means were sufficient to satisfy her bent.

Fortune has greatly spited me in interrupting the noble structure of the new bridge of our great city, and robbing me of the hope of seeing it in full use before I die.

Moreover, to the subjects, spectators of these triumphs, it appears to be their own wealth that is displayed before them, and that they are feasted at their own expense. For the people are apt to suppose of kings, as we do of our servants, that they should make it their care to provide us in abundance with all that we need, but that for their part they should never lay hands on it. And therefore it was that the Emperor Galba, pleased with the performance of a musician whilst he was at supper, sent for his casket and gave him a handful of coins which he fished out of it, with these words, ' This is not out of the public purse, but my own.'

At all events, it most often happens that the people are right, and that their eyes are feasted on what should go to feed their bellies.

Liberality itself is not in its right setting in the hands of a sovereign ; private individuals have more right to be liberal. For, precisely speaking, a king has nothing that is properly his own ; he owes even himself to others.

Justice is administered, not in favour of him who administers it, but of him to whom it is administered. A superior is never appointed for his own benefit, but to benefit the inferior ; and a physician for the patient, not for himself. All authority, as every art, has its end outside of itself ; *no art is concerned with itself* (Cicero).

Wherefore the governors of young princes, who make it a point to instil into them this virtue of lavish generosity, and preach to them that they should be unable to deny anything, and to think nothing so well spent as what they give (an instruction that in my time I have heard highly commended), either look to their own profit rather than that of their master, or they do not quite realize to whom they are preaching. It is too easy a matter to inculcate liberality into one who has ample means to practise it at others' expense. And as the esteem in which he is held is proportioned, not to the measure of the gift, but to the measure of the means of him who bestows it, it comes to nothing in hands so powerful. They become prodigal before they are liberal.

Therefore it is a virtue little to be recommended in comparison with other royal virtues ; and it is the only one, as Dionysius the Tyrant said, that goes well with tyranny itself. I would rather teach him this little saying of the ancient labourer, *To obtain a good crop, you must sow with the hand, not pour out of the sack* (Plutarch). He must scatter the seed, not spill it ; and since he must give, or, more properly speaking, since he must pay and restore to so many people according to their deserts, he ought to be a fair and discreet dispenser. If the liberality of a prince is without measure and discrimination, I would rather he were a miser.

Royal virtue seems to consist chiefly in Justice ; and, of all the branches of justice, that best stamps a king which is accompanied by liberality. For this they have particularly taken into their own keeping, whilst every other kind of justice is generally administered through others.

Extravagant liberality is a feeble means of acquiring goodwill ; for it alienates more people than it wins. *The more you have formerly obliged, the fewer you will be able to oblige in the future. What greater folly is there than to disable yourself ever after from doing that which you delight in ?* (Cicero.) And if it is exercised without regard to merit, it shames him who receives, and is received ungraciously. Tyrants have been sacrificed to the hatred of the people by the hands of the very men they have unjustly advanced ;

for that kind of man thinks he will secure himself in the possession of property received without being earned, by showing hatred and contempt for the man from whom he holds it. Thereby he rallies to the opinion and judgement of the majority.

The subjects of a ruler who is lavish in gifts become lavish in asking ; they assess themselves, not according to reason, but to example. We have indeed often cause to blush for our impudence ; in justice we are overpaid when the reward equals our service, for do we owe nothing to our princes, by natural obligation ? If he bears our expenses, he does too much ; it is enough if he contributes to them. The surplus is called benefit, and cannot be exacted ; for the very name Liberality suggests Liberty.

From our point of view, he has never done ; what we have received is no longer taken into account. We love only liberality to come ; wherefore the more a prince exhausts himself in giving, the poorer he grows in friends. How can he assuage desires that grow the more they are fulfilled ? He whose thoughts are bent on taking no longer thinks of what he has taken. Nothing is so properly allied to greed as ingratitude.

The example of Cyrus will not be amiss in this place, to serve the kings of our time as a touchstone to know whether their gifts are well or ill bestowed, and make them see how much more happily that Emperor invested them than they do ; whereby they are reduced to borrowing of unknown subjects, and rather of those they have wronged than those they have benefited, and receive aid that is gratuitous only in name.

Croesus blamed him for his extravagance, and calculated what his treasure would amount to if he had been less openhanded. Cyrus desired to justify his liberality, and sent dispatches in all directions, to the grandees of his State whom he had particularly advanced, begging each one to assist him with as much cash as he could afford, for an urgent necessity, and send him particulars. When all these notes were brought to him, he found that each of his friends had considered it insufficient to offer him no more than he had received through Cyrus's munificence, but had added much more of what was his very own ; so that the total amounted to very much more than Croesus' estimate of what he would have saved by being less generous. Whereupon Cyrus said, ' I am not less in love with riches than other princes ; rather I am more careful of them. You see at how small a cost I have gained the inestimable treasure of so many friends ; and how much more trusty treasurers they are to me than any mercenary fellow, without obligation, without affection, would have been. And my fortune is better harboured than in chests, that would call down upon me the hatred, envy and contempt of other princes.'

The Emperors found some excuse for the superfluity of their public games and shows in the fact that their authority depended to some extent (at least in appearance) on the will of the Roman people, who had from time immemorial been accustomed to be flattered by extravagant spectacles of that description. But it was the private individuals who had kept up this custom of gratifying their fellow-citizens and friends, chiefly out of their own purse, by that great profusion and magnificence. It had quite a different flavour when it was the masters who came to imitate them. *The transferring of property from its rightful owners to others who have no claim to it should not be regarded as liberality* (Cicero).

Philip taunted his son in a letter, for trying to purchase the goodwill of the Macedonians with gifts, in these words, ' What, do you wish your subjects to regard you as their purse-bearer and not as their king ? Would you bribe them ? Bribe them with the benefits of your virtue, not with the benefits of your coffers.'

It was, however, a fine thing to transport and plant in the amphitheatre a great number of big trees with all their branches in full verdure, to represent a large and shady forest, disposed in fine symmetry, and on the first day to let loose into it a thousand ostriches, a thousand stags, a thousand wild boars, and a thousand fallow deer, and leave them to be scrambled for by the people ; on the next day to have a hundred big lions, a hundred leopards, and three hundred bears butchered in their presence ; and for the third day to make three hundred pairs of gladiators fight to the bitter end, as did the Emperor Probus.

It was also a fine thing to see those great amphitheatres faced with marble on the outside, adorned with statues and ornaments, the interior glittering with many rich and rare gems :

> The circle here behold with gems inlaid,
> The porches all in gold ! (CALPHURNIUS.)

all the sides of this vast space filled and environed, from top to bottom, with three or fourscore tiers of seats, also of marble, covered with cushions :

> ' Out you go, for very shame, he says ;
> These cushioned seats are only for the Knights
> Who pay the lawful tax ' ; (JUVENAL.)

where a hundred thousand people could dispose themselves and sit in comfort.

The arena, where the shows took place, would be in the first place artificially opened and split into chasms, representing caves that vomited forth the animals intended for the spectacle ; then, secondly, it would be flooded with a deep sea, wherein swam store of marine monsters, and laden with armed vessels, to represent a naval battle ; and thirdly, dried and levelled again for the combat of the gladiators ; and for the fourth show, strewn with vermilion and storax instead of sand, arranged for a ceremonial banquet for all that endless number of people ; the last act of a single day.

> How oft have we beheld the floor sink in,
> When from the open chasm there emerged
> Wild beasts ; and from the same retreat there grew
> Forests of trees with gold and saffron bark.
> And sylvan monsters not alone we saw,
> But seals and bears locked in a deadly strife ;
> And, though no horse, yet horse-like is he named,
> The huge and shapeless hippopotamus. (CALPHURNIUS.)

Sometimes they created a high mountain covered with fruit and other trees in full leaf, from the summit of which gushed a rivulet, as from the mouth of a living spring. At other times they sailed on it a big ship, which opened up and came to pieces of itself, and, after vomiting from its belly four or five hundred fighting beasts, closed up again and vanished without assistance. Again from the floor of the place they caused springs and spurts of water to shoot up into the air, and, at that immense height, sprinkled and perfumed the great multitude.

To shelter themselves from harm by inclement weather, they stretched over that immense space awnings made of purple and worked with the needle, or of silk of one colour or another, which were drawn back or forward in a moment, as they had a mind :

> The awnings, though the sun doth scorch the skin,
> Are, when Hermogenes appears, drawn in.[1]

The nets too which were hung before the spectators to protect them from the violence of the animals that were let loose, were worked in gold :

> The woven nets refulgent are with gold. (CALPHURNIUS.)

If there is anything excusable in these extravagances, it is that the inventiveness and the novelty excite our wonder, more than the expense.

Even in those vanities we discover how fertile those ages were in wits differing from those of our time. It is with this kind of fertility as with all other productions of Nature. That is not to say that she exhausted all her resources in those times. We do not move forwards ; we rather prowl about, turning this way and that. We retrace our steps. I fear that our knowledge is deficient in all directions ; we do not see very far ahead, nor very far behind us. It embraces little and is shortlived ; short in extent of time and extent of matter :

> For many have lived who were valiant in fight,
>   Before Agamemnon ; but all have gone down,
> Unwept and unknown, in the darkness of night,
>   For lack of a poet to hymn their renown. (HORACE.)

> Long, long before the Theban war, and Troy
> And its sad fall, were there not other bards
> To sing of those old days ? (LUCRETIUS.)

And Solon's account, which he had from the Egyptian priests, of the long life of their State, and their manner of learning and recording the history of other countries, is not, I think, a testimony to be despised in this connexion. *If we could view that unbounded extent of space and time into which the mind, plunging and spreading itself, travels so far and wide that it can find no end, no extremity to arrest its*

[1] From an epigram of Martial. Hermogenes was a notorious thief and picker-up of unconsidered trifles, as handkerchiefs, table-cloths, awnings.

*course, we should, in that immensity, discover an endless
number of forms* (Cicero).

Even if all that has been handed down and reported to
us concerning the past, until our own time, were true and
known to some person, it would be less than nothing compared with what is unknown. And of this same image of
the world which glides along while we live upon it, how
limited and contemptible is the knowledge even of the most
curious ! Not only of particular events, which by chance
often become exemplary and important, but of the condition of great governments and nations, a hundred times
as many escape us as come to our knowledge. We raise
our hands in admiration over the miracle of our invention
of artillery and our printing-press ; other men, at the other
end of the world, in China, used them a thousand years
before us. If we saw as much of the world as we do not see,
we should perceive, as may well be believed, a perpetual
multiplication and vicissitude of forms.

There is nothing single and uncommon as regards Nature,
but there is indeed with regard to our knowledge, which
is a poor foundation for our rules, and is apt to give us
a very wrong idea of things. As vainly as we now conclude
the decline and decrepitude of the world, from arguments
based on our own weakness and decay :

> This age is broken down, the earth outworn ; (LUCRETIUS.)

so vainly did that poet argue its birth and youth from the
vigour he saw in the minds of his time, abounding in
novelties and inventions in the different arts :

> The truth I think is this :
> The universe is new, quite fresh the world,
> Nor long ago begun. Why, there are arts
> Which even now receive the final touch,
> Even now advance ; how much is now being learned
> Of ships ! (LUCRETIUS.)

Our world has of late discovered another (and who will
warrant us that it is the last of its brothers, since the
Demons, the Sibyls, and we moderns had been hitherto
ignorant of this one), no less big and full-limbed than himself, yet so fresh and infantile that he is still being taught
his ABC. It is not fifty years since he knew neither letters,
nor weights and measures, nor clothes, nor corn, nor vines.

He was still quite naked at the breast, and lived only on what his nursing mother provided.

If we are right in our conclusions with regard to the end of the world, and this poet is right with regard to the youth of his own age, this other world will be only coming into the light as we are leaving it. The universe will fall into paralysis ; one limb will be shrunken, the other in full vigour.

I very much fear that we shall have greatly hastened the decline and downfall of the latter by our contact ; and that we shall have made him pay us very dearly for our ideas and our arts. It was an infant world, and yet we have not whipped it and subjected it to our discipline, with all our advantages in valour and natural strength ; nor have we won it over by our justice and goodness, nor subdued it by our magnanimity. Most of their replies in our dealings with them are witness that they were by no means behind us in native clearness of wit and pertinence.

The astounding magnificence of their cities, Cuzco and Mexico, and among many other like things, that King's garden where all the trees, fruits, and all the herbs were exquisitely formed in gold, of the same size and so arranged as in an ordinary garden, as well as, in his cabinet, all the animals that are native to his states and in his seas ; and the beauty of their workmanship in jewellery, feathers, cotton, and painting, prove that neither did they yield to us in industry. But with regard to their piety, observance of the laws, goodness, liberality, loyalty, and openness, it served us well that we had not as much as they ; by this advantage over us they lost, sold, and betrayed themselves.

In respect of hardihood and courage, of firmness, steadfastness, fortitude in bearing pain and hunger and death, I should not fear to oppose the examples I could find amongst them to the most famous examples in ancient times that we find recorded in our hither world. For, take away from their conquerors the tricks and artifices which they practised to deceive them, and the natural amazement of those people on seeing the so unexpected arrival of men with beards, differing from them in language, religion, shape and countenance, from so remote a region of the world, where they had never imagined that there could be any inhabitants, mounted on big, strange monsters, opposed

to men who had never seen, not only a horse, but any
animal whatever trained to carry and support a man or
any other burden ; provided with a hard and shining skin
and a sharp and glittering weapon against men who, for
the marvel of a shining mirror or a knife would barter great
wealth of gold and pearls, and who had neither the knowledge nor the material with which, even with time at their
disposal, they could pierce our steel ; add the thunder and
lightning of our cannon and musketry, enough to disturb
even Caesar, if he had been surprised with so little experience
and at that hour, against people who were naked, except
where they had risen to the invention of some sort of
cotton tissue, with no other arms, at the most, but bows,
stones, staves, and wooden bucklers, people taken at a disadvantage, under colour of friendship and good faith, by
curiosity to see strange and unknown things. Place to the
account of the conquerors, I say, all this superiority, and
you will deprive them of all credit for so many victories.

When I look upon the indomitable ardour with which so
many thousands of men, women, and children so often
came forward and plunged into inevitable dangers, in
defence of their gods and their liberty, their noble stubbornness in suffering every extreme hardship and even
death, rather than submit to the dominion of those who
had so shamefully deceived them ; some of them, after
being captured, choosing to waste away with hunger and
fasting rather than accept food at the hands of their enemies
who had been so basely victorious ; I can foresee that if
any one had attacked them on equal terms in respect of
arms, experience, and numbers, it would have been as
hazardous, or more hazardous, a war than any we know of.

Why did not so noble a conquest fall to the lot of Alexander, or the ancient Greeks and Romans ; why did not
this great change and transformation of so many empires
and nations fall into hands that would have gently refined
and cleared away all that was barbarous in them, and
fostered and propagated the good seeds that Nature had
there produced ; not only mingling with the cultivation of
their lands and the adorning of their cities the arts of our
hemisphere, so far as might have been necessary, but also
blending the Greek and Roman virtues with those of the
natives of that continent ?

What a compensation it would have been, and what an improvement for the whole of this earthly globe, if the first examples of our conduct offered to those people had called them to the admiration and imitation of virtue, and established between them and us a brotherly fellowship and understanding ! How easy it would have been to turn to profit minds so fresh, so hungry to learn, which had, for the most part, naturally made so good a beginning !

On the contrary, we took advantage of their ignorance and inexperience, to bend them more easily to treachery, luxury, avarice, and to every kind of inhumanity and cruelty, by the pattern and example of our manners. Who ever set so high a value on the utility of trade and commerce ? So many cities razed to the ground, so many nations exterminated, so many millions of people put to the edge of the sword, and the richest and most beautiful part of the earth turned upside down, for a traffic in pearls and pepper ! Wretched machine-made victories ! Never did ambition, never did national enmities impel men one against the other to such horrible acts of hostility and such miserable calamities.

Certain Spaniards, coasting the sea in search of their mines, put to shore in a pleasant and fertile region, thickly peopled, and made their usual professions to the inhabitants: ' That they were peaceable men, come from distant countries by sea, sent on behalf of the King of Castile, the greatest Prince on the habitable globe, to whom the Pope, representing God on earth, had given the lordship over all the Indies. That if they would be tributary to him, they should be treated very kindly.' They demanded of them provisions for their sustenance, and some gold to use in some medicine or other. They besides expounded to them their belief in one God, and the truth of our religion, which they advised them to accept ; to this they added a few threats.

The reply was as follows : ' That, as to being peaceable, if that was so they did not look like it. As to their King, since he begged he must be needy and indigent, and the man who parcelled out things in that way must be fond of broils, to go and give to another person what did not belong to him, and set him by the ears with the ancient possessors. With regard to provisions, they would supply

them ; of gold they had little, and it was a thing they
valued not at all, since it was of no use to them in their
daily life, their only care being to pass it happily and
pleasantly. They might, however, boldly take all they
could find, except what was used in the service of their
Gods. As to the one God, what they had said pleased them
well ; but they had no wish to change their religion, which
had so long served them so well ; and they were not
accustomed to take counsel but of their friends and acquaintances.

' As to their threats, it was a sign of want of judgement to
go threatening those with whose nature and means they
were unacquainted. So let them make all speed to quit
their territory, for they were not wont to take in good part
the professions and civilities of armed and strange men ;
if not, they would treat them as they had treated these
others,' showing them the heads of some men executed
around their city.

There we have an example of the babbling of these
children. But so it is, neither here nor in several other
places where they did not find the merchandise they were
in search of, did the Spaniards make any stay or attempt
any violence, in spite of any other advantages they found
there ; witness my Cannibals.

Of the two most powerful monarchs of that hemisphere,
and perhaps of this, kings of so many kings, the last they
drove out, the King of Peru, having been taken in a battle,
and put to so excessive a ransom that it surpasses all belief,
and this having been faithfully paid, and he having in negotiation shown signs of a frank, liberal and undaunted spirit,
and a clear and logical mind, the desire seized the victors,
after extorting a million three hundred and twenty-five
thousand five hundred weight of gold, besides silver and other
things that amounted to no less, so that their horses never
went but shod with solid gold, to discover besides, by any
treacherous means they could think of, what the remainder
of this King's treasures might come to, and freely to take
possession of what he had in reserve. They set up a false
accusation and false proofs that he was plotting to raise an
insurrection in his provinces to set him free. Whereupon,
in a delightful judgement pronounced by the very men who
had contrived this treachery, he was condemned to be

publicly hanged and strangled, after making him buy off
the torment of being burned alive, by the baptism they
gave him at the moment of execution. A dreadful and
unprecedented crime, which he, however, suffered without
betraying himself either by look or word, with truly royal
demeanour and gravity ! And then to soothe the people,
alarmed and bewildered by such strange doings, they
counterfeited great sorrow at his death, and appointed him
a sumptuous funeral.

The other, the King of Mexico, after a prolonged defence of
his beleaguered city, during which he showed what endurance
and perseverance are capable of, if ever prince or nation did
so, had the misfortune to fall alive into his enemies' hands,
it being stipulated that he should be treated as a King (nor
did he in his captivity exhibit anything unworthy of that
title). When, after this victory, they did not find all the gold
they had promised themselves, after turning up and ran-
sacking everything, they set about to obtain information,
by inflicting the most cruel tortures they could think of upon
the prisoners in their power. But, having got nothing out of
these, and finding that the courage of the victims was stronger
than their torments, they became at last so enraged that,
against their given word and every human right, they condemned the King himself and one of the chief lords of his
court to be put to the torture in each other's presence.

This lord, finding himself overcome with the pain, surrounded by red-hot braziers, at last turned piteous eyes
towards his master, as if to ask his pardon for not being
able to endure it. The King, proudly and sternly fixing
his eyes upon him, to reprove his cowardice and pusillanimity, spoke only these words, with rude and firm voice,
' Do you think that I am in a bath ; do you think that I
am more comfortable than you ? ' The other immediately
succumbed to his anguish, and died on the spot. The King,
half roasted, was carried from thence, not out of pity (for
what pity ever touched the soul of a man who, for the
dubious revealing of some gold vessel to be pillaged, had
a man grilled before his eyes, not to speak of a King so
great in fortune and merit), but because his fortitude made
their cruelty more and more shameful. They hanged him
afterwards, for having bravely attempted to deliver himself
by force of arms from so long a captivity and subjection ;

and he ended his life in a manner worthy of a great-souled Prince.

On another occasion they made a fire in which they burned alive, at one time, four hundred and sixty men ; the four hundred being of the common people, the sixty being the principal lords of the province, mere prisoners of war.

We have the accounts of these atrocities from themselves ; for they not only admit them, but they boast of them and preach them abroad. Can it be for a testimony of their justice, or zeal for their religion ? Truly those are ways and means too contrary and hostile to so sacred a purpose. If it was their purpose to spread our faith, they should have considered that it does not spread by possession of territory but by possession of men, and they should have been more than satisfied with the murders that war's necessity brings with it, without adding an indiscriminate butchery, as of so many wild beasts, and as universal as fire and sword could attain to ; since they purposely kept alive only so many as they meant to make miserable slaves of, for the working and service of their mines.

So far did they exceed that many of the captains were punished with death on the scene of their conquests by command of the Kings of Castile, who were justifiably shocked by their horrible crimes ; and almost all of them were hated and despised. God justly rewarded them by allowing those great spoils to be swallowed up by the sea in transit, or by the intestine wars in which they devoured one another ; and the most part of the men buried one another on the scene of their crimes, without enjoying any fruits of their victory.

With regard to the fact that the revenue, even in the hands of a thrifty and prudent King,[1] answers so little to the expectations given of it to his predecessors, and to that abounding wealth which they originally came across on landing in that new world (for, although they obtain a great deal from thence, we can see that it is nothing compared with what they should expect), the reason is that the use of money was quite unknown, and that their gold was consequently all collected together, since it was of no use except for show and ostentation, as if it were a piece of

[1] Philip II, who was then ruling in Spain.

furniture preserved from father to son by many powerful kings, who were ever draining their mines for creating that vast heap of vessels and statues to adorn their palaces and temples. Whereas our gold is all in circulation and trade. We cut it up small and adulterate it in a thousand ways, then we scatter and disperse it.

Imagine our Kings accumulating in that way all the gold they could lay hands on during several centuries, and keeping it idle !

The inhabitants of the kingdom of Mexico were somewhat more civilized and artistic than the other nations of that continent. They too believed, with us, that the world was nearing its end, and accepted as a sign of it the desolation we brought upon them. They believed that the existence of the world was divided into five ages, and into the life of five consecutive suns, four of which had already run their time, and that the one that gave them light was the fifth. The first perished with all other creatures by a general inundation of water. The second by the heavens falling upon us and stifling every living thing ; to which age they assigned the giants, whose bones they showed to the Spaniards, according to the proportions of which the stature of men amounted to twenty handbreadths. The third by fire, which burned and consumed all. The fourth by an agitation of air and wind which levelled even many mountains ; the human beings did not die therein, but were changed into baboons (what ideas will not human credulity accept in its imbecility !). After the death of this fourth sun the world was for twenty-five years in perpetual darkness, in the fifteenth of which a man and woman were created, who restored the human race. Ten years later, on a certain day of their calendar, the sun appeared newly created, and from that day begins the reckoning of their years. On the third day after its creation the old gods died ; the new ones have been born since, from day to day. In what manner they think this last sun is to perish my author did not learn. But their number of this fourth change coincides with that great conjunction of the stars which produced, some eight hundred years ago, according to the calculation of the astrologers, many great alterations and innovations in the world.

With regard to the pomp and magnificence which led me

to this subject, neither Greece nor Rome nor Egypt has any work to compare, either in usefulness or difficulty or grandeur, with the road which is seen in Peru, levelled by the kings of the country, which connects the cities of Quito and Cuzco (three hundred leagues in length), straight, even, twenty-five paces wide, paved, enclosed on either side by fine, high walls, and running alongside, within the walls, two perennial streams of water, bordered with handsome trees which they call *Molly*. When they met with rocks and mountains, they cut through and levelled them, and filled up the valleys with stone and chalk. At the end of each day's journey there were fine palaces, furnished with provisions, clothes and arms, both for travellers and for the armies that had to pass that way.

In calculating this work I have considered the difficulty of it, which is unusually formidable in that place. They built with stones no less than ten feet square, and had no other means of transporting them but the strength of their arms, to draw their loads ; they had not even the art of scaffolding, knowing no other cunning but to raise so much earth against the building as it gradually rose, and afterwards removing it.

Let us return to our coaches. Instead of these or any other kind of vehicle, they had themselves carried by men, and on their shoulders. That last King of Peru, on the day when he was taken, was thus carried in the midst of his battle-army, seated in a gold sedan-chair, supported on golden shafts. As many of these carriers as they killed, to bring him to earth (for they wished to take him alive), so many others strove in emulation to take the place of the dead ; so that they could never bring him down, however many of his men they massacred, until a horseman seized him round the body and pulled him to the ground.

CHAPTER 7

OF THE DISADVANTAGE OF GREATNESS

SINCE we cannot reach it, let us avenge ourselves by disparaging it. Yet to find defects in a thing is not absolutely to disparage it ; there are defects in all things, however beautiful and desirable.

Greatness has as a rule this evident advantage, that it

can descend from its height when it pleases, and can well-nigh choose between either condition. For one does not fall from every height ; there are more from which one can descend without falling.

It really seems to me that we think too highly of it, and that we also think too highly of the resolution of those men who, in our own experience or from hearsay, have despised it and laid it down of their own accord. Its advantages are not so essentially manifest that one may not refuse it without performing a miracle.

I should think it needs great strength to bear adversity ; but in being content with a mediocre degree of fortune and avoiding greatness I can see nothing to make a stir about. That is a virtue to which I think I myself, who am but a noddy, could attain without a great effort. What effort can it need in those who also consider the glory attending such a refusal, wherein there may lurk more ambition even than in the desire for and enjoyment of greatness ; since ambition never better follows its own bent than along out-of-the-way and unused paths ?

I urge on my heart to patience ; I rein it in to desire. I have as much to wish for as another, and allow my wishes as much freedom and indiscretion ; and yet it has never occurred to me to wish for empire or royalty, nor for the eminence of those high and commanding fortunes. My aim lies not in that direction ; I love myself too well. When my thoughts are bent on growth, it is a humble growth, a restricted and mean-spirited growth, of a more personal nature, towards firmness, wisdom, health, beauty, and even wealth. But such renown, such mighty authority, crushes my imagination. And, quite contrary to that other,[1] I would perhaps rather see myself the second or third at Périgueux than the first in Paris ; at least, without feigning, rather the third than the first in authority in Paris. I would neither wrangle, a wretched nobody, with a door-keeper, nor have a crowd of worshippers make room for me. I am

---

[1] There is a story that as Caesar was crossing the Alps, he passed through a wretched barbarian town with very few inhabitants. When his companions humorously observed that they did not suppose there were any contests for honours in such a place, Caesar replied seriously, ' I would rather be the first man here than the second in Rome.'— Plutarch, *Life of Julius Caesar.*

accustomed, both by lot and by inclination, to a middle station. And I have shown, in the conduct of my life and my undertakings, that I have rather avoided, than not, climbing beyond the degree of fortune at which God placed me at my birth.

Everything that is constituted according to Nature is equally right and easy.

My soul is so indolent that I do not measure good fortune by its height ; I measure it by its facility.

But if my heart is not big enough, it is proportionably open, and commands me boldly to publish its defects. Should any one ask me to compare the life of L. Thorius Balbus, a gentleman, handsome, learned, healthy, intelligent, with a superfluity of all kinds of pleasures and opportunities, leading a peaceful existence quite at his own disposal, his mind fully armed against death, superstition, grief, and other obstacles to human needs, ending his life in battle with sword in hand, in the defence of his country, on the one hand ; and on the other, the life of M. Regulus, so great and eminent that it is known to all men, and his admirable end : the one without a name and without honours, the other so exemplary and famous as to excite wonder, I should certainly speak of them as Cicero does, if I could speak as well as he.[1]

But if I had to measure them by my standard, I should also say that the first is as much within my reach, and according to my desire, which agrees with my reach, as the second is far beyond it ; that to the latter I can only attain by veneration ; the former I could easily attain in practice.

Let us return to our temporal greatness, from which we started.

I have a dislike for mastery, either active or passive. Otanez, one of the seven who had a claim to the throne of Persia, took a step which I could easily have taken : he renounced to his competitors his possible right to come to it by election or by lot, provided that he and his family might live in that empire free from all subjection and mastery,

---

[1] ' You call this man happy ? As for me, I will not venture to name the man I prefer to him. Virtue herself shall speak for me, and she will not hesitate to rank Marcus Regulus before this happy man of yours.'— Cicero, *De Fin*, ii. 20.

saving that of the ancient laws, and could enjoy every freedom that was not prejudicial to these ; averse either to commanding or being commanded.

The hardest and most difficult trade in the world is, to my mind, to play the part of a King worthily. I can excuse more of their faults than people usually do, in consideration of the terrible weight of their burden, which confounds my reason. It is difficult to observe measure in a power so unmeasured.

And yet, even in men of a less excellent nature, it is a singular incitement to virtue to be seated in a place where you can do no good action that is not recorded and placed to your account ; where the smallest good action affects so many people, and where your excellence, like that of a preacher, chiefly appeals to the people, no very exacting judges, easy to deceive and easily satisfied.

There are few things on which we can pass a sincere judgement, because there are few things in which we have not, in one way or another, a particular interest.

Superiors and inferiors, masters and subjects, are bound to be naturally envious of and hostile to one another ; they must be perpetually robbing one another. I trust neither, when the rights of the other party are in question. Let us leave the decision to Reason, who is inflexible and impassive when we can get at her.

Less than a month ago I was perusing two books written by Scotchmen, who were debating this subject. The democrat makes the King out to be in a worse plight than a carter ; the monarchist lodges him a few fathoms above God in power and sovereignty.

Now the disadvantage of greatness, which I have been led to discuss here by an event that has lately put me in mind of it, lies in this : There is perhaps nothing more pleasing in human intercourse than those trials of strength we make against one another, in rivalry of honour and worth, whether in exercises of the body or those of the mind, in which those in supreme power can have no true share. Indeed it has often seemed to me that through over-much respect princes are in this regard treated contemptuously and insultingly. For what used to offend me mightily as a boy, namely that those who competed with me in bodily exercises refused to take me seriously, because they thought

I was not worth their exerting themselves for, is what we see every day happening to princes, since every one thinks himself unworthy to use his best efforts against them. If they are observed to have the least desire to gain the victory, there is no man who will not do his best to let them have it, and who will not rather betray his own honour than offend theirs ; he only exerts his strength so far as is necessary to save his reputation.

What share can they have in the fray in which every one fights on their side ? They remind me of those Paladins of olden times who entered the tournaments and battles with enchanted bodies and weapons.

Brisson, running a race against Alexander, only pretended and hung back ; Alexander scolded him for it, but he should have had him flogged.

In this connexion Carneades used to say ' that the sons of kings learn nothing well except the management of horses ; since in every other exercise every man gives way to them and yields them the victory. But a horse, who is neither a courtier nor a flatterer, will throw the son of a king as soon as the son of a porter.'

Homer was constrained to consent to Venus, so sweet a saint and so frail, being wounded at the battle of Troy, to show her courage and daring, virtues which never fall to the share of those who are immune against danger. The gods are made to show anger, to fear and run away, to give way to jealousy, grief, and passion, in order to honour them with the virtues which, in human beings, are built up on these imperfections.

He who does not share in the danger and difficulty can claim no interest in the honour and pleasure which attend dangerous actions.

It is a pity when a man is so powerful that everything gives way to him. His fortune removes him too far from the society and company of his fellow men ; it plants him too far out of the way. That ease and facility, that needs no effort, in making everything bow to you is an enemy to every kind of pleasure. It is to slide, not to walk ; to sleep, not to live. Imagine a man accompanied by omnipotence, you engulf him ; he must entreat of you, as an alms, impediments and opposition ; his being and substance lie in indigence.

Their good qualities are dead and wasted; for these are only felt by comparison, and they are disqualified from competing. They can little know true praise, being deafened with such perpetual and uniform approval. If they have to deal with the most stupid of their subjects, they have no means of gaining an advantage over him. If he says ' it is because he is my king ', he thinks he has given a sufficient reason for lending a helping hand to his own defeat. That royal quality stifles and consumes the other real and essential qualities; they are drowned in royalty. And it leaves them nothing to recommend themselves by but those actions which directly concern and interest it, the duties of their charge.

It is so much to be a king, that he only exists as such. That external light that surrounds him hides and steals him from us; our sight is broken and dissipated by it, being filled and arrested by this strong glare.

The Senate allotted the prize of eloquence to Tiberius; he refused it, judging that he could derive no honour from so unfree an award, even if it had been just.

As we yield to them every advantage of honour, so we encourage and authorize their vices and defects, not only by approval, but even by imitation. Every one of Alexander's followers carried his head on one side, as he did; and the flatterers of Dionysius used to collide with one another in his presence, and kick and upset things at their feet, to make believe that they were as shortsighted as he. Even a rupture of the bowels has at times served as a recommendation to favour. I have known deafness to be affected. And Plutarch saw courtiers who repudiated their wives, although they loved them, because the master hated his.

What is more, we have known lechery to be in fashion for that reason, and every kind of dissoluteness, as well as disloyalty, blasphemy, cruelty, nay heresy, superstition, irreligion, cowardice, and worse, if worse there can be. Their example was even more dangerous than that of the flatterers of Mithridates who, when their master was most anxious to be reputed a good physician, brought him their limbs to be slashed and cauterized; for the others allowed their souls to be cauterized, a nobler and more delicate part.

But to end where I began. When the Emperor Hadrian was disputing with the philosopher Favorinus about the interpretation of some word, the latter soon yielded him the victory ; and to his friends who expostulated with him, he said, ' You cannot be serious ; would you not have a man be more learned than I who can command thirty legions ? '

Augustus wrote some lines against Asinius Pollio. ' And I, said Pollio, will hold my tongue ; it is not wisdom to enter the links as a scribe with one who has the power to proscribe.' And they were right ; for Dionysius, because he was no match for Philoxenus in poetry and Plato in prose, condemned the one to the quarries, and sent the other to be sold for a slave in the island of Aegina.

CHAPTER 8

OF THE ART OF CONVERSING

IT is a custom of our justice to condemn some as a warning to others.

To condemn them because they have done wrong would be stupidity, as Plato says. For what is done cannot be undone. But they are condemned that they may not go wrong again in the same way, or that others may avoid following their example.

We do not correct the man we hang ; we correct others through him. I do the same. My errors are sometimes natural and incorrigible ; but whereas honest men benefit the public by setting an example, I may perhaps benefit them by making them avoid my example :

> Look, boy, he'ld say, at Albius' son,
>   Observe his sorry plight ;
> And Barrus, that poor beggar there !
>   Say, are they not a sight
> To warn a man from squandering his patrimonial means ?
> (HORACE.)

If I disclose and publish my imperfections, some will learn to fear them. The qualities I most value in myself derive more honour from my self-accusation than from my self-commendation. That is why I so often fall back and dwell upon them. But when all is summed up, a man never speaks of himself without losing thereby. His self-accusations are always believed ; his self-praise disbelieved.

There may be some who are constituted like me, who

learn more by avoiding the faults of others than by imitating their example ; by flight than by following. That was the kind of teaching that the elder Cato had in mind when he said that the wise have more to learn of fools, than fools of the wise ; and that ancient player on the lyre, of whom Pausanias tells us, that he used to make his pupils go to hear a bad performer who lived over the way, where they might learn to hate his discords and faulty phrasings.

The horror of cruelty impels me more to clemency than any model of clemency could draw me on. A good rider does not improve my seat as well as an attorney or a Venetian on horseback ; and a bad style of speaking improves mine more than does a good one.

Every day the foolish demeanour of another warns and admonishes me. That which irritates will affect and arouse us more than that which pleases. These times are only good for reforming us backwards ; more by disagreement than by agreement ; more by difference than by similarity. Since I learn little by good examples, I make use of the bad, which give me daily lessons. I have tried to make myself as agreeable as I see others disagreeable ; as energetic as I see others feeble ; as mild as I see others fierce ; [as good as I see others wicked]. But I set up unattainable standards.

In my opinion the most profitable and most natural exercise of our mind is conversation. To me it is a more agreeable occupation than any other in life ; and for that reason, if I were at this moment obliged to choose, I would sooner consent, I think, to lose my sight than my hearing or speech. The Athenians, and still more the Romans, held this practice in great honour in their Academies. To this day the Italians preserve some traces of it, and greatly to their benefit, as may be seen if we compare ourselves with them in intelligence.

The study of books is a feeble and languid action which does not warm us, whilst conversation instructs and exercises us at the same time. If I converse with a man of strong mind and a stiff jouster, he will press on my flanks, prick me to right and left ; his ideas will give an impetus to mine. Rivalry, vainglory, strife, stimulate me and lift me above myself. And agreement is an altogether tiresome element in conversation.

As our mind is strengthened by communication with

vigorous and well regulated minds, it is not to be imagined how much it loses and deteriorates by continual intercourse and association with vulgar and feeble-minded people. There is no infection which spreads like that. I know well enough by experience how much a yard it costs.

I love to discuss and dispute, but in a small company of men, and in private. For to exhibit oneself before great people, and to parade one's wit and cackle in rivalry with others, is to my mind a trade very unbecoming a gentleman.

Foolishness is an unfortunate quality ; but to be unable to endure it, to be vexed at and worry over it, which is my case, is another kind of infirmity that is not much less tiresome than foolishness. And it is this that I am about to condemn in myself.

I can enter into a conversation and debate with great freedom and ease, since opinions find in me a soil very hard to penetrate and strike deep roots. No propositions astonish me, no belief offends me, however much opposed to my own. No idea is so frivolous or so extravagant but it appears to me naturally produced by human wit. We others,[1] who deny our judgement the right of deciding, look indulgently upon opinions differing from our own ; and if we do not lend credence, we readily lend an ear to them.

When one scale of the balance is entirely empty, I let the other waver under the weight of some old woman's superstitious fancies. And it appears to me excusable if I accept an odd rather than an even number ; if I prefer a Thursday to a Friday ; if I would rather make a twelfth or a fourteenth than the thirteenth at table ; if, when I am travelling, I am more pleased to see a hare skirting than crossing my path ; and rather offer my left than my right foot to be booted first.

All such idle fancies, which obtain credit around us, deserve at least a hearing. For me they weigh just more than nothing, but they do weigh. Vulgar and unfounded opinions are besides, as regards weight, other than nothing in nature. And one who will not yield so far may perhaps, whilst avoiding the error of superstition, fall into that of opinionativeness.

Opinions then that are opposed to mine do not offend or estrange me ; they only arouse and exercise my mind.

[1] We Pyrrhonians.

We dislike correction ; we should meet it half-way and welcome it, especially if it comes in the form of conversation and not of a school-lesson. At every contradiction we do not consider whether it be just, but by what means, fair or foul, we may get rid of it. Instead of extending our arms, we extend our claws to it.

I could endure hard knocks from my friends : ' You are a fool ; you are dreaming ! ' Among gentlemen I like bold expressions of opinion, and to have them speak as they think. We must fortify and harden our ears against that delicate and ceremonious sound of words. I love a strong and manly fellowship and familiarity, a friendship that delights in the rudeness and vigour of its intercourse, as love does in bites and scratches that draw blood.

It is not vigorous and generous enough if it is not quarrel-some ; if it is all civility and art ; if it fears a shock and walks in constraint. *For there can be no discussion without reprehension* (Cicero).

When a man opposes me he arouses my attention, not my anger ; I meet him half-way if he contradicts and corrects me. The cause of truth ought to be the cause common to both of us. What will he reply ? The passion of anger has already knocked his judgement on the head. Confusion has usurped the place of reason.

It would be a boon if our disputes were decided by way of wager, and if there were a substantial mark of our losses, that we might keep them in mind ; and if my serving-man could say to me, ' Your ignorance and wilfulness on twenty occasions last year cost you a hundred crowns.'

I hail and welcome the truth, in whatever hand I find it ; I cheerfully surrender and tender my vanquished sword to her, as soon as I see her approach in the distance.

And, as long as it does not come with too overbearing and schoolmasterly a mien, I encourage criticism of my writings ; and I have often altered them more from civility than because they were improved by it ; preferring, by readily giving way, to gratify and foster their freedom to admonish me ; yea, even at my own expense.

And yet it is difficult to draw the men of my time into it ; they have not the courage to correct because they have not the courage to suffer correction, and always speak with dissimulation in presence of one another. I take so much pleasure in being known and criticized that it is almost a matter of indifference to me which of the two forms it takes. My imagination so often contradicts and condemns itself that it is all one to me if another do it, chiefly in view of the fact that I allow his criticism only as much authority as I please. But I shall fall out with him who holds his head too high, as does one man I know, who thinks his advice is thrown away if it is not taken seriously, and takes it as an insult if you do not immediately follow it.

That Socrates always welcomed with a smile the contradictions offered to his arguments was due, we might say, to his strength ; and that, the advantage being certain to fall to his side, he accepted them as occasions for fresh triumphs. But we may, on the other hand, observe that there is nothing that makes us so delicately sensitive to contradiction as the feeling we have of our adversary's superiority, and his contempt of us ; and that, in reason, it is the part of the weaker rather to accept with a good grace the opposition which corrects and sets him right.

In fact I seek the society of those who drub me rather than of those who fear me. It is a flat and harmful satisfaction to have to do with people who admire and give way to you. Antisthenes recommended his children ' never to regard with gratitude or favour the man who praised them '. I feel much prouder of the victory I gain over myself when, in the very heat of the combat, I make myself give way to the force of my adversary's argument, than I feel gratified by the victory I gain over him through his own weakness.

In short, I accept and admit any kind of blow that is delivered according to the rules of the game, however weak it may be ; but I am much too intolerant of those that are given irregularly. I care little about the matter, and all opinions are the same to me ; and I am pretty indifferent as to who wins. I can argue peaceably for a whole day, if the debate is carried on according to the rules.

It is not so much force and subtlety that I expect, as order ; the order that we may see any day in the altercations of shepherds and shop-boys, never with us. If they go wrong, it is in want of civility ; and so it is with us. But their turbulence and impatience never put them off their theme ; their argument keeps its course. If they speak out of their turn without waiting for the other to finish, they at least understand one another.

To my mind a man answers only too well if he answers to the purpose. But when the discussion becomes confused and disorderly, I leave the subject to take care of itself, and, losing my temper and my head, I cling to the form ; I fall into a testy, spiteful, and overbearing style of debate, for which I have afterwards to blush.

It is impossible to deal honestly with a fool ; not only my judgement but also my conscience is vitiated at the hands of so impetuous a master.

Our wranglings ought to be forbidden and punishable like other verbal crimes. How much vice they always stir and pile up, when ruled and governed by anger ! We quarrel, first with the reasons, and then with the men. We learn to debate only that we may contradict ; and when every one contradicts and is contradicted, it follows that the fruit of debate is to suppress and nullify the truth. So Plato, in his Republic, forbids debates among fools and ill-bred people.

What is the good of starting in quest of truth with one who has no pace and no walking-power to speak of ?

We do no wrong to the subject when we leave it in order to find a better method of treating it ; I do not mean a scholastic method, a method according to the rules, but a natural method, carried out with a sound understanding.

What will be the end of it all ? One will go East, the other West ; they drop the main point and lose sight of it among a crowd of incidental questions. After an hour's storming they forget what they are after ; one shoots low, the other high, the other wide. One catches at a word and a simile. Another forgets his opponent's point, so intent is he on steering his own course ; he can only think of following up his own reasons instead of yours. Another, finding he is weak in the back, is afraid and declines all argument ; at the very outset he mixes up and confuses the issues. Or, in the thick of the debate, he stops dead, holds his tongue and sulks, in spiteful ignorance, affecting a proud contempt, or a silly modesty in giving up the struggle.

Provided that he gets in his blow, one man does not care how much he lays himself open. Another counts his words and weighs them as if they were so many reasons. Another only takes advantage of his voice and lung-power. Here we have one who sums up against himself, and another who deafens you with futile preambles and digressions. This one arms himself with downright insults, and seeks a Dutch quarrel to rid himself of the society and conversation of a wit who presses too hard upon him. This last can see nothing in reason, but keeps you enclosed within the barriers of his logical clauses and the formulas of his art.

Now who will not begin to distrust the sciences and doubt if he can derive any substantial gain from them for the needs of life, when he considers the use we put them to ? *Learning which cures nothing* (Seneca). Who has ever gained any intelligence from Logic ? Where are her fine promises ? *She teaches neither to live any better, nor to reason any more pertinently* (Cicero). Do you hear any worse jumble in the cackle of herring-wives than in the public debates of the professors of Logic ? I would rather my son learned to speak in the taverns than in the talking schools.

Take a Master of Arts,[1] converse with him ; why does he not make us sensible of excelling in those arts, and captivate the ladies and ignoramuses like ourselves with admiration for the solidity of his reasons and the beautiful arrangement of his matter ? Why can he not use his powers of persuasion and guide us at his pleasure ? Why is a man with all his advantages in learning, and in conducting a debate, unable to fence without getting furiously angry and insulting his opponent ? Let him put away his hood and gown and his Latin, and cease to beat his quite raw and undigested Aristotle about our ears, and you will take him for one of us, or worse.

When they become entangled and involved in the words with which they drive us into a corner, they remind me of a juggler ; their sleight of hand imposes upon and vanquishes our senses, but it does not by any means shake our belief. Leave out their legerdemain, and what they do is but commonplace and mean. They may be more learned than we, but they are none the less fools.

I love and honour learning as much as those who possess it ; and, if rightly used, it is the noblest and most powerful

[1] i. e. a professor of the Humanities and Philosophy.

human acquisition. But in those (and there is an endless number of their kind) who make it the ground of their worth and excellence, who appeal from their understanding to their memory, *covering under the shelter of others* (Seneca), who are powerless without their book, I hate it, if I may venture to say so, a little more than I do stupidity.

In my country, and in my time, learning often enough mends the purse, but rarely the soul. If it lights upon a mind that is dull and heavy, like a crude and undigested mass it makes it duller and heavier, and chokes it up ; if upon an acute mind, it usually purifies, clarifies, and subtilizes it, even to exhaustion. It is a thing of almost indifferent quality ; a very useful accessory in a naturally gifted mind, pernicious and harmful to another. Or rather it is a thing of very precious use, which is not to be purchased at a low price ; in some hands it is a sceptre, in others a fool's bauble.

But to proceed. What greater triumph can you expect than to teach your enemy that he is not your match ? When you gain the advantage by the substance of your argument, it is the truth that wins ; when you gain the advantage by your method of conducting it, it is you who win.

I am of opinion that, in Plato and Xenophon, Socrates debates more for the sake of the debaters than for the sake of the debate, and more to teach Euthydemus and Protagoras to know their own irrelevance than the irrelevance of their art. He lays hold of the first matter that comes to hand, as one who has a more useful purpose than to clear it up, namely, to clear up the minds he undertakes to direct and exercise.

The excitement of the chase is properly our quarry. We are not to be pardoned if we carry it on badly or foolishly ; to fail to seize the prey is a different matter. For we are born to search after the truth ; to possess it belongs to a greater power. It is not, as Democritus said, hidden in the depths of chasms, but rather raised to an infinite height in divine knowledge.

The world is but a school of research. The question is not who shall hit the ring, but who shall run the best course. He can be as great a fool who speaks true, as he who speaks false ; for we are concerned with the manner, not the matter, of speaking. It is my nature to regard the form as much as the substance, the advocate as much as the cause, as Alcibiades ordained that we should.

And every day I spend time in dipping into authors without any care about their learning ; in searching their style, not their matter. Just as I eagerly seek the society of any man renowned for his intellectual qualities ; not that he may teach me, but that I may know him [and knowing him, imitate him, if he is worthy of it].

Any man may speak truthfully ; but to speak methodically, with wisdom and talent, is given to few. So the errors that proceed from ignorance do not offend me ; it is the foppery of it. I have broken off several transactions which might have profited me, because of the impertinent protestations of those with whom I was transacting.

I do not once in a year excite myself over the faults of those over whom I have authority ; but when they stupidly and obstinately persist in their brutish and asinine assertions, excuses and defences, we are every day ready to fly at each other's throats. They neither understand what is said to them nor why, and reply accordingly ; it is enough to drive one to despair.

My head only hurts when it comes into rough contact with another. And I can sooner put up with the vices of my men than their want of thought, their unreasonableness and stupidity. Let them do less, provided they are capable of doing. You live in hopes of warming up their willingness. But we cannot hope to get any good out of a log.

But what if I take things otherwise than they are ? It may be so ; and therefore I condemn my intolerance and hold, firstly, that it is equally a blemish in one who is right and in one who is wrong. For it is always a sign of an arbitrary and sour nature to be unable to suffer any way of thinking differing from our own ; and besides, there can be no worse, no more obstinate and more eccentric fatuity than to be annoyed and exasperated by the fatuities of the world. For it irritates us chiefly with ourselves. And that philosopher [1] of olden times would never have lacked an occasion for shedding tears as long as he had himself to look at.

Miso, one of the Seven Sages, who was of a Timonian and

---

[1] Heraclitus, called the ' weeping philosopher '.

Democritian [1] humour, being asked why he was laughing to himself, replied, ' Because I am laughing to myself.'

How frequently I make remarks and replies every day that appear foolish to myself ; therefore how much more commonly and frequently they must appear so to others ! If I bite my lips over it, what must they do.

In short, we must live among the living, and let the river flow under the bridge, without caring, or at least without being upset by it.

True, but why can we meet a man with a crooked and deformed body without being moved, when we cannot bear to meet with an illogical mind without getting angry ? The hardness of the judge is here more to blame than the fault.

Let us ever keep that saying of Plato on our lips : ' If I find a thing unsound, is it not because I am myself unsound ? Am I not myself at fault ? May not my observations reflect upon myself ? ' A wise and divine refrain, which scourges the most common and universal error of mankind ! Not only the blame we cast at one another, but also our reasons and arguments and matters in dispute may usually be turned against us ; we wound ourselves with our own weapons. Of which antiquity has left me pregnant examples enough. This was cleverly said, and much to the purpose, by him who first thought of it :

> Every man's ordure well
> To his own sense doth smell. [2]
>
> (ERASMUS, slightly altered.)

Our eyes can see nothing behind us. A hundred times a day we laugh at ourselves when we laugh at our neighbours ; and we detest in others the faults which are much more glaring in ourselves, and with marvellous impudence and thoughtlessness we express our astonishment at them. Only yesterday I had the opportunity to hear a man, an intelligent and well-mannered person, ridiculing with as much humour as aptness, the fatuity of another who pesters everybody with his pedigrees and his alliances, which are more than half imaginary (for they are most ready to pounce upon this silly subject whose quality is most doubtful and least certain). And this man, if he had retired within him-

[1] The humour of Timon of Athens, the Misanthrope, and Democritus, the Laughing Philosopher.
[2] A good specimen of Florio's doggerel rhymes.

self, would have seen that he was hardly less extravagant and tedious in publishing and extolling his wife's family prerogatives. Oh, the meddlesome presumption with which the wife sees herself armed by the hands of her own husband ! If they understood Latin we might say to them :

> As if she were not mad enough already,
> You now provoke her to a greater madness. (TERENCE.)

I do not mean that no man should judge unless he himself be spotless, for then no man could judge ; not even if he were free from the same kind of blemish. But I do mean that our judgement, when laying blame on another who is in question, should not save us from self-judgement. It is a charitable office in one who cannot rid himself of a fault to endeavour none the less to rid another of it, in whom it may have taken less deep and stubborn root.

Nor do I think it a proper answer to one who apprises me of a fault, to say that he also has it. What of that ? The warning is still true and useful. If our sense of smell were good, our ordure should stink the more in our nostrils because it is ours. And Socrates is of opinion that if a man and his son and a stranger were guilty of some violence and injustice, he should begin by offering himself to be condemned by justice, and implore, for his purgation, the help of the executioner's hand ; secondly for his son and in the last place for the stranger. If this precept strikes rather too high a note, he should at least present himself first for punishment to his own conscience.

The senses are our first and proper judges, which perceive things only by external accidents ; and it is not to be wondered at if in all the parts of the service of our social life there is so perpetual and universal a mingling of ceremonious and superficial appearances ; so much so that therein consists the best and most effective part of our regulations. It is, after all, man with whom we have to do, whose condition is wonderfully corporeal.

Let those who, in these latter years, have tried to establish for us so contemplative and immaterial a practice of religion,[1] not wonder if there are people who think that it would have melted and slipped through their fingers, if it had not held together amongst us as a mark, title, and

[1] The Protestant Reformers.

instrument of division and faction, more than by its own power.

So in conversation the gravity, the gown, and the fortune of the speaker often gain credit for his empty and foolish remarks. It cannot be supposed that a gentleman so formidable and with such a following should not have inside him more than ordinary talents ; and that a man so arrogant and supercilious, who has been trusted with so many offices and missions, is not more able than this other who salutes him from afar, and whom nobody will employ. Not only the words, but even the grimaces of these people are pondered and weighed, and every one labours to discover some fine and deep meaning in them. If they condescend to familiar talk, and if you do not approve and bow to everything they say, they will knock you down with the authority of their experience : they have heard this, they have seen that, they have done the other ; you are crushed with examples. I should be inclined to say to them that the result of a surgeon's experience is not the history of his patients, and the recollection that he has cured four plague-stricken and three gouty people, unless from that experience he has been able to draw conclusions wherewith to form his judgement, and has given us reason to believe that he has become the wiser in the practice of his profession.

So in an instrumental concert we do not hear a lute, a spinet, and the flute ; we hear a general harmony, the effect of the blending of the whole band.

If their travels and their experience in office have improved them, they should make it apparent in the product of their intelligence. It is not enough to sum up their experiences, they should weigh and sort them ; they should have digested and distilled them, in order to extract from them the reasons and conclusions they admit of.

There were never so many historians. It is always good and profitable to give ear to them, for they keep us fully provided with good and commendable instruction from the store-house of their memory ; they assist us no doubt, for a great part, in the conduct of life. But that is not what we ook for at present ; we seek to know if those tellers and gatherers are themselves commendable.

I hate any kind of tyranny, whether of words or deeds. I commonly battle against those unreal surroundings that

delude our judgement through our senses ; and, when I keep
a strict watch on those who have risen to any extraordinary
eminence, I find that they are for the most part only men,
like the rest of us :

> In those high places common sense
> Is rarely to be found.　(JUVENAL.)

Perhaps in our estimation they appear smaller than they
are, by reason of their attempting more and being more in
evidence than others ; they are not equal to the burden
they have taken on their shoulders.　There must be more
strength and power in the porter than in the load.　He who
has not fully tried his strength leaves you to guess if he has
any power left, and if he has been tested to his utmost ; he
who sinks under his burden, betrays his measure and the
weakness of his shoulders.　That is why we see so many
incapables among the scholarly, outnumbering the capable.
They might have made good husbandmen, good tradesmen,
good artisans.　Their natural powers were cut out to those
proportions.

Knowledge is a thing of great weight, and they sink under
it.　Their mental machine is not powerful nor manageable
enough to spread out and distribute that noble and powerful
matter, to use it and derive help from it.　It can only dwell
in a strong nature, and strong natures are very rare.　And
the weak, says Socrates, by their handling mar the dignity
of philosophy.　It appears not only useless but harmful
when it is badly encased.　See how they prejudice and undo
themselves !

> As when an ape, the counterfeit of man,
> By grinning schoolboy dressed in silken coat,
> Leaving his backside bare, is ushered in
> To amuse the dining guests !　(CLAUDIAN.)

So too it is not enough for our rulers and administrators,
who hold the world in their hands, to have no more than an
ordinary intelligence, no more ability than we.　They are
very much below if they are not very much above us.　As
they promise more, so they owe more.

And therefore their silence not only gives them an air of
solemnity and gravity, but it is often profitable and econo-
mical.　For Megabysus, visiting Apelles in his studio, stood
a great while without speaking a word.　Then he began to

deliver his opinion of the painter's work, and received this rude snub, ' As long as you held your tongue, I thought you somebody out of the common, because of your chains and your fine clothes ; but now that I have heard you speak, there is not a boy in my workshop who does not despise you.' His gorgeous attire, his elevated rank, were no excuse for being ignorant with a common ignorance, and for speaking impertinently of painting. He should have kept his external and presumptive abilities under a mask of silence.

For how many foolish souls, in my time, has not a frigid and taciturn demeanour served as a mark of wisdom and capability !

Dignities, offices, are necessarily conferred more by fortune than according to merit ; and we are often wrong when we blame the King for it. Rather is it a marvel that they are so successful, when they have so little skill in it :

A Prince's virtue is his folk to know. (MARTIAL.)

For Nature has not given them eyes to take in so many people, to discern our pre-eminence and penetrate our bosoms, where lies the knowledge of our intentions and our greatest worth. They must sift us by conjecture and experiment, by family, wealth, learning, the voice of the people : very feeble testimonies. If any man could discover a means of judging and choosing men correctly and rationally, he would, by that act alone, establish a perfect form of government.

' Yes, but he has conducted this great business with success.' That is something, but it is not enough ; for this is a maxim which is rightly accepted : ' That we must not judge the plan by the issue.'

The Carthaginians punished the badly-laid plans of their generals, although they were set right by a happy issue ; and the Roman people often refused a triumph for a great and very advantageous victory, because the conduct of the commander did not correspond with his good fortune.

We may commonly observe, in the actions of this world, that Fortune, to apprise us of her power in all things, and because she takes a pleasure in confounding our presumption, being unable to make a blockhead wise, makes him successful, to spite the virtuous ; and she is fond of stepping in and favouring those actions in which she has done most of the weaving. Hence we may see every day that the simplest of us may successfully carry through an important affair, either public or private. And, as Siramnez the Persian replied to some one who wondered that his affairs should turn out so badly, seeing that he planned them so wisely : ' That he was sole master of his plans, but that of the success of his affairs Fortune was mistress ; ' these may answer the same, but with a contrary bias.

Most part of the things of this world work themselves out of their own accord :

> For the Fates will find a way. (VIRGIL.)

The issue often justifies a very foolish conduct. Our intervention is little more than a routine, and most commonly we consult custom and example rather than reason. Being once astonished at the greatness of some affair, and having learned from those who carried it through their motives and their proceedings, I found that their schemes were no more than commonplace. And the most commonplace and time-worn are perhaps also the surest and most adapted to the purpose, in practice if not in appearance.

What if the shallowest reasons are the most suitable ; the loosest, most commonplace and threadbare the best adapted for affairs ? For the king's Council to maintain its authority, outsiders should not be allowed to join it, or to see further than the nearest barrier. It must command respect on trust and in the lump, if it would keep up its reputation.

In my deliberations I outline the matter a little, and consider it cursorily in its first aspect ; the main and chief part of the business I usually entrust to heaven :

> All else unto the Gods I leave. (HORACE.)

Good and bad fortune are, in my opinion, two sovereign powers. It is folly to imagine that human wisdom can play the part of Fortune. And vain is his undertaking who has the presumption to embrace both causes and consequences, and to lead the progress of his affair by the hand ; especially vain in military deliberations.

There was never more caution and circumspection in military matters than is observed at times in this country. Can it be that they are afraid of losing themselves on the way, and reserve themselves for the catastrophe of that drama ? I go further, and say that our wisdom itself and our deliberation follow, for the most part, whither chance leads them.

My will and my reason are stirred now by one breath, now by another ; and many of these movements take place without my guidance. My reason is impelled and stirred by accidental causes varying from day to day :

> The phases of their minds are changed ; their breasts
> Conceive emotions now far otherwise
> Than when the storm-wind drove the scudding clouds. (VIRGIL.)

If you will observe who are the most influential people in the cities, and who are most successful in business, you will usually find that they are the least talented. It has fallen to the lot of women, of children and madmen, to rule great states equally well with the most able princes ; and the gross-witted, according to Thucydides, are usually more successful than the clever. We attribute to their wisdom the results of their good fortune.

> He makes his way who uses Fortune right,
> And all the world calls, ' What a clever man ! ' (PLAUTUS.)

Wherefore I confidently say that in every way results are a poor testimony of our worth and ability.

Now I was about to say that we have but to look at a man who has been raised to dignity. Although we knew him three days before as a man of very little account, there steals imperceptibly into our minds a picture of greatness and excellence, and we are persuaded that, having grown in pomp and reputation, he has grown in merit. We estimate him, not according to his worth, but after the manner of counters, according to the prerogative of his rank. Let his luck turn, let him fall again and mingle with the crowd, every one will ask with wonder what it was that lifted him to such a height.

' Is this the man, they will say ; did he know no more about it when he was there ? Are princes so easily satisfied ? We were in good hands, forsooth ! '

That is a thing I have often seen in my time. Yea, and the mask of greatness they put on in stage-plays affects and deludes us to a certain degree.

What I myself reverence in kings is the crowd of their reverers. All obeisance and submission is due to them except that of the understanding ; my reason is not trained to bow and bend, it is only my knees.

Melanthius, being asked what he thought of Dionysius' tragedy, said, ' I did not see it, it was so obscured by words.' So most of those who judge a great man's speeches might say, ' I did not understand his meaning, his discourse was so obscured by solemnity, grandeur and majesty.'

Antisthenes one day advised the Athenians to order their asses to be used for field-labour, as well as their horses ; whereupon somebody replied that that animal was not born for such service. ' That does not matter, he replied ; your order will be sufficient, for the most ignorant and incapable man you appoint to a command in your wars, immediately and invariably becomes most worthy of it, just because you appoint him.'

Which comes very near the custom in so many nations of canonizing the King they have elected from among themselves ; not satisfied with honouring, they must also worship him. The Mexicans, as soon as the ceremony of crowning their King is over, dare no more look him in the face ; nay, as if his royalty had raised him to the gods, with the oaths they make him take to maintain their religion, their laws, and their liberties, to be valiant, just, and mild, he also swears to make the sun run its course with its accustomed light, to make the clouds drop their water at the proper seasons, to make the rivers flow in their channels, and cause the earth to bring forth all things necessary for his people.

I am opposed to this common way of treating them, and I am inclined rather to doubt a man's ability when I see it attended by exalted fortune and the popular favour. We must be on our guard and think how much it means, when a man is able to speak at his own time, to choose his points, to interrupt the course of a discussion or to change it, with a magisterial authority, to defend himself against opposition of others by a motion of the head, by a smile or by silence, in the presence of an assembly trembling with reverence and respect.

A man of prodigious fortune, putting in his word in a certain trifling discussion that was running its even course at his table, began with these very words, ' He can only be a liar or an ignoramus who says otherwise than, &c.' Follow up this philosophical point with a dagger in your hand !

Here is another observation which I find very useful :

That in discussions and conversations, not all the sayings which we approve of should be immediately accepted. Most men are rich in borrowed excellence. It may very well happen that a man will make a good point, give a good answer, cite a good maxim and put it forth, without perceiving the force of it.

(That a man does not possess all that he borrows may perhaps be verified in my case.)

We must not always grant it, whatever truth or beauty it may contain. Either we must oppose it seriously, or retire under colour of not understanding it, to feel on all sides how it came into the head of the man who gave utterance to it. We may happen to run upon the point of his sword and assist his stroke, although we were out of his reach.

Sometimes, when forced to it and hard pressed in the combat, I have employed a riposte that told beyond my intention and expectation. I only gave it by measure, and it was received by weight. Just as, when disputing with a strong man, I delight in meeting his conclusions half-way, relieving him of the trouble of explaining himself, and anticipating his idea whilst still unformed and nascent (the order and precision of his understanding warning and threatening me from afar) ; in the case of those others I do quite the contrary : I am obliged to understand and presume nothing but what they say. If they give their opinion in general terms, ' This is good, that is not good,' and they happen to hit the mark, see if it is not Fortune that hits it for them. Let them circumscribe and limit their judgements a little : why it is so, how it is so.

Those sweeping judgements which are so common are meaningless. They are like men who salute a whole crowd of people in the mass. Those who really know them salute and take notice of them individually and by name. But it is a hazardous experiment. For I have observed, more often than every day, that a man with a poor intellectual foundation, trying to show off his cleverness when reading a book, by remarking upon some fine passage, will fix his admiration with so poor a choice, that instead of showing up the excellence of the author, he only betrays his own ignorance.

After hearing a whole page of Virgil, it is safe to exclaim, ' That is fine ! ' In that way the artful save their faces.

But when you attempt to follow him line by line, and, with positive and discriminating judgement, to point out where a good author surpasses himself, where he rises to sublime heights, weighing his words, phrases, ideas, one after the other, away with you ! *We must consider not only what each one says, but what he thinks, and why he thinks it* (Cicero).

Every day I hear stupid people saying things that are not stupid.

They say [1] a good thing ; let us know how far they understand it ; let us see whereby they grasp it. We assist them when they use this fine maxim and that fine argument, which is none of theirs ; it is only in their keeping. They will have brought it out at a venture and diffidently ; it is we who give it value and credit. You lend them a hand. What is the good ? They do not thank you for it, and only become more foolish. Do not back them up, let them go ; they will handle this matter like people who are afraid of burning their fingers ; they dare not alter its setting and light, nor probe its meaning. Shake it ever so little, and it will escape them ;- they will give it up to you, be it never so strong and beautiful. They are fine weapons, but they are ill-hafted. How often I have had this experience !

Now, if you happen to enlighten them and corroborate them, they will catch at it and forthwith rob you of the advantage of your interpretation : ' That is what I was about to say ; that was exactly my idea, and if I failed to make myself so clear, it was only for want of words.' Blow your hardest ! One must employ even cunning to correct this arrogant stupidity.

Hegesias' dogma, ' That we should neither hate nor condemn, but instruct,' is reasonable in other cases, but in this case it is unjust and inhuman to help and set him right who stands in no need of it, and is the worse for it. I like to leave them sticking in the mud and becoming more entangled than ever, and so deeply, if it is possible, that they will at last come to acknowledge their error.

Stupidity and a confused mind are not to be cured by a word of admonition ; and we may fitly say of this kind of correction what Cyrus replied to one who urged him to harangue his army when on the point of entering into

[1] i. e. those who are ' rich in borrowed excellence ' ; see the last paragraph but six.

battle, ' That men are not suddenly made brave and warlike by a fine harangue, any more than a man immediately becomes a musician after hearing a good song.' It needs a preliminary apprenticeship, a long and continued education.

This attention, this assiduity in correcting and instructing, we owe to our families ; but to go preaching to the first passer-by, to be schoolmaster to the ignorance and stupidity of any chance person, is a thing I greatly grudge. I rarely do so even in private conversation with another ; and rather give up the whole thing than impart pedantic instruction to such backward people. I am naturally no more adapted to speak than to write for beginners. But when things are said in company or before others, however false and absurd they may appear to me, I never interfere either by word or sign.

Moreover, nothing exasperates me so much in a stupid person as that he is more self-satisfied than any reasonable person can reasonably be. It is a pity that wisdom forbids you to be satisfied with yourself and to trust your own judgement, and always dismisses you discontented and diffident ; whilst a bold opinionativeness always fills its possessors with delight and assurance. It is the most empty-headed who look at other men over their shoulders, and always return from the combat full of glee and triumph. And besides, as a rule their arrogant language and cheerful looks make them the victors in the eyes of the audience, who are usually of weak intelligence and incapable of judging and discerning on which side the advantage really lies.

Obstinacy and heat in sticking to one's opinions is the surest proof of stupidity. Is there anything so cock-sure, so immovable, so disdainful, so contemplative, so solemn and serious as an ass ?

May we not include under the heading of conversation and intercourse the quick and smart repartees that mirth and intimacy introduce among friends, pleasantly and wittily chaffing and poking fun at each other ? A sport for which my natural gaiety makes me fit enough. And if it is not so strained and serious as the other exercise I have spoken of, it is no less subtle and intellectual, and, as Lycurgus thought, no less profitable.

For my part I contribute to it more licence than wit, and have therein more luck than originality. But in patience

I am perfect, and can bear a retaliation that is not only rude but impertinent, without being moved. And when attacked, if I have not a brisk retort ready to hand, I do not waste time in following up that point with feeble and tiresome persistence, bordering on obstinacy ; I let it pass, cheerfully letting my ears drop and deferring my revenge to some better opportunity. There is no merchant who always gains.

Most people change countenance and raise their voices when their strength begins to fail ; and with unreasonable anger, instead of getting their revenge, only betray their weakness and their impatience at the same time. In this mirthful mood we sometimes pluck some secret string of each other's imperfections, which, in a more sober mood, we cannot touch without offence. And we profitably give one another a hint of our defects.

There are other kinds of rough play, which are unwise and cruel, after the French manner, for which I have a deadly hatred ; for I have a tender and sensitive skin. I have seen in my time two Princes of our royal blood brought to their graves as a consequence of them.[1] It is an ugly thing to fight in play.

For the rest, when I wish to size up a man, I ask him how far he is satisfied with himself, how much he is pleased with his conversation and his work. I will have none of those fine excuses : ' I only did it in play ;

> This work unfinished from the anvil comes ;   (OVID.)

I was not an hour over it ; [2] I have not looked at it since.' Well then, I reply, put this piece aside ; give me one that does you full justice, by which you would like to be measured. And then, what do you consider best in your work ; is it this passage, or this ? Is it the charm, or the matter, or the idea, or the judgement, or the learning ?

---

[1] According to Motheau this can only refer to King Henry II and to Henry de Bourbon-Montpensier, both of whom died of wounds received in the last two tournaments that were held in France, one at Paris in 1559, the other at Orleans in 1560.

[2]   *Oronte.*   Au reste, vous saurez
          Que je n'ai demeuré qu'un quart d'heure à le faire.
  Alceste.   Voyons, Monsieur ; le temps ne fait rien à l'affaire.

Molière, no doubt, remembered this passage when he wrote that wonderful ' sonnet scene ' in the *Misanthrope*.

For I observe generally that men are as wide of the mark in judging their own work as in judging that of others, not only by reason of the affection that creeps in, but for want of capacity to know and discriminate it. The work, by its own power and fortune, may second the workman, and outstrip him, beyond his own inventiveness and knowledge.

For my part, I do not judge of the value of another's work less clearly than my own ; very changeably and hesitatingly I rate the Essays now low, now high.

There are many books that are useful by reason of their subject, for which the author earns no praise ; and there are good books, as well as good works, which shame the workman. I may write of the fashions of our dinner-parties and our clothes, and write without enthusiasm ; I may publish the edicts of my time, and the letters of Princes, which will pass into the hands of the public ; I may make an abridgement of a good book (and every abridgement of a good book is a foolish abridgement), and the book itself may be lost ; and the like things. Posterity may derive singular benefit from such compositions ; but what honour shall I gain, except through my good fortune ? A good number of famous books are in this plight.

When, some years ago, I read Philip de Commines, truly a very good writer, I noticed this for no common remark : ' That we must take good care not to serve our master so well as to make it difficult for him to requite us adequately for our services.' I ought to have commended the idea, not the writer. I came across it, not long ago, in Tacitus : *Benefits are only so far acceptable as they appear capable of being returned ; if they pass much beyond that limit, they reap hatred rather than gratitude.* And Seneca says with vigour : *The man who thinks it disgraceful not to pay back, would rather have no man for a creditor.* And Q. Cicero,[1] from a meaner point of view : *The man who thinks he cannot requite you can in no way be your friend.*

The subject, according to its nature, may gain a man a reputation for learning and a good memory ; but in order to appreciate those qualities in the book which are most original and most valuable, the power and beauty of the writer's mind, we must know how much of it is original, how

[1] Quintus Cicero, brother of the great orator, known for the letter of advice he addressed to the latter, ' On Standing for the Consulship '.

much not. And, with respect to what is not original, how much we owe him in consideration of the choice, the disposition, embellishment and style which he has contributed to it. What if he has borrowed the matter and impaired the form, as so often happens ? We others who have little acquaintance with books are in this strait that, when we come across some beautiful idea in a new poet, some forcible argument in a preacher, we dare not commend them for it until we have been informed by some man of learning whether that element is their own, or some other's. Till then I always stand on my guard.

I have just run through Tacitus' *History* without a break (a thing that seldom happens with me ; it is twenty years since I have devoted a whole hour at a time to a book) ; I did so at the instigation of a gentleman who enjoys great esteem in France, both for his own worth, and for a consistent kind of excellence and goodness which he shares with several brothers.

I know no writer who introduces into the annals of public affairs so many reflections on the manners and dispositions of private persons. And I totally disagree with him when he says that, having made it his special task to trace the lives of the Emperors of his time, so abnormal and so outrageous in every direction, and to tell of the many remarkable deeds which their cruelties in particular called forth in their subjects, he had a more solid and attractive material on which to build his narrative and his reflections, than if he had had to tell of battles and general insurrections. So that often I find him sterile, hurrying over those noble deaths, as if he feared to weary us with their number and length.

This form of history is by far the most useful. Public movements are more dependent on the guidance of Fortune ; private ones on our own.

It is rather a summing up than an historical narrative ; there are more precepts than stories. It is not a book to read, it is a book to study and learn ; it is so full of maxims, that they seem to have been brought in by hook and by crook. It is a nursery of ethical and political dissertations, for the benefit and improvement of those who hold a place in the management of the world.

He always pleads with strong and solid reasons, in pointed

and subtle fashion, in accordance with the affected style of that age ; they were so fond of inflated language that when they could find no point or subtlety in things they borrowed them of words.

He writes not unlike Seneca ; he appears to me more fleshy, Seneca more pointed. His services were better adapted to a sick and disturbed state, as ours is at present ; you might often think he were describing us and criticizing us.

They who doubt his sincerity plainly betray themselves as ill-disposed to him on some other account. His opinions are sound, and he leans to the right side in Roman affairs. Yet I blame him a little for having judged Pompey more harshly than is consistent with the opinion of the honest men who lived at the time and had dealings with him ; and for placing him entirely on a par with Marius and Sylla, except in so far as he was more close. In aiming at the government of affairs he was not acquitted of ambition and a feeling of revenge ; and even his friends feared that victory would have carried him beyond the bounds of reason, but not to so unbridled a degree.[1] There was nothing in his life to suggest a threat of such purposeful cruelty and tyranny. Besides we should not weigh suspicion against evidence ; so I do not agree with Tacitus in that matter.

That his narrative is simple and straightforward may perhaps be argued even from this, that it does not always fit in with the conclusions his judgement comes to, which he follows according to the bias he has taken, often beyond the matter he is presenting to us, which he has not deigned to twist in the least degree.

He needs no excuse for having countenanced the religion of his time, in accordance with the laws which commanded him to do so, and of having been ignorant of the true faith. That was his misfortune, not his fault.

I have considered chiefly his judgement, and am not very clear about it in every case. For example, those words in the letter which Tiberius, sick and aged, sent to the Senate : ' What to write, Conscript Fathers ; in what terms to express myself, or what to refrain from writing, is a matter of such perplexity, that if I know how to decide, may the just Gods and the Goddesses of Vengeance doom me to die

[1] As Marius and Sylla.

in pangs worse than those under which I linger every day ! '
I cannot see why he so positively attributes them to a
poignant remorse tormenting Tiberius' conscience ; at
least I did not see it when I was best able to do so.[1]

This too appeared to me a little mean-spirited, that
having occasion to mention a certain honourable office that
he filled at Rome, he excuses himself by saying that it is not
out of ostentation that he mentions it. This seems to me a
cheap thing to say, coming from a mind like his ; for not to
dare to speak roundly of oneself betrays some want of spirit.
A man of staunch and lofty judgement, who judges soundly
and surely, will unhesitatingly use himself as an example,
as if he were some other person, and give as frank testimony
of himself as of anything else. He should override those
common rules of politeness for the sake of truth and
liberty.

I dare not only to speak of myself, but to speak only of
myself ; when I speak of other things I wander away and
escape from my subject. I am not so inordinately in love,
so wholly bound and mixed up with myself, that I cannot
consider and distinguish myself apart, as I do a neighbour
or a tree. Not to see how much we are worth is as great
a fault as to tell more of ourselves than we are able to discover. We owe more love to God than to ourselves, and we
know him less well ; and yet we speak of him to our heart's
content.

If the writings of Tacitus in any way reflect his character,
he was a great man, upright and courageous, not of a superstitious, but of a philosophic and generous virtue. We may
think him venturesome in his testimony, as when he tells
of a soldier, who was carrying a load of wood, that his hands
were so stiffened by cold, that they stuck to the wood, and
there remained fixed and dead, having come away from his
arms. In such matters I usually bow to the authority of
such great witnesses.

And when he says that Vespasian, by the grace of the god
Serapis, cured a blind woman of Alexandria by anointing
her eyes with his spittle, and I know not what other miracle,
he follows the example and duty of all good historians.
They keep a record of important events, and among
matters of public interest are to be numbered popular

[1] ' When I read the text ', is perhaps what Montaigne meant.

rumours and ideas. It is their part to cite common beliefs, not regulate them. That part concerns divines and philosophers, the directors of consciences.

Very wisely too his fellow-historian, a great man like himself, said : *Indeed I set down more things than I believe ; for I neither affirm things I doubt, nor suppress what I have heard* (Quintus Curtius). And this other : *These are things we need not be at pains either to affirm or refute ; we must abide by report* (Livy). And, writing in an age when the belief in prodigies was beginning to decline, he says he will not on that account forbear to insert in his *Annals* and lend currency to things accepted by so many worthy men, and with so much reverence for antiquity. That is very well said. Let them deliver history as they receive it rather than as they believe it.

I, who am monarch of the matter I treat of, and am accountable for it to no man, yet do not trust myself with regard to everything ; I often venture on intellectual flights of fancy which are suspicious to myself, and certain verbal quibbles at which I shake my ears. But I let them run their chance. I observe that some are praised for such things ; it is not for me alone to judge. I present myself standing and lying, front and back, right and left, and in all my natural attitudes.

Minds, even if alike in strength, are not always alike in tastes and inclinations.

That is what my memory of Tacitus pictures to me in the gross, and with uncertainty enough. All generalizations are loose and imperfect.

CHAPTER 9

OF VANITY

THERE is perhaps no more manifest vanity than to write of it so vainly. What the Deity has so divinely said of it ought to be carefully and continually meditated by intelligent people.[1]

Who does not see that I have chosen a path along which I shall wander, without cease and without labour, as long as there is ink and paper in the world ? I cannot keep a record

---

[1] See Ecclesiastes, or the Preacher.

of my life by my actions ; Fortune places them too low. I keep it by my ideas. So I knew a gentleman who only communicated his life by the operations of his bowels ; at his house you might have seen on view a row of chamber-pots of seven or eight days' use. That was his study, his conversation ; all other talk stank in his nostrils.

Here, a little more decently, you have the excrements of an old mind, now hard, now loose, and always undigested. And when shall I have done reflecting a continual movement and change in my thoughts, whatever the matter they light upon, seeing that Diomedes filled six thousand books with nothing but grammatical subjects ? [1] What should be the output of garrulity, since the untying of the tongue and mere prattle stifled the world under such a horrific load of volumes ! So many words for mere words ! O Pythagoras, why did you not conjure this tempest ! [2]

One Galba [3] of olden times was reproved for living idly ; he replied, ' Every man should render an account of his actions, not of his leisure-hours.' He was mistaken, for justice also notices and censures those who keep holiday.

But there should be some kind of coercion on the part of the laws of those who write futile and unprofitable things, as there is of vagrants and idlers. Both I and a hundred others would be banished from the hands of the people.

I am not jesting. The mania for scribbling appears to be one of the symptoms of an unruly age. When did we write so much as in these disturbed times ? When did the Romans write so much as at the time of their downfall ? Besides, intellectual subtlety does not imply a greater wisdom in a government ; that busy idleness proceeds from this, that every man takes a lax interest in the duties of his office, and is easily led away from them.

The corruption of the times is made up of the individual contributions of each one of us ; some contribute treachery, others injustice, irreligion, tyranny, avarice, cruelty, according as they are more or less influential ; the weaker sort

[1] According to Seneca, Didymus (not Diomedes) the Grammarian wrote four thousand books on futile questions connected with literature, such as ' Who was Aeneas' real mother ? ' ' Was Anacreon more a lecher than a drunkard ? '

[2] Pythagoras is supposed to have imposed a silence of two or five years on his disciples.

[3] According to Suetonius, the Emperor Galba.

bring to it folly, vanity, idleness : of these am I. It would seem as if unprofitable things were in season, when the hurtful weigh heavily upon us. At a time when wicked deeds are so common, merely unprofitable deeds are almost praiseworthy.

I find comfort in the reflection that I shall be one of the last on whom they must lay hands. Whilst they see to the more urgent cases, I shall have leisure to mend. For I think it would be contrary to reason to hunt down the petty evil-doers when the country is infested with great ones.

The physician Philotinus said to one who came to him to have his finger dressed, but who, as he perceived from his complexion and his breath, had an ulcer on his lungs, ' My friend, this is no time to busy yourself with your nails.'

And yet, speaking on this subject, a few years ago I saw that a man whose memory I hold in particular esteem, at the height of our great disorders, when there was no more law or justice, nor any magistrate who did his duty, than there are at this moment, publicly suggested some pitiful reforms or other in our dress, cookery, and law-practice. Those are diversions with which they feed an ill-used people, to make them believe that they are not entirely forgotten.

It is the same with those others who zealously waste their time denouncing forms of speech, dancing, and games, in a people abandoned to all sorts of execrable vices. It is no time to wash and clean up when we are attacked by a high fever. Only the Spartans could afford to set about combing and dressing their hair when about to rush headlong into some extreme danger to their lives.[1]

For my part, I have this other worse habit, that if one of my pumps is trodden down, I am equally neglectful of my shirt and my cloak ; I scorn to mend by halves. When I am in evil plight, I revel in my misfortune ; I abandon myself to despair, and let myself go to the dogs, throwing, as the saying is, the helve after the hatchet. I persist in growing worse, and no longer think myself worth caring for ; either entirely well or entirely ill.

It is in my favour that the desolation of this State coincides with the desolation of my age ; I can more readily suffer that my ills should be increased, than that my wellbeing should be disturbed by it. The words I utter in

[1] An allusion to the battle of Thermopyle.

misfortune are words of anger ; my courage bristles up
instead of drooping.

And, contrary to others, I am more devout in good than
in evil fortune, following Xenophon's precept, if not his
reason,[1] and more generally make eyes at Heaven to give
thanks than to beg.

I take more pains to improve in health when it smiles
upon me, than to recover it when I have mislaid it.

Prosperity is my teacher and instructor, as adversities
and rods are to others.

As if good fortune were incompatible with a good conscience, men never become good but in evil fortune.

Good fortune is to me a singular spur to temperance and
humility.

A prayer wins me, a threat repels me ; favour makes me
bend, fear stiffens me.

Among human attributes this is common enough, that we
are better pleased with things of others than with our own,
and that we love change and motion :

> The day flows onward in a grateful stream,
> Because the steeds are changed at every hour.[2]   (PETRONIUS.)

I have my share in it. Those who go to the other extreme,
of being satisfied with themselves, of valuing what they
possess above all other things and admitting nothing to be
more beautiful than what they see, are indeed happier if
not wiser than we. I do not envy their wisdom, but certainly
their good fortune.

This greedy craving for the new and unknown greatly
helps to foster in me the desire to travel ; but there are
enough other circumstances that contribute to it. I am
content to turn aside from the ruling of my household.
There is a certain gratification in being in command, though
it were only of a barn, and in being obeyed by one's people ;
but it is too dull and humdrum a pleasure. And besides, it
is necessarily attended by many tiresome considerations ;
now it is the indigence and oppression of your tenants, now

---

[1] ' The most likely person to obtain favour from the Gods (as well as
from men) is not he who, when he is in distress, flatters them servilely,
but he who, when he is most prosperous, is most mindful of them.'—
Xenophon, *Cyropedia*.

[2] There appear to be two metaphors involved in this Latin quotation,
that of the water-hourglass, and of Apollo's steeds.

a quarrel among your neighbours, now the trespasses they make upon you, that give you trouble :

> Whether your vines be smit with hail;
> Whether your promised harvest fail,
>   Perfidious to your toil;
> Whether your drooping trees complain
> Of angry winter's chilling rain,
>   Or stars that burn the soil ; (HORACE.)

and that God hardly once in six months sends you a season that fully satisfies your steward, and which, if good for the vines, does not harm the meadows :

> The sun above with burning heat destroys,
> Or sudden showers and icy frosts lay low,
> And blasts of storms with furious whirlwinds vex. (LUCRETIUS.)

Add to this the new and well-shaped shoe of the man of olden times that hurts your foot.[1] And that a stranger does not understand what it costs and how much you sacrifice to keep up that show of order that is seen in your household, and which perhaps you pay too dearly for.

I was late in taking up husbandry. Those whom Nature sent into the world before me for a long time relieved me of that burden. I had already taken another bent, more suitable to my humour. However, so far as my experience goes, it is an absorbing rather than a difficult occupation ; whoever is capable of anything else will be easily capable of this. If I sought to become rich, that way would seem to me too long ; I might have served kings, a more fertile traffic than any other. Seeing that I only aspire to the reputation of having acquired nothing, as I have wasted nothing, conformably to the rest of my life, being unable to do any good or any ill, and that I only desire to pass, I can do that, thank God, without any great exertion.

If it comes to the worst, always hasten to meet poverty half-way by retrenching your expenses ; that is what I strive to do, and to mend my ways before I am forced to it. I have, moreover, sufficiently thought out in my mind the different stages of doing with less than I have ; I mean

---

[1] A certain Roman having divorced his wife, his friends remonstrated and asked him, ' Was she not chaste ? Was she not fair ? Was she not fruitful.' He held out his shoe and replied, ' Is it not handsome ? Is it not new ? Yet no one knows where it pinches but he that wears it.'—Plutarch, *Life of Paulus Emilius.*

contentedly. *Not by your income, but by your living and style, is your wealth really to be calculated* (Cicero).

My real need does not so wholly take up all I have but that Fortune may find something in me to nibble at, without biting to the quick.

My presence, in spite of my ignorance and apathy, affords great help in my domestic affairs ; I busy myself with them, but grudgingly. Besides that in my house, although I burn the candle at my end, the other end is by no means spared.

Travelling does me no injury except in regard to the expense, which is great and beyond my means ; and I am accustomed to travel with not merely a necessary, but a handsome retinue. I am obliged to make my journeys the shorter and less frequent, and spend on them only the skimmings and the reserve fund, delaying and putting off according as they come in.

I do not wish the pleasure of my wanderings to spoil the pleasure of my retreat ; on the contrary I intend that they shall nourish and favour one another. Fortune has been helpful to me in this, that, since my chief aim in this life was to live comfortably and idly rather than busily, she has relieved me of the necessity of multiplying riches to provide for a multitude of heirs. As for the one I have, if that does not suffice her which has so plenteously sufficed me, so much the worse for her ; if she is improvident she will not deserve that I should wish her any more. And, after the example of Phocion,[1] every man sufficiently provides for his children who provides for them in so far as they are not unlike him. I should certainly not agree with Crates, or do as he did. He left his money in the hands of a banker, with this condition : ' If his children were fools, he was to give it to them; if they were clever, he was to distribute it among the most foolish of the people ; ' as if fools, for being less able to do without riches, were more capable of using them !

At all events, the loss that is caused by my absence does not, as long as I am able to bear it, appear to deserve that I should refuse to seize any opportunity that offers of taking a holiday from the labours that my presence entails.

There is always something that goes wrong ; you are

---

[1] ' If my children are like me, my little estate will be enough for them ; if not I will not encourage and increase their expensive habits at my cost.'—Cornelius Nepos, *Phocion*.

plagued by business, now about one house, now about another. You pry too closely into everything ; your perspicacity is harmful to you in this, as it often enough is in other things. I avoid any occasions for annoyance, and try to ignore things that go amiss ; and yet I cannot manage so well but that at every hour when at home I experience some unpleasant jar. And the rogueries they most carefully keep from me are those I know best. There are some we must ourselves help to conceal, that we may suffer less. Harmless pin-pricks ; harmless sometimes, but still pin-pricks. The pettiest and minutest troubles are the most keenly felt ; and as small letters hurt and tire the eyes most, so do little matters most irritate us. The petty ills that crowd upon us are more worrying than a single big one, however severe. Coming thick upon us with their delicate points, these domestic thorns prick us the more sharply and without warning, easily taking us unawares.

I am no philosopher ; evils crush me according to their weight ; and they weigh as much in proportion to their form as to their matter, and often more. I have more insight into them than the vulgar, and so suffer them more patiently. In short, if they do not wound me, they hurt me.[1]

Life is a delicate thing, and easily disturbed. From the moment that I am inclined to be ill-humoured—*for after yielding to the first impulse we cannot resist it* (Seneca)—however absurd the cause of it, I incite my humour in that direction ; it then nurses [2] and exasperates itself of its own accord, attracting and accumulating matter upon matter whereon to feed :

The drippings from the eaves will scoop the stone. (LUCRETIUS.)

These frequent little droppings eat into my soul. Everyday annoyances are never light. They are continual and irreparable, especially if caused by the continual details inseparable from household management.

---

[1] The edition of 1588 had this passage in place of the last paragraph : 'Now Homer shows us well enough the power of surprise, when he makes Ulysses weep at the death of his dog and not at his mother's (wife's ?) tears. The first accident, trivial as it was, got the better of him since it attacked him unawares ; he bore the second and more violent attack because he was prepared for it. They are slight causes, which however disturb our lives.'

[2] 'Nursing her wrath to keep it warm.'—BURNS.

When I consider my affairs from a distance and in the lump, I find, perhaps because I do not remember them very exactly, that they have till now continued to prosper beyond my expectation and calculations. I seem to get more out of my estate than there is in it ; the success of my affairs is deceptive. But when I am in the midst of the drudgery, when I see all those little things in progress,

> Then is my soul with care on care distraught, (VIRGIL.)

a thousand things give me cause to desire and fear. To forsake them entirely I find very easy ; to give my attention to them without anxiety, very hard. It is a pitiful thing to be in a place where everything you see gives you concern and trouble. And I think I enjoy with a lighter heart and with a purer relish the comforts of another man's house.

Diogenes answered according to my humour when, being asked what sort of wine he liked best, he said, ' Another man's.'

My father loved building at Montaigne, where he was born ; and in the management of all my domestic affairs I love to follow his example and his rules ; and I will interest my successors in them as far as I am able. If I could do more for him, I would. I make it my boast that his will is in active operation through me. God forbid that I should fail to repay so kind a father by resembling him in any way whatever !

Whenever I have taken in hand to complete some bit of old wall, or rectify some badly-squared farm-building, I have thought more of his intentions than of my own satisfaction. And I blame my indolence that I have not gone any further towards completing the things he so handsomely commenced in his house, the more so as I am in all likelihood the last possessor of my race, and the last to put a finishing hand to it.

For, with regard to my own inclinations, neither this pleasure of building, which is said to have so much fascination, nor the chase, nor gardening, nor any of those other pleasures of a secluded life, are much of a pastime to me. That is a thing for which I blame myself, as I do for all other notions that I find inconvenient. I do not care so much whether they be vigorous or learned, so long as they are easily adaptable to life ; they are true and sound enough, if they are useful and pleasing.

They do me a mortal wrong who, when they hear me
declare my incompetence in matters of husbandry, whisper
into my ears that it is disdain, and that I am careless about
knowing the implements of field labour, its season, its order,
how my vines are dressed, how they are grafted, the names
and shapes of plants and fruits and the preparation of the
viands on which I live, the names and prices of the materials
with which I am clothed, because my heart is set upon some
higher knowledge. That would be folly and stupidity rather
than vanity. I would rather be a good horseman than a
good logician :

> Why not apply yourself to useful tasks,
> Plait wicker crates and baskets of soft reeds ? (VIRGIL.)

We entangle our thoughts with general questions, universal causes and the conduct of universal affairs, which will
go forward very well without our assistance, and we neglect
our own business, and Michael, who concerns us much more
nearly than man in general.

Now I do indeed stay at home for the most part ; but I
should like to take more pleasure in staying at home than
in going abroad :

> May it the haven be, I pray,
> For my old age to wear away ;
> Oh, may it be the final bourne
> To one with care and travel worn ! (HORACE.)

I know not whether I shall bring it about. I could wish
that instead of some other part of his possessions, my father
had left me that passionate love he had in his old age for his
household. He was very happy in being able to adapt his
wishes to his fortune, and to be satisfied with what he had.
I care not how much political philosophy may condemn the
meanness and sterility of my occupation, if I can once take
a liking for it, as he did. I am of this opinion, that the most
honourable occupation is to serve the public, and to be
useful to many. *We best employ the fruits of genius, virtue
and all excellence, when we are able to bestow them on our
fellow-men* (Cicero). For my part, I stand aside ; partly for
conscience' sake (for whenever I consider the weight of
obligation attaching to such employments, I also perceive
how little I am able to bear it ; and Plato, a master-worker
in all political government, none the less kept aloof from

it) ; partly through indolence. I am content to enjoy the world, without busying myself with it ; to live no more than an excusable life, a life that will be no burden to myself or others.

Never did any man more fully and weakly allow himself to be cared for and ruled by another than I should do, if I could find somebody. One of my wishes at this moment would be to find a son-in-law who would comfortably spoon-feed me in my old age, and rock me to sleep ; to whose hands I might entrust, with full power, the management and use of my property, that he might dispose of it as I do, and get at my expense what I get, provided he did so with a truly grateful and loving heart. But no, we live in a world where loyalty in our own children is unknown.

Whoever has charge of my purse when I travel, has it purely and without control ; and so he might cheat me in the reckoning. And if he is not a devil, my reckless trust obliges him to deal honestly by me. *Many, in their fear of being cheated, have taught how to cheat ; and by their suspicions have justified another's crimes* (Seneca). My trust in my people is generally founded on my ignorance of their faults ; I do not presume any vice in them until I have seen it, and I place more trust in the younger, whom I consider to be less corrupted by evil examples.

I would rather be told, at the end of two months, that I have spent four hundred crowns, than to have my ears drummed every night with three, five, seven. Yet I have as seldom as any man been a victim to this kind of petty larceny. It is true that I lend a helping hand to my own ignorance ; I purposely keep my knowledge of my money somewhat uncertain and muddled ; up to a certain point I am quite content to be able to doubt. You must leave a little margin for the disloyalty or improvidence of your servant. If on the whole we have enough to make ends meet, let that overplus of Fortune's liberality run a little more at her mercy : the gleaner's portion. After all I do not so much prize the fidelity of my people as I despise the injury they can do me.

O what a vile and ridiculous study it is to study one's money, to take a pleasure in fingering, weighing, and counting it over and over again ! That is the way by which avarice makes its approach.

During these eighteen years that I have governed my estate, I have not been able to bring myself either to look at a title-deed or to examine my principal affairs, which have necessarily to pass under my knowledge and attention. This is not a philosopher's contempt for transitory and mundane things ; my taste is not so clarified, and I appreciate them at least at their true value ; but it is certainly inexcusable and puerile sloth and negligence.

What would I not do rather than read a contract, rather than go and disturb those dust-laden documents, a slave to my business, or, still worse, to another's business, as so many are for money payment ? Nothing costs me so much as trouble and anxiety ; and I only seek to throw off care and live in idleness.

I believe I was better adapted to live on another man's fortune, if that were possible without obligation and subjection. And yet I know not, on looking more closely into it, whether, with my disposition and my lot, what I have to suffer from business and at the hands of servants and familiars, does not bring more humiliation, trouble, and bitterness, than I should feel in the retinue of a man, of higher birth than myself, who would steer my course for me in comfort. *Slavery is the subjection of a broken, abject mind, lacking free will* (Cicero).

Crates did worse, who took refuge in the freedom of poverty, to rid himself of the cares and drudgery of household management. That I could not do (I hate poverty equally with pain), but what I could do is to exchange this kind of life for another less showy and less busy.

When absent from home I can throw off all such thoughts, and would feel the ruin of a tower less than I do, when present, the fall of a tile. My mind easily becomes free at a distance, but when at home it suffers like that of a vine-grower. A bridle wrongly adjusted, a stirrup-leather beating against my leg, will keep me in bad humour a whole day. I screw up my courage well enough against discomforts, my eyes I cannot.

The senses, ye Gods, the senses !

At home I am responsible for all that goes amiss. Few masters (I mean those of medium condition like mine, and if there be any such, they are more fortunate) are able to rely so much upon a second, but that a good part of the burden will still rest upon their shoulders. That generally makes me less gracious in entertaining any chance visitors (and some perhaps have been induced to stay for the sake of my good table rather than my gracious manners, as is the way with bores), and takes away much of the pleasure I should derive from the visits and meetings of my friends in my house.

The most absurd figure a gentleman cuts is to be seen in his own house worrying over the details of housekeeping, whispering to one footman, threatening another with his eyes. Things should glide smoothly and imperceptibly and reflect their ordinary course.

And I think it a hateful custom to talk to your guests about the fare you are providing for them, whether to excuse it or to boast of it.

I love order and cleanliness,

> Your cup and salver such that they
> Yourself unto yourself display, (HORACE.)

as much as I do abundance ; and at home I am very particular about the needful, and care little for display.

If in another man's house a footman begins fighting, if a dish is upset, you merely laugh at it. You go to sleep while Monsieur is arranging with his butler about your to-morrow's entertainment.

I speak of these things as I myself think, not omitting to consider, in a general way, what a pleasure to certain natures it is to have a peaceful, thriving household, carried on with order and regularity : and not wishing to fasten my own errors and defects to the matter, or give Plato the lie, who esteems it the happiest occupation for every man ' to carry on his own affairs without wronging others '.

When I travel, I have only myself to think of, and the employment of my money ; that is disposed of by a single precept. For amassing wealth too many qualities are needed ; I have no skill in it. I understand a little how to spend, and how to make the most of what I spend, which is indeed its chief use. But I set about it too ambitiously, which renders it unequal and distorted, and immoderate besides in both respects.[1] If it makes a show and accomplishes

---

[1] In economy and prodigality.

its purpose, I let myself go injudiciously ; and just as injudiciously do I tie up my purse-strings if it does not
shine and does not please me.

Whatever it be, whether Art or Nature, that implants
that idea in our minds that we must defer to others as to
how we live, does us much more harm than good. We
defraud ourselves against our own interest, in order to make
appearances fit in with public opinion. We care not so
much what we are in ourselves and in reality, as what we
are in the estimation of other people. Even intellectual
advantages and knowledge appear fruitless to us, if we alone
enjoy the benefit of them, if they are not displayed to the
eyes and approval of others.

There are some men whose gold flows in broad streams,
through underground places, imperceptibly ; others hammer
it all out into thin plates and leaves, so that to the one a
farthing is worth a crown, to the other the reverse ; and the
world judges of the use and the value according to the show.
All anxious care about wealth savours of avarice ; so also
does the spending and lavishing of it, when it is too syste-
matic and artificial. It is not worth such painful vigilance
and solicitude. He who tries to be too exact in his spending
makes it pinched and narrow. Hoarding and spending are
in themselves indifferent things, and assume no colour of
good or bad but according to the application of our will.

The other cause that invites me to these excursions is
that I cannot put up with the present moral condition of
our State. I could readily console myself for this corruption
as far as regards the public interest :

> Times more evil than the Iron age,
> Whose misdeeds even Nature cannot name,
> Or find a metal to compare them to ; (JUVENAL.)

but in regard to my own, no. I in particular suffer too much
from them. For in my neighbourhood we are, through the
long-continued licence of our civil wars, almost grown old
in so riotous a form of government,

> A place where right and wrong unseat each other, (VIRGIL.)

that it is in truth a marvel how things can hold together :

> In arms they plough the furrow, and evermore
> Amass new plunder, and by rapine live. (VIRGIL.)

In short I can see by our example that human society will hold and keep together at whatsoever cost. In whatever position you place human beings, they will shake up and arrange themselves in stacks and heaps, just as uneven bodies, bundled into a sack without any order, will themselves find the means of uniting and settling down together, often better than they could have been arranged by art.

King Philip made a collection of the most wicked and incorrigible men he could find, and settled them all in a city which he had built for them, and which took its name from them.[1] I imagine that out of their very vices they established among themselves a civil constitution, a regular and decent society.

I see not one action, or three, or a hundred, but a commonly accepted state of morality so unnatural, especially as regards inhumanity and treachery, which are to me the worst of all sins, that I have not the heart to think of them without horror ; and they excite my wonder almost as much as my detestation. The practice of these egregious villainies bears as much the mark of strength and vigour of soul as of error and disorder.

Necessity reconciles men and brings them together. This accidental union afterwards takes shape in laws. For there have been laws as ferocious as any that the human mind could give birth to, which have yet been as healthy in body and as long-lived as any that Plato and Aristotle could draw up. And indeed all those outlines of government as imagined by art [2] are found to be absurd and unfit to be put into practice.

Those long and tedious debates on the best forms of society, and on the most suitable laws for binding us, are only adapted for exercising the mind ; as in the liberal arts there are many subjects which have their being only in discussion and controversy, outside of which they have no existence. Such a description of a form of government might be in place in a new world ; but we are assuming people already bound and brought up to certain customs. We do not create them, like Pyrrha or like Cadmus.[3]

Though we may have the power, by some means, to im-

---

[1] Poneropolis, the City of Rogues.   [2] Such as Plato's *Republic*.
[3] Pyrrha, after the deluge, repeopled the world by throwing stones ; Cadmus sowed dragon's teeth, from which sprang men ready-armed.

prove and redispose them, we can hardly twist them out
of their accustomed bent without breaking all. Some one
asked Solon if he had drawn up the best possible laws for
the Athenians. ' Yes, indeed, he replied ; the best they
were capable of receiving.'

Varro excused himself in like manner : ' That if he had
to write of religion, if it were quite new, he would say what
he thought of it ; but seeing that it is already formed and
accepted, he will speak of it according to custom rather
than according to nature.'

Not in theory only, but in truth, the best and most
excellent form of government for every nation is that under
which it has maintained itself. For its form and essential
suitability it is dependent on custom. It is usual for men
to be discontented with their actual condition. I maintain,
however, that to wish to replace a Republic by an Oligarchy,
or a Monarchy by a different kind of government, is foolish
and wrong :

> The government approve, be it what it will ;
> If it be Royal, then love Monarchy ;
> If a Republic, yet approve it still,
> For God himself thereto subjected thee.   (PIBRAC.)

Good Monsieur de Pibrac,[1] whom we have recently lost, a
man of so noble a mind, such sound opinions, such pleasing
manners ! His death, and that of Monsieur de Foix, which
fell about the same time, were a grievous loss to our crown.
I doubt whether there remains in France another couple to
be compared to these two Gascons in honesty and ability,
to supply their places in our King's Council. Theirs were
beautiful souls in different ways, and truly, as the times go,
rare and beautiful, each in its kind. But how did they come
to be set down in this age, being so out of proportion and
harmony to these our corrupt and tempestuous times ?

Nothing presses so hard upon a state as innovation ;
mere change gives scope to injustice and tyranny. When
some part becomes loosened, it may be propped ; we may
guard against the alteration and corruption natural to all
things carrying us too far from our beginnings and prin-

[1] Guy du Faur de Pibrac, 1529–84, author of *Quatrains Moraux* and
a few other poems. He defended the Protestants in Parliament, and was
imprisoned in the Bastile ; but afterwards wrote a political apology for
the massacre of St. Bartholomew. Good M. de Pibrac !

ciples. But to undertake to put so great a mass back into the melting-pot, to renew the foundations of so great an edifice, is to efface a picture in the cleaning, to reform particular defects by a general confusion, to cure a disease by killing the patient, *to be not so much for changing as for overturning everything* (Cicero).

The world is incapable of curing itself ; it is so impatient of the weight that oppresses it, that it only aims at getting rid of it without considering the cost. We may see by a thousand examples that it usually cures itself to its own prejudice. To throw off a present evil is no cure, if there be not an all-round improvement in condition.

The surgeon's ultimate aim is not to kill off the diseased flesh ; that is but the first step in his cure. He looks beyond, to make the natural flesh grow again and to restore the limb to its normal state. Whoever purposes to remove only what galls him will fall short, for the good does not necessarily succeed the evil ; another evil may succeed it, and a worse one, as happened to Caesar's assassins, who brought the Republic to such a pass, that they had reason to repent having meddled with it. The same thing has since happened to many, even down to our times. The French, my contemporaries, could indeed tell a tale about it.

All great changes shake up a state and throw it into confusion.

If any man should aim straight at a cure and take counsel with himself before taking action, he would be likely to cool down about setting his hand to it. Pacuvius Calavius corrected the fault of such a method by a signal example : His fellow-citizens had risen up in revolt against their magistrates. He, a person of great authority in the town of Capua, one day contrived to imprison the Senate in the palace, and, calling the people together in the market-place, he said to them that the day was now come when they were at full liberty to take their revenge on the tyrants who had so long oppressed them, and whom, isolated and disarmed, he had at his mercy. He gave them this advice, that, after being drawn by lot, these men should be let out one after another, that the case of each should be considered separately, and that the decision they came to should be executed on the spot ; with this additional proviso, that they should at the same time appoint some honourable man to fill the place of the condemned, that there might be no vacancy in the office.

They had no sooner heard the name of one Senator, when there arose a general outcry of dissatisfaction against him. ' I very well see, said Pacuvius, that this man must be dismissed ; he is a wicked man ; let us have a good man in exchange.' There was a prompt silence, every man being at a loss whom to choose. When the first man, with more effrontery than the rest, nominated his candidate, there was a still louder and more unanimous chorus of rejection ; they found a hundred imperfections and just causes for refusing him. These contradictory humours growing more heated, it fared still worse with the second Senator, and the third ; as much disagreement in the election as agreement in the dismissal.

Having fruitlessly worn themselves out in this disturbance, they began gradually, one here, one there, to steal out of the meeting, each one having come to this conclusion in his mind, ' That the oldest and best known evil is after all more bearable than one that is new and untried.'

Because I see that we are pitifully agitated (for what have we not done ?)

> O we repent us of our scars and sins
> 　And brothers' blood. What wickedness unplanned
> Has our hard generation left ? Within
> 　What bounds restrained itself ? Whence did its hand
> Our youth in reverence for the Gods refrain ?
> 　What altar spare ? (Horace.)

I do not immediately jump to the conclusion that

> 　　The very genius of Success
> 　　Could not this household save. (Terence.)

Yet we are not perhaps at our last term. The preservation of States is a thing that in all likelihood surpasses our understanding. A civil government is, as Plato says, a mighty thing, and hard to dissolve. It often holds out against fatal and internal diseases, against the mischief of unjust laws, against tyranny, against the encroachments and ignorance of the authorities and the licence and sedition of the people.

In all our fortunes we compare ourselves with what is above us, and look towards those who are better off ; let us measure ourselves with what is below. There is no one so ill-starred but he will find a thousand examples to comfort him.

It is a human weakness that we are not so pleased to see a man going ahead of us as we are pleased to see one lagging behind us.

Solon said that ' if we were to heap together all the ills, there is no man who would not rather take back with him his own ills than agree to a lawful division with all other men, and take his share.'

Our government is in a bad way ; yet others have been in a more advanced stage of sickness without dying.

The gods play at ball with us, and knock us about in all directions :

> Truly the Gods play with us as with balls. (PLAUTUS.)

The stars fatally destined the Roman State for an exemplar of what they could do in this way. In it are comprised all the forms and vicissitudes that affect a state ; all that order can do, and disorder, and good and evil fortune. What state need despair of its condition, seeing the shocks and commotions by which Rome was disturbed ? And yet she withstood them. If extent of dominion be the health of a state (of which I am by no means persuaded ; and Isocrates pleases me when he instructs Nicocles not to envy princes who have wide dominions, but rather those who are well able to keep those they have inherited), the State of Rome was never so well as when it was least well. She was happiest when she was at her worst.

Under the first Emperors we can hardly distinguish the face of any kind of government ; it was the darkest and most dreadful confusion conceivable. And yet she endured it, and continued in it, preserving, not a monarchy confined within its boundaries, but all those many nations, so diverse, so remote, so ill-affected, so loosely governed and unjustly conquered :

> For to no nation Fortune gives the task
> To vent her hate against the Roman people,
> Masters of land and sea. (LUCAN.)

Not everything that totters, falls. The frame of so great a body is held together by more than one nail. It is held together even by its antiquity ; like an old building whose foundations are worn away by age, without cement and mortar, which yet lives and is supported by its own weight ;

> Or, like a mighty trunk, with no firm roots,
> Safe in its own bulk. (LUCAN.)

Moreover it is not a good plan to reconnoitre only the flank and the moat ; to judge of the security of a fortress, we must know from which side an approach can be made, and the condition of the attacking party.

Few ships sink of their own weight, without outside violence.

Now let us turn our eyes in all directions ; all is crumbling around us. In all the great States that are known to us, whether of Christendom or elsewhere, use your eyes and you will discover evident menace of change and ruin :

> For they too have their ills ; the storm hath swept o'er all.
> (Adapted from VIRGIL.)

The astrologers have an easy game when they warn us, as they do, of great and imminent changes and revolutions ; their prophecies are present and palpable ; no need to go to the stars for that.

There is not only consolation to be derived from this universal aggregation of evils and menaces, but even some hope for the duration of our State ; since naturally where all falls, nothing falls. Universal sickness is individual health ; conformity is antagonistic to dissolution. For my part, I am not going to despair about us, and I think I see ways of saving ourselves :

> Perhaps a God, by happy change,
> May yet our bliss restore. (HORACE.)

Who knows but that God intends it to be as with bodies, that are purified and restored to a better state of health by long and grievous maladies, which will bring them to a cleaner and more perfect health than that they took from them ?

What troubles me most is that, in counting up the symptoms of our malady, I see as many that are due to natural causes, and sent by Heaven itself, as of those attributable to our disorders and our human unwisdom.

It would seem as if the very stars have ordained that we

have endured long enough beyond the ordinary term. And this too troubles me, that the evil which most nearly threatens us is not an alteration in the entire and solid mass, but its dissipation and disintegration ; the extremest of our fears.[1]

In these rhapsodies too I fear the treachery of my memory, lest by inadvertence it has made me record a thing twice over. I hate seeing my own reflection, and never, unless compelled, read again what has once escaped me. Now I bring here no new discoveries. They are common ideas, and, having perhaps conceived them a hundred times, I fear I have already set them down. Repetition is tiresome everywhere, even in Homer ; but it is disastrous in things that have only a superficial and transitory appearance. I dislike the habit of rubbing things in, even wholesome things, as Seneca does ; and I dislike that habit of his Stoical school of reiterating on every matter, and in all their length and breadth, the principles and postulates of general bearing, and of restating over and over again their common and universal reasons and arguments.

My memory grows cruelly worse every day :

> As though with thirsty throat I'd quaffed
> The cups which bring Lethean sleep. (HORACE.)

Instead of seeking time and opportunity, as others do, to think over what I have to say, I must henceforward (for hitherto, thank God, nothing much amiss has happened) avoid all preparation, for fear of binding myself to something I have to depend on. To be tied and bound puts me quite out, as well as to depend on so weak a tool as my memory.

I never read the following story without indignation, and a natural feeling of personal resentment : Lyncestes, accused of conspiracy against Alexander, on the day when he was brought before the army, according to custom, to be heard in his own defence, had in his mind a studied speech of which, stammering and hesitating, he uttered a few words. As he became more and more confused and was struggling with his memory and trying to jog it, the soldiers

---

[1] The note of pessimism in this last paragraph, which is a manuscript addition, appears out of harmony with the more optimistic view expressed a few lines above.

nearest to him charged him and killed him with their pikes, concluding that he had convicted himself. His confusion and silence was to them a sign of confession. Having had so much leisure to prepare himself in prison, it was not in their opinion his memory that failed him ; it was conscience that tied his tongue and robbed him of its power.

That is all very fine, indeed ! The place, the audience, their expectation, have a paralysing effect, even when it is only a question of ambition to make a good speech. What can a man do when life or death depends on the speech ?

For my part, the very fact of being tied to what I have to say is enough to put me off it. When I wholly trust and commit myself to my memory, I lean so heavily upon her that I bear her down ; she is dismayed at the weight. As long as I rely upon her, I lose my head and am put out of countenance ; and on some days I have been at pains to conceal my slavish dependence upon her, whereas my object in speaking was to appear perfectly cool and collected, using casual and unpremeditated gestures suggested by the occasion. I would as soon make an insignificant speech as make it evident that I have primed myself with a good one : a thing unbecoming especially in a man of my profession,[1] and which arouses too many expectations for a man who cannot satisfy them. Preparation raises more hopes than it can fulfil. A man often foolishly strips himself of his doublet, to leap no further than he would have done in his cassock. *There is nothing so unfavourable to those who wish to please as to raise expectation* (Cicero). It is recorded of the orator Curio that when he declared his intention of dividing his speech into three or four parts, or announced the number of his arguments and reasons, it often happened that he forgot one or two, or added one or two more. I have always carefully guarded against falling into that awkward situation, being loath to promise or tie myself in that way ; not only because I distrust my memory, but because that method savours too much of the artificial. *A simple style becomes a soldier* (Quintilian). Enough that I have henceforward decided with myself not again to undertake to speak on ceremonious occasions. For, as to reading one's speech, besides that it is unnatural, it is very disadvantageous

---

[1] As a knight Montaigne was a soldier, though he was not properly speaking of the military profession.

to those who are naturally able to give effect to it by action and gesture. And I am still less able to cast myself at the mercy of my improvisation ; my mind works slowly and confusedly, and is not equal to sudden and momentous emergencies.

Reader, permit this test-piece also to pass muster, and this third addition to the other parts of my portrait.[1] I add, but I do not correct. Firstly, because it appears reasonable that one who has handed his work over to the world has no further claim on it. Let him state his views better elsewhere, if he can, and not adulterate the work he has sold. If he does so, nothing of his should be bought until after his death. Let him thoroughly think out his subject before publishing. Why such haste ?

My book is always one. Except that at every new edition (that the buyer may not go away quite empty-handed) I take the liberty to add an occasional ornament over and above, since it is only a piece of badly-joined marquetry. They are but over-weights, which do not contradict the first form, but, by a little ambitious subtlety, impart some particular value to each of those that follow. Whence, however, some transposition of chronology may easily slip in. My stories take their place according to their opportuneness, not always according to their age.

Secondly, because, as concerns myself, I fear to lose by the change ; my understanding does not always advance, it also goes backwards. I do not distrust my thoughts less because they are the second or third, than because they are the first, or my present less than my past thoughts. Besides, we often correct ourselves as foolishly as we correct others.

My first Essays were published in the year 1580. I have since grown older by a long stretch, but I have certainly not grown an inch wiser.[2] Myself now, and myself a little while ago, are indeed two. But whether I am better I really cannot say. It would be a fine thing to be old if we only progressed towards betterment. It is a drunkard's walk,

---

[1] i. e. the third book, first published in 1588. When Montaigne says that he does not correct, he is not strictly accurate ; but most of his corrections were made after 1588.

[2] In the 1588 edition we read ' but I doubt whether I have grown an inch wiser '. Montaigne becomes more modest as he grows older.

reeling, giddy, uncertain ; or the motion of reeds stirred by the wind at its pleasure.

Antiochus had written strongly in favour of the Academy ; in his old age he adopted a different view. Whichever opinion I followed, should I not still be following Antiochus? To attempt to establish the certainty of human opinions after doubting it, was not that to create doubt and not certainty, and to give promise that, had he been given another life to live, he would always have been likely to change his mind, not so much for the better as for something different ?

My favourable reception by the public made me a little bolder than I expected. But what I fear most is to surfeit my readers ; I would rather provoke than weary them, as a learned man of my time has done.

Praise is always agreeable, let it come from whom, or on what account it will ; and yet, if our satisfaction is to be justified, we must find out why we are praised. Even imperfections have a way of recommending themselves. Vulgar and popular favour is seldom seen to be happy in its choice ; and in my time I am much mistaken if it is not the worst writings that have been borne highest by the breath of popular applause.

Truly I render thanks to those good-natured people who are pleased to approve of my feeble efforts.

Nowhere are the faults of style so apparent as in a matter which in itself has nothing to recommend it.

Do not blame me, reader, for the errors that slip in here through the caprice or inadvertence of others ; every hand, every workman [1] contributes his own. I do not meddle either with orthography, only suggesting that the old spelling be followed, or with punctuation ; I am little expert in either.

When they wholly break the sense, I am little concerned, for at least they relieve me of responsibility ; but when they substitute a false one, as they so often do, and twist my

---

[1] Presumably every compositor. The earlier editions of the Essays were, it seems, very carelessly printed, and full of errors. Montaigne did not approve of the spelling ' reform ' of the etymologists, who overloaded words with unnecessary letters found in the (often supposed) Latin originals. He himself adopts a simple spelling, but most of his editors did not fall in with his views, so that, for example, when Montaigne writes *avec* we almost invariably find *avecques* in the printed editions.

meaning to their own conception, they ruin me. However, when the thought is not vigorous and proportioned to my capacity, a sensible man must decline to take it as mine. Any one who knows how little laborious I am, how framed after my own fashion, will easily believe that I would rather reindite as many more essays than subject myself to the toil of reading these through again, for so puerile a correction.

I was recently saying then, that, being planted in the deepest mine of this new metal,[1] not only am I deprived of any great familiarity with men of opinions and ways differing from my own, in which they are bound together by a tie that flees every other tie ;[2] but I am besides not free from danger among men to whom everything is equally permissible, and most of whom cannot henceforth make their case worse in the eyes of our justice ; so that licence is now carried to its extreme. Summing up all the particular circumstances concerning myself, I know no man of my country who pays more dearly for the defence of the laws, both in *cessant gain* and *emergent loss*, as the lawyers say, than I do. And many there are who boast of their zeal and fortitude who, if weighed in a correct balance, do much less than I.

As a house that has always been free, very accessible, and at the service of all (for I could never be induced to make it an implement of war, in which I would rather be engaged when it is as far as possible from my neighbourhood), mine has sufficiently deserved the affection of the people round about ; and it would be a very difficult matter to defy me on my own dunghill. And I regard it as a wonderful and exemplary masterpiece that it still continues a virgin from blood and pillage under so prolonged a storm, with so many changes and disturbances round about me. For, to tell the truth, it was possible for a man of my nature to escape one constant and continued form of danger, whatever it might be ; but the invasions and incursions, first by one side and then by the other, and the alternations and vicissitudes of Fortune, around me, have hitherto more exasperated than mollified the temper of the country, involving me over and over again in insuperable dangers and difficulties.

I escape ; but it is unpleasant to think that this is due to

---

[1] The unknown new metal that should characterize this wicked age ; see p. 420.   [2] The tie of religion.

chance, nay also to my own prudence, rather than to justice ; and it makes me sad to think that I am outside the protection of the laws, and under any other safeguard than theirs. As matters stand, I more than half live by the grace of others ; which is a hard obligation. I am loath to owe my safety either to the goodwill and kindness of the great, who approve of my respect for the laws and my independence, or to the easy-going manners of my predecessors and my own.

For, supposing I were different ? If my conduct and my open dealings lay my neighbours or my kinsmen [1] under obligation, it is cruel that they should be able to pay off their debt by allowing me to live, and to say : ' We freely pardon him for continuing his divine service in the chapel of his house, after all the churches round about have been ruined and laid waste by us ; and we grant him his life and the use of his property, since he shelters our wives and our cattle in times of need.'

For a long while past my house has shared the praise given to Lycurgus the Athenian, who was depositary-general and guardian of his fellow-citizens' purses.

Now I maintain that we should live by right and authority, not as a reward and a favour. How many gallant men have preferred losing their lives to being indebted for them ! I would rather not subject myself to any kind of obligation, but especially one that binds me by a duty of honour. Nothing appears to me so dearly bought as what is given me, and that for which my will is pledged under the name of gratitude ; and I am more willing to accept such services as are for sale. I think I am right ; for the latter I give only money, for the others I give myself.

The tie that holds me by the law of honesty appears to me more insistent and binding than that of legal constraint ; a bond drawn up by a notary binds me more loosely than I do myself. Is it not right that my conscience should be much more strongly pledged when it has been trusted in all simplicity ? In other cases my fidelity owes nothing, for nothing has been lent to it ; let them use the assurance and security they have taken by outside means. I should much sooner break the prison of a wall or of the laws than that of my word.

[1] Some of Montaigne's relations, including his mother and one of his brothers, were of the Protestant faith.

I am scrupulous, even to superstition, in keeping my promises, and in all matters I prefer to make them vague and conditional. To those of no great weight I give weight by adhering jealously to my rule, which plagues and burdens me with its own interest. Nay, even in actions in which I alone am concerned and in which I have a free hand, if I once say a thing I feel as if I were bound by it, and that to make it known to another is to command myself to do it. When I say a thing I feel as if I had promised it. Therefore I seldom divulge my plans.

The sentence I pass upon myself is stronger and stiffer than that of any judge, who only considers my case from the point of view of an ordinary obligation ; that which my conscience imposes upon me is more strict and severe. I lag behind in those duties to which I should be dragged if I did not go to them. *The most just action is only just in so far as it is voluntary* (Cicero). If the action have not some glamour of freedom it has neither grace nor honour.

Where law commands, my will is in abeyance. (TERENCE.)

When necessity draws me I am content to let the will go. *For what is imposed by a higher power is imputed to him who commands rather than to him who obeys* (Cicero). I know some who follow this rule even to injustice, who will sooner give than restore, sooner lend than pay ; who are more niggardly in doing good to one to whom they are beholden. I do not go so far as that, but I come very near it.

I am so disposed to throw off debts and obligations, that I have sometimes counted as profit the ingratitude, the affronts and indignities put upon me by men to whom, by nature or accident, I owed some friendly duty ; seizing upon this occasion of their offence as an acquittance and discharge of my debt. Although I continue to pay them the outward civilities reasonably enjoined by society, I find it a great saving to do in the name of justice what I once did through affection, and to relieve myself a little of the tension and solicitude of my inward will—*It is the part of a wise man to restrain, as he would a chariot, the first impulse to friendship* (Cicero)—which in me is a little too urgent and pressing when I take to a person, at least for a man who has no wish to force his friendship. And this husbanding of my feelings consoles me a little for the imperfections of those in

whom I am interested. I am very sorry that they are less
worthy, but the fact remains that I am spared some of my
attentions and obligations towards them.

I do not blame the man who loves his son less for being
scurfy and hunchbacked, and not only when he is ill-
tempered, but also when he is ill-favoured and ill-born (God
himself abated that much from his natural value and estimation) ; provided that in his coolness towards him he
bears himself with moderation and strict justice. With me
nearness of blood does not lessen imperfections, but rather
aggravates them.

After all, as far as I understand the science of benefits and
gratitude, which is a complicated and very useful science,
I know of no man who is freer and less indebted than I have
been hitherto. What I owe I owe by ordinary and natural
obligations. In other respects no one is more absolutely
clear :

> The gifts of Princes are to me unknown. (VIRGIL.)

Princes are liberal to me when they take nothing from
me, and do me sufficient good when they do me no ill ; that
is all I ask of them. Oh, how much I am beholden to God
that he was pleased that I should receive all I possess immediately by his grace, and that he specially reserved to himself my whole debt of gratitude ! How earnestly I beg of
his holy mercy that I may never owe thanks to any man
for the essentials of life ! Blessed liberty which has carried
me so far ! May it continue to the end !

I endeavour to have no express need of any one :

> All my hope is in myself. (TERENCE.)

It is a thing that any man may do for himself, but more
easily one whom God has sheltered from natural and urgent
necessities. It is a very pitiful and hazardous lot to be
dependent on another. We ourselves, on whom we can
most justly and surely rely, have not made ourselves
sufficiently sure. I have nothing of mine except myself,
and yet the possession is in part defective and borrowed.
I fortify myself, both in courage, on which is the strongest
reliance, and also in fortune, in order to have enough to
satisfy me, though all else should forsake me.

Hippias of Elis furnished himself not only with learning,

that he might in the lap of the Muses dispense gaily, at need, with all other company ; not only with the knowledge of philosophy, to teach his soul to find contentment in herself and manfully to do without outward comforts, when Fate would have it so. He was so careful besides as to learn how to cook, to shave himself and cut his own hair, to make his own clothes and shoes, and his rings, to be as self-dependent as he could, and dispense with all outside help.

We enjoy borrowed goods much more freely and more heartily when the enjoyment is not forced and constrained by want, and when we have, in our will and fortune, the power and means to live without them.

I know myself well ; but I find it difficult to imagine any so pure liberality, any so free and genuine hospitality in any person, but that I would think it disastrous, tyrannical and tainted with reproach, if I were entangled in it by necessity.

As giving denotes ambition and a wish to rise to pre-eminence, so taking is a mark of submission : witness the insulting and aggressive manner in which Bajazet refused the presents that Timour sent him. And those that were offered in the name of the Emperor Solyman to the Emperor of Calicut so angered him, that he not only rudely declined them, saying that neither he nor his predecessors were accustomed to take, and that it was their part to give ; but he even had the ambassadors sent for that purpose cast into a dungeon.

When Thetis, says Aristotle, flatters Jupiter ; when the Lacedemonians flatter the Athenians, they do not refresh their memory with the good they have done them, which is always a hateful thing to be reminded of, but recall the benefits they have received from them. Those whom I see so freely making use of all and every man, and laying themselves under obligation to them, would not do so [if they relished, as I do, the sweetness of a pure liberty, and] if they considered, as much as a wise man should do, the weight of an obligation ; it is perhaps sometimes repaid, but it is never dissolved. A cruel bondage for one who loves free elbow-room on all sides.

My acquaintances, both above and below me in station, are able to say whether they have known a man [less importuning, soliciting, entreating and] who is less of a burden to others. If I surpass all present-day examples in this respect, it is no great wonder, seeing how many characteristics I have that contribute thereto : a little natural pride, inability to bear a refusal, moderate desires and projects, incapacity for all kinds of business, and my most favoured qualities, idleness and freedom. From all these together I have contracted a deadly hatred of being bound to another or by another than myself. Before enjoying another's favours I should leave no stone unturned to do without them, however slight or important the occasion.

It is to me an intolerable nuisance to be asked by a friend to ask of a third person. And I think it hardly less costly to acquit one who is indebted to me, by making use of him, than to become indebted for a friend to one who owes me nothing. With that exception, and provided also that they do not desire anything of me that requires negotiation and anxiety, for I have declared war to the death against all anxiety, I am accommodating and ready to help any one in need.[1]

I have oftener avoided receiving than sought occasions for giving ; and that is much easier, according to Aristotle. My fortune has seldom allowed me to benefit others, and what I have given has met with little thanks. If I had been born to take a high rank among men, I should have been ambitious to be loved, not to be feared or admired. Shall I put it more arrogantly ? I should have thought as much of the pleasure I gave as of the good I was doing.

Cyrus, very wisely, and by the mouth of a very good general and a still better philosopher,[2] places his bounty and good deeds far above his valour and his conquests in war. And the first Scipio, whenever he tries to set himself in a favourable light, lays more stress on his mild and humane qualities than on his prowess and victories ; and ever has this boast on his lips : ' That he has given his enemies as much cause to love him, as his friends.'

I mean to say then, if we must owe something in this way, it ought to be by a more lawful title than that of which I speak, to which the necessity of this wretched war pledges

---

[1] The edition of 1588 also contained this passage, which was afterwards deleted : ' I have very gladly sought occasions for doing good and attaching others to myself ; and it seems to me that we cannot make any better use of our money.'

[2] Xenophon.

me ; and not of so big a debt as that of my total preservation ; that is too crushing.

I have a thousand times gone to bed in my own house,
with an apprehension that I should be betrayed and struck
dead that same night, compounding with Fortune that it
might not be a terrible and lingering death. And after my
Paternoster I would exclaim :

> Shall these my fields, so fairly dressed,
> By godless soldiers be possessed ? (VIRGIL.)

Where is the remedy ? It is my birthplace, and that of
most of my ancestors ; on it they fixed their affection and
their name.[1] We become inured to everything we are
accustomed to. And, in a wretched state such as ours,
habit has become a very kind gift of Nature, which benumbs
our senses to the suffering of many ills. A civil war is worse
than other wars in this, that it makes each of us turn his
house into a watch-tower :

> How sad with gate and wall our life to guard,
> And scarce be safe ! (OVID.)

It is an extreme hardship to be threatened in one's very
household and domestic peace. The district in which I live
is always the first and last battle-ground in our disturbed
times, where peace never shows her full face :

> Even when peace is here, we quake in fear of war. (OVID.)

> So often as Fortune breaks the peace, 'tis here
> War stalks apace. O better had it been
> To dwell beneath the scorching Eastern vault,
> Or wander homeless in the frozen North ! (LUCAN.)

At times I seek the means of combating these thoughts in
indifference and carelessness. They also lead some way to
fortitude. With a kind of pleasure I often imagine myself
in danger of death and awaiting it ; in a dull stupor I plunge
headlong into it, without considering or recognizing it, as
into a dark and silent abyss that swallows me up at one
leap, and in an instant wraps me in a profound slumber,
without pain or feeling of any kind.

And in this kind of sudden and violent death I am more
comforted by the reflexion of what follows after it, than
alarmed by the fear of dying.

---

[1] Not quite correct ; his family took their name of Montaigne from the
place, and not vice versa.

They say that as life is no better for being long, death is the better for not being long. I am not so averse to the idea of being dead but that I meet death itself with confidence. I wrap myself up snugly in this catastrophe which must blind and carry me away with the fury of an attack so sudden that I shall not feel it.

If it were only true, as some gardeners say, that roses and violets spring up more fragrant in the proximity of garlic and onions, since these suck and imbibe the bad odours of the soil ; and that those depraved natures also absorb all the venom of my air and climate, and make me so much better and purer by their proximity that I should not be wholly a loser ! That is not so ; but there may be something in this, that goodness is more beautiful and attractive when it is rare ; and that contrariety and diversity stiffen and compress well-doing within itself, and kindle it by the jealousy of opposition and the desire for approbation.

Thieves, when left alone, have no particular spite against me. Have I any more spite against them ? I should have to hate too many people. The like consciences abide under different kinds of fortune, the like cruelties, disloyalties, robberies. And they are all the worse for being more meanly and securely hidden under the shadow of the laws. I hate a wrong done openly less than one done treacherously ; under the cloak of war than in peace. Our fever [1] has attacked a body that is not much the worse for it. The fire was there, it has burst into flames ; the noise is greater, not so much the evil.

To those who ask me why I travel I usually reply, ' I know well what I am fleeing from, but not what I am in search of.' If they tell me that there may be just as little health among foreigners, and that their ways are no better than ours, I reply firstly, that that is hardly likely :

> Wickedness assumes a thousand forms
> Where wars are raging. (VIRGIL.)

Secondly, that there is always gain in changing an evil for an uncertain state ; and that others' misfortunes should not affect us as painfully as our own.

I will not forget to mention this, that I am never so

[1] The Civil Wars.

exasperated against France that I cease to have a kindly feeling for Paris ; she has had my heart since my boyhood. And, as in the case of all excellent things, the more I have since seen of other fine cities, the more does the beauty of this one impress me and gain on my affection. I love her for herself, and more in her own being than overladen with foreign pomp. I love her tenderly, even her warts and blemishes. I am a Frenchman only through this great city, great in its people, great in the happiness of its site ; but above all great and incomparable in variety and diversity of amenities, the glory of France and one of the noblest ornaments of the world. May God keep our discords far from her ! [1] Entire and united, I think she will be safe against all other violence. I warn her that of all parties the worst will be that which sets her at variance. For her I only fear herself ; and truly I fear for her as much as for any other part of this State. As long as she endures, I shall not want a retreat wherein to give up the ghost, sufficient to compensate me for the loss of any other retreat.

Not because Socrates has said it, but because it is really in my nature, and perhaps a little more than it should be, I look upon all men as my fellow-citizens, and would embrace a Pole as I would a Frenchman, subordinating this national tie to the common and universal one. I am not enamoured of the charms of my home atmosphere. Quite new and quite personal friendships appear to me fully as good as those other chance acquaintances with one's neighbours, that are shared by all. Friendships that are purely of our own acquiring usually carry the day against those which join us by the common tie of blood and climate.

Nature has given us to the world free and unfettered ; we imprison ourselves in certain narrow districts, like the Kings of Persia, who bound themselves to drink no other water but that of the river Choaspes, foolishly renouncing their right to the use of any other stream, and turning the rest of the world, as far as they were concerned, into a waterless desert.

As to what Socrates did towards his end, in regarding a sentence of banishment against him as worse than a death sentence, I shall never, I think, be so broken up or so

[1] Montaigne's prayer was not fulfilled ; after 1588 the discord was more violent in Paris than anywhere else.

closely wedded to my country as to agree with him. The
lives of such divine men offer sufficient models which I can
embrace by esteem rather than affection. And some are
so sublime and wonderful that they are even above my
esteem, since they are above my conception.

That was a very tender feeling in a man who looked upon
the world as his city. It is true that he disdained travel,
and had hardly even set foot outside Attic territory.

What are we to think of his grudging his friends' money
to buy off his life, and his refusing to leave his prison with
the help of others, that he might not disobey the laws, and
that at a time when they were so corrupt ? These examples
are of the first kind for me ; of the second there are others
that I could discover in this same person. Many of these
rare examples exceed my power of action, but some even
exceed my power of imagination.

Besides the reasons I have given, travel appears to me
a profitable exercise ; the mind is continually exercised by
observing new and unknown things. And I know no better
school, as I have often said, for modelling one's life, in that
it continually brings us face to face with so many other
lives, ideas, and customs, and gives us a relish for human
nature in so perpetual a variety of forms. The body is
therein neither idle nor fatigued ; and that gentle excitement keeps it in breath.

In spite of my colic I can keep in the saddle, without dis-
mounting and without weariness, for eight or even ten hours,

> Beyond the strength and ordinary lot of eld. (VIRGIL.)

No season is hostile to me except the fierce heat of a burning sun. For umbrellas, which have been in use in Italy
since the time of the old Romans, weary the arm more than
they relieve the head.[1]

I should like to know by what contrivance the Persians,
so long ago and when they first fell into luxurious ways,
obtained fresh air and shade at their pleasure, as Xenophon
tells us.

I love rain and mud as much as the ducks do. Change
of air and climate does not affect me ; every sky is the
same to me. I am only vanquished by the changes in my

---

[1] It seems that they weighed about five pounds. Umbrellas did not
come into use in France until the end of the seventeenth century.

internal arrangements ; and these are not so frequent when I travel.

I am not easy to move, but once on the way, I go as far as you please. I shy as much at a little as at a great undertaking, and at preparing for a day's excursion or to visit a neighbour, as for a real journey. I have learned to arrange my day's journey after the Spanish fashion, making one stage of it : long and reasonable journeys ; and in excessive heat I make them by night, from sunset to sunrise. The other method of stopping to bait and dining on the way, in hurry and confusion, is inconvenient, especially when the days are short.

My horses are the better for it. Never did any horse fail me that was able to hold out the first day's journey with me. I water them everywhere, and only see to it that they have time enough after their last watering to work it off.

My laziness in rising gives my attendants time to dine in comfort before starting. For my own part it is never too late for me to eat ; my appetite comes with eating, and not otherwise. I am never hungry but at table.

Some people blame me for continuing to take a pleasure in this exercise, now I am married and well on in years. They are wrong. The best time to leave your family is when you have put them in the way of carrying on without you ; when you have left the home in such good order as to correspond with its former government. It is much more unwise to depart and leave your house to a less faithful guardian, who is less careful to provide you with the needful.

The most useful art, and the most honourable occupation for a woman, is the art of housekeeping. I know some who are miserly, but very few good managers. It is her mistress quality, which one should seek before any other, as the only dower that helps to ruin or save our houses.

Don't tell me ! Experience has taught me to value in a married woman, above every other virtue, the housekeeping virtue.

I give my wife an opportunity of bearing me out by leaving her, during my absence, in full control of my affairs. It vexes me to see, in many households, Monsieur coming home about noon, fretful and worried by business troubles, to find Madame still doing her hair and titivating herself in her dressing-room. That is all very well for

a Queen ; and yet I am not so sure. It is absurd and unfair
that our wives should be kept in idleness by our sweat and toil.

No person, if I can help it, shall enjoy my goods more
easily, more tranquilly, and more free of obligation, than I.
If the husband provides the matter, Nature herself ordains
that the wife shall provide the form.

As to the duties of marital love being prejudiced by my
absence, as some people think, I do not agree with them.
On the contrary, it is a relationship that a too continual
presence is easily liable to cool, and that is impaired by too
assiduous attentions. Every strange woman appears to us
agreeable to associate with. And we all find by experience
that being continually together cannot equal the pleasure
of parting and meeting again at intervals. These interruptions fill me with a fresh love for my family, and make
the resumption of my home-life more pleasurable. The
alternation warms my appetite for the departure, and then
for the return.

I know that the arms of friendship are long enough to
reach and join from one end of the world to the other,
and especially this kind, in which there is a continual
interchange of services, which reawaken its obligations and
memory. The Stoics say truly that there is so close a bond
and relation between the sages, that one who dines in
France nourishes his friend in Egypt ; and that if one of
them merely holds out a finger, wherever he may be, all the
sages in the habitable globe will feel its help.

Enjoyment and possession are chiefly a matter of imagination. It embraces more warmly what it is in quest of than
what we hold, and more continually. Cast up your daily
musings and you will find that you are most absent from
your friend when he is in your company ; his presence
releases your attention and gives your thoughts freedom to
absent themselves at any time and for any occasion.

From distant Rome I hold and control my house and the
goods I have left there ; I see my walls, my trees, and my
rents growing, and diminishing as well, within an inch or
two, as when I am there :

> Before mine eyes the vision of my home
> Hovers, and all the once familiar spots. (OVID.)

If we enjoy nothing but what we touch, farewell our

crowns when they are in our coffers, and our boys when
they are gone a-hunting. We would have them nearer.
In the garden, is that far ? Half a day's journey away ?
What about ten leagues, is that far or near ? If it is near, how
about eleven, twelve, thirteen? and so on, step by step. Truly
if there be a woman who prescribes to her husband the howmanieth step that ends the near, and the howmanieth step
that begins the far, I advise her to fix it between the two :

> Name some fixed term, all cavil to arrest . . .
> Myself of the concession I avail ;
> As from a horse's tail we pluck out hairs,
> I take off one league, then another league,
> Till you are vanquished by the very force
> Of my sorites. (HORACE.)

And let them boldly call Philosophy to their aid, in whose
teeth it might be cast that, since she sees neither one end
nor the other of the joint between the too much and the
little, the long and the short, the light and the heavy, the
near and the far ; since she recognizes neither the beginning
nor the end of it, she is a very uncertain judge of the middle.
Nature has given us no knowledge of the limits of things (Cicero).

Are those not still wives and mistresses of the deceased,
who are not at the end of this, but in the other world ?
We embrace both those who have been, and those who are
not yet, not only the absent. We did not bargain, when we
married, to be continually joined together by the tail, like
some little insects or other that we see, or like the be-
witched people of Karenty,[1] in canine fashion. And a wife
should not have her eyes so greedily fixed on her husband's
front that she cannot endure to see him turn his back upon
her, if need be.

But may not these words, by so excellent a painter of
their humours, be aptly quoted here, to show the cause
of their complaints ?

> Your wife, if you should stay out late,
> At once thinks you are toying with a girl,
> Or she with you ; that at the public-house
> Or elsewhere you enjoy yourself ; in short
> That you have all the fun, and she has all the cares.
> (TERENCE.)

[1] A reference to a passage in the *History of Denmark* of Saxo Gram-
maticus.

Or may it not be that opposition and contradiction are in themselves meat and drink to them ; and that they are comfortable enough if they can make you uncomfortable ?

In true friendship, of which I am a good judge, I give myself to my friend more than I draw him to me. Not only would I rather benefit him than that he should benefit me, but also that he should benefit himself rather than me ; he benefits me most when he benefits himself. And if absence be either agreeable or profitable to him, it is much more acceptable to me than his presence. And you cannot rightly call it absence when you have the means of communicating with one another.

I used to find our separation profitable and agreeable. We possessed our lives more fully and more extensively by keeping apart ; he lived, he enjoyed, he saw for me, and I for him, as fully as if he had been present. One part of us remained idle when we were together ; we were blended into one another. The distance of place made the conjunction of our wills richer. That insatiable hunger for the bodily presence rather betrays weakness in the enjoyment of souls.

With regard to my old age which they urge against me, it is, on the contrary, for the young to subject themselves to public opinion, and constrain themselves for others. They are able to satisfy the demands of both the public and themselves. We have only too much to do to satisfy ourselves. As our natural resources fail us let us maintain ourselves by artificial means. It is unfair to excuse youth for pursuing its pleasures and forbid old age to seek them. When I was young, I concealed my gay passions by caution ; now that I am old I dispel my joyless ones by distractions. Besides, the Platonic laws prohibit travelling before the age of forty or fifty, in order that travel may be more profitable and instructive. I should more readily [1] agree to that other second article of the same laws, which forbids it after sixty.

' But at such an age you may never return from so long a journey.' What do I care ? When I start upon it I think neither of the return, nor of the goal. I only undertake it to keep myself on the move, as long as I like movement.

---

[1] Coste suggests that Montaigne meant to write *plus mal volontiers*, ' less readily ', instead of *plus volontiers*, in consideration of the following sentence.

I only ride for the sake of riding. Those who run after a benefice or a hare do not run ; they only run who run in prisoner's base, or to practice running.

My design is divisible throughout : it is not grounded on any great hopes ; each day's journey forms the end of them. And my life's journey is carried on after the same manner. And yet I have been in many distant places where I could have wished that I had been induced to remain. Why not, if Chrysippus, Cleanthes, Diogenes, Zeno, Antipater, so many wise men of the most surly school,[1] left their country, without any reason for being dissatisfied with it, and only for the enjoyment of a different atmosphere ? Indeed what displeases me most in my peregrinations is that I cannot bring myself to decide on settling in a place that takes my fancy ; and that I must always make up my mind to return, to fall in with conventional ideas.

If I were afraid to die in any other place but that of my birth, if I thought I should die less comfortably away from my family, I should hardly go out of France ; I should not go outside my parish without terror. I can feel death continually clutching me by the throat or the reins. But I am differently made ; death is the same to me everywhere. Yet if I had the choice I think I would rather die in the saddle than in a bed, away from my home, and far from my people.

There is more heart-break than comfort in taking leave of our friends ; I willingly neglect that social duty. For of friendly offices that is the only unpleasant one, and I could as willingly dispense with that great and eternal farewell. If there is any advantage in being surrounded by your friends, there are a hundred disadvantages. I have seen some die very piteously, besieged by all those dependants ; the crowd stifles them. They think it contrary to duty and a testimony of little affection and little care, to allow you to die in peace ; one torments your eyes, another your ears, another your tongue ; there is not a sense or a limb that they do not shatter. Your heart is wrung with pity to hear your friends' lamentations, and perhaps with vexation to hear the feigned and counterfeit laments of others.

[1] The Stoic school. These philosophers all came from distant parts and settled in Athens.

When a man has always had delicate sensibilities, they are still more so now that he is in this weak state. In this great extremity it needs a gentle hand, in accordance with his feelings, to scratch him just where he itches ; otherwise touch him not at all. If we need a wise woman [1] to bring us into the world, we have great need of a still wiser man to help us out of it. The services of such a man, and a friend to boot, are worth buying at any cost on such an occasion.

I have not reached that pitch of disdainful vigour that finds fortitude in itself, that nothing can either assist or disturb ; I am a peg lower. I shall try to steal away and hide from this manner of passing out, not through fear, but by artifice. I have no intention, in this act of dying, to give a proof or make a show of fortitude. For whom should I do so ? At that moment all my right and interest in making a reputation will cease. I shall be satisfied with a calm, collected, and solitary death, all to myself, in harmony with my retired and private life.

Quite contrary to the superstition of the Romans, who esteemed a man ill-fated who died without speaking and had not his nearest relations at his side to close his eyes, I shall have enough to do to comfort myself without having to console others, enough thoughts in my brain without need of others suggested by the circumstances, enough matter to reflect upon without borrowing.

To die is not to play a part in society ; it is the act of a single person. Let us live and laugh among our friends ; let us die and sulk among strangers. For money payment you will find some one to turn your head and rub your feet, who will not press you more than you wish, who will turn indifferent eyes upon you, and leave you to your own reflections and allow you to groan as much as you please.

Every day I try to conquer by reason that puerile and unfeeling disposition that makes us wish to stir the compassion and sympathy of our friends for our misfortunes. We exaggerate our ills beyond measure, to draw their tears. And the fortitude to support their adverse fortune which we commend in all others, we blame and condemn in our friends, when the misfortune is our own. We are not content that they should be sensible of our woes, unless

[1] *Une sage-femme,* the French term for a midwife.

they are also grieved by them. We should spread joy, but, as far as we can, repress sorrow.

He who excites pity without cause deserves not to be pitied when there is cause. To be ever complaining is the way to be never pitied ; to put on piteous airs so often is to be pitiable to none. He that makes himself out to be dead when he is alive is in danger of being thought alive when he is dying. I have known some who would take it in dudgeon to be told that they had a ruddy complexion and a steady pulse ; restraining their mirth because it betrayed their recovery, and hating health because it did not arouse pity. And, what is much more strange, they were not women !

I describe my ailments at the most as they are, and avoid words of evil omen and made-up exclamations. If not gaiety, at least a serene countenance is appropriate in those attending on the sick sage ; he does not pick a quarrel with health because he is in the opposite condition ; he likes to contemplate it sound and robust in others, and to enjoy at least its company. Though he finds himself sinking, he does not entirely put away all thoughts of life, nor avoid ordinary conversation.

I am prepared to study sickness when I am well ; when it is present it will make its impression real enough, without the help of my imagination. We make our preparations beforehand for the travels we are about to undertake, and have made up our minds about them ; we leave it to our attendants to decide when we are to take horse, or we put it off for their convenience.

I have felt this unexpected advantage from the publication of my conduct of life, that in some sort it serves me as a rule. I sometimes consider whether it would not be better not to disclose the history of my life. This public disclosure of it obliges me to keep to my path, and not to give the lie to the picture I have drawn of my qualities, which are usually less distorted and contradictory than the malicious and unhealthy judgements of these times will admit of. The uniformity and simplicity of my character makes it appear easy of interpretation ; but the shape of it being rather novel and unusual, calumny has an easy game. Yet so it is, that to any one who is inclined to abuse me by legitimate means, my known and avowed imperfections

will, I think, afford sufficient opportunity to bite me to his
heart's content, without skirmishing with the wind. If he
thinks I am drawing his teeth by anticipating his revelation
and condemnation of them, it is but reasonable that he
should exercise his right of amplifying and extending
(offence has its rights outside of justice) ; of magnifying
the roots of the vices which I reveal in myself until they
have become trees, and of using for that purpose not only
those that possess me, but also those that merely threaten
me : prejudicial vices, both in quality and number ; let
him belabour me with them.

I could frankly follow the example of the philosopher
Bion. Antigonus was beginning to taunt him on the subject
of his origin. He stopped his mouth with these words : ' I
am the son of a slave, a butcher, branded, and a prostitute,
whom my father married by reason of her humble lot.
They were both punished for some misdeed. An orator
who took a liking for me as a boy, bought me, and at his
death left me his whole fortune. Having transferred my
possessions to this city of Athens, I devoted myself to
philosophy. Historians may save themselves the trouble
of seeking information about me ; I will tell them how the
case stands.'

A free and generous confession takes the sting out of
reproach and disarms calumny.

Yet it is true that, taking one thing with another, it
seems to me that I am as often praised as dispraised beyond
reason ; it also seems to me that from my youth up I have
been given a rank and degree of honour rather above than
below what was my due.

I should be more at home in a country where those orders
of precedence were either regulated or despised. Among
men, as soon as an altercation on precedence in walking or
sitting exceeds three replies, there is an end of politeness.
I am not afraid of ceding or preceding out of my order, to
avoid such tiresome disputes ; no man ever desired to
precede me but I permitted him to do so.

Besides the benefit I reap from writing about myself,
I hope for this other advantage, that if there happens to
be any worthy man who approves and agrees with my
humours, he will endeavour before I die to come into touch
with me. I am giving him a great advantage over me ;

for, all the knowledge he might have gained by a long acquaintance and intimacy during several years, he will obtain in three days from this record, and that more surely and accurately.[1]

An amusing idea! Many things that I would not say to a single person I say to the public; and for my most secret knowledge and thoughts I send my most faithful friends to a bookseller's shop!

> My very heart I open to men's view. (PERSIUS.)

If I knew for a certainty of a man who was of the same mind with me, truly I would go a very long way to find him out; for we cannot, I think, pay too much for the delight of having a companion who is in sympathy and agreement with us. O for a friend! How true is this old saying, ' that the possession of a friend is sweeter and more necessary than the elements of fire and water.'

To return to my story. There is no great evil in dying away from home and alone. Do we not consider it a duty to withdraw apart for natural actions that are less unsightly and less ghastly than this? Besides, those who are reduced to dragging out a prolonged and lingering existence should not perhaps wish to involve a large family in their miseries. For that reason the Indians of a certain region thought it right to kill a man who had reached that unfortunate state; and in another region they abandoned him to himself, to survive as best he could.

To whom do they not in the end become tiresome and insupportable? Ordinary duties do not go to that length. You forcibly teach your best friends to be cruel; by long familiarity with your ailments your wife and children become hardened and cease to feel for you and pity you. The groans that my colic forces from me have ceased to alarm anybody. And though we may derive some pleasure from their company (which is not always the case, by reason of the disparity of conditions, which easily begets contempt or envy for anybody whatever), is it not too much to abuse their good nature for such an age? The more I saw them cheerfully putting a restraint upon themselves for my sake,

---

[1] Montaigne's hope was partially fulfilled by Mademoiselle de Gournay, who called upon him when, for the purpose of seeing his new edition of the Essays through the press, he went for the last time to Paris.

the more sorry should I be for their pains. We are justified in leaning, but not in lying so heavily, upon others, and propping ourselves to their detriment. Like the man who had the throats of little children cut, to make use of their blood to cure some disease he had.[1] Or that other who was provided with young and tender virgins to keep his old limbs warm at night, and mingle the fragrance of their breath with his own rank and fetid exhalations.[1]

I could willingly choose Venice for my retreat when reduced to that feeble condition of life.

Decrepitude is a condition that requires solitude. I am sociable to excess. And yet it appears to me reasonable that I should henceforth withdraw my troublesome person from the eyes of the world, and brood over it in solitude ; that I should shrink and retire into my shell, like a tortoise. I am learning to see people without clinging to them ; that would be outrageous in so steep a pass. It is time to turn my back on the company.

' But on so long a journey you may be miserably detained in some hole of a place where you will lack everything.' Most of the necessary things I carry about with me. And then we cannot run away from Fortune, if she resolves to attack us. When I am ill I need nothing out of the common ; if Nature has no power over me, I have no mind to trust to a pill. At the very beginning of my agues and the maladies that lay me low, whilst I am yet whole and near to health, I reconcile myself with God by means of the last Christian offices ; and I feel the more easy and relieved, and seem to have got the better of the malady.

Of notaries and their advice I have less need than of doctors. If I have not settled my affairs when quite well, I cannot be expected to do so when ill. What I wish to do for the service of death is always done ; I would not venture to defer it for a single day. And if nothing is done, it means either that hesitation kept me from making a choice (for sometimes not to choose is to choose well), or that I had quite resolved to do nothing.[2]

---

[1] Tiberius, according to one commentator, Louis XI, according to another. The second example is obviously King David.

[2] We have an example of Montaigne's foresight in one of the very few notices of him in contemporary records. In a Commentary on the customs of Bordeaux, under the heading of *Wills*, Bernard Anthoine

I write my book for few people, and for few years. If I had expected a long life for my Essays, I should have committed them to a more settled language.[1] Seeing the continual changes that have taken place in our tongue to this day, who can expect that fifty years hence it will be used in its present form ? Every day it slips from our hands, and during my lifetime it has altered by one half. We say that at this moment it is perfect ; every century says the same of its own. I hesitate to believe that, as long as it escapes us and changes its forms as it does. It is for the good and useful writings to rivet it to themselves, and its credit will follow the fortunes of our State.

Therefore I do not fear to insert a few private items, interest in which will be confined to people now living, and which deal with things known to certain individuals who will see further into them than the ordinary intelligence. After all I do not wish to be discussed in the way I often hear people raking up the memories of the dead, saying : ' This is what he thought ; this is how he lived ; this is what he meant ; if he had spoken when he was dying, he would have said this, he would have given that ; I knew him better than any man.' Now, as far as decency permits I here make my inclinations and feelings known ; but I do it more freely and readily by word of mouth to any one who wishes to know them. In any case, if any one examines these memoirs, he will find that I have said everything, or hinted at everything. What I cannot express I point at with my finger :

> But for the keen eye these mere footprints serve
> Whereby thou mayest know the rest thyself. (LUCRETIUS.)

I leave nothing concerning myself to be desired or to be guessed at. If people must be talking about me, I would have it to be truthfully and justly. I would willingly return from the next world to contradict any man who described me other than I was, although he did it to honour me. I have observed that even the living are always

writes : ' The late Montaigne, author of the Essays, feeling his end drawing near, got up in his shirt, put on his dressing-gown, opened his cabinet, called all his servants and legatees, and paid them the legacies he had left them by his will, foreseeing the difficulty his heirs would make in paying them.'

[1] Latin, which, being a dead language, is not liable to change.

misrepresented. And if I had not with all my power upheld the reputation of a friend I have lost, he might have been torn to pieces and represented in a thousand contradictory lights.[1]

To make an end of speaking of my poor humours, I confess that in my travels I seldom reach my night's lodging but the thought comes into my mind whether I could be ill or die there in comfort. I prefer to be lodged in a place which has been appropriated to my own particular use, neither noisy, nor dirty, nor smoky, nor stuffy. I endeavour to flatter death by these trivial details ; or, to be more exact, to rid myself of all other encumbrances, that I may give my whole mind to it, since it will probably lie heavy enough upon me without any other load. I would like death to have her share in the ease and comforts of my life. Death is a great and important piece of life, and I hope from this day that mine will not belie the past.

Death assumes shapes of which some are easier than others, and takes on different properties according to each one's imagination. Among natural deaths that which results from weakness or stupor appears to me gentle and pleasant. Among violent deaths I can less easily fancy falling down a precipice than a ruin crushing me, and dying by a sword-cut than by a musket-shot. And I would sooner have drunk Socrates' potion than stabbed myself as Cato did. And, although it all comes to the same thing, yet my imagination sees as much difference between leaping into a fiery furnace and into the channel of a shallow river, as between death and life. So foolishly does our fear regard the means more than the end ! It is but an instant ; but it is of so much importance that I would willingly give many days of my life to pass it in my own way.

Since every one's imagination discovers a more or a less in its bitterness ; since every one has some choice in the manner of dying, let us try a little further to find one that is free from all pain. Might we not make it even voluptuous,

<hr />

[1] The friend was presumably La Boëtie. The edition of 1588 had this passage : ' I know well that I shall not leave behind me any man who will take my part with anything like the same affection and the same understanding of me as I do his. There is no man whom I would fully trust to represent me faithfully ; he alone possessed my true portrait, and took it away with him. That is why I reveal myself so carefully.'

as did the ' companions in death ' of Antony and Cleopatra ?
I will not speak of the cruel deaths which are the result of
philosophy and religion, and which are held up as examples.
But among men of little mark there have been found some,
such as a Petronius and a Tigellinus, at Rome, who, pledged
to take their own lives, lulled death to sleep as it were by
the luxury of their preparations. They made it pass and
glide away amid their customary effeminate pastimes, in
the company of girls and boon companions ; no words of
consolation, no mention of wills, no ambitious affectation
of fortitude, no talk about their future state, but amidst
games, feastings, jestings, ordinary conversation on topical
subjects, music and erotic poetry.

Could we not imitate that resoluteness in a more seemly
fashion ? Since there are deaths good for fools and deaths
good for wise men, let us discover some that are good for
those who are neither the one nor the other. My imagination suggests to me one or two forms of death that are easy
and, since we must die, desirable.

The Roman tyrants considered that they were giving a
criminal his life when they gave him the choice of his death.
But was not Theophrastus, so delicate, modest, and wise
a philosopher, obliged by his reason to dare to say this line,
which was latinized by Cicero :

Fortune, not Wisdom, rules the life of man ?

How greatly Fortune has helped me to keep with ease the
bargain of my life by placing me in such a position that it is
henceforth neither necessary nor cumbersome to anybody !
It is a condition that I would have accepted at any season
of my life, but now that I am ready to pack up for good
and turn up my toes, I find a more particular satisfaction in
the thought that I shall not give anybody either much
pleasure or much pain by dying. By an artistic compensation she has brought it about that those who may expect
some material benefit from my death will at the same time
suffer some material loss. Our death often bears hard upon
us because it is painful to others, and brings us almost as
much harm through the harm it does them, and sometimes
even more.

Among the comforts I look for in mine inn I include
neither magnificence nor abundance ; I hate them rather ;

but a certain simple neatness which is more often met with
in places where there is less of art, and which Nature has
adorned with some charm entirely her own. *A meal in
which not abundance but cleanliness prevails* (quoted by
Nonius). *More wit than luxury* (C. Nepos).

And then, it is those who are compelled, in the depth of
winter, to travel on business through the Grisons who are
overtaken on the way by those extreme discomforts. I,
who most often travel for my pleasure, do not steer myself
so badly. If it is unattractive on the right, I take the left
turning. If I feel unfit to ride, I stay where I am. And
by so doing I really cannot see that it is not as pleasant
and commodious as being at home. It is true that I always
find superfluity superfluous, and notice that even dainty
food and abundance occasion trouble.

If I have left anything unseen behind me, I go back ; it
is still on my way. I draw no fixed line, either straight or
crooked. If I do not find, at the place I go to, what I have
been told of, as it often happens that others' opinions do
not agree with mine and have generally turned out to be
erroneous, I do not regret my trouble ; I have learned that
what I was told of was not there.

My bodily nature is as adaptable, and my tastes are as
catholic, as those of any man living. The different customs
I find in one nation after another please me by their very
diversity ; each custom has its reason. Whether the plates
be of tin, of wood, or of earthenware, whether the meat be
boiled or roast ; whether they give me butter or oil, whether
nut-oil or olive-oil ; whether dishes be hot or cold, it is all
one to me ; and so much one that, as I grow older, I find
fault with this liberal disposition, and feel the need of a
more discriminating choice to arrest my immoderate appetite, and sometimes to ease my digestion.

When I have been outside of France, and people have
asked me, out of politeness, whether I would like to be
served with French dishes, I laughed at the idea ; and
I always sought the tables that were most thick with
foreigners.

I am ashamed when I see my countrymen steeped in that
silly prejudice which makes them fight shy of any customs
that differ from their own ; when they are out of their
village, they seem to be out of their element. Wherever

they go they keep to their own ways, and abominate those of foreigners. If they come across a fellow-countryman in Hungary, they celebrate the happy meeting. See them hobnobbing and joining forces, and railing at all the barbarous customs they see around them ! Why not barbarous, since they are not French ? And yet those are the cleverest, who have taken sufficient notice of them to revile them. Most of them start on their travels with no thought but to return. They travel reserved and self-centred, wrapped in a taciturn and unsociable caution, on the defensive against the infection of any strange atmosphere.

What I say of these reminds me of what I have sometimes observed in our young courtiers, in similar circumstances. They associate with none but those of their own kidney, regarding us with contempt or pity, as people of another world. Deprive them of the opportunity of talking of court intrigues, and they are like fish out of water ; as green and ignorant to us as we appear to them. It has been very well said that a well-bred man is an all-round man.

I, on the other hand, start on my wanderings very much fed up with our ways. I do not look for Gascons in Sicily (I have left enough of them at home) ; I would rather meet Greeks and Persians. With these I enter into conversation, and I study them. To them I offer and lend my services. And, what is more, I seem to have met with few customs that are not as good as ours.

I do not risk much ; for I have hardly lost sight of my weathercocks.[1]

For the rest, most of the company one casually meets with on the road causes more embarrassment than pleasure ; I do not cultivate their acquaintance, and less so now that old age makes me particular and somewhat inclined to avoid the customary formalities. You feel for others, or others feel for you ; both are painful discomforts, but the latter seems to me the ruder.

It is a rare chance, but of inestimable solace, to meet with a well-bred man, of solid good sense, agreeing with you in tastes, who takes a pleasure in your company. I have been greatly in need of such a man on all my travels. But

---

[1] As this was written after Montaigne had been as far as Rome, it must be taken metaphorically ; perhaps he means that he sees many familiar objects in foreign parts.

such company must be chosen and acquired before you leave home.

I relish no pleasure that I cannot communicate. I never have even a merry thought without being vexed at having to keep it to myself, with nobody to share it. *If I were offered wisdom on condition that I must keep it to myself, and not communicate it to others, I would have none of it* (Seneca). This other has tuned it to a higher note : *If the life of a wise man were so arranged, that with an abundance of all things he might have full leisure to consider and contemplate all things worth his study, yet if his solitude were such that he could see no man, he must give up his life* (Cicero).

I agree with Archytas when he says ' that it would be undesirable to be even in Heaven, and to wander about those great and divine celestial bodies, without the companionship of a friend '.

But it is still better to be alone than in stupid and tiresome company. Aristippus preferred to live a stranger everywhere.

> Had Fate vouchsafed me of mine own free will
> My course to shape,   (VIRGIL.)

I should choose to pass my life with my seat on the saddle,

> Where scorching suns the long day fill,
> Where mists and snows and tempests chill
> Hold reckless bacchanal. (HORACE.)

' Have you no more restful pastimes ? Of what have you any lack ? Is not your house in a beautifully airy and healthy situation, sufficiently furnished and more than sufficiently capacious ? Royal majesty with its train has more than once found room in it.[1] Are there not more families below yours in orderliness than there are above you in eminence ? Is there any local, extraordinary, indigestible thought that eats into your heart,

> That is now burning in thy troubled breast,
> And ne'er will suffer thee to be at rest ? (ENNIUS.)

Where do you expect to live without constraint, and undisturbed ? *Fortune's favours are never unmixed* (Q. Curtius). Do you not see that you alone stand in your own way, and

---

[1] King Henry of Navarre stayed at the Château of Montaigne on two occasions.

that you will follow your own inclination everywhere, and that you will grumble everywhere ? For there is no satisfaction here below except for brutish or divine souls. With so much just cause to be contented where do you think to find contentment ? How many thousands of men there are who limit their wishes to such a condition as you enjoy ! You must just amend your own ways, for you are able to do that to any extent ; whereas you have no right but to be patient in the face of Fortune. *There is no peace and quiet except that which Reason has conferred* (Seneca).'

I see the reasonableness of this homily, and I see it very clearly ; but it would have been briefer and more pertinent to have said in one word, ' Be wise.' Such a resolution is beyond wisdom ; it is she that brings about and produces that state. It is like the physician who keeps shouting after a poor lingering patient, ' Be cheerful ; ' his advice would not sound quite so foolish if he said, ' Be well.' For my part, I am but a man of the baser sort. This is a wholesome precept, sure, and easily understood, ' Be content with what you have,' that is to say, with your reason. But to carry it out is no more in the power of the wisest than it is in mine. It is a popular saying, but terribly far-reaching ; what does it not comprehend ? All things are subject to discrimination and qualification.

I know well that, to speak by the letter, this pleasure in travelling is a testimony of restlessness and instability ; and indeed these are our ruling and predominating qualities. Yes, I confess to it, I see nothing, not so much as in a dream, in a wish, whereon I could set up my rest ; variety alone satisfies me, and the enjoyment of diversity, at least if anything satisfies me. When I travel I am sustained chiefly by this idea, that I can give up travelling without inconvenience, and that I have a place where I can comfortably dispense with it.

I love a private life, because it is by my own choice that I love it, not because I am unfit for public life, for which I am perhaps by nature just as well suited. I can serve my Prince the more cheerfully because I can do so by the free choice of my judgement and reason, without any particular obligation ; and because I am not thrown back upon it or forced to it in consequence of being inadmissible and unwelcome to any other party. So of the rest. I hate the morsels that necessity carves for me. Any commodity on which I had solely to depend would stick in my throat :

> Let me in water plunge one oar,
> And with the other rake the shore. (PROPERTIUS.)

One cord will never hold me fast enough. 'There is vanity, you will say, in this amusement.' But where is there not ? And those goodly precepts are vanity, and all wisdom is vanity. *The Lord knoweth the thoughts of the wise, that they are vain* (Paul to the Corinthians). Those fine-spun subtleties are only for the pulpit ; they are admonitions that would send us ready saddled into the next world. Life is a material and corporeal movement, an action imperfect in its own essence and irregular ; I make it my business to serve it in its own way.

> We suffer each our ghostly punishments. (VIRGIL.)

We must act in such a way as not to contravene the universal laws of Nature ; that rule being observed, we must follow our own nature (Cicero). What end is served by those lofty heights of Philosophy, on which no human being can sit, and those rules which exceed our strength and our use ?

I often hear a man proposing an ideal form of life, which neither he nor his hearers have any hope, or what is more, any desire to follow. From the same sheet of paper on which he has just written the sentence delivered upon an adulterer, the judge will tear a scrap for a billet-doux to his colleague's wife. The lady with whom you have just been in illicit contact will presently, even before you leave her, abuse her friend for the same fault more bitterly than a Portia [1] might have done. And many will condemn men to death for crimes which they do not even regard as faults,

In my younger days I have known a gentleman offer the public with one hand poems excelling in beauty and licentiousness, and with the other, at the same moment, the most contentious work on theological reform that the world had breakfasted upon for many years.

So it is with men. They let the laws and precepts follow their own way ; we take another road, not only because we are of dissolute habits, but often because we disagree with them. Listen to a lecture on Philosophy ; your mind

---

[1] Portia, daughter of Cato of Utica, killed herself on hearing of the death of her husband Brutus at the Battle of Philippi.

is at once stirred and affected by the originality, the eloquence, the pertinence of the remarks, but they have no power to tickle and prick your conscience. It is not your conscience that is spoken to. Is that not true ? And so Aristo says ' that neither a hot bath nor a lecture is of any avail unless it cleans away and removes the dirt '. One may busy oneself about the rind, but not till after the pith has been extracted ; just as after draining the good wine out of a beautiful cup we examine the engraving and workmanship of it.

In all the workshops of ancient Philosophy we shall find this, that one and the same worker will publish rules of temperance, and at the same time publishes erotic and licentious writings. And Xenophon, in the bosom of Clinias, wrote against Aristippic sensuality. It is not a question of a miraculous conversion stirring them by fits and starts. But it is as with Solon, who portrays himself now in his own person, now in the shape of a law-giver ; now he speaks for the multitude, now in his own name. And for himself he adopts free and natural rules, feeling assured of perfect and robust health.

> For dubious maladies call in
> A doctor of repute. (JUVENAL.)

Antisthenes permits the sage to love, and do in his own way what he thinks convenient, without paying any attention to the laws ; since he is better advised than they, and has a greater knowledge of virtue. His disciple Diogenes said : ' To agitation oppose Reason ; to Fortune, confidence ; to the laws, Nature.'

For delicate stomachs are needed precise and artificial prescriptions. A good digestion simply follows the prescriptions of its natural appetite. So do our doctors, who eat melon and drink new wine, whilst they keep their patients tied down to syrups and slops.

' I know nothing about their books, said Laïs the courtesan, or their wisdom, or their philosophy ; but I know that these men knock at my door as often as any others.' Since our licence always carries us beyond what is lawful and permitted, the precepts and laws which rule our lives have often been made stricter than universal reason requires.

> No man is satisfied if he transgress
> No further than the laws permit. (JUVENAL.)

It were desirable that there were more proportion between the command and the obedience ; and it seems unjust to set the goal further than we can reach. There is no man, good as he may be, who, if all his thoughts and actions were submitted to the scrutiny of the laws, would not deserve hanging ten times in his life ; yea, many a man whom it would be a very great loss and very unjust to punish with death.

> It is no business of yours
> What he or she do with their skins. (MARTIAL.)

And many a man who has never offended against the laws not only does not deserve to be commended for honesty, but would be very justly scourged by Philosophy. So confused and unjust is the proportion !

We take no heed to be good men according to God's laws. We cannot be so according to our laws. Human wisdom never yet came up to the duties she has prescribed for herself, and if she did come up to them, she would prescribe others beyond them, to which she would ever aim and aspire ; so hostile to consistency is our human condition !

Man has ordained that he shall necessarily be at fault. He does not show much discrimination when he carves out his duties to the measure of another being than his own. For whom does he prescribe that which he expects no man to do ? Is he wrong in not doing what it is impossible for him to do ? The laws which condemn us not to be able, themselves accuse us of not being able.

At the worst this distorted liberty of presenting ourselves in two ways, the actions after one manner, the reasonings after another, may be allowable in those who speak of things, but it cannot be so for those who speak of themselves, as I do ; I must walk with my pen as I do with my feet. The life of the public man ought to have some relation to other lives. The virtue of Cato was vigorous beyond the measure of his time ; and for a man who took upon himself to govern others, a man dedicated to the public service, the rightness of it may be said to have been, if not wrong, at least a vain and unseasonable rightness.

My own conduct of life, which hardly deviates by the width of an inch from that of the generality of people, yet makes me somewhat shy and unsociable to my age. I do

not know if I am unreasonably disgusted with the world
I frequent ; but I know well that it would be unreasonable
for me to complain of the world being more disgusted with
me than I am disgusted with the world.

The virtue assigned to the affairs of the world is a virtue
with many bends, angles, and elbows, to join and adapt
itself to human frailty ; mixed and artificial, not straight,
clear, constant, nor purely harmless.   Our annals to this
day blame one of our Kings for yielding too simply to the
conscientious persuasions of his confessor.   Affairs of state
have bolder precepts :

> Let him who would be pure from courts retire.   (LUCAN.)

I once tried to adapt to the service of conducting public
affairs ideas and rules of life as rude, fresh, unpolished, and
unpolluted as they were either born with me, or derived
from my education, which serve me, if not commodiously,
at least safely, in my private concerns : the virtue of a
schoolboy and a novice.   I found them unsuitable and
dangerous in such matters.   A man who enters a crowd
must go now this way, now that, keep in his elbows, retreat
or advance, nay he must quit the straight path, according
to what he encounters.   He must live not so much according
to himself as according to others ; not according to what
he proposes to himself, but according to what is proposed
to him, according to the times, according to the men,
according to the business in hand.

Plato says that the man who escapes with clean hands
from the management of the world's affairs, escapes by
a miracle.   He also says that when he places his philosopher
at the head of a government, he has not in mind a corrupt
government like that of Athens, and still less a government
like ours, in which Wisdom herself would lose her Latin.
Since a herb, transplanted to a soil differing greatly from
that which suits it, rather adapts itself to the soil than
corrects the soil to suit itself.

I feel that if I had to direct my mind entirely to such
occupations, I should need a great deal of change and
reclothing.   And even though I could prevail upon myself
to do so (and why could I not, with time and diligence ?),
I would not.   The little experience I have had in that trade
disgusted me with it.   At times I feel a certain temptation

to ambition arising like vapour in my soul ; but I stiffen myself obstinately to resist it :

> Be thou, Catullus, firm unto the last ! (CATULLUS.)

I am seldom called upon, and as seldom do I offer myself. Independence and laziness, which are my ruling qualities, are qualities diametrically opposed to that trade.

We are unable to distinguish between the faculties of different men ; they are minutely divided and limited, and difficult to choose between. To conclude that, because a man is competent in private life, he will be competent in public service, is to conclude badly. Many a man guides himself well who cannot guide others well ; and produces Essays who cannot produce deeds. A man will direct a siege well who would badly direct a battle ; and discourse well in private who cannot address a crowd or a prince. Nay, to be able to do the one is perhaps rather evidence, than not, that he is unable to do the other.

I observe that great minds are hardly more fitted for little things than little minds for great things. Can it be believed that Socrates gave the Athenians food for laughter at his expense, because he had never been able to count up the votes of his tribe, and report upon them to the Council ? Truly the veneration I have for that great man's perfections deserves that my chief imperfections should be excused by the magnificent example which he was fated to set me.

Our talents are cut up into small pieces ; mine have no breadth and are miserably few. Saturninus [1] said to the men who had set him at the head of the army, ' Fellow-soldiers, you have ruined a good captain to make a bad general.'

If any man flatters himself that, in a diseased age like the present, he can employ in the service of the world a pure and spotless virtue, he either does not know what virtue is, since morality and our ideas of morality deteriorate in the same ratio (indeed, hear them describing virtue, listen to most of them glorying in their conduct and laying down the law ; instead of painting virtue they paint injustice and vice pure and simple, and offer this false image as an example for princes) ; or, if he does know, he flatters

---

[1] One of the thirty tyrants who rose up in the time of the Emperor Gallienus.

himself wrongfully, and, whatever he may say, he does a thousand things of which his conscience accuses him.

I would willingly take Seneca's word with regard to his experience on a like occasion, provided that he would speak candidly. The most honourable mark of uprightness in such a difficulty is freely to acknowledge one's error, and that of others ; to restrain and resist with all one's might the inclination to evil, to follow that bent reluctantly, to hope and desire something better.

I observe, in this dismemberment of our country and these divisions into which we are fallen, that every man labours to defend his cause, but even the best of them does so with lies and dissimulation. Whoever should write bluntly about them would be a bold man, and vicious. The most just party is still a member of a putrid and worm-eaten body ; but in such a body the member that is least diseased calls itself sound, and with good reason, since our qualities have no name except by comparison. Political innocence is measured according to places and times.

I should like to have seen Xenophon commending Agesilaus for this action :[1] Being entreated by a neighbouring Prince, with whom he had once been at war, to allow him to pass through his territory, he granted him permission, giving him free passage through the Peloponnesus, and not only did he not imprison or poison him when he had him at his mercy, but he received him courteously [as bound by his promise], and did him no harm. To a man of Xenophon's way of thinking there was nothing remarkable in this ; elsewhere and in another age such an action will be specially recorded for its generosity and magnanimity. Our wretched schoolboys would have laughed it to scorn ; so little does Spartan innocence resemble the French kind.

We have no lack of virtuous men ; but it is according to our standard. If there be a man whose morals are tuned to a higher key than that of his age, let him either twist or blunt his rules of conduct, or (which I would rather advise him to do) let him retire into private life, and not mix with us. What could he gain by it ?

An upright and a blameless man appears
More wondrous than a boy with double limbs,

[1] This is written ironically ; but it seems that Xenophon did commend Agesilaus in his Life of that King.

> Than fishes found by ploughing husbandman,
> Or mule that 's big with foal. (JUVENAL.)

We may regret better times but we cannot flee from the present ; we may wish for different men in authority, but we must nonetheless obey those we have. And there is perhaps more merit in obeying the bad than the good. As long as a reflexion of the old and accepted laws of this monarchy shines in any corner, there will I abide. If they unfortunately happen to thwart and contradict one another, and produce two factions of doubtful and difficult choice, I shall readily choose to avoid and escape the storm. In the meantime Nature or the hazards of war may lend me a helping hand. Between Caesar and Pompey I could have openly declared myself. But with those three robbers who came after,[1] either I should have had to hide, or follow with the wind ; which I consider permissible when Reason is no longer at the helm.

> Whither from the course so wide ? (VIRGIL.)

This padding has carried me a little away from my theme. I go out of my way, but rather through licence than inadvertance. My ideas follow one another, but sometimes at a distance ; and they look at one another, but askance.

I have cast my eyes over a certain dialogue of Plato,[2] divided into two halves like a fantastic motley garb, the upper part treating of love, all the lower part of eloquence. They are not afraid of these quick changes, and with wonderful charm they allow themselves thus to roll before the wind, or they seem to.

The headings of my chapters do not always embrace the matter of them ; often they only indicate it by some mark, like those other titles, the ' Maid of Andros ', ' The Eunuch '[3] or these other names, Sylla, Cicero, Torquatus.[3]

I love the poetic gait, by leaps and bounds. It is, as Plato says, a light, fleet-footed, divinely inspired art.

In some of his dissertations Plutarch forgets his theme ; and the drift of his argument is only incidentally found, quite drowned in foreign matter. See how he wanders in

---

[1] Octavius, Antony, and Lepidus.   [2] The *Phaedrus*.
[3] The first are the names of two comedies of Terence ; the latter respectively personify the Dictator, the Orator and the Cruel father.

the ' Daemon of Socrates '. My word, what charm there is in those frolicsome sallies and those digressions ! And the more charming, the more careless and casual they appear to be !

It is the negligent reader who mislays my subject, not I ; a word or two on it may always be discovered in some corner, which will not fail to be sufficient, though it may be hard to find.

I am fond of change and variety, unwisely and impetuously fond, and my style and mind have the same vagabond nature.

A man must be a little mad if he would not be more foolish,[1] as the precepts of our masters tell us, and still more their examples.

A thousand poets flag and languish prosaically ; but the best ancient prose (and I scatter it here indifferently as if it were verse), shines throughout with the vigour and boldness of poetry, and reflects some touch of poetic frenzy. And we must certainly allow that poetry has the mastery and pre-eminence in speaking. The poet, says Plato, seated upon the tripod of the Muses, in his frenzy pours out whatever rises to his lips, like a spouting fountain, without weighing and ruminating it ; and things escape him of varied hues, of contrary substance, and in a broken stream. Plato himself is poetic throughout, and the old theology is poetry, so the scholars tell us, and the first philosophy. It is the original language of the gods.

I would have my matter distinguishable of itself ; that it should sufficiently show where it changes, where it concludes, where it begins, where it is resumed, without interlacing it with joining and connecting words introduced for the benefit of feeble or inattentive ears ; and without my having to write my own glosses.

Where is the man who would not rather not be read than read sleepily or hastily ? *Nothing, however useful it may be, can be useful when treated negligently* (Seneca). If to take up a book were to take it in, if to look at it were to consider it, if to run through it were to grasp it, I should be wrong to profess to be quite as ignorant as I do.

---

[1] *Il faut avoir un peu de folie qui ne veut avoir plus de sottise.* Hazlitt translates, ' He must fool it a little who would not be deemed wholly a fool.'

Since I am unable to fix the reader's attention by the weight of it, it is a point gained if I chance to fix it by my intricacies. ' True, but he will afterwards repent of having puzzled over them.' No doubt ; but after all he will have puzzled over them. And besides, there are men of that nature, who despise what is intelligible, who will think the better of me for not understanding what I say ; they will infer the depth of my meaning from its obscurity, which, to tell the truth, I very much hate, and would avoid if I could avoid myself. Aristotle somewhere boasts of affecting it ; a mistaken affectation !

As the cutting up of my work into so many chapters, a method which I adopted at the beginning, appeared to me to break and destroy, before arousing, the reader's attention, since it would disdain to settle down and collect itself for so little, I have taken to making them longer, and such as need a firm determination and leisure on his part. In this kind of occupation, to a man to whom you will not give a single hour you will give nothing. And you do nothing for a man for whom you do only whilst you are doing something else. Besides which I have perhaps some particular reason for speaking only by halves, for speaking confusedly and discordantly.

I was about to say that I am out of humour with that kill-joy Reason ; and as to those extravagant ambitions that torment one's life and those superfine opinions, if there is any truth in them, I think it too dearly bought and too inconvenient. I am rather out to champion the cause of vanity even, and asininity, if they bring me any pleasure ; and let myself follow my natural inclinations, without examining them too closely.

I have seen elsewhere ruined houses, and statues, both of heaven and the earth ; [1] they are men, when all is said. All that is true ; and yet I cannot so often revisit the tomb of that great and powerful city, [2] but it always excites my wonder and awe.

Care for the dead is a duty imposed upon us. Now I was brought up from childhood with these dead ; I was familiar with the affairs of Rome long before I was with those of my own house. I knew the Capitol and its position before I knew the Louvre, and the Tiber before the Seine. I have

---

[1] i. e. of gods and men.   [2] Rome.

meditated more on the conditions and fortunes of Lucullus, Metellus, and Scipio than I have about any of our own men. They are dead. So indeed is my father ; he is as absolutely dead as they, and as far removed from me and life, after eighteen years, as they are after sixteen hundred. And yet I do not cease to cherish and keep alive his memory, his love and companionship in a perfect and very living union.

Nay, I am naturally inclined to be more serviceable to the departed ; they cannot help themselves, and therefore seem to be more in need of my help. It is just here that gratitude shows in its best light. A benefit is less generously bestowed where there is hope of its being returned and reflected.

Arcesilaus, going to see Ctesibius who was ill, and seeing that he was poorly off, softly slipped the money he had intended giving him under his pillow ; by concealing it he besides acquitted him from acknowledging his thanks.

Those who have deserved love and gratitude at my hands never lost it through being no longer on the spot ; I have repaid them better and more carefully in spite of their absence and ignorance of my gratitude. I speak more affectionately of my friends when they have no longer any means of knowing it.

Now I have started a hundred quarrels in defence of Pompey and for the cause of Brutus. This friendship still endures between us ; we have no hold even on present things except through the imagination. Finding myself of no use to this age, I hurl myself back into that other, and am so infatuated with it, that the state of that ancient Rome, when free, just and flourishing (for I love her neither at her birth nor in her old age) arouses my passionate interest. Wherefore I cannot so often revisit the sites of their streets and houses, and those deep ruins extending to the Antipodes, but I must muse over them.

Is it by nature or through an error of the imagination that the sight of places we know to have been frequented and inhabited by men whose memory is held in honour, affects us somewhat more strongly than to hear tell of their deeds or to read their works ? *Such is the power of places to call up memories ! And in this city they are endless ; for wherever we tread we set our foot on some piece of history* (Cicero).

I take a delight in reflecting on their faces, their bearing and their clothes. I ruminate those great names between my teeth and make them resound in my ears. *I pay reverence to them, and always rise in honour to such great names* (Seneca). Of things that are in some part great and admirable I admire even the common parts. I should delight in seeing them talk together, taking their airing, and at supper. It would be ungrateful in me to despise the remains and statues of so many honourable and valorous men whom I have seen live and die, and who by their examples give us so many good instructions, if we but knew how to follow them.

And then, this same Rome that we see deserves our love, having been so long and by so many ties allied to our own crown : the only common and universal city. The supreme authority who rules there is equally acknowledged in other countries ; it is the metropolitan city of all Christian nations. Spaniard or Frenchman, every one is at home there. To be one of the Princes of that state, it is but necessary to be of Christendom, wherever it may be. There is no place on this earth that has been so much and so constantly under the protection and influence of Heaven. Her very ruins are replete with glory and pomp :

The dearer for her memorable ruins. (SIDONIUS APOLLINARIS.)

In her very tomb she still retains the marks and reflexions of empire. *That it may be clearly manifest that in this place of all others Nature rejoiced in her handiwork* (Pliny).

Some would reproach themselves and feel an inner revolt at their being tickled by so vain a pleasure. Our inclinations are not too vain if they are agreeable. Let them be what they may, if they constantly satisfy a man capable of common sense, I should not have the heart to find fault with him.

I owe much to Fortune, in that to this day she has done me no great wrong, at least not more than I was able to bear. May it not be her way to leave those in peace who do not trouble her ?

> The more a man himself denies,
> The more to him the Gods will give.
> Naked I seek the camp of those
> Who covet nought . . .
> Much they lack who much demand. (HORACE.)

If she continues, she will dismiss me very well contented and satisfied :

> I importune the Gods for nothing more.   (HORACE.)

But beware the shock ! There are thousands who go to pieces in the very harbour.

I can easily console myself for what will happen here when I am gone ; present things keep me sufficiently busy :

> The rest I leave to Fortune.   (OVID.)

Besides, I have not that strong tie that is said to attach men to the future through the children who bear their name and honour.[1] And I ought perhaps to desire them the less if they are so desirable. I am too much attached as it is to the world and to this life, through myself. I am content to be in the clutches of Fortune with regard to the circumstances that are properly necessary to my existence, without in other ways extending her authority over me ; and I have never thought that being without children was a drawback that should render life less complete and less contented. A sterile occupation also has its advantages. Children are among the things that are not strongly to be desired, especially in this age when it would be so difficult to make them good men. *Nothing good can be brought forth now, so corrupt are the seeds* (Tertullian). And yet they are just the things whose loss, when they have been acquired, is to be regretted.

He who left me in charge of my house prophesied that I was likely to ruin it, considering how little I had of the stay-at-home disposition. He was mistaken ; here I am as I was when I first entered into possession, if not a little better off. And yet I have neither official position nor church living.

For the rest, if Fortune has done me no violent or extraordinary injury, neither has she done me any particular favour. All the gifts she has bestowed on my house go back more than a hundred years. For my own part I am not beholden to her liberality for any essential and solid benefits. She has granted me a few airy favours, of an honorary and titular nature, without any substance ; and these she did not, to tell the truth, grant, but offer to me ;

---

[1] Montaigne means that he has no sons.

to me who am, God knows, grossly material, who am only satisfied with realities, and very massive realities ; and who, if I dared to confess it, would think avarice rather more pardonable than ambition, and pain more to be shunned than disgrace, and health more desirable than learning, and wealth than nobility.

Among her empty favours there is none that gives so much pleasure to this silly conceit of mine which feeds upon it, as an authentic patent of Roman citizenship, which was granted me on my recent visit to that city, magnificent with its seals and gilt letters, and granted with all gracious liberality. And as these patents are worded differently, in more or less gracious style ; and as I myself, before I set eyes on one, would have been very glad to be shown a formula of it, I will, for the satisfaction of any person who is suffering from the same curiosity as I, transcribe it here in full :

' On the report made to the Senate by Orazio Massimi, Marzo Cecio, Alessandro Muti, Conservators of the city of Rome, concerning the right of Roman citizenship to be granted to the most illustrious Michel de Montaigne, Knight of the Order of St. Michael, and Gentleman of the Chamber in ordinary to the Most Christian King, the Senate and People of Rome have decreed :

' Considering that, by ancient usage, those have ever been adopted amongst us with ardour and eagerness, who, distinguished by virtue and nobility, have served and honoured our Republic, or might do so in the future ; We, full of respect for the example and authority of our ancestors, consider that we should imitate and follow this laudable custom. Wherefore, the most illustrious Michel de Montaigne, Knight of the Order of St. Michael, and Gentleman of the Chamber in ordinary to the Most Christian King, most zealous for the Roman name, being by the rank and distinction of his family, and by his personal qualities, highly worthy to be admitted to the rights of Roman citizenship by the supreme judgement and suffrage of the Senate and People of Rome : it has pleased the Senate and People of Rome, that the most illustrious Michel de Montaigne, adorned with every kind of merit, and very dear to this noble People, should be inscribed as a Roman citizen, both in regard to himself and his posterity, and admitted to enjoy all the honours and advantages reserved for those who were born Citizens and Patricians of Rome, or who have become such by right of their good title thereunto. And herein the Senate and People of Rome consider that they are less conferring a gift, than paying a debt, and that it is less a service they render than a service they receive from him, who, in accepting this Citizenship, honours and gives lustre to the City itself. The Conservators have caused this Senatus-Consultus to be transcribed by the secretaries of the Roman Senate and People, to be deposited among the archives of the Capitol, and have drawn up this act, sealed with the common seal of the City. A. U. C. 2331, A.D. 1581, 13th March.

ORAZIO FOSCO,

Secretary of the Sacred Senate and of the Roman People.

VINCENTE MARTOLI,

Secretary of the Sacred Senate and of the Roman People.'

Being a burgess of no town, I am very pleased to be one of the noblest city that ever was and ever will be. If others were to examine themselves attentively, as I do, they would, as I do, find that they are full of vanity and foppery. I cannot do away with it without doing away with myself. We are all steeped in it, one as much as the other ; but those who are sensible of it are in a better way ; and yet I am not so sure.

That common habit of mind of looking elsewhere than at ourselves has stood us in good stead. We are an object that fills us with discontent ; we see nothing there but misery and vanity. In order not to discourage us, Nature has very fittingly thrown the action of our sight outwards. We go forward with the current ; but to turn our course back upon ourselves is a painful movement ; thus the sea, when thrown back upon itself, falls into confusion and gets in its own way. Observe, says every one, the motions of the heavens, observe the people, the quarrel of this man, the pulse of that, the last testament of another ; in short, keep on observing, high or low, on one side, or before, or behind.

It was a paradoxical command that was given us in ancient times by that God at Delphi. ' Look into yourself ; know yourself ; lay hold on yourself ; call back your mind and will, which are expending their powers elsewhere, to themselves ; you are running out, you are diffusing yourself ; concentrate yourself ; resist yourself ; you are being betrayed and dispersed and robbed of yourself. Dost thou not see that this world keeps its sight concentrated upon itself, and its eyes open to contemplate itself ? It is always vanity for thee, within and without ; but it is less vanity when less extended. Saving thyself, O man, said that God, each thing studies itself first, and, according to its need, sets limits to its labours and desires. There is not a single thing so destitute and needy as thyself, who embracest the universe. Thou art the searcher without knowledge, the magistrate without authority and, when all is said, the fool of the comedy.'

CHAPTER 10

OF HUSBANDING ONE'S WILL

BY comparison with the common run of men, few things give me concern, or, more correctly speaking, gain a hold upon me. For it is reasonable that they should concern, provided they do not possess us. I do my best, by study and argument, to increase this privilege of insensibility, which I have by nature in a high degree. There are consequently few things that I passionately espouse. My sight is clear, but fixed on few objects ; my sensibilities are soft and tender. But my powers of apprehension and application are dull and hard. I find it difficult to pledge myself to a thing.

As far as in me lies, I give all my attention to myself ; and even here I would willingly curb my feelings and keep them from plunging too deeply into an object that I possess by the favour of others, and over which Fortune has more right than I. So that even as regards health, which I value so highly, it would be well if I did not so passionately desire and dote upon it as to make sickness insupportable.

We should find a mean between hatred of pain and love of pleasure ; and Plato prescribes a middle course of life between the two.

But to the feelings that draw me away from myself and attach me elsewhere, I certainly offer all the resistance in my power. My maxim is ' that we should lend ourselves to

others, and give ourselves only to ourselves '. If I were
easily led to pledge and devote myself, I should not hold
out against it ; I am too soft, both by nature and habit :

> Averse to all affairs and born
> In idleness and ease. (OVID.)

Obstinately contested disputes in which my adversary
in the end had the better of me, the shame of having
pursued my point too hotly to an issue, would perhaps
rankle too cruelly within me. If I rose to the bait as
readily as others do, my soul would never have the strength
to bear the terrors and emotions which attack those who
espouse so many things. It would be straightway unhinged
by that inward excitement.

If at times I have been driven to take up the management
of other people's affairs, I have promised to take them in
hand, but not into my lungs and liver ; to take them upon
my shoulders, not to identify myself with them ; to look
after them, yes ; to take them passionately to heart,
certainly not. I give my attention to them, but I do not
brood over them. I have enough to do to order and dispose
the throng of domestic cares which I foster in my bowels
and veins, without harbouring and being crushed by a
throng of other men's affairs ; and am sufficiently concerned
with my own natural and necessary affairs, without inviting
others that are foreign to me.

Those who know how much they owe to themselves, how
much they are in duty bound to themselves, discover that
Nature has given them this charge, which will keep them
fully enough occupied : ' Thou hast ample business at home ;
do not abandon it.'

Men hire themselves out. Their faculties are not exercised for themselves, but for those to whom they become
slaves. Their lodgers make themselves at home in their
house, not they themselves. This common humour is not to
my liking. We must husband the freedom of our soul, and
not let it out except on lawful occasions, which are very
few, if we judge sanely. Observe the people who are accustomed to let themselves be seized and carried away ; they
do so on all occasions, in little matters as well as great,
in those which do not concern them as well as in those
that do. They thrust themselves forward indiscriminately

wherever there is work to do and anything to bind them. Not to be in a state of bustle and excitement, is to them death. *They seek business only for business' sake* (Seneca).

Not that they wish to be on the move so much as that they cannot keep still ; any more or less than a stone which, started on its downward course, does not stop until it comes to its resting-place.

To be busy, for a certain class of people, is a mark of efficiency and dignity. Their minds seek repose in the swing, like infants in the cradle. They may be said to be as serviceable to their friends as they are troublesome to themselves.

No man deals out his money to others ; every man deals out his time and his life. Of nothing are we so prodigal as of those things in which alone avarice would be useful and commendable.

I am of quite the opposite disposition. I retire within myself ; what I desire, and that is little, I generally desire with no great ardour. So too I am rarely busy and occupied, and then calmly.

Whatever they will and carry out they do with all their will-power and intensity. There are so many slippery places that, for greater safety, we must glide rather lightly and superficially over this world ; we must slide over it, and not break through. Even sensual pleasures are painful when they are intense :

> You tread on fires that lurk beneath the treacherous ashes.
> (HORACE.)

Messieurs [1] of Bordeaux elected me Mayor of their town when I was far from France, and still farther from any such thought. I begged to be excused, but they told me I was wrong, since the King also intervened with his command. It is a charge that should appear the more honourable as there is no remuneration or profit attached to it, other than the honour of administering it. The duration of the office is two years, but it may be extended by a second election, which very rarely happens. It was so extended in my case, and only twice before : a few years previously in the case of Monsieur de Lanssac, and recently of Monsieur de Biron,

---

[1] The *Jurats* or Aldermen. Montaigne was at the time at the baths of Lucca in Italy.

Marshal of France, to whose place I succeeded ; and I left mine to Monsieur de Matignon, likewise Marshal of France. Smart in such noble company !

> Both able ministers in peace and war. (VIRGIL.)

Fortune desired to have a hand in my promotion by that particular circumstance which she put in of her own. By no means vain ; for Alexander flouted the Corinthian ambassadors who offered him the citizenship of their town. But when they proceeded to explain to him that Bacchus and Hercules were also on that register, he graciously thanked them.

On my arrival I portrayed myself faithfully and conscientiously, such as I feel myself to be : without memory, without vigilance, without experience and without energy ; without hatred too, without ambition, without avarice, and without strong passions ; that they might be informed and advised of what they were to expect of my service. And since in their choice of me they had only been instigated by their knowledge of my late father and the honour in which they held his memory, I further gave them very clearly to understand that I should be very sorry that anything should affect my feelings as strongly as his had formerly been affected by their municipal affairs, whilst he was administering them in this same office to which they had called me.

I remembered as a boy having seen him, in his old age, his soul cruelly distressed by those bickerings over public affairs, neglecting the sweet atmosphere of his home, to which he had long before become attached in his declining years, his household affairs and his health ; and truly thinking little of his own life, which he came near losing in consequence, obliged as he was to make long and laborious journeys on their behalf. Such was he, and this devotion of his proceeded from his great natural goodness of heart ; there never was a more benevolent and public-spirited soul.

This proceeding, which I commend in others, I am not inclined to follow ; and I am not without excuse. He had been told that we ought to forget ourselves for others ; that the individual was of no importance whatever when the general public interest was concerned.

Most of the rules and precepts of the world aim at pushing

us out of ourselves, and driving us into the market-place, for the benefit of public society. Their authors imagined they had done a great thing in diverting and distracting us from ourselves, assuming that we were but too firmly and naturally wedded to ourselves ; and they have not been sparing of words to tell us so. For it is no new thing for the wiseacres to preach things as they serve, not as they are.

Truth has its hindrances, disadvantages, and incompatibilities with us. We are often obliged to deceive, lest we deceive ourselves, and to seal our eyes, deaden our understanding, in order to redress and amend them. *For it is the ignorant who judge and must often be deceived, lest they fall into error* (Quintilian).

When they command us to love three, four, or fifty degrees of things before ourselves, they reflect the skill of the archer, who, to hit the mark, takes his aim far above the bull's eye. To straighten a bent piece of wood we bend it the other way.

I believe that in the Temple of Pallas, as we may see in all other religions, there were open mysteries to be shown to the people, and others, more occult and sublime, to be shown only to the initiated. In these is to be found, in all likelihood, the right degree of love that every man owes to himself. Not a false love that makes us embrace glory, knowledge, wealth, and such things, with a paramount and immoderate affection, as parts of our being ; nor a languid and indiscriminate love, whose effect we see in the ivy, that decays and ruins the wall it clasps ; but a healthy and well-regulated love, equally beneficial and agreeable.

He who knows the duties of this love and practises them is truly of the cabinet of the Muses ; he has reached the summit of human wisdom and human happiness. Such a man, knowing exactly what he owes to himself, finds it written down in his part that he should make the ways of other men and the world serve his purpose ; and to do this, that he must contribute to public society the duties and services that he owes to it.

He who does not live in some degree for others, hardly lives for himself. *Know that he who is his own friend is a friend to all the world* (Seneca).

The principal charge we have is ' to every one his own conduct ' ; and it is for that that we are here.

As the man who should neglect to live a good and godly life, thinking he was discharging his duty by guiding and training others to do so, would be a fool ; so the man who, for his own part, abandons a healthy and cheerful life to help others to live it, takes, in my opinion, a wrong and unnatural course.

I would not have a man, when he takes up an office, spare his attention, his pains, his eloquence, his sweat, and his blood, if need be :

> Not he for his friends whom he loves, or the land
> Of his fathers, will dread to surrender his breath ;   (HORACE.)

but only by way of loan, and incidentally, his mind being ever at rest and in health, not indeed inactive, but un-affected by excitement and strong emotions. To be simply acting costs the mind so little, that it is active even in sleep. But it should be set going discreetly. For the body receives the loads laid upon it just as they are ; the mind makes them greater and heavier, often at its own cost, giving them what proportion it pleases.

The same things are done by different men with different degrees of effort and exertion of will-power. The one goes very well without the other.[1] For how many men every day risk their lives in a war which is of no concern to them, and rush into the dangers of a battle the loss of which will not disturb their next night's sleep ! Many a man in his own home and far from those dangers, which he would not have had the courage to face, will be more passionately interested in the issue of that war, and more harried in his soul, than the soldier who gives his life and blood to it.

I was able to discharge public duties without departing from myself a nail's breadth, and to give myself to others without robbing myself of myself.

Those eager and passionate desires hinder rather than advance the execution of what we undertake ; they fill us with impatience when things do not turn out or progress as we wish, and with bitterness and suspicion against those with whom we have to deal. We never carry out a thing well that entirely possesses and rules us :

> In all things passion is an unsure guide.   (STATIUS.)

The man who uses only his judgement and his discretion

---

[1] The action goes very well without the passion.

in those matters proceeds more cheerfully. He dissembles, he gives way, he puts off very readily, according to the need and the occasion. When he fails to attain his purpose he is neither grieved nor worried, unscathed and ready for a fresh attack. He always walks with the reins in his hand.

In the man who is drunk with purposes so passionate that they tyrannize over him we necessarily observe much unwisdom and wrongheadedness. He is carried away by the impetuosity of his desires. They are reckless movements and, unless Fortune lends a strong helping hand, of little fruit.

Philosophy wills that we put away anger in punishing for injuries received ; not that the vengeance may be less, but, on the contrary, that it may be better directed and fall more heavily ; which, she thinks, will be frustrated by such impetuosity. Not only does anger turn aside, but of itself it also wearies the arm of him who chastises. This passionate heat benumbs and wastes its strength. As in hastiness, *more haste, less speed* (Q. Curtius). Haste trips itself up, shackles and arrests itself. *Speed gets in its own way* (Seneca). To give an example from what I have observed in everyday life, greed has no greater disturbing element than itself. The more it strains its powers, the less fertile it is. Commonly it grasps wealth more quickly when hidden under the mask of liberality.

A gentleman, a very worthy person and my friend, was in danger of going out of his mind by a too passionate affection and too assiduous attention to the interests of his master, a Prince. This master thus portrayed himself to me : ' That he can estimate the gravity of misfortunes as well as any man ; but when he sees there is no remedy, he decides at once to bear them. In other cases, after giving the necessary orders, which he is enabled to do promptly by reason of the quickness of his intellect, he calmly awaits the issue.'

Indeed I have seen him at work, very cool and collected, maintaining his freedom of action and his serenity in the midst of very great and thorny affairs. He appears to me greater and more capable when Fortune frowns than when she smiles upon him. His defeats are more honourable to him than his victories, and his sorrows than his triumphs.

Consider that even in actions that are vain and frivolous,

in chess, tennis, and similar games, the ardent and eager intrusion of passionate desire straightway throws the mind and the limbs into a state of disorder and a disability to discriminate ; we are blinded and hampered by our action. The man who bears himself more soberly towards gain and loss has always his wits about him ; the less excited and impassioned he is over the game, the more safely and advantageously will he play it.

For the rest, we hinder the mind's hold and grip by giving it too many things to seize. Some things should be merely presented to her, others fastened upon her, others incorporated with her. She may see and feel all things, but she must feed only on herself ; and she must be taught what properly concerns her, and what is properly of her having and substance.

The laws of Nature teach us exactly what we need. When the sages have told us that no man is poor according to Nature, and that every man is poor in the opinion of the world, they thus make a subtle distinction between the desires which are natural and those which are the result of our disorderly imagination. Those whose bounds are in view are Nature's ; those which flee before us and which we cannot catch up with, are ours.

Poverty in worldly goods is easily cured ; poverty of the soul is impossible of cure :

> If what for man's enough enough could be,
> It were enough ; but that not being so,
> How can I e'er believe that any wealth
> Will ever fill my mind with real content ? (LUCILIUS.)

Socrates, seeing a great quantity of riches, jewels, and costly furniture, being paraded through his city, remarked, ' What a number of things there are for which I have no desire ! '

Metrodorus lived on twelve ounces a day, Epicurus on less. Metrocles slept in winter among the sheep, in summer in the porticoes of the temples. *Nature provides for all that Nature needs* (Seneca). Cleanthes lived by the labour of his hands, and boasted that Cleanthes, if he would, could maintain yet another Cleanthes.

If that which Nature exactly and originally requires of us to keep us alive is too little (and indeed, how little it is, and how cheaply our life may be supported, cannot be better expressed than by this consideration, that it is so little that by its littleness it escapes the grip and shock of Fortune), let us allow ourselves something over and above. Let us also call the habits and condition of each one of us, Nature ; let us rate and treat ourselves by this standard ; let us stretch our appurtenances and our calculations thus far. For thus far, it seems to me, we have some excuse. Habit is a second Nature, and no less powerful. What my habit lacks, I seem to lack myself. And I would almost as soon be deprived of life as that the style of living which I have so long enjoyed should be greatly diminished and curtailed.

I am no longer in a condition for a great change, nor inclined to plunge into a new and untried course of life, not even a better one. It is too late for me to become other than I am. And as, if some great windfall were at this moment to drop into my hands, I should feel aggrieved that it had not come at a time when I was able to enjoy it :

> Of what advantage wealth to me,
> If I to use it am not free ? (HORACE.)

so I should deplore any inward acquisition.

It were almost better never to become an honest man than so late, or to have learned to live well when there is no life left in us. I, who am about to take my departure, would readily resign to any man who came to me all the worldly wisdom I am acquiring for human intercourse. Mustard after dinner !

I have no use for the blessings I am no longer able to turn to account. What is the use of knowledge to one who has no head left ? It is wrong and unkind of Fortune to offer us gifts which fill us with righteous anger that they failed us in their due season. Guide me no more, I can go no further.

Of all the qualities of an excellent character patience is enough for us.

Give the capacity of an excellent treble voice to a singer with rotten lungs, and eloquence to a hermit consigned to the deserts of Arabia !

It needs no art to fall ; the end is found of itself at the conclusion of every affair. My world is at an end, my form emptied ; I belong entirely to the past, and am bound to authorize it and conform my departure to it.

I mean this [by way of example], that the recent eclipse of ten days by the Pope [1] has so taken me aback, that I cannot quite become reconciled to it. I belong to the years in which we counted differently. A custom so ancient and time-honoured claims me and calls me back to it. I am constrained to be something of a heretic on that point, unable to tolerate any innovation even for the better. My imagination, in spite of my teeth, keeps thrusting me ten days forward or backward, and grumbling into my ears, ' This rule concerns those who are to come.'

Even if health, sweet as it is, happens to revisit me now and again, it is rather to give me cause for regret than possession of it ; I have now no place to harbour it. Time forsakes me, without which nothing can be possessed. O how little account I should make of those great elective dignities which I see in the world, and which are given only to men who are about to leave it, in which the chief consideration is not how fit they are to fulfil their duties but how short a time they will do so ! At their very entry others look to their exit.

In short, here I am in course of finishing this man, not remaking another. By long habit this form of mine has passed into substance, and Fortune into Nature.

I say then, that every one of us feeble creatures is excusable for regarding as his own that which is comprised under this measure. But beyond those limits too all is confusion ; it is the largest extent we can grant to our claims. The more we enlarge our needs and our possessions, the more do we expose ourselves to the blows of Fortune and adversity. The range of our desires ought to be circumscribed and restricted to a short limit of the nearest and most contiguous commodities ; and their course ought, moveover, to be directed not in a straight line that ends elsewhere, but in a circle, the two points of which, after a short circuit, meet and terminate in ourselves.

Actions which are performed without this reflexion, I mean near and essential reflexion, like those of the avaricious and ambitious and so many others who run straight ahead, whose course bears them ever forward, are erroneous and diseased actions.

[1] An allusion to the reform in the calendar made by Pope Gregory XIII in 1582.

Most of our professions are histrionic. *All the world's a stage*.[1] We must play our part as we should, but as the part of a borrowed personage. We must not make a reality out of a mask and outward appearance, nor of a strange person, our own. We cannot distinguish between the skin and the shirt. It is enough to paint [2] the face without painting the heart. I see some who transform and transubstantiate themselves into as many new shapes and new beings as the offices they take upon themselves ; who strut and swell to the very liver and bowels, and carry their dignity even to their closet. I could not teach them to distinguish between the bonnetings intended for their person and those intended for their office, or their retinue or their mule. *They are so wrapt up in their fortunes that they unlearn their nature* (Q. Curtius). They swell and puff up their souls and their natural speech to the height of their seat of authority.

The Mayor and Montaigne have always been two, very distinctly separated. Though we are lawyers or financiers we must not ignore the knavery there is in those callings. An honest man is not accountable for the vices or the follies of his profession, and therefore need not refuse to practise it. It is the custom of his country, and there is profit in it. We must live by the world and make the best of it, such as we find it. But the judgement of an Emperor ought to be above his imperial power, and should look upon and consider it as an extraneous accident ; and he himself ought to know how to enjoy a separate existence and reveal himself like any Jack or Peter, at least to himself.

I cannot pledge myself so deeply and so entirely. When my will has commanded me to take a side I am not so forcibly bound to it that my understanding is infected. In the present broils of our State my interests have not made me blind to the laudable qualities of our adversaries, nor the reprehensible qualities in the leaders of my own party. It is usual to worship everything on one's own side ; for my part I do not even pardon most of the things done on mine. A good work does not lose its charm for arguing against my cause.

[1] Mundus universus exercet histrioniam (Petronius).
[2] Literally ' whiten with flour ', after the manner of the stage Pierrots.

Except with regard to the knot of the controversy[1] I have kept myself in a state of equanimity and absolute indifference. *And beyond the requirements of war I bear no special hatred.* Which is a source of satisfaction to me, since I observe that most men sin in the opposite direction. *Let him who cannot appeal to reason appeal to the passions* (Cicero). Those who extend their anger and hatred beyond the dispute in question, as most people do, show that it is due to some other, some personal, reason ; just as, when a man has been cured of an ulcer, and the fever continues, it is clear that it must have another more hidden cause.

The fact is that they have no feeling against the cause in general, and in so far as it injures the interest of all and of the State. But they hate it only in so far as it galls them in their private interests. That is why they are stung to a particular passion, to a degree beyond justice and common sense. *They did not agree in blaming all things, but each carped at such as interested him personally* (Livy).

I would have the advantage on our side, but I am not beside myself with anger if it is not. I adhere firmly to the soundest of the parties, but I have no ambition to be specially remarked as an enemy of the others, and more hostile than is consistent with common sense.

I very strongly condemn this vicious form of reasoning : ' He is of the League, for he admires the charm of Monsieur de Guise ; He is astonished at the King of Navarre's activity, therefore he is a Huguenot ; He picks holes in the King's morals, so he must be a rebel at heart.'[2] And I did not even admit the authorities to be right in condemning a book, because the author classed a heretic among the best poets of this century.[3]

Dare we not say of a thief that his hair is nicely parted ? And because she is a prostitute, must she also be syphilitic ? Did they, in the wisest ages, revoke the proud title of Capitolinus, which they had previously given to Marcus Manlius, as the preserver of public religion and liberty ? Did they suppress the memory of his liberality and his feats of arms, and the military rewards granted to his

---

[1] The religious question.   [2] Montaigne was guilty of all three crimes.
[3] Montaigne evidently means the Papal authorities in Rome, who dragged him over the coals for having spoken so highly of a French poet who was not a Catholic.

valour, because he afterwards aspired to royalty, to the prejudice of his country's laws ?

Take a dislike to a barrister and to-morrow you will deny his eloquence. I have elsewhere touched upon the zeal which drives good people to similar faults. For my part I am quite able to say, ' He does this wickedly, and that virtuously.' So too, when prognostics are falsified and affairs turn out unluckily, they will have it that every one, in his own cause, is blind and dull-witted ; that our convictions and judgements should subserve, not the truth, but our plans and desires. I would rather err towards the other extreme ; so greatly do I fear to be misled by my desires. Besides, I am rather tenderly distrustful of the things I wish.

I have in my time been astounded to see with what wonderful and indiscriminating ease the people have allowed themselves to be led by the nose and manœuvred into believing and hoping whatever has pleased, and served the purpose of, their leaders, in spite of a hundred mistakes one on top of the other, despite dreams and phantasms. I am no longer astonished at those who were cozened by the tomfooleries of Apollonius [1] and Mahomet. Their sense and understanding are entirely drowned by their passions. Their judgement leaves them no choice but that which smiles upon them and flatters their cause.

I had observed this in a supreme degree in the first of our feverish factions. The other,[2] which has since been born in imitation of it, surpasses it. From which I conclude that it is an attitude inseparable from popular errors. When the first error has started on its course others follow, and they drive one another forward, like the waves following the wind. Whoever is able to gainsay them, and does not wander with the common herd, is not a member of the body.

But, indeed, we wrong the just side when we try to bolster it up with fraud. I have ever been against that practice. That is a remedy that is of no avail except for sick brains ;

---

[1] ' Apollonius of Tyana was born about the same time as Jesus Christ. His life is related in so fabulous a manner by his disciples that we are at a loss to discover whether he was a sage, an impostor, or a fanatic ' (Gibbon). Froude also gives a short account of him in his *Short Studies*.

[2] Respectively, the Protestants and the League.

for the healthy there are not only more honest but surer ways for keeping up our spirits and explaining away mishaps.

Heaven has not seen, and will not again see in the future, so serious a discord as that between Caesar and Pompey. Yet in those noble souls I observe, if I am not mistaken, great moderation in their dealings with one another. It was a rivalry in honour and power, which did not transport them to a blind and furious hatred, and was free from malice and detraction. In their sharpest encounters I can discover some remnant of respect and goodwill ; and so I conclude that, if it had been possible, each of them would have liked to effect his purpose without, rather than with, the downfall of his competitor.

How different is the case of Marius and Sylla ! Think it over !

We must not pursue our passions and interests so madly. As in my younger days I used to resist the progress of love which I felt to be gaining too rapidly upon me, and strove to prevent it becoming so pleasing as in the end to vanquish and hold me at its mercy ; so I do likewise on all other occasions whenever desire gets the better of my will. I lean to the opposite side of its inclination, as I see it plunging ahead and making itself drunk with its own wine. I avoid feeding its pleasure to such a degree that I cannot get the better of it without cruel loss.

The souls that, through their dullness, only half see things, enjoy this happiness, that noxious things are less hurtful to them ; it is a spiritual leprosy that has some semblance of health, and such health as Philosophy does not in any way despise. That is no reason, however, for calling it wisdom, as we often do. And so somebody, in ancient times, made sport of Diogenes who, in the depth of winter and stark naked, was hugging a snow-figure to test his endurance. Seeing him in this attitude the man said, ' Are you very cold now ? ' ' Not a bit,' replied Diogenes. ' Then why do you think it so difficult and so exemplary to do what you are doing ? '

To measure fortitude we must necessarily know suffering.

But as for those souls which are to meet with adversities and the outrages of Fortune in all their depth and sharpness, to feel all their weight and taste their natural bitterness, let them do their best to avoid piling up the causes, and to parry their advances.

What did King Cotys do ? He paid liberally for the beautiful and costly vessel that had been offered to him ; but seeing that it was particularly fragile he straightway broke it himself, to remove betimes so easy an occasion for anger against his servants. In like manner I have generally avoided having my affairs mixed up with others', and have not been anxious to have my estate adjoining those of my relations and others with whom I am to be linked in close friendship ; which usually gives rise to estrangement and disagreement.

I used to be fond of games of chance with cards and dice. I have long given them up for this sole reason that, however well I appeared to bear my losses, I could not help feeling inwardly annoyed.

A man of honour, who must take to heart a contradiction or an affront, who is not ready to take a foolish answer as payment and consolation for his loss, should avoid being mixed up with any dubious affair and any dispute that might lead to a quarrel.

I avoid any man of melancholy disposition and a surly temper as I would the plague ; and, unless forced by duty, I do not meddle with a subject that I cannot discuss disinterestedly and without excitement. *It is easier not to begin than to stop* (Seneca). The surest way then is to be prepared beforehand for every occasion.

I know well that some wise men have chosen another way and have not feared to clutch and come to grips with many subjects. Those men are confident in their strength, under which they take shelter in all kinds of adverse fortunes, making their power of endurance wrestle with disaster :

> Even as a rock
> That juts far out into the mighty main,
> Bare to the winds' brunt, a target for the sea,
> All stress, all menace both of sky and deep
> Outfaces, and itself remains unmoved. (VIRGIL.)

Let us not attempt to imitate these examples ; we should not succeed. They will steadfastly and resolutely, without any emotion, witness the destruction of their country, which once commanded and possessed all their affection. That is too difficult and rude a task for ordinary souls like

ours. Cato gave up to it the noblest life that ever was.
We other little men must fly the storm long before it
comes ; we must obey our apprehensions and not trust to
endurance, and dodge the blows we cannot parry.

Zeno, seeing Chremonides, a youth whom he loved,
approaching to sit beside him, immediately started up.
When Cleanthes asked him the reason he said, ' I have
heard that the doctors especially prescribe tranquillity, and
forbid excitement, for all kinds of risings.'

Socrates does not say, ' Do not surrender to the charms
of beauty ; resist it, do your best to oppose it. Fly from
it, he says, avoid either seeing or meeting it, as if it were
a powerful poison that darts and strikes from a distance.'
And his good disciple,[1] imagining or recounting, but I think
recounting rather than imagining, the rare perfections of
the great Cyrus, makes him distrustful of his power to
withstand the attractions of the divine beauty of that
illustrious Panthea, his captive, and charging another, who
had less liberty than he, to visit and guard her.

And the Holy Ghost in like manner : ' Lead us not into
temptation.' We do not pray that our reason may not be
combated and vanquished by lust, but that it shall not
even be put to the proof ; that we may not be brought
to a pass in which we have even to suffer the approaches,
the solicitations and temptations of sin. And we entreat
our Lord to keep our conscience at peace, fully and completely delivered from all dealings with evil.

Those who say that they have gained the mastery over
their passion for revenge, or some other kind of troublesome
passion, often tell the truth as things are, but not as they
were. They speak to us now that the causes of their error
have been developed and advanced by themselves. But
go further back ; recall those causes at their beginning ;
there you will take them unawares. Do they mean to
say that their sin is less for being of longer duration,
and that of a wrong beginning the sequel can be
right ?

Whoever desires the good of his country, as I do, without
fretting or pining, will be pained, but not stunned, to see
it threatened either with ruin or with a no less ruinous

_____
[1] Xenophon.

continuance. Poor vessel, that the waves, the winds, and
the pilot toss and worry with such contrary intention !

> Dragged in different ways
> By master, waves and winds. (BUCHANAN.)

He who does not gape after the favour of Princes, as after
a thing he cannot do without, is not greatly piqued by the
coolness of their reception and countenance, nor by the
inconstancy of their affections. He who does not brood
over his children or his honours with slavish fondness, will
manage to live comfortably after he has lost them.

He who does good chiefly for his own satisfaction will
not be much put out when men judge his actions contrary
to his merit. A quarter of an ounce of patience will be
a sufficient remedy against such troubles. I find that
recipe effectual, making up for the beginnings as cheaply
as I can ; and by its means I find I have escaped much
trouble and many difficulties. With very little effort I arrest
the first swing of my emotions, and abandon the subject which
begins to be troublesome, and before it carries me away.

He who does not arrest the start has no power to arrest
the course. He who cannot shut them out will not expel
them once they are in. He who cannot accomplish the
beginning will not accomplish the end. Nor will he resist
the fall who has not been able to resist the push. *For, once
severed from reason, the passions rush headlong ; human
frailty trusts in itself, heedless it ventures into the open sea,
and can find no harbour in which to anchor* (Cicero).

I feel betimes the low winds, forerunners of the storm,
rumbling and searching for an entry into me. *The soul is
shaken long before it is vanquished.*

> As rising winds that, in the forest caught,
> Murmur, and, rolling a dull roar along,
> Bode storm to sailors. (VIRGIL.)

How often have I done myself a very manifest injustice,
to avoid the danger of having a worse done me by the judges
after an age of vexations, of vile and dirty practices, more
hostile to my nature than fire and torments ! *We must shun
lawsuits by all legitimate, and even a little less than legitimate,
means. It is not only generous, but sometimes even profitable,
to yield a little of our right* (Cicero).

If we were really wise we should rejoice and boast, like

a certain young gentleman of very noble family, whom I one day heard, very naïvely and with great glee, telling everybody that his mother had lost her lawsuit, as she might have lost her cough, her fever, or some other thing very troublesome to keep. Even the favours which Fortune may have bestowed on me, through my being related to or friendly with people of supreme authority in such things, I have to the best of my powers carefully and conscientiously avoided employing to the prejudice of others ; and I have never rated my pretensions above their real value.

In short, I have laboured so hard that (may I say with the help of luck !) I am to this day virgin of lawsuits, though on many occasions I have been tempted to make use of the law, having very good rights on my side, if I had been inclined to give ear to the temptation ; and virgin of quarrels. I shall soon have spent a long life without having either given or received serious offence, and without ever hearing worse than my own name ; a rare grace of Heaven !

Our greatest disturbances have ridiculous springs and causes. How disastrous to our last Duke of Burgundy was a quarrel about a cartload of sheepskins ! [1] And was not the engraving of a seal the primary and principal cause of the most dreadful upheaval that this machine has ever suffered ? For Pompey and Caesar are only the offshoots and the sequel of the other two. And I have seen in my time the wisest heads in this realm meeting, with great ceremony and at great public expense, to discuss treaties and agreements which were meantime really and absolutely decided by the chattering ladies in a boudoir, and the whim of some little woman.

The poets very well understood this when they put Greece and Asia to fire and sword for an apple.[2]

Ask this man why he stakes his honour and life on his sword and dagger ; let him tell you where is the source of the quarrel ; he cannot do so without blushing, so frivolous is the occasion.

Before beginning a thing, only a little discretion is needed ; but once you are embarked, all the tackle is on

---

[1] A reference to the war between Charles the Bold and the Swiss in 1476. The next sentence refers to the civil war between Marius and Sylla.
[2] Allusion to the Judgement of Paris, which was the primary cause of the Trojan war.

the stretch. Greater, more difficult and important measures are needed.

How much easier it is not to enter in, than it is to come out again !

Now, our proceeding should be the opposite of that of the reed, which at its first springing sends up a long straight stem, but afterwards, as if it were weary and out of breath, forms frequent and thick knots, as it were so many pauses, which show that it has lost its first vigour and firmness. We must rather begin coolly and leisurely, and keep our breath and strenuous efforts for the stress and completion of the business.

We guide a business at the beginning, and hold it at our mercy ; but afterwards, when set going, it is the business that guides us and drags us along, and we have to follow.

Yet I do not mean to say that this plan of conduct has relieved me of all difficulty, and that I have not often been at pains to curb and bridle my passions. They are not always to be ruled according to the magnitude of the causes, and often enter into us violently and unexpectedly. In any case one may save and gain a great deal by it, except those who, in doing good, are not content with any gain, if there is no reputation to be made by it. For in truth such a result is only valued by each one in himself. You are better contented, but not more esteemed, for having reformed before joining in the dance, and before the matter was in sight. Yet not in this only, but in all other duties of life, the path of those who aim at honour is very different to that followed by those whose aim is order and reason.

I see men who rashly and furiously enter the lists, and slacken as they run. As Plutarch says that those who, owing to bashfulness, are weak and ready to grant whatever may be asked of them, and afterwards as ready to break their word and recant ; so he who enters lightly into a quarrel is apt to get out of it just as lightly. This same difficulty which keeps me from cutting in would spur me on when I was once in the swing and heated. It is a bad principle : when once in it, go on or die miserably.

' Undertake coldly ', said Bias, ' but pursue hotly.' For want of prudence, men are in danger of wanting heart, which is still less tolerable.

Most of the settlements of our quarrels nowadays are disgraceful and full of deceit ; we only seek to save appearances, and at the same time we betray and disown our true intentions. We plaster the fact ; we know how and with what meaning we have declared it, and those who are present know it, as well as our friends whom we wanted to make aware of our advantage. At the expense of our sincerity and honour and courage we disown our intention and seek to hide our heads in falsehood in order to come to an agreement. We give ourselves the lie to save a lie we have given.

You must not consider whether your action and your word may admit of another interpretation ; you must henceforth uphold your true and sincere interpretation, whatever it may cost you. Your virtue and your conscience are appealed to ; they are not things to be hidden behind a mask. Let us leave those mean shifts and expedients to the chicanery of the Law Courts.

The excuses and reparations I see made every day to purge away the want of judgement appear to me more hateful than the want of judgement itself. It would be better to offend your adversary a second time than to offend yourself by giving him such reparation. You defied him when excited and angry, and you are about to appease and flatter him in your cooler and better mood ; thus you give way to him more than you had advanced.

Nothing a gentleman can say appears to me so wicked as his unsaying of it appears discreditable to him, when it is a recantation that is wrested from him by authority ; since obstinacy is more excusable in him than pusillanimity.

I find it as easy to avoid passions as I find it difficult to moderate them. *They are more easily rooted out of the soul than held in check.* If a man cannot attain that noble impassibility of the Stoics let him take refuge in the bosom of this vulgar callousness of mine. What those men did through virtue I bring myself to do by temperament. The middle region harbours storms ; the two extremes, those of the philosophers and rustics, concur in tranquillity and happiness :

> Happy was he whose wit availed to grasp
> The origin of things, who trampled low
> The thronging horrors of unpitying Fate,
> And roarings of unsated Acheron !
> Blest too is he who knows the rural Gods,
> Pan and grey-haired Sylvanus and the Nymphs,
> Sweet sisters !　(VIRGIL.)

All things are weak and tender at their birth. Wherefore we should have our eyes open to the beginnings of a thing. For, as in its littleness we can discover no danger, so when it is grown it is too late to discover the remedy. I might have found it harder to digest a million troubles that I should have encountered every day in an ambitious career, than to arrest the natural inclination which bore me to it :

> I shrink with dread
> From raising too conspicuously my head. (Horace.)

All public actions are liable to be interpreted uncertainly and differently, for there are too many heads to judge them. Some say of this civic function of mine (and I am glad to say a few words about it, not that it is worth mentioning, but to serve as an example of my conduct in such matters), that I behaved as one who is not easily enough stirred to action and shows too languid an interest ; and they were by no means far wrong. I endeavour to keep my soul and my thoughts at rest. *At all times calm by nature, and more so as the result of age* (Q. Cicero). And if at times they break out into a rude and cutting attack it is, indeed, against my will.

Yet from this natural listlessness it would be wrong to infer any proof of incapacity (for lack of diligence and lack of sense are two different things), and still less any want of recognition or ingratitude towards those citizens, who did their very utmost to testify their goodwill to me both before and after they had come to know me, and did me much more honour by my re-election [1] than by their first conferring that office upon me. I wish them all possible good, and, indeed, if opportunities had offered I should have spared no pains to be serviceable to them. I have been as active in serving them as on my own behalf. They are good people, warlike and generous, therefore amenable to obedience and discipline, and, if well guided, capable of being made good use of.

They also say that my term of office passed without leaving any trace or mark. That is good ! They accuse me of inaction at a time when almost everybody else was convicted of doing too much. I have an impatient activity when

---

[1] On the expiration of his first term of office, Montaigne was re-elected Mayor in 1583.

my will carries me along. But that kind of eagerness is hostile to perseverance. If a man would expect a service of me in conformity with my character let him employ me in a business that needs vigour and freedom, where a direct, short, and even hazardous conduct is necessary ; there I might do something. If it is to be a lengthy business, needing cunning, labour, artifice, and tortuous methods, he would do better to apply to some other.

Not all important offices are difficult. I was prepared to be a little more energetic if there had been great need of it. For it is in my power to do something more than I do, or than I care to do. So far as I know I never neglected to move in a matter when duty really required it of me. I readily neglected those things in which ambition mingles with, and hides under the name of, duty. Those are the things that most often fill the eyes and ears of people, and satisfy them. Not the thing but the semblance pays them. If they hear no noise they think we are asleep.

My humour is the opposite of a noisy humour. I could easily check a disturbance without being disturbed, and punish a piece of irregularity without changing countenance. Do I stand in need of anger and heat ? I borrow it and put it on like a mask. My manners are blunt, rather tame than fierce. I do not condemn a magistrate when he goes to sleep, provided that those under his charge sleep with him. The laws sleep too. For my part I commend a gliding life, without bustle or glitter, *neither abject and submissive, nor puffed up* (Cicero). My fortune will have it so. I was born of a family which has lived quietly, without brilliance and without bustle, and from all times particularly ambitious of a character for probity.

The men of our day are so bred up in excitement and ostentation that goodness, moderation, equability, steadiness and such unobtrusive and obscure qualities are no more appreciated. Uneven bodies make themselves felt ; the smooth and polished may be handled without feeling them. Sickness is felt ; health, little or not at all, nor are the things which relieve us, compared with those which grieve us.

We work for our own reputation and private advantage, not for the public weal, when we reserve for the public square what we can do in the Council-chamber, and in the full glare of noonday what we might have done the night before ; and when we are jealous of doing ourselves what our colleague can do equally well. So some of the surgeons in Greece were wont to perform the operations of their art on platforms in sight of the passers-by, to attract more custom and patients. They imagine that good rules cannot be heard except to the blare of trumpets.

Ambition is not a sin for little fellows, and for such endeavours as ours. Some one said to Alexander, ' Your father will leave you a great empire, easy to govern and peaceful.' The boy was envious of his father's victories, and of the justice of his rule. He would not have wished to possess the whole universe in peace and inactivity.

Alcibiades, in Plato's Dialogue, prefers to die young, handsome, rich, noble, and eminently learned, rather than not to advance beyond his present condition.

This malady is perhaps excusable in so strong and full a soul. When these puny and dwarfed little souls flatter themselves, baboonlike, and think to spread their name for having delivered a correct judgement or continued to change the guards at the city gates, the more they hope to raise their heads the more do they show their backsides. These petty services have neither body nor life ; they vanish in the first telling, and are only carried from one street corner to another. Tell it boldly to your son and your valet, like that ancient who, having no other auditor of his praises and witness of his valour, boasted to his housemaid, exclaiming, ' O Perrette, what a brave and excellent man is your master ! ' [1] Tell yourself of it, for want of a better, like a councillor of my acquaintance who, having disgorged a boatload of paragraphs, with as much effort as inappropriateness, retired from the Council-chamber to the Palace urinal, and was heard mumbling very devoutly between his teeth, *Not unto us, O Lord, not unto us, but unto thy name give glory* (Psalms). If he cannot get it out of another, let him pay himself out of his own purse.

Fame does not prostitute herself so cheaply. The rare and exemplary deeds which deserve her would not tolerate the company of that numberless crowd of little everyday actions. The marble will exalt your titles as much as you

[1] ' Dionysia, see how I am no longer proud and vainglorious ! ' Plutarch, according to Amyot.

please for having patched up a bit of old wall or cleaned out a public gutter ; but men who have any sense will not. Renown does not follow all good actions unless they are accompanied by rarity and difficulty. Nay, according to the Stoics esteem is not even due to every action born of virtue ; and they will not admit that we should even approve a man who, from temperance, abstains from a blear-eyed old woman.

Those who have known the admirable qualities of Scipio Africanus deny him the honour that Panaetius gives him of having kept his hands off money gifts, since it was an honour that he shared with all his age.

We have the pleasures suitable to our lot ; let us not usurp those of greatness. Ours are more natural, and the more substantial and sure for being more humble. Since we do not refuse ambition for conscience' sake let us at least refuse it for ambition's sake. Let us despise that low and beggarly craving after honour and renown that makes us cringe for it to all sorts of people. *What praise is that which is to be sought in the market-place* (Cicero), by abject means and at any price however degrading ? It is dishonour to be so honoured.

Let us learn not to be more greedy than we are deserving of fame. To be puffed up with every useful and harmless deed is good enough for people with whom such deeds are uncommon and extraordinary ; they will value them at the price they cost them.

According as a good deed is more brilliant I discount its goodness, since I suspect that it has been performed for its brilliance rather than for its goodness ; displayed is half sold. Those works are more graceful which slip from the hands of the workman, heedlessly and noiselessly, and which are afterwards picked up by some honest man and rescued from obscurity, to be thrust into the light for their own sake. *To me all things appear more praiseworthy that are done without vainglory and unwitnessed by the people* (Cicero), said the most vainglorious man in the world.

I had but to continue and conserve, which are noiseless actions, passing unperceived. Innovation makes a great show but it is out of the question in these days when we are hard pressed and when innovation is just what we have to stand up against.

Abstention from doing is often as noble as doing, but is less exposed to the light of day ; and the little good there is in me lies almost entirely in that direction.

In short, in my term of office as Mayor, opportunities were in keeping with my disposition, for which I am very thankful to them. Is there any one who wishes to be ill that he may see his physician at work, and would not a physician deserve corporal punishment who wished the plague upon us that he might practise his art ? I never shared that wicked and common enough feeling that would desire a disturbed and diseased state of affairs in the city, that my administration might be magnified and honoured ; I heartily lent a shoulder to relieving and lightening them.

If any man refuses to give me credit for the order, the even and silent tranquillity which accompanied my administration, he cannot at least deprive me of the share that belongs to me by right of my good fortune. And I am so built that I would as soon be lucky as wise, and as soon owe my successes purely to the grace of God as to the intervention of my action.

I had explained elaborately enough to the world my unfitness for such public duties. There is something in me worse than my unfitness, which is that I hardly regret it, and hardly try to cure it, in view of the course of life I have mapped out for myself. I did not satisfy myself any more than I did others in this business ; but I almost succeeded as far as I had promised myself, and greatly exceeded the promises I had given to those with whom I had to deal. For my promises are usually of such a nature that I can keep them better than I expected, and perform more than I promise.

I am sure that I left no cause for offence or hatred behind me. As for leaving regret and desire, at the very least I know well that I did not greatly aspire to it :

Would'st thou have me put faith in such a monster,
Mark not the sea's smooth face and tranquil waves ? (VIRGIL.)

CHAPTER 11

OF CRIPPLES

TWO or three years ago the year was shortened by ten days in France. How many changes were expected to follow this reform ! It was literally moving heaven and earth at the same time. And yet nothing has budged from its place : my neighbours find the right moment for sowing and reaping, for their business opportunities, their harmful and lucky days, at the very same times that had been assigned to them from time immemorial. We were not sensible of any error in our habits, nor are we now sensible of any improvement. So much uncertainty is there in all things ; so gross, obscure, and obtuse is our perception !

They say that this correction might have been carried out in a less inconvenient way by following the example of Augustus and leaving out, for several years, the bissextus, which in any case is an awkward and troublesome day, until we had made a full settlement of the debt (which has not even been done by this correction, for we still remain a few days in arrears). And so by the same means we could provide for the future by arranging that after the revolution of so many years that supernumerary day might be eclipsed for good ; then our miscalculation would henceforth not exceed twenty-four hours.

We have no other computation of time but by years. The world has employed it so many centuries, and yet it is a measure we have not yet succeeded in fixing, and of such a nature that we are every day in doubt what form other nations have variously given to it, and what used to be their custom.

What if it be true, as some say, that the heavens, as they grow older, contract and come nearer to us, throwing us into an uncertainty even of hours and days, and of months, since Plutarch says that even in his time Astrology had not been able to determine the motion of the moon ? We are in a pretty way to keep a record of past events !

I was just ruminating, as I often do, on this theme, What a free and vague instrument is the human reason ! I generally observe that, when a matter is set before them, men are more ready to waste their time in seeking the reason of it than in seeking the truth of it. They leave the things to take care of themselves and trifle over the causes. Amusing triflers ! [1]

The knowledge of causes concerns only him who has the guidance of things, not us who only have to suffer them, and have the full and absolute use of them according to our nature, without penetrating into their origin and essence. And wine is not any more agreeable to the man who knows its primary properties. On the contrary ; both body and soul disturb and sophisticate their right to enjoy the world by bringing in the pretensions of science. [We are concerned with effects, not at all with means.] To determine and to know is the part of the ruler and master, as well as to give ; that of the inferior, the subject, the learner, is to enjoy and accept.

Let us return to our habit. They stride over facts, but they diligently investigate their consequences. They usually begin thus, ' How can that be ? ' They should say, ' But is it so ? ' Our reason is capable of furnishing a hundred other worlds and discovering their beginnings and structure. It lacks neither matter nor foundation. Let it run on. It will build as well on the void as on the full, out of nothingness as out of matter :

> Fit but to give solidity to smoke. (PERSIUS.)

I find that in almost every case we might say, ' That is not so.' And I should often make use of that reply, but I dare not ; for people will exclaim that that is an attempt to avoid discussion, the result of mental feebleness and ignorance. And I am generally reduced to join the company in juggling with words and discussing trivial subjects and tales which I entirely disbelieve. Besides that it is certainly rather rude and aggressive to flatly deny a stated fact. And few men will resist the temptation, especially when they find a difficulty in persuading, to declare that they have seen the thing, or to cite witnesses whose authority will put a stopper on our contradiction.

In this way we know the foundations and causes of a thousand things that never were ; and the world skirmishes

[1] *Ils laissent là les choses et s'amusent à traiter les causes. Plaisants causeurs !* Montaigne's fondness for playing on words sometimes leaves the translator stranded.

with a thousand questions of which both the *pros* and the *cons* are false. *The false is so much akin to the true that a wise man should not trust himself in so dangerous a position* (Cicero).

Truth and falsehood are alike in face ; they walk and carry themselves alike, and they taste alike ; to us they appear the same. It seems to me that we are not only loosely on our guard against deception but that we court and invite its trammels. We love to embroil ourselves in unreality, as being conformable to our being.

I have witnessed the birth of many miracles in my time. Even though they are smothered as soon as born we are none the less able to foresee the course they would have taken if they had lived to their full age. For it is only a matter of finding the end of the string, then we may unravel as much as we please. And the distance is greater from nothing to the smallest thing in the world than from this to the greatest.

Now the first who are imbued with the strangeness of the thing, when they begin to circulate their story, find, from the opposition they meet with, where the difficulty of persuasion lies, and proceed to caulk up that place with some spurious piece. Besides that, *through the appetite innate in man industriously to feed rumours* (Livy), it naturally goes against our conscience to give back what has been lent to us without a little interest, and some addition of our own. The private error first creates the public error, and in its turn the public error afterwards creates the private error.

Thus it comes about that this whole edifice goes on being built up and shaped by one hand after another in such a way that the remotest witness knows more about it than the nearest, and the last informed believes it more firmly than the first. It is a natural progression. For whoever believes a thing thinks it a work of kindness to persuade another to believe it ; and for that purpose he is not afraid to add out of his own invention as much as he sees to be necessary to his tale to meet the resistance or the lack of imagination he expects in others.

I myself, though I am singularly conscientious about lying, and am not particularly anxious to give credibility and authority to what I say, observe none the less that, when I become excited over some matter in hand, either through another's opposition or my own heat in the telling, I magnify and inflate my theme by voice and gesture, by the force and energy of words, as well as by extension and amplification, not without prejudice to the naked truth. On the understanding however that, for the first who pulls me up and asks for the plain and unvarnished truth, I straightway drop my ardour and give it to him without exaggeration, without bombast or padding. A lively and noisy style of speaking, as mine is usually, is apt to run into hyperbole.

There is nothing to which men are ordinarily more prone than to push their beliefs ; when ordinary means fail us, we add command, violence, fire, and sword. It is a misfortune to have come to such a pass that the best touchstone of truth is the multitude of believers, in a crowd where the fools so much outnumber the wise. *As if there were anything so common in the world as error !* (Cicero.) *A fine evidence of sanity is the multitude of the insane !* (St. Augustine.)

It is a difficult thing to set up a decided judgement in the face of commonly prevailing opinions. The first persuasion, taken from the subject itself, seizes the simple ; from them it spreads to the clever, under authority of the number and antiquity of the testimonies. For my part, in a matter on which I would not believe one, I would not believe a hundred and one. I do not judge opinions by age.

It is not long since one of our Princes, in whom the gout had spoiled a fine nature and a cheerful disposition, allowed himself to be so strongly persuaded, on the strength of a report which had reached him of the marvellous operations of a priest who, by means of words and gestures, cured all maladies, that he made a long journey to see him, and, by the power of his imagination, so persuaded his legs that he sent them to sleep for some hours, and obtained from them the service they had long forgotten.

If Fortune had allowed five or six such incidents to accumulate, they were capable of making this miracle a natural thing. They afterwards found so much simplicity and so little cunning in the architect of those works, that he was thought too contemptible to be punished.[1] As

[1] He was probably in danger of being accused of witchcraft.

would be thought of most such things, if we traced them back to their home. *We wonder at the things that deceive us by their distance* (Seneca). So our sight often presents us strange phenomena at a distance, which vanish as they come nearer. *Rumour is never quite cleared up* (Q. Curtius).

It is wonderful from what unreal beginnings and trifling causes such widespread ideas usually proceed ! That alone makes investigation difficult. For whilst we seek out solid and weighty causes and purposes, worthy of so great a fame, we miss the real ones ; they escape our view by reason of their littleness. And, indeed, such researches need a very wise, diligent and keen inquirer, one who is impartial and unprejudiced.

To this hour all those miracles and strange phenomena have hidden from me. I have seen no more evident monstrosity and miracle in the world than myself. By use and time one becomes familiar with all things strange ; but the more I associate with and know myself the more does my deformity astonish me and the less do I understand myself.

It is a privilege chiefly reserved to chance to bring such incidents to light and into repute. As I was passing, the day before yesterday, through a village about two leagues from my house, I found the place still quite warm with a miracle that had lately failed of success, which had kept the neighbourhood talking for several months and was beginning to excite the adjoining provinces ; all sorts of people were flocking thither in great numbers. A young fellow of the place had one night amused himself by counterfeiting the voice of a spirit in his own house, with no more thought or aim than to enjoy his joke for the moment. Having succeeded rather better than he expected he took a girl of the village, a very stupid and silly lass, into partnership to help him extend his operations. In the end there were three of them, all of the same age and equally intelligent ; and after preaching to their families they preached to the public, hiding under the church-altar, speaking only at night, and forbidding any light to be brought.

From words aiming at the conversion of the world and threatening a day of judgement (for those are the subjects under whose authority and reverence imposture most easily lurks) they proceeded to apparitions and actions, more silly, ridiculous and clumsy almost than anything you could imagine in the playing of children. Yet if Fortune had favoured them ever so little who knows how far their foolery would have gone.

These poor devils are now in prison, and will probably bear the penalty for the foolishness of the community ; and who knows but some judge will take vengeance on them for his own folly ?

Here the imposture, which has been discovered, is clearly seen ; but in many things of a like nature, which have escaped our knowledge, it seems to me that we must suspend our judgement before either rejecting or accepting.

Many of the delusions of the world, or to speak more boldly, all the delusions in the world, are begotten of our being taught to be afraid of professing our ignorance, and thinking ourselves bound to accept everything we cannot refute. We speak of all things in an authoritative and dogmatic style. It was distinctive of the Roman style that even that which a witness deposed to having seen with his own eyes, and what a judge decided of his most certain knowledge, was drawn up in this form of speech : ' It seems to me.' It makes me hate accepting things that are probable when they are held up before me as infallibly true. I prefer these words which tone down and modify the hastiness of our propositions : ' Perhaps, In some sort, Some, They say, I think,' and the like. And if I had had to train children I should have so accustomed them to adopt this inquiring, doubting mode of reply : ' What does that mean ? I do not understand ; It might be so ; Is that true ? ' that they would rather have kept up the appearance of learners at the age of sixty than put on the airs of a learned doctor at ten, as they do.

Whoever will be cured of ignorance, let him confess it.

Iris is the daughter of Thaumas.[1] Wonder is the foundation of all philosophy ; research, the progress ; ignorance, the end. There is, by heavens, a strong and generous kind of ignorance that yields nothing, for honour and courage, to knowledge : an ignorance to conceive which needs no less knowledge than to conceive knowledge.

In my younger days I read of a trial which Corras, a

[1] i. e., the Rainbow is the daughter of Wonder. ' For she is so wonderfully beautiful, that she is rightly said to be the daughter of Thaumas.' (Cicero.)

Counsellor of Toulouse, had printed, concerning a strange incident, in which two men personated one another. I remember (and that is all I remember) that he seemed to me to have made out the imposture of the man he judged to be guilty, so marvellous and so far surpassing all our knowledge and his, who was judge, that I thought it was a very rash sentence that condemned him to be hanged. Let us accept some form of sentence which says, ' The Court understands nothing of the matter ; ' more freely and ingenuously than the Areopagites did who, finding themselves perplexed by a case they could not unravel, ordered the parties to appear again after a hundred years.

The witches of my neighbourhood are in danger of their lives when any one brings fresh witness to bear to the reality of their visions. To reconcile the examples which Holy Writ gives us of such things, most certain and irrefutable examples, and to bring them into comparison with those that happen in modern times, since we can see neither the causes of them nor the means by which they took place, needs a greater ingenuity than ours. That almighty witness is perhaps alone able to say to us, ' This is a miracle, and that ; but not this other.' God must be believed ; that is, indeed, very reasonable. Not however one of ourselves, who is amazed at his own telling (and he must necessarily be amazed, if he is not out of his wits), whether he is denouncing another or witnessing against himself.

I am dull-witted, and rather stick to what is substantial and probable, avoiding the reproaches of the ancients : *Men bring a stronger faith to the things they do not understand* (Anon.). *By a mental twist we are more ready to believe what is obscure* (Tacitus). I see, indeed, that people get angry ; and I am forbidden to doubt upon pain of execrable punishment : [1] a new kind of persuasion !

Thank God I am not to be cuffed into believing. Let them rail at those who condemn their opinions as false ; I only condemn them for being rash and hard to believe,

---

[1] This may be aimed at Jean Bodin (for whom, by the way, Montaigne had great admiration) who, in his *Démonomanie* (1580), having proved the existence of sorcerers from the Bible, called down the utmost rigours of the law, not only upon those who practised witchcraft, but upon those who disbelieved in it. Montaigne had the courage of his opinions.

and am quite as ready as they to condemn those who affirm the opposite, if not so imperiously. *Let it be said that they appear likely; only let them not be affirmed positively* (Cicero).

The man who tries to establish his arguments by domineering bluster shows that his reasoning is weak. In a wordy and scholastic altercation they may appear to be as much in the right as their contradictors; but in the actual conclusions they draw the latter have greatly the advantage.

When it is a question of killing people a clear and shining light is needed; and our life is too real and essential to warrant these supernatural and fantastic chances. As to drugs and poisons, I leave them out of my reckoning; they are homicidal, and of the worst kind. However, even in this matter they say we must not always attach too much weight to the confessions of those people against themselves, for they have sometimes been known to accuse themselves of having killed persons who turned out to be alive and in good health.

In regard to those other extravagant accusations I should be inclined to say that it is as much as we can do to believe a man, however high he may stand in our estimation, on human matters; in matters that are beyond his conception and of a supernatural kind, we should believe him only when he has supernatural sanction and approval. This privilege that God has been pleased to give to some of our testimonies ought not to be cheapened and lightly communicated.

My ears are assailed by a thousand tales such as these: ' Three saw him on such and such a day in the Levant, three saw him next day in the West, at such and such a time, in such and such a place, and dressed in such and such a way.' To tell the truth I would not believe my own eyes in such a case. How much more natural and likely it seems to me that two men are lying than that a man could travel with the wind in twelve hours from the East to the West! How much more natural that our judgement should be misled by the flightiness of our disordered mind, than that one of our kind, in flesh and bones, should be borne away by a strange spirit up the chimney on a broomstick.

Let us not look for outside and strange delusions, when

we are perpetually disturbed by our own home delusions. I think we may be pardoned for disbelieving in a prodigy, at least as long as we are able to turn down and avoid the supernatural explanation. And I agree with Saint Augustine when he says ' That it is better to lean towards doubt than towards assurance, in matters hard to prove and dangerous to believe.'

Some years ago I was passing through the territory of a ruling Prince, who, as a favour to me and to beat down my incredulity, graciously allowed me to see, in his presence and in a private place, ten or a dozen prisoners of that kind,[1] and among others an old woman, a regular witch in ugliness and deformity, whose reputation in that profession was of long standing. I saw both proofs and free confessions, and some hardly perceptible mark or other [2] on that miserable old creature. I questioned and talked as much as I pleased, giving the soundest attention I could to their replies ; and I am not the man to allow my judgement to be captivated by preconceived ideas. In short and in all conscience I should rather have prescribed them hellebore [3] than hemlock. *With them it seemed to be a case of madness rather than crime* (Livy). Justice has its corrections proper for such maladies.

With regard to the objections and arguments which honest men have raised up against me, both on this subject and often on others, I have not heard any that could put me to silence, and that do not always admit of a more likely solution than their conclusions. Very true it is that the proofs and reasons that are founded on experience and fact I do not attempt to unravel ; they have in fact no end, and I often cut them as Alexander did his knot.[4] After all it is rating one's conjectures at a very high price to roast a man alive on the strength of them.

Among divers other examples it is related by Prestantius of his father that, having fallen into a coma deeper and heavier than an ordinary sleep, he imagined he was a mare, and was being used by some soldiers as a pack-horse ; and what he imagined, he was. If the sorcerers dream in this

[1] Persons, probably women for the most part, accused of witchcraft.
[2] Witches were supposed to have some mark or stigma on their bodies, imprinted by the Devil. [3] Hellebore was supposed to cure insanity.
[4] The Gordian knot, tied by the Phrygian King Gordius. The oracle declared that the man who untied it should rule all Asia.

material way ; if dreams can thus sometimes assume a body and become realities, still I cannot believe that our will should be accountable to justice.

This I say, neither as a judge nor as an adviser of kings, of being which I esteem myself very far from worthy, but as a man of the common sort, naturally pledged to obey common sense, both in words and deeds. If any man should take my idle talk seriously and act upon it to the prejudice of the pettiest law, belief or custom of his village, he might get himself into trouble, and me just us much. For in what I say I guarantee no other certainty, except that that is what I had in my mind at the time ; a turbulent and vacillating mind !

When I speak of all kinds of things it is by way of chat, and by no means to impart information. *And I am not ashamed, as they are, to confess ignorance of what I do not know* (Cicero). I should not speak so boldly if it were likely that people would follow my advice ; and this was the answer I gave to a great man who complained that my preachings were too harsh and arbitrary : ' Seeing you bent and prepared to go in one direction, I propose to you the other, with all the diligence and care I am capable of, to enlighten your judgement, not to force it. God holds your heart in his hands, and he will provide you with the means of choosing. I am not so presumptuous as even to wish that my opinions should turn the scale in a matter of such importance ; I was not fated to direct them to such high and influential decisions.'

Truly, I have not only a great many propensities, but also enough opinions, which I would gladly make my son dislike, if I had a son. What if the truest opinions are not always the most suitable to man ; so untamed is his disposition !

Apropos, or malapropos, it matters not which, it is a common proverb in Italy that he does not know Venus in her perfect sweetness who has not lain with the cripple. Chance or some particular incident has long ago put this saying into the mouths of the people ; and it applies to males as well as females. For the Queen of the Amazons replied to the Scythian who invited her love, ' *The lame do it best* ' (Greek proverb). In that feminine State, to escape the domination of the males, they used to cripple them in their earliest childhood ; arms, legs, and other parts which gave them an advantage, were lamed, and the men were only used for the purpose for which we use the women over here.

I might have said that the disjointed motions of the cripple add some new kind of pleasure to the business, and a certain agreeable titillation to those who try it. But I have lately learned that the old Philosophy had even decided the question. It says that, as the legs and thighs of the lame woman do not, by reason of their imperfection, receive their due aliment, it follows that the genital parts, which lie above, are fuller, better nourished and more vigorous. Or perhaps that, as this defect prevents them taking exercise, those who are tainted with it do not waste so much strength and come fresher to the sports of Venus. Which is also the reason why the Greeks denounced the women-weavers as being hotter than others, by reason of their sedentary occupations which they perform without much bodily exercise. What can we not prove by arguing at this rate ? Of the latter I might also say that the tremor which their work imparts to them, while thus seated, arouses and excites their feelings, as the shaking and jolting of their coaches does the ladies.

Do not these examples serve to make good what I said at the beginning : That our reasonings often anticipate the fact, and extend their jurisdiction so infinitely far that they judge and meddle even with things that have no substance and no existence ? Besides the versatility of our invention in forging reasons for all sorts of delusions, our imagination is equally ready to take false impressions from very trifling outward signs. For example, on the mere authority of the ancient and general use of that proverb, I once made myself believe that I received more pleasure from a woman because she was not straight, and accordingly put down that deformity among the number of her charms.

Torquato Tasso, in the comparison he draws between France and Italy, says he observed that we have more slender legs than the Italian gentlemen, and attributes this to the fact that we are continually on horseback. From the same fact Suetonius draws quite the opposite conclusion ; for he says, on the contrary, that Germanicus' legs became thicker through continual exercise of that nature.[1]

---

[1] Which Holland, in a note to his translation of Suetonius's *Life of*

Nothing is so supple and erratic as our understanding ; it is the shoe of Theramenes,[1] fitting both feet. And it is double and diverse ; and the matters are double and diverse. ' Give me a silver drachma,' said a Cynical philosopher to Antigonus. ' That is not a kingly gift,' he replied. ' Then give me a talent.' ' That is not a gift for a Cynic.'

> Or whether the heat unlocks
> New passages and secret pores, whereby
> Their life-juice to the tender blades may win ;
> Or that it hardens more and helps to bind
> The gaping veins, lest penetrating showers,
> Or fierce sun's ravening might, or searching blast
> Of the keen North should sear them.[2]

Every medal has its reverse (Italian proverb). That is why Clitomachus said of old that Carneades had exceeded the labours of Hercules, in that he had eradicated assent, that is to say, opinionativeness and rashness in forming judgements, out of men's minds. This so vigorous idea of Carneades was, in my opinion, suggested by the impudence of those men who in olden times professed to know, and by their inordinate overweeningness.

Aesop was exhibited for sale with two other slaves. A buyer asked the first of them what he could do ; and he, to enhance his price, promised mountains and marvels, saying he could do this and that and the other. The second promised as much, and more. When it came to Aesop's turn to answer what he could do he replied : ' Nothing, for these two have forestalled me, and can do everything.'

So it happened in the school of Philosophy : the arrogance of those who attributed to the human mind the capacity to know all things gave rise in others, through spite and emulation, to the belief that it is capable of nothing. The one side go to the same extreme of ignorance as the other of knowledge ; so making it undeniable that man is immoderate in all things, and can never stop but of necessity and through his inability to proceed further.

Caligula (1606), explains as follows : ' For they used then no stirrops, therefore the bloud and humours wold descend to the legges.'

[1] According to Plutarch, Theramenes was nicknamed *Kothornos* or ' the Buskin ' on account of his liability to change sides ; the buskin being a boot that would fit either foot.

[2] Virgil's reasons for setting fire to the barren fields and burning the stubble ; see *Georgics*, I. 89.

CHAPTER 12

OF PHYSIOGNOMY

ALMOST all the opinions we hold are taken on authority and trust. There is no harm done ; we could not make a worse choice than our own in so feeble an age. The sayings of Socrates, as reflected in the works which his friends [1] have handed down to us, gain our approval only out of respect to the universal approval that has been accorded to them, not as the result of our own knowledge. They are not in accordance with our way of thinking. If at this moment anything of the same kind should appear there are few men who could appreciate it.

We can perceive no beauties that are not emphasized, puffed out and inflated by artificial means. Those which glide in their native purity and simplicity easily escape so gross a sight as ours. It is a delicate and hidden beauty ; it needs a clear and well-purged sight to discover their hidden light.

Is not simplicity, as we conceive it, germane to silliness, and an object of scorn ? Socrates makes his mind move with a natural and familiar motion. A peasant says this, a woman says that. He never speaks but of charioteers, joiners, cobblers and masons. His inductions and similes are drawn from the most common and best-known activities of men ; everybody understands him. Under so humble a form we should never have recognized the nobility and splendour of his admirable ideas ; we who think all ideas mean and shallow that are not set off by learning, and can perceive no riches but in pomp and show. This world of ours is only formed for ostentation ; men only puff themselves up with wind, and move by leaps and bounds, like balloons.

Socrates' purpose was not vague and fanciful ; his aim was to furnish us with things and precepts that are really and more directly serviceable to life,

> Observe due measure, keep one's end in view,
> And ever follow Nature's course. (LUCAN.)

He was besides always one and the same, and raised him-

[1] Plato and Xenophon.

self not by fits and starts, but by his natural temperament, to the highest pitch of vigour. Or, to speak more correctly, he raised nothing, but rather brought down, reduced and subjected vigour to his natural and original pitch, as well as all asperities and difficulties. For, as regards Cato, we see very clearly that he goes a strained pace, far beyond the ordinary ; in the brave exploits of his life, and in his death, we always feel that he is riding the high horse. The other skims the ground, and, at a gentle and ordinary pace, treats of the most useful matters ; and, both in the face of death and over the thorniest obstacles that may come in his way, follows the ordinary course of human life.

It has turned out fortunate that the man most worthy to be known, and to be offered to the world as an example, is the man of whom we have most certain knowledge. He has had a clear light thrown upon him by the most clear-sighted men that ever lived ; the testimonies we have of him are admirable for fidelity and fullness.

It is a great thing to have been able to put such order into ideas as pure as those of a child that, without altering or stretching them, he produced from them the finest results of our mind. The mind he shows us is neither exalted nor richly furnished, only healthy, but assuredly with a health that is very brisk and sound. With those common and natural resources, with those ordinary and everyday ideas, without being animated or excited, he erected not only the best regulated, but the most sublime and vigorous set of beliefs, actions and morals that ever were.

It was he who brought human Wisdom down again from heaven, where she was wasting her time, and restored her to man, with whom her most normal and most laborious and most useful business lies.

Hear him pleading his causes before his judges. See with what reasons he rouses his courage in the hazards of war ; with what arguments he fortifies his patience in the face of calumnies, tyranny, death and against his wife's temper. There is nothing borrowed from art and science ; the simplest may there discover their own means and strength ; it is not possible to mount higher and descend lower. He has done human nature a great kindness by showing how much it can do of itself.

We are, every one of us, richer than we think, but we are

trained to borrow and beg ; we are accustomed to make
more use of what is another's than of our own. Man can
never stop and be satisfied with the needful ; of pleasure,
wealth, power, he grasps at more than he can hold ; his
greed is not capable of being moderated.

I have observed that he is the same in his curiosity to
know ; he cuts out much more work for himself than he can
do, and much more than he needs to do, imagining that the
utility of knowledge extends as far as its matter. *In learning, as in all things else, we observe no moderation* (Seneca).
And Tacitus is right in commending the mother of Agricola
for curbing in her son a too eager appetite for learning. If
we look at it steadily it is a blessing in which, as in other
blessings enjoyed by man, there is much trifling and
weakness, proper and natural to itself, and it costs very
dear.

The purchase of it is far more dangerous than that of any
other food or drink. For, in the case of other things, what
we have bought we carry home in some vessel or other, and
there we have leisure to examine its worth, and to consider
how much of it, and when, we shall consume. But learning
we can at the outset stow into no other vessel but our mind ;
we swallow it at the moment of buying, and leave the
market-place already either contaminated or improved.
Some of it, instead of nourishing us, only clogs and over-
loads our stomach ; and some of it besides, under colour of
curing, poisons us.

I was once delighted to meet, in some place or other, men
who had, in the name of religion, taken a vow of ignorance,
as well as of chastity, poverty and penitence. That too is a
castration of our unruly appetites, a muzzling of that
cupidity which spurs us on to the study of books, and depriving the mind of the voluptuous complacency which
tickles us with the idea that we know something. And it is
abundantly carrying out the vow of poverty to add to it
that of the mind.

We need but little learning to live happily. And Socrates
tells us that we have it in us, and instructs us how to find
it and make use of it. All these acquisitions of ours that
exceed the natural are well-nigh vain and superfluous. It
is enough if they do not burden and cumber us more than
they do us good. *Little learning is needed to form a healthy*

mind (Seneca). They are feverish excesses of our mind, which is a restless and meddlesome instrument.

Concentrate your thoughts ; you will find in yourself the true arguments of Nature against death, and the fittest to serve you in times of necessity. It is they which enable a farm-labourer, and whole nations, to die with as much fortitude as a philosopher.

Should I have died less cheerfully before I had read the Tusculans ?[1] I think not. And when I think it over I feel that my tongue is the richer, but certainly not my heart. This is as Nature forged it for me, and it arms itself for the conflict in a natural and ordinary way. Books have been of service to me not so much for instruction as to exercise my mind.

What if knowledge, whilst trying to arm us with new defences against natural misfortunes, has rather impressed our mind with the magnitude and weight of them than furnished it with arguments and sophistries to shelter us from them ? They are sophistries, indeed, with which she often alarms us to little purpose. Look at even the wisest and most concise writers, how many frivolous and, if we examine them closely, bodyless arguments they scatter around a single good one. They are but wordy quibbles, made to deceive us. But as long as they do so profitably I will not sift them any further. There are enough of that kind in divers parts of this book, either borrowed or imitated.

So we ought to be a little on our guard against calling power what is mere prettiness, or solid what is merely acute, or good what is only beautiful, *which is pleasanter to taste than to swallow* (Cicero).

Not all that pleases, appeases, *when it is a question of the soul, and not the wit* (Seneca).

To see how Seneca strives to prepare himself for death, to see him sweating with anguish to stiffen himself, and struggling so long to gain assurance on his pedestal, I should be inclined to shake his reputation if he had not very valiantly maintained it at his death. His agitations, so burning and frequent, show that he was naturally impetuous and passionate. *A great soul expresses itself more calmly and cheerfully. . . . The soul and the intellect are not differently*

[1] Cicero's *Tusculan Disputations*, the first Book of which deals with the ' Contempt of Death '.

coloured (Seneca). He has to be convinced at his own cost. They also show in some sort that he was hard pressed by his enemy.

Plutarch's style, though more offhand and less strained, is in my opinion the more virile and convincing ; I could easily believe that his soul's movements were more confident and more orderly. The one, sharper, pricks and makes us start up ; he touches the spirit more. The other, more sober, consistently forms us, sets us up and comforts us ; he touches the understanding more. The former carries off our judgement, the latter wins it.

I have likewise seen other writings, still more honoured, which, in depicting the conflict they sustain against the goads of the flesh, paint them so sharp, so powerful and invincible that even we, who are of the dregs of the people, cannot help wondering as much at the strangeness and uncommon vigour of their temptation, as at their resistance.

To what purpose do we go arming ourselves with this laboriously acquired learning ? Let us look down there, at the poor people we see scattered about on the face of the earth, their heads bowed over their labours, who know neither Aristotle nor Cato, neither example nor precept ; from them Nature every day extracts deeds of fortitude and endurance, purer and more vigorous than those we study so diligently in the schools. How many I see every day who ignore poverty, how many who wish for death, or who meet it without fear and without distress ! This man who is digging my garden has this morning buried his father or his son.

Even the names by which they call their maladies mitigate and sweeten their bitterness ; phthisis is to them a cough, dysentery a looseness of the bowels, pleurisy a cold ; and as they mitigate their names so they support them more easily. It must be a very serious ailment that will interrupt their ordinary labours ; they take to their beds only to die.

This simple virtue, that is within the reach of all, has been converted into an obscure and mysterious science (Seneca).

I was writing this about the time when a great load of our troubles had for months descended straight upon me with all its weight. On the one hand I had the enemy at my gate, on the other the freebooters, a worse kind of enemy :

they fight not with arms but with crimes : and I had a taste of every kind of outrage inflicted by the soldiery at the same time :

> To right and left the dreaded foe appears,
> And present danger threatens all around. (OVID.)

A monstrous and unnatural war ! Other wars act outwardly, this also against itself, eating away and destroying itself with its own venom. It is of so malignant and ruinous a nature that it ruins itself together with everything else ; in its fury it tears itself limb from limb. More frequently we see it dissolving of itself than through any dearth of necessary things, or by the power of the enemy. All discipline flies from it. It comes to cure sedition, and is full of it ; it professes to chastise disobedience and sets an example of it. And, being employed for the protection of the laws, plays its part in rebelling against its own laws. To what a pass we have come when our medicine carries infection !

> Our evil mounts the more, grown worse with healing. (VIRGIL.)
> All right and wrong, with awful frenzy blent,
> Estranged from us the righteous-minded gods. (CATULLUS.)

In the beginning of these diseases that attack the people we can distinguish the sick from the sound ; but when they come to stay, as ours does, the whole body is infected from head to heels ; no part is exempt from corruption. For there is no air that is inhaled so greedily, that so spreads and penetrates, as the air of licence. Our armies no longer join and hold together except with a foreign cement ; no longer is it possible to form a regular and reliable army-corps of Frenchmen.

O the shame of it ! There is no discipline but that we see in borrowed soldiers ; as to ourselves, we follow our own lead, not that of the leader. Every one goes his own way. The general has more to do within than without. It is his part to follow, to pay court and crook his back. He alone obeys ; all the rest are free and dissolute.

I am not sorry to see that ambition is reduced to such unmanly and mean-spirited, such abject and servile actions, to attain its end. But this I am sorry to see, that good and generous natures, capable of uprightness, are every day corrupted in their administration and guidance of this confused State.

Prolonged toleration begets habit ; habit, consent and imitation. We had ignoble souls enough without spoiling the good and generous. Wherefore, if we continue at this rate, there will hardly be left a man to whom we may entrust the health of this State, in case Fortune should restore it.

> This youthful Prince forbid ye not at least
> To save a fallen generation.[1] (VIRGIL.)

What has become of that old precept, ' That soldiers ought to fear their general more than the enemy ' ? And that wonderful example of the apple-tree which happened to be enclosed within the precincts of a Roman army-camp, and was found the day after the army had broken up, leaving the owner in possession of the full tale of his ripe and delicious apples ?

I could wish that our young men, instead of spending their time in less profitable peregrinations and less honourable apprenticeships, would put in the half of it in witnessing naval warfare under some good Captain-commander of Rhodes, and the other half in observing the discipline of the Turkish armies ; for it differs greatly from ours, and greatly to its advantage. For example, our soldiers become more licentious on warlike expeditions, whilst the Turkish soldiers become more restrained and timid ; for the offences or thefts committed upon the poor, which in times of peace are punished with the bastinado, become capital offences in war-time. For an egg taken without payment the penalty is, according to a fixed tariff, fifty strokes with a stick. For any other thing, however small, not necessary for food, they are impaled or beheaded without delay.

I was astonished to read in the history of Selim, the most cruel conqueror that ever was, that when he subjugated Egypt the wonderful gardens, abounding in delicious fruits, surrounding the city of Damascus, were left virgin of the hands of the soldiers, unenclosed and open to all as they were.

But is there any disease in a State so bad that it deserves to be fought with so fatal a drug [2] ? Not even, said Favonius, the usurping of possession of the State by a tyrant.

---

[1] Virgil refers to Augustus, and no doubt Montaigne had in his mind the King of Navarre, afterwards Henry IV of France.
[2] As civil war.

Plato too will not consent to have the peace of his country violated in order to cure it, and will not accept reformation at the cost of the blood and destruction of the citizens. He lays it down as the duty of a good man in that case to leave things alone, only entreating God to lend extraordinary aid ; and he seems to be angry with his great friend Dion for having gone about it somewhat differently.

I was a Platonist on this point before I knew there had been a Plato in the world. And if such a man is to be absolutely barred from our fellowship, who, for the clearness of his conscience, deserved at the hands of the divine favour to penetrate so deeply into the light of Christianity, through the universal darkness in which the world of his time was involved, I do not think it fitting that we should be taught by a Pagan, how great an impiety it is not to look to God for any succour simply his own, and without our co-operation.

I often doubt whether, among so many men who meddle in such a business, any one is to be˙ met with of so weak understanding as to be seriously convinced that he was on the way to reformation through the worst of deformations ; that he was advancing towards his salvation by roads that most positively lead to certain damnation ; that by overthrowing the government, the authorities and the laws, under whose protection God has placed him, by dismembering his mother and giving her limbs to be devoured by her old enemies, by filling the hearts of brothers with fratricidal hatred, by calling devils and furies to his aid, he could assist the most holy sweetness and justice of the divine word.

Ambition, avarice, cruelty, revenge, have not sufficient natural fury of their own ; let us set a match to them and fan the flames under the glorious pretext of justice and religion ! It is not possible to imagine a worse outlook than when wickedness becomes lawful and, with the permission of the authorities, puts on the cloak of virtue. *Nothing is more deceptive in appearance than a false religion, in which the will of God is made a cloak for crimes* (Livy).

The extreme of wrong, according to Plato, is reached when what is wrong is held to be right.

The lower classes suffered very largely at that time, not only present losses,

Such wide confusion fills the countryside ; (VIRGIL.)

but also future losses. The living had to suffer, and so had
those who were yet unborn. They robbed them, and consequently myself, even of hope, snatching from them all the
means they had for providing for their livelihood for many
years to come :

> All that they cannot bear or lead away
> The brutal horde maliciously destroys ;
> And harmless cottages are burnt to ashes. (OVID.)
>
> In walls there is no trust, and fields
> Lie all untilled and desolate. (CLAUDIAN.)

Besides this shock I suffered others. I incurred the
penalties that moderation brings with it in that kind of
epidemic. I was fleeced on all hands. To the Ghibelline I
was a Guelph, and to the Guelph a Ghibelline. One of my
poets has put that very well, but I do not remember where
it is. The situation of my house and my intimacy with the
people in my neighbourhood made me appear with one face,
my life and my actions with another.[1]

They made no formal accusations, for there was nothing
they could lay their teeth on. I never go outside the laws ;
and if any man had proceeded against me he might have
found that he was more guilty than I. There were only
mute suspicions moving under the surface, for which there
is never a lack of apparent grounds in so mixed and confused a state of affairs, any more than there is of envious and
foolish minds.

I myself generally lend a hand to the offensive presump-
tions that Fortune scatters abroad against me, by a way
I have always had of being loath to justify, excuse and
explain my actions ; thinking that to plead on behalf of my
conscience was to endanger it. *For the clearness of a case is
clouded by argument* (Cicero). And, as if every one could see
as clearly into me as I do myself, instead of withdrawing
from an accusation I advance towards it, and rather improve
upon it by an ironical and scornful confession, if I do not
absolutely hold my tongue, as if it were something unworthy
of reply.

But those who regard this attitude as too arrogant and
self-confident show me hardly less ill-will than those who

[1] M. Villey explains that in the Périgord the majority were Protestants,
and Montaigne was by some taken for a Protestant.

look upon it as the weakness of an indefensible cause ;
especially the Great, in whose eyes want of submission is
the great sin ; hard upon all self-conscious rectitude that
is not humble, servile and suppliant. I have often run my
head against that pillar.

However that may be, what I suffered then would have
made an ambitious man hang himself ; and a miser would
have done the same. I have no anxiety whatever to
acquire wealth :

> Let me possess
> The goods that now I have, or even less ;
> Live for myself the days I have to live,
> So please the Gods a few more days to give ! (HORACE.)

But the losses that befall me through others' wrongdoing,
whether by theft or violence, hurt me almost as much as
they would a man who is sick and tormented with avarice.
The injury is infinitely more bitter than the loss.

A thousand different kinds of misfortune assailed me in
single file ; I could more cheerfully have suffered them in
a throng.

I was already considering to which of my friends I could
commit a needy and ill-fated old age ; after turning my eyes
in all directions I found myself stripped to my shirt. When
a man falls plumb, and from so great a height, it must be
into the arms of a strong and firm affection that is favoured
by Fortune ; such an affection is rare, if there be any. In
the end I saw that it was safest to rely upon myself in my
distress ; and if it should so fall out that Fortune was too
cold in offering me protection, to entrust myself more to
my own and fix my eyes and thoughts more firmly on
myself.

On all occasions men are too ready to throw themselves
into other people's arms, to save their own, which alone are
reliable and powerful, if they can make use of them. Every
man rushes elsewhere and into the future, because no man
has turned to himself.

And I came to the conclusion that my misfortunes were
beneficial, since, Firstly, a bad learner must be taught with
the rod, when reason is insufficient ; as by means of heat
and the force of wedges we restore a piece of warped timber
to straightness. I have so long been urging myself to rely
on my own strength and be independent of strangers, and

yet I still keep turning my eyes to one side. The favour of a great man, a gracious word, a condescending glance, tempt me ; and God knows how little scarcity there is of such in these days, and how little they mean ! I can still listen without wrinkling my brows to the flattering offers that are made me to draw me into the open ; and I resist them so feebly that I appear rather willing than not to be vanquished by them. Now so indocile a spirit needs a beating ; and when this cask begins to split, and crack, and leak, and fall to pieces, it needs some good sound strokes of the mallet to force down and tighten the hoops.

Secondly, this misfortune might be to me a profitable experience, to prepare me for a worse, in case I, who hoped through the kindness of Fortune, and as a consequence of my own attitude, to be among the last, should be one of the first to be caught in the storm ; that I might learn betimes to restrict my mode of life, and set it in order for a new state of things.

True liberty is to be able to control one's own actions. *The most powerful man is he who has power over himself* (Seneca).

In ordinary peace times we prepare for ordinary and reasonable accidents, but in this state of confusion which has existed for these last thirty years every Frenchman, whether as an individual or as a member of the community, may expect at any moment an entire upheaval of his fortune. All the more reason why he should keep his heart well stored with strength and courage. Let us be grateful to Fate that we do not live in an effeminate, idle and languid age. Many a man who could never have become so by other means may become famous by his misfortune.

As I seldom read in history of those upheavals in other States without regretting that I had not been present, to have a better view of them, so my curiosity makes me congratulate myself in some sort for being able to witness with my own eyes this notable spectacle of our public death, its form and symptoms. And, since I am unable to prevent it, I am pleased that I was destined to be a spectator of it, and gain instruction from it.

Thus do we eagerly desire to see, even in pictures and in dramatic fictions, the tragedies of human fortune performed before our eyes. Not that the things we hear do not excite our compassion ; but, those pitiable events being so un-common, we take a pleasure in having our feelings worked upon by them.

Nothing tickles without hurting. And the wise historian skims over the accounts of peaceful events as he would stagnant water and dead sea, to come back to wars and seditions to which he knows that we beckon him.

I doubt whether I can honestly enough confess with how very mean a sacrifice of my peace of mind and tranquillity I have lived more than half my life whilst my country was in ruins. I exercise my patience a little too cheaply over the misfortunes that do not affect me personally ; and when I feel inclined to pity myself, I think less of what I have been robbed of than of what I have saved, both inwardly and outwardly. There is some comfort in dodging now one, now another of the evils that are successively taking aim at us, and that hit others round about us. Also in this, that when public interests are concerned the more widely my sym-pathy is scattered the weaker does it become. To which may be added that this is almost certainly true, *that we only feel public calamities in so far as they affect us personally* (Hannibal, according to Livy) ; and that the health with which we parted was so poor that any regret we might feel for the loss of it is lessened. It was health, but only by comparison with the sickness that followed.

We have not fallen from a very great height. The corrup-tion and brigandage that is found in high quarters and is the order of the day seems to me the least supportable. Robbery is less offensive in a wood than in a place of safety. It was a universal conjunction of limbs severally diseased, and each one more so than the other, and for the most part with inveterate ulcers, which no longer admitted of cure or desired it.

This general collapse then certainly stimulated me more than it crushed me, with the help of my conscience, which was not only at peace but bore itself proudly ; and I found no reason to be dissatisfied with myself. Besides, as God never sends us mortals either good or evil quite unmixed, my health at that time held out unusually well ; and, as I can do nothing without health, there are few things that I cannot do with it. It afforded me the means of calling up all my resources to ward off the plague, which might possibly have come nearer to me. And I found that with my endurance I could keep a firm seat against the attacks of Fortune, and that it would need a great shock to throw me out of the saddle.

I do not say this in order to provoke her to make a more vigorous attack upon me. I am her humble servant, and hold out my hands to her and entreat her, in God's name, to be satisfied.

Do I feel her attacks ? Yes, indeed. As one who is possessed and stricken with grief will yet at intervals be tickled by some witticism and coaxed into a smile, I too can control myself sufficiently to keep my mind usually in a state of equanimity and free from painful ideas ; yet every now and again I am suddenly bitten by those unpleasant thoughts, which attack at the moment when I am putting on my armour to struggle with and repel them.

But now came another aggravation of evils which arrived on top of the others. Both outside and in my house I was welcomed by the plague, virulent above all others. For, as robust bodies are liable to more serious maladies, which alone have any power over them, so the very salubrious air around me, where no infection had within living memory gained a foothold, although it had come very near, became poisoned, and produced uncommon results :

> Old and young promiscuous crowd the tomb ;
> No head is spared by ruthless Proserpine. (HORACE.)

I was reduced to that absurd state [1] that the sight of my house became terrible to me. All that was in it was unguarded, and left to the mercy of any man who had a mind to take it. I myself, who am so hospitable, was reduced to the painful necessity of begging for a retreat for my family, a lost and wandering family, a source of fear to their friends and even to themselves, bringing terror wherever they sought to settle, obliged to shift their abode as soon as one of the company began to complain of a sore finger. At such times every malady is concluded to be the plague ; people

---

[1] *Cette plaisante condition.* Most of the French commentators, headed by Coste, are scandalized that Montaigne could make a jest of so serious a matter. But the word *plaisant* has various shades of meaning in Montaigne, such as ' amusing ', ' ridiculous ', ' humorous ', ' witty '. My predecessors ignore any difference, and generally translate it ' pleasant '.

do not waste time to investigate it. And the irony of it was that, in accordance with the rules of the faculty, whenever the danger approaches, you are for forty days in a panic terror of that sickness ; imagination meanwhile makes havoc of your feelings in its own way, and even turns your health into a fever.

All this would have affected me less if I had not had to feel for the sufferings of others, and for six miserable months to pilot this caravan. For I carry my antidotes within myself, which are resolution and patience. I am not greatly troubled by apprehensions, which are particularly to be dreaded in this disease. And if I had been alone and allowed myself to catch it, it would have been a much more cheerful and distant flight.[1] It is not one of the worst kinds of death in my opinion ; it is usually short, numb, painless, comfortable by reason of being shared by many ; no fuss, no mourning, no crowd of onlookers.

But, with regard to the people about us, not a hundredth part of the inhabitants had any hope of escaping :

> Behold the shepherds' realms a waste,
> And far and wide the fields untenanted. (VIRGIL.)

In this place the best part of my revenue depends on manual labour ; the land that a hundred men cultivated for me long lay fallow.

What an example of fortitude did we not then see in the simplicity of all these people ! All and every one gave up caring about life. The grapes remained hanging on the vines, which form the principal wealth of the country. All unconcernedly prepared for and expected death that evening or the morrow, showing so little alarm, either in countenance or voice, that they seemed to have resigned themselves as to a necessity, and regarded it as an inevitable and universal sentence of death.

Death is always inevitable. But on how little depends the resolution to die ! Distance and a few hours' difference, the mere consideration of having company, makes one feel quite differently towards it. Look at these people : because they die in the same month, children, young people, old

---

[1] Meaning, I think, that he would have died cheerfully. M. Villey apparently takes the sentence to mean, ' If I had wished to run away I should have done so cheerfully, and well out of danger.' But the words that follow seem to agree better with my interpretation.

men, are no longer alarmed by it, they cease to lament for themselves. I saw some who dreaded being left behind, as in a dreadful solitude ; and I generally observed them to have no other anxiety than about their burial. They were troubled to see the bodies scattered about in the fields, at the mercy of wild animals that immediately swarmed thither.

How the ideas of men diverge ! The Neorites, a nation subdued by Alexander, throw the bodies of their dead into the deepest parts of their forests, there to be devoured ; the only happy sepulture in their eyes.

Here and there a man, still in good health, was already digging his own grave ; others, still alive, lay down in theirs. And one of my day-labourers, as he was dying, scraped the earth over himself with his hands and feet ; was that not like covering himself up in order to sleep more comfortably ? A heroism almost as sublime as that of the Roman soldiers who, after the Battle of Cannae, were found with their heads thrust into holes, which they had made and filled in with their own hands whilst they smothered. In short, a whole nation was, by habit, soon reduced to adopt a course which for doggedness yields in no wise to any studied and premeditated determination.

Most of the teachings of the learned which are intended to put heart into us are more showy than forcible, more ornamental than effectual. We have abandoned Nature and presume to give lessons to her who used to guide us so happily and surely. And meanwhile from the traces of her teaching, and what little remains of her image, by the favour of ignorance, imprinted on the lives of these unpolished rustics, learning is constrained every day to borrow for its disciples, to serve as models of fortitude, innocence and tranquillity. It is edifying to see how these disciples, with all their fine knowledge, are reduced to copying those foolish and simple people, and to copying them in their elementary actions of virtue ; and how our sapience may derive from the very animals the most useful teachings for the greatest and most necessary concerns of our life : how to live and how to die, how to husband our property, how to love and bring up our children and how to maintain justice : a singular testimony of human infirmity; and how our reason, which we use as it suits us, ever finding

something different and something new, leaves in us no
apparent trace of Nature.

And men have treated Nature as perfumers treat oil :
they have sophisticated her with so many arguments and
far-fetched reasons, that she has become variable and individual to every man, and has lost her own constant and
universal look ; so that we must seek in animals any
evidence of her that is not liable to favour, corruption or
diversity of opinions.

For it is, indeed, true that even they do not always strictly
follow the path of Nature, but they swerve so little from it
that you can always perceive her tracks. So a horse that is
led by hand indulges in much kicking and plunging, but
no further than the length of its halter, and yet always
follows the steps of the man who is leading it ; and so a
hawk takes its flight, but under restraint of its leash.

*Meditate upon exile, tortures, wars, diseases, shipwreck, that
no disaster may find you a novice* (Seneca).

What good will it do to anticipate so carefully all the ills
of human nature, and prepare ourselves with so much pains
to encounter even those which will perhaps never come our
way ? *The possibility of suffering makes us as unhappy as
the suffering itself* (Seneca). We are frightened not only
by the blow, but by the wind and the crack. Or why must
you go this very moment, like the most fanatic, for, indeed,
it is fanaticism, and ask to be birched, because Fortune may
some day have a rod in pickle for you ? Why take to your
furred gown in Midsummer because you will need it at
Christmas ?

' Make haste and try the evils that may befall you,
especially the worst of them ; test your powers, they say,
and make sure that you can bear them.'

On the contrary, the easiest and most natural way would
be to banish them even from your thoughts.

' They will not come soon enough, and will not afflict you
long enough in their true essence ; your mind must prolong
and magnify them and become united with them beforehand, and make much of them, as if they were not sufficiently
painful to our senses.'

' They will be painful enough when they come, said one of
the masters, not of some tender sect, but of the hardest.[1]

[1] Seneca the Stoic.

Meantime, indulge yourself ; believe what you like best. What good can it do you to welcome and anticipate your ill-fortune, and to lose the present through fear of the future ; to make yourself miserable now, because you are to be so in time.' Those are his words.

Learning does us a great service, forsooth, in telling us the exact dimensions of evils,

> Whetting the minds of men with care on care. (VIRGIL.)

What a pity that any part of their magnitude should escape our sense and knowledge !

It is certain that to most men the preparation for death has been a greater torment than the suffering of it.

It was once said very truly by a writer of great judgement : *the senses are less affected by physical suffering than by the apprehension of it* (Quintilian).

The feeling that death is present sometimes of itself inspires us with a sudden resolution not to evade a thing that is quite inevitable. Many gladiators in olden times, after fighting faint-heartedly, were seen to swallow death bravely, offering their throat to the adversary's sword and inviting it.

The prospect of death in the future needs a courage of long duration, and consequently hard to acquire.

If you do not know how to die, do not let it trouble you ; Nature will give you full and sufficient instructions when the time comes. She will do the business for you at the precise moment ; do not burden your mind with the thought of it :

In vain, O mortal man, you seek to know
The hour when death shall come, and by which way. (PROPERTIUS.)

Less painful 'tis to suffer sudden death ;
Much harder then to live in constant dread ! (MAXIMIANUS.)

We trouble our life by the thought of death, and death by the thought of life. The one gives us a feeling of regret, the other terrifies us.

It is not for death that we prepare ; that is too momentary. A quarter of an hour of suffering, without any hurtful consequences, does not deserve any particular instruction. If we would confess the truth, it is for the preparations for death that we prepare.

Philosophy exhorts us to keep death ever before our eyes, to foresee and meditate upon it before the time comes, and then gives us rules and precautions to provide against that foresight and meditation doing us any hurt. That is what those physicians do who bring sickness upon us in order to have a subject on which to practise their skill and test their drugs.

If we have not known how to live it is wrong to teach us how to die, and to make the end differ from the whole. If we have known how to live bravely and tranquilly we shall know how to die bravely and tranquilly. They may brag as much as they please, that *the whole life of a Philosopher is a meditation on death* (Cicero). But it seems to me that it is, indeed, the end, but not the aim of life ;[1] it is its finality, its extremity, not however its object. It ought to be its own drift, its own purpose ; its rightful study is to order, to direct, to suffer itself.

Among the many other duties comprised under this general and important heading of ' Knowing how to live ' is this article of ' Knowing how to die ' ; and one of the lightest, if our fear did not weigh it down.

Judging them by their usefulness and by the naked truth, the lessons of simplicity yield little to those which learning teaches to the contrary. Men differ in inclination and power ; they must be guided to their own good, according to their nature, and by different ways.

Where wind and weather waft me, there I'm borne. (HORACE.)

I never met a farm-labourer in my neighbourhood who meditated how, and with what face and assurance, he should spend his last hours. Nature tells him not to think of death until he is dying. And then he will do so with a better grace than Aristotle, whom death oppresses with a double weight, both with itself and with so long a foresight. Therefore it was Caesar's opinion that the happiest and easiest death is the least premeditated. *He grieves more than is necessary who grieves before it is necessary* (Seneca).

The bitterness of this imagination springs from our curiosity. So we always shackle ourselves when we try to outdistance and control what Nature prescribes. It is only

---

[1] *C'est bien le bout, non pourtant le but, de la vie.* As remarked, Montaigne is fond of playing on words.

for the doctors, when in good health, to look glum at the spectre of death and to dine with less enjoyment. The common people have no need of physic or of comfort except when the blow falls, and they think of it no more than just as they feel.

Is it not as we say, that it is the dullness and want of apprehension of the common people that gives them that power to endure present ills, and that profound indifference to the mishaps that may be impending in the future ; that their souls, through being gross and obtuse, are not so easily penetrated and moved ? If that is so let us in God's name henceforth keep a school of stolidity. This result to which stolidity so imperceptibly guides its disciples is the utmost that learning can promise us.

We shall not lack good teachers, interpreters of the simplicity of Nature. Socrates shall be one. For, as far as I can remember, he speaks something to this purpose to the judges who are about to dispose of his life :

' I fear, my friends, that if I entreat you not to put me to death, I shall involve myself in the indictment of my accusers, which is that I claim to know more than others, as if I had some more secret knowledge of things that are above and below us. I have had no association or acquaintance with death, nor have I known any one who has had experience of its nature, and could give me information. They who fear it presume that they know it. As for me, I neither know what it is nor what the other world is like. Death may be an indifferent thing, or it may be desirable.

' We may believe however that, if it is a migration from one place to another, it will be a gain to go and live with so many departed great ones, and to have nothing more to do with unjust and corrupt judges. If it is an annihilation of our being, it will still be a gain to enter upon a long and peaceful night. Nothing in life is sweeter than a deep and tranquil rest and sleep, without dreams.

' The things I know to be wicked, such as wronging our neighbour and disobeying our superior, whether it be God or man, I carefully avoid. Those as to which I do not know whether they be good or evil, I cannot fear.

' If I am to depart and leave you alive, the Gods alone can see which of us, you or I, will fare the better for it. Wherefore, as far as I am concerned, you may dispose of

me as you please. But, following my custom of advising
just and profitable things, I will yet say that, for the sake
of your conscience, you will do better to set me free, unless
you can see further than I do into my case. And, if you
consider my past actions, both public and private, if you
consider my intentions, if you consider the profit that so
many of our citizens, young and old, derive every day from
my conversation, and the good I have done you all, you
cannot duly repay me for my deserts except by ordering
that, in view of my poverty, I be maintained at the public
cost at the Prytaneum, a privilege I have often known you,
with less reason, to grant to others.

'Do not impute it to obstinacy or disdain if I do not
follow the custom of supplicating you and trying to move
you to pity. I have friends and kinsmen (not being, in the
words of Homer, born of stocks and stones, any more than
others) who might appear before you in mourning and tears,
and I have three disconsolate children to move you to
compassion. But I should disgrace our city, at my age and
with the reputation for wisdom of which I am accused, to
demean myself so abjectly. What would be said of the
other Athenians ?

'I have always admonished my hearers not to redeem
their lives by a dishonourable action. And in the wars of
my country, at Amphipolis, at Potidaea, at Delium, and
others in which I took part, I proved by deeds how far I was
from securing my safety by disgracing myself. Moreover,
I should make you depart from your duty and invite you to
do hateful things ; for not my entreaties, but pure and solid
reasons of justice, should persuade you.

'You have sworn to the Gods to bear yourselves thus.
It would seem as if I were suspecting and retorting upon you
that you do not believe there are Gods. And I should
testify against myself that I did not believe in them as I
should, if I mistrusted their guidance and did not commit
my affair entirely to their hands. I wholly rely upon them,
and hold for certain that they will dispose of this matter as
will be best for you and for me. No good man, either in life
or after death, has any cause to fear the Gods.'

Is not that a sound and sober pleading, but at the same
time artless and familiar, inconceivably highminded, candid,
truthful and honest beyond all example ? And in what a

pressing need it was spoken ! Truly he was right to prefer it to that which the great orator Lysias had written for him, which was admirably couched in forensic style, but unworthy of so noble a criminal. If we had heard from the lips of Socrates a single supplicating note that proud virtue would have struck sail at the height of its fame.

And should his rich and powerful nature have entrusted its defence to cunning, and, in its greatest ordeal, renounced truth and simplicity, the ornaments of his speech, to deck and disguise itself with the embellishments and pretences of a discourse committed to memory ? He acted very wisely, and in accordance with his character, not to corrupt the tenor of an incorrupt life, and so sanctified a model of human nature, in order to prolong by a year his old age, and impair the immortal memory of that glorious end. He owed his life, not to himself, but, as an example, to the world. Would it not have been a public disaster if he had ended it in idleness and obscurity ?

Assuredly, this carelessness and indifference to his own death deserved that posterity should make more of it on his behalf ; as, indeed, they did. And no justice was ever so just as that which Fortune had in store for him, to his glory. For the Athenians held those who had been the cause of his death in such abomination, that they shunned them as excommunicated persons. Everything they had touched was looked upon as polluted. No man washed with them at the baths, no man saluted or accosted them, so that at last, unable any longer to support the general hatred, they hanged themselves.

If any one should think that, among so many examples of the sayings of Socrates I had to select from to suit my purpose, I have made a bad choice ; and if he judges this speech to be too exalted for ordinary conceptions, I may say that I have purposely selected it. For I judge otherwise, and regard it as a speech that ranks, in naturalness, far behind and below common conceptions. It reflects with unstudied and artless boldness and a childlike assurance the simple and primitive idea and ignorance of Nature. For it may be believed that we are naturally afraid of pain, but not of death in itself. Death is a part of our existence, no less essential than life.

Why should Nature have engendered in us a hatred and

horror of it, seeing that it ranks so highly with her for its usefulness in fostering the continuance and alternation of her works, and that, in this universal republic, it conduces more to birth and increase than to loss or destruction ?

> For evermore is thus renewed
> The total sum of things. (LUCRETIUS.)
> A thousand lives are born of one decease. (OVID.)

The decay of one life is the passage to a thousand other lives.

Nature has implanted in animals an instinct to look after themselves and keep out of harm's way. They go no further than fear of injury, of knocks and wounds, of being fettered and beaten by man, accidents which their senses and experience teach them to avoid. But they cannot fear being killed by us, nor have they the faculty to imagine and conclude such a thing as death. So it is also said that they not only suffer it cheerfully (most horses neigh at their death, and swans celebrate it in song), but that, when urged by necessity, they seek it, as has been often exemplified in the case of elephants.

Besides, is not the method of arguing that Socrates adopts in this case equally admirable for its simplicity and its power ? Truly it is much easier to speak like Aristotle and to live like Caesar than to speak and live like Socrates. There lies the extreme degree of perfection and difficulty ; art cannot attain to it. Our faculties have not been trained to such a pitch. We neither test them nor do we know them ; we invest ourselves in those of others, and let our own lie idle.

Any one might therefore say of me that in this book I have only made up a bunch of other people's flowers, and that of my own I have only provided the string that ties them together. I have certainly given way to public opinion in wearing these borrowed plumes. But I have no intention that they shall cover me and hide me ; that is the very opposite of my purpose, for I wish to make a show of nothing but what is my own, and what is my own by Nature ; and if I had followed my own inclination I should at all hazards have drawn entirely on my own resources. I burden myself with them more and more every day, going beyond my intention and my original practice, following the fashion of the day and other people's advice. If it is unbecoming in me, as I think it is, no matter ; it may be of use to some other person.[1]

Many a man quotes Plato and Homer without ever having seen the originals ; and I have often enough taken passages elsewhere than from their source. Without trouble and without learning, being surrounded by a thousand volumes of books in the room in which I am writing, I could presently, if I pleased, borrow from a dozen such patch-makers, men whose books I seldom look into, the wherewithal to enamel this treatise on Physiognomy. I need only turn to the preliminary epistle of some German to stuff myself with quotations. In this way we go begging a dainty reputation, and tricking a silly world.

Those pasties of commonplaces, with the help of which so many men economize their studies, are of little use except for commonplace themes ; and they only help us to show off our learning, not to regulate our conduct : a ridiculous outcome of learning which Socrates belabours so humorously when arguing against Euthydemus. I have seen books compiled on subjects neither studied nor understood by the writer, who deputed various learned friends of his to look up this and that matter to build it up with, being content, for his share, with planning the work and industriously piling up that heap of undigested material ; the ink and paper at least are his. That is in all conscience to buy or borrow a book, not to make one. That is the way to teach men not that you can write a book, but that you cannot write one, about which they may have been in doubt.

A President boasted in my presence that into one of his presidential judgements he had packed two hundred and so many passages from foreign sources. By publishing this fact to all and sundry he was, it seems to me, robbing himself of the glory he might have gained by it. A fatuous and ridiculous boast, to my mind, for such a feat and such a person !

[I do the contrary] ; and when so many things are borrowed, I am glad to be able to filch a thing now and then, disguising and altering it for some new purpose. At the

---

[1] It may be noted, in explanation of the foregoing, that the original editions of the Essays, published in 1580 and 1582, contained very few quotations. Many of them were added when the third Book appeared in 1588, and more subsequently.

risk of its being said that I failed to understand its original application, I give it some particular turn of the hand, that it may be less purely inappropriate. The others make a show of their pilferings and take credit for them, and so are more pardonable for them than I.[1]

We followers of Nature think that the honour of invention is greatly and incomparably to be preferred to the honour of quotation.

If I had wished to speak learnedly I should have spoken earlier ; I should have written at a time nearer to my study-period, when I had more wit and memory, and I should have trusted more to my vigour at that age than at this, if I had wished to become a writer by profession.

Moreover, such kind favour as Fortune perhaps offered me through the mediation of this book would then have lighted upon a more propitious season.[2]

Two of my acquaintances, great men in this profession, have in my opinion lost by half through refusing to publish at forty years of age and waiting till they were sixty. Maturity has its drawbacks, as well as the green years, and worse. And old age is as unfit a time for this kind of work as for any other. He who puts his decrepitude under the press plays the fool, if he hopes to squeeze out of it any ideas that do not smack of the disagreeable, the drowsy and visionary. Our brains, as they age, become constipated and stagnant.

I dispense my ignorance abundantly and ostentatiously, my learning meagrely and sparingly ; the latter accidentally and secondarily, the former positively and authoritatively. The only things I treat adequately are things of no account, and all my knowledge betrays want of knowledge.

I have chosen the time when my whole life, which I have to portray, lies before me ; what remains of it is more allied to death. And of my death I should probably give an

---

[1] In the 1588 edition we read here : ' Like a horse-thief I paint the mane and tail, and sometimes blind them in one eye ; if the first owner used it as an ambler I make a trotting horse of it ; and if it was a saddle-horse I turn it into a pack-horse.'

[2] This is taken to be an allusion to Montaigne's friendship with Mademoiselle de Gournay, whom he met in Paris in 1588, when he was seeing his book through the press. In all the printed editions it appeared in an altered form.

account to the public only if I happened to be loquacious, as others are, at the time of my departure.

It grieves me that Socrates, who was a perfect model of all great qualities, chanced to have so ill-favoured a body and face, as they say he had, and out of harmony with the beauty of his soul ; when he was so enamoured of, so infatuated with beauty. Nature did him an injustice.

There is nothing more likely than the conformity and relation of the body to the spirit. *It is of no little consequence in what body the soul is lodged ; for there are many things which depend on the body that give an edge to the soul, and many which blunt it* (Cicero). Cicero is thinking of an unnatural ugliness and deformity of limbs. But we also call ugliness an incongruity that is visible at the first glance, which lies chiefly in the face, and which often arouses our dislike on very slight grounds : the complexion, a scar, a rugged countenance, some inexplicable cause, whilst the limbs are symmetrical and perfect.

The ugliness which clothed a very beautiful soul in La Boëtie was in this category. This superficial ugliness, which is however very impressive, affects the state of the mind less prejudicially, and makes people uncertain about it. The other kind, which is more properly called deformity, is more material, and more generally strikes inwardly. Not only every shoe of soft leather, but every well-shaped shoe, shows the shape of the foot within.

So Socrates said of his, that it would have betrayed just as much ugliness in his soul, if he had not corrected it by training. But in saying that I think he was jesting, according to his wont ; and never did so excellent a soul fashion itself.

I cannot often enough repeat how much I look upon beauty as a quality that gives power and advantage. He called it ' a short tyranny ' ; Plato, ' Nature's privilege '. Man has no quality that stands in higher repute. It ranks highest in human intercourse ; it is the first that attracts notice, it seduces and prepossesses our judgement, exercises great influence, and makes a wonderful impression.

Phryne would have lost her case, although conducted by an eminent counsel, if she had not torn open her tunic and corrupted her judges by her dazzling beauty.

And I observe that Cyrus, Alexander and Caesar, those three masters of the world, did not disdain it in carrying out their great enterprises ; nor did the elder Scipio. One and the same word in Greek embraces both the good and the beautiful ; and the Holy Ghost often calls those good whom it would call beautiful.

I would readily agree to range the blessings of this life in the order in which Plato found them in a song, taken from some ancient poet, which he says was current in his time : Health, Beauty, Wealth.

Aristotle says that to the handsome belongs the right to command, and, if there are any whose beauty approaches that of our idea of the Gods, that veneration is also their due. To one who asked him why one associated longer and more frequently with handsome people, he replied, ' That question could be asked only by one who is blind.'

Most of the Philosophers, and the greatest of them, paid for their schooling, and acquired wisdom, by the favour and mediation of their beauty.

Not only in the men who serve me, but also in animals, I regard it as within two fingers' breadth of goodness. Yet it seems to me that that cut of the face, those features and lineaments from which they argue a certain inner disposition, and foretell our future fortunes, are not things that may be simply and directly classed under the heading of beauty and ugliness. No more can we say that every good odour and clearness of atmosphere promise health, and every closeness and offensive smell bode infection, in times of pestilence.

Those who accuse the fair sex of contradicting their beauty by their character do not always hit the truth ; for in a face that is not too well fashioned there may dwell an air of honesty that inspires confidence ; as, on the other hand, I have at times read in a lovely pair of eyes threats of a dangerous and mischievous nature. There are physiognomies that promise friendliness, and when surrounded by victorious enemies you will immediately choose from among a number of strangers one rather than another to whom you will surrender and trust your life ; and not exactly in consideration of his beauty.

The face is a weak surety ; yet it deserves some consideration. And if I had the punishment of the wicked I would more severely lash those who belie and betray the promises that Nature has implanted on their brows ; I would more harshly chastise knavery under a meek and mild aspect.

It seems as if some faces were happy, and others ill-starred. And I believe that it needs some skill to distinguish between the gentle and the silly, the stern and the rugged, the ill-natured and the downcast, the contemptuous and the melancholy, and such other bordering qualities. There are types of beauty that are not only proud but repellent ; there are others not only sweet but, beyond that, insipid. As to foretelling from them their future fortunes, that is a matter I leave undecided.

As I have said elsewhere, I have for my part adopted, very simply and crudely, this ancient rule, ' That we cannot go wrong if we follow Nature ', and that the sovereign precept is, ' To conform to her '. I have not, like Socrates, by the force of reason, corrected my natural propensities, and have not in the least interfered with my inclinations by art. I let myself go as I have come ; I combat nothing. My two ruling qualities live, of their own accord, in peace and harmony ; but my nurse's milk was, thank God, passably wholesome and temperate.

May I say this by the way, that I observe that we attach an undue value to a certain conception, almost the only one in vogue with us, of scholastic probity, a slave to precepts, cramped by hope and fear ? I would have it, not formed, but perfected and authorized by laws and religions, sensible of being able to stand without help, springing up within us from its own roots, from the seed planted by universal reason in every man not corrupt by nature. This reason, which straightens Socrates from his vicious bend, makes him obedient to the men and gods who rule in his city, brave in death, not because he has an immortal soul, but because he is a mortal man. It is a teaching that is destructive to all government, and much more harmful than ingenious and subtle, which persuades the people that religious belief alone, without morality, is sufficient to satisfy the divine justice. Experience tells us that there is an enormous difference between piety and conscience.

My bearing is friendly, both in itself and as interpreted by others :

> Is, did I say ?   Nay, Chremes, it once was.   (TERENCE.)
>
> Alas ! of this old worn-out body
> Thou seest but the bones ;   (MAXIMIANUS.)

and offers an example that contrasts with that of Socrates. It has often happened that, on the strength of my looks and presence only, people who had no knowledge of me have placed great confidence in me, whether in their own affairs or in mine ; and in foreign parts they have won me particular and unusual kindness.   But the two following experiences perhaps deserve telling in detail.

An individual who shall be nameless planned to make a surprise attack upon me and my house. His scheme was to arrive alone at my gates and rather earnestly request to be let in. I knew him by name and had reason to trust him, since he was a neighbour and distantly related to me by marriage. I opened to him, as I do to everybody. There I found him in a great state of terror, his horse panting and worn out. He entertained me with this fiction : ' That he had just had an encounter, half a league away, with an enemy of his, whom I also knew, and I had heard of their feud ; that his enemy had made him clap on his spurs to some purpose, and having been taken unprepared and in- ferior in numbers, he had sought safety at my gate ; that he was very troubled about his men, whom he concluded to be either taken or dead.'

In my innocence I tried to comfort and reassure him, and put new heart into him. Presently four or five of his soldiers turned up with the same look of terror, and were let in, and then more and still more, well armed and mounted, until there were twenty-five or thirty of them, all pretending that the enemy were at their heels.

This mystery was beginning to arouse a little suspicion. I did not forget in what age I was living, how greatly my house might be coveted ; and I remembered several ex- amples of others of my acquaintance who had had similar misadventures. However, seeing that there was nothing to be gained by beginning to use them kindly if I did not go through with it, and that I could not get rid of them without bringing matters to a head, I took the most natural and simple course, as I always do, and bade them come in.

Besides, to tell the truth, I am by nature little given to suspicion and mistrust, and am easily inclined to admit excuses and the most favourable interpretation. I take men to be pretty much all alike, and, unless I am forced to do so by overwhelming evidence, I cannot believe in such perverse and unnatural intentions, any more than I believe in prodigies and miracles. And I am, moreover, a man who readily trusts to Fortune and throws himself heedlessly into her arms. And I have hitherto had more reason to applaud than blame myself for so doing, having found her more prudent and more friendly to my affairs than I am myself.

There have been several actions in my life the conduct of which might justly be called suspicious, or, if you prefer it so, circumspect ; of these same, supposing the third part may be set down to my credit, the other two-thirds are abundantly due to her. It seems to me that we sin in that we do not sufficiently trust ourselves to Heaven, and expect more from our own conduct than we are entitled to. Therefore it is that our plans so often miscarry. Heaven is jealous of our yielding so much to the claims of human wisdom, to the prejudice of its own ; and the more we extend them the more does it cut them down.

These men remained on horseback in my courtyard, whilst the leader was with me in my hall ; he would not have his horse stabled, saying he would have to depart as soon as he had news of his men. He saw that he was master of the situation, and nothing remained but the execution of his enterprise. He has since often said, for he was not ashamed to tell the tale, that it was my face and my ingenuousness that snatched the treachery out of his hands. He remounted his horse, whilst his men continually had their eyes upon him to see what signal he would give them, greatly astonished to see him depart and abandon his advantage.

On another occasion, relying upon some truce between our armies that had just been proclaimed, I started upon a journey through an uncommonly ticklish part of the country. My departure was no sooner winded than three or four parties of horsemen started from different points to seize me. One caught me up on the third day, when I was attacked by fifteen or twenty gentlemen with masks, followed by a swarm of troopers. There I was captured and surrendered, drawn into the thick of a neighbouring forest, dismounted, rifled, my coffers searched, my money-box seized, horses and armour divided amongst new masters. We were a long time in this thicket, disputing the matter of my ransom, which they rated so high that it was very evident that they did not quite know who I was. They had a lively dispute over my life. Indeed, there were many threatening circumstances which showed the danger I was in:

> Now, Trojan, for a stalwart heart and true,
> Firmness and steadiness ! (VIRGIL.)

I persisted in standing on my rights under the truce, only relinquishing the gain they had made in despoiling me, which was not to be despised, without promise of any other ransom. After we had been there two or three hours, and after they had set me on a nag of whose escape there was no danger, and committed me to a special escort of fifteen or twenty musketeers, my men being divided among others, and orders given that we should be led prisoners by different routes, and I being already two or three musket-shots on the way,

> Invoking the aid of the Heavenly Twins, (CATULLUS.)

behold a sudden and very unexpected change of mind in my captors ! I saw the leader return to me with milder words, taking the trouble to collect my scattered belongings from among the company, and restoring to me as many as he was able to recover, including even my money-box. The best present they made me was after all my freedom ; the rest did not give me much concern at that time.

The true cause of so strange a change of mind and conduct, due to no apparent impulse, and of so miraculous a repentance at such a time, in an enterprise that had been deliberately planned beforehand, and which by custom had become quite the right thing to do (for at the outset I openly confessed to them what party I belonged to, and what road I was going), I cannot, indeed, understand to this day. The most conspicuous among them, who removed his mask and told me his name, repeated to me several times that I owed this deliverance to my face, my freedom and firmness of speech, which made me undeserving of such ill-treatment, and asked to be assured of a like treatment if occasion should offer.

It may be that the divine goodness willed to make use of this trivial means for my rescue. It also protected me the very next day from still worse ambushes, against which those men themselves had warned me.

The latter is still above ground to tell the tale; the former was killed not long ago.

If my face did not answer for me, if the innocence of my intentions were not to be read in my eyes and voice, I should not have survived so long without quarrels and without harm, seeing the indiscreet freedom with which I say, right or wrong, whatever comes into my head, and give utterance to rash opinions on things. This habit may reasonably appear uncivil and little in keeping with our usage, but I have never met any one who thought it insulting or ill-natured, or who took offence at my candour, if he had it directly from my lips. Repeated words have a different sound and a different sense.

Nor do I hate any man; and I am so disinclined to do any one a wrong, that I cannot do so even should reason require it. When occasions required me to sentence a criminal I rather sinned against justice. *Whilst I would not have crimes committed, I lack the heart to punish them when they have been committed* (Livy).

It is said that Aristotle was blamed for having been too merciful to a wicked man. ' It is true, he said, that I was merciful to the man, but not to his wickedness.'

The judgement of the ordinary man is provoked to exercise vengeance by the horror of the misdeed. That itself is enough to cool mine. Horror of the first killing makes me fear a second; and hatred of the first cruelty makes me hate any imitation of it. To me who am but a knave of clubs,[1] may be applied what was said of Charilaus, King of Sparta : ' He cannot be good, since he is not hard on the wicked.' Or rather thus, for Plutarch puts the matter in these two ways, as he does a thousand other things, variously and contradictorily : ' He must needs be good, since he is good even to the wicked.' As I am loath to proceed even lawfully against a man who would resent my action, so, to tell the truth, I am not sufficiently conscientious to refrain from an illicit action with one who acquiesces in it.

[1] A person of no importance. The expression *valet de carreau*, knave of diamonds, is also used in the sense of a ' contemptible fellow, mean wretch '.

CHAPTER 13

OF EXPERIENCE

THERE is no more natural desire than the desire for knowledge. We try all ways that may lead us to it. When reason fails we resort to experience :

> By various proofs Experience art has made,
> Example pointing out the way ;   (MANILIUS.)

which is a more ineffectual and less worthy means. But the truth is so great a thing that we should despise no means that may lead us to it. Reason has so many shapes that we know not which to lay hold of : experience has no fewer. The inference we try to draw from the likeness of events is uncertain, because they are always unlike.

No quality is so universal, in the appearance of things, as diversity and variety. To express the highest degree of similarity, both the Greeks and Latins, as well as ourselves, use eggs as an example. Yet there have been men, and notably one at Delphi,[1] who could distinguish marks of difference in different eggs so well that he never mistook one for another. And although he had a great number of hens he was able to tell which of them laid a particular egg.

Dissimilarity intrudes of itself into our works ; no skill can attain similarity. Neither Perrozet [2] nor any other can smoothe and whiten the backs of his cards so carefully that no gamester can distinguish between them on merely seeing them slipping through another's hands. Resemblance does not make things so much alike as difference makes them unlike. Nature has obliged herself to make nothing other that was not unlike.

Therefore I do not much like the opinion of the man [3] who thought that to multiply the laws was to curb the authority of the judges, by cutting up their meat for them. He did not realize that there was as much liberty and latitude in interpreting the laws as in the making of them. And they fool themselves who think they can lessen and put a stop to our disputes by referring us to the actual words of the

[1] A slight inaccuracy : Cicero, who was probably the source of Montaigne's information, notes that there were many people at Delos who had this power.

[2] Presumably the name of a maker of playing-cards.

[3] Justinian, Emperor and legislator.

Bible, since our mind finds the field no less spacious for controverting another's meaning than for urging its own. As if we showed less animosity and tartness in commenting than in inventing !

We see how much he was mistaken. For in France we have more laws than all the rest of the world together, and more than necessary to rule all the worlds of Epicurus. *As formerly we suffered from crimes, so now we suffer from the laws* (Tacitus). And yet we have left so much to the opinions and decisions of our judges that there has never been such complete liberty and licence.

What have our legislators gained by selecting a hundred thousand particular cases and actions, and applying to them a hundred thousand laws ? This number is quite out of proportion to the infinite variety of human actions. By multiplying our invented cases we shall never arrive at the number and variety of possible cases. Add to them a hundred times as many more, and yet no future case will ever be found so to tally with, so exactly to fit and match another of the many thousands of selected and registered cases, that there will not remain some circumstance and diversity that will require a separate consideration and decision.

There is little relation between our actions, which are perpetually changing, and fixed and unchangeable laws. The most desirable laws are those which are most rare, most simple and general ; and I still believe it would be better to have none at all, than to have them in such numbers as we have.

The laws that Nature gives us are always happier than those we give ourselves. Witness the Golden Age as depicted by the poets, and the condition in which we see those nations to be living which have no other laws.

Here we have a people who have no judges, but call upon the first traveller who passes through their mountains to decide their quarrels for them.[1] And these others elect one from among themselves, on market-days, to settle all their suits on the spot.

Where would be the danger if the wisest should thus

---

[1] According to Coste, Montaigne was thinking of the little community of San Marino in Italy, which was enclosed within the Papal States. In the Middle Age the custom mentioned prevailed generally in the republics of Lombardy.

settle ours, according to the circumstances and at sight, without being tied to precedents and issues ? To every foot its shoe.

When King Ferdinand sent colonists to the Indies he wisely provided that they should take with them no men learned in the law, for fear lest law-suits might breed in that new world, since it is a branch of learning that of its nature generates altercations and divisions ; deciding, with Plato, that 'lawyers and doctors are a bad provision for a country.'

Why is it that our common language, so easy for all other uses, becomes obscure and unintelligible in wills and contracts, and that this language that can express itself so clearly, whatever it may say or write, here finds no way of declaring its meaning that does not involve doubt and contradiction ? Unless it be that the princes of that art, applying themselves with a particular attention to picking out solemn words and contriving artful formulas, have so carefully weighed each syllable and so accurately analysed every kind of combination that we see them trammelled and embroiled in the endless number of figures and such minute partitions that they cease to fall within any rule and prescription, and to convey any definite meaning. *Whatever is beaten into powder becomes confused* (Seneca).

Have you ever seen a boy attempting to divide a quantity of quicksilver into a certain number of parts ? The more he works and squeezes it, and tries to bring it under control the more does he provoke the freedom of that noble metal ; it escapes his ingenuity, and keeps dispersing into small particles beyond all reckoning. So it is here ; for by subdividing those subtleties they teach men to increase their doubts ; they put us into a way of magnifying and diversifying the difficulties ; they lengthen them out and disperse them. By scattering questions abroad and cutting them up they make the world to fructify and abound in uncertainties and quarrels ; as the earth is made more fertile the more deeply it is dug up and crumbled. *It is learning that creates difficulties* (Quintilian).

We are perplexed by Ulpian ; we are still perplexed by Bartolus and Baldus.[1] We should blot out all traces of these

[1] Ulpian, a jurist of the second and third centuries ; Bartolus and Baldus, Italian jurists of the fourteenth century, all commentators of Justinian.

innumerable differences of opinion, instead of using them
to show off our learning and swelling the heads of posterity
with them. I know not what to say to it, but experience
tells us that so many interpretations disperse the truth and
destroy it.

Aristotle wrote to be understood ; since he was expressing
his own ideas, if he did not succeed, still less will another
succeed who is not so clever as Aristotle. We open the
matter, and spread it out by diluting it ; of one subject we
make a thousand, and by multiplying and subdividing fall
again into the infinity of atoms of Epicurus.

Never did two men judge alike on the same matter ; it is
impossible to find two opinions exactly agreeing, not only
in different persons, but in the same person at different
times. I commonly find matter for doubt in a thing of
which the commentator has disdained to take notice. I am
most apt to trip on smooth ground, like certain horses that
I know, that more often stumble on a level road.

Who would not say that glosses increase doubt and ignorance, since there is no book about which the world busies
itself, whether of human or divine origin, of which the
difficulties evaporate by interpretation ? The hundredth
commentator hands it on to his successor, more knotty and
slippery than the first had found it. When did we ever
agree that ' this book has been sufficiently commented upon,
that there is henceforth nothing more to be said about it ? '

This is best seen in law-practice. We attribute legal
authority to an endless number of doctors, an endless
number of judgements and as many interpretations. And
yet do we see any end to the need of interpreting ? Do we
see any progress and advance towards peace ? Do we need
fewer lawyers and judges than when this great body of law
was yet in its first infancy ? On the contrary, we darken
and bury the understanding ; we discover it only hidden
behind so many hedges and barriers.

Men do not realize the natural infirmity of their mind ;
it does nothing but ferret and hunt around, incessantly
wheeling about, contriving, involving itself in its own work,
like a silkworm, and there suffocating. *A mouse in a barrel
of pitch* (Latin proverb).

It thinks it sees in the distance something like a glimmer
of light and imaginary truth ; but, while it is hastening

thither, its path is crossed by so many difficulties, so many obstacles and so many new quests, that it goes off the track and becomes dazed. Not much unlike the dogs in Aesop's fable who, discovering something resembling a dead body floating on the sea, and unable to come near it, set to work to drink up the water and lay the passage dry, and choke themselves.

What a certain Crates said of the writings of Heraclitus may be aptly quoted, ' that they needed a reader who was a good swimmer,' if, owing to the depth and weight of his learning, he is not to sink and drown.

It is only particular weakness that makes us content with what others, or we ourselves, have discovered in this pursuit of knowledge. A more able man will not rest content with it. There is always room for a successor, yea and for ourselves, and another road to travel. There is no end to our researches. Our end is in the other world. It is a sign of contraction of the mind when it is content ; or of lassitude. No noble spirit stays within itself ; it ever aspires and rises above its strength. It soars beyond its deeds ; if it does not advance and does not press forward, and does not back and does not clash with itself, it is only half alive. Its pursuits are boundless and formless, its food is wonder, the chase, ambiguity.

This was sufficiently declared by Apollo, who always spoke to us with a double, obscure and oblique meaning ; not satisfying us, but keeping us always occupied and busy. It is an irregular, perpetual movement, without model and without aim. Its inventions excite, pursue and produce one another :

> So in a running stream one wave we see
> After another roll incessantly.
> And as they glide, each will successively
> Pursue the other, each the other fly :
> By this wave that is e'er pushed on, and this
> By that continually preceded is :
> The water still does into water go,
> Still the same brook, but different waters flow. (LA BOËTIE.

It is more of a business to interpret the interpretations than to interpret the things, and more books have been written on books than on any other subject ; we do nothing but gloss one another.

All the world swarms with commentaries ; of authors there is a great dearth.

Does not the chief and most reputed learning in our present age consist in learning to understand the learned ? Is not that the universal and final end of all studies ?

Our opinions are grafted one upon the other. The first serves as a stock to the second, the second to the third. Thus, we mount stairwise from step to step. So it comes about that he who has mounted highest has often more honour than he deserves, for on the shoulders of the last but one he is only one barley-corn higher.

How often, and perhaps foolishly, I have enlarged my book to make it speak of itself ! Foolishly, if for no other reason than this, that it should remind me of what I say of others who do the same, that their so frequent oglings of their own work testify that their heart thrills with love of it, and that even the offhand roughness with which they beat it is only the mincing dissembled love of a fond mother ; according to Aristotle, for whom prizing and mis-prizing of self often have their origin in the same arrogance. For, as to my excuse, that I ought herein to have more elbow-room than others, since I write specifically of myself and my writings, as well as of my other actions, and that my theme turns upon itself, I doubt whether it will be generally accepted.

I have observed that in Germany Luther had left as many divisions and disputes concerning the uncertainty of his beliefs, and more, as he raised concerning the Holy Scriptures.

Our disputes are about words. I ask what are Nature, Pleasure, Circle and Substitution. The question is one of words, and with words it is answered. A stone is a body, but if you urge any further, ' And what is a body ? '— ' Substance.'—' And what is substance ? ' and so on, you will end by driving the respondent to exhaust his dictionary. We exchange one word for another, and often for a less-known word. I know better what Man is than I know what Animal is, or Mortal, or Rational. To satisfy one doubt they give us three ; it is the Hydra's head.

Socrates asked Meno, ' What is virtue ? '—' There is, replied Meno, the virtue of a man and the virtue of a woman, the virtue of a magistrate and the virtue of a private individual, the virtue of a boy and the virtue of an old man.'—' This is very fine, said Socrates ; we were in search of a virtue, and here you bring us quite a swarm of them.'

We put a question, and they give us a hive-full. As no event and no shape exactly resembles another, neither do they entirely differ ; an ingenious mixture on the part of Nature. If our faces were not similar we could not distinguish man from an animal ; if they were not dissimilar, we could not distinguish one man from another. All things hold together by some similarity or other ; every example limps, and the connexion that is drawn from experience is always faulty and imperfect. And yet comparisons join at some corner or other. And so do the laws serve and adapt themselves to each of our affairs, by the same wrested, forced and biased interpretation.

Since the ethical laws, which are concerned with the individual duties of every man in himself, are so difficult to establish, as we see them to be, it is no wonder if those which govern so many individuals are more so. Consider the form of this justice which rules us ; it is a true testimony of human feebleness, so full is it of errors and contradictions. What we regard as partiality and severity in justice—and we find so much of them, that I doubt whether impartiality is as often met with—are sickly parts and unjust members of the very body and essence of justice.

Some countrymen recently informed me in great haste that they had just left, in a wood that belongs to me, a man with a hundred wounds, still breathing, who entreated them for pity's sake to give him water and help him to rise. They said they did not dare to go near him, and ran away for fear the officers of justice might catch them there, and (as happens with those who are found near a murdered person) they should be made accountable for that mischance, which would be their undoing, since they had neither the ability nor the money to defend their innocence. What could I say to them ? It is certain that that act of humanity would have brought them into trouble.

How many innocent people we have known to be punished, I mean without the fault of the judges ; and how many are there that we have not known of ! This happened in my time : Certain men are condemned to death for murder ; the sentence, if not pronounced, is at least decided and fixed.

At that point the judges are informed, by the officers of an inferior court near by, that they hold several men in custody who openly confess to that murder, and are able to throw a light on the whole business that admits of no doubt. And yet they deliberate whether they shall interrupt and defer the execution of the sentence passed upon the first accused. They consider the novelty of the case, and its consequence for suspending judgements ; that the sentence is juridically passed, and the judges have no reason to repent of it. To sum up, those poor devils are sacrificed to the forms of justice.

Philip, or some other, dealt with a like dilemma in this way : He had pronounced judgement on a man and condemned him to pay a heavy fine to another. The true facts of the case having come to light some time after, it was found that he had condemned him wrongfully. On the one side was the right of the cause, on the other the right of judicial forms. He in some sort satisfied both by allowing the sentence to stand, and making up the loss to the condemned out of his own purse.

But he had to do with a retrievable miscarriage ; my men were irretrievably hanged. How many condemnations I have witnessed more criminal than the crime !

All this brings to my mind these ancient theses : That he must needs do wrong in detail who would do right wholesale, and injustice in little things if he would achieve justice in great ;

That human justice is formed after the model of medicine, according to which all that is profitable is also right and honest ;

That, as the Stoics hold, Nature herself, in most of her works, goes against justice ;

That, as the Cyrenaics contend, there is nothing just of itself ; that customs and laws make justice ;

That, according to the Theodorians, the wise man is right to commit theft, sacrilege, every kind of lechery, if he knows it to be profitable to him.

There is no remedy. I agree with Alcibiades, and will never, if I can help it, place myself in the power of a man who can dispose of my head, when my honour and life depend on the skill and activity of a solicitor more than on my innocence. I would risk a kind of justice that would take account of my good actions as well as my bad ; that would give me as much cause to hope as to fear. To be indemnified is not sufficient coin for a man who does better than not to go wrong. Our justice offers us only one of her hands, and that is the left. Let him be who he may, he comes off with loss.

In China, a kingdom whose governments and arts, having had no contact with or knowledge of ours, offer examples that surpass ours in many excellent features ; from whose history I learn how much wider and more diverse the world is than either the ancients or we moderns have been able to conceive, the officers deputed by the ruler to inspect the condition of the provinces, whilst punishing those who are guilty of corruption in administering their office, also reward, from pure liberality, those whose conduct has been more than ordinarily honourable, and more so than mere duty required. These men come forward not only to answer for their conduct but to gain ; not to be simply paid but to receive a present.

No judge has yet, thank God, spoken to me as a judge in any cause whatsoever, whether my own or another's, whether criminal or civil. No prison has ever received me, not even as a visitor.[1] Imagination makes even the outside of a jail odious to me. I am so hungry for freedom that if any one were to forbid me access to some corner of the Indies I should feel my life to be a little more constrained. And as long as I can find earth and air free and open elsewhere, I will never lurk in a place where I must hide.

Good heavens, how I should chafe if I were reduced to the condition of so many people I know of, riveted to a district of this kingdom, deprived of the right to enter the chief towns and courts and to make use of the public roads, for having quarrelled with our laws ! If those laws I observe were to threaten only the tip of my little finger I should immediately go in search of others, wherever they may be. All the little caution I possess, in these Civil wars in which we are engaged, is exercised to prevent their curtailing my freedom of coming and going.

---

[1] In 1588 Montaigne did actually become acquainted with the inside of the Bastile, having been arrested at the instigation of the Duc d'Elbeuf as a reprisal for some wrong done to a kinsman, but after four hours' detention he was set free by authority of the Queen-mother.

Now the laws maintain their credit not because they are just but because they are laws. That is the mystic foundation of their authority, and they have no other. And that is, indeed, their advantage. They are often made by fools ; more often by men who, in their hatred of equality, are wanting in equity ; but always by men, vain and unsteadfast authors. Nothing is so clumsily and widely, nor so ordinarily, faulty as the laws. Whoever obeys them because they are just does not obey them for the reason for which they should rightly be obeyed.

Our French laws, by their irregularity and formlessness, rather lend a helping hand to the confusion and corruption that we see in their administration and execution. Their authority is so confused and inconsistent that in some sort it excuses both disobedience and mistakes in their interpretation, administration and observance. Whatever then may be the fruit of experience, that which we derive from foreign examples will make us little wiser if we profit so little from that which we have of ourselves, which is more familiar to us, and certainly sufficient to tell us what we need.

I study myself more than any other subject ; that is my Metaphysics, that is my Physics ;

> With how much skill this mighty world is ruled ;
> Whence comes the rising moon, and where she sets ;
> How 'tis she joins her horns, and every month
> Comes to the full ; where winds surmount the sea ;
> What regions Eurus seizes with his blast ;
> Why waters turn to clouds ; if ever a day
> Will come, when all these earthly towers
> Are overthrown : let them inquire whose minds
> Are moved to know the secrets of the world.
>
> (PROPERTIUS and LUCAN.)

In this universe of things I allow myself to be ignorantly and carelessly guided by the general law of the world. I shall know it well enough when I feel it. My learning cannot make it alter its course. It will not modify itself for my sake. It is folly to expect it, and greater folly to be disturbed about it, since it is necessarily the same for all of us. The goodness and capability of our Pilot must relieve us fully and absolutely from all anxiety about steering.

The researches and meditations of the philosophers only

serve to feed our curiosity. The philosophers very rightly refer us to the laws of Nature ; but these laws are not concerned with such sublime knowledge. The philosophers falsify them, and show us Nature with a painted face, too high in colour and too sophisticated ; whence spring so many different portraits of so uniform a subject. As she has provided us with feet to walk with, so she has given us wisdom to guide us through life : a wisdom not so ingenious, robust and showy as that they have devised, but correspondingly easy and wholesome, which very well performs what the other promises, if we are fortunate enough to be able to live it simply and fitly, that is to say, naturally. To trust to Nature most simply is to trust her most wisely.

O what a soft and easy and wholesome pillow is ignorance and freedom from care to rest a well-screwed-on headpiece !

I would rather know myself well by studying myself than Cicero. The experience I have of myself I find sufficient to make me wise if I were a good scholar. He who calls to mind the excess of his past anger, and remembers how he was carried away by his passion, will see the hatefulness of it better than in Aristotle, and will have more reason to hate it. He who remembers the evils he has suffered, and those which have threatened him, the slight causes which have disturbed his state of mind, is by them prepared for future changes, and for the knowledge of his condition.

The life of Caesar can offer us no more examples than our own ; and whether it be the life of an Emperor or that of a proletarian, it is still a life that is subject to all human accidents. Let us only give ear to it ; we tell ourselves all that we chiefly need. If a man remembers how many and many a time he has been mistaken in his own judgement, is he not a fool if he does not ever after distrust it ? When I have been convinced by another's arguments that I have held a wrong opinion ; what I have learned is, not so much the new thing he has told me, and the fact that I was ignorant in one particular (that would be no great gain), but that I am generally feeble-minded and that my understanding is a treacherous guide ; whence I draw the conclusion that my whole mental process needs reforming. I do the same in the case of all my other errors, and find this a very profitable rule in life. I regard not the species and the individual, as I should a stone over which I have stumbled ;

I learn to distrust my steps throughout, and am careful to place them aright.

To learn that we have said or done a foolish thing, that is nothing ; we must learn that we are but fools : a much fuller and more important lesson.

The mistakes that my memory has so often led me into, even when it was most confident of itself, have not been wasted upon me ; she may swear to me at this moment, and assure me to her heart's content, I shake my ears. The first opposition her testimony meets with will give me pause ; I would not dare to trust her in a matter of importance, nor answer for her in another's concerns. And were it not that what I do for lack of memory others do still more often through want of good faith, I should always accept the truth, concerning a matter of fact, from another's lips rather than from my own.

If every one would closely watch the effects and circumstances of the passions that sway him, as I have done of the one that has fallen to my lot, he would see them coming, and would a little break their course and impetuosity. They do not always fly at one's throat with one leap ; they threaten us by degrees :

> As when a wave beneath the rising gale
> 'Gins whiten, slowly heaves the sea, and rears
> Its billows higher, then from lowest deep
> Mounts in one mass to heaven. (VIRGIL.)

The judgement holds a masterful sway with me ; at least it carefully endeavours to do so. It leaves my feelings to go their own way, both hatred and love, even the love which I bear to myself, without change or corruption. If it cannot convert the other parts as it would, at least it does not allow itself to be perverted by them ; it plays its own game by itself.

The advice given to every man, ' Know thyself ', should have very great influence, since the God of light and learning had it engraved on the front of his temple,[1] as comprising all that he had to counsel us.

Plato says besides that wisdom is no more than the carrying out of this command, and Socrates, according to Xenophon, proves it in particular cases.

The difficulties and obscurities of every science are only

[1] The temple of Apollo at Delphi.

perceived by those who have entered upon it. For it still
needs some degree of intelligence to be able to remark our
ignorance ; we must push a door before we know it is
closed. Whence arises this Platonic subtlety, ' Neither
those who know need inquire, since they know, nor those
who know not, since in order to inquire they must know
what they are inquiring about.'

So in the matter of ' knowing oneself ', the fact that every
man is so cocksure and self-satisfied, and thinks he knows
enough about himself, shows that he does not know himself
in the least ; as Socrates, in Xenophon, impresses upon
Euthydemus.

I, who make no other profession, find in myself such
infinite variety and depth, that the only result of my learning is that I feel how much I still have to learn. I owe it to
my weakness, which I so often admit, that I am inclined
to be modest, to bow to the beliefs that I have been taught,
to be consistently cool and moderate in my opinions, to hate
that overbearing and quarrelsome arrogance that causes
a man to believe and trust entirely to himself ; a deadly
enemy of learning and truth.

Hear them laying down the law ; as soon as they open
their mouths to utter some foolish thing, you would think
they were prophets and legislators. *Nothing can be more
discreditable than to assert and acquiesce in a thing before we
know and understand it* (Cicero).

Aristarchus said that in former times there were scarcely
seven wise men in the world, and that in his own time he
could scarcely find seven ignorant men. Could we not say
the same with more reason of our times ?

Affirmation and opinionativeness are positive signs of
stupidity. This man may have fallen on his nose a hundred
times in one day, and yet here we see him riding the high
horse, as positive and headstrong as ever. You would
think he had since been inspired with some new soul and
intellectual vigour, and that, like that old son of the earth,
he renewed his strength and courage with each new fall : [1]

> Whose weakened limbs, touching his Mother Earth,
> Forthwith exult in renovated strength. (LUCAN.)

---

[1] The giant Antæus, a famous wrestler who could not be thrown, as he
regained his strength whenever he touched his Mother Earth ; eventu-
ally defeated and killed by Hercules, who suspended him in mid air.

Does not this incorrigibly pig-headed fellow think he has picked up a new wit because he has picked up a new argument ? It is personal experience that makes me accuse the world of ignorance, the consciousness of which is, in my opinion, the surest means of schooling the world. Those who will not conclude their ignorance from so vain an example as mine, or as theirs, let them acknowledge it with Socrates. He was the teacher of teachers ; for the philosopher Antisthenes said to his pupils, ' Come, you and I will go and hear Socrates ; there I shall be a pupil with you.' And, maintaining this doctrine of the Stoic sect, ' that virtue sufficed to make a life completely happy, wanting nothing whatever,' he added, ' excepting the strength of Socrates.'

Having so long and attentively studied myself I am also qualified to form a passably good estimate of others ; and there are few matters on which I can speak more happily and pardonably. I am often able to observe and discern the nature of my friends more accurately than they do themselves. I have surprised one or two by the aptness of my description ; and I have warned them against themselves. Through having trained myself from youth up to see my own life reflected in that of others, it has become a natural propensity to study that subject ; and when I give my mind to it, there are few things in the faces, humours and talk of the persons around me that escape my notice, if they are likely to be instructive to me.

I study everything : what I must flee, what I must follow. So from the outer manifestations of my friends I discover their inner natures ; not in order to marshal those infinitely varying, motley and disconnected actions under fixed headings and categories, to distribute my lots and sections into distinct and recognized classes and degrees ;

> How many kinds, and what their names,
> There is no telling. (VIRGIL.)

It is only learned scholars who divide and mark off their ideas more specifically and in detail. I, who see no further into things than I have been taught by using my eyes, and that without any method, present my ideas in the gross, and tentatively. As in this : I express my meaning in disjointed clauses, as a thing that cannot be said all at once and in the lump. A mean and commonplace mind like ours is unable to connect and relate. Wisdom is a complete and substantial structure, each part of which keeps its place and bears its mark. *Wisdom alone is contained wholly in itself* (Cicero). I leave it to artists, and I know not whether they will bring it about, in a matter so mixed, so subtle and uncertain, to marshal into bands that endless variety of aspects, to resolve our inconsistencies and arrange them in order. I find it not only difficult to reconcile our actions with one another, but I find it difficult, taking each one singly, to properly designate it by some leading quality, so ambiguous and motley do they appear from different points of view.

What is remarked as uncommon in Perseus, King of Macedon, ' That his mind, fixing itself to no one condition, wandered through every kind of life, reflecting a character so flighty and erratic, that neither he himself nor any other knew what kind of a man he was,' seems to me to apply to nearly the whole world.

And above all I know another of his kidney, to whom I think this description would still more fittingly apply : no middle attitude, being always carried away from one extreme to another by causes not to be guessed at ; steering no kind of course without being crossed, and changing its direction in a surprising manner ; no one simple and unmixed quality ; so that the likeliest supposition that may be some day put forth about him is that he affected and studied to make himself known by being unknowable.

It needs very strong ears to hear yourself frankly criticized ; and since there are few who can bear it without being mortified, those who boldly venture to censure us show their friendship in a remarkable degree. It is a sign of a healthy affection to undertake to offend and wound us for our good. It taxes my powers to give my opinion of a man in whom the bad qualities outnumber the good.

Plato requires three qualities in a man who undertakes to examine another's soul: Knowledge, Benevolence, Boldness.

I was once asked what I thought I was fit for, if any one had thought of employing my services whilst I was young enough to be of use :

> While better blood gave strength, before the snow
> Of envious age was sprinkled on my brows. (VIRGIL.)

' For nothing,' I said. And I generally excuse myself by

saying that I can do nothing that would enslave me to another. But I would have told any master of mine the plain truth, and would have watched over his conduct, if he had allowed me. Not in the gross, by lecturing him like a schoolmaster, which I cannot do (and I do not observe that those who can do so effect any real improvement), but by observing him step by step, at every opportunity, keeping a close watch upon him, bit by bit, simply and naturally, letting him know what the public thought of him, and opposing his flatterers.

There is not a man of us who would not be worse than a king, if he were continually being pampered, as a king is, by those rapscallions. What can we expect when Alexander, so great both as king and philosopher, was unable to resist them ?

I should have had fidelity, judgement and candour enough for that. It would be a nameless office, else it would lose its effect and its grace. And it is a part that cannot be played by all indiscriminately. For even the truth is not privileged to speak at all times and in every kind of way ; the exercise of it, noble as it is, is limited and circumscribed. It often happens, as the world wags, that the truth slips into the ears of a Prince, not only fruitlessly, but prejudicially and even wrongfully. And no one will make me believe that a righteous remonstrance cannot be viciously administered ; and that the interest of the substance must not often yield to the interest of the form.

For this business I would have a man who is content with his fortune,

> Who likes that present state of his,
> And would not be but what he is,   (MARTIAL.)

and of middle rank by birth, because, on the one hand, he would not be afraid of touching his master's heart to the quick or of deeply offending him, and so losing his chance of preferment ; and on the other hand, being of middle station, he would more probably be in communication with all classes of people. I would have him to stand alone, for to spread the privilege of this freedom and intimacy among several would beget a harmful irreverence. And certainly in that man I would require above all things the fidelity of silence.

A king is not to be believed when, for fame's sake, he

boasts of his bravery in standing his ground against the attack of the enemy, if he cannot, for his own good and improvement, stand the liberty of speech of a friend, which has no other power but to penetrate his ear, the rest of its effect being in his own hand. Now there is no kind of man that stands in such great need of true and sincere warning as a king. He has to endure to live in the public eye, and to satisfy the notions of so many onlookers, that, as those about him are wont to conceal from him everything that frustrates his plans, he finds himself involved, without being conscious of it, in the hatred and detestation of his people, often on grounds he might have avoided, even without prejudice to his pleasures, if he had been informed and set right in time. His favourites commonly look to their own interests more than to those of their master ; and it answers them well, since, indeed, most of the duties of true friendship towards the sovereign are put to a rude and dangerous test ; so that there is need, not only of great affection and freedom, but also of courage.

In fine, all this farrago that I am scribbling here is nothing but a record of the experiences of my life, which, in regard to spiritual health, is exemplary enough if the instruction to be derived from it is reversed. But in regard to bodily health no man can furnish more useful experience than I, since I offer it unadulterated, quite uncorrupted by art and theory. In the realm of medicine experience is, so to say, a cock on his own dunghill, since reason must entirely give way to it.

Tiberius used to say that the man who had lived twenty years ought to be responsible to himself for all the things that were harmful or wholesome for him, and be able to take care of himself without medical aid.[1]

He might have learned this of Socrates, who recommended his pupils to look carefully after their health as a most important study, and added that an intelligent man who took exercise, and was careful about his eating and drinking, could not fail to know better than a physician what was good or bad for him.

---

[1] According to both Suetonius and Tacitus, Tiberius said, in other words, that ' a man at thirty is either a fool or a physician ' ; Plutarch makes him say that ' the man is a fool who offers his pulse to a doctor after sixty '.

And, indeed, medicine always professes to make experience the touchstone of its actions. So Plato had reason on his side when he said that to be a genuine physician it would be necessary for the practitioner to have passed through all the diseases he professes to cure, and to be familiar with all the accidents and circumstances on which he is to give an opinion. It is but right that he should catch the pox if he would know how to treat it.

I should certainly trust such a man. For the others guide us like a man who should paint seas and rocks and harbours seated on his table, with the model of a ship passing in all safety before his eyes. Put him to the real thing and he will not know how to set about it.

They describe our diseases like a town-crier trumpeting the loss of a horse or a dog : such and such colour, such and such a height, such and such ears ; but bring it to him he will not recognize it.

By heavens ! if only medicine should some day give me real and perceptible relief, you should see how I would exclaim in good earnest :

> At length to potent science I surrender. (HORACE.)

The arts that promise to keep our body in health and our soul in health promise much ; but at the same time there are none that keep their promise less. And in our time and our country the men who profess these arts can show fewer results than any other. The best we can say for them is that they sell medicinal drugs ; but that they are medical men we cannot say.

I have lived long enough to be able to give an account of the habits that have carried me so far. For any man who has a mind to try them I have tasted them as if I were his cupbearer. Here follow a few details, as my memory shall supply me with them. I have no habits that I have not varied according to circumstances, but I record those that I have oftenest observed to prevail, and that have hitherto taken most hold of me.

My mode of life is the same in sickness and in health : the same bed, the same hours, the same food and even the same drink, serve my purpose. I make no change whatever except that I observe more or less moderation, according to my strength and my appetite. With me health means keeping up my accustomed way of living without discomfort. I find that sickness upsets my balance in one direction ; if I take the advice of the doctors they will upset it in the other ; so what with fortune and art I have quite lost my way.

Of nothing am I more certain than of this, that nothing harms me that I have been so long accustomed to.

It is the part of habit to shape a man's life according to its pleasure ; in this it is all-powerful. It is Circe's draught that varies our nature as seems good to her.

In how many countries, and only three steps from here, it is regarded as a ridiculous fancy to dread the night-dew which appears so hurtful to us ! And our watermen and peasants laugh at it.

You will make a German ill if you give him a mattress to sleep on, as you will an Italian on a feather-bed, and a Frenchman without curtains or a fire. A Spaniard's stomach cannot stand our way of eating, nor ours to drink like the Swiss.

A German at Augsburg amused me by arguing against the disadvantages of our open fire-places with the very same reasons for which we condemn their stoves. For, indeed, that stifling heat, and the smell of the heated material of which they are made, give most of those who are not accustomed to them a headache ; but not me. After all, this heat being even, constant and general, without light, without smoke, and without the draught that is caused by our open chimneys, it may very well bear comparison in other respects with ours.

Why do we not copy the Roman architecture ? For it is said that in ancient times the fires were made, not inside the houses but on the outside, and at the foot of them, whence the heat was drawn through the whole dwelling, through pipes which were contrived in the thick walls and embraced the rooms that were to be warmed ; which I have seen plainly described somewhere in Seneca.

My German, hearing me praise the beauties and amenities of his town, which certainly deserve the praise, began to pity me because I had to leave it ; and among the chief disadvantages he mentioned to me was the heaviness of head that the fire-places elsewhere would cause me. He had heard somebody complain of this discomfort, and fixed it upon us, habit having made him unable to detect it at home.

All heat that comes from a fire makes me feel weak and heavy. And yet Evenus said that fire was the best condiment of life.[1]   I prefer any other way of escaping the cold.

We are afraid of the wine at the bottom of the cask ; in Portugal they commend it for its delicious bouquet, and call it the drink of princes. In short, every nation has many habits and customs which to any other nation are not only strange but amazing and barbarous.

What can we do with those people who will admit of no evidence that is not in print, who will not believe a man who is not in a book, or the truth unless it is of suitable age ?

We dignify our stupidities when we send them to the printers.

To say ' I have read it ' carries very much more weight with them than if you say ' I have heard it '. But as for me, who would no more disbelieve a man's mouth than his hand, who know that people write with as little judgement as they speak, and who esteem this age as highly as one that is past, I would as soon quote one of my friends as I would Aulus Gellius or Macrobius, and what I have seen as what they have written.

And, as some have said of Virtue that it is no greater for being of long standing, so I hold of the Truth that it is no wiser for being older.

I often say that it is mere foolishness that makes us run after outlandish and bookish examples. They flourish quite as well at this moment as in the time of Homer and Plato. But is it not true that we seek to gain more credit for the action of quoting than for the truth of what we quote ? As if it were more to the purpose to borrow our proofs at the shop of Vascosan or Plantin,[2] than from what we may see in our village.

Or is it not rather true that we have not the wit to pick out and turn to account the things that pass before our eyes, nor the acumen to estimate their fitness to serve as examples ? For if we say that we lack authority to win belief for our testimony, we say so without reason ; since, in my

---

[1] Or, according to Amyot's translation ' the best sauce in the world '. no doubt on account of its culinary properties.

[2] Two well-known printers of the day.

opinion, if we could set them in their proper light, the most ordinary, trite and commonplace things might form the subject of the greatest wonders in Nature, and provide us with the most surprising examples, especially in the matter of human actions.

Now, in this connexion, setting aside the examples I know from books, and the case of Andro of Argos, who, according to Aristotle, crossed the sandy deserts of Libya without drinking, a gentleman, who had acquitted himself very creditably in several charges, said in my presence that he had travelled from Madrid to Lisbon in the middle of summer without drinking. He is very robust for his age, and there is nothing extraordinary in his mode of life except this, that he will go two or three months, and even a year, so he told me, without drinking. He feels the thirst, but he allows it to pass, and maintains that it is a craving that easily becomes weaker of itself ; and he drinks more from caprice than from need or for pleasure.

Here is another : Not long ago I found one of the most learned men in France, and a man of no mean fortune, studying in the corner of his hall which had been partitioned off by tapestries, whilst his servants, under no restraint whatever, were creating a regular hubbub around him. He told me, and Seneca says pretty much the same about himself, that this pandemonium suited him. It would seem that, stunned by the noise, he could better retire within himself, become more collected and meditate the better ; as if this storm of voices drove his thoughts inward. When he was a scholar at Padua, he studied so long in a room that was exposed to the rattle of coaches, and the tumult of the market-place, that he had trained himself not only to ignore the noise but to find it necessary for his studies.

Socrates replied to Alcibiades, who wondered how he could stand the perpetual din of his wife's scolding tongue, ' I am like those who are accustomed to the regular sound of the water-drawing wheels.'

I am quite the contrary : my mind is sensitive, and is apt to wing its flight ; when it is absorbed in itself the mere buzzing of a fly will torment it to death.

Seneca, in his youth, being sorely bitten by the example of Sextius to eat nothing that had been killed, abstained from animal food for a year, and with pleasure, as he said. He left off the habit only because he did not wish to be suspected of borrowing that rule of some new religions that were propagating it. At the same time he followed the precept of Attalus not to lie on any bedding that gave way under his weight, and continued even in his old age to sleep on a bed that did not yield to his body. What was accounted an austere habit in his day would now be put down to effeminacy.

Look at the difference between the life-habits of my hinds and my own. The Scythians and Indians are not more remote from me in ways and capabilities. I remember having rescued boys from a life of beggary and taken them into my service, who soon after left me and gave up my kitchen and their livery, only to return to their former life. And I found one of them afterwards picking up mussels out of the midden for his dinner, whom neither by entreaties nor threats I could reclaim from the relish and delight he took in want.

Beggars have their sumptuousness and their sensual pleasures as well as the rich, and, so they say, their civil ranks and orders.

These are the results of Habit. She can not only mould us into any shape she pleases (' wherefore, as the sages say, choose the best, and habit will soon make it easy for you '), but also teach us to change and vary, which is the noblest and most useful thing we can learn from her.

The best thing about my physical constitution is that it is pliable and not very stubborn. Some of my inclinations are more personal and usual, and more agreeable than others ; but I can depart from them with very little effort and easily glide into the opposite habit.

A young man should break in upon his rules, to stir up his energy and keep it from becoming mouldy and lazy ; for no course of life is so foolish and feeble as that which is carried out according to rules and discipline :

> Before she takes a drive of half a mile
> Her almanac must tell the proper hour ;
> If she but chafes the corner of her eye,
> No salve must touch it ere she can consult
> Her horoscope. (JUVENAL.)

If he will take my advice, he will occasionally even run into excess ; otherwise the least dissipation will upset him, and he will become disagreeable and unfit for company. The most repugnant quality in a gentleman is to be over-fastidious and tied down to certain particular ways ; and they are particular if they are not yielding and pliable. It is a disgrace for a man to refrain from what he sees his friends doing, because he cannot or dare not follow their example. Let such a man keep to his own kitchen. It is unbecoming in every other man, but in a soldier it is an intolerable fault ; for, as Philopoemen said, he should harden himself to all the changes and ups and downs of life.

Although I was trained, as far as possible, to be easily pleased and independent, yet so it is that, having, through indifference as I grew older, become more settled in certain habits (at my age I am beyond learning, and I have hence-forth no other prospect but to keep my course), habit has already unconsciously impressed its stamp upon me, in cer-tain things, to such a degree that I call it excess to deviate from it. And I cannot, without trying myself, either sleep by day, or take snacks between meals, or breakfast, or go to sleep without a long interval, of about three hours at least, after supper, or procreate except before sleep, or standing, or carry my sweat, or quench my thirst with either water or wine unmixed, or remain long bareheaded, or have my hair cut after dinner ; and I should be as un-comfortable without my gloves as without my shirt, or without washing when I rise from table or get up in the morning, or without a canopy and curtains to my bed ; which to me are all very necessary things.

I could dine without a table-cloth, but very uncomfort-ably without a clean napkin, in the German fashion ; I soil them more than they or the Italians do, as I make little use of spoon or fork. I am sorry they did not keep up the fashion which was begun in my day, following the royal ex-ample, of changing the napkin with the plates at every course.

We are told by that hard-working soldier, Marius, that he became dainty in his drinking as he grew older, and that he drank only out of one particular cup of his own. I too have dropped into the habit of using a glass of a certain shape, and do not care to drink out of a common glass, nor when served by a common hand. I dislike all metal in comparison with a clear and transparent material. My eyes must also taste to the best of their capacity.

I owe many such weaknesses to Habit. Nature, on the other hand, has also brought me her share of them, such as being unable to bear two full meals a day without overloading my stomach, or abstaining entirely from one of those meals without becoming flatulent, drying up my mouth and taking the edge off my appetite ; and suffering from long exposure to the night air. For during the last few years, in the drudgeries of the war, when they continue all through the night, as they often do, after five or six hours my stomach begins to give me trouble, with violent headache, and before daybreak I am obliged to vomit. When the others go to breakfast I go to sleep, and after that I am as fresh as ever.

I had always understood that the evening dew only fell at nightfall, but having during these latter years been long and intimately acquainted with a lord who was imbued with the belief that the evening air is keener and more dangerous towards the decline of the sun, an hour or two before it sets, when he carefully avoids it whilst despising the night air, he has almost communicated to me not so much his belief as his feeling.

What if our imagination should even be so affected by doubt and inquiry as to cause a change in our health ? Those who suddenly yield to these fancies will entirely ruin their health. And I pity several gentlemen who, through the foolish advice of their doctors, though still young and in perfect health, have made close prisoners of themselves.[1] It would after all be better to suffer from a cold than by disuse to forfeit for ever the pleasures of life in common by giving up so widespread a habit.[2]

What a disagreeable science to run down the most agreeable hours of the day ! Let us hold on to the utmost of our powers. Most often we may harden ourselves by persistence, and correct our constitutions, as Caesar did his epilepsy by dint of despising and fighting it.

We should adopt the best rules, but not become slaves to them ; except to those, if there are such, to which obligation and slavery are beneficial.

Kings and philosophers obey Nature's call, and ladies too.[3]

---

[1] *Se sont mis en chartre ;* which might also mean, as Florio translates it, ' fallen into a decline or consumption '.

[2] The habit of going out at night.

[3] *Les Roys et les philosophes fientent, et les dames aussi.*

A man who lives in the public eye is obliged to observe the conventions ; I, who am an obscure and private individual, enjoy every dispensation that Nature allows. As a soldier and a Gascon I may be allowed a little indiscretion. Wherefore I will say of that action that it must be relegated to certain fixed and night hours, to which we should force and subject ourselves by habit, as I have done ; but not, as I have done in my declining years, pamper ourselves by being tied for this function to a particularly comfortable place and seat, and make it a burden by prolongation and luxury.

And yet in the dirtiest functions is it not in some measure excusable to require more care and cleanliness ? *Man is by nature a cleanly and dainty animal* (Seneca). It is the one function of Nature that I can least bear to put off. I have known many soldiers to be inconvenienced by the irregularity of their bowels ; whilst I and mine never miss the moment of our assignation, which is on leaping out of bed, unless we are disturbed by some urgent occupation or some serious malady.

I cannot think therefore, as I said before, where a sick man can better find safety than in quietly continuing the course of life to which he has been reared and trained. Change of every kind is disturbing and hurtful. Will any man believe that chestnuts will hurt a native of Périgord or Lucca, or milk and cheese a mountain-dweller ?

They keep ordering us not merely a new diet, but the very opposite to that we are accustomed to ; a change that not even a healthy man can suffer. Order a Breton of seventy to drink water ; shut up a sailor in a hot-house ; forbid a Basque footman to walk : you deprive them of movement, and in the end of air and light.

Is mere existence then so very sweet ? (ANON.)

We must perforce renounce our dearest things,
And give up life that we may merely live.
Can he be said to live to whom we grudge
The air we breathe and light that gives us life ? (MAXIMIANUS.)

If they do no other good they do this at least, that they prepare their patients betimes for death, by gradually undermining and cutting off their enjoyment of life.

Both in health and sickness I have generally yielded to

my urgent appetites. I allow my desires and inclinations
to have a great say in the matter. I have no wish to cure
one ill with another ; and hate the remedies which are more
unpleasant than the malady. To be subject to the stone,
and to subject myself to abstaining from the pleasure of
eating oysters, are two evils instead of one. The disease
twinges us on the one side, the rule on the other. Since we
risk making a mistake let us rather risk the pursuit of
pleasure. The world goes the contrary way to work, and
thinks nothing beneficial that is not painful ; it is suspicious
of facility.

My appetite has in many things happily enough adapted
itself of its own accord, and fallen in with the health of my
stomach. Sharp and pungent sauces were agreeable to me
when I was younger ; my stomach having since then turned
against them, my palate has forthwith followed suit. Wine
is hurtful to the sick ; it is the first thing my mouth takes a
dislike to, and an invincible dislike. Whatever I take that
is disagreeable to me, disagrees with me.

Nothing disagrees with me that I do greedily and
heartily. I have never taken harm from any action in which
I found great pleasure. And so I have made every medical
decision to yield very largely to my pleasure. And as a
young man,

When young Dan Cupid, gay in saffron shift,
Would hover round me with his playful wiles, (CATULLUS.)

I yielded, as wantonly and thoughtlessly as any other, to the
desire that held me captive ;

And, not without some glory, held my own. (HORACE.)

My love, however, was more constant and enduring than
vigorous ;

I scarce remember once attaining six. (OVID.)

It is, indeed, distressing and wonderful to me to have to
confess at what a tender age I first chanced to come under
Cupid's subjection. It was, indeed, a chance, for it was long
before the age of choice and knowledge. I cannot remember
so far back. And my lot may be wedded to that of Quar-
tilla,[1] who had no recollection of her maidenhood.

Precocious hairs and beard soon blossomed forth,
A mother's admiration. (MARTIAL.)

[1] See Petronius's *Satyricon*.

The physicians modify, usually with good results, their rules according to the vehemence of their patients' cravings. The great desire in question must be put down to Nature, however monstrous and vicious we may imagine it to be. And then, how much does it need to satisfy the imagination? In my opinion that faculty is all-important, at least more so than any other. The most grievous and the most common ills are those that fancy puts upon me. I like this Spanish saying from several points of view, *God defend me from myself*.

When I am ill I am sorry not to have some craving that will give me this pleasure of satisfying it ; medicine would find it hard to turn me from it. I feel the same when I am well ; I see hardly anything more to hope and wish for. It is pitiful when even the power of wishing becomes weak and languid.

The medical art is not so cut and dried that we cannot find some authority for doing whatever we please. It changes according to climate and according to the moons ; according to Fernel and l'Escale.[1] If your doctor does not think it good for you to sleep, to drink wine, or to eat of a particular dish, do not worry ; I will find you another who will not agree with him.

The various medical arguments and opinions assume every kind of form. I saw a wretched sick man faint and dying with thirst, for his cure, who was afterwards laughed at by another doctor, who condemned that treatment as hurtful. Had he not had all his torments for nothing ?

One of the faculty recently died of stone in the bladder, who resorted to starvation to combat his malady ; his colleagues say, on the other hand, that his fast had dried him up and baked the gravel in his kidneys.

I have observed that when sick, or wounded, talking excites me and hurts me as much as any other irregularity that I may commit. The use of my voice tires me, and I have to suffer for it, for it is loud and strong ; so much so that when I used to entertain the ears of eminent men with weighty affairs, they would often anxiously entreat me to moderate my voice.

This story deserves a digression : Some one in a certain

---

[1] Fernel or Farnel and l'Escale, better known as Scaliger, two famous physicians of the day.

Greek school was speaking in a loud voice, as I do ; the master of the ceremonies sent him a request to speak lower. ' Let him send me, he said, the tone in which he wishes me to speak.' The other replied, ' That he should take his tone from the ears of him he was speaking to.' That was well said, provided it was meant in this way : ' Speak according to the matter you have to discuss with your hearer.' For if he meant, ' Let it be enough that he hears you,' or ' Adapt your voice to his hearing,' then I do not agree with him. The tone and movement of the voice help to express and signify my meaning ; it is my part to govern it in order to make myself understood.

There is a tone for teaching, a tone for wheedling, a tone for scolding. I wish my voice not only to reach him, but perhaps to impress him, to force its way into him. When I rate my footman in a sharp and bitter tone, it would be a fine thing if he said to me, ' Master, speak lower, I can hear you very well.' *There is a kind of voice adapted to the hearing, not so much by reason of its volume, as its quality* (Quintilian). Speech is half his who speaks, and half his who hears. The latter must prepare to take it according to the impetus it receives. As with tennis players, he who takes the ball must shift his position and make ready according to the movement of the striker, and according to the nature of the stroke.

Experience has also taught me this, that we undo ourselves by impatience. Misfortunes have their life and their limits, their sickness and their health.

Maladies are constituted after the model of living creatures. Their destiny and their length of days are limited from their birth. He who arbitrarily and forcibly attempts to cut them short in the middle of their career, will prolong and multiply them, and will incense instead of appeasing them. I agree with Crantor, that we should neither obstinately and frantically oppose them, nor weakly succumb to them ; but naturally give way to them, according to their condition and our own.

We ought to give maladies free access to us ; and I have found that they stay a shorter time with me, who give them a free hand. And some have left me, even of those reputed among the most tenacious and stubborn, dying of their own decay, without the help of the art of medicine, and in spite of its rules. Let us allow Nature a little free play ; she knows her business better than we do.

' But so and so died of it.' So will you, if not of that disease, of some other. How many have died in spite of having three doctors at their backsides !

Example is a clear looking-glass, universal and all-embracing.

If the physic is pleasant, take it ; it is always so much present gain. I will not boggle at the name or the colour, if it is delicious and appetising. Pleasure is one of the principal elements in the benefit.

I have allowed colds, gouty discharges, looseness, palpitations, megrims, and other ailments to grow old in me and die a natural death ; they would leave me when I had half accustomed myself to keep them. They are better conjured by courtesy than by defiance.

We must meekly endure the laws of our nature. We are born to grow old and weak, to fall into sickness, in spite of all medicine. It is the first lesson that the Mexicans read their children, when they thus salute them after they have come out of their mother's womb : ' Child, you have come into the world to endure ; endure, suffer, and hold your peace.'

It is wrong to complain that a thing happens to any one of us that may happen to all of us. *You may complain if anything is unjustly decreed against you alone* (Seneca).

Look at an old man praying to God to keep him in perfect and robust health, that is to say, to restore his youth :

Why prayest thou, fool, such childish prayers in vain ? (OVID.)

Is it not madness ? His state does not admit of it. The gout, the stone, indigestion, are symptoms of a long life, as heat, rain and winds of a long voyage.

Plato does not believe that Aesculapius would have taken the trouble to treat a wasted and crazy body and prolong the life of one who was of no use to his country, unequal to his calling, and unable to beget healthy and sturdy children ; nor does he think it consistent with divine justice and wisdom to concern itself with such matters, its duty being to direct all things to usefulness. My good man, it is all over with you. You cannot be set up again ; at the most

you may be a little patched up and propped ; your misery
may be prolonged for an hour or two :

> Like one who, eager to defer a while
> Impending ruin, props the tottering pile,
> Till in short space the house, the props and all
> Together in awful devastation fall. (MAXIMIANUS.)

What cannot be cured must be endured. Our life is
made up, like the harmony of the world, of contrary things,
also of different notes, soft and loud, sharp and flat, high
and low. What could the musician express who liked only
the one kind ? He must be able to use them in common
and blend them. And we too must take the evil with the
good, which are consubstantial with our life. We cannot
exist without that blending, and the one set is no less
necessary to it than the other. To try to jib against the
law of Nature is to copy the folly of Ctesiphon, who tried
to match his mule in kicking.

I seldom consult the doctor when I feel myself getting
worse, for those gentlemen take advantage of you when
they have you at their mercy ; they deafen you with their
forebodings. Formerly, taking me unawares when I was
weakened by my ailment, they would deal harshly with me,
what with their dogmatic assertions and their masterful
airs, threatening me now with acute pain, now with approaching death. Though they knocked and pushed me,
they could not upset me and make me lose my balance.
If my power of judgement was not impaired or disturbed,
it was at least troubled ; there is always agitation and
a struggle.

Now I treat my imagination as gently as I can, and
would relieve it, if I could, of all trouble and conflict. It
must be helped and coaxed, and cheated when possible.
My mind is well fitted for that service. It has no lack of
good reasons for all things. If it could convince as well as
it preaches, it would be a very happy assistance to me.

Would you like an example ? My mind says to me, ' It
is for your good that you have the stone ; at your age the
edifice has naturally to suffer some leakage. It is the season
when it begins to become loose and give way. That is the
common lot, and you cannot expect a new miracle to be
worked in your favour. In this way you pay the tribute
due to old age, and you could not have got off more cheaply.

' You must find comfort in the idea that you are in company, since you have fallen into the most common infirmity of men of your time of life. On all sides you see men afflicted with the same kind of disease, and it is an honourable fellowship, since it most commonly attaches itself to great people. There is something noble and dignified in it.

' Few men who are afflicted with it get off more cheaply ; and then they have to pay the penalty of an offensive diet, and the daily swallowing of loathsome medicinal drugs ; whilst you owe your better state purely to your good fortune. For a few ordinary decoctions of eryngo and rupture-wort that you have swallowed three or four times, to oblige the ladies who, with more kindness than your pain was sharp, offered you the half of theirs, seemed to you as easy to take as they were ineffectual. The others have to pay a thousand vows to Aesculapius and as many crowns to their doctor for an easy and abundant ejection of gravel, which you often owe to the kindness of Nature.

' Even your decent behaviour in everyday company is not disturbed by it ; you can carry your water ten hours, and as long as another.

' You used to be terrified by this disease, says my mind, before you were acquainted with it ; the shouts of despair of those who aggravated it by their impatience begot a horror of it in you.

' It is a malady that chastises those of your members through which you have most sinned ; you are a man of conscience.

> That punishment alone should be resented
> That we have least deserved. (OVID.)

' Look at the punishment ; it is very mild compared with that of others, and inflicted with a paternal tenderness. Consider how late in life it has come ; it only seizes and troubles you at a time of your life that, in any case, will be henceforth barren and wasted, having, as if by agreement, left your youth free to enjoy its wanton pleasures.

' The fear and sympathy that people feel at the sight of this malady is for you a cause of vainglory, a feeling of which, even if you have purged your judgement and cured your words of it, your friends will yet discover some tincture in your disposition. It is gratifying to hear people say of you : there is strength of mind indeed, there is patience ! They see you sweating in agony, turning pale, red, trembling, vomiting your very blood, suffering strange contractions and convulsions, your eyes sometimes dropping big tears, passing water that is thick, black and dreadful to look at, or having it stopped by some rugged and sharp-edged stone that pricks you and cruelly flays the neck of your penis ; meanwhile talking to the bystanders in your usual way, jesting at intervals with your servants, taking your share in a connected conversation, making excuses for your pain and minimizing your sufferings.

' Do you remember those men of olden times who so greedily courted pain, to keep their virtue in breath and exercise ? Put the case that Nature is bearing and forcing you into that vainglorious school, which you would never have entered of your own accord. If you tell me that it is a dangerous and fatal disease, what others are not so ? For it is a trickery of the doctors to make exception of some, which they say do not make a bee-line for death. What matter if they lead thither by accident, and if they easily glide and turn into the path that takes you there ?

' But you do not die because you are ill ; you die because you are alive. Death will kill you right enough without the help of sickness. And maladies have kept death away from some who have lived the longer for thinking they were dying. Besides, there are maladies, as there are wounds, that are medicinal and health-bringing.

' The stone is often no less tenacious of life than you. We see men with whom it has stayed from their childhood to their extreme old age ; and if they had not left it in the lurch, it was ready to accompany them still further. You kill it more often than it kills you. And though it should confront you with the idea of imminent death, would it not be a kind service to a man at that age to bring him to meditate upon his end ?

' And, what is worse, you have no longer any reasons for desiring to be cured. In any case the common lot will call you away at the first opportunity.

' Consider how artfully and imperceptibly she makes life distasteful to you and detaches you from worldly things. She does not subject you to a continual tyranny, like so

many other infirmities that afflict old people, which keep
them perpetually shackled, without any relaxation of weakness and pain ; but by warnings and instructions, repeated
at intervals, interrupted by long pauses of rest, she seems
to give you the opportunity to repeat and meditate over
her lessons at your leisure.

' To give you the means of forming a sound judgement
and of resigning yourself like a brave man, she brings before
you every different condition of health, at its best and its
worst. On one and the same day your life may be at one
moment of the gayest, and the next moment quite unbearable.

' Once a month, if you do not embrace death, you at least
shake hands with him. Wherefore you will have more
reason to expect that he will one day catch you without
any warning, and that, being so often led to the port,
trusting you are still in your usual state, you and your
trust will some morning find that you have unexpectedly
crossed the water.[1]

' We have no reason to complain of a disease which
loyally divides the time with health.'

I am beholden to Fortune for having so often attacked
me with the same kind of weapons ; she fashions and trains
me by use to resist them, she hardens and habituates me.
Henceforth I know within a little how much it will cost me
to be quit of them.

For want of a natural memory I make one of paper ; and,
as any new symptom appears in my ailment, I write it
down. Wherefore now, having had experience of almost
every kind, if I am threatened by some unforeseen disaster,
by turning over these little disconnected notes, like the
Sibylline leaves, I never fail to find, in my past experience,
some favourable prognostic to comfort me.

Habit is also of use in giving me better hopes for the
future. For these ejections having so long continued at the
same rate, it may be taken for granted that Nature will
not change the rate, and that nothing worse will happen
than what I have already experienced. Besides, this
infirmity is of such a nature that it is not out of keeping
with my hasty and impetuous temper. When the attack
is mild it makes me afraid, because then it has come to

[1] The river Styx.

stay for some time. But normally the attacks are brisk, vigorous and extreme ; they shake me to pieces for a day or two.

My kidneys held out for an age [1] without any change for the worse ; it is nearly another age [1] since their condition did change. Evil things as well as good have their periods ; perhaps this infirmity is drawing near its end. Age diminishes the heat of my stomach ; the digestion being the less perfect, it passes this crude matter on to my kidneys. Why cannot the heat of my kidneys be likewise diminished, in definite rotation, that they may cease to petrify my phlegm, and Nature find some other way of purging me ? Age has evidently caused some of my rheums to dry up. Why not the excrements which provide matter for the gravel ?

Moreover, is there anything so delightful as the sudden change, when, after extreme pain, by ejection of the stone I recover, as in a flash of lightning, the beautiful light of health, so full and so free, as happens in our sudden and sharpest attacks of colic ? Can the agony we have suffered for a moment counterbalance the pleasure of such a sudden improvement ? How much more beautiful health appears to me after the illness, when they come so near and are in such close contact, that I am able to confront them in their full armour ; when they appear as two rivals defying and opposing one another.

Just as the Stoics say that vices have been beneficially introduced into the world as a set off and an aid to virtue, we may say, with better reason and less bold conjecture, that Nature has given us pain that we may the better appreciate pleasure and painlessness.

When Socrates, after being relieved of his irons, felt the dainty and pleasurable itching in his legs caused by their weight, he was delighted to think what a close alliance there was between pain and pleasure, how they are linked together by a necessary connexion, so that they follow and beget one another by turns. And he exclaimed to the good Aesop that this consideration might have provided him with a fitting theme for a fine fable.

The worst of other maladies that I know is that their immediate effects are not so serious as their consequences.

[1] The edition of 1588 has respectively ' forty years ' and ' fourteen years '.

It takes a year to recover from them, always a year of weakness and dread. There is so much risk, there are so many stages before one is brought back to safety, that there is no end to it. Before you have doffed your kerchief, and then your skull-cap, before you are again allowed to enjoy the fresh air, wine, your wife, and melons, you are lucky if you do not have a relapse into some new misery. My malady has this privilege, that it carries itself clean off, whilst the others always leave their mark and some change for the worse, which renders the body susceptible to catching a new disease ; they lend a hand to one another.

These diseases may be pardoned that are content with immediate possession of us, without extending their tyranny and introducing their sequelae ; but courteous and gracious are those whose passing benefits us in some way. Since I have had the stone I find myself free from other ailments, more so I think than before ; and I have not since then had any fevers. I conclude that the frequent and violent fits of vomiting that I suffer purge me ; and on the other hand, my loss of taste and appetite, and the unusual fastings I keep, digest my peccant humours, and Nature ejects in the form of these stones the superfluous and hurtful matter.

Do not tell me that the physic is too dearly sold ; for what will you say of all those stinking draughts, those cauteries, incisions, sudorifics, setons, dietings, and all those methods of cure which, being more powerful and violent than we can bear, often bring us to death's door ? So, when I have an attack I take it as a physic ; when I am free I take it as being a full and certain deliverance.

Here is another benefit peculiar to my malady : that it almost plays its game by itself, and allows me to play mine, unless I lack the courage to do so. When I have been in the greatest throes I have held out for ten hours in the saddle. If you can only support it you have no need of any other regimen : play, dine, run, do this and do that, if you can ; your dissipation will do you more good than harm. You cannot say the same of one who has the pox, the gout or a rupture.

The other maladies impose a more general constraint ; they fetter our actions much more strongly, they disturb all our arrangements, and their consideration involves the whole condition of our life. Mine only pricks the skin ; it leaves the understanding and the will wholly at your disposal, as well as the tongue, the feet and the hands. It rouses rather than dulls your faculties. The mind is affected by a burning fever, struck down by an epileptic fit, and dislocated by a violent sick-headache, and in short turned upside down by all the maladies that hurt the main body and the noblest parts of it. In this case the mind is not attacked. If it goes wrong it has itself to blame ; it betrays, abandons, breaks itself up.

Only fools allow themselves to be persuaded that that hard and solid body that is baked in our kidneys can be dissolved by drinking ; therefore, once it is shaken up, there is nothing to be done but to give it passage ; and for that matter it will make one for itself.

I have also observed this particular advantage, that it is a disease that gives little scope for guessing. We are relieved of the uneasiness which other infirmities give us by reason of our uncertainty with regard to their cause, their condition and progress ; an extremely painful uneasiness. We have no need to consult the doctors and listen to their explanations ; our senses tell us what it is, and where it is.

By such arguments, both weak and strong, I endeavour to lull and beguile my imagination and anoint its wounds, as Cicero did the infirmity of his old age.[1] If to-morrow they become worse, to-morrow we will provide other loopholes.

For proof of what I say, since I wrote the above,[2] this new development has taken place, that the slightest movement forces the pure blood out of my kidneys. What of that ? I move about no less than before, and I gallop after my hounds with the ardour and arrogance of youth. And I find that I make great capital out of so momentous an accident, which costs me only a dull heaviness and uneasiness in that region. It is some big stone that bruises and consumes the substance of my kidneys and my life, which I void by degrees, not without some natural pleasure, as an excrement that is now troublesome and superfluous.

Do I feel a little shaky ? Do not suppose that I waste

---

[1] In his treatise *On Old Age*.
[2] This paragraph is one of the marginal additions to the edition of 1588.

my time feeling my pulse and inspecting my urine, in order to take some tiresome precautions or other ; I shall feel the pain soon enough, without prolonging it by the pain of fear.

He who fears he will suffer, already suffers because of his fear.

Moreover, the uncertainty and ignorance of those who presume to interpret the workings of Nature and her inner progress, and explain away all the wrong prognoses of their art, should make it clear that her ways are infinitely inscrutable. There is great uncertainty, variety and obscurity in both her promises and threats. Saving old age, which is an undoubted sign of the approach of death, I can detect few signs in any other of our ills on which to found a forecast for the future.

I only judge of my condition by actual sensation, not by reasoning. What would be the good, since I intend to do nothing but wait patiently ? Would you know how much I gain thereby ? Look at those who act otherwise and are swayed by so many different opinions and counsels ; how often they are plagued by their imagination, in which the body has no share. Many a time when I felt safe and free from those dangerous attacks, I have felt a malicious pleasure in communicating the symptoms to the doctor, as if they were just beginning. Most cheerfully did I suffer the dreadful doom to which their conclusions condemned me, and was the more beholden to the grace of God, and the more convinced of the futility of the art of medicine.

There is no better recommendation to youth than to be active and wide-awake. Our life is all movement. I am hard to move, and am slow in all things : in rising, going to bed, and at meals. Seven o'clock is early for me, and where I have a say in the matter I never dine before eleven nor sup till after six. I used to attribute the fevers and other ailments to which I was subject to the dullness and heaviness caused by long hours of sleep, and always repented dozing off again in the morning.

Plato disapproves of excess in sleep more than he does of excess in drinking.

I like to sleep hard and alone, even without my wife, in regal style, and rather well covered up. My bed is never warmed, but since I have grown old they give me, when I need it, woollen wraps to warm my feet and stomach.

They used to upbraid the great Scipio with being a sluggard ; for no other reason, I think, than because it vexed them that he was the only man in whom they could find no fault.

If I am at all particular in my manner of living, it is in this matter of sleep more than in anything else ; but as a rule I am able to adapt myself and yield to necessity as well as any other. Sleep has absorbed a good part of my life, and I still continue, at my age, to sleep eight or nine hours at a stretch. I am weaning myself with advantage from this lazy propensity, and am visibly the better for it. I find the change a little hard ; but in three days it is done. And I know of few men who can live with less sleep when necessary, or who take more constant exercise, or who are less affected by prolonged hard work.

My body is capable of enduring constant, but not violent and sudden movement. From now I avoid violent exercises, and such as make me perspire ; my limbs grow tired before they are heated. I can stand a whole day long, and do not tire of walking ; but on paved roads I have always, from my earliest days, preferred to ride. When on foot I am splashed up to the buttocks with mud ; and in our streets a little man is apt to be jostled and elbowed, for want of presence. And I have preferred to rest, either lying or sitting, with my legs as high or higher than my seat.

There is no more agreeable calling than that of the soldier ; a profession noble in its exercise (for valour is the highest, most generous and superb of all the virtues) and noble in its cause. No service is more useful, better justified and more universal than that which is devoted to the protection of one's country's peace and greatness. You take a pleasure in the society of so many noble and active young men, the often recurring tragic sights, the freedom of intercourse without any artificiality, the manly and unceremonious way of living, the many and varying feats of arms, the stirring harmony of the martial music which delights your ears and rouses your soul, the honour of the service with all its hardships and difficulties, of which Plato makes so light that, in his *Republic*, he makes women and boys share them. As a volunteer you may yourself offer to play your part in particular exploits and hazards, according to their importance and the kudos that you

think you may derive from them ; and you may see, when
life itself is staked for good reasons, that

> 'Tis beautiful to die with sword in hand. (VIRGIL.)

To fear the risks that are shared in common by so great
a number, not to dare what is dared by so many men of all
classes, is the mark of an incalculably mean and craven
spirit. Even children are reassured by company. If others
surpass you in knowledge, in charm, in strength, in fortune,
you have other causes to blame for it ; but if you yield to
them in stoutness of heart you have only yourself to blame.

Death is more despicable, more lingering and painful in
bed than in battle ; fevers and catarrhs are as distressing
and fatal as a musket-shot. One who is equal to enduring
bravely the accidents of everyday life would have no need
to swell his courage to become a soldier. *To live, my
Lucilius, is to fight* (Seneca).

I do not remember ever having been troubled with the
itch. Yet to scratch oneself is one of Nature's most agreeable gratifications, and as ready to hand as any. But repentance follows too intrusively upon its heels. I mostly scratch
the insides of my ears, which are at times liable to itch.

I came into the world with all my senses sound and
almost perfect. My digestion is good enough for ordinary
purposes, as well as my head and my breathing, and they
generally hold out all through my fevers. I shall soon have
passed my fifty-sixth year, an age which in some countries
was, not without reason, fixed upon as so reasonable a term
of life that they allowed no one to exceed it. Yet I still
have occasional, though brief and fickle, returns of youth-
fulness, so bright that they fall little short of the health
and freedom from pain of my young days. I do not mean
vigour and sprightliness ; it is not to be expected that they
should accompany me beyond their limits :

> No more can I endure the wind and rain
> To serenade my mistress 'neath her casement. (HORACE.)

My face, and my eyes too, immediately reveal the state
of my health ; all the changes I undergo begin there, and
they appear rather worse than they are in reality. My
friends often pity me before I am sensible of the reason.
My looking-glass does not alarm me, for even in my youth
I have more than once put on a muddy complexion and

look that boded mischief, without anything serious happening ; so that the doctors, finding no internal cause to account for the outward change, ascribed it to the mind and some secret passion that was gnawing at my heart. But they were mistaken. If I could control my body as well as I do my soul, we should get along together a little more comfortably. My mind was then not only free from troubles, but full of glee and contentment, as it commonly is, half by disposition, half by design :

> No sickness of the mind did e'er
> Affect my body's health. (OVID.)

I am of opinion that this temperament of my soul has many a time lifted the body after a fall. The latter is often in a low state ; but the other, if not gay, is at least tranquil and at rest. I had a quartan fever for four or five months, which quite disfigured me ; the mind held its course, not only calmly but in good humour. If the pain is outside of me, the weakness and languor do not much sadden me.

I have observed that there are many bodily infirmities the very name of which excites horror, but which I should fear less than a thousand mental sufferings and troubles which I see around me.

I have made up my mind that I cannot run any more ; it is enough if I crawl along. And I no more complain of the natural decay that holds me back,

> We marvel not in Alpine heights to see
> The tumid goitre ; (JUVENAL.)

than I regret that my life is not as long and as sound as that of an oak.

I have no reason to complain of my imagination. I have seldom in my life had thoughts which even interrupted the course of my sleep ; except perhaps desires which would excite without distressing me.

I seldom dream ; if I do, I dream of extravagant and grotesque things, usually the result of humorous and absurd, rather than distressing, thoughts. And I believe it to be true that dreams are faithful interpreters of our inclinations ; but it needs some skill to sort and understand them :

> No wonder 'tis if in our dreams
> The acts and thoughts, the cares and sights
> That occupy our waking hours
> Appear again. (ACCIUS, quoted by Cicero.)

Plato says, moreover, that it is a wise precaution to draw from them hints for divining the future. I see nothing in that, if it were not for the marvellous experiences on the subject of dreams related by Socrates, Xenophon, Aristotle,[1] men of unimpeachable authority.

Historians tell us that the Atlantes never dream, and that they eat nothing that has been killed. I add this detail, since that is perhaps the reason why they do not dream ; for Pythagoras prescribed certain preparations of food to induce appropriate dreams.[2]

My dreams are mild and make me neither restless in body nor talk in my sleep. I have known of many in my time who have been strangely disturbed by them. Theon the philosopher walked in his sleep ; as did also Pericles' slave, on the very roof and tiles of the house.

I exercise little choice at table, and take the first and nearest thing ; and I do not readily change from one flavour to another. I dislike a crowd of dishes and courses as much as I do any other crowd. I am easily satisfied with few dishes, and I entirely disagree [3] with Favorinus when he says that at a feast a dish should be removed as soon as you have taken a fancy to it, and a fresh one substituted ; that it is a niggardly supper at which the guests have not had their fill of the ' pope's nose ' of different birds, and that the beccafico is the only bird that deserves to be eaten whole.

I often eat salt meats, and yet I prefer bread with no salt in it, and my baker at home serves me with no other at my table, contrary to the custom of the country. In my childhood the chief fault they found to correct in me was my refusal to eat the things that children commonly love best at that age, sweetmeats, preserves, pastry. My tutor would combat this aversion to dainty things as if it were a form of daintiness. And, indeed, it is nothing more than a kind of fastidiousness, whatever be the object of it. If you cure a child of a particular and obstinate liking for

[1] As related by Cicero, De Divinatione, i. 25.

[2] See Cicero, De Divinatione, ii. 58, who tells us that among other things Pythagoras advised his disciples to abstain from beans. Cicero adds : In short I know nothing so absurd as not to have found an advocate in one or other of the philosophers.'

[3] Montaigne should have said that he agreed with Favorinus, who condemned the practices mentioned.

brown bread, bacon or garlic, you cure him of a kind of epicurism.

There are some who put on the patient airs of a martyr if deprived of beef and ham when partridges abound. They are well off : that is the daintiness of the dainty ; it is the taste of an easy fortune that is palled by usual and accustomed things, *by which luxury would escape the tedium of wealth* (Seneca). Not to make good cheer where another does so, to be very particular about what you eat and drink is the essence of this vice :

> And if you fear not homely fare
> Served up on plainest earthenware. (HORACE.)

There is, indeed, this difference, that it is better to restrict your desires to the things that are easiest to procure ; but still it is wrong to restrict them. I once called a kinsman of mine fastidious who had in our galleys learned to dispense with a bed and go to sleep without undressing.

If I had sons I should like them to have the same advantages that I enjoyed. The good father that God gave me, whom I can only repay with gratitude, but certainly a very hearty gratitude, for his goodness, sent me to be reared from my cradle in a poor village of his,[1] and kept there as long as I was at nurse, and longer. I was trained to the humblest and most common mode of life. *A well-behaved stomach is a great part of liberty* (Seneca).

Never take upon yourselves, and much less give up to your wives, the charge of bringing up infants. Leave them to be shaped by Fortune, subject to the laws of Nature and the people ; let them be trained to frugal and austere habits, that they may rather come down from hardships than rise to them.

His whim had yet another aim, to unite me with the lower class and that condition of people who need our assistance, holding that I was in duty bound rather to look to the man who extends his arms to me than to the one who turns his back upon me. And for this reason I was held over the baptismal font by people of the lowliest fortune, that I might feel obliged and attached to that class.

His plan succeeded by no means badly. I generally feel

[1] According to tradition the village of Papessus, about three kilometres from the Château of Montaigne.

drawn towards the lower class, whether on account of the greater credit, or by a natural compassion, a feeling which has great influence with me. The faction which I should condemn in our wars I should much more severely condemn when it is flourishing and prosperous; it will somewhat reconcile me to it when I see it miserable and crushed.

How greatly I admire the generous spirit of Chelonis, daughter and wife of Spartan kings! As long as Cleombrotus her husband had the better of her father Leonidas during the civil war of her city, she played the part of the dutiful daughter, and joined her father in his exile and poverty, in opposition to her victorious spouse. Did Fortune turn? We see her affections changing with Fortune; she bravely stands at her husband's side, whom she attended whithersoever his ill-fortune led him, having, as it seems to me, no other choice but to join the side where she was most needed, and where she could best show her compassion.

I am more naturally inclined to follow the example of Flaminius, who gave himself to those who had need of him instead of to those who could benefit him, than that of Pyrrhus, who was given to cringe to the powerful and to be arrogant with the weak.

Long drawn-out meals are irksome to me, and disagree with me; for, perhaps because I acquired the habit as a boy, for want of something better to do, I eat as long as I am at the table. Therefore, when at home, although the meals are of the shortest, I generally sit down a little time after the others, after the manner of Augustus. But I do not copy him in rising from table before the others; on the contrary, I like to rest a good while after and listen to the conversation, as long as I take no part in it. For it tires me and disagrees with me to talk on a full stomach, whilst I find that to shout and argue before a meal is a very wholesome and pleasant exercise.

The ancient Greeks and Romans had more sense than we in setting apart for eating, which is an important action in life, several hours and the better part of the night, unless they were prevented by some other unusual business; eating and drinking less hastily than we do, who perform all our actions post-haste, prolonging this natural pleasure with more leisure and with greater benefit, and combining therewith various social duties of a profitable and agreeable nature.

Those whose duty it is to look after me could cheaply deprive me of what they think will do me harm ; for in such things I never covet nor feel the absence of what I do not see. But again, they waste their time if they preach abstinence from the things that are set before me. Therefore, if I wish to fast they must keep me away from the supper-table, and put before me just so much as is necessary for the small repast that has been prescribed ; for if I sit down to table I forget my resolution. When I order any dish to be prepared differently my family know what it means : that my appetite is gone and that I shall not touch it.

The meat that will admit of it I like underdone, and very tender ; and some I like high, even smelling. Toughness alone I cannot endure as a rule (with regard to any other quality I am as indifferent and long-suffering as any man I have known), so much so that, contrary to prevailing tastes, I even find some kinds of fish too fresh and firm. Not that my teeth are at fault, for they have always been exceptionally good, and are only now being threatened by age. From childhood I have been accustomed to rub them with my napkin, both in the morning and on sitting down and rising from table.

God is kind to those from whom he takes life by degrees ; that is the only blessing of old age. The final death will be less complete and hurtful ; it will dispatch only the half or quarter of a man.

Here is a tooth that has just come out without any pain and without an effort ; it was the natural term of its duration. And this part of my being, and several others, are already dead, others half-dead, even of those that were most active and ranked highest during my years of vigour. Thus do I melt and steal away from myself. What a folly it would be in my understanding to feel the height of this fall, already so far advanced, as if it were from the very top ! I hope it will not.

Indeed, when I think of death I derive my best comfort from the reflexion that it will be normal and natural, and that any favour I may henceforth require or hope from Destiny will be undeserved.

Men hug themselves with the belief that in olden times

they were taller and longer-lived. But Solon, who belongs to those times, cuts down the extreme duration of life to seventy years. How can I who have in all things been such a devotee of the *golden mean* of ancient times, and have regarded the average measure as the most perfect, how can I expect an immeasurable and unnatural old age ? Whatever runs contrary to the course of Nature may be disagreeable, but whatever is in accordance with her should be ever pleasing. *All things that are done according to Nature should be accounted good* (Cicero).

Wherefore Plato says that the death that is brought on by wounds or disease may be accounted violent, but that which, guided by old age, overtakes us, is the easiest of all, and in some ways pleasant. *Young men are taken away by force, old men fall like ripe fruit* (Cicero).

Death even mingles and is confounded with all our life ; decay anticipates its hour and thrusts itself even across the course of our progress. I have portraits of myself taken at twenty-five and thirty-five years of age, and compare them with that taken at the present moment. In how many ways they are no longer myself ! How much more remote is my present face from those, than it will be from that of my end ! What an abuse of Nature to drag her along so far that she will be obliged to quit us, to leave our guidance, our eyes, our teeth, our legs, and the rest, to the mercy of assistance begged of others, and, weary of accompanying us, resign us to the hands of art !

I am not excessively fond of salads or fruit, with the exception of melons. My father hated every kind of sauce ; I like them all. Eating too much makes me uncomfortable ; but in respect of its properties I am not yet very certain that any kind of food disagrees with me. Nor have I noticed that I am affected by full or new moons, by autumn or spring.

We are subject to fickle and inexplicable changes. For example, radishes, which I first found to agree with me, afterwards disagreed, and now they agree again. In several things I have found my stomach and palate to vary in the same way : I have changed more than once from white wine to claret, and back again from claret to white wine.

I have a dainty tooth for fish, and the meatless days are my meat-days ; my fasts are my feasts. Besides, I believe that it is, as some people say, more easily digested than meat. As it goes against my conscience to eat meat on fish-days, so my taste rebels against mixing meat and fish ; the difference seems to me too wide.

From my youth up I have occasionally skipped a meal ; either to sharpen my appetite for the next day (for, as Epicurus used to fast and make lean meals in order to accustom his greed to dispense with plenty, I do so, on the contrary, in order to train my greed to take better advantage of plenty and to enjoy it more cheerfully) ; or I used to fast to keep my strength for the performance of some mental or bodily action ; for both my body and mind are made cruelly sluggish by repletion. (And especially do I hate the foolish idea of coupling so healthy and active a goddess with that little pot-bellied, belching god, all swelled up with the fumes of his liquor). Or again, to cure my ailing digestion ; or for want of congenial company ; for with that same Epicurus I say that we should not so much look to what we eat as to whom we eat with. And I applaud Chilo, who would not promise to accept Periander's invitation to a feast until he was informed who were the other guests.

To me no dressing is so acceptable, and no sauce so appetising, as that derived from good company.

I think it is more wholesome to eat more at leisure, and less, and to eat oftener. But I would give hunger and appetite their due ; I should take no pleasure in dragging through three or four wretched repasts a day, restricted by doctors' orders. Who will assure me that I can recover at supper-time the good appetite I had this morning ? Let us old men especially take the first opportunity that comes our way. Let us leave the making of dietaries to doctors and almanac-makers.

The best fruit of my health is sensual pleasure ; let us seize the first that is present and known. I avoid consistency in these laws of fasting. He who wishes to benefit by a habit, let him avoid continuing it. We become hardened, our powers are dulled by it ; six months after your stomach will be so inured to it, that all the advantage you have gained will be to have lost the freedom of doing otherwise except to your prejudice.

I do not cover my legs and thighs more in winter than in

summer : simple silk hose. For the relief of my colds
I gave way to the habit of keeping my head warmer, and
my belly on account of the colic. But in a few days my
ailments became accustomed to them and scorned my
ordinary precautions : from a cap I advanced to a kerchief,
and from a bonnet to a lined hat. The wadding of my
doublet is now only ornamental. All that would be of no
avail unless I added a hare's skin or a vulture's plumage,
with a skull-cap for the head. Continue this gradual progress and you will go a long way. I shall take care not to
do so, and would gladly go back to where I began, if I
dared.

'Have you developed a new ailment ? Is the remedy
no longer of any avail ? You have grown accustomed to it ?
Then try another.' In this way they ruin their health who
allow themselves to be fettered by enforced rules, and
superstitiously adhere to them ; they need more and more,
and after that more again. There is no end.

To suit our occupations, and for pleasure, it is much more
convenient to lose one's dinner, as the ancients did, and
defer making good cheer till the time of retirement and rest,
instead of cutting up the day : that is what I used to do.
For health's sake, on the other hand, I have since found by
experience that it is better to dine, and that I digest better
when awake.

I am not very subject to thirst, whether I am well or ill ;
in the latter case I very often have a dry mouth, but
without thirst, and as a rule I only drink from the desire
which comes with eating, and when the meal is well advanced. I drink pretty well for a man of ordinary build ;
in summer, and with an appetizing repast, I not only
exceed the limits of Augustus, who drank only three times
and no oftener, but, in order not to violate Democritus'
rule, which forbade stopping at four as an unlucky number,
I slide on, if need be, to the fifth : about three half-pints.
For little glasses are my favourites, and I like to drain them,
a thing which others avoid as unbecoming.

As a rule I dilute my wine with half, sometimes a third
part of water. And when at home, following an old custom
which my father's doctor recommended to him and himself
followed, the wine I need is mixed in the buttery, two or
three hours before it is served.

It is said that Cranaus, King of the Athenians, first introduced the custom of mixing wine with water ; whether beneficially or not has been a matter for debate. I think it more seemly and more wholesome for children not to take wine before they are sixteen or eighteen years of age.

The best mode of life is that which is most usual and common ; I think all singularity should be avoided. And I should hate to see a German putting water into his wine as I should to see a Frenchman drinking his pure. General use lays down the law in such things.

I fear a confined atmosphere, and have a mortal dread of smoke (the first repairs I set about in my house were those of the chimneys and the privies, which are commonly defective in old buildings, and not to be tolerated) ; and among the discomforts of war I include the thick clouds of dust in which we are buried in the hot weather for a whole day's march.

My breathing is free and easy, and my colds generally pass off without a cough, and without injury to the lungs.

The rigour of summer is more hostile to me than that of winter ; for, besides the discomfort caused by the heat, which is less easily to be remedied than that of cold, and the force of the sunbeams that strike upon my head, my eyes are afflicted by any dazzling light. I cannot even now sit down to dinner opposite a brightly burning fire.

To counteract the whiteness of the paper, when I used to read more than I do now, I laid a piece of glass upon my book, and felt great relief from it. To this moment [1] I am ignorant of the use of spectacles, and can see as far as I ever did, and as any other person. As the day declines my eyes certainly begin to feel a little dim and weak when reading, an exercise that has always tried them, but especially at night-time.

That is a step backwards, but very hardly perceptible. I shall be retiring another step, from the second to the third, from the third to the fourth, so softly that I must needs become really blind before I feel the age and decay of my sight. So cunningly do the Fates unwind our life's thread !

And so I doubt whether my hearing is hesitating on its way to hardness, and you will see that, before I have half lost it, I shall still blame the voices of those who are speaking

[1] The edition of 1588 adds : ' at fifty-four years of age '.

to me. We must, indeed, put great pressure on the soul to make it feel how it ebbs away.

My step is quick and firm ; and I know not which of the two, my mind or my body, I have had most difficulty in arresting at the same point. The preacher who can hold my attention during a whole sermon is very much my friend. On solemn occasions, when the faces of all are so rigid, and when I have seen ladies keep even their eyes so steady, I could never succeed in keeping some part or other of me from ever wandering ; though I may be seated, I am anything but settled.[1]

As the house-slave of Chrysippus the philosopher said of her master that he was only drunk in his legs (for he had the habit of moving them about, in whatever position he was in ; and she said it when the others were excited by wine and he felt no effects from it), it might have been said of me too that from my childhood I had madness in my feet, or quicksilver, so restless and fidgety are they, wherever I place them.

It is unmannerly, besides being prejudicial to health and even to one's pleasure, to eat greedily, as I do. I often bite my tongue in my haste, and sometimes my fingers. Diogenes, meeting a boy who was eating in that way, gave his tutor a box on the ear. There were people at Rome who taught others to masticate, as well as to walk,[2] gracefully. This habit leaves me no time for talking, which gives so agreeable a relish to the dinner-table, provided that the conversation be in keeping, agreeable, and brief.

There is jealousy and envy between our pleasures ; they clash and counteract one another. Alcibiades, a man who understood the art of entertainment, banished even music from his tables, lest it should disturb the pleasure of conversation, for the reason that Plato ascribes to him, ' that it is the custom of vulgar men to call singers and instrumentalists to their feasts, for want of good conversation and agreeable entertainment, with which intelligent men know how to regale each other.'

Varro makes the following requirements for a banquet :

---

[1] The edition of 1588 adds : ' And as to gesticulation, I am never without a switch in my hand, riding or walking.'

[2] *A mascher comme à marcher.* Montaigne cannot keep away from his *jeux de mots.*

' A company of persons of handsome presence and pleasing conversation, who must be neither dumb nor loquacious ; cleanliness and daintiness in the food and in the chamber ; and fine weather.' It needs no little skill to provide good entertainment, and it is attended with no little pleasure. Neither great generals nor great philosophers have disdained the knowledge and practice of good eating. My imagination has given three repasts to my memory's keeping, which chanced to be particularly pleasant to me, at different times of my greater prime. For each of the guests brings the principal charm with him, according to the good temper of body and mind in which he happens to be at the time. My present condition excludes me from those pleasures.

I who am but of the earth earthy, dislike that inhuman sapience which would have us despise and hate the care of the body. I think it equally wrong to be out of love with natural pleasures and to be too much in love with them.

Xerxes was a coxcomb who, lapped in all human delights, offered a prize to the man who should invent others ; but not much less of a coxcomb is a man who cuts himself off from those that Nature has invented for him. We must neither pursue nor flee them ; we must accept them. I accept them a little more generously and graciously, and allow myself more readily to follow the bent of Nature.

We have no need to exaggerate their emptiness ; it makes itself sufficiently felt and manifest, thanks to our morbid, kill-joy mind, which disgusts us with them as well as with itself. It treats both itself and all that it takes in, now well, now ill, according to its insatiable, erratic and versatile nature.

> Unless the vessel you would use be sweet,
> 'Twill sour whatever you may pour therein. (HORACE.)

I who boast of embracing so eagerly and particularly all amenities of life, find in them, when I look at them thus closely, little more than wind. But what would you have ? We are all wind throughout. And the wind too, more wisely than we, loves to bluster and shift about, and is content with its own functions, with no desire for stability and solidity, which are none of its properties.

The unmixed pleasures of the imagination, as well as its unmixed pains, are, as some say, greater than all others, as hinted at by Critolaus and his scales.[1] It is not to be wondered at, since she composes them at her own sweet will, and cuts them out of the whole cloth. Of this I see every day notable and perhaps desirable examples. But I, who am of a mixed and coarse grain, cannot so fully bite at this single and so simple object presented by the imagination, but that I let myself go, in all my grossness, after the present pleasures prescribed by human and universal laws, intellectually perceptible and perceptibly intellectual.

The Cyrenaic philosophers hold that, like bodily pains, so also bodily pleasures are the more powerful, as being both twofold [2] and more rational.

There are some who with savage stupidity, as Aristotle says, express disgust of pleasures ; I know some who do so from ambition. Why do they not also forswear breathing ? Why do they not live on their own breath, and refuse the light, because it shines gratis, and costs them neither invention nor strength ? Let them try to find sustenance in Mars or Pallas or Mercury, and see what happens, instead of Venus, Ceres, and Bacchus. Are not those the sort of people who will try to square the circle when perched on their wives ?

I hate to be told that my spirit should be in the clouds whilst my body is at table. I would have the spirit not nailed down to it, nor sprawling upon it, but attending to it ; it should sit at it, and not lie upon it.

Aristippus stood up for the body alone, as if we had no soul ; Zeno embraced only the soul, as if we had no body. Both of them mistakenly. They say that Pythagoras followed a philosophy that was all contemplation, Socrates one that was all conduct and action ; Plato found the adjustment of it between the two. But they say that to make up a tale. And the true adjustment is found in Socrates, and Plato is much more Socratic than Pythagorean ; and it becomes him better.

When I dance, I dance ; when I sleep, I sleep. Aye, and

---

[1] ' Supposing all the goods of the mind to be put into one scale, and the goods of the body into the other, Critolaus thought the goods of the mind would outweigh the others so far, that they would require the whole earth and sea to equalize the balance.'—Cicero, *Tusc. Quaes*, v. 17.

[2] i. e., both physical and mental.

when I take a solitary stroll in a beautiful garden, if some part of the time my thoughts dwell on outside events, for some other part I recall them to my walk, to the garden, to the sweetness of the solitude and to myself.

Nature has, with motherly care, observed this rule, that the actions she has laid upon us for our need should give us pleasure ; and she invites us to them, not only through our reason but also through our desire. It is wrong to infringe her rules.

When I see both Caesar and Alexander, in the thick of their great labours, so fully enjoying natural, and therefore necessary and reasonable pleasures, I do not call it a relaxing of their minds ; I call it a stiffening of their minds to subordinate, by strength of spirit, their strenuous occupations and heavy thoughts to the usages of everyday life. Wise they would have been if they could have believed that the latter was their ordinary, the former their extraordinary vocation.

What fools we are ! ' He has spent his life in idleness,' we say ; ' I have done nothing to-day.' What, have you not lived ? That is not only the fundamental but the most honourable of your occupations. ' If I had been given an opportunity to manage great affairs, I might have shown what I can do.' Have you been able to meditate and manage your own life ? Then you have performed the greatest work of all. In order to show herself and get to work, Nature has no need of a great destiny ; she will show herself equally in all ranks, both behind a curtain and without one.

It is our duty to compose our character, not to compose books, and to win, not battles and provinces, but order and tranquillity for our conduct of life.

Our great and glorious masterpiece is to live to the purpose ; all other things, ruling, laying up treasures, building, are at the most but appendicles and adminicles.

I delight in contemplating an army-general, at the foot of a breach he is about to attack, devoting himself entirely and free from cares to his dinner and to his table-talk among his friends. And Brutus, with heaven and earth conspiring against him and Roman liberty, stealing an hour or two from his nightly rounds, to read and epitomize Polybius in all security. It is the part of a little soul, buried

under the weight of business, not to be able to get clean
away from it, to lay it aside and take it up again :

> Now ye brave hearts that have weathered
> Many a sorer strait with me,
> Chase your cares with wine—to-morrow
> We shall plough the mighty sea ! (HORACE.)

Whether it be in jest or in earnest that the wine of the
Divines [1] and the Sorbonne has become proverbial, like
their banquets, I think it reasonable that they should dine
more agreeably and cheerfully for having been usefully and
seriously employed in the morning teaching their classes.
The consciousness of having made good use of the other
hours is the right savoury sauce for the table.

Thus did the Sages live. And that inimitable straining
after virtue which excites our admiration in both of the
Catos, that austere turn of mind that is carried to obtrusive-
ness, has thus tamely and complacently submitted to the
laws of human nature, and of Venus and Bacchus ; in
accordance with the teachings of their school, which require
the perfect sage to be as skilled and experienced in the
enjoyment of natural pleasures, as in any other of life's
duties. *A wise palate should go with a wise judgement*
(Cicero).

The power to relax and assume easy manners is highly
honourable, I think, and the most becoming trait in a strong
and generous soul. Epaminondas never imagined it to be
derogatory to the honour of his glorious victories and the
perfect purity of his morals to mingle with the dance of
the boys in his town, and to sing, play an instrument, and
give his whole mind to these recreations.

And among the many admirable actions of Scipio, the
grandfather,[2] a man worthy to be reputed of celestial
origin, there is none that shows him in such a charming light
as to see him strolling along the beach with Laelius, playing
the fool like a careless boy, picking up and selecting shells
and playing ducks and drakes ; and in bad weather amusing

---

[1] *Vin Théologal* : notable good and strong wine ; or the best wine, of
what kind soever.—Cotgrave.

[2] The original reading of the 1588 edition was ' of the younger Scipio
(when all is considered, the first of the Romans) '. Montaigne seems to
have forgotten that it was the younger Scipio who was contemporary
with Laelius and Terence.

and tickling himself with reproducing in written comedies the commonest and most vulgar actions of the people ; [1] and, with his thoughts taken up with that wonderful expedition against Hannibal and Africa, visiting the schools in Sicily and attending lectures in Philosophy, thus arming the teeth of the blind envy of his enemies at Rome.

And there is nothing more remarkable in the life of Socrates than that he found time in his old age to learn to dance and play on instruments, and thought it was time well spent.

This same man was once seen standing for a whole day and night in a trance, in the presence of the whole Greek army, his mind caught and carried away by some deep thought. He first, among so many valiant men of the army, ran to the help of Alcibiades, when the latter was overwhelmed by the enemy, covered him with his body and by main force of arms extricated him from the throng. And he first, among all the Athenians, who, like him, were incensed by so shameful a sight, came forward to rescue Theramenes, who was being led to his death by the satellites of the Thirty Tyrants. And, although he was joined by only two other men, all told, only at the instance of Theramenes himself did he desist from this bold undertaking. Although he was run after by a fair lady with whom he was in love, he was known, in spite of pressing need, to observe strict chastity. At the battle of Delium he was seen to pick up and save Xenophon, who had been thrown by his horse. He was always seen to march to war and tread the ice barefoot, to wear the same gown winter and summer, to surpass all his comrades in enduring hardships, and to eat no more at a banquet than at his ordinary. He was seen for twenty-seven years to endure, with unchanged countenance, hunger, poverty, the perverseness of his children, his wife's clawings, and in the end, calumny, tyranny, imprisonment, fetters, and poison.

But if ever he was challenged to a drinking-bout, he

---

[1] Montaigne was quite convinced that Scipio and Laelius wrote the comedies of Terence ; see Book I, ch. 4. The 1588 edition had this passage, afterwards deleted. ' I am exceedingly vexed that the lives of those two great men, Epaminondas and the younger Scipio, by common consent of the world, the one the first of the Greeks, the other the first of the Romans, the finest pair of lives that Plutarch wrote, should have been among the first to be lost.'

accepted as a matter of civility, and of all the army he was the man who came off best. And he never disdained to play at knuckle-bones with the boys or to ride with them on a hobby-horse, and he did it all gracefully ; for all actions, says Philosophy, are equally becoming and honourable in a sage. We have material enough, and we should never weary of presenting the picture of this great man as a pattern and ideal of perfection in all things.

There are very few examples of a pure and perfect life, and our education is all wrong when every day we are shown such crazy and defective models, scarce to be commended for any quality, which rather pull us backward ; corrupters rather than correctors.

People generally go wrong : it is much easier to go along the side-path, where the boundary serves as a check and guide, than by the broad and open middle way, to be guided by art rather than by Nature ; but also much less noble and less commendable.

Greatness of soul consists not so much in soaring high and in pressing forward, as in knowing how to adapt and limit oneself. It regards as great all that is sufficient, and shows its distinction in choosing the mean things rather than the eminent.

There is nothing so noble and so right as to play the man well and fitly, nor anything so difficult to learn as how to live this life well and according to Nature ; and the most inhuman of our diseases is to despise our being.

If you would send your soul abroad, do so by all means, if you can, when your body is in a bad way, in order to escape the contagion. At other times, however, let her be kind and helpful to the body, and, with wifely sympathy, not disdain to share his natural pleasures ; bringing moderation to them, if she be the wiser of the two, for fear lest, through want of discretion, they be confounded with pain.

Intemperance is the bane of sensual pleasure, and temperance is not its scourge but its seasoning. Eudoxus, for whom pleasure was the sovereign good, and his fellow-philosophers, who set so high a value upon it, savoured it in all its charm and sweetness, by reason of their temperance, which they practised in an uncommon and exemplary degree.

I bid my soul to look upon pleasure and pain with a sight equally well-balanced—*for the dilation of the soul in joy is as blameworthy as its contraction in sorrow* (Cicero)—and equally firm ; but to regard the one gaily, the other severely, and, as far as in her lies, to be as anxious to extinguish the one as to extend the other.[1]

To take a sane view of good naturally means to take a sane view of evil. And pain has something unavoidable in its gentle beginnings, as pleasure has something to be avoided in its excessive end. Plato couples them together and holds that it is equally the duty of courage to fight against pain and against the immoderate charms and blandishments of pleasure. They are two springs, at which all who draw, whence, when and how much they need, whether they be city, man or beast, are very fortunate. The first must be taken in the way of physic and when needed, but more sparingly ; the other for thirst, but not to intoxication.

Pain, pleasure, love, hatred, are the first things a child feels ; and if they conform to Reason, when she comes, that is Virtue.

I have a vocabulary all my own. I ' pass the time ' when it is wet and disagreeable.[2] When it is fine I do not wish to pass it ; I ruminate it and hold on to it. We should hasten over the bad, and settle upon the good. Those ordinary phrases ' pastime ' and ' pass the time ' reflect the habit of those wiseacres who think they cannot make a better use of their life than to let it slide and to escape from it, to while it away, to dodge it, and as far as in them lies to ignore it and run away from it, as if it were an irksome and contemptible thing.

But I know it to be otherwise, and find it agreeable and worthy to be prized, yea even in its last stage, in which I now enjoy it. Nature has given it into our hands, trimmed with so many and such happy surroundings, that we have only ourselves to blame if we feel it a burden, and if we waste it unprofitably. *The life of the fool is joyless, agitated, and wholly given to the future* (Seneca).

And yet I am resigned to lose it without regret ; but as

---

[1] *D'en esteindre l'une que d'estendre l'autre.*

[2] *Je passe le temps quand il est mauvais, &c.* The word *temps* means both ' time ' and ' weather '.

a thing that is by its nature losable, not as if it were a troublesome burden.

Not to hate the idea of death is properly becoming only in those who enjoy life.

It needs good management to enjoy life. I enjoy it doubly as much as others, for the measure of enjoyment depends upon the more or less attention we give to it. Especially now that I feel mine to be so brief in time I try to increase it in weight ; I try to arrest the speed of its flight by speedily laying hold of it, and, by the zest of my enjoyment to make up for its hasty ebbing. The shorter my possession of life the fuller and deeper must I live it.

Others feel the sweetness of contentment and well-being ; I feel it as well as they, but not in letting it pass by and slip away. Rather should we study, relish and ruminate it, in order to give adequate thanks to him who bestows it upon us.

They enjoy other pleasures, as they do that of sleep, unconsciously. I used to enjoy being disturbed in my sleep in order to get a glimpse of it, and not allow it so senselessly to slip away.

I meditate over a thing that gives me pleasure ; I do not skim over it, I go to the bottom of it and force my reason, now grown peevish and hard to please, to welcome it. Am I in some situation where I feel at rest ? Is there some sensual pleasure that tickles me ? I do not allow my senses to cheat me of it. I make my soul to share in it, not in order to be drawn into it, but to find it acceptable ; not to lose, but to find herself in it. And I induce her, for her part, to mirror herself in this fortunate state, to weigh and appreciate its happiness, and to magnify it. She will estimate how far she owes it to God that she is at peace with her conscience, free from other inner passions, that her body is in its natural healthy state, fitly and properly enjoying the exercise of the agreeable and soothing functions with which he of his grace is pleased to compensate her for the afflictions with which his justice chastises us in its turn ; how much it means to her to be so situated that, whithersoever she casts her eyes, the heavens around her are serene ; that no desire, no fear or doubt disturbs her atmosphere ; that there is no difficulty, past, present, or future, over which her imagination may not roam without harm.

Much light is thrown upon this consideration by comparison of my state with that of others. Thus, I can picture to myself in a thousand aspects those who are carried away and tossed about by Fortune or their own errors, as well as those who, more like me, so languidly and indifferently accept their good fortune. Those are the people who really ' pass their time ' ; they overpass the present and what they possess, to be slaves to hope, and for the shadows and vain images that their imagination dangles before their eyes,

> Like phantoms that, folk say, flit after death,
> Or visions that befool the slumbering sense ;   (VIRGIL.)

which speed and prolong their flight the more they are pursued. The fruit and aim of their pursuit is to pursue ; as Alexander said the end of his labour was to labour ;

> Thinking naught is done, if aught is left to do.   (LUCAN.)

For my part then, I love life and cultivate it such as it has pleased God to grant it to me. I do not go about wishing that it might be relieved of the necessity of eating and drinking, and I should think it no less pardonable a sin to wish that necessity to be doubled—*the wise man eagerly desires the treasures of Nature* (Seneca) ;—or that our life could be sustained by merely putting into our mouth a little of that drug with which Epimenides took away his appetite, and kept himself alive ; or that we could obtusely beget children by the fingers or heels (nay, in reverence be it spoken, that we could rather beget them voluptuously by the fingers and heels) ; or that the body should be without desire and incapable of being titillated.

Those would be ungrateful and wicked complaints. I accept heartily and gratefully what Nature has done for me ; and I am proud and well pleased with myself that I do so. For we wrong that great and all-powerful giver when we reject, destroy, and disfigure her gift. Being all good, she has made all things good. *All things that are according to Nature are worthy of esteem* (Cicero).

Of philosophical opinions I more readily embrace those which are most solid, that is to say, most human and most our own ; my words, in keeping with my actions, are mean and humble.

Philosophy appears to me very childish when she rides the high horse, and preaches to us that it is a barbarous alliance to marry the divine with the earthly, the reasonable with the unreasonable, the severe with the indulgent, the honest with the dishonest ; that sensual pleasure is a brutish thing, unworthy to be enjoyed by the sage ; that the only pleasure to be derived from the enjoyment of a fair young bride is the conscientious pleasure of performing an orderly action, like putting on one's boots for a business ride.   May her followers have no more right or nerve or sap in ravishing their wives than in learning her lessons !

That is not what Socrates, her master and ours, says. He prizes, as he should, the pleasures of the body ; but he prefers those of the mind, as being more powerful, more enduring, more easy to come by, more varied and dignified. The latter by no means go alone, according to him (he is not so fanciful), but only come first.   With him temperance is the moderator, not the enemy of pleasures.

Nature is a gentle guide, but not more gentle than she is wise and just.   *We must penetrate into the nature of things, and see exactly what it demands* (Cicero).   I try to follow her footsteps in all things ; we have confounded the traces by artificial means.   And the sovereign good of the Academics and the Peripatetics, which is to ' live according to her ', becomes for that reason difficult to limit and explain ; as does also that of the Stoics, which, related to the other, is to ' acquiesce in Nature '.

Is it not a mistake to regard some actions as less worthy because they are necessary ?   Yet they will not knock it out of my head that the marriage of pleasure with necessity (with which, as an ancient says,[1] the Gods always conspire) is a very proper marriage.   Why do we dismember by divorce a fabric woven of so close and brotherly a correspondence ?   Rather, let us knit it again by mutual offices. Let the mind rouse and quicken the dulness of the body, and the body check and steady the levity of the mind. *He who exalts the nature of the soul as the sovereign good, and condemns the nature of the flesh as an evil thing, truly both carnally desires the soul and carnally flees the flesh ; since he is inspired by human vanity, not by divine truth* (Saint Augustine).

In this gift of God there is no part that is unworthy of our attention ; we must account for it even to the last hair.

[1] Simonides.

And it is not a merely formal charge to man to direct man according to his nature ; it is positive, simple, and of prime importance, and the Creator has given it to us seriously and sternly.

Authority alone has any weight with an ordinary intellect, and weighs still more heavily in a foreign tongue. Let us here renew the attack. *Who will not say that it is the nature of the fool to do lazily and reluctantly what is to be done ; to urge the body one way and the soul another ; to be divided between wholly different movements* (Seneca).

Come now, to prove it, let such a man some day tell you the diversions and fancies he fills his head with, for which he diverts his thoughts from a good meal, and regrets the hour he spends over his eating. You will find that there is nothing so insipid in all the dishes on your table as the fine things with which he is entertaining his mind (for the most part it would be better fairly to go to sleep than to keep awake for the thoughts of our waking hours) ; and you will find that all his talk and all his aspirations are not worth your savoury stew.

Though they were the raptures of Archimedes himself, what of it ? I am not here concerned with that riff-raff of men that we are, or those aimless desires and thoughts that divert us from more serious things, nor am I confounding them with those venerable souls, lifted by pious and religious ardour to a constant and conscientious meditation on divine things, who, anticipating, by dint of a lively and passionate hope, the enjoyment of the heavenly food, the final aim and last step of Christian desires, the only constant and incorruptible pleasure, scorn to give their minds to our beggarly, fleeting, doubtful goods, and readily leave it to the body to provide and enjoy sensual and temporal fodder. It is a study for the privileged.[1]

Between ourselves, I have ever observed that super-celestial ideas and subterrestrial conduct are singularly suited to each other.

Aesop, that great man, saw his master making water as he walked. ' What ! he said, must we void ourselves as we run ? ' Use our time as best we may, yet a great part

---

[1] In 1588 the following was added and deleted : ' Our studies are all of this world, and of the things of this world the most natural are the most right.'

of it will still be idly and ill spent. Our mind has probably not enough other time to spare in which to do its business, unless it dissociates itself from the body for that brief space that it requires for its needs.

People try to get outside of themselves, and escape from the man. That is foolishness : instead of transforming themselves into angels, they transform themselves into beasts. Instead of raising they degrade themselves.

Those transcendental fancies overawe me, like high and inaccessible places ; and nothing is for me so hard to swallow in the life of Socrates, as his trances and his possessions by his daemon ; and nothing in Plato is so human as that for which they say he was called Divine.

And of our sciences those appear to me most terrestrial and low which have soared to the greatest heights. And I can see nothing more contemptible and mortal in the life of Alexander than his fancies about his immortalization. Philotas taunted him wittily in his rejoinder. He had congratulated him by letter on his elevation to the Gods by an oracle of Jupiter Ammon. 'For your sake I am glad ; but those people have reason to be pitied who will have to live with and obey a man who exceeds and is not satisfied with human proportions.'

> You rule the world because that you
> Confess the God's supremacy. (HORACE.)

I quite agree with the pretty inscription with which the Athenians welcomed Pompey on his entering their city :

> So far you may be deemed a God
> As you confess yourself a man. (PLUTARCH.)

A man who can rightly and truly enjoy his existence is absolutely and almost divinely perfect.

We seek other conditions because we know not how to enjoy our own ; and go outside of ourselves for want of knowing what it is like inside of us. So it is no use raising ourselves on stilts, for even on stilts we have to walk on our own legs. And sitting on the loftiest throne in the world we are still sitting on our behind.

The most beautiful lives, in my opinion, are those which conform to the model of common humanity, with order, but with nothing wonderful or extravagant.

Now old age needs to be treated a little more tenderly. Let us commend it to that tutelary God [1] of health and wisdom, but a gay and sociable wisdom:

> Give me but health, Latona's son,
> To enjoy what I possess ;
> Give me but this, I ask no more,
> This and a mind entire—
> An old age not unhonoured, nor
> Unsolaced by the lyre ! (HORACE.)

[1] Apollo.

THE END

INDEX

PRINTED IN ENGLAND AT THE
UNIVERSITY PRESS, OXFORD
BY JOHN JOHNSON
PRINTER TO THE UNIVERSITY